EDGAR CAYCE ✐ P9-BXX-739

An American Prophet

continued . . .

"So many authors have claimed to be the definitive expert on Cayce, often co-opting his teachings to fit their own agendas, that Cayce the man . . . has all but disappeared into folklore. Sidney D. Kirkpatrick is the first author to have been granted full access to [Cayce's 14,145 documented spiritual readings], as well as all correspondence in [Cayce's] archives. [He] details many ill-fated business relationships that Cayce, ever naive and prone to depression, entered into against the advice of others, particularly his long-suffering wife, Gertrude. In fact, Kirkpatrick's account of the Cayces' often strained relationship offers the first glimpse into the toll his gift took on their personal lives."

—*The Cleveland Plain Dealer*

"This biography of Edgar Cayce, a veritable twentieth-century Nostradamus, is a fascinating look at the man who had visions of the future."

—*The Sunday Oregonian*

"Our culture has put mysticism down. A few giants like Edgar Cayce broke through."

—Matthew Fox,
author of *Sins of the Spirit, Blessings of the Flesh*

"Sidney D. Kirkpatrick does an excellent job of giving a complete chronicle of Cayce's life. He holds us spellbound with an engrossing narrative of this remarkable man, who has always been my hero."

—Sylvia Browne,
author of *The Other Side and Back*

"[A] curious and controversial man."

—*The Washington Times*

"The story of Edgar Cayce has inspired me from the time I was twelve years old. As one of the first well-studied medical intuitives, his work and his life helped blaze the path for the future of medicine."

—Christiane Northrup, M.D.,
author of *Women's Bodies, Women's Wisdom*

RIVERHEAD BOOKS

NEW YORK

EDGAR CAYCE

An
American
Prophet

SIDNEY D. KIRKPATRICK

Most Riverhead Books are available at special quantity discounts for bulk purchases for sales promotions, premiums, fund-raising, or educational use. Special books, or book excerpts, can also be created to fit specific needs.

For details, write: Special Markets, The Berkley Publishing Group, 375 Hudson Street, New York, New York 10014.

RIVERHEAD BOOKS
Published by The Berkley Publishing Group
A division of Penguin Putnam Inc.
375 Hudson Street
New York, New York 10014

Copyright © 2000 by Sidney D. Kirkpatrick
Book design by Amanda Dewey
Interior and insert photographs courtesy Edgar Cayce Foundation Archives
Cover design by Royce M. Becker
Cover photograph courtesy Edgar Cayce Foundation Archives/Corbis/Bettmann

Published simultaneously in Canada.

First Riverhead hardcover edition: September 2000
First Riverhead trade paperback edition: November 2001
Riverhead trade paperback ISBN: 1-57322-896-6

Visit our website at www.penguinputnam.com

The Library of Congress has catalogued
the Riverhead hardcover edition as follows:

Kirkpatrick, Sidney.
Edgar Cayce : an American prophet / Sidney Kirkpatrick.
p.   cm.
ISBN 1-57322-139-2
1 Cayce, Edgar, 1877–1945.
2. Psychics—United States—Biography.   I. Title.
BF1027.C3 K57   2000   00-027975
133.8'092—dc21
[B]

PRINTED IN THE UNITED STATES OF AMERICA

10   9   8   7   6   5   4   3   2   1

To Nancy, in gratitude for the love and light
she has brought into my life

There are no unnatural or supernatural phenomena,
only very large gaps in our knowledge of what is natural.

—EDGAR MITCHELL
Apollo 14 Astronaut

Contents

Introduction:

The Open Door

Nine years after the turn of the twentieth century, a photographer named Edgar Cayce stepped off a Pullman onto a crowded passenger platform in Hopkinsville, Kentucky. Edgar might normally have paused to greet acquaintances at the station or warm himself beside the coal stove in the ticket office, but he had more pressing business on that cold February night. He pulled up the collar on his thin cotton jacket and ventured into the downpour to meet a waiting carriage.

The driver, Lynn Evans, quickly ushered Edgar inside his cab. As chief ticket agent and superintendent at the Hopkinsville depot, Lynn was the natural choice to be on the lookout for his brother-in-law's arrival on the northbound local from Guthrie, Kentucky. Knowing the urgency of Cayce's visit, Lynn likely reached for the horse's reins the moment the tall, lanky photographer emerged from the cloud of steam billowing out from under the eighty-two-ton locomotive.

Framed in the yellow halo of light from the overhead oil lamps on East Ninth Street, Edgar looked too young to be a church deacon or the owner of one of Kentucky's most respected photography studios. His shy, pensive smile and clean-shaven face gave him the youthful appearance of a college sophomore coming home for the holidays. His tousled brown hair was cut short, accentuating his high forehead, deep-set blue-gray eyes, and receding chin. His large feet and hands seemed better suited to an awkward boy on the verge of manhood than a thirty-two-year-old husband and father.

A closer look at Cayce revealed the truth of his age and occupation. Having spent much of the last decade in a darkroom, his complexion was pale and his fingers were stained brown from the chemicals he handled routinely in the developing baths. The acrid odor of those chemicals still clung to his clothes as Edgar knocked the mud from his high-top leather shoes and climbed into the carriage for the 1¼ mile trip through Hopkinsville to a house known to Edgar and Lynn as "The Hill."

The journey was familiar territory for both men. Edgar had traveled it many times on foot and by bicycle during his courtship with Lynn's sister, Gertrude, and though he now had the luxury of taking a horse and carriage, Cayce knew the unpaved streets of the city and its squat two- and three-story redbrick buildings as intimately as he knew the darkroom in his photographic studio in Bowling Green, Kentucky.

Behind the teardrop spire on the train station was the downtown business district where Edgar had once clerked at the Hopper Brothers Bookstore. To the east was the block-long tobacco planters' warehouse, which had been built by his great-uncle George, and which housed the crop that gave Hopkinsville and greater Christian County the distinction of being the largest producer of pipe and chewing tobacco in the nation. Beyond the clock tower on the fire station shone the lights of the Hotel Latham, where he had photographed Theodore Roosevelt during his campaign for president.

Lynn Evans drove the carriage east on the Russellville Road, passing the ivy-covered boys' dormitory at South Kentucky College on Belmont Hill. The grand Victorian homes lining the road were painted in rich pastels and were festooned with scalloped shingles, copper weather vanes, flag poles, and white picket fences. The farther they went from the center of town, the less ornate the homes became. The asphalt soon gave way to an unpaved road where the massive wrought-iron gates of the Hopkinsville mental asylum, Christian County's largest building, dominated the bleak landscape. The carriage rattled past a few lonely stands of ash and elder trees, shorn of leaves, and the dirt road became two muddy lanes running between the rolling brown hills and the still bare tobacco fields that were the primary source of Hopkinsville's wealth.

The house called The Hill sat on a high promontory a few hundred feet within the city limits. It was a single-story, four-bedroom home of classic antebellum design, painted gun-metal gray and dominated by four white Doric columns. The front of the house had a large open veranda shaded by oak and maple trees. At the rear of the property, separated from the main house by a carriage walk and rose garden, were the kitchen, smokehouse, chicken coop, barn, and dog run. The many outbuildings, like the home itself, had been designed and constructed by Dr. Samuel Salter, Lynn and Gertrude's maternal grandfather, a respected civil engineer, an unlicensed physician, and one of the county's leading building contractors.

It had been the late Salter's dream that The Hill would always be a safe haven for his family and their progeny, and he had seen to it that the house, its adjoining orchard, and ten acres of farm land were free of debt before his death. He had assembled an extensive library of technical and reference books, kept a full store of medical supplies in a large cedar chest in the dining room, and stored enough food in the root cellar and smokehouse to feed a family of eight for an entire year. It wasn't enough, however, that his family be materially independent. In the spirit of Franklin and Jefferson, he wanted all five of his children—three daughters and two sons—to become free thinkers. He sent them all to college, where they studied Plato and Shakespeare, and urged them to read newspapers, attend rallies, and engage in intellectual discussion. Their opinion counted, no matter what political or social cause they chose to support.

To Edgar Cayce, who had been born in a tiny frame cottage on a remote Christian County farm, who had ended his formal education at the age of sixteen in a single-room schoolhouse, and whose mother and sisters didn't dare to express an opinion of their own, The Hill held an attraction that went beyond his love for Gertrude and his affection for Lynn Evans. The Hill was an intellectual hothouse that both stimulated and challenged his deeply felt notions of religion and spirituality. At The Hill, Edgar didn't feel the need to confine his creative interests to the darkroom or conform to rules preached by the church elders. He could freely explore a part of himself that he had kept hidden from his pastor and from his clients at the photo studio. At The Hill, he was free, as Lynn liked to say, "to experiment."

As the carriage approached the main entrance, Edgar felt the familiar sense of security that accompanied all of his trips to The Hill. Lynn brought the horse to a halt, and as he tended to the carriage, Edgar walked quickly up the muddy path to the veranda where he was greeted by Hugh Evans, Lynn's older brother. The two briefly exchanged pleasantries before entering the parlor, where the rest of the family was gathered around the fireplace. Lynn's mother, Elizabeth, was there, along with their aunt Kate and her son Hiram, and their aunt Carrie and her husband, Dr. Thomas House. Everyone's attention was focused on Carrie and Thomas's infant son, Thomas House Jr., who lay on a small, white, embroidered pillow in his mother's lap.

The infant had been suffering convulsions since his premature birth three months earlier. The convulsions had become so frequent that they now occurred every twenty minutes, leaving the helpless child too weak to nurse from his mother's bosom or to wrap his tiny hands around her fingers. Tommy House was on the verge of death from malnutrition and lack of sleep, a diagnosis confirmed by the child's father, a doctor, and by the family's two personal physicians, Dr. Jackson, a general practitioner in Hopkinsville, and Dr. Haggard, a pediatric specialist from Nashville who had been attending the child since birth. Although the three doctors disagreed about what treatment they should provide, all agreed that Thomas House Jr. had little or no chance of living through the night.

They now turned to Edgar Cayce, a photographer with an eighth-grade education and no medical training, to save little Tommy's life. Carrie wasn't sure Edgar could help her son—no more than Edgar himself was—but she wanted him to try. In previous "experiments," Cayce had demonstrated a remarkable ability to put himself into a hypnotic trance and obtain medical and other information beyond the grasp of ordinary people.

Even as a child, Edgar only had to close his eyes to locate a lost ring or pocket watch. He could read a deck of playing cards that were facedown on a table or recite the contents of a closed book or sealed envelope. By merely thinking about someone he could wake the person up from a deep sleep, induce him or her to make a telephone call or write a letter, or in the case of young children, hold them in a particular pose long enough to have their portraits taken. He had solved a murder, found missing persons, diagnosed illness and disease, and recommended cures. He didn't use a crystal ball, playing cards, or a Ouija board. Nor did he belong to a temple or arcane spiritual fraternity. He needed only to close his eyes, as if putting himself to sleep, and after a short period of quiet and meditation, he was able to help any person who asked for it. The greater the person's need, and the more sincere their motivation, the more astonishing were the results.

The mere arrival of Cayce at The Hill was enough to provoke Dr. Haggard to pack his bags and leave. Like many doctors in the area, he had heard accounts of Cayce's alleged powers and wanted no part of his "trickery." Dr. Jackson shared his colleague's skepticism, but as the family's longtime physician, he had seen Cayce do things that he could not readily explain. Dr. House was also skeptical, but he also knew Cayce too intimately to believe that trickery was involved. The Cayces were simple tobacco farmers from the rural hamlet of Beverly, and Edgar was the least educated and most unassuming of the lot. House had reluctantly agreed to call Edgar to The Hill only because House's headstrong wife, Carrie, had insisted he be consulted.

Doctors House and Jackson accompanied Edgar from the parlor into the master bedroom across the hall. Inside, Edgar took off his jacket and shoes, removed his tie and collar, and laid himself down on the embroidered linen bedspread covering the large oak bed. He pulled a down comforter over his stocking feet, adjusted himself on his back, and then, feet together, hands across his chest, he lay back in bed and stared at the ceiling.

More than a minute passed. In a silence broken only by the rain pounding on the roof and the weak cries of the dying child in the next room, Edgar's breathing deepened and his eyes closed. "You have before you the body of Thomas House Jr. of Hopkinsville, Kentucky," Dr. House said. "Diagnose his illness and recommend a cure."

By all appearances, Edgar was fast asleep—his arms crossed, legs straight, eyes closed, breathing slowly—but Dr. House knew better. He had once seen the young photographer go into a trance so deep that fellow physicians thought he was in a coma. When one of House's colleagues had jabbed the blade of a knife under one of Cayce's fingernails and another had stuck a hypodermic needle into his foot, he had not even flinched. And yet, the "sleeping" Cayce could answer questions as if he were wide awake.

Cayce began to speak in his normal voice: a deep, rich baritone with a distinctly southern accent. At first his words were garbled, almost a hum, and then, like a phonograph needle that has found the groove on a record, his voice cleared and his words became well modulated and easy to understand. "Yes, we have the body and mind of Thomas House Jr. here," he said.

Cayce proceeded to report the infant's temperature, blood pressure, and other physical and anatomical details of his body. He described the child's condition in such a cool, calm, and detached manner that an observer would have been left with the impression that he was a physician describing to fellow colleagues an examination he was in the process of conducting. In this case, however, the physician had his eyes closed and his patient was cradled in his mother's arms in the next room. Cayce appeared to have the ability to see right into his patient's body, to examine each organ, blood vessel, and artery with microscopic precision.

Doctors House and Jackson listened intently as Cayce described an epileptic condition that had caused severe infantile spasms, nausea, and vomiting—evidently the outcome of the child's premature birth—which in turn had been the result of his mother's poor physical condition during the early months of her pregnancy. Cayce prescribed a measured dose of belladonna, administered orally, to be followed by wrapping the infant in a steaming hot poultice made from the bark of a peach tree. Cayce ended the trance session himself when he stated, "We are through for the present."

House instructed the "sleeping" Cayce to regain consciousness. Cayce dutifully followed instructions and awoke, only to find himself alone in the bedroom. In the two or three minutes it took him to open his eyes and stretch his arms, the two doctors, deep in discussion and agitated by what he had said, left the room and returned to the parlor.

As unbelievable as the source of the information was, House and Jackson both agreed that the diagnosis sounded perfectly reasonable. It was the recommended cure that upset them, for the sleeping Cayce had prescribed an unusually high dose of a toxic form of deadly nightshade. Even if the peach-tree poultice could somehow leach the poison out of the infant's system, administering such a large dose of belladonna to a child as small and weak as Thomas House Jr. was tantamount to murder. Jackson expressed his sentiments to his colleague and the child's mother in no uncertain terms: "You'll kill little Tommy for sure," he said.

Tommy's father had no choice but to agree. Although homeopathic belladonna was sometimes used to treat lung and kidney ailments, *pure* belladonna, in the form Cayce recommended, was used only in topical ointments and was certainly not something to spoon into the mouth of a three-month-old child.

Edgar joined the two doctors in the parlor but couldn't contribute to the discussion taking place. He had never been able to remember anything he had said or heard in a trance state and had little more than a rudimentary knowledge of medicine in his waking state. Even so, he grew more and more concerned as he listened to the doctors' ensuing debate. Until now, his sessions had been an experiment—a way of seeing if his abilities could help the people who came to him. He now had to face the grim reality that something he had said in a trance might result in the death of a family member.

It was the child's mother who made the decision to administer the drug. Having seen Cayce work miracles in his sleep, she believed that he was touched by the Divine, that a heavenly spirit spoke through him when he was in a trance. In previous experiments, she herself had been advised not to undergo an abdominal surgery recommended by her doctors, which indeed turned out to be unnecessary. Cayce had also predicted that she would become pregnant, something that her husband and two specialists had said was physically impossible. He also foretold the date of birth and said she would deliver a boy. And the spiritual message accompanying this information—that God's love and forgiveness must be foremost in her heart—had inspired her to minister to the patients at the Hopkinsville asylum. Now, she believed, God's mercy, love, and compassion were reaching out to her. If Edgar Cayce said that she had to poison her son in order to save his life, then that was what she was going to do.

Dr. House could not make the same leap of faith. As a highly respected general practitioner with aspirations to become the county health commissioner, everything he had seen and heard in the bedroom ran contrary to his training, experience, and common sense. Although he was aware of the experiments at The Hill, he hadn't condoned them nor given them much credence. He had permitted his wife to participate because she derived pleasure and comfort from them. He had looked upon Edgar's activities as entertainment, a mere parlor game. But what he had just seen and heard in the bedroom a few moments earlier terrified him. Cayce hadn't spoken in terms that were open for interpretation. Without physically examining Tommy, Cayce had recited the child's blood pressure and temperature, figures that House knew to be correct because he and Jackson had taken them a few minutes before Edgar's arrival at The Hill. Cayce had also described body organs with the expertise of a skilled surgeon conducting an autopsy. House didn't dare let himself speculate why Cayce had used the plural form "we" when conducting his trance examination, or why he apparently needed to contact little Thomas's "mind" as well as his "body" before the examination could proceed.

At his wife's insistence, and despite his very great reservations, House ultimately agreed to prepare the belladonna. He justified the decision by saying that his son would surely die anyway if nothing else were done. He and Dr. Jackson might be able to prolong the infant's life by a few hours, but they were powerless to keep him alive through the night. At the very worst, giving little Tommy belladonna would put the child out of his misery.

Edgar and Lynn Evans went outside to collect the ingredients for the poultice that had been recommended in the treatment. By the light of an oil lamp, Edgar climbed a peach tree in the orchard behind the barn. Using a penknife, he skillfully cut the bark from around the youngest shoots he could reach, then handed them down to Lynn Evans. They took the bark to the kitchen at the rear of the house where Aunt Kate had put a kettle on the stove to boil.

Aunt Kate prepared the hot poultice and then carried it into the parlor where Dr. House had already measured out the belladonna. He dissolved the white powder into a spoonful of water, and Carrie forced her son to swallow it. Edgar didn't join the others in the parlor to see what would happen, because, as he later said, he "couldn't stand the thought of seeing Tommy House die in his mother's arms."

Medical records do not exist to describe the child's physiological reaction to the belladonna, or to the steaming hot towels dipped in peach-tree solution in which the naked child was immediately wrapped. All that is known is that the crying stopped as soon as the mother spooned the poison into her child's mouth, and that he fell into his first deep and uninterrupted sleep since birth. Thomas House Jr. awoke hours later, drenched in sweat, cheeks pink, and breathing steadily. He was never to have a convulsion again.

No one at The Hill that night knew who or what had intervened to save the child's life. They knew only that their lives, like that of little Tommy House, had been irrevocably changed. There was no turning back. The tears in their eyes and the pounding in their hearts told them that what they had experienced could neither be ignored nor denied. Edgar Cayce had saved the child's life.

Dr. House had witnessed something that would make it impossible for him to return to the medical profession as he knew it. Twenty years later, he would close his practice and dedicate the remainder of his career to operating a hospital devoted to Edgar Cayce and his healing arts in Virginia Beach, Virginia. Carrie House would become the Cayce Hospital's supervising nurse and an outspoken proponent of the Divine "message" that she believed was being communicated through the man to whom the hospital was dedicated. Thomas House Jr. would grow up and spend his adult life designing and building innovative medical technology based on Cayce's trance readings, and, at great personal expense, would frequently drive hundreds of miles to deliver readings to patients unable to come to Virginia Beach.

Edgar Cayce also had undergone a change: he had once again proven to himself that good might come from his special talents. He had taken one of his first apprehensive and faltering steps away from the refuge of his darkroom and closer to the moment he would, as he later said, "step out into the light" and turn himself over to what became known simply as "Cayce's work," or "the work." Foremost among his many challenges would be overcoming the fear and trepidation he experienced every time he went into a trance: never knowing what might happen when he closed his eyes, what he might say while he was "under," and whether or not he would be able to open his eyes when the session ended.

In the years ahead, the work became such an integral part of Edgar Cayce's life that it was impossible to separate the man from his trance-induced communications. There were times when the readings threatened to tear his family apart, and times when they were all that held it together. Edgar Cayce would be catapulted to national prominence on the front page of the *New York Times* and then vilified by the *Chicago Examiner.* He would be championed as a savior and reviled as an agent of the Devil. But he would continue giving readings, twice a day, nearly every day, on topics as diverse as organ transplants, cures for breast cancer and treatments for arthritis to the design of the universe and the purpose of man's existence on earth. No subject was off limits. He provided trance commentary on Jesus and His disciples, the role of women in the founding of Christianity, and the secret of the sphinx. He offered insights into how to improve relations between men and women, the spiritual role that parents play in choosing the child that will be born to them, and the possible causes of homosexuality. During his forty-three-year career, which ended on September 17, 1944—three months before his death—Edgar Cayce gave 14,145 fully documented readings for 5,744 people. Transcripts of these readings—which sometimes run as long as twenty single-spaced typed pages—and the approximately 170,000 pages of correspondence, diaries, medical reports, and notes documenting the work now comprise what is the most unusual and voluminous archive that has ever existed on a practicing psychic.

The only consolation Edgar would have in his long and frequently perilous journey out of the darkroom was knowing that he had the unqualified love and support of those closest to him. Despite Gertrude's worry that her husband was slowly going insane and might, one day, have to be put into the Hopkinsville asylum, she devoted her life to conducting his trance sessions and battling the ever-present financiers and speculators who sought to exploit him. Accompanying Edgar on his journey was a young woman from Alabama named Gladys Davis, a stenographer and secretary who became an indispensable part of the work by making verbatim transcripts of everything Cayce said while in trance, and whose appreciation and love for the "messenger" as well as his "message" raised the level of Edgar's trance readings to that of an art form.

Edgar Cayce's partners through the years included physicians, stockbrokers, inventors, soldiers, film producers, and Texas oilmen. These men would help build the Cayce Hospital in Virginia Beach and establish the first and only university whose faculty underwent psychic scrutiny before being hired. Despite the fact that these partnerships sometimes ended in costly and humiliating lawsuits, they also brought Cayce many hundreds of grateful recipients of his trance counsel. As his son, Hugh Lynn Cayce, once said, "Edgar was like an open door into another dimension. People were attracted to the light."

Master magician Harry Houdini, having dedicated himself to exposing the fraudulent practices of hundreds of occult mediums and spiritualists, failed to debunk or explain the Cayce phenomenon, and neither did police and FBI agents who launched an investigation into how he was able to accomplish the seemingly impossible. That Cayce didn't charge admission to witness his trance sessions, that he didn't conjure ectoplasm or summon phantom spirits in a darkened room, presented unique and entirely unfamiliar challenges. That he built no church, had no disciples, and avoided the limelight confounded and confused them. As the novelist and psychic researcher Arthur Conan Doyle said of Cayce: "He was in a class all his own."

From hundreds of pages of documents and correspondence that have never before been made public, it is now clear that such scientific luminaries as Thomas Edison and Nikola Tesla were given trance readings by Cayce, as were engineers at RCA, IBM, Delco, and the president and founder of the Goodyear Tire and Rubber Company. The inventor Mitchell Hastings credited Cayce with helping him to develop FM radio. NBC founder David Sarnoff and his family had secret readings. Innovative electronic technologies designed by Cayce in trance are now used in almost every large hospital and airport in the world.

Edgar Cayce gave readings for Irving Berlin, George Gershwin, Gloria Swanson, and the concerned mother of Ernest Hemingway, who consulted Cayce about her son's writing career. Marilyn Monroe practiced beauty aids recommended by Cayce in trance. Business tycoon Nelson Rockefeller and labor organizer George Meany availed themselves of Cayce's medical advice. High-ranking foreign diplomats and church leaders consulted Cayce, as did government agents and politicians whose trance readings were conducted and transcribed privately. And although the details remain unclear, circumstantial evidence suggests that Cayce conducted psychic readings for President Woodrow Wilson, as he sought to make peace in the aftermath of the "war to end all wars." Cayce predicted the failure of prohibition, the great stock market crash, the beginning and end of two world wars, the deaths of two presidents, and made startling assertions about the second coming of Christ and the next millennium.

Despite the overwhelming success of his medical readings, and despite the fact that the recipients of many of these readings were some of the richest and most influential people in the country, Edgar Cayce would spend much of his adult life living in poverty, moving from home to home, constantly under threat of being persecuted for fortune-telling or practicing medicine without a license. His readings were often conducted in makeshift conditions and sometimes had to be transcribed on sheets of recycled wrapping paper. At times, he didn't have enough money to feed his children and had to rely on his friends and in-laws to bail him out of debt—or even jail.

That Edgar Cayce persevered and continued giving readings for four decades was perhaps the greatest miracle of his life. And however inseparable the readings became from the man who gave them, it was not his trance communications that endeared him most to family and friends. A humble, kind, gentle, and affectionate man, Edgar preferred the company of children over and above his many rich and famous acquaintances. He invented card games to entertain visitors, bottled his own preserves, kept a dazzling garden, and maintained a lively correspondence with a vast array of people whom he had never met—from child prodigies and bank presidents to railway conductors and undertakers. Though demands on his time were so great that appointments sometimes had to be scheduled months in advance, he rarely missed his weekly Bible study class and never turned anyone away who was in genuine need.

Like the engine on the locomotive that had brought him from Bowling Green to Hopkinsville to treat Thomas House Jr., a powerful force drove Edgar out of what might otherwise have been a comfortable and ordinary existence as a church deacon, photographer, and husband. Exactly where he was going and what he would find when he arrived were questions he hadn't yet answered on that cold February night—nor had he, in fact, even begun to ask them. That his journey would be helpful to others was not in doubt. The life of Thomas House Jr. was evidence of that. That he had the courage to overcome his fears and, as he said, "step out into the light," made his journey all the more remarkable, given how frightening and blinding the glare of that light could sometimes be. His life became a series of sometimes joyful, often excruciating steps toward self-discovery, and although he may have never fully grasped the unimaginable forces that had chosen him as a messenger, he would one day discover what he believed to be the real purpose of his work.

As Edgar Cayce himself, in trance, once said: "There are no shortcuts to knowledge or wisdom or understanding . . . these must be lived and experienced by each and every soul."

PART ONE

A Christian in
Christian County

A Most
Unusual Child

Thomas Jefferson Cayce, a handsome and successful farmer, was purported to love his bourbon nearly as much as the red and black rolling hills of his native Christian County. The fact that his choice of liquor and the earth that produced it were the same color was merely evidence of what he knew in his heart: that he, like his corn whiskey and the lush dark leaves of the tobacco plants that grew in his fields, were merely an extension of the rich soil that had been his birthright. And Tom and his family had much to be proud of. From the Liberty Church on the Palmyra Pike near the crossroads village of Beverly, Kentucky, Tom could walk the seven miles into Hopkinsville without leaving property owned by a Cayce or their neighbors, the Majors. And as everyone in Christian County knew, the Cayces and the Majors had married so often and generated so many children that there practically wasn't a Cayce in the county who didn't have a Major as a family member.

The Kentucky branch of the Cayce clan believed that the family had originally come from France before settling in Cumberland County, Virginia. Their Virginia ancestors, however, have genealogical records that indicate their earliest known descendant had come to colonial America from

Scotland. The Virginia Cayces had fought with distinction at Yorktown during the Revolutionary War, helped build the Library of Congress, and were stone masons for the Washington monument. The Kentucky branch of the family, led by pioneers William and Betsy Cayce, established themselves in Beverly on 29¼ acres purchased for $145 in 1827. All ten of William and Betsy's children, including the youngest, Thomas Jefferson, became corn, wheat, and tobacco farmers, and collectively increased the family's holdings to over 4,500 acres in less than a decade. Unlike their Virginia cousins, the variety of tobacco that they raised was dark fired, which was used primarily for chewing and pipe smoking as opposed to the burley tobacco used in cigarettes. The success of that crop in the limestone-rich soil of Christian County did much to ensure the prosperity of the Cayces and Majors, and made the region the dark tobacco capital of Kentucky, as it remains to this day.

Tom Cayce became one of the best farmers and businessmen in the county, second only, perhaps, to his brother George, who was twenty-two years his elder and outlived him by sixteen years. In addition to an original farm consisting of 205 acres, Tom owned and farmed 122 acres that he acquired through extensive land trading and was also partners with George in the highly successful Hopkinsville tobacco planters' warehouse.

In 1851, Tom married his cousin, Sarah Thomas, from Piney Fork, Tennessee, and during their thirty-year marriage the couple had seven sons and one daughter: Edgar, Leslie, Ella, Clint, Matthew, Robert E. Lee, Lucian, and Delbert. Their home grew larger as each son married, for Tom and Sarah required their newlywed children to live with them for their first year of marriage.

Tom's neighbors, Howard and Uriah L. Major, were brothers who had moved to Kentucky in 1828 from Madison County, Virginia. Family legend held that Uriah, who was known as U. L., built his home out of bricks he had imported from England, though this story is probably not accurate given that Christian County produced some of the finest red-clay bricks in the country. Howard constructed his house entirely out of wood, with hand-hewn and pegged-oak shingles. U. L.'s youngest daughter, Carrie Elizabeth Major, married Tom's second son, Leslie, and they would later become the parents of Edgar Cayce Jr.

Along with his large home, Tom Cayce built a smokehouse, two barns for curing tobacco, and stables so large that his men could drive a team of four horses through any door and turn them around inside. His children remember Tom as being as proud of these buildings as he was of the land they were built upon. Everything had to be kept neat and orderly and was always properly maintained. As Thomas Jefferson, after whom Tom Cayce had been named, said: "The greatest fertilizer that a field can experience is the shadow of its owner."

Tobacco's importance to Tom Cayce, and to his grandson Edgar Jr., cannot be overstated. Tom raised tobacco his entire life. Edgar did so until he was sixteen. And they lived in a community where social status was determined by their skills as tobacco farmers and where the entire community attended churches that passed the collection plate once at the end of each year, when the fall tobacco harvest had been sold.

Tom loved the lore and conversation of tobacco growing as much as he loved the smell of tobacco smoke. He also adored the social aspects of it: the pooling of family resources and labor during the harvesting and planting, when all the Cayces came together to help each other get the job done. These times of hardest work were also times of the largest meals, when long tables filled with ham, hominy, corn cakes, and beans were set out in the yard. There was always much conversation, laughter, music, and dipping of the ladle into the whiskey barrel.

There was no doubt that Tom liked to drink. Edgar Jr. mentions it in his letters, and describes Tom Cayce as "a grand, good man," but also says that Tom, "like so many of the Cayces, was his own worst enemy. He would take too much now and then causing anxiety and even want in many ways." However, Tom didn't become abusive or mean-spirited when he drank, and this was not the reputation that followed him beyond the grave. What people remembered Tom Cayce for most was his alleged psychic ability, which Sarah Cayce called "the gift of the second sight." Exactly what this "second sight" was remains something of a mystery, for unlike his grandson, Tom Cayce's "gift" was never tested in a formal setting, or even discussed beyond family circles.

The talent that Tom had as a "water witch," or dowser, has never been disputed. He would cut a forked limb from a peach tree, grasp a branch in each hand, and, holding the limb in front of his chest, walk back and forth over a parcel of land until he felt the "vibrations" that told him where a well should be dug. The fact that he was particularly good at this, however, is not proof that he used psychic powers to locate water. And as any Christian County farmer will point out, the land around Beverly is full of underground streams and hidden pools. Anyone could pick a spot, dig deep enough, and eventually find water.

Beyond being a good dowser, however, Tom is alleged to have had psychokinetic powers—the ability to move objects without touching them. Edgar said that his grandfather could make a broom appear to "dance" by merely holding his hand over it, or move a table without touching it. According to Sarah, Tom's wife, he rarely used the "energy" in his hands to move inanimate objects, choosing instead to channel his energy to make plants grow, "as God intended," and to make animals behave. A deeply religious man, he believed it was evil to use it in any other way, and that the Lord would take the power away from him if he used it to do tricks for entertainment purposes.

However exaggerated the accounts of Tom's unusual "psychic" powers might have been, the fact remains that he and his extended family believed he could do things that were beyond the abilities of normal human beings. This is not only important to his own story, but to that of his grandson, for it went a long way toward creating an environment that was not hostile to behavior that might otherwise have been seen as abnormal or even evil. As Edgar's devoted mother repeatedly admonished her son, "The Lord works in mysterious ways. It's not ours to question His intentions."

Of course, the rural farming communities of Kentucky had many beliefs and practices that would be characterized today as superstitious. These included the hour and day a hog should be butchered, the way a corpse was prepared and displayed for burial, the significance of an owl hooting in the daytime, and certain odors in a smokehouse before a rainstorm. They also believed that the dead sometimes appeared as spirits, as evidenced by the rich and varied ghost stories that circulated throughout the region in the late 1800s. A favorite story was that of an unfortunate black servant who had been raped and murdered on a farm outside of Hopkinsville. Her face was said to have appeared in a tree that grew out of her grave.

There was also a long tradition of using clairvoyance to solve problems and heal the sick. Two notable psychics of the time were Dr. Schlatter of Henderson, Kentucky, who healed by the laying on of hands, and Blind Mary, a sightless black medium who lived outside of Hopkinsville on the Clarksville Pike. Blind Mary was so well respected that the mayor of Hopkinsville routinely consulted her on business and family decisions.

It is doubtful that Tom Cayce ever used his talents as Blind Mary did. He didn't take his powers for granted, but he also didn't make a show of them. The fact that Tom had been attending Liberty Church since before the church had a regular pastor, and that he had publicly pledged his faith and was baptized in front of his friends and family a few months before his fiftieth birthday, is further indication that he saw no conflict between his faith in the Lord and his special gifts.

Leslie Burr Cayce, Tom's second-born son and Edgar's father, manifested no such psychic ability, and except for his drinking and good looks, shared little if anything in common with his father. Although Tom Cayce enjoyed farming and the fields of his youth, his son Leslie was more at home in the smoke-filled public meetings held behind the Liberty Church, playing cards at the Beverly Store, or gambling with tobacco futures at the planters' association meeting room. It was perhaps as a result of volatile disagreements at the planters' association meetings, or fistfights in his teenage years, that Leslie was reported to have had nearly every bone in his body broken at least once before his twenty-first birthday.

Leslie Cayce was a man of neat appearance, with clothes always well pressed, shoes shined, and, except for a neatly waxed handlebar mustache, a clean-shaven face. His brothers described him as a man who was always looking for new inventions, and in several instances he took exclusive sales rights for items such as butter churns and gate locks. He was a good speaker, loved to debate, and by all accounts, enjoyed life. "I wish I could be as optimistic as my dad used to be," Edgar later wrote of his father. "He was a very unusual man in many ways, and his expressions 'as good as new' and 'tip top' are still voiced by many who knew him."

Leslie married Carrie Elizabeth Major on June 10, 1874, when he was not yet twenty and she barely seventeen. Photographs of Carrie show a thin, plain-looking young woman with a large, prominent nose and dark hair that she tied in a bun. People who knew her, however, have been more generous with their compliments of her physical appearance. They describe her as quite attractive—almost radiant—and tall to the point of being statuesque. There is no doubt that she had a warm and generous personality with a deep love for children. Edgar would later describe her as "genteel and courteous on the one hand, loving, forgiving, compassionate, and God fearing on the other."

By all accounts, Tom Cayce and the rest of the Cayce clan considered Leslie's choice to be a good one, for she was a Major first and foremost, and the daughter first in line to inherit a few hundred acres of her father's prosperous farm. The Major family may not have viewed the union quite as favorably as the Cayces. Although they would presumably have approved of her marriage to a Cayce, Leslie was not a good farmer and was generally considered to be a spendthrift and a playboy. As best as can be inferred from the historical record, Carrie must have been swept off her feet by her fast-talking, easy-living suitor. The fact that her own father was an alcoholic perhaps numbed her to the fact that Leslie drank to excess. She conceived her first child within days of their wedding night.

The joy of their union was short-lived. Leslie ultimately spent much of his time away from home, presumably chasing other women and get-rich-quick schemes. Debts quickly piled up. For a girl who had grown up the center of attention of an adoring father and four brothers, and who had been waited upon by her own servant, the shock of finding herself doing the housework as well as managing the farm must have been daunting. Moreover, Leslie, who had an eighth-grade education and an inflated opinion of himself, made and enforced the rules of the house. Carrie, who had attended the Baptist-run Bethel Female College in Hopkinsville, was permitted no decision-making power. Her sole comfort was in her children, whom she doted upon, and her close friendship with Leslie's sister, Ella Cayce Jones.

There is no doubt that Leslie was a poor farmer. Repeated attempts to farm the 166 acres that Carrie inherited from her father proved futile, and the property was turned over to creditors soon after the birth of their first child. A few months later, she and Leslie were renting a two-room cottage behind the Beverly Store, located near the intersection of the Palmyra Pike and LaFayette Road. The reason offered by the Cayce family for Leslie's failure as a farmer was not his inability to raise crops, but rather an obsessive fear of snakes dating back to childhood. According to his brothers, snakes were strangely attracted to Leslie. It didn't seem to matter if they were harmless garter snakes or deadly water moccasins. If he put his hat down on the ground a snake would crawl into it or curl around the crown. If he stood still long enough they wrapped themselves around his ankles or crawled up a pant leg. They apparently never harmed him, they just liked to be near him.

Leslie always said that this "vexing" attraction of snakes greatly contributed to his desire to drink. Upon encountering a snake, he was said to take a shot of whiskey to calm his nerves. But where Tom Cayce was said to love his bourbon, his son Leslie sometimes let the bottle take control of him. When drunk, he was angry and belligerent and sometimes took a whip to his children.

The most notable incident involving his drinking occurred on December 24, 1875, the night his and Carrie's first child, Leila Beverly Cayce, was born and died. They were living in a home on Carrie's brother's farm because the land Carrie inherited hadn't come with a house on it. No specific details of what happened on that Christmas Eve night exist except for a reference in a letter, which Edgar would write years later to an old family friend, that said that Leslie got "mad" drunk and stormed out of the house. The next morning the child was found dead in her crib. Family members have long alluded to a connection between his drinking and the child's death, but no evidence exists to support or deny such a claim.

Leslie's brothers often referred to Leslie in their correspondence as "selfish" and "self-centered," and took him aside for heart-to-heart talks. It was they who convinced him to lease the Beverly Store, located in a quarter-mile-long settlement of homes and other buildings that included a blacksmith shop, a doctor's office, a church, and a one-room schoolhouse. Leslie traded what remained of his wife's inheritance for dry goods and other inventory.

Despite the fact that the store didn't do very well under Leslie's management, he clearly took more pleasure and pride in it than he had in farming. The store carried everything from buggy whips to potato mashers. Leslie sold shoes for $2, a bushel of meal for 40 cents, and a pound of coffee for 20 cents. For each dollar spent on dry goods, a customer was entitled to one drink from a barrel of whiskey. Leslie's duties not only included managing the store and its merchandise, but being post master and justice of the peace, which is how he came to be known as "Squire Cayce."

Edgar Jr., named after his father's older brother, was born at 3:20 P.M. on Sunday, March 18, 1877, fourteen months after the death of his sister, Leila. Dr. John L. Dulin, one of Beverly's two resident physicians, assisted with the birth. The delivery went smoothly and nothing unusual was noted about the condition of the child or his mother. He was called Edgar Jr., not because he was technically a Jr., but to distinguish him from his uncle Edgar, who was a regular visitor to the house.

Leslie had nothing but praise for his son. "He was, we thought, an exceptionally fine baby, healthy, with large brown eyes, fat and rosy cheeks, and a remarkably cheerful face," he later reminisced. However glowing his report, Leslie's powers of observation left room for improvement. His son's eyes were not brown, but a blue that grew darker in passing years.

During his first month, Edgar cried incessantly and only stopped when Patsy Cayce, a former slave of Tom Cayce's, who now had a room of her own in his house, treated him for "milk breast," a common malady resulting from a hormonal imbalance at birth. The hormones passed on to the child from the mother cause the child's breasts to become enlarged. Patsy took a sterilized needle and pricked each of Edgar's nipples, whereupon a milk-colored fluid came out. Leslie noted that the child rarely ever cried after that and soon began "cooing" or making a "jolly sort of grunt" whenever someone entered the room.

Once Edgar began to crawl, he would not stay still. Leslie remembers coming home from his store one rainy day for lunch. After sitting down to chat with Carrie and to play with Edgar, he returned to the store, leaving Edgar to crawl about. Carrie went back to her household duties. But soon afterward, she heard a loud cry from outside the front door and ran to find Edgar lying outside on the ground, with sheets of rain water from the porch gutter pouring over him. Evidently he had gotten out the door and fallen off the porch while trying to follow Leslie to work.

A far more serious accident occurred on May 27, 1880, when Edgar, now three years old, fell headfirst off a fence post onto a board with a nail protruding out of it. The nail went so deeply into his head that it reportedly punctured his cranium and entered his brain cavity. Leslie, who had seen the accident happen, immediately ran to him and removed the nail. Carrie was following close behind. After the initial trauma of the fall, Edgar appeared to be perfectly fine. Turpentine was poured onto the open wound, the head was bandaged, and the child eventually resumed his normal play.

The degree to which this injury may have left lasting physiological damage or altered Edgar's normal brain development is not known. It must be pointed out, however, that other psychics, among them Dutch-born Peter Hurkos, attributed the development of their psychic abilities to similar blows they suffered to the head, which they believe stimulated their pineal or pituitary glands. Little or nothing is said about this incident by those who knew or wrote about Edgar in his later years, perhaps because Cayce himself believed that his gifts were given him from God and were not of physiological origin.

A final episode of Edgar's early childhood is worth noting. At the age of three, he had gone wading out into a pond at his grandfather's house after a heavy rainstorm. He discovered many fish that had been stranded in the shallows. Edgar was busily catching them in his hands and putting them into deeper water when he lost his footing and fell in over his head. A former slave who worked for his grandfather came to Edgar's rescue and was credited with saving his life.

Carrie gave birth to another daughter, Annie Cayce, in 1878, and would subsequently give birth to four more children; Thomas, Ola, Mary, and Sarah. With her hands full, and with Leslie at the store, she hired an eleven-year-old nephew, Edward Cayce, to look out for Edgar. This was an arrangement, Leslie said, that proved "quite satisfactory."

Not long after Edgar's "big brother" came on board, Dr. Dulin, the physician who assisted at Edgar's birth, came to take meals with the Cayces. He was a bachelor who lived alone and operated out of an office adjacent to the Beverly store. Most of the Cayces and Majors believed that he disliked children, so it was only natural that Leslie and Carrie were not certain that he would ever consent to being seated at the dinner table with their son. While Dulin initially protested, he did agree to give the arrangement a try. To everyone's surprise, Dulin not only became reconciled to the situation, but actually came to enjoy Edgar's company.

By the time Edgar had begun to talk, at age two, Dr. Dulin had begun showing him around his office, introducing him to patients and remarking that Edgar was the "best" and "most interesting" child he had ever known. Dulin would talk and joke with him, sometimes imitating Edgar's mannerisms. He was the first to call Edgar "old man," a nickname that stuck throughout his early childhood. Edgar didn't mind it. In fact, he seemed to like it better than his own name, although he preferred Eddy, or simply Cayce.

As he grew older, Edgar often visited his father's store, where he quickly became familiar with the inventory and could, when asked, retrieve items for customers. When business was slow, Edgar was quite content to sit quietly among the barrels and boxes and listen to the men discuss politics and farming. He also liked the occasional talk of women as they bought yards of cloth, barrels of sugar, sacks of rice, herbs, tea, or medicine. Most of the customers were cousins, uncles, aunts, or people from the Major farms. They liked little Eddy and paid him quite a bit of attention, although it did seem to them that he was quite precocious. One uncle described Edgar as a "grave, skinny, intense little boy," given to long periods of quiet. He acted, quite literally, like an "old man."

Nevertheless, Edgar's inquisitive nature was much in evidence. His favorite toy was a mechanical circus with two clowns, a ringmaster, several horses and their riders, and a small crowd of spectators that spun slowly around in a circle. Edgar liked to wind the toy up and turn it off and on, and it was not long before he wanted to take it apart to see what was inside. Leslie and Carrie knew ahead of time that he wouldn't be able to get it back together, but they let him dismantle it anyway because they were impressed by the "deep thought" he put into it.

In 1881, when Edgar was four years old, a real circus came to Hopkinsville, and Edgar was determined to go. Leslie was reluctant to close the store early and asked one of his brothers to take Edgar on ahead in his buggy. They would meet up later on. Upon arriving and throughout the show, Leslie and Carrie searched for Edgar and his uncle but couldn't find them. Afterward, when they still hadn't appeared, his parents became concerned. They eventually located Edgar's uncle, who said that Edgar had spotted his parents during the performance and had gone to join them. They immediately organized a search of the grounds and tent area. Shortly afterward, Edgar—not the least bit concerned—walked out of one of the tents deep in discussion with a neighbor from home.

Indeed, Edgar demonstrated remarkable independence, but his preference to play alone soon became a source of concern for his parents. He loved nothing better than to entertain himself in the garden behind the store where he built a teepee out of a row of butterbeans that were held up with cross sticks. It was here that he played with what he described as the "little folk." His parents thought of them as imaginary playmates, but they were intensely real to little Edgar. In fact, they would remain a part of his life for decades to come.

In a trance reading conducted forty years later, Edgar suggested that he had indeed been visited by spirit "entities," who at the time appeared in a form that would not frighten or threaten him. Their purpose, according to this reading, was to prepare him for the trials and tribulations to come, and many of these entities, if not all, were alleged to have been later reincarnated as people who became closely associated with the work.

All Leslie and Carrie knew about the "little folk" was what Edgar told them about the games they played in the vegetable garden. There were never more than seven or eight of them, boys and girls, all about his own age. They had names, personal backgrounds, and distinct personalities. The only things that apparently troubled Edgar was that they didn't appear to get wet when it rained and didn't like being seen by other people.

Edgar could become quite upset if a parent or another child interrupted his play time with the "little folk" and would sometimes cry. On one occasion his mother humored him by saying that she too saw his playmates and that they were outside waiting for him in the garden. Hearing this pleased Edgar greatly, and he immediately rushed to the vegetable garden to see them. From that moment on, Edgar believed that his mother actually saw his playmates.

Leslie never humored his son the way Carrie did, but he didn't mind listening to the curious stories Edgar told when visiting the Beverly Store. Leslie and his customers often remarked about the sophistication of Edgar's imagination—his "make-believe" friends weren't Kentucky farm children, they came from places that people in Beverly didn't talk about, let alone visit, such as Egypt and Persia. Leslie remembered one day when he sat next to Edgar in the family garden. Instead of becoming infuriated, as was often the case when he was interrupted during play, his son broke out in unexpected laughter. Leslie asked him what was so funny. Edgar turned and pointed to someone or something that only he could see.

Leslie and Carrie fully believed that their son's imaginary playmates would go away when his father gave up the Beverly Store and the family moved. Business was not as good as they had hoped, primarily because too many customers sat around and drank whiskey instead of shopping. Leslie decided to try his luck farming again and in 1880 he sold the store and moved into the Benjamin Thompson house, which was located on one of the Cayce farms about 2½ miles from Beverly and a short walk to the home of

Tom and Sarah Cayce, Edgar's grandparents. The Thompson house was much bigger than the tiny one they had lived in behind the store. In addition to seven bedrooms in the main house, there was a large barn for curing tobacco and a stable where Leslie kept a fine white stallion, which he used to ride to Hopkinsville. Behind the stable was an old cemetery, nestled among a stand of cedar trees.

Edgar's baby-sitter was no longer needed at the new house since Tom Cayce was pleased to watch over his grandson. Carrie was relieved to have the extra help, as was Leslie. Besides, Tom and Edgar took to one another instantly. They didn't just spend an hour or two together at a time, but three or four days in a row. They were, as old family friends would later contend, "cut from the same tree." And although no one came out and said as much, the suggestion has always been that old Tom Cayce's talent for handling his grandson was much like his talent for handling the forked limb from the peach tree he kept by the family hearth, which he used to locate water wells. "That boy literally came alive in his hands," one of Leslie's brothers once remarked.

Leslie had never seen his son so content. According to him, Edgar often napped in Tom's arms and was never happier than when he was wrapped in Tom's long coat. On the nights that he stayed over at his grandparents' house, Edgar would curl up and sleep next to Tom. Sarah said that she would wake up and see little Edgar clutching his grandfather's beard in his little fists. In addition to teaching Edgar to fish and ride horseback, Tom helped Edgar build playhouses out of the tall grass and brush that grew along the banks of the Little River. Their favorite place was the barn where Tom cured tobacco. In the fall, Edgar and his grandfather would watch as farmhands burned great slabs of hickory, and the thick smoke rose through the tiers on which the stalks of tobacco hung. Both he and his grandfather loved the pungent scent of the dark tobacco being fired. They also liked the smell in the smokehouse, where the burning hickory mixed with sassafras chips created an incense that drifted to the meat hanging from the rafters.

During one of their many rides together, Tom Cayce had a terrible accident. It is not known for certain whether Tom had been drinking or not, although it has long been rumored that he had. The date was June 8, 1881. Edgar, just four years old, was riding behind Tom on a favorite mare. Heading for the machinery house, where Edgar's uncle Lucian was repairing a binder, they stopped to water the horse at the pond near the barn and Tom let Edgar down to catch minnows, his favorite pastime.

As the story goes, Tom's horse was startled by what may have been a water moccasin emerging from under a buried tree root. The horse bolted, plunged into the water, and swam to the other side. Tom managed to remain in his saddle. The horse, reaching the other side of the pond, tried to jump a fence, failed, and then turned back. At that point the horse stumbled, throwing Tom into the water. Edgar, on the other side of the pond, looked on as the horse reared up and brought its hoofs down on Tom's chest. Lester Major, Tom's young neighbor, was soon at the scene. Edgar had to show him where Tom had disappeared into the water. Dr. Alexander Kenner, a physician who lived nearby, was called for help, but Tom was surely dead before they were able to pull him out of the water. Tom had either been knocked unconscious and drowned or had died from having his chest crushed under the horse's hoofs.

Tom's body was brought inside the house that same day. As was the custom, his sons and brothers washed and dressed him. Then the body was laid out on a long "cooling board," fully clothed, except for shoes. The lower part of the body was draped with a dark cotton cloth. Edgar watched as all the Cayces arrived by carriage and buckboard at his grandfather's house for the funeral. His uncles Edgar, Clint, Matthew, Robert E. Lee, Lucian, and Delbert all were there, along with his granduncles; George Washington, James Monroe, and Franklin Pierce. His aunt Ella Jones was there as were his uncles on the Major side.

An undertaker arrived from Hopkinsville with a large oak coffin that had metal handles and a thin pane of glass set into the top. Tom's body was taken off the cooling board, placed inside, and then they closed the lid. Although Edgar saw his grandfather go into the coffin, he didn't get to see the coffin going into the ground. Patsy Cayce stayed with him while his uncles and aunts went around to the family cemetery in the garden behind the house.

Despite the close relationship that had developed between Edgar and his grandfather, Edgar seemed less perturbed by the tragedy than might have been expected. This could be attributed to his youth. But it was also true that even as a young child, Edgar's perception of his grandfather's death wasn't the same as it was for other family members. Not long after the funeral, Edgar's parents found him standing in the tobacco barn "conversing" with his deceased grandfather.

2.

❖

Little Friends
and Little Anna

Reports that Edgar could allegedly speak to his dead grandfather remained a closely guarded family secret until the child went to stay with his aunt Lou. Edgar temporarily moved into the home of Lulu Boyd Cayce and her husband, Clint, so that Carrie could more easily care for Leslie's mother, who had been injured in a fire that destroyed the top floor of the old family home. Although her injuries were minor, Leslie decided that it was best that his mother, Sarah Cayce, stay in Edgar's bedroom until her health improved and the family home could be repaired. The arrangement proved suitable for everyone concerned. Edgar enjoyed the company of Aunt Lou and Uncle Clint, and since they had no children of their own at that time, the young couple was free to lavish the kind of attention on their young nephew that Edgar would otherwise have had to share with his two siblings. Edgar also got to see his mother and father frequently since his aunt and uncle lived nearby in a small home on a farm owned by Leslie's great-uncle James Monroe Cayce.

The subject of Edgar's conversations with his dead grandfather was first raised on a warm afternoon when Edgar and his Aunt Lou were outside gathering wild mustard greens for supper. Lulu asked Edgar why he spent so much time alone in the tobacco barn. Edgar told her that he wasn't alone—he was visiting his grandfather. Edgar told her that "grampa" came to the barn to help the farmhands hang the tobacco. He didn't talk to the farmhands as he did with Edgar, but worked alongside them, helping without their knowing it by reminding them of chores that needed to be done. Edgar went on to say that grampa could sometimes be hard to see, that he appeared in "beams of light" that shone from between the rafters in the ceiling, and that if Edgar looked really hard, he could see right through him. Grampa's favorite place to sit was under the eaves, near where a robin had built a nest. Edgar offered to show it to his aunt, but she declined.

Edgar's claims upset and frightened his aunt Lou because he also told stories about the Cayce family's distant past. These stories were not the kind easily produced by the overactive imagination of a five-year-old. They were authentic stories about the Cayce family's early years in Virginia and Kentucky—stories that only Tom and his generation would be likely to know. After repeatedly questioning Edgar, Lulu Cayce advised his parents that they should take Edgar to see a doctor, or at the least a priest. "He's got the Devil in him," she told Leslie. "No good can come of this."

Leslie and Carrie did not heed Lulu's advice, despite the concern from other family members about Edgar. His younger sister Annie had become so frightened by her brother's behavior that she didn't like to play with him. It wasn't just his alleged conversations with his dead grandfather, but his ongoing activities with imaginary playmates.

According to Edgar, the "little folk" appeared at Aunt Lulu and Uncle Clint's farm in even greater numbers than they had back at the Beverly Store. They now had parents, brothers, and sisters, first and last names, and were less interested in playing games with him than they were with talking to him and teaching him things. Their favorite place to meet was under a tent of vines and branches that Edgar had built beneath the cedar trees at the old family cemetery. Here they would talk to Edgar as he searched for small pieces of colored glass between the tombstones.

It must have been quite a relief to Edgar's parents when their son made friends with a neighborhood girl, little Hallie Seay, who was a year older than Edgar. She was the daughter of Hallie and Barney Seay, from whom Leslie had taken over the Beverly store. Barney and his wife had bought the property across the road from the Thompson house, torn down the existing structure, and built a quaint three-bedroom home, which is still standing today. Petite, dark-haired Hallie was born in April 1876, and was called Little Anna to differentiate her from her mother.

Little Anna and Eddy became inseparable. In the winter they would run through the fields trying to catch snowflakes in their mouths or play games around the covered bridge near his uncle Frank Cayce's house. Their summer activities included chasing dragonflies and collecting violets in the pasture behind the Liberty Church, playing along the banks of the Little River, or watching the farmers haul corn to Steger's Mill on the road near Pat Major's farm. Most important to Edgar, the "little folk" liked Anna as much as he did. And she—according to Edgar—got to know them better than he because she was always plying them with questions.

Edgar and Anna's favorite place to play was in the barn adjacent to the Thompson house. Perched on the upper beams of the barn, they had great fun leaping onto the haystack and then sliding down the side. They also hollowed out a hiding place inside the haystack, which they entered through a narrow tunnel. This was where they would "play house" together. Edgar would be the husband, she would be the wife, and the little folk would be their children.

Their greatest adventure was during a trip to the Little River. They came upon a boat that had come loose from its mooring and drifted downstream, and Edgar and Anna availed themselves of the opportunity to take a boat ride. They paddled out into the current until they came to a small island near a fork in the river. As Edgar later related the story in his memoirs, the little folk joined him and Anna on the island, where they introduced the two children to creatures who were smaller than the little folks, but larger than insects. Edgar described these creatures to his parents as fairies or "sprites" and said they came in a variety of shapes and colors. He and Anna didn't get to spend much time with the creatures because they reportedly didn't like to play with children. They wanted nothing to do with human beings, whom they viewed as interfering in their affairs.

Edgar's family naturally dismissed the notion of fairies as yet another figment of their child's ever-expanding imagination. But Edgar would never agree that he hadn't really seen them. He just learned not to talk about them, a lesson he carried with him when he later had visions of angels and other "spiritual guides." Many years would elapse before he would describe to friends his belief that these colorful "energy forms" lived in and among plants and trees and played an integral role in their growth process. Like the little folk he played with under the butterbeans, the colorful bundles of energy were transformed into shapes and forms to which a young child could relate. It is interesting to note—given the many parallels that Cayce's later work shared with those of Rudolf Steiner, the spiritual psychologist and

Cayce's Austrian contemporary—that Steiner also reported childhood visions of gnomes and elves, as did Eileen Garrett, the famous Irish-born psychic.

Edgar's parents described the eighteen months he spent with Little Anna as the happiest of his childhood, and although she was older than he, her companionship clearly enhanced any psychic or imaginative powers that the young Cayce exhibited. Unfortunately, their relationship ended all too quickly. In December 1882, Edgar's father uprooted the family once again, the result of a poor tobacco harvest, and over the next eight months they moved three times. Their first move was from the Thompson house back to the Beverly Store, where in addition to assuming his previous duties as postmaster and justice of the peace, Leslie also shared part-time responsibilities with his brother Lucian as a schoolteacher. Business turned out to be even more difficult for the Squire the second time around—Carrie's brother George Major had opened another general store across the road, greatly cutting into Leslie's share of the crossroads trade. Unable to make the store profitable, Leslie moved the family back to his parent's home, and then into a small cabin that he and his brothers built in a stand of trees nearby. Edgar was 5½ years old.

It was more than just the move back to the store that made their last winter at the Thompson house emotionally difficult for the family. Carrie had given birth to another son on November 19, 1882, whom they named Thomas, after Leslie's father. There is no record if Carrie carried the child to term, nor are any details known about the circumstances of the child's birth, only that Thomas lived for ten days and was buried beside his grandfather in the small cemetery under the cedars.

Edgar's mother fell into a depression that lasted throughout the winter, during which time she became quite frail and developed asthma, an affliction that would plague her until her death thirty-five years later. She took to her bed for three or four days at a time, sometimes coughing so loudly that she could be heard outside. No one in the family, least of all Carrie herself, spoke openly about the tragedy, and in the years to come, the name of her infant son never appeared in their correspondence.

Edgar's recollections of his mother's anguish at the loss of her baby were vivid, and he often referred to this period in his family's life as a particularly troubling one. He described seeing his mother unexpectedly burst into tears in the middle of the day, drop to her knees, and ask the Lord for His blessings and His help. Having never before seen her cry, nor pray, the sight left an indelible impression. He soon began to pray with her. The experience must have been a powerful healing force for both mother and son because it was an activity that they were to practice frequently in the years to come, and prayer was a subject that would ultimately engage Edgar for the rest of his life.

His brother's death was not the only tragedy for which Edgar and his mother sought solace in prayer. The move away from the Thompson house had separated him from Little Anna, and their separation was made permanent when she later contracted and died of pneumonia in January 1892. Edgar, then fourteen, is reported to have walked several miles through the snow to be with his childhood friend when the end came. She was buried in a small coffin near her home, where she was soon joined by her father, Barney Seay, who died a day later from pneumonia contracted while nursing her. Like Edgar's dead grandfather, Little Anna would reappear in Edgar's life, but not for many years to come, and not as the delicate brown-haired young girl with whom he had explored Little River.

Anna's death touched Edgar in ways that his parents could only speculate, for it coincided with the disappearance of the little folk. Though Edgar would continue to build special places in the woods where he could be alone, his spirit companions stopped visiting him. And although Edgar returned to the old tobacco barn many times, his grandfather no longer appeared under the robin's nest in the eaves. Tom Cayce's appearance in the barn would become no more than a distant memory of Edgar's childhood.

There is no record of whether or not Edgar's parents were aware of the loneliness that engulfed their son during the difficult years of his childhood. Perhaps the first time they would have sensed that something was wrong was when he enrolled in the Beverly School in the fall of 1883, at the age of six.

Like other subscription schools of its day, the Beverly School, which was located behind the Liberty Church, was built and operated by the families of its students. It was not uncommon for one family to supply the timber for the building, another the school books, and a third the room and board for the teacher. Because all the families in the community relied upon the tobacco crop, the school term coincided with the planting and harvesting seasons. Children from the ages of six to sixteen attended, and for the vast majority, this school was the only formal education they would receive. The schoolhouse had two entrances, one for girls and one for boys. Inside were four rows of hard-backed wooden desks with inkwells. At the front of the room was a large black-slate chalkboard and a rectangular oak desk for the teacher. A coal stove sat in one corner, a dunce's chair in the other.

It was the dunce's chair where Edgar would soon find himself. The problem wasn't that he misbehaved or was a slow learner. Edgar was simply unable to concentrate on anything for more than a few minutes at a time and developed a reputation as being "strange." Even when he did apply himself to his studies, he was out of step with his classmates, too shy and ill-equipped to handle himself in a social setting.

Lela Cox, his first teacher, considered Edgar to be a daydreamer. She punished him for not paying attention and frequently embarrassed him by making him stand while other students were permitted to sit. Edgar was already self-conscious about his height, and the increased attention only made matters worse. At the age of seven he was already well over four feet tall, and his thin, gangly legs kept getting tangled under his desk.

The situation didn't improve when the Beverly School closed and the Beverly Academy opened its doors near the Beverly Store. Residents viewed the new school as an improvement, for although there were still only one teacher and one room, the building accommodated twice as many students. It was the last school that Edgar would attend.

From the moment he entered the new school in September 1889, Edgar was constantly getting into fights. His aunt Lou and his mother had taught him to be careful about what he said about himself, but Edgar's reputation had preceded him. Everyone in the class, including his new teacher, U. L. Clardy, a cousin of Edgar's on his mother's side, had heard stories about him talking to ghosts. The fact that Edgar had no apparent interest in playing baseball, shooting marbles, or any of the other popular school games aggravated an already tense situation. The only saving grace was that two-thirds of the school was either Cayces or Majors, and for every brawl that Edgar got into, he had a cousin to come to his rescue. But even they couldn't save him from the teacher. Clardy routinely whipped Edgar for not paying closer attention to his studies.

Reading was the only subject that interested him. This was triggered by a conversation that Edgar had had with a black woodcutter who lived on his grandfather's old farm, and who may have been the same hired hand and former slave who had saved Edgar from drowning in the pond when he was just a toddler. People in Beverly called the woodcutter "Crazy Bill," because he was, as Edgar himself later said, "not quite right in the head."

Edgar happened to talk to Bill on the road on his way home from school one day when Bill was removing a tree that had fallen across the road. "I'm feeling as strong as Samson," Bill said as he wielded his ax. Edgar didn't know who Samson was, so Bill proceeded to recount the Old Testament story of how Samson was strong enough to pull a house down, and that he killed a thousand men with the jaw bone of an ass. No sooner had Edgar arrived home than he wanted to know all about the Bible, the people in it, and what went on in church, where people read it. The family didn't have a Bible at the time—theirs had been destroyed with other family heirlooms in the fire at the old homestead—nor did his parents attend church regularly, though Leslie, in later years, frequently told journalists that he and his family had come from a long line of churchgoers. The truth is that Edgar's immediate family didn't start attending services regularly until late 1886, when their nine-year-old son unrelentingly pestered them to take him.

The first Bible that Edgar ever held in his hands was quite large and heavily illustrated, and belonged to his aunt Ella. She showed him a black-and-white woodcut depicting Samson pulling down the pillars of the temple. Bolts of lightning from heaven captured the ferocity of Samson's strength and illustrated God's power. Edgar couldn't take his eyes off the picture as Ella read him the story, and no sooner had he returned home than he hounded his father to get him a Bible of his own. Leslie stopped at the Hopper Bookstore on his next trip into Hopkinsville and told its owner, Elijah Hopper, that his adolescent son wanted a Bible more than anything else. Impressed, the elderly Hopper presented Leslie with a Bible for Edgar. It was inscribed on the day of the gift, January 14, 1887.

Edgar immediately tried to read it. At first he couldn't pronounce the names and had to have his mother and father follow along with him. Frequently they would take turns reading and would end each scripture session with a prayer. By early the following year Edgar could read many passages of the Bible without help and soon was reading it entirely on his own. For the rest of Edgar's life, a Bible was seldom out of his reach, and as numerous pastors willingly attested, no one they had ever met could quote scripture or knew its stories as thoroughly as Edgar did.

A painful accident that occurred on January 9, 1888, would ultimately allow him to devote many hours to his program of home Bible study. While walking in the woods early one evening, Edgar tripped and fell onto the sharp end of a stick. The point pierced his trousers and went right through one of his testicles. He was treated that same evening by both of Beverly's doctors, Dulin and Kenner, but had great difficulty recuperating because of an infection that spread throughout his groin area. Excused from chores and school, he spent much of that entire year in bed, alternately suffering from chills and fever, and reading his Bible. By the time he had returned to his daily routine of farm chores, he had read the Old and New Testament three times in their entirety.

Dulin and Kenner were unable to effect a complete cure for Edgar. The person who would eventually come to his aid was Emily Cayce, the daughter of Patsy Cayce. Using a time-tested folk remedy, she provided Edgar with the only comfort he had known since the accident. She had him drink an elixir she had prepared from spiderwebs. Edgar later described the cure to doctors by jokingly telling them that he had been "hoodooed" by his "colored mammy." All humor aside, the injury was the most painful physical trauma of his life, and, much as his mother had sought to bury the anguish she felt at Thomas's death, Edgar never would speak openly of his suffering.

Once he was finally up and out of bed, Edgar continued to read the Bible. He carried it with him everywhere he went and eventually asked his mother to sew what he called a "hind pocket" on his overalls so that it could be transported more easily and safely.

Edgar naturally took an interest in the Old Testament stories about what might now be termed supernatural or psychic phenomena, though it would be many years before Edgar himself ever used those terms. One Bible story that held particular interest for the young Cayce was that of Moses, who, when sent into Egypt to deliver the chosen people, was told to take his shepherds crook, and with Aaron his brother, go before Pharaoh, and God would show His mighty wonders. As Moses went before the Pharaoh he cast his rod down and it turned into a serpent. The Pharaoh's magicians cast their rods down and they turned to serpents too, but Aaron's serpent ate them all up. To Edgar, God moved in mysterious ways, just as He had when He sent a whale to swallow Jonah or provided David the strength to subdue Goliath.

Edgar's interest in the Bible naturally led him to take a more active role in the Liberty Church, which he began attending the first Sunday in January 1887, and where, on November 13, 1888, he pledged his faith and was baptized by immersion in the Little River. During the next eight years, Edgar would miss only two services.

Liberty Church was a simple white-frame building with clapboard siding and had been built in 1856, when the congregation had outgrown the original Liberty meeting house from which the church took its name. The services each Sunday lasted approximately two hours and typically consisted of congregational prayers, a sermon, celebration of the "Lord's Supper," and hymn singing. No musical instruments were played. Although the collection plate was routinely passed among the parishioners, most of the contributions to the maintenance of the church came once each year, when the Beverly tobacco crop was sold.

Liberty Church was part of the immensely popular Christian Church, later known as the Disciples of Christ, which broke away from the Presbyterian Church during a revival in Lexington, Kentucky, in 1834. The original purpose of the Christian Church was to bring all Protestant churches and denominations together into one faith. The principal difference between it and the Presbyterian Church was that members of the Christian Church practiced open communion. They believed that Christ died for all who freely accepted Him as their savior, not just the "elect," as defined by the Presbyterians. The Christian Church also rejected all "man-made" creeds and accepted the Bible alone as its full and final authority.

The congregation numbered between seventy-five and a hundred during the years Edgar attended. Though it was not unusual for a ten-year-old to join the church, it was quite extraordinary for a child of that age to take such a keen interest in issues of doctrine and church management as Edgar did. He eagerly sat through the two-hour services, attended Sunday School, adult Bible study, and the meetings of the church elders, where he surprised the adults with his ability to quote long passages and interpret scripture. To many visiting pastors he expressed his firm and simple conviction that everything in the Bible was literally true. The miracles of old, he told a minister from Hopkinsville, were still possible.

Brother Granville Lipscomb, a church elder who had begun preaching when he was quite young, was so impressed by Edgar's sincerity that he appointed Edgar as the church sexton, a position that had never before or since been held by a child. This fact made Leslie a pleased and proud father, and for a short time, he took to teaching Sunday School and leading his family in evening Bible reading sessions. One of Edgar's fondest memories of his father was of the night when Leslie's younger brother Lucian came to the door of their house, calling to them several times to let him inside. Leslie adamantly continued reading scripture, only stopping to let him into the house when the requisite hour-long Bible reading session had ended.

Although Edgar had responsibilities at home, he took his duties at church quite seriously. He walked the quarter mile to church every Saturday, swept it out, cleaned the two outhouses, and filled a bucket with lime for parishioners to use in the outhouse. On Sundays he would arrive before sunrise. If it was winter, his first task was to stock the coal bin and build a fire in the stove. He would then prepare the communion table, draping the linen cloth over the table and putting out the "emblems"; the common cup for the wine and the communion plate for the bread. For eight years, Edgar's mother would bake bread to be used for the services at the Liberty Church.

Whenever the church officers got together it was usually Edgar who initiated Bible discussions. During one meeting, he heard a church elder—most likely Edgar's older cousin Jim Adams—declare that he had "read the Bible from cover to cover ten times." Immediately, Edgar determined that he would read it through once for each year of his life. His mother promised to help him.

Edgar's enthusiasm did not wane, but became more acute as his knowledge of the Bible increased. With this increase in knowledge came ever-greater curiosity and more difficult questions, which were not easily answered by the church elders or the visiting circuit-riding "brothers" who came to preach. Among the many questions Edgar had for the church elders was why his mother couldn't become an elder or deacon. Though she baked the bread for communion and understood the teachings better than he, she couldn't join the pastor or the elders at the communion table. The fact that Edgar didn't receive what he felt was an adequate explanation for this question didn't cool his interest in the church but inspired him to hound members of the congregation into adopting new practices. One former church elder recalled taking a different route to church each Sunday just to avoid being stopped and "interrogated" by Edgar.

The most pressing question that occupied his interest concerned prayer. Edgar couldn't understand how a person could call himself a true disciple of the Lord if he talked and talked to God and He didn't answer. Edgar fully expected and believed God would, and should, answer anyone who sincerely asked something of Him. It was this belief that undoubtedly led to what Edgar later described as the single most profound experience of his childhood: a visit by an angel.

This incident occurred in 1889, by which time Edgar and his family had moved to yet another house. The "cottage," or "little house in the woods," as Edgar later described this home, was located a short walk down a dirt road from the site of the old homestead and had been built the previous summer by Leslie with the help of his brothers. Edgar liked this home better than any of the others because it stood in the midst of a grassy meadow full of wildflowers and herbs and was surrounded on three sides by a stand of hickory, ash, elm, maple, poplar, and dogwood trees. Edgar selected a quiet spot under a gnarled willow tree a few hundred feet behind the house to build a retreat out of a crude canopy of saplings and vines covered with bark. Adjacent to the willow was a natural spring, which Leslie later tapped for water to save himself from digging a well. Beside the spring grew violets, jack-in-the-pulpits, crocuses, and jonquils. Edgar, who prided himself on learning all the names of plants and flowers in Beverly, was quite excited the morning he found a mandrake plant mentioned in the Bible.

Edgar spent many hours in his new retreat. His primary activities were reading from the Bible, praying to God, and watching the squirrels, birds, and other animals that came to drink out of the spring. Many accounts of

Edgar's childhood state that it was here, under the willow tree, that an angel appeared, causing Edgar to have the revelation that was the inspiration for his later career. Edgar himself, however, said that the angel appeared to him in his bedroom, after he had spent a long day reading his Bible in the woods and asking himself how he could be of service to the Lord. He had eaten dinner and, as usual, went to bed after helping his mother with the chores. His sisters were fast asleep in beds adjacent to his own when he suddenly awoke in the night and perceived what he described as a powerful light coming through the doorway.

"I felt as if I were being lifted up," Edgar later wrote. "A glorious light as of the rising morning sun seemed to fill the whole room, and a figure appeared at the foot of my bed. I was sure it was my mother and called [out], but she didn't answer. For the moment I was frightened, climbed out of bed, and went to my mother's room. No, she hadn't called. Almost immediately, after I returned to my couch, the figure came again. Then it seemed all gloriously bright—an angel, or what, I knew not, but gently, patiently, it said: 'Thy prayers are heard. You will have your wish. Remain faithful. Be true to yourself. Help the sick, the afflicted.' "

Edgar slept very little that night. Once the vision had faded, he rushed outside to his favorite tree, and through its branches the moon seemed to shine more brightly than he had ever seen it. He knelt beside the tree and thanked God for answering his prayers. In the morning, as the sun began to rise, he awoke to find himself still sitting under the tree. A squirrel came down from one of the branches and searched for nuts in Edgar's pocket. Edgar felt a sudden sense of joy and release, as if the mysteries of his early childhood had come into sharp focus. It was at that moment that Edgar believed he had obtained his first true insight into the life that lay ahead of him. He would be doing "God's work," though exactly what he was to do, and how he was to prepare himself were questions he hadn't yet begun to address.

3.

In the Company
of Angels

Edgar didn't immediately tell his mother and father about the angel. To have done so would surely have raised questions similar to those asked him by his aunt Lou. And even if he had felt up to facing an interrogation at home, and the one that would inevitably have followed at Liberty Church, he didn't feel he had the skills to convey the intense personal nature of his vision or to avoid public mockery and skepticism. "I had no way of knowing which was more real," he later confessed, "the vision of the lady or the pillow I rested my head upon."

More than three years would elapse before he summoned the courage to tell anyone about the angel's visit, and many more years passed before he was able to understand his vision in the broader context of his early childhood experiences. Ultimately, Edgar concluded that he, like his grandfather, had been born with special abilities, that as a youth he frequently had glimpsed a reality that could not normally be perceived through the five senses, and that the greatest challenge he faced during his early years was to translate what he perceived into something meaningful to his adolescent mind. The fact that the angel in his bedroom bore a striking resemblance to an illustration in his aunt's Bible didn't invalidate the experience or make its message less meaningful; it was merely the means for a young child—steeped in Christian mysticism—to experience what Edgar, as an adult, would sometimes experience when he entered a trance.

The fact that Edgar had what was later perceived to be psychic talents was becoming more apparent to him with each new year. A highly reported example occurred in 1890 when he was at the Beverly Academy and his uncle Lucian was his teacher. All previous accounts place this event as occurring the morning after Edgar experienced his angelic vision. Documentary evidence, however, suggests that the incident took place a year later, when Edgar was thirteen.

By Edgar's own admission, he was already quite "dull" and "backward" at school. He couldn't seem to concentrate on his lessons. "The voice of my uncle Lucian seemed very far away," Edgar later wrote. "The voice of the angel was quite near."

As part of his daily lessons, Lucian asked him to spell the word "cabin." Edgar couldn't do it and was asked to stay after school to write the word five hundred times on the chalkboard. While Edgar stayed behind at school, Lucian visited Leslie to inform him that Edgar was years behind where he should be in all his academic subjects. Leslie was furious. After Edgar got home and they had had dinner, Leslie took the spelling book and sat down "to help" Edgar with his next day's lesson.

Edgar read the words in his McGuffy's Reader and then spelled them out loud. But when the book was taken from him he was still unable to get the spelling right. Leslie became increasingly annoyed at his son's failure to learn such a simple lesson. Furious, he slapped Edgar two or three times with the back of his hand, then knocked him out of his chair. It was almost eleven o'clock at night. Edgar was tired. He wanted to cry. He told his father that if he had a few minutes to rest he knew he could do better. Leslie, tired himself by the struggle, agreed to a five-minute recess.

Edgar put the book down on the desk and laid his head down on it while his father went into the kitchen. When Leslie returned, Edgar told him he felt refreshed. Leslie put the first word to him, and Edgar spelled it correctly. He also correctly spelled the second word, then the third, and the fourth.

Initially, his father was pleased that all his work had apparently paid off. But as Edgar proceeded to spell the entire lesson correctly without so much as pausing, Leslie could only conclude that Edgar had cheated, or imagined that his son had pulled a practical joke at his expense—that he had known the lesson the entire time and had merely feigned ignorance.

Leslie leafed through the speller, picking out words at random. Edgar knew them all. Before long Edgar was telling his father where to find the words on the page. He knew exactly what column they were on and what words came before and after them. All he said he had to do was to close his eyes and he could picture exactly what the page looked like. Frustrated and confused, Leslie hit Edgar in the head for "fooling" with him—the last reported time Leslie would ever strike his son. Nothing more was said about the incident until the next day, when the truth of the matter was revealed to his uncle Lucian and his forty-eight classmates. All Edgar had to do, it seemed, was place a book against his forehead and he knew its contents perfectly.

From that day on, Edgar advanced rapidly in school. No one was able to keep up with him in any of his subjects. Edgar became so good at memorizing facts that the church elders gave him a column in the church program in which he answered difficult biblical questions. His ability to remember the contents of books was witnessed by many, and thanks to his father's bravado, was put to an unusual test. Leslie had a childhood friend, Congressman Jim McKenzie, who had recently been appointed the U.S. ambassador to Peru by President Cleveland. He and Leslie met in Hopkinsville to have a drink and celebrate the honor. Not to be outdone by his friend's success, Leslie bragged about Edgar. "My son can remember anything if he is allowed to sleep on it." McKenzie demanded proof, and Leslie wagered ten dollars that his son could memorize a 110-page speech that McKenzie had delivered in Congress. Moreover, he wasn't going to allow Edgar to hold or touch the speech.

Leslie read the speech aloud to Edgar before he went to sleep that night. The next day, he read it to him again. On the third night, standing alone on a raised dais, Edgar would recite all 110 pages in front of the entire school, assorted parents, and America's new ambassador to Peru. The recital took over one hour. Upward of fifty people, including two future mayors of Hopkinsville, and various teachers and visiting businessmen, witnessed the event, and an account later appeared in the *Kentucky New Era*.

Within a single year, fourteen-year-old Edgar Cayce moved from the third grade to the sixth grade. By this time, Lucian was no longer his teacher. He had been replaced by Bernardino Emelio Thom, who had been born in Mexico and spent his teen years in Fredericksburg, Virginia. Thom was not only to become Edgar's favorite teacher, but a much-admired educator who taught throughout Christian County and neighboring communities for over forty years.

Thom soon became aware of Edgar's unusual ability and took him aside to talk with him about it. Edgar's immediate reaction at being singled out was one of fear. He was already sensitive to the fact that he was not like his other classmates and was sure that Thom would think him unbalanced. But Thom put Edgar at ease. He listened intently to Edgar's description of how he could close his eyes and "visualize" each page of any given document.

Thom nodded approvingly and told a story about his father, Captain Thom, who had served as a marine on the iron-clad vessel *Merrimac* during the Civil War. According to Edgar's teacher, Captain Thom had a dreamlike vision in which he saw a plan and was given instructions for armor-plating his ship. Thom left his young student with the impression that what Edgar had been given was a "gift," something to be cherished and used. He also insisted that Edgar run out and play with the other boys, and for his own good, to do his best to try and "fit in."

One day Edgar was following Thom's suggestion by participating in a ball game similar to monkey in the middle. When it was Edgar's turn to stand in the middle, between the two other players, he was struck in the lower part of his spine by the baseball. He blacked out and remained unconscious until the next morning, when he woke up in his bedroom and saw Dr. Kenner standing over him. Along with Kenner were Edgar's grandmother and other family members who had held an all-night vigil.

There are slight variations in the various accounts of what transpired between the time Edgar passed out and the moment he awoke in bed. The one thing shared by all accounts is that during his blackout, Edgar appeared to be conscious but acted strangely, as if he had suddenly become possessed by a demon. His sister Annie, who was on the playground when the accident happened, provided what appears to be the most reliable account.

According to her, Edgar didn't seem to be physically hurt. After falling down, he got up, dusted himself off, and returned to the classroom when recess had ended. This was when he began to act "queerly," as Annie described it. He upset the routine at school by making rude remarks and speaking out of turn. On his way home from school he rolled on the ground, jumped in ditches, and stood in the middle of the road with his hands upraised to stop riders and carriages. He had a devilish grin on his face, suggesting a mischievous sort of pleasure.

At home his mother was roasting green coffee beans in a pan on the kitchen stove. He took the pan in his hands, unmindful of its heat, and went into the yard where he sowed the coffee as if it were seed. His strange behavior continued through dinner, where he threw food at his sisters and laughed uproariously. Angry, Leslie sent him to bed.

As soon as Edgar's head hit the pillow, he began to speak strangely. He talked about Professor Thom and his intimate relationship with the superintendent of the school, recounting information that Edgar—according to his father—couldn't possibly have known. At some point in Edgar's rambling diatribe he announced the outcome of the next presidential election, which was then in progress. "Hooray for Cleveland!" he shouted.

Indeed, Cleveland was winning the election at approximately the time Edgar let out his cheer. There were no telephones or telegraphs that could have relayed the information to the Cayce farm. Suddenly, Edgar became very earnest. He began to issue instructions to his father and mother to fix a poultice for the back of his head. Although the exact recipe was not put down on paper, all accounts agree that it consisted of corn meal, onions, herbs, and other things readily available in the Cayce pantry. "Do that and I'll be all right," he told Leslie and Carrie. But his parents, fearful that this was some trick or work of the devil, didn't act. It was Sarah Cayce, his grandmother, who collected the ingredients, prepared the poultice, and put it on the back of Edgar's head.

Dr. Kenner and the Cayce's other neighbors were confident that Edgar had lost his mind. But the next morning Edgar appeared to be fine. He climbed out of bed, dressed, and ate a large breakfast.

"He cured himself!" Leslie told neighbors.

4.

A Voice
from Beyond

The fact that he was different from other children had always been a source of insecurity and irritation to Edgar Cayce. As a teenager, it became an outright problem. This became clear during the summer after he turned fifteen and fell in love with sixteen-year-old Bessie Kenner, the daughter of Dr. Alexander and Mary Kenner, and the granddaughter of William E. Mobley, Liberty Church's most beloved minister.

Edgar had known Bessie his whole life, for she and her parents and her older brother lived in a house across the road from the Beverly Store. Bessie had dark brown hair and green eyes and was, without a doubt, the most popular girl at the Beverly Academy. Edgar had been secretly in love with her for a year before he more openly courted her at picnics and parties. During the last days of school in the spring of 1893, he wrote her a short letter. She responded by sending him a brief reply, which he tucked into his Bible until he had a chance to read it in private. Her note made him think that she liked him too, or at least she didn't mind his advances.

It took all of Edgar's courage to make his feelings clear to her during a church picnic held in the woods behind the Cayce cottage. Bessie and Edgar wandered off together to the little glen where he liked to dream and read his

Bible. He told her about the times he had spent there in his youth, and about the dreams he had for himself as an adult. It was no secret by now that Edgar wanted to be a preacher, to do "God's work." He was certain that Bessie, of all people, would appreciate his career choice because her grand-father was a minister. Edgar went even further to suggest that she could be-come his wife, and that they might have a church like Liberty, along with a farm where they could grow tobacco and other crops. "And a flower garden and horses to ride, too," Edgar added.

Bessie laughed. She did like him, but her interest in him had been more curiosity than a love relationship. The fact that he wasn't "right in the head," as her father put it, made marriage to him unthinkable. Edgar was shocked: not only did she not share his love, she thought that he was unworthy of her. Upset, he visited Dr. Kenner to ask him if he truly believed that he had mental problems. Edgar was convinced that Kenner, who was a Confederate Army veteran, a respected elder at the church, and—besides Dr. Dulin—the most educated man in Beverly, would tell him the truth.

Kenner showed Edgar into his office. Edgar didn't wish to talk about his affections toward Bessie, he only wanted to know if the doctor agreed with his daughter. Kenner didn't mince words. Indeed, he thought Edgar was unfit to be a husband and a father. Not only was there the question of whether or not he would be able to have children—the result of his testicles being injured in his youth—but there was an even greater concern about his mental health. "I should know," Kenner told him. "I was there that day you got hit with a baseball." Edgar already suspected that Kenner would have preferred Bessie to take on a different suitor, but he hadn't been prepared for total rejection from both father and daughter. Deeply hurt and humiliated, he could neither stand the thought of returning to school to face Bessie, nor going to church where he would surely see the whole Kenner family.

As Edgar would do many times in the years to come, he turned his back on this difficult and unpleasant situation. Later, he would say that he had dropped out of school because his family needed him in the fields. But this was not entirely the truth. He never set foot in the classroom after this meet-ing with Dr. Kenner and came close to resigning as sexton of Liberty Church. Nor is there any record of him ever speaking to Bessie Kenner again until three years later, when she married Edgar's cousin, George Major.

It was Edgar's grandmother who convinced him to continue at Liberty Church, but there was nothing she or Professor Thom could say to convince him to remain in school. Despite his remarkable academic progress and a generous offer by a Hopkinsville businessman to finance a college education,

Edgar dropped out of school and took a job growing tobacco for his uncle Edgar.

Edgar's decision was not only the result of his plummeting self-esteem, but came from a desire to please his mother, who knew it was only a matter of time before the "freak" from the Beverly Academy would come to the attention of greater Christian County. And apart from the scrutiny she believed Edgar would receive if he stayed in school, Edgar's mother truly needed him at home. She was soon to give birth to her seventh and last child—another girl. The income from Edgar's job would help see the large Cayce clan through the winter. No doubt Leslie desired the extra income as much as his wife, though he claimed that the decision was made as a "curative" measure. Hard physical labor, he believed, was the best "tonic" for his "strange" son.

Edgar was determined, as never before, to turn his back on what he had come to view as his childhood preoccupation with "fairies, imps, and angels." He desired nothing less than to be normal. To him, this meant playing cards, dating girls, and drinking corn whiskey. The fact that these things didn't come naturally to him was not going to stop him. He intended to learn.

Up until this time, Edgar's only vice had been smoking a pipe, which he had begun to do when he was about fourteen. Now he began rolling his own cigarettes, too. He also became an avid quail and rabbit hunter. His equipment consisted of an old muzzle loader, powder horn, shot flask, and newspaper for wadding. If he didn't pack the gunpowder tight enough with the newspaper, the wadding would stream out when the gun went off, catch fire, and burn like a Roman candle. But despite the primitive equipment, Edgar was apparently such a good hunter that he hired himself out as a local guide to Hopkinsville businessmen.

Edgar also went in search of older and more worldly boys with whom he could be friendly, or as he later said, "from whom I could learn the ways of the world." He found a suitable model in Tom Andrews, a handsome and gregarious young man who temporarily boarded with the Cayces. Tom had come from out west, where he had worked as a cowboy. He told tales of roundups and riding the range that fascinated everyone who heard them. Intrigued, Edgar plied Tom with questions, followed him around, and eventually became his friend. Under Tom's mentorship, Edgar read the *Louisville Courier Journal*, played poker, and learned to dance.

Tom surprised Edgar in many ways—he didn't lead the life Edgar associated with that of a cowboy. Tom didn't drink and discouraged others from it. He also didn't court girls, as Edgar imagined cowboys would. Tom teased girls. He would frighten them by riding too close on a fast horse, or spin them around too quickly while dancing a Virginia reel. Nor did Tom pick fights and get put in jail. Like a real cowboy, however, Tom did wander the countryside, visiting saloons, pool parlors, dance halls, and any place that suited his fancy. Edgar often accompanied Tom, joining him on a horse that had only recently been broken in.

Edgar and Tom were passing a dance hall one night when they stopped to watch a crap game that was going on outside. A disagreement arose and people started shooting. Edgar was hit in the shoulder as he and Tom were making their escape. Rather than return to Beverly, where Dr. Dulin or Dr. Kenner would surely inform Edgar's parents, they rode to a doctor five miles away. The bullet was removed and the shoulder bandaged in such a way that the dressing would not show through his coat. Edgar's family didn't learn of the incident until a year later, although their son proudly displayed the scar as proof that he had earned the status of a "real" man.

Edgar didn't get to know Andrews as well as he would have liked because his friend left Beverly in the fall of 1893 with a girl from California who had come to Beverly to visit her married sister. Although Tom was out of his life, Edgar was determined to continue on the path to manhood he had begun. During one of Edgar's forays into Hopkinsville he entered a saloon and asked for a drink. The bartender, however, recognized him from church and refused to serve him. "I'll not be responsible for giving a boy like you your first drink," the bartender reportedly told him.

Another time, when Leslie was out of town, Edgar took the day off to visit the John Robinson Circus, which had come to Hopkinsville. He saddled up his favorite white Mexican pony and started for town with the intention of doing everything that he perceived a normal boy would do, even if that meant picking a fight and having to spend a night in jail. Riding past the Beverly Store on his way out of town he met an elderly farmer, A. L. Carter, who was standing on the porch. Carter, who was related to the Cayces by marriage, was one of the most prosperous farmers in the county, a devoted member of the Liberty Church, and a member of the Masonic lodge. As Edgar rode past him, Carter motioned for him to stop, asking him if he was on his way to the circus. When Edgar answered affirmatively, Carter responded: "That's too bad," and proceeded to lecture him on the evils of associating with the kind of individuals who were attracted by such entertainment. He begged Edgar not to go. "You're too good a boy to undertake such a trip alone and at night."

Edgar said he was going anyway. After a moment of consideration, Carter said that it would cost Edgar fifty cents admission, twenty-five cents to stable the pony, and at least another twenty-five cents to get something to eat.

That came to a dollar. Carter offered to give him a dollar if he would turn around and go home. Edgar thanked Carter, and rode on. But before he had gone much farther, his pony balked. However much he pushed and pulled, he couldn't get the pony to move forward. He eventually discovered that a rock had lodged under the pony's horseshoe. By that time, however, Edgar had decided to return to the store, where Carter handed him the dollar, put his hand on Edgar's head, and said a short prayer.

Edgar's now bedridden grandmother had started saying prayers on Edgar's behalf. She sent for him on June 8, 1893, the anniversary of her husband's death. Edgar dutifully came. He remembered the visit in great detail, for it was the day, at age sixteen, he decided not to be someone he wasn't and to move out of his parent's home and live with his grandmother. He broke off the associations he had been trying to cultivate at dance halls and saloons, returned to reading his Bible, and opened his heart and mind to whatever it was that "the good Lord" had in store for him.

In Edgar's later correspondence it is clear that the conversations he had with his grandmother that summer went a long way toward helping him accept the fact that he would never be able to live the kind of life that others would expect of him. Edgar and his grandmother discussed Edgar's dream of becoming a pastor, but mostly they talked about the special gifts that Sarah believed the Lord had bestowed on his grandfather and on him. "Don't be afraid of it [the power] and don't misuse it," she told him. "If you hear voices, compare what they say to what Jesus says in the Bible. Then you won't go wrong. Don't be afraid, and don't be proud."

Before Edgar left her bedside that day in June 1893, she had elicited a promise from him not to look upon those he met in life's journey as adversaries who would do him harm, but as people, like himself, searching for their rightful place in God's kingdom. The Lord's blessings were meant for everyone. A person had only to eat of the fruit of the tree, and Edgar could be instrumental in bringing that fruit to them. As if seeking a more tangible means of expressing her sentiments, the bedridden woman, wrapped in a shawl, asked that Edgar fetch a peach from one of the trees that his grandfather had planted. Edgar did as he was told. He skinned the peach, cut it in quarters, and fed it to her himself.

Edgar was alone with her, holding her hand, when she died a month later. The last thing she said to him was that everything was all right. "I see your grandfather coming for me," she said. Although Edgar, by now, could no longer see his grandfather, he believed that, indeed, Tom Cayce had come for her.

However painful Sarah's passing was for the Cayces, her estate eased the financial stress that the family had been under since the previous winter, when Leslie had lost heavily by investing in a wagon load of dark tobacco. Prices had been high when he had the tobacco prepared for auction in Clarksville, Tennessee, but the bottom dropped out of the market before he could sell. Leslie had come home $18,000 in debt. The family lost everything of value they owned, including their cottage and the family's only horse and buggy. Leslie and Carrie were forced to move to the big redbrick house where Carrie had spent her girlhood. To Edgar, like his four sisters, the move was a punishment beyond anything they had previously experienced— alcohol had gotten the best of their maternal grandfather, and their maternal grandmother experienced bouts of insanity that frequently required her to be locked in an upstairs bedroom.

Edgar felt more sorry for his mother than anyone else. She had been raised in luxury. She had gone to school each day accompanied by her maid. Now she worked harder than any servant. Leslie left home for many days at a time, leaving her to care for their five children as well as nurse her mentally unstable mother. And when Leslie was home, he spent all of his time in bed or hanging around the Beverly Store, concocting schemes to get rich. Even politics no longer interested him. Edgar was not only the sole breadwinner, he had taken on his father's judicial responsibilities.

No reason has been given by the family for Leslie's inability to perform even the most minor of his obligations as a husband and father. References in family correspondence merely say that he was "sick," and unable to work. But later reports reveal that Leslie had contracted a venereal disease that periodically caused open sores around the genitals and made walking or riding a horse painful.

Thus, it was only natural that Leslie's family would decide to move to Hopkinsville. Money left from Leslie's mother's estate would go a long way toward paying off the family debts. And in Hopkinsville, Leslie could make a new start for himself and the girls would be able to continue their education beyond the eighth grade, the highest grade level offered at the Beverly Academy.

It was a cold day late in December 1893 when the family packed their belongings, sold what they couldn't take with them, and moved into town. Edgar drove the family cow, a gift from his aunt Ella, behind their one wagon. They moved into a log home on Seventh Street, which they rented from John Young, the owner of the local hardware store. The house has been described as a pleasant one, with a stable and a barn at the back, and a kitchen separated from the main house to lessen the risk of fire spreading to the living quarters. Facilities included an outhouse next to the barn and a well from which they would draw their water.

Edgar helped his family unpack and get settled. As much as he loved the warmth and chatter of his younger sisters, and although he desperately did not want his father to be the sole male in the household, he was determined not to stay in Hopkinsville. Edgar found the sight of Hopkinsville's crowded muddy streets, teeming with strangers, frightening. It reminded him of a day in his early youth when he had accompanied his father to Hopkinsville and had seen a man gunned down on the wooden sidewalk just a few yards in front of him.

In her own quiet way, Edgar's mother supported her son's decision, perhaps for the same reason she desired to have him drop out of school. Hopkinsville was no place for a boy whose unconscious mind could seemingly absorb the printed contents of anything coming into contact with it. He was better off with a plow share and a Bible than dabbling in tobacco futures or handling the works of Charles Darwin.

Edgar returned to the country and took a job working for his uncle Clint on what was called the "old" Anderson farm. He went to Hopkinsville only on weekends to visit his family and attend Sunday school at the Ninth Street Christian Church, a towering edifice that resembled a medieval fortress. Although Edgar eventually became a member of that church, he kept a much lower profile than at Liberty, and fellow parishioners remembered him as a quiet boy who sat in a back pew and kept to himself.

Edgar took as much pleasure in his work on the farm as he did in the company of his handsome and outgoing Uncle Clint. During the seven months they spent together, Clint and Edgar became quite close and would remain that way for many years to come. And Clint would, in fact, be the only member of the greater Cayce clan to openly embrace their prodigal son when a Hopkinsville doctor later made public what generations of Cayces in Beverly considered the "family secret."

Clint admired Edgar and saw in him a humble Christian and hard worker. The responsibilities he gave the young man on his hundred-acre farm included tending the flocks of ducks and geese, brushing and feeding the mules and horses, spreading manure, plowing the fields, seeding and harvesting the crops, and curing tobacco. In the evenings, Edgar, Clint, and Clint's wife, Lulu Boyd Cayce, would take turns reading aloud from the Bible.

Life was quiet on the farm, which was how Edgar liked it. The cycles of plowing, fallowing, and planting were a comfort and gave him lots of time to think about what he would do with his life. Almost over night he had found himself to be a grown man. His body was now better proportioned, lean, and strong from heavy physical labor. His hands were callused, and his complexion burnished by the sun. And each morning when he climbed out of bed before sunrise, he now had to shave as well as dress and groom himself for the day. His Bible study had taken him through the "good book" five times, and he could recite to himself—during lonely hours out in the fields—many passages upon which he chose to reflect. The hours he spent alone in the fields also gave him time to think about a dream he had had many times since his parents moved to Hopkinsville.

In his dream, he was walking through a wood composed of small, pyramid-shaped trees. The ground was blanketed with vines bearing small white flowers. A girl walked with him, clinging to his arm. Her face was veiled. They were happy, content, and in love. The ground sloped downward to a stream of clear water running over white sand studded with pebbles. They crossed to the other side, where they met a male figure, who was bronze-skinned, nude except for a loin cloth, and had wings at his feet and shoulders. He carried a rectangular piece of gold cloth. "Clasp your right hands," he told them. Over their clasped hands he laid the cloth. "United you may accomplish anything," he said. "Alone you will do very little."

The winged man disappeared and Edgar continued walking through the forest with the veiled woman until they came to a muddy road. Edgar and the girl were looking at it, wondering how best to cross it without soiling their clothes, when the brown-skinned male figure appeared again. "Use the cloth," he said, then disappeared once again.

Edgar and the veiled woman waved the cloth in the air and then found themselves on the other side of the road. Eventually they came to a cliff. Here they found a sharp knife, which Edgar used to cut steps into the soft rock, which he and his companion used to climb higher and higher up the side of the cliff. There the dream ended.

Each time Edgar had this dream he would ponder its meaning. For many years he thought the veiled female represented the woman who would become his wife. Later, however, he would interpret the dream's symbols using guidelines suggested in his own trance readings and come to believe that the veiled woman was not a flesh-and-blood wife who would make his life complete, but rather, a metaphor for his own psychic ability. The winged man was a messenger of the Gods, directing him to make peace with this aspect of himself if he was to accomplish anything. He had to truly unite with his psychic abilities if his life was to be worthwhile.

In June 1894, Edgar Cayce, now seventeen, did in fact, act upon what he believed to be a message from above. He had just returned from lunch to a field where he had been mending a broken plow. As he knelt to continue to make repairs, he heard a humming. A sense of pleasantness or well-being came over him. Edgar recognized it. He was going to hear again the voice of the angel he had heard years ago in his bedroom. "Leave the farm," the voice said. "Go to your mother. Everything will be all right."

Edgar did as the voice commanded. He drove his mules back to the house and led them into the pasture. Then he went inside and informed his uncle that he was leaving for Hopkinsville immediately. His uncle protested, but to no avail. Edgar packed his Bible and a few other possessions and started off on the seven-mile journey to Hopkinsville by foot. Meanwhile, his uncle, who had decided he shouldn't have given Edgar a hard time about letting him go, had left on horseback in search of him.

Edgar was nowhere to be found. His uncle then drove his carriage into town to his brother's house. Edgar showed up later that night. He had not taken the Palmyra Pike as Clint had supposed, but cut across Pat Major's fields and followed the old Indian trail up the north fork of the Little River and into Hopkinsville.

Edgar hadn't changed his mind about leaving the farm. He was in town to stay. Like his father, he was giving up farming for good. But that didn't mean he knew what he wanted to do with his life. The voice had directed him to Hopkinsville. It hadn't told him what to do when he got there.

PART TWO

Hoptown and Louisville

5.

Hopper Brothers
Bookstore

For a country boy who had probably never eaten in a restaurant, traveled by train, or journeyed beyond Christian County, Edgar found "Hoptown" alive with unusual sights and sounds. It had pistol-carrying "country boys," scantily clad dance girls, gamblers in bowler hats and pinstriped suits, tobacco-chewing tradesmen, three funeral parlors, a store that sold just hats, a tea room, and a baseball field where the Hopkinsville Moguls played. Holland Opera House contained the first stained glass window Edgar had ever seen that didn't depict a scene from the Bible. The wide, unpaved streets were frequently buried in a cloud of dust churned up by the wheels of buggies and the high-stepping trotters that pulled them or by the slower mule-driven livery wagons hauling tobacco to the giant planters' warehouses. And yet, for all its robust growth, Hopkinsville was still a city where roosters crowed in the mornings and packs of dogs roamed the streets.

None of these sights and sounds could match the delight Edgar felt when he first stepped off Main Street and into the Hopper Bookstore one day in late June 1894. It was the first bookstore he had visited, and inside he found everything he could imagine, and more. His first surprise came from the books themselves. Although he had seen various editions of the Bible, he had no idea that books were published in such a variety of sizes and bound in paper as well as leather. The store also carried stationery, pictures, moldings for picture frames, rolls of wallpaper, window shades, vases, urns, statuary, fancy pillows, wall mottoes, and art supplies. As Edgar later wrote, "I had spent much of my life working for the material things for sustaining of the physical man. Here in the store they had the things for sustaining the mental man."

Edgar spent much of the morning browsing around the store. Finally he worked up the courage to ask one of its owners for a job. The man he spoke to was Will Hopper, a kind, gentle-looking man who stood six feet tall and had dark hair and eyes. Will, whom Edgar came to call W. L., ran the bookstore with his older brother Harry, and it had been their father, now deceased, who had presented the Bible to Edgar six years earlier. Edgar explained his connection to their store and was greeted warmly by Will. Edgar offered to come and work for them, but was told that they didn't need any more employees than they already had.

Disappointed, he left the bookstore and went across the street to speak with Charles M. Latham, who owned a dry goods store, and with whom he had also had previous contact. Latham was a brother to the rich banker John C. Latham, who some sources said had once been Jefferson Davis's private secretary. The story circulating around Hopkinsville was that John Latham had absconded with a fortune in Confederate gold, which he used to open a New York commodities exchange after the war. Besides the Hotel Latham, which was only one of the family's business interests in Hopkinsville, they owned a large tobacco warehouse, which would later become the target of firebombing by the infamous Night Riders, a marauding band of tobacco farmers who tried to break the American Tobacco Company's monopoly on pricing.

Edgar had never met John Latham, but he knew Charles, whom he had met a few years earlier on a trip to town he had made on behalf of his father. During their previous meeting, Latham had noticed that Edgar was not dressed properly for the cold and had thoughtfully showed him how to stuff newspaper under his clothing to help keep himself warm. He had also given Edgar a pair of mittens. Latham remembered Cayce fondly and assured him that he would help him get a job once the young man made up his mind what he wanted to do. Edgar thanked him for his generosity and told him he would stop back after he'd had a chance to look around at more of the shops.

Next, he went to R. C. Hardwick's Jewelry Store, which was next door to Latham's. He asked the owner of this store for a job, and being turned down, again walked up the street to Garner's Drug Store and then on to Wall's Clothing Store, which was at the corner of Main and Seventh Streets. He next went across the street to the Bank of Hopkinsville, Hoosier's Tailor Shop, and three or four other stores before finding himself back out in front of Hopper Brothers, which he decided would be the most interesting place to work.

Inside, Edgar this time approached Harry Hopper, Will's older brother, who was now seated behind the cash register. Harry has been described as an austere man, about five feet ten inches tall, with fair hair and a blond handlebar mustache. Will had already spoken to Harry about Edgar and was surprised to see him back in the store. Exhibiting a tenacity that bordered on arrogance, Edgar insisted that Hopper Brothers was where he wanted to work and made them a deal that they couldn't refuse. He would work for nothing. If after a month they didn't value his help, he would leave. The Hopper brothers agreed with this arrangement and told him to show up for work the following Monday.

The first morning when Edgar arrived for work, the janitor told him that Harry Hopper hadn't arrived yet, and that Will Hopper was still in his bedroom, which was located in an apartment above the store. Will soon came down. He told Edgar that he should acquaint himself with the stock, and that he would find most everything marked. He also showed Edgar the combination to the cash drawer, telling him that he was leaving to eat breakfast at the family home, where his brothers and sister lived just outside of town. Edgar watched him ride off on the bicycle he kept in the back of the store. Harry, Edgar learned, looked after other properties as well as the bookstore, and only came to the store a few hours each day.

Edgar got started on the job by inspecting and dusting the store from one end to the other. At its entrance was a wide, open space where framed pictures were displayed. Behind this were the bookcases containing best-sellers, popular literature, and classics. Then came schoolbooks and school supplies—not only for the two public schools in Hopkinsville, but for the South Kentucky College, the Bethel Female College, and Ferrell's Military High School for Boys. At the opposite side of the store were bins containing umbrellas, plaster busts, and stationery with delicate floral imprints. Then came samples of moldings for pictures, rows of plaster busts, and a large rack in which unframed pictures were kept. In the rear of the store were display racks for wallpaper, Will Hopper's desk, and a very large cast-iron safe.

Edgar worked hard to acquaint himself with the books and the stock. He also did his best to charm the customers. Since no one knew of his special talents he decided to keep that quiet and to emulate the manner of the shoppers who came into the store: stylish men with pin collars and three-piece suits and ladies draped in silks and satins who seemed to know where they were going and what they intended to do with their lives.

Harry and Will quickly came to appreciate Edgar. At the end of the first month they bought him a new suit of clothes to replace his outdated and threadbare Sunday best. At the end of the second month they gave him ten dollars, which would become his monthly salary for the first year. He ended up staying at the store for three years in all.

Edgar's decision to work at the bookstore must have brought many sleepless nights for his mother, who feared the "vexing" influence popular literature might have on her impressionable son. The store's shelves not only carried Charles Darwin, but Henry James, Mark Twain, and Harriet Beecher Stowe. There were Latin and Greek classics. Gilbert and Sullivan operettas, New York tabloids, and an ever-swelling inventory of dime novels with titles like *The Pirate Priest*, and *Deadwood Dick's Defiance*. But Carrie's fear of losing her son in the morass of 1890s popular culture was ultimately unwarranted. Although Edgar Cayce read and reportedly "slept on" hundreds of books, the Bible remained his one true love, and much to the exasperation of some of his friends, the scriptures were the central topic of virtually all of his literary discussions.

One morning, while dusting merchandise on an upper shelf, Edgar came to learn how different the two Hopper brothers were. Harry, the older of the two brothers, stopped to tell him to be careful. "Don't break anything," was his admonition. Later that morning Will came in and said: "Good morning, I see that you are busy. Be careful. Don't hurt yourself." It was Will's concern for him that endeared him to the young clerk more than anything else. Edgar came to love him as a brother and was grateful for his mentorship during the first few years of his life in Hopkinsville. He would have loved to share with him details of his unusual childhood, but instead talked to him about his real passion, the Bible.

For Edgar, the only unpleasant side of the business was collecting bills. Never before had he ever presented a bill to anyone, and he felt uncomfortable doing so now. This turned out to be the only area in which he did not excel. It offered him, as he later said, ample opportunity to become a "laggard."

The bookstore also offered him the opportunity to meet people of his own age, who, like the Hopper brothers, knew nothing of his previous reputation. He especially liked the young college students who had so many varied interests and seemed so full of life. Edgar naturally tended to strike up conversations with people he recognized from church. His seemingly inexhaustible knowledge of the Bible was immediately apparent, and in 1896, when the Yale educated Harry D. Smith took over the pulpit at the Ninth Street Christian Church, Edgar was given a Sunday school class to teach and took on a prominent part in organizing the local chapter of Christian Endeavor, a worldwide interdenominational outreach program founded in the early 1880s. The Ninth Street Christian Church was then undergoing a renaissance and attracted a wide spectrum of Hopkinsville residents, tripling its congregation during Smith's tenure. Edgar's Sunday school class became so popular that he eventually had thirty-eight students from several different churches.

Most memorable for Edgar during this time were the many interesting and fascinating people he got to know. Among them was a two hundred pound, six-foot deputy Christian County sheriff and a Southern Railway detective named Will Starling, who pitched for the Hopkinsville Moguls and later joined Teddy Roosevelt's Rough Riders, eventually becoming the head of the secret service and protector of five American presidents. Hallie Rives, whose nationally syndicated columns and books of etiquette would later make her famous, also shopped frequently at Hopper's and would become one of Edgar's friends.

One afternoon when Edgar was alone in the store, a very dignified gentleman came in. He asked Edgar what was good to read among the bestsellers. Edgar named several titles, but told him that the one that was particularly interesting was *The Jucklins*, by author and lecturer Opie Percival Read. He took the book off the shelf, showed it to the man, and then proceeded to detail the plot. Edgar may well have quoted an entire passage from the book verbatim, for the young salesman made a strong impression. The customer listened intently, then said, "Very interesting." He went on to introduce himself as the author and said that he was lecturing that night at the 2,500-seat Sam Jones Tabernacle, named for the charismatic preacher who frequently spoke there. He gave Edgar a free pass. Later that night, Edgar and the two Hopper brothers were surprised to hear the author sing the praises of the young store clerk who had given such a remarkably detailed account of his book.

Edgar spent another interesting evening at the Holland Opera House, where he was invited onto stage by a professional hypnotist—Stanley Hart—who billed himself as *Hart the Laugh King,* and who usually came to town for ten days to two weeks at a time, or until the crowds began to dwindle. A medium-sized man with light-brown wavy hair, and hazel green eyes, Hart wore no robes and used no colored lights or the other paraphernalia often used by magicians and stage entertainers popular at the opera house. He credited his powers to the "new science" of hypnotism and clairvoyance, which, at the time, had generated great interest across America and Europe. Although Hart was an ardent spokesman for the alleged powers of hypnotism to cure headaches, treat alcoholism, and eliminate self-destructive behaviors, it was the entertaining aspects of his "art" that drew crowds to his performance. He invited members of the audience onto the stage, put them into a hypnotic trance, and ordered them to do embarrassing things such as play hopscotch, imitate fish, climb nonexistent ladders, crochet imaginary doilies, and sing silly show tunes.

Hart also had a professional troupe of performers, including a man who, when hypnotized, would lie down and allow a large rock to be put on his chest. Another member of the troupe, using a blacksmith's hammer, would then pound on the rock until it broke. Hart's performances usually began the afternoon before the stage performance, when he would have a local volunteer hide an object somewhere in town. Then Hart, blindfolded and sitting in a carriage, would hold his guide's wrist and retrace the route telling the driver what turns to take until he eventually found the hidden object. He also walked around town generating interest by "reading" people's minds and claiming that he could cure them of bad habits, such as cigarette smoking, drinking, or other addictions. Hopkinsville residents had great faith in Hart because he made a number of prominent citizens do things that they would never have otherwise considered doing on stage in front of others. After the performance, he would invite subjects backstage, where he would try to help them break bad habits or put on private demonstrations.

Edgar was invited on stage during a main performance and Hart swore just by looking at him that he would make the ideal hypnotic subject. To everyone's disappointment, Hart was unable to put Edgar into a trance and eventually he asked him to leave the stage. This was not, however, the last Edgar Cayce would see of Hart, for he would later figure prominently in the discovery of the talent for which he became best known.

While Hart and other vaudeville acts held some fascination for Edgar, it was the preachers that moved him the most. Besides seeing Sam Jones at the Tabernacle, he heard and met noted evangelists like George B. Pentecost, George Stewart, and Mordecai Ham, who was the preacher who converted Billy Graham at a revival meeting in North Carolina. He may have also heard Booker T. Washington, Carrie Nation, and William Jennings Bryan, all of whom lectured or preached in Hopkinsville at the time Edgar was living there.

The religious leader who made the greatest impression on Edgar was Dwight L. Moody, arguably the most popular and charismatic preacher of his generation. Moody had been brought to Hopkinsville by the Bethel Baptist Association on April 5, 1898, and his appearance there was one of the last great revival meetings of Moody's long and illustrious career. Moody had just returned from a second tour of England, where he drew crowds of twelve and thirteen thousand people. Like the Christian Church of which Edgar

was a part, Moody sought to bring unity to the various Protestant denominations. He taught the brotherhood of man and preached eloquently against
anarchy, greed, extortion, and hate.

On the morning that Edgar met Moody, he had risen early as usual and
was preparing to do his morning chores when he discovered that the family
cow was missing from the barn. Edgar followed her tracks through an open
gate, across a meadow, and down along the riverbank some hundred or so
yards behind the barn. After he followed the creek a little way up the other
bank, he came upon a middle-aged, overweight man seated on a log. The
man had a great beard, which had begun to turn white, like his hair. Edgar
couldn't help but notice that he held a Bible in his hands.

"Good morning, young man," the stranger said. "I'll venture you are
seeking this cow here just behind me. She must have come up this way from
the path you came over." Edgar asked him how he knew he was looking for
the cow—he didn't think he looked like a farmer. It was the anxiety in his
face that gave him away, Dwight Moody said. He and Edgar got to talking
and their conversation turned to the Bible, the bookstore, and Edgar's desire
to become a preacher. Moody explained that he had come to Hopkinsville to
hold a meeting, which was scheduled to begin that night, and would run an
entire week. Moody asked if he wanted to go, and Edgar said he did.

Edgar showed up that night and was very impressed. He sat in the front
row amidst a standing-room-only crowd. The text that night was from the
Gospel of Luke, 10:25. Edgar had read it many times and heard various interpretations, but he had never heard it treated in quite the same way as
Moody presented the subject. Edgar communicated his excitement to Moody
the next morning when he found the evangelist waiting for him at the same
place he had found him the day before. They continued to meet like this for
Moody's entire visit to town.

During one of these sessions, Edgar asked Moody the same question that
he had put to many different pastors. He asked Moody if God had ever spoken to him. Moody responded by asking Edgar what had prompted the question. In a rare moment of confession, Edgar poured out his heart as he had
not done since speaking to Bessie Kenner, saying things that he had been too
frightened to admit even to his own parents or to his pastor. Perhaps Edgar
felt safe with Moody. For whatever reason, he told the evangelist about the
little folk, and about the angel who had visited him in his bedroom and the
voice he had heard in the field at his uncle's farm. Edgar, no doubt, was
worried about what Moody might think. As Edgar's own reading of the
Bible revealed, the Devil often spoke through spirits.

Moody shocked Edgar by saying that other people had told him of having experiences such as Edgar had. These people received messages in all sorts of ways. Moody felt sure they were sincere in their beliefs, and that it was genuinely the Lord that spoke to them, not the Devil. "You can tell a tree by its fruit," he reminded Edgar. Moody went on to quote from various passages in the Bible that described experiences that people had, hearing spirits or seeing angels. He pointed out that although many biblical passages condemned such communications, one verse in particular authoritatively stated otherwise. He quoted the Book of Numbers, in which God speaks to Aaron and Miriam regarding Moses. The voice of God says: "Hear now my words: If there be a prophet among you, I the Lord will make myself known unto him in a vision, and will speak unto him in a dream."

Moody went on to describe his own experience on a trip to Cleveland to hold a revival meeting. The visit was to last a few weeks and a large audience was expected. But something started to nag at Moody soon after he arrived: he had a dream in which he was told to close his meeting at once and go to London, England. Moody had never been to England before, nor had anyone from there ever shown any unusual interest in his efforts. However, Moody was faithful to the vision, for he believed it to be an expression of the will of God. The next evening he announced that the meeting was closed. Many of his associates thought him foolish, for he was just starting out at the time and didn't have the enormous popularity that later made him such a sensation. Moody wouldn't explain to anyone other than his closest friends just why he felt impelled to close the meeting.

Moody felt like a stranger in London when he first arrived. He wandered the streets, asking himself if he was sure that he knew what he was doing. Perhaps his vision hadn't been authentic. He was strolling through a poor section of the city when he happened to notice a window box on a nearby tenement in which a geranium bloomed. It was a color he liked very much. As he walked over to take a closer look, he heard an angelic voice singing one of his favorite hymns. He stopped to listen. After a few minutes he felt impelled to climb the stairs of the tenement. At the top of the stairs a door was open. He could hear the singing come from inside. There he saw a young lame girl. As soon as he looked in, the girl said, "Oh, Mr. Moody. It's you. I knew God would answer my prayer and send you here. I read of you in one of our papers and have been praying for you to come to London." At that moment, Moody knew that it had been God who had spoken to him. He didn't know what manner or channel the Lord had used, but the prayers of the child had reached him. He began a prayer meeting in that child's room, which eventually touched the lives of a quarter of a million or more people in England. "I know it was God who spoke to me," Moody told Edgar.

Edgar would cherish his morning conversations with Moody as much as he did the evangelist's sermons in the evenings. In those sermons, he would find what seemed like hidden or veiled references to what they had spoken of in their morning sessions. Just to listen to Moody sent chills up his spine. On the last morning that he and Moody met, Edgar had arrived before sunrise and found the evangelist making marks in the soil with a stick. Moody asked Edgar what he was going to do with his life. Edgar told him he still wished to be a minister. Moody advised him to be true to that vision, but to know that there were many different ways to serve God besides being a pastor. He could do so in missionary work, or by merely persuading others to read the Bible.

Years later, after Moody had died, Edgar would reflect on the hours he spent with the evangelist as one of the most moving experiences of his life. Although he would never meet Moody again in person, the evangelist would appear in his dreams. The most intriguing was a recurring dream that made such an impact he recorded it for later study and reflection.

"I was sitting alone in the front room playing solitaire when there was a knock at the front door," Cayce wrote. "When I went to the door a gentleman whom I did not recognize said, 'Cayce, I want you to go with me to a meeting this evening.' At first I said, 'But I seldom go out in the evening . . .' He insisted I should go with him and I did. As I went out I realized that another person was waiting for us in the street. We walked . . . on as if into the air, up and up, until we came to where there seemed to be a large circus tent . . . We approached the flap of the tent and as he pulled the flap back, I for the first time, realized that the two men with whom I had been walking were the evangelists Dwight L. Moody and Sam Jones . . ."

In Cayce's dream, he, Moody, and Jones entered the tent, which was filled to overflowing with inspirational religious leaders, some of whom Edgar recognized, and some he did not. And then, Cayce remembered: "It seemed that there was . . . lightning in the distance. With the lightning there was a noise, not of thunder but of wind, yet nothing seemed to stir . . . When I asked one of my companions what it was, I was told 'The Lord our God will speak to us.' Then a voice, clear and strong, came as from out of the cloud and the lightning and said, 'Who will warn my children?' Then from out of the throng before the throne came the Master . . . He spoke saying, 'I will warn My brethren.' The answer came back, 'No, the time is not yet fulfilled for you to return . . .' Then Mr. Moody spoke and said, '. . . send Cayce, he is there now.' Then the Master said, 'Father, Cayce will warn My brethren.' "

6.

The Young Lady
from The Hill

Edgar Cayce had begun to feel that the world and all its possibilities was finally opening up to him. In many respects, it was. Not long after he began at the bookstore, Edgar received an invitation to attend his first party, what was then called a "moonlight." The party was to be held at a house just outside of town, which local residents called The Hill. This first invitation to The Hill was extended by Ethel Duke, a Hopkinsville elementary schoolteacher who had heard Edgar deliver the McKenzie speech, and whom he had known from Beverly. Photos reveal her to be a tall, shapely woman with wire-rimmed glasses and a full head of thick brown hair, which she kept in a bun. Edgar recognized her immediately when she stepped into Hopper Brothers to purchase supplies. They spoke for a few minutes before she asked if he wanted to come to a moonlight at the old Salter house, which was east of town on the Russellville Road. Edgar eagerly said he would come, though he later admitted that the thought of being in such high company made him feel "uncouth and uneducated."

Leslie, who had been supportive of Edgar's initiative at finding a job, didn't share his son's enthusiasm at the prospect of him attending a party at The Hill. He forbid him to go. The reasons are not now known, but it is logical to believe that Leslie, being a conservative, didn't think it was proper for his son to attend a party in a home belonging to liberals, especially those who openly espoused such radical notions as a woman's right to vote and to hold public office. Practically everyone in town had heard at least one story of how the three Salter girls virtually ran The Hill, and how their dinner guests included Jews, blacks, and Hindus. Leslie suspected that all kinds of subversive things occurred at The Hill and wanted Edgar to have no part of it.

Edgar unhappily abided by his father's decision. However, this didn't keep him from finding out everything he could about life at that large gray house on the outskirts of town. Harry Hopper's girlfriend, Mary Greene, who taught at the South Kentucky College, had known the Salter family for years and told him everything he wanted to know.

At the head of the household was old Samuel Livezey Salter, who had been born and raised in Philadelphia, where he had trained to be a doctor, but who ultimately earned a reputation as an architect and builder. He and his partner, John Orr, had come to Hopkinsville as contractors and had built many of Christian County's homes and buildings, all noted for their sturdy construction, elaborate woodwork and handsome stairways. During the war, Samuel Salter married Susan Jones and they proceeded to raise a family together. Even then, the Salter patriarch had what might be considered radical or alternative notions about how life should be lived. His medical training led him to raise plants and herbs for medicinal purposes, which he prepared himself for his patients and his livestock. Although he had ample funds to buy an elegant town house, he preferred to build a farmhouse where he could experiment with various crops and could always be assured of having food on the table. Due to his overriding interest in the arts and history, he assembled a large personal library and entertained many distinguished thinkers and musicians who visited Hopkinsville. All five of their children were sent to college, studied a foreign language, and were taught the skills to perpetuate The Hill into the next generation and beyond. Their legacy did in fact live on, for not only did all of their children attend college, but so did their grandchildren.

The Salters had five children: Elizabeth, Katherine, William, Hiram, and Caroline. Elizabeth Ella, or Lizzie, their first child, would grow up extremely bright and well read. She married Sam Evans, the owner of the Hopkinsville coal yard and eventually had three children, Hugh, Lynn, and Gertrude, the youngest, who was born on February 22, 1880. The children were still infants when their father died suddenly from a burst appendix. Lizzie immediately sold their holdings in the coal yard and built a small house immediately adjacent to The Hill. Though Hugh, Lynn, and Gertrude didn't live in the main house, they were there practically all the time.

The youngest of the Salter children was Caroline Bennetta, or Carrie, who was considered the most beautiful and charming in the family. A part-time art teacher at the Hopkinsville asylum, she loved to paint, sketch, do embroidery, and collect old silver, linens, and furniture. Although she was not as outspoken as Lizzie and could not write poetry or play music as well as Kate, she seemed to have inherited the full range of her father's talents as well as his fierce sense of independence. Edgar knew Carrie and some of her young nieces and nephews because they frequently stopped into the book-store for school supplies while they were attending the South Kentucky Col-lege. In addition to schoolbooks, they purchased a wide assortment of reading material. According to Mary Greene, no subject was off limits. The more Edgar learned about the intellectual freedom at The Hill, the more dis-appointed he became at having missed the party.

When Ethel came to the store to issue a second invitation, this time she brought along her best friend and second cousin, who, unbeknownst to Edgar, had been the one who had prompted the first invitation to him. It was not Ethel Duke who was interested in Edgar, but Gertrude Evans, Lizzie's daughter. Ethel invited Edgar to come outside to meet Gertrude, who was seated in the back of Duke's buggy, which was parked on Main Street.

Edgar was immediately impressed by Gertrude's beauty. She had just turned fifteen and had silky brunette hair, large brown eyes, an oval face, porcelain white skin, and fine, delicate features. She stood only five foot three inches tall and weighed less than eighty pounds. "A mere slip of girl," was the way Edgar later described her. Edgar recognized Gertrude from ear-lier visits she had made to the store to buy freshman textbooks for her col-lege classes, but they had never spoken before Ethel introduced them that day. "I want you to meet my cousin, Gertrude," Ethel Duke had said.

Edgar was again invited to attend another moonlight at Gertrude's grand-father's house on a Friday night at eight o'clock. This time, he said nothing to his parents. He polished his shoes, oiled his hair, and set off for The Hill on foot. It took him the better part of an hour to reach the house. He was sure that he had found the correct address: just past the wire fence that sep-arated the property from the Russellville Road, Edgar saw paper lanterns hung from the maple trees and many people milling about on the front lawn sipping lemonade and eating cookies and small sandwiches.

Edgar had been in homes that were larger and had more land than The Hill, but he had never been more impressed than he was by the Salter home. It was a cornucopia of colors and textures: oriental carpets, thick brocade upholstery, house plants in Chinese porcelains, wicker chairs, fans, umbrellas, musical instruments, colored glass oil lamps, and a library of newspapers, magazines, and books. He liked nothing better than to run his hands over the needlepoint pillows, drink in the rich colors of the sashes and the dried flowers. But best of all he liked the scents that seemed to permeate the house: perfume, talcum powder, and honeysuckle—smells that he would forever associate with the feminine charms of the ladies who ruled The Hill.

Ethel Duke greeted him at the door and made introductions. The eldest of the clan was Samuel Salter, a tall, gray-haired, handsome man with great personal charm. Sarah, his wife, was equally handsome, but seemed more austere. Together they held court in what the family called the library, which was at the entrance to the house and contained two giant oak secretaries.

Twenty-year-old Carrie Salter was seated in the parlor surrounded by a group of adoring young male suitors. This scene gave Edgar his first hint that life at The Hill was truly different from most other homes, for he quickly saw that it wasn't for lack of opportunity that Carrie hadn't married—she just hadn't found the right man yet and wasn't willing to settle for second best just because she was no longer a teenager.

Edgar was also introduced to Lizzie Evans, Gertrude's mother, who was as petite and dark-haired as her daughter. It was she, Edgar would later learn, who supervised the planting and harvesting of the vegetable gardens and the orchard and who saw to it that the home was always full of flowers and color. She also saw to it that The Hill was a forum for political discussion and that the house had its doors open to all elected or aspiring policy makers. Through her voluminous correspondence, she met or exchanged letters with many of the most important political figures of her day.

Edgar met many others that night at The Hill: clergymen from the Methodist church, railroad engineers, and practically the entire junior class from South Kentucky College. The one thing everyone seemed to have in common was that they liked to talk and seemed to converse more easily than Edgar, who felt that he didn't have much to say except when the discussion turned to the Bible. However, he was a good listener, which seemed to be all right with Ethel Duke, who happily filled in any gap in their conversation.

By the time Edgar began to sort the family members out from the invited guests, he found himself face to face with Gertrude. Ethel Duke had quietly disappeared. Gertrude took his hand and they walked down the carriage path past the rose garden to an open space between the trees where she said they would have the best view of the moon.

Edgar remembers not being able to take his eyes off of her long enough to look at the sky. She had a single red rose in her brunette hair and wore a beautiful ankle-length gingham dress that Carrie had purchased for her at a department store in Springfield. To him, the red rose epitomized the beauty that radiated from her, and in the years to come, he never planted a garden that didn't feature at least one rose bush.

Edgar didn't say much to her that first evening. Since his debacle with Bessie Kenner, he hadn't been able to summon the courage to speak privately with anyone of the opposite sex. Nevertheless, that night he and Gertrude talked about books and Edgar's job at Hopper Brothers. Gertrude told him she liked books more than anything else and flattered Edgar by suggesting that he was probably so good at what he did that he would someday own a bookstore himself. Edgar couldn't be certain but he got the impression that she knew more about him than he did about her. Ethel Duke could well have filled Gertrude in about the specifics of his childhood experiences at the Beverly Academy. How much Gertrude knew about his unusual abilities or about the little folk he couldn't say and was too embarrassed to ask.

Edgar left The Hill that night not knowing if Gertrude liked him as much as he liked her, or if indeed she had been the one behind his invitation to the party. If Edgar hadn't known then, he certainly would become aware of it, for he soon began to receive numerous invitations to parties and social gatherings. Gertrude was at every one of them. Despite these overtures, Edgar was so insecure about himself and his station in life that he had trouble believing that a girl like Gertrude, from a family like the Salters, could accept him for who he was. Every time Edgar saw Gertrude he was unsure that he would ever get to see her again, until the day she invited him to join her and her cousin Stella Smith for a picnic at Pilot Rock, a famous Christian County landmark.

In customary fashion, an elderly couple—the Hisgens—accompanied them. They loaded a wagon with fried chicken, beaten biscuit, fresh tomatoes, cake, and demijohns of iced tea. That day Edgar caught a glimpse of Gertrude's delicate ankle as they hiked to the top of the limestone cliffs for a view of Christian and Todd Counties. A photograph, presumably shot that afternoon, shows the happy gathering on Pilot Rock.

Soon, Edgar was going everywhere with Gertrude: parties, church socials, and performances at the Holland Opera House. They also liked to attend baseball games, especially those of the Hopkinsville Moguls, for whom Lynn Evans played shortstop. Every Sunday, after he attended the Christian Church and Gertrude the Methodist Church, Edgar went to The Hill, where they sat out on the large front porch or joined others in playing games in the parlor or reading out loud from books that he brought from Hopper Brothers. Among other volumes, he presented her with a complete set of the novels of the popular author E. P. Roe, her favorite.

Although Edgar felt completely accepted by the family, the truth was that Gertrude's Aunt Kate and the older Salters didn't consider him an ideal suitor for Gertrude. They were far too polite, however, to let him know. The younger generation of the Salter clan, which consisted of Gertrude's brothers Hugh and Lynn, and Kate's sons, Porter and Raymond, treated him with genuine affection—like a brother.

All of the Salter family came to know about Edgar's ability to memorize books held to his head. Ethel Duke was his most enthusiastic fan, and Carrie couldn't stop questioning him about the things he said and did as a child. The fact that the family didn't seem to mind what they learned about him was reassuring, and subsequently Edgar revealed more about himself to the Salters than he had to his own family. He told them about his curious dreams and how he could sometimes see colors or patterns of colors around people when the person was feeling strong emotions. Ethel Duke and Carrie, who must have read press accounts of the Fox sisters' seances in Hydesville and Rochester, New York, shared the popular interest in the spiritualist movement, which was then just beginning to spread beyond its New England roots.

Edgar's stories captivated the ladies at The Hill. Hugh and Lynn also came to share their aunt's and cousin's interest when they tested Edgar with a deck of cards. He was reported to have correctly read the cards from front to back without turning them over. Edgar also helped them to find lost objects or items that they had hidden in the house. It seemed that he had only to go to sleep thinking about the location of a lost ring or a personal possession and he would wake up in the morning knowing where it was. Although it is rumored that some form of seance may have taken place at The Hill, there is no mention of it in any of the Cayce or Salter correspondence. Nor is it likely because then, as later, Edgar's fundamentalist upbringing would have prevented him from participating in something that clearly violated his understanding of proper Christian conduct. It was one thing to receive spiritual help, but quite another to summon spirits deliberately. The activities of the Fox sisters and later, mediums like Madame Blavatsky, were no more than of mild interest to Cayce. The Bible was all the excitement he needed or wanted.

Edgar couldn't be quite sure of what Gertrude thought about the experiments that took place. She was quiet at the times when he and the others discussed the subject and her eyes revealed nothing. Edgar knew, however, that there were times when she looked at him, he said, as if he were "a strange fish that ought to be thrown back." He eventually asked her directly what she thought of his unusual abilities. Not one to mince her words, she responded, "I don't like it." Edgar said that he didn't like it either. And after that, they seemed to get along better.

Two incidents occurred, however, that gave everyone reason for concern. The first took place late one Sunday evening when Edgar was dozing off in one of the arm chairs in the parlor. The last thing that Gertrude remembered telling him was that he should go to sleep. This is apparently just what he did, only he didn't wake up that night or the next morning. Nothing anyone did to try to wake him seemed to do any good. He appeared to be in some kind of a coma. It was well into the next day when Gertrude, out of sheer frustration and concern, "ordered" him to wake up. He immediately opened his eyes and stretched, not realizing anything unusual had taken place.

A second incident occurred at the Cayce family home on Seventh Street. As Edgar later told the story, he and an old school friend had just returned home from one of Sam Jones's revival meetings at the Tabernacle. His friend was expecting Edgar to share his bedroom with him when they realized that a houseful of Cayce relatives had unexpectedly dropped in from Beverly and were spending the night. Edgar's room had been requisitioned for the visitors and there was no place for him or his friend to sleep. Edgar lost his temper. This was his room and he was paying the lion's share of the rent on the house. In the ensuing uproar, Leslie and Edgar had a few cross words and Edgar's friend slipped out of the house unnoticed. Edgar fell asleep later that night on the sofa in the living room.

Edgar himself couldn't say whether or not his mental state had anything to do with the events that later transpired, but this has long been the assumption. Apparently he went to sleep without undressing, except for his shoes and coat. Then, not long after the house had quieted down, the sofa that Edgar was sleeping on burst into flames. The smoke and fire woke him up. Edgar dashed outside and rolled in the snow, putting out his burning clothes, and then hauled the sofa out the front door to extinguish its flames, too. Since Edgar had not been smoking, nor had the sofa been near anything hot, the cause of the fire remained a mystery.

There were, of course, various possible explanations: Edgar had done something in his sleep to cause the fire, a hot coal had shot out of the stove at the other end of the room and rolled under the couch, or one of the visitors from Beverly had been smoking and accidentally left a burning cigarette between the cushions. The trouble with all of these scenarios was that the fire hadn't started under the couch or between the cushions. The evidence suggested that the fire had started in Edgar's clothes.

Family members apparently didn't give the matter much thought. The fire had been put out, and that was all. At The Hill, however, the incident was much discussed and took on considerable importance. Carrie and Gertrude, like others who came to know Edgar intimately, had become aware that unusual or unexplained things frequently happened around him. More often than not, these things occurred when Edgar was angry or upset. Papers would fly off desks as if an invisible breeze had blown through the room. Books sometimes would fall off shelves. The Seventh-Street fire would be the first of four inexplicable fires involving Edgar.

The fire had a chilling effect on Gertrude, but despite this, Edgar continued coming to The Hill on a regular basis. Leslie was still adamantly opposed to Edgar's romance, but his headstrong son wouldn't listen. And since it was Edgar, not his father, who was the primary wage earner in the family, the younger Cayce felt justified in following his own heart's desire. His mother, Carrie, did not publicly express an opinion on the subject—at least not in front of Leslie. But in private, Edgar knew that she supported him and always wished him to look his best when he went "calling" on Gertrude. Oftentimes Edgar would travel to The Hill by horseback or on foot. But soon his salary at the bookstore was raised from ten to fifteen dollars and Edgar acquired a bicycle he rode even when it was raining or snowing.

On one particularly cold day—March 7, 1897 just days before his twentieth birthday—Edgar Cayce would propose to seventeen-year-old Gertrude Evans. He told her he loved her and wanted to spend the rest of his life with her. To Edgar's surprise, Gertrude didn't reject him immediately and was at least willing to consider his proposal. "It's true that I love you," she told him. "But I will have to think about it." Edgar naturally wanted to know when he would have an answer. Gertrude went to a calendar in the parlor, closed her eyes, and put her finger on a date. "I'll tell you on the twelfth." That was five days away. Edgar said he would be back then.

On the night of the twelfth Edgar arrived on horseback, in a driving rain. Gertrude told him that night that she had given the matter much consideration and she had decided to accept his proposal. Edgar was pleased, honored, and filled with joy. Once she had accepted, an awkward silence ensued as she stood waiting for him to kiss her. She asked him why he hesitated, and when Edgar admitted to her that he had never kissed anyone before, she proceeded to show him how. Then, as later, Edgar would find her to be an extremely sensual woman, far more gifted in the art of love than himself. It wasn't that she gave herself over to passion or the heat of the moment. She had a dancer's knowledge of her body and a natural grace that left him breathless.

Less than a week later, Edgar would present her with a small diamond for her engagement ring. Unable to restrain his exuberance, he sent the stone to be cut and mounted in Romania where, he had been told, the finest diamond cutters could be found. Gertrude feared that the ship that carried the diamond might sink or that the stone would get lost or stolen. But the ship stayed afloat and the diamond was delivered on time. By the summer of 1897, Gertrude had a ring on her finger, and they were discussing a date for their marriage. No sooner had they set a date, however, than it had to be postponed. Edgar lost his job at the bookstore.

Harry Hopper broke the news to Edgar at the end of that summer. He and his brother were taking on a partner at the store, and Edgar's services would no longer be needed. "I was so astonished I hardly knew what to do," he later wrote of his dismissal.

At first, he didn't tell Gertrude. He decided he would get another job before breaking the news. He went next door to see Charles Latham, who immediately made him a sales clerk in his dry goods store. But that job only lasted through the beginning of the fall and he was back out looking for another. He applied for other jobs without success. One day as he was out job hunting he happened to follow a large crowd into Richard's Department Store, which was having a sale.

As Edgar told the story later that day to friends and family, he was standing in the shoe department when a man asked him for a pair of shoes. Edgar sold him a pair, enjoyed making the sale, then looked around for another customer. It didn't take long before the department manager noticed. He asked Edgar his name, then told him to go to the bank and get some change for the cash register. Edgar worked through the rest of the day and then showed up for work the next morning. Asked why he had come to work without even applying for a job, Edgar explained the truth, "somebody asked me for something and I just gave it to them."

Edgar Cayce would work at the department store for the next twelve months, but didn't take the same joy in the experience as he had at the bookstore. It was Gertrude's Aunt Carrie who finally told him he should strive to do more with his life. She suggested he look for a job in a city larger than Hopkinsville, in a position where he could better use his talents. "Expand your horizons," she instructed him.

7.

Margaret
of Louisville

In the summer of 1898, Edgar Cayce decided to look for a job in Louisville, the largest city in the state, where he knew there was a major wholesale book distribution and printing company. The John P. Morton Company had a catalog of books, publications, and other merchandise that was many times larger than the Hopper brothers' store. Edgar wrote to the distributor immediately, only to receive a polite reply from the manager saying that his application had been received and would be put in a file until a position opened.

However shy Edgar could sometimes be, he was also headstrong, a quality no doubt spurred on by his eagerness to settle himself in a new job so that he could marry Gertrude. He would not take no for an answer. Cayce obtained letters of recommendation from everyone who did business at the Hopper Bookstore. It didn't matter if they were traveling salesmen, clergymen, or college students. He flooded the J. P. Morton Company's mailbox with such a stream of letters that after three days he received a telegram signed by the manager, Howard Griswold, ordering him to stop sending recommendations and report for work on Monday morning, August 1, 1898. This gave Edgar two days to pack, say good-bye to Gertrude, and find a place to live.

Edgar borrowed money, bought a linen suit, and spent his last evening in

Hopkinsville at The Hill. Though no records exist documenting the last hours he spent in Gertrude's company, it is not hard to imagine Edgar's unusually large hands cupping Gertrude's own small and delicate hands as they sat together on the porch swing overlooking the rose garden. It would be the first time that the two would be separated since their engagement, and as much as she must have shared his excitement at the prospect of his new job, their parting must have been a bittersweet moment. Louisville was 180 miles away, and the nine-hour journey by train and the $2.59 fare would make weekend trips home for Edgar impossible. Nor would Gertrude be able to go to see him, for even with an elderly escort, it would be unseemly for an unmarried young lady to visit a bachelor in another city, especially since they were engaged. Edgar, no doubt, kissed her good-bye—as Gertrude instructed—and promised to write.

The record of the sixteen months Edgar spent in Louisville is rich in color and texture, thanks primarily to a personal journal he kept to document his Christian Endeavor work for the First Christian Church of Louisville. The journal begins with Edgar's arrival in Louisville and his initiation into a city that was as different for him from Hopkinsville as Hopkinsville had been from Beverly. Though both Hopkinsville and Louisville had the good fortune of being in the tobacco trade during the most lucrative years of that industry's growth in Kentucky, Louisville, with its cobblestone streets, tall buildings, and dignified coachmen, was distinctly metropolitan. There were no howling dogs in the alleyways or roosters crowing from barnyards. Louisville prided itself on offering the latest and best of everything, and what cost a dollar in Hoptown went for nearly twice that in Louisville.

Edgar's journal tells of arriving at the station, when he took the advice of a family friend to rent a room at a boarding house on Second Street. The idea of paying for his room and meals was an entirely new concept to the young man, made all the more real when he learned the cost would be $5 a month, to be paid in advance. Edgar had no idea what his salary would be at J. P. Morton, but he knew it wouldn't cover much more than room and board. Edgar grudgingly paid over the $5—virtually all the money he had brought with him—and set about unpacking his small trunk.

Later that same day he began to appreciate the communal and cosmopolitan atmosphere of his new lodgings. At dinner he was introduced to the kinds of people he believed could truly "expand his horizons." There was a medical student, a government worker, a musician, a journalist, a railroad clerk, and a professional artist. Their conversation at the table was just as lively and unrestrained as at The Hill, only here, their talk was peppered with unfamiliar terms and risqué stories. Edgar himself later admitted that they must have found the young sales clerk—who quietly listened to their conversations—something of an enigma.

The owner of the house, who had once lived in Hopkinsville, went out of his way to make Eddy—as Edgar now called himself—feel at home. He knew all of Edgar's family, asked about each one, then gave advice on how Edgar could quickly make new friends. Edgar began following his advice the very next morning when 11 o'clock services were convened at the Louisville First Christian Church. Again, Edgar found himself much impressed by the "ways of the big city."

Membership at First Christian Church of Louisville, on the corner of Fourth and Walnut, was four times the size of his two previous churches combined. The Louisville church was also considerably richer, with sizable endowments coming from families who owned large interests in two tobacco companies, Brown and Williamson and Philip Morris. Edgar had never seen so many well-dressed people seated together in one place. The men all wore dark jackets with high, starched collars and ties. The women wore fine dresses with layers of petticoats and carried silk parasols. To Edgar's surprise, a number of the women also wore makeup. Their faces were powdered and rouged, and their lips reddened. Edgar was enthralled.

Much to his delight, Edgar discovered an old friend. Dr. Edward Lindsay Powell, the minister of the Louisville Church, had briefly been the minister at First Christian Church in Hopkinsville before moving on to Maysville and then Louisville. Edgar remembered how impressed he had been by his sermons. Now, however, Powell had truly reached his prime. By all accounts, he was one of Louisville's most dynamic and motivational speakers, and a social activist under whose tenure the Louisville Church nearly doubled in size in a few short years. His sermons were often published in full by the *Louisville Courier-Journal*.

Edgar introduced himself to Powell at the end of the first service. Powell remembered him from Hopkinsville and was pleased to have him in Louisville. He invited Edgar to join the minister's study class that met at regular intervals throughout the week and to teach Sunday school. Dr. Powell also engaged Edgar in what has been described as one of the most active Christian Endeavor movements in Kentucky's history. It would be through his work with Powell and Christian Endeavor that Edgar would meet most of the important people in Louisville, including John H. Whallen, the Tammany Hall–style chief of police who also owned an interest in Louisville's largest brothel, and Annie Fellows Johnston, one of Louisville's most famous authors and, like Powell, a social activist.

Edgar's first morning at the J. P. Morton Company proved to be as interesting as his first church service. His fellow clerks at the store received him with great curiosity and interest, and Mr. Griswold, the company manager and nephew of the company's founder, immediately plied Edgar with questions about why he had come to Louisville in the first place. He thought that Edgar must have surely gotten into some kind of trouble at home, or why else would he leave a community where so many people loved and admired him. The clerks came out to look at him. All stood in line to shake his hand and ask his advice, for never had someone come to the store with such glowing recommendations. Rather than put a damper on the already exaggerated expectations of his fellow employees, Edgar put on a performance that rivaled anything that they could imagine. He recited the entire fall catalog: every book, author, product, and price. Impressed, the manager gave Edgar a rooming allowance of $1.50 a week along with his regular salary of $5 a month.

Although Edgar had been hoping for more, he quickly found other means of increasing his income. An artist who lived in the rooming house introduced him to the owner of a gallery where she sold her paintings. Using experience he had gained at the Hopper Brothers Bookstore framing pictures, he did some moonlighting for the gallery and was able to double his income. Edgar also made friends with the railroad clerk who lived at the same rooming house. The clerk found Edgar temporary work taking tickets on the L&N night shift in exchange for free railroad passes, which he could use to visit Gertrude on long weekends and holidays.

It wasn't long before Edgar's co-workers at J. P. Morton accused him of being the boss's pet: he not only earned a higher income than his fellow co-workers, but he was quickly being accorded privileges that others were not. Fellow co-workers couldn't complain, however, because practically everyone in the store at one time or another turned to him for help on a particular book, author, or product. He also had become instrumental in preparing the new catalog and in answering the many questions put to him by the company's traveling salesmen who routinely stopped by to pick up supplies and process orders.

The longer he worked at the store, the more impressive his knowledge became. One day, Mr. Griswold assigned him to the showroom to wait on a particularly important customer. In his Christian Endeavor journal, Edgar only refers to this woman as "Margaret," but circumstantial evidence suggests that she may have been a grandchild or niece of James Phelps, a rich Louisville tobacco merchant who amassed a family fortune in Hopkinsville and greater Christian County.

Edgar waited upon Margaret, who purchased several hundred dollars worth of merchandise, including vases, toilet articles, and books. Like so many others whom Edgar had waited on, she was impressed and curious at his astonishing knowledge of everything in the store. Margaret peppered him with questions until he admitted that he had memorized the store's entire inventory. But this was not all that impressed Margaret. There was an artless, boyish quality about Edgar that endeared him to her, and when it came time to pay, she handed him an embossed business card and asked for his own, which he gratefully provided. The sales manager was thrilled when Edgar later processed the order. The client, he said, was the wealthiest girl in the city.

The next afternoon Edgar was called into Griswold's office and complimented for his efforts. Griswold himself had tried, unsuccessfully, for years to entice Margaret's family into doing business with J. P. Morton. Edgar had not only landed their family's account, but made such a good impression that Edgar and John Morton received an invitation to Margaret's house for dinner that night. After the initial surprise at receiving the invitation had worn off, Edgar realized that he had nothing appropriate to wear, and consequently didn't think he should go. His single pair of shoes looked like they belonged to a farmer, not to a clerk looking to make good in the wholesale distribution business. Griswold smiled and said that he would be pleased to arrange for a tailor to fit him for a new suit that same afternoon and that he would send a carriage to pick Edgar up at his boarding house later that evening. In addition, Griswold gave him a raise. Edgar would now be making $10 a month.

As promised, a carriage arrived and transported Edgar Cayce, dressed in his new suit, to what turned out to be a palatial mansion in the most exclusive section of Louisville. There were doormen to greet the carriage, servants in uniforms, and a sitting room where he was served a glass of imported wine before dinner. Everything seemed unreal to Edgar, especially Margaret, his charming and beautiful hostess for the evening. His worst fear was that he would have nothing interesting to say to Margaret or her parents, and that what he did have to say would reveal him to be the simple farm boy he felt himself to be. But as it turned out, Margaret was a member of the Glad Helpers, part of the same Christian Endeavor organization that he had joined in Louisville. They also knew many of the same people in the Christian Endeavor organization and seemed to have much in common. And Margaret's father, Edgar discovered, had made his fortune in dark tobacco. Throughout the meal Edgar entertained the family with stories about Tom Cayce's farm and the subtleties of tobacco cultivation. After dinner, when Edgar's boss went into the next room to talk business with Margaret's father, Edgar and

Margaret strolled the house and grounds. A few weeks after this evening, Margaret's father footed the bill for a major building expansion and renovation of the store. Edgar was given an office of his own and another salary raise. Now he was earning the exorbitant sum of $40 a month.

At no point in Edgar's memoirs does he admit to being in love with anyone other than Gertrude. In correspondence and other writings, however, Edgar does mention a "secret flame" and acknowledges that the deep, mutual friendship that began between him and Margaret threatened to end his engagement with Gertrude. That she was more refined and worldly than Gertrude is not in doubt. And what she may have lacked in sensual charm, she must have compensated for in other ways. As one journalist of the time described families such as hers, "Plenty of people know how to get money, but not many know what best to do with it. To be rich properly is indeed a fine art. It requires culture, imagination, and character."

Instinctively, Gertrude must have known that Edgar's promise of getting married as soon as he got settled in Louisville wasn't going according to plan. Perhaps she even knew something of his infatuation with another girl, for Gertrude dropped out of college—never to return—soon after Edgar began seeing Margaret and took to her bed, much like a widow in mourning. Her already meager weight dropped precipitously. Her shoulders drooped, and lines formed at the corners of her eyes. Edgar surely knew what was going on, for more than anyone in his life, Gertrude's physical appearance was a barometer of her mental well-being. A photo of Gertrude, taken at any given moment, could accurately reflect the tide of her emotions just beneath the surface.

Family friends assumed that Gertrude truly was in mourning, first over the passing of her grandfather, followed in rapid succession by that of her grandmother. But Gertrude's aunt Carrie and others in the household knew or suspected the truth. There had been a gradual decline in the number of letters home from Edgar, and despite his salary increases, he wasn't putting any money aside for their life together. While Gertrude took to her bed, Edgar and Margaret spent nearly every Sunday together.

The majority of the young couple's activities revolved around their work for Christian Endeavor, and at Sunday school, where Margaret was a pupil and Edgar the teacher. The class he taught was apparently more appealing for women than for men since there were twelve girls but only two boys. In striking contrast to the picnics and church socials that he and Gertrude had attended, Edgar and Margaret's work in Christian Endeavor involved visiting the county jail and hospital once each week, where they would conduct prayer services and minister to the weak and infirm.

Besides his trips to the hospital and jail, Edgar attended the theater with Margaret. His favorite play was *When Knighthood was in Flower,* starring Julia Marlow and E. H. Sothern. On one memorable night, he and Margaret managed to attend three events: a heavyweight prize fight, a Salvation Army meeting, and a vaudeville show.

Edgar had been invited to the vaudeville show by a hypnotist called Herman the Great, whom he had met in the J. P. Morton showroom. Like many carny showmen of the time, Herman the Great performed card and sleight-of-hand tricks as well as his hypnotist routines. He had come into J. P. Morton to buy playing cards, and Edgar happened to wait on him. When Herman went to pay for the cards he appeared to take the money from Edgar's pocket. He then said that these cards were being sold at such a reasonable price that he would buy a dozen packs and proceeded to take the money from the mouth of the astonished J. P. Morton cashier. Before leaving the store, he told Edgar that he thought the young clerk would make an ideal subject for hypnotism, and with permission from his manager, would put Edgar "under." Edgar agreed to be hypnotized, but advised Herman that Hart the Laugh King had had no success in putting him into a trance a few years earlier, no matter how hard he had tried. Herman told Edgar something that Hart had also told him: the more often a person was hypnotized, the easier it became to put him under and the deeper he went. Herman set about hypnotizing Edgar right there on the spot.

There is no record of exactly what Herman did to Edgar, but it is presumed that he had Edgar concentrate on a spot on the wall or some object that was held up in front of him while Herman repeatedly made suggestions that he relax and go to sleep. The next thing that Edgar remembered, he was lying on a countertop surrounded by fellow co-workers. Edgar, it seemed, had not only gone under, he had been the perfect subject and had done everything that the hypnotist told him to do. Edgar laughed about the experience and promptly forgot all about it. However, the incident took on significance later when Edgar was hypnotized a second time.

The second time occurred early the next year when Edgar accompanied his father on a business trip to Madisonville, Kentucky, a small town about thirty miles north of Hopkinsville, where Leslie—now working as a field agent for the highly successful Woodman of the World Life Insurance Society—sought to sell group policies to the Madisonville branch of the Odd Fellows fraternal organization. They had been in Madisonville only a few hours when state health officials arrived at their hotel and ordered its doors closed. The hotel was being quarantined due to an outbreak of smallpox, and no one could come or go for three days. By coincidence, a fellow guest at the hotel was a hypnotist who volunteered to entertain fellow guests until the quarantine was lifted. Edgar was one of the guests who agreed to be hypnotized.

Like Herman the Great, the hypnotist succeeded in putting Edgar into a trance. Again, he had no memory of what happened because he lost consciousness the moment the hypnotist put him "under." Edgar knew only what Leslie and the other hotel guests told him when he woke up. According to them, the hypnotist suggested that Edgar play the piano.

The hypnotist's intention was to amuse the fellow guests at Edgar's expense. At best, he expected Edgar to play off key, but more likely, to bang at the keys like a child pretending to make music. Edgar not only took the hypnotist's suggestion, he allegedly exhibited a skill far beyond what would normally be expected of a young man who had never had a piano lesson in his life. To much applause, Edgar sat down at the piano bench and began to play beautiful music. The hypnotist, no doubt, was greatly impressed, believing that he had helped the young man to discover a latent ability. The truth, however, was more astonishing than even the hypnotist could have imagined, for playing the piano skillfully was merely one of the many extraordinary "latent" talents possessed by Edgar Cayce.

For the time being, Edgar didn't pursue the matter any further. Earning a living and making plans for his future were utmost on his mind. He could stay in Louisville, marry Margaret, and in all likelihood become an owner and manager of the J. P. Morton Company—or he could return to Gertrude and face an uncertain future in Hopkinsville. The need for Edgar to make this decision reached a crisis by Christmas of 1899, when he returned home to Hopkinsville for the holidays, bearing beautifully wrapped presents that Margaret and her family had sent from Louisville.

Edgar could see that Gertrude had become a mere shadow of her former self. Her skin, Edgar said, was pale from lack of sun, and her weight had dropped to less than seventy pounds. The engagement ring he had purchased for her more than a year and a half ago was so large on her finger that he could easily slip it off and on. There is no record of the discussion that ensued between the two of them. It is reasonable to believe that their talk occurred at The Hill, during one of their private moments together in the parlor or sitting room, perhaps after their Christmas dinner and before candlelit vespers at the church. The house would have been full to overflowing with the many aunts and uncles who traditionally gathered at The Hill to sing carols and decorate their tree. Nevertheless, the family would have arranged time for Gertrude to be alone with Edgar. Then, as later, Edgar would have given Gertrude picture postcards, or perhaps a book. Gertrude liked both, and she was known to have kept an indexed collection of post-cards from around the world in a Chinese lacquer box by her bed.

Gertrude's sentiments about their future were made evident by the fact that both of their families interceded on her behalf to help Edgar to, in his own words, remain "true to his promise." Edgar's father offered him a job as his traveling field agent for Woodman of the World, and Gertrude's mother, Lizzie, promised them a place to live in the quaint cottage adjacent to The Hill when they eventually married.

It is interesting to speculate what may have happened had he decided to return to Louisville and not remain in Hopkinsville after the holidays. In a dream Edgar would have while giving a trance reading in 1941, he was permitted to visit a great hall of records, which housed bound volumes of recorded events both past and future. The records not only told of what was, but what might have been. According to this dream, had he not married Gertrude Evans, she would have died of tuberculosis in 1906. And Edgar, himself, would have died, in 1914, from a debilitating stomach condition. No mention was made of what would have become of Margaret.

As it was, Edgar and Gertrude celebrated the turn of the new century in one another's arms, amidst a fireworks display that dazzled all of Hop-kinsville. Despite many trips back to Louisville in the days to come, Edgar would never see Margaret again. Biographical records in Louisville provide not a single clue as to what became of her, though it's quite likely that she later married and continued her much celebrated work for Christian Endeavor and other social outreach programs in Louisville.

8.

Miraculous
Recovery

Twenty-three-year-old Edgar Cayce made a great insurance salesman when he put his mind to it. As his father's field representative for Woodman of the World, a company based in Omaha, Nebraska, he had total recall of prices and sales options and could easily anticipate a potential customer's want or needs. The money he made selling insurance, coupled with additional income he received selling mail-order items from the J. P. Morton catalog, amounted to approximately $50 a month, the equivalent of nearly $5,000 a month by today's standards. The trouble for Edgar was keeping his mind on his business. From the beginning of January through March of the new year, he suffered from a series of migraines that prevented him from concentrating on his work or getting a full night's sleep.

It wasn't until March 1914, when Edgar underwent surgery for appendicitis, that the cause for his headaches became known. As a result of the injury to his testicle as a child, a blood-clot had begun to form in his pelvis. This had now hardened into a lesion, causing pain along his spine and his head when he was cold or under mental stress. During the winter of 1900, he was suffering from both.

As a salesman for his father, he was traveling by train from one city to the next during the coldest months of the year. Besides this, Edgar was also feeling much guilt at having betrayed Gertrude's trust, as well as the stress of having left a high-paying and secure job in Louisville for the insecurity of being in business with an unreliable partner whose politics Edgar found as distasteful as the partner. Unaware of the physiological reason for his headaches, Edgar blamed his condition on what he considered his own poor behavior over the past year and half. As he revealed in one of his attempts to write his own memoir, he felt "ashamed" for not having been true to Gertrude. He also believed that he was not treating the angel of his childhood vision in the manner that was expected of him—for he was now applying his God-given talents to selling life insurance. Equally disturbing to Edgar, his father had radically different ideas about the insurance business and the good that might come from their mutual endeavors. An avowed racist, his father took it as a matter of pride and honor that his policies were sold to "whites only" and made this one of the principal selling points to his customers.

In keeping with the generally accepted precepts of "polite society" in turn-of-the-century Kentucky, it was the responsibility of the members of the "pure race" to see that "coons" or "niggers" not overstep their boundaries. Though Leslie did, in fact, make reference in letters to Hopkinsville's law-abiding Negroes, he also endorsed the practice of taking the "unruly" others out to a hanging tree behind the jail on East Seventh Street. Leslie apparently saw no contradiction in the fact that the livelihood of generations of Cayces had been dependent upon "nigger town" for their farm labor.

To Edgar, the notion that only whites should have insurance was something that ran counter to his fundamental belief in equality and justice. A black man had saved Edgar from drowning as a child. His black nanny had healed the infection from the wound he had suffered in his testicles, which doctors Kenner and Dulin had been unable to do. And a black man had been the first person to inspire him to read the Bible. As evidenced by the many comments made by businessmen who would later be in partnership with the younger Cayce, it is clear that Edgar couldn't in good faith join a company whose charter was based on the "purity of the white race."

Thus, to Edgar's mind, it was "Divine punishment" that brought on his headaches, and "destiny" that resulted in the event that made it impossible for him to remain in his father's business for more than a few months. The incident that brought their partnership to an end occurred on April 18, 1900, when Edgar was on a business trip in Elkton, a small town about twenty miles east of Hopkinsville. He had stopped into a doctor's office for a sedative to relieve the pain from his headaches. The doctor gave him a white powder and told him to dissolve it in a glass of water. Edgar went back to his hotel and swallowed the drug. When he woke up, Edgar was lying in bed at his parents' home in Hopkinsville being treated by Dr. Jackson and his associate, Dr. A. C. Hill. The two physicians were quite concerned about their patient, for Edgar had been found wandering around the Elkton railroad station by Ross Rogers, a longtime friend of the Cayce family. According to Rogers, Edgar had been acting strangely at the station, quite like he had reportedly acted when he was hit in the spine by a baseball years before.

The doctors didn't know how to treat him, except to put him to bed. They were pleasantly surprised when he woke up the next morning and seemed to be fine. There was only one problem: Edgar could only speak in a whisper. The two doctors were not concerned at this point because they believed this was only a temporary condition, resulting from a shock to his system from the too-strong sedative. Either that or he had caught cold wandering around Elkton without a coat or hat. Edgar was given a solution with which to gargle and told that his voice would soon improve. Gertrude dedicated herself to seeing him get well.

But Edgar's voice did not improve. Days passed, then weeks, and eventually months. His voice seemed only to get worse. A throat specialist, Dr. Manning Brown, made an examination and declared him to be suffering from ophonia or laryngitis, and believed that it would soon heal itself. Margaret, back in Louisville, heard about Edgar's condition and paid to have a European specialist visit Hopkinsville to examine him. But this just exacerbated his condition. He could still speak only in the faintest of whispers and after three months was convinced that he would never be able to speak normally again. Not even Gertrude's patience or the aromatic tea her mother prepared from herbs in the garden would help.

Edgar Cayce believed his life was in ruins. He certainly couldn't sell insurance, or return to his job at the J. P. Morton Company in Louisville. Nor did there seem to be any point in continuing his engagement to Gertrude. In a moment of self-loathing and pity, he begged her to release him from his obligation, saying that she deserved more from a potential husband than he could ever deliver.

Gertrude would not consider letting him back out of their engagement. Her love for him appeared to be unconditional and would remain as steadfast during this crisis as it would in the even greater challenges that lay ahead of them. "She was his strength and will to carry on," a close family friend said. "She didn't give up on him when he would have preferred that she do so, and when she had every reason to want to."

The situation in the Cayce household was complicated by the fact that without Edgar to sell policies, his father's insurance business was failing.

Leslie spent an ever-increasing amount of time on the road hoping to improve the situation, but appears to have lost more money than he made. In
a letter to creditors he squarely put the blame on "some members" of his
family who were "sick." Lack of income forced the family to move to a
smaller home on Jessup Avenue, and then into a third rental on Seventh
Street, which Edgar's mother, Carrie, turned into a boardinghouse. To help
make ends meet, Annie and Mary, two of Edgar's sisters, dropped out of
school and took jobs making hats at the J. H. Anderson Department Store.
William R. Bowles, a friend of the Hopper brothers, came to Edgar's temporary relief by giving him a job as an apprentice in one of Hopkinsville's
only photo studios, which was located upstairs over Coleman's Shoe Store on
East Ninth and Virginia Streets.

It is ironic, given Edgar Cayce's later career as a photographer, and his
skill in producing museum-quality photographs, that he didn't take readily
to his job with Bowles. He exhibited none of the enthusiasm he had when
first clerking at the Hopper Brothers Bookstore, or the childish glee he took
at selling his first pair of shoes at the department store. In his unfinished
memoirs, all he said about his apprenticeship was that it permitted him to
concentrate on something besides himself and Gertrude and his own continuing poor health.

Under Bowles's direction, Edgar learned to develop using different photo
stocks and revived some of the skills he picked up at Hopper's bookstore by
assembling frames in which to display the finished photographs. The job
didn't pay very much, but it did provide a modicum of income while requiring a minimum of communication. In June of 1900, as part of his in-
ternship with Bowles, twenty-three year old Edgar was sent to Louisville to
take a brief course in the rudiments of photography at the Bryant and Strat-
ton Business College. The new profession he had fallen into turned out to be
a good one, for photography was one of the fastest growing businesses in the
country, and with few handheld cameras on the market, studios such as the
one Bowles operated were in high demand.

Edgar made a name for himself right from the start of his career. Although he would become known for his studio portraits, he also covered a
number of local events, including Republican vice presidential candidate
Theodore Roosevelt's arrival at the Union Tabernacle on October 13, 1900.
Edgar eagerly joined a large crowd to see Roosevelt—all teeth and smiles,
and wearing his famed Rough Rider hat—step out of a carriage that had
taken him from the train station to the Hotel Latham. Edgar photographed
Roosevelt exiting his carriage. In the photograph immediately to Roosevelt's
left, with his back to the camera, stands a young man who quite possibly was

Hopkinsville's own Will Starling, who had joined Roosevelt in his siege on San Juan Hill.

By this time, practically everyone in town knew about Edgar's condition. Friends urged Cayce to consult Stanley Hart, "The Laugh King," when he next visited Hopkinsville. Though Hart had tried unsuccessfully to put Edgar into a trance, he was willing to try again. When he heard about Edgar's condition, he was certain he could affect a cure and was undoubtedly pleased at the prospect of doing just that on stage in front of a paying audience.

On the night of his first performance, Hart invited Edgar onto the stage of the opulent opera house. The oil burning footlights were dimmed. Hart, expensively dressed in a black tuxedo, stood directly in front of Edgar, telling him to concentrate on an object—most likely a ring or pocket watch—which he dangled in front of Edgar's eyes. Unlike Hart's previous attempt, Edgar slipped easily into a trance.

There is no record of what words Edgar spoke, but from the moment he opened his mouth, the whisper was gone. The audience gasped, and then began to cheer. Everyone in town had heard the story of how he had lost his voice and now saluted Hart for working his magic. No doubt Gertrude, along with Hugh and Lynn, were among the cheering crowd. However, a problem soon became evident. Once Edgar was released from Hart's hypnotic suggestion, his voice returned to a faint whisper, despite Hart's instructions otherwise.

Backstage after the performance, Hart explained what he thought had occurred: Edgar could not go past the "third stage" of hypnosis and could therefore not take "posthypnotic suggestions." Hart concluded that the problem was not the power of his suggestions, but Edgar's inability to go deep enough into trance to affect the cure. Hart was sure, however, he could make the cure permanent and promised that for $200 he would keep trying until he got it right. Edgar agreed, though it was not clear how he or his family were going to come up with the $200. It is reasonable to conclude that the editors of the *Kentucky New Era*, Hopkinsville's largest newspaper, agreed to contribute this amount because Hart reportedly met with Edgar and the editor and publisher before adjourning to the office of Manning Brown, the Hopkinsville throat specialist who had previously examined Edgar, and who now agreed to examine Cayce both before and after the hypnotic session.

As promised, Hart quickly put Edgar into a trance. Again, Edgar began to speak in a normal voice. But as soon as Hart gave the command for his subject to wake up, Edgar could speak only in a whisper. As it was later revealed, Hart's appraisal of Edgar's condition was correct in that his laryngitis—though physiologically triggered—was prolonged by his psychosomatic doubts about himself and his purpose in life. However, Hart failed to understand how "special" his subject was. The truth was that Edgar actually could go into a deep trance. In fact, he could go into a trance that was perhaps deeper than any of the other subjects Hart had worked with.

Frustrated, Hart boarded a train and continued his tour in other cities. Although he had failed to help Edgar, he had provided an important insight that would later be used to restore the young man's voice. Hypnotism did indeed have a strange and powerful effect upon Edgar Cayce. Exactly what it was Hart did not know—but he knew from reports from previous hypnotic trances that Edgar had undergone in Louisville and Madisonville that his subject was capable of doing some extraordinary things while in a trance state. Hypnotizing Edgar seemed to bring out a power that was somehow related to his ability to "read" closed books in his sleep or locate lost objects.

There was, of course, much talk at The Hill on the subject. A former professor of Gertrude's, Dr. William Girao, who taught German and psychology at South Kentucky College, had seen the demonstration at the Holland Opera House and became fascinated by the phenomenon. A small man with large, deep-set eyes and a mustache, he was as intensely interested in clinical research as he was in establishing a name for himself. Thus, Edgar's "condition" was a challenge he could not pass up.

No records exist to indicate what possible role, if any, Gertrude may have played in Girao's entrance into the Cayce story, but it is logical to assume that her desire to see Edgar cured overcame her fear that he was being treated as a test subject rather than as a patient, and that she may well have encouraged Girao to get involved. In the days to come, when Girao would begin giving press interviews and would subsequently arrange to have Edgar hypnotized while on display in the front window of a Hopkinsville funeral home, Gertrude's opinion of Girao would change.

After discussions with Edgar and his family, Girao sent newspaper clippings about Edgar, along with his personal observations about his case, to a doctor in New York, unfortunately named John D. Quackenboss. A leading practitioner of hypnotherapy and an ardent believer that all illness could be healed by directing the unconscious mind of the sufferer to heal the body, Quackenboss took a special interest in Edgar's case and requested more details. Girao supplied them. Much to the surprise of Edgar, who was not informed of Quackenboss's interest in his case, the eminent hypnotherapist arrived by train in Hopkinsville, determined to succeed where Hart had failed. But unlike Hart and Girao, he was more interested in the medical implications of the phenomena than he was in putting on a performance or collecting a reward.

Quackenboss was reported to be a quick-moving, sharp-featured man with a kindly attitude toward his patient. He asked many penetrating questions, listened to Leslie's account of Edgar's childhood experiences, and took copious notes of everything he saw and heard. Edgar was taken back to Dr. Brown's office, where Quackenboss was quickly able to put him into a trance. But getting him into trance was a great deal less difficult than restoring his voice. Quackenboss was no more successful than Hart had been. Hypnotized, Edgar could speak normally. Awake, he could only whisper.

Unwilling to give up, Quackenboss decided to try a different kind of experiment. In trance, he asked Edgar to put himself to sleep for twenty-four hours. To everyone's surprise, Edgar took the suggestion quite literally, just as he had previously done at The Hill when Gertrude told him to sleep. He went instantly to sleep and could not be awakened for exactly twenty-four hours—precisely to the minute. Though the experiment was viewed as another failure—Edgar was again without his voice when he woke up— another important insight had been gained. While under trance, Edgar could and would do exactly what he was told.

Like Hart before him, Quackenboss gave up and returned home. Girao, however, was still intrigued. He studied Edgar intensively. The experiments had convinced him that hypnotism was still the solution to Edgar's problems—if only the right suggestions could be put to him. The problem, Girao believed, was finding the right combination of suggestions. Adamant about continuing the experiments, he enlisted the help of Al Layne, the only person he knew in Hopkinsville who had training in hypnotism, and who already knew about Edgar through his wife, who employed Annie Cayce at J. H. Anderson's Department Store.

A middle-aged man suffering from chronic malnutrition, Layne had become interested in hypnotism and osteopathy as a means of improving his health. When Edgar first met Layne he was in his late thirties, had a pencil-thin gray mustache, and a predominant bald spot on the top of his head. He was a delicate man, weighing less than a 120 pounds, in contrast to his wife, Ada, a heavy, large-breasted, robust woman.

Like Hart, Layne was part of a groundswell of public interest in what today might be considered alternative medicine. Unlike Hart, however, he wasn't interested in the entertainment aspects of hypnotism's alleged power to control behavior and cure disease. He viewed hypnotism as merely one aspect of a medical treatment that also included osteopathy, the science of manipulating or realigning human vertebrae and other bone structures to permit the body to heal itself, and homeopathy, a system of treatment based on the use of natural remedies that in minute doses produce symptoms similar to those of the disease being treated, thus triggering the body's own immune response. Layne, like Professor Girao, was an ardent believer in a popular slogan of the day: "Every man his own doctor."

Layne and Girao were by no means alone in their thinking. In 1900, the year Layne learned osteopathy through a mail-order course, there were twenty-two homeopathic medical schools in the United States and more than fifteen thousand homeopaths in practice throughout the country. The American School of Osteopathy was eight years old, and the first college of "naturopathy" was at that very moment being established. Although Layne called himself a doctor, in reality he had nothing but a correspondence degree and until this point hadn't had much success in either of his two chosen sidelines.

Throughout the month of February and the beginning of March 1901, Layne and Girao had no trouble putting Edgar into a trance, at which time he would speak in a normal voice. It was during this time, in the midst of numerous hypnotic experiments conducted by Girao and Layne, that Edgar was put on display in the window of a funeral home on Eighth and Main Streets. Gertrude may well have been the one to quickly put a halt to this public demonstration. In many respects, however, the damage had already been done. Edgar now had the dubious distinction of having been both center stage at the Holland Opera House and on view at the local funeral parlor in the same year. Gertrude could well imagine that the circus might be next.

Despite their many experiments, and the interest that their funeral home display may have generated, the results were the same. As soon as Edgar came out of trance, the laryngitis returned. The only thing new about these experiments was that Edgar was more talkative in his trance state when Layne put him under than when previous hypnotists had worked with him. In addition to being able to make him do virtually anything Layne asked of him, Layne was reportedly able to have had long conversations with Edgar. Edgar would stop talking only when the suggestion was made that he go into a deeper trance, at which point communication would cease altogether.

Layne put his and Girao's various findings into another letter to Quackenboss. In return correspondence, Quackenboss noted a similar tendency about Edgar: a willingness to do what he was told. At a certain point in putting Edgar under there was a moment when Edgar's unconscious self seemed to "take charge." Perhaps, Quackenboss suggested, Layne should put Edgar "under" and ask his unconscious self what he thought should be done to restore his voice.

Layne decided to give it a try. Edgar's mother and father were initially reluctant to let their son undergo further experimentation. Their reasons were obvious. Edgar's weight had gone from 165 to a mere 85 pounds, and by his own admission, he was a "nervous wreck." The family was tired of the constant hypnosis with no results. Meanwhile, Gertrude seemed to be in no better health. Although she had her voice, she was still underweight and rarely ventured out into public, not even to attend Edgar's hypnotic sessions with Girao and Layne. No doubt she regretted having ever given her blessing for her future husband to mount the stage at the Holland Opera House.

Layne pleaded for one more chance. Edgar was willing to continue the experiments and in a brief note urged his parents to give Layne their permission. He likely wrote a similar note to Gertrude. Notes were necessary now because his whisper had gotten so painful that he could say no more than a few words at any one time. Along with his Bible, he now carried a pencil and pad. Reluctantly, his parents agreed. Leslie, Carrie, Edgar, and Layne met at the Cayce home on Sunday afternoon, March 31, 1901. Edgar lay down on the family couch, a horsehair sofa that had been part of his grandmother's wedding suite. Leslie sat in a chair near the sofa. Carrie was standing alongside Layne. Edgar, resting on his back, began to put himself into trance, as he had learned to do from having undergone so many previous hypnotic sessions. Layne made his first suggestion just as Edgar looked like he was going "under."

An exact transcript was never made of the proceeding, but based on subsequent readings, notes made by Leslie, and the recollections of Carrie, the session started with Layne saying: "You are now asleep and will be able to tell us what we want to know. You have before you the body of Edgar Cayce. Describe his condition and tell us what is wrong." Edgar began to mumble, then his throat cleared and he spoke. "Yes," he said. "We can see the body."

Layne told Edgar's father to write down what was being said. Leslie, too excited by what was happening to realize that his son had paper and pencil in his coat pocket, rushed into the kitchen and retrieved the pencil that was tied to the grocery list. Even then, he was too flustered by what was happening to write anything coherent down on the paper. The later report of what he said is pieced together from the recollections of Layne and the Cayce family.

"In the normal physical state," Edgar said, "this body is unable to speak due to partial paralysis of the inferior muscles of the vocal cords, produced by nerve strain. This is a psychological condition producing a physical effect and may be removed by increasing the circulation to the affected parts by suggestion while in this unconscious condition. That is the only thing that will do it. Suggestion to the body forces the circulation through it here and as the circulation passes along it takes that away, puts new life to it, makes the supply to the nerve force go, you see."

Layne, curious that Edgar should be addressing himself in the third person, and doing so in an unfamiliar and almost conversational tone, put another command to him. "Increase the circulation to the affected parts."

Edgar replied: "The circulation is beginning to increase. It's increasing."

Leslie, Layne, and Carrie leaned over to look at Edgar. Just as the "sleeping" Cayce had said, the circulation to his throat actually appeared to increase. They could see his neck begin swelling with blood to the point that Leslie felt compelled to lean over and unbutton his son's shirt collar. The upper portion of his chest, then throat, slowly turned pink. The pink deepened to rose, then to bright red. Twenty minutes passed before he cleared his throat and spoke again. "It's all right now," Cayce said, still in trance. "The condition is removed. The vocal chords are perfectly normal now. Make the suggestion that the circulation return to normal, and that after that the body awaken."

Layne did as Cayce instructed. "The circulation will return to normal," Layne said. "After that the body will awaken."

They watched while the red around Edgar's neck faded back to rose then to pink. Edgar woke up a few minutes later, sat up, reached for his handkerchief, coughed, and spat blood. The blood that came out was not just a drop or two, but enough to soak through the thin cotton cloth, turning it a crimson red.

"Hello," he said, in a clear voice. "Hey, I can talk," Edgar grinned.

Everyone in the room was quite moved by the experience. Edgar's mother was in tears. His father couldn't control himself, pumping Layne's hand and repeating, "Good boy, good boy, good boy!"

Edgar's sisters, Annie and Mary, who had been eavesdropping through the keyhole, also found "brother's experience," as they called it, "quite exciting!"

Edgar was elated. He wanted to be told over and over every detail of what had happened. He wanted to know exactly what had been said, who said it, and how he had looked when Layne told him to increase the circulation to his neck and his father had to unbutton his collar. The bloodstained handkerchief was evidence of how remarkable the cure had been.

Thus began and ended Cayce's first documented trance reading. The "door," as Cayce's psychic ability would later be described, had opened. And once opened, it could not be easily closed.

PART THREE

Psychic Diagnostician

9.

A Child in Need

Edgar Cayce's recovery was spectacular, but his cure was not yet complete. Approximately once a month for the next year his voice would become a whisper, making further treatments by Layne necessary. During these treatments, it was only natural that more experimentation take place. "If you can do this for yourself," Layne said, "I don't see any reason you can't do it for others."

Layne became the first patient. He had a debilitating gastrointestinal condition that he had been suffering from for more than a decade and which caused an irritating inflammation of his nose and throat. Edgar was skeptical that he could do anything about Layne's condition but was willing to try.

Edgar went into trance exactly as he had done before and answered questions about Layne as readily and easily as he had about himself. What astonished Layne the most was that Cayce—in trance—spoke about his condition with the same confidence and knowledge as a physician who had studied this particular case for years. Also interesting was the fact that Cayce would not be aware of anything he had said in trance until Layne told him afterward. Layne showed Edgar a detailed list of the stretching exercises and various medications that he had recommended. And indeed, this was apparently exactly what Layne needed: the symptoms of his illness vanished upon instituting the recommended treatment.

It was not long before everyone in Hopkinsville was talking about how Edgar's voice had returned to normal and how Layne's stomach problems had been diagnosed and cured. A few brave souls—the majority of whom were personal friends—began to approach them for help. Florence Cayce, a first cousin of Edgar's whose illness was described only as "a woman's disease," was one of their first patients. Another was one of Edgar's future in-laws, William Salter, star of the Hopkinsville Moguls, whom Edgar diagnosed as having a complex kidney disease. Salter's physician, Thomas House, who was still living in Springfield at the time, was given the diagnosis, but not told until much later how the diagnosis was obtained or who had provided it. Both patients were reported to have been completely cured upon applying the treatments Cayce recommended.

Thus began an informal arrangement between Edgar Cayce and Al Layne. Layne set up a small office in the upstairs of his wife's millinery shop, which contained little more than a desk, a cot, and a few file cabinets. Layne conducted all of the business and booked requests, and Edgar stopped in once or twice a week to let Layne hypnotize him. A stenographer, Miss Addie P'Pool, was occasionally asked to join them to take down a written record of what transpired. The cases that she recorded were as varied as the treatments that were prescribed.

Of the estimated eighty or more trance readings that Layne conducted during the first year of their informal partnership, nearly all involved medical problems. This is not known for certain, because Addie P'Pool, unaware of the long-term value of the readings, destroyed them after she left Edgar's employ. All that exists are the recollections of those present, who, for the most part, included Layne himself, sometimes Leslie, and anyone who happened to be in the millinery shop when the readings were conducted.

That Cayce could apparently diagnose illness came as less of a surprise to Layne than it did to Edgar himself, for Layne was a great believer in the power of hypnotism, and through his correspondence course had read about Marquis de Puysegure, the controversial French physician who first experimented with hypnotism in the late 1700s. De Puysegure's most famous subject, Victor, an otherwise illiterate peasant, had allegedly shown remarkable intelligence and apparent powers of clairvoyance when hypnotized. Layne may have also read accounts of Andrew Jackson Davis, the son of a Poughkeepsie, New York, shoemaker who earned an international reputation diagnosing illness much like Edgar Cayce was doing in Hopkinsville.

Layne conducted no scientific studies of what happened when Cayce

went into a trance, but through trial and error made some interesting observations. Cayce had difficulty going under after he had eaten. He couldn't
seem to concentrate on a full stomach, and if he did manage to put himself
into a trance state, he invariably woke up with a bad case of indigestion.
Layne also learned that the patients who received trance readings would
not necessarily have to be in the same room or even in the same county as
Cayce for him to make a diagnosis. Cayce—in trance—would only have to
be told where a patient was at the time of the reading, and sometimes even
this would not be necessary. In one much-discussed case, Cayce would say
that the patient he was being asked to diagnose hadn't gotten home yet but
had been delayed by talking to a friend, something that was later reported
to be true. In another reading, he would say that the patient wasn't in the
farmhouse where her husband said she would be. The husband, who was
standing beside Layne while the reading was being conducted, interrupted
Cayce by saying, in effect, "She has to be around there somewhere." At this
point in the reading, Cayce hesitated, as if mentally searching for the man's
wife, then said, "Yes, she's in the root cellar."

Layne was of the belief that it was Edgar Cayce himself who was doing
the diagnosing, or perhaps more accurately, Edgar's "higher self." Later experiments would not entirely support this conclusion, but rather would suggest that it wasn't only Edgar's higher self doing the diagnosing, but that his
higher self was the conduit or channel for someone or something else. The
Source, as Layne began to call Edgar's higher self, used language that wasn't
in Edgar's regular vocabulary and seemed to have its own distinctive personality and sense of humor. At one point during a trance reading the Source
was reported to have commented on the poor behavior of a patient's pet, and
at another time paused to mention the lovely view from the subject's window and the fact—later substantiated by the patient—that a rooster was
crowing in the yard.

A frequently discussed case was that of a Hopkinsville physician's daughter who couldn't breathe properly. She had been examined by various physicians and x-rayed at the hospital, but no one had been able to ascertain the
cause of her problem. Layne put the question to Cayce, who, in trance, said
that a small collar button had lodged in the girl's throat. He went on to explain precisely the point at which the button could be found in her wind-
pipe. Indeed, physicians located the button. It hadn't appeared on the X rays
because it was made of celluloid.

A Hopkinsville druggist was also an early patient. For two years he had
been steadily losing weight as doctors tried in vain to help him. In trance,
Cayce recommended that the druggist drink a large quantity of onion juice

each day. After hearing the reading, the druggist bluntly stated that he never ate onions, did not like them, and would not drink onion juice. According to a report by Leslie, who knew the patient, the druggist's health continued to decline. Finally, persuaded by his family and friends, and the doctor who had been treating him, the druggist began the recommended treatment and his condition quickly improved.

The case of an invalid from Nashville also proved to be quite revealing. Help was requested for the man by his son, and the reading was conducted in front of several local physicians and pharmacists. At the conclusion of the reading, the pharmacist said that the prescription could not be filled because the drugs would not compound. The young man, who had said that the reading accurately described his father's condition, was dejected, and left for the train station to return home. This, however, was not the end of the story. Intrigued by the reading, one of the pharmacists decided he would try to prepare the remedy anyway. That same day he returned to Layne's office to say that the compound was indeed possible, and further, that his search through medical books contained references to that particular combination of drugs, saying that the compound was an excellent treatment for the condition that Cayce had diagnosed. The pharmacist found the young man at the train station and gave him the good news. The young man returned to Nashville and gave his father the medicine. Just as the reading had suggested, the man got well.

The first known example of Cayce diagnosing illness from a long distance was the case of Bill Andrews of New York, who was the managing director of the Mechanicsburg Railroad. He had heard of Edgar Cayce through New York hypnotists with whom Layne had been corresponding, and who were as enthusiastic as Layne about the medical possibilities of the Cayce phenomena. Because of the patient's high profile, a stenographer was hired to take the reading, which was conducted in Layne's office in the millinery shop. Cayce diagnosed a stomach disorder and prescribed "clarawater." Although Layne had never heard of clarawater, he supposed it to be a commercial product that was readily available, much like the many other remedies and ointments that Cayce had prescribed.

Andrews wrote back from New York saying that the diagnosis agreed in all points with physicians that he had consulted, and that he intended to follow the treatment as outlined. He had been unable to find a pharmacy that carried clarawater, but was advertising for it in the *Journal of American Medicine*. He eventually wrote Layne a second letter saying that he had still been unable to find clarawater.

Edgar Cayce went back into a trance. This time he provided Andrews with the recipe. He was to use distilled water as the base into which he should dissolve garden sage, ambergris, grain alcohol, syrup, cinnamon, and Gordon's gin, No sooner had the recipe been sent to Andrews than the New York businessman wrote back saying that he had received in the same mail a letter from Paris from a reader of the medical journal who said that his father had manufactured and sold a product by the same name fifty years ago. He enclosed his father's formula so that Andrews could make it for himself. It was identical to the formula that Layne had obtained in the reading.

At around the same time that Andrews first wrote to them, friends of Layne's made a trip to France to see the Paris Exposition. Among them were two of Edgar Cayce's most staunch critics. As a test, Layne asked them to keep a written record of their activities while at the exposition. Upon their return, Layne requested a trance session to describe their itinerary. Layne then took the subsequent reading and reported to his friends that on a certain day and hour they had visited the Art Building at the exposition and admired particular paintings, which he described in detail. Far more impressive—and quite embarrassing for the Paris travelers—Layne went on to recount Cayce's report on the details of an evening when they visited a striptease show.

The success of this reading prompted another man to approach Edgar Cayce for help—this time to locate some hidden treasure. Cayce's reading ended as abruptly as it began. He said: "This land and this treasure does not belong to you and it would not be right to give you the information." Another nonmedical reading was conducted when a friend of Layne's approached Cayce with an advertisement he had clipped from a newspaper requesting information concerning the whereabouts of the missing wife of a Pittsburgh steel magnate. It offered a considerable reward for the information but stated that the woman must not be arrested or detained.

In trance, Cayce provided the address of the hotel where the woman was staying. Along with this information came the address of the home she left and the station where she had boarded a train to reach the hotel. The woman was described in detail: Cayce told of her weight, height, the color of her hair and eyes, a birthmark, and other physical marks and scars on her body. Layne's friend wired the husband with the information. He received a return wire that a private detective would be arriving in Hopkinsville shortly to find out how Cayce could have had such detailed information about the woman's anatomy. The detective arrived and Cayce gave another reading, this time tracking the woman from her original hotel to yet another. The woman was eventually found there.

Given the fact that Layne was conducting upward of ten or more trance readings a month, it is ironic how little direct knowledge Edgar himself had about them in his waking state. Layne conducted the majority of readings privately and usually Edgar knew only what Layne took the time to tell him, which usually wasn't much. Nor were Gertrude or Edgar's mother aware of how many or what type of readings were being given. It can only be presumed from the records that this is how Edgar wanted it, for he clearly found the entire business of "experimenting" with the readings unpleasant and admitted in his correspondence that he actually felt "ashamed" of them, feeling that they were not the occupation of a dignified person. He didn't mind an occasional experiment or two, but he disliked the kind of attention he was receiving.

It was for this reason, and with Gertrude's blessing, that he took every opportunity he could to leave Hopkinsville, first as a traveling photographer for Bowles, then as a studio photographer in Bowling Green, where he would end up spending the next eight years. Even then—months before the news of his supposed talents spread beyond Hopkinsville and greater Christian County—he sought to separate himself and Gertrude from the public scrutiny he knew would result from his work with Layne.

Edgar's first assignment as a traveling photographer took him to Pembroke, a town about ten miles southeast of Hopkinsville. Edgar spent three days there setting up a temporary studio in the back hall of a rented space near the Baptist Church. Bowles supplied the equipment and helped Edgar make advance appointments—mostly shooting school pictures and family portraits. Many of these early photographs are still in existence and are the earliest work of the man who would soon be recognized as the finest photographer in the state.

At the end of April 1902, Edgar moved his operation to LaFayette, approximately eighteen miles south of Hopkinsville and the home of the LaFayette Milling Company, whose "Magnolia" brand flour was sold throughout Kentucky. He had been there for only three days when he received a call from Frank Bassett, a businessmen with whom he had become friends. Bassett had been in discussions with Lucian Potter, whose bookstore in Bowling Green was one of the oldest and finest bookstores in southern Kentucky. Potter was looking for someone who could help him run the store. Edgar, eager to establish himself in a more permanent location, agreed to help Potter on the condition that he could supplement his income by running a small photo studio at the back of the store. Potter loved the idea and hired him before they had even met.

Edgar felt happier than he had in years. He not only had his voice back, but the prospect of operating a photo studio in a popular bookstore was everything he could have asked for in a job. Gertrude was also regaining her health and in frequent letters assured him of the place he held in her heart. She couldn't have been more pleased by the prospect of his new job, for it would provide a steady income and more stable environment. And the only traveling she anticipated him doing was the train ride back and forth to Hopkinsville to visit her.

Equally important to Edgar and Gertrude's well-being, Edgar's new situation seemed to give them a future to look forward to. There was plenty of room at Potter's Bookstore to expand both the photography and book businesses. And Bowling Green, at an important junction on the Louisville and Nashville Railroad, with a population of over 10,000 people, had great potential. It was, as Edgar later said, "a city that was literally overrun with students." Nearby Ogden College had been founded by a wealthy resident of Bowling Green who believed that all students in the county interested in higher education should go to college free of charge. Also nearby was the Bowling Green Business University, which at one time had the reputation of being the Harvard College of the Midwest. Potter's Bookstore was also perfectly located on State Street in front of the picturesque town square, Fountain Park, where students gathered every afternoon to sit by the fountain or stroll under the shade trees.

As in Louisville, Edgar did exceptionally well and in a short time was able to open a savings account at the First National Bank of Bowling Green. His easy and humble manner endeared him to the bookstore's longtime clientele, and his extensive and intimate knowledge of store inventory made him an instant success with the ever-changing college crowd. Despite the fact that the Clark Photo Studio was upstairs from the bookstore, Edgar managed to bring in a great deal of business, mostly portraits and school photos. And for the first time, he began taking landscape photographs, one of which includes a photo of Fountain Park after a snowstorm. By any standards, this photograph was a work of art, beautifully capturing the interplay of light and darkness on the newly fallen snow. Potter liked the photo so much that he gave Edgar a bonus and published it on a Christmas card that sold several thousand copies that holiday season.

Edgar took a room at a boardinghouse where he could live cheaply and walk to work. Potter had recommended that he go to the Hollins Boarding House on State Street, on the north side of Fountain Park, and introduced him to Mrs. Hollins, the widow who ran it. Hollins was a short, stout woman, with laughing, twinkling eyes that made everyone "feel at home," as Edgar would frequently say. His room was quite large and overlooked the park. Edgar shared it with a young doctor, Hugh Beazley, an eye, ear, nose, and throat specialist to whom he took an immediate liking. He was a short man, barely over five feet tall, and exceptionally thin. Edgar remembered him as being quite nimble and a thoroughly devoted Christian. Another boarder at the house was James Blackburn, a dentist, and his brother John Blackburn, a general practitioner who wore a full Van Dyke beard in what Edgar considered a "failed attempt to look older than his age." The others in the house included Louis Darter, a secretary at the Young Men's Christian Association, Robert Holland, who worked in a department store, and O. A. Roup, who was a circuit court judge and newspaper publisher who stayed at the boardinghouse only a few nights each month. All of the men—except for the judge—were in their early twenties, and Edgar, now twenty-five, liked them enormously.

Edgar soon joined the First Christian Church of Bowling Green on Tenth Street, where he was immediately given membership by letter of transference from the First Christian Church of Hopkinsville, and where later, by popular demand, he was made a deacon. As in Louisville, Edgar became active in the Christian Endeavor and Bible Study program, which was later renamed the "Crusaders." Although the church was not as active in their outreach program as Edgar's previous church in Louisville had been, Edgar and other members were engaged in activities such as paying hospital bills for underprivileged parishioners and collecting food for Christmas baskets. Also, as he had done in Louisville, Edgar taught an immensely popular Sunday school class.

Edgar joined a committee headed by Louis Darter to organize socials and parties at the YMCA. During one of the YMCA committee meetings that he had attended with Darter and an art teacher named George Putnam, Edgar devised a card game he called "The Pit" or "Board of Trade." The idea came to Edgar when he was listening to Beazley, Blackburn, and Blackburn's brother talking at dinner about trading options in the commodity market, where options on such things as wheat, sugar, and coffee were bought and sold. The object of Edgar's game was similar: to corner the market in commodities and become rich. Each of the sixty-four cards he had Putnam draw represented various commodities. Ultimately the game became so popular that Darter had special decks printed for YMCA members and urged Edgar to submit it to one of the big game companies.

Edgar sent a sample to Parker Brothers, in Salem, Massachusetts. He received a cordial letter in response, along with a check for six dollars, thanking him for the idea. The Pit was soon being distributed nationwide. All Edgar received for his efforts were a dozen decks of the cards, with the company's compliments, and two articles about his contribution, which appeared in the Bowling Green newspapers. He wrote Parker Brothers asking for a percentage of sales of the game, then visited an attorney when they refused his request, but he didn't pursue the matter further. Parker Brothers retains the copyright on the popular game, and The Pit cards are still being sold today.

Edgar had far more success claiming the reward in a nationwide crossword puzzle contest being run by one of the large New York newspapers. There is no evidence to suggest that he used his psychic abilities to "sleep" on the puzzle, but he did come up with all the correct answers in record time. He took first place and proudly carried the gold watch that he won as a trophy.

Edgar was doing so well in Bowling Green that he didn't even mind the occasional visits by Layne, who would come to treat his voice and would then inevitably have follow-up readings on his various patients. At Edgar's request, the purpose of the visits was kept secret. Layne merely introduced himself at the boardinghouse as a friend and conducted readings in the privacy of Edgar's bedroom when Beazley was not there. Layne kept trying to impress upon Edgar how successful the readings were, but Edgar didn't want to hear any of it. The only reading he gave during this time that had a lasting impact on him was one conducted on behalf of six-year-old Aime Dietrich, whose reading would become the most heavily researched and documented of Cayce's early career.

Edgar became involved in the case in early August 1902, when Layne had approached Professor Charles H. Dietrich on a street corner in downtown Hopkinsville. Dietrich, one of the best-educated and most-respected residents of Christian County, had originally come to Hopkinsville from Ohio when he took over as superintendent of schools. He literally turned the school system upside down, lobbied to pass a bond issue, and as a result, gave the Hopkinsville school system a reputation for being far ahead of any town of its size south of Columbus, Ohio. He had recently resigned as superintendent and had accepted a position with the American Book Company in Cincinnati. Although he now worked in Ohio, his family was still living in Hopkinsville and he frequently visited them. Practically everyone in town had heard at least one story about his daughter Aime's tragedy. His six-year-old had had a bad case of diphtheria as a toddler, which was believed to have caused her brain to stop developing. Doctors considered her mentally retarded.

Having met Dietrich on the street one day, Layne inquired of Aime's status. When told that her condition hadn't improved, Layne volunteered Edgar's services. Dietrich thought the entire idea was patently absurd, but agreed to have Cayce give a reading since Layne was so insistent, and since he and his wife had tried just about everything else. Layne immediately called Bowling Green, and Edgar agreed to meet him at the Hopkinsville train depot the next morning.

Layne met him at the station, and they walked through the back alleys along Coleman Street to the Dietrich house on Walnut Street and then entered the kitchen through the stable. They had taken the circuitous route at Dietrich's request so that a neighbor, James West, a prominent member of their own Presbyterian Church, wouldn't see Edgar entering their house.

Inside their elegantly furnished home, Dietrich asked Edgar if he wanted to see the child. Edgar said that he didn't know whether or not he should. Except for Layne and a few family members, he had never met any of his patients. Minnie Dietrich, the child's mother, made the decision. She showed Edgar into a playroom where a healthy-looking six-year-old was on the floor playing with building blocks. A nurse sat near her in a chair watching. Edgar said hello, but the child barely looked up to meet his eyes.

Edgar said he didn't wish to examine Aime, in fact, saw no point in doing so, because he wasn't a physician. Layne led them into the living room where they spoke to Aime's father and mother for a few minutes before he lay down on the sofa and Layne guided him into a trance. Twenty minutes later, when Edgar woke up, Mrs. Dietrich was in tears. Mr. Dietrich was later described by Layne as looking to be in a state of shock. He and his wife said they had never seen or heard anything like what they had just experienced. Between her sobs, Minnie Dietrich said, "You've given us the first hope we've had for a normal baby."

Edgar asked what he had said, admitting that he hadn't even known what was wrong with the child when Layne called him to their house. She had looked normal enough when he saw her on the floor playing with blocks. Mrs. Dietrich described her condition. Aime suffered from diphtheria when she was two years old, apparently resulting in convulsions in which she would fall down suddenly and her body would stiffen. The convulsions had ended some time ago, but her mind had stopped developing. Although she looked like a healthy six-year-old, she had the mind of a two-year-old and was quickly losing even that. Mrs. Dietrich and her husband had taken her to specialists as far away as Florida and New York. But this had all been to no avail. The latest doctor, in Cincinnati, had diagnosed a rare brain disorder that would soon result in death.

Professor and Mrs. Dietrich felt hopeful about Cayce's reading because it was unlike any medical report they had ever received. In trance, he had told them that her condition wasn't directly related to the diphtheria. According to him, she had received an injury to her spine before becoming sick. This had occurred as she was stepping down out of a carriage and slipped, injuring her back on the carriage steps. The germs that caused her convulsions had settled in the damaged area along her spine. The body naturally undertook to protect itself by forming a membrane around the damaged area. Over time, this membrane had begun to thicken and thus impeded the circulation of blood to her head. In trance, Cayce recommended that Layne make osteopathic adjustments, which would relax the muscles along her spine and soften the membrane. "Then nature will take its course," he had told them. "She will recover."

Edgar looked skeptically at Layne. The osteopathy Layne knew had been learned in a correspondence course. This, however, didn't stop Layne from treating her. He made his first adjustments the same night that the reading was given and made a second treatment the next morning. At the Dietrichs' request, Edgar agreed to stay the night and do a follow-up reading to see if Layne was making the proper adjustments. When he woke up from the second trance, Mrs. Dietrich was smiling. She told them that Edgar would have to stay at the house a third day because Layne—according to the trance reading—hadn't made all the adjustments correctly and would have to try again. After three tries, Layne succeeded in performing the adjustments to the satisfaction of the sleeping Cayce.

Edgar returned to Bowling Green not expecting to hear from the Dietrichs again—and was afraid that if he did, it wouldn't be good news. But a week later, Mrs. Dietrich telephoned the bookstore to tell him that Aime had called the name of her favorite doll—a major step forward for a child who had lapsed into "baby talk." Another few days passed and Aime called her mother by name, and then her father. Within three weeks she was able to sit in a chair and cut out pictures with a pair of scissors. Then, within three months, the Dietrichs had a normal six-year-old daughter. In the years after that, Aime would grow up strong and healthy, and eventually would graduate at the top of her class in college.

The Dietrich reading, more than any other, compelled Edgar to continue working with Layne. It also gave him the first "legitimacy" he had known since Layne set up his small office in the millinery shop. The Dietrich family never again asked Edgar to enter their house through the stable door. He was treated with the respect and honor accorded a doctor who had saved the life of their child. Mrs. Dietrich wanted to shout Edgar's praises from the rooftops. Instead, she went to the newspapers.

Edgar's reaction to the short article that ran in the *Hopkinsville Ken-*

tuckian was mixed. He was obviously elated that what he had done had been helpful and that others would know about it. However, it brought the kind of notoriety that he knew from his childhood years at the Beverly Academy could be dangerous.

Gertrude didn't want to know anything about his trance activities and was horrified by the account in the paper. Edgar's abilities were something that they rarely discussed, and when the subject came up, Gertrude viewed it as an intrusion on their personal lives. She much preferred to daydream about the conventional lifestyle they both yearned for, and the wedding they had been planning for the last five years. Gertrude envisioned herself as one of the dignified ladies in long skirts who pushed their babies in perambulators through Fountain Square. Edgar, dressed in a dark suit and high-starched collar, would join her on his lunch breaks for a stroll around the square before eating sandwiches she made for him.

With Edgar's career going so well, a marriage license or "bond" was obtained in Bowling Green and preparations were begun for a wedding to be held on June 17, 1903. Three hundred invitations were sent out. The Hill and its adjoining property were put in shape by a team of gardeners, and cooks were hired to help out in the kitchen. The food had to be gathered and prepared, final additions were made to Gertrude's hope chest, and her wedding dress was made. Gertrude's dress would not be the long flowing dress appropriate to a church wedding but rather a more practical white "traveling gown," which she could wear around the gardens, in a carriage, and on the train en route to their new home in Bowling Green. Her dowry was modest, the most valuable asset being a hundred dollars worth of gold coins that her mother had given her. Owing to Edgar's still-modest income, there would be no honeymoon.

The wedding took place as planned and the day was bright and sunny. The Hill, one guest said, "had never looked finer." Hugh Beazley and Robert Holland, Edgar's housemates, arrived from Bowling Green. Also attending were Gertrude's brothers, Hugh and Lynn, who together with Hugh Beazley and Robert Holland, were the best men. Leslie, Carrie, and Edgar's four sisters were naturally present, along with what seemed like the entire population of Edgar's aunts, uncles, and cousins from Beverly and the surrounding area. The Evans side of the family was also well represented. There was Carrie Salter with her new beau Dr. Thomas House, Stella, Aunt Kate and Mrs. Evans, Will and Hiram. Conducting the ceremony was Harry D. Smith, the minister at the Ninth Street Christian Church in Hopkinsville.

The wedding photos, compliments of the Potter Studio, show Gertrude looking more radiant than at any other point in her life. Her face was flush and full, and she wore a white rose in her bonnet. By contrast, Edgar, sitting beside her, looks bewildered and almost afraid.

The twenty-three-year-old bride and twenty-six-year-old groom received their guests in the rose garden. The reception was held on the lawn at the rear of the house, where long tables were filled with cooked hams, bread pudding, turkey, sweet potatoes, and bowls of lemonade. Following the reception, Edgar and Gertrude were bundled into a carriage and escorted to Guthrie, a small village on the Louisville and Nashville train line. There, before boarding the 8:35 P.M. train for Bowling Green, they ate another meal, compliments of one of Edgar's childhood friends, Tommy Crawford.

It was after 10:15 P.M. when they finally arrived at the Bowling Green station. To their surprise and utter delight, the depot platform was crowded with people assembled to welcome Edgar and his new bride. The young couple stepped off the train into a shower of rice and hoots and hollers. More than a hundred young people from Edgar's church and Christian Endeavor group were there to greet them. Among them was Carrie Redd, the future Mrs. Hugh Beazley, who would become a dear and devoted friend to Gertrude, and who would help to see her through the first of many difficult years of marriage to Edgar.

The young Cayces, unable to remain at the singles'-only Hollins house, moved into a boardinghouse directly across the street. It was run by a Mrs. McCluskey, whose husband worked as a mail clerk for the railroad. Her boardinghouse, like the Hollins house, was a very large wooden frame building painted in shades of white. Inside, a parlor, or music room, was to the right of the main hall, and a sitting room was to the left. The stairway in the hall that took them upstairs was circular, which Gertrude took as a sign of good luck since her grandfather had brought just such a stairway to Kentucky as a decorative feature for the Hopkinsville asylum. The young couple lived in a room on the second floor that had a view of State Street.

The luck of the spiral stairway, if indeed there had been any, didn't last more than a few days, for Layne was constantly calling on Edgar in Bowling Green, begging him to relocate back to Hopkinsville where he envisioned them opening a "psychic medical practice." Layne was so sure that their partnership would be a success, and that they could actually charge a fee for what they were presently doing for free, that he offered Edgar Cayce a guaranteed weekly salary of $40, about $2,000 annually.

Gertrude wanted the entire matter of Edgar's trance readings kept quiet, but she knew there was trouble ahead when Layne showed up a few days after the wedding during their first Sunday dinner in Bowling Green, at the Hollins house. No sooner had he arrived than he promptly started into conversation with Judge Roup. Roup, like others at the boardinghouse, had wondered about Layne's visits and was curious to know what went on when he and Edgar disappeared into his room together.

Layne told Roup that he had come to give Edgar therapy for his voice. This answer didn't satisfy Roup, who asked why Cayce would consult an unlicensed medical practitioner with a correspondence degree when his best friend, Hugh Beazley, was a specialist. It was there that Layne, perhaps egged on by the insult, told Roup that he had not only put Edgar into a trance and that he "cured" himself, but that Edgar had also helped cure some of his other patients.

Gertrude, who had been listening to the conversation with growing concern, burst into tears and fled from the room. Edgar, however, did not follow her. Despite the heartfelt words Edgar would later use to comfort her, it seemed to the young bride that her husband valued the work he was doing with Layne more than he shared his wife's concern for the impact it might have on them and their marriage.

At the dining table, with so much already said, Edgar was forced to describe their "experiments." He, Beazley, Roup, Layne, and the Blackburn brothers then crowded into Beazley's room. Edgar answered questions about the Dietrich case and described some of his earlier childhood experiences. Had the men not known and respected Edgar as much as they did prior to receiving these revelations, they would undoubtedly have thought the claims ludicrous and dismissed Edgar as a fake, a fraud, or just out of his mind. But all the men had witnessed Edgar's honesty and integrity over the past year and if anyone in the room believed that fraud was involved, such doubts were directed at Layne, not Edgar.

Layne suggested they witness a reading for themselves, which they readily agreed to. They couldn't do the reading right away because Edgar had just eaten, so the group spent the next two hours talking about various cases Edgar had diagnosed. After adequate time for digestion had passed, he went into trance and proceeded to make diagnoses, offer treatments and conduct follow-up readings on a number of Layne's patients. When he awakened, the room was silent. Edgar's friends looked at him with speculation and wonder. It wasn't only that he had made what sounded like bona fide medical diagnoses. He had recommended three completely different kinds of treatments—that medicine be given to one patient, electromagnetic therapy to a second, and osteopathy to a third. He reportedly described in detail the location of blood clots in one patient's lung and addressed several other cases of lesser importance. The doctors in the room were astonished at how knowledgeable Cayce had appeared to be—and not just in one particular field of

medicine, but in all fields. And along with his recommendation for electromagnetic therapy, he had prescribed an as yet untested state-of-the-art treatment being practiced by only a few physicians.

Dr. Blackburn asked Layne if he was planning to do what had been recommended in the reading. Layne said that he was—that he had no reason
not to. Though he only had a mail-order degree, Layne was now not only
practicing medicine, but openly doing so out of the millinery shop. And unknown to Edgar, Layne now had a sign hanging over the door to his office
that advertised Layne as a doctor.

Edgar didn't stay to listen to what transpired between Layne, Roup, and
the physicians. He returned to his room to find Gertrude packing her clothes
into her hope chest to leave. It took all of Edgar's power of persuasion to convince her to stay.

Her concerns were many. The man Gertrude had fallen in love with was
gentle and sensitive, with a deep compassion and love of nature and of people. The man who had slipped into the back door of the Dietrich home to
give little Aime a trance reading, and who now "performed" for Blackburn
and the others was a mystery—a man with a strange voice that seemed to
come out of some dark place. That voice was not that of Edgar, or at least the
Edgar Cayce she knew and loved. That voice was distant, clinical, and although it exhibited humor, it had an almost impersonal or omniscient outlook on life, and not someone or something that could love or be loved as a
man loves a woman or a woman loves a man. That strange voice, that other
man who emerged when her husband went into trance, brought with it
problems that would prevent her and her husband from living the normal
life they had both hoped for and believed in. This first Sunday in Bowling
Green, Gertrude came to recognize that she was not able to have one man
without accepting the other.

Gertrude's decision to stay in Bowling Green that night was a pivotal
moment in their marriage, for no matter what crisis or challenge they would
encounter in the years to come, or how estranged their marital relations became, Gertrude steadfastly remained at his side. Edgar turned his back on
many other people in his life, and at least once, tacitly turned his back on
Gertrude, as he had done in Louisville, but Gertrude would always stick
with him no matter how difficult things got. And difficult times were right
around the corner. There would be no quiet strolls through Fountain Square,
with babies in carriages, for early the next week they were greeted by the
first of two front-page stories about Edgar in the *Bowling Green Times-
Journal*, both written by Judge Roup.

In Roup's first story, dated June 24, 1903, just one week after their wedding, both Edgar's place of employment and his church were named, along with details of his schoolboy experiences and a summary of the Aime Dietrich reading. The next day, the Nashville papers picked up the article and it ran in papers throughout Kentucky and Tennessee. Any thoughts Edgar and Gertrude may have had about remaining anonymous were dashed for good.

At work, Edgar was treated with sudden distrust and suspicion, as if he had betrayed Potter's confidence by not letting him in on his secret life as a psychic healer. The same people who had come out only days before to greet him and his bride at the Bowling Green train platform now avoided their company. The young couple was asked to leave the boardinghouse, and at Potter's request, Edgar was asked to look for another job.

In a letter home, Edgar referred to the various accusations made about him at church and at the bookstore as being "very ugly," suggesting that he was being called the same names that had been used by his classmates and their families at the Beverly School: Edgar was a "freak," and his trance abilities the work of the Devil. He was summarily asked to leave the First Christian Church of Bowling Green.

Al Layne faired no better than Edgar and Gertrude. Not long after the newspaper article ran, he was asked by the state medical board to close his office in Hopkinsville. Feeling guilty for their part in creating such unpleasant circumstances, the two Blackburn brothers interceded on Layne's behalf with the medical board, and through their efforts he gained entrance to the Southern School of Osteopathy in Franklin, Kentucky, from which he eventually graduated.

Layne's entrance to medical school, however, was of only slight consolation to Edgar, and none at all to Gertrude. They were beginning to feel as if their life together was over before it had even begun.

10.

Mind Is
the Builder

In July of 1903, Edgar and Gertrude returned to The Hill as they would invariably do again and again in the difficult years ahead. Here, they could be assured of acceptance, a roof over their heads, and sound advice from three loving and caring aunts who had only the couple's best interests at heart.

Gertrude's Aunt Carrie, now married to the debonair Dr. Thomas Burr House, was the first to try and talk sense into Edgar and her niece. Packing their bags and leaving for another city wasn't going to solve their problems, nor would ignoring the "special gift" that she believed the Lord had given to Edgar. His trance readings, she told Gertrude, would be no more accepted in Bowling Green than in Dallas, Chicago, or anywhere else. The young couple would have to make a life for themselves despite what others said about them, and there was no reason not to do it in Bowling Green. Carrie and her sisters felt so strongly about Edgar and Gertrude remaining in that city that they did something that they had once vowed to their own father never to do. They mortgaged The Hill to raise capital so that Edgar could open his own photo studio. It was a magnanimous gesture that touched Edgar and Gertrude very deeply.

He and Gertrude did everything they could to live up to the family's expectations. Acting as if they were confident and unperturbed by the events that had transpired earlier, they returned to Bowling Green and moved into a modest cottage on upper Twelfth Street owned by Mrs. Ernest A. Vick. Although small, it had a wide and well-groomed yard with tall sugar maple trees. Edgar took great pleasure sitting out on its lawn with Gertrude in the late afternoons.

Joe Darter, Edgar's friend from the YMCA, petitioned the elders at the Bowling Green Christian Church for a hearing to discuss Edgar's reinstatement as Sunday school teacher and deacon. Church records do not reveal the exact details of the private meeting, but it is clear that Darter, an enthusiastic and articulate public speaker, and himself a second-generation member of the church, convincingly argued Edgar's case before the elders. There is every reason to believe that Darter cited no less an example than Alexander Campbell, the co-founder of the Disciples of Christ Church, who was reported to have had a number of psychic visions and examples of precognition. In 1807, while he and his family were sailing to America, he had a dream in which their ship, the *Hibernia,* was sunk. As he had predicted, their ship was wrecked and Campbell and his family were safely taken to shore. During Campbell's college years, he was visited by an angel who told him much about his life to come: his travels, his two marriages, and the large audiences to whom he would preach. All of what she told him came true.

Thanks to Darter, Edgar was welcomed back into the church. Various members of the congregation still voiced their concerns and sometimes made the young couple's church experience unpleasant. Edgar had such a long and distinguished history of service though, that no one dared to ask Edgar or his wife to leave the church again. Nor, for another forty years would this type of problem recur. Records indicate that attendance in Edgar's Bible study class at the Bowling Green Christian Church actually increased as a result of the newspaper articles and subsequent controversy.

Edgar had an easier time than he had anticipated in restoring his reputation in the business community. In a wise business decision, no doubt prompted by Gertrude's savvy financial instincts, they chose Frank Potter, a distant cousin of Lucian Potter, Edgar's former employer, as a partner in the new photo studio. Frank, an extrovert, knew a great many people from his previous job as assistant county court clerk. He was a tall blond man with an amicable personality, and his integrity was beyond question. On July 22, 1904, using money from the mortgage on The Hill, together with a lump sum from Potter, they purchased the former Harry L. Cook Studio,

Edgar's former competitor in the Gerard Building on College Street, facing Fountain Square. Except for the fact that that they shared the building with a mortuary—a horse-drawn hearse was frequently parked in front of their office—it was an ideal location.

At Potter's insistence, Edgar attended a refresher photography course in McMinnville, Tennessee, where he learned the most modern techniques. During the eight weeks that Edgar attended school, Potter set about redecorating and organizing the studio, which was in an upstairs suite with a large glass skylight. It had shades on rollers that could be adjusted to provide just the right amount of light. Off to one side were canvas screens with scenes painted on both sides to serve as backdrops and various types of furniture to seat portrait subjects. In the back of their suite was a large room where the chemical fixing baths and washing trays were kept, along with long wooden frames on which the glass negatives were set out to dry. The printing room, with a state-of-the-art overhead projector, was in an adjoining suite. There were also two front offices to greet customers, and each came complete with its own coal stove.

The studio was a financial success from the start, with much credit going to Gertrude's family, who had not only provided the financial backing but who sent customers too. The first holiday season Edgar was in business, practically everyone who had ever been to The Hill gave themselves portraits for Christmas. But Edgar could take some of the credit, too, for many of their clients commented on how well he treated his customers and the skill with which he handled portrait subjects, especially children. He quickly earned a reputation for being able to get even the most wriggly, hyperactive children to sit quietly. "I don't know how he made Junior sit so still," one family friend later told a reporter.

One of the portraits Edgar took that fall of 1904 was of Mrs. McKenzie Moss and her young son, who were members of a very prominent Bowling Green family. Potter and Edgar had the good sense to put the photo in their display case in front of the studio. In July of 1905, Elbert Hubbard, a noted lecturer and journalist, happened to see the photo when he was walking through town after giving a graduation speech at the Bowling Green Business College. Hubbard came into the studio and suggested Edgar enter the picture into the annual *Ladies Home Journal* contest for mother and son photos. Edgar entered and won first prize, not realizing until much later that Hubbard had been one of the judges.

That same year Edgar attended the annual meeting of the National Association of Photographers held in St. Louis, Missouri—the longest trip that Edgar had ever taken. Gertrude was happy to stay home and spent her days entertaining one or two close friends or sitting in the back room at the photo studio balancing the company's books. For Edgar, on the other hand, traveling not only provided an opportunity to see more of the country, but gave him a chance to meet and make new friends. His trip to St. Louis also gave him the opportunity to display his art photographs at the convention, where he won three honorable mentions in the national competition sponsored by the association. A year later he took first place—the highest honor in his profession—with a portrait photo, possibly one of Gertrude, entitled "A Kentucky Belle."

The Cayce Studio, as it had now come to be known, did such brisk business that its only serious remaining competitor, the Clark Studio in the Mitchell Building on State Street, offered to sell Edgar its studio. Expanding their operation seemed like a good idea, especially since the location of the Clark Studio, directly above Potter's Bookstore, provided Edgar and Gertrude the pleasure of succeeding at the same location he had been asked to leave less than eighteen months before. To bankroll the purchase Edgar and Gertrude took on two new partners, Gertrude's brother Lynn, and Joe Adcock, a friend of the Salter and Evans families.

The State Street studio was larger than the one on College Street. It not only extended over the bookstore, but over most of the saddle and harness shop next to the bookstore as well as adjacent to Callis Brothers Drug Store. The front of the space housed an office, a studio, and a frame shop, all in one large room, each separated by dividers. Lynn Evans was put in charge of the operation, with Joe Adcock and an employee, Tom Barnes, shooting and developing photographs. Potter remained at the College Street studio, where Gertrude worked as the receptionist, and Edgar split his time between the two locations.

The College Street studio now became the Cayce Art Company. Gertrude, who had shown a natural talent for watercolors and needlepoint, took up hand-tinting photographs, a skill at which she became quite adept, and which fulfilled her growing need to play a greater role in her husband's business endeavors. As far as the rest of the family was concerned, they felt Gertrude should have been given sole responsibility for running the financial end of the business, leaving Edgar to confine his talents to picture taking. This certainly would have pleased members of the Salter clan who later complained that "Cayce would literally give his prints away if Gertrude wasn't watching over him." Nor was Edgar willing to actively collect debts owed the studio or conscientiously collect or pay the tax on his sales.

Had it not been for Edgar's continued need for treatments for his voice, he might have stopped doing trance readings altogether. But at least once a month, his voice was reduced to a whisper, requiring what were now routine treatments by Layne. Previously, Layne had traveled to see Edgar. Now Edgar visited Layne, often taking a morning train to Franklin, Kentucky, where Layne was attending medical school. During one of these visits, two of Layne's classmates solicited the help of a professor in an effort to expose Layne and Edgar as frauds.

The classmates had read the newspaper articles written about Cayce and Layne. They also naturally felt some resentment that the Blackburn brothers and other Bowling Green associates of Edgar's had used their influence to allow Layne to skip the first two years of medical school. The Blackburn brothers had justified their actions by pointing out that Layne already had much practical training in anatomy and osteopathy through his correspondence course and by working with Edgar. But Layne's classmates didn't see the situation in quite the same terms.

The plan to expose Cayce involved luring him and Layne into a classroom on the pretext of diagnosing a patient in the school infirmary who was being used by school officials to test the students' diagnostic competence. Once the reading was in progress, one of the students would open a door to an adjoining classroom where Dr. Robert Bowling, the school's dean and one of the most highly respected osteopaths in the country, was scheduled to teach a class. It was presumed that Bowling, who was clinically blind, would hear what Cayce was saying, realize how he and the school had been duped, and toss Cayce and Layne out on the street.

Everything went according to the plan, right up until the end. Dr. Percy Woodall, the instructor whom Layne's detractors had chosen to assist them, successfully lured Layne and Cayce into one of the classrooms and proceeded to obtain a reading on the patient in the infirmary. In the middle of the reading, one of Layne's classmates opened the door between the two classrooms. Dr. Bowling, who stood in the next room, stopped speaking when he heard Cayce's voice and began to listen intently to what he was saying. He was fascinated by Edgar's unusual discourse and the treatment he recommended. He then asked who was lecturing in the next room. A student who was party to the scheme said he didn't know. When Layne noticed that Bowling was listening from the next room, he realized what was going on and immediately instructed Cayce to awaken. Not knowing what to expect, Layne then tried to explain to Bowling what he had heard and how the other students had tricked him into having Cayce give the reading. At first, Bowling didn't say anything. He waited for Edgar Cayce to wake up and then proceeded to question him on his education and specifically, his medical training.

Just when Layne's classmates thought that Bowling would dismiss Cayce and Layne as frauds, the esteemed physician announced that he had never heard such a fine and accurate diagnosis. He considered it "perfect." Furthermore, he said Edgar Cayce's anatomy was "flawless." Even more impressed was Dr. Woodall, the professor who had been party to the plan from the start. He too had never heard such a remarkable diagnosis. To the astonishment of Layne's classmates, instead of being thrown out of the school, Cayce and Layne were introduced to the school's founder and the father of osteopathy, the esteemed Andrew Taylor Still.

Edgar would keep in touch with Doctors Bowling and Woodall for many years after this episode, but shortly after returning to Bowling Green he decided to stop making trips to Franklin. He turned for help instead to his friend, Dr. John Blackburn. If Layne could put suggestions to him, he figured there was no reason why someone else could not do it. He and Layne had made a small leatherbound book to write down the suggestions that could be used to treat his occasional bouts with laryngitis. More important, the book contained notes explaining how to conduct one of Cayce's trance readings.

The first of Blackburn's readings took place in his office. Blackburn read from the black book. Edgar Cayce remembered going into trance as he normally did and upon waking to have his voice back. But when Edgar looked around, he saw Blackburn standing at the door, pale and trembling. He asked Edgar to join him for a walk in Fountain Square while he regained his composure. As Edgar soon learned, Blackburn had used the opportunity to ask him questions not related to Edgar's voice.

Blackburn didn't tell Edgar the questions that he had asked during that trance reading, but the answers had shaken him, giving Edgar every reason to believe that he had asked questions of a personal nature: things that only Blackburn himself could have known. As a result of this reading, Blackburn became as committed to Edgar as Layne had been. That same day Blackburn insisted that a team of doctors be assembled to study the phenomena. Edgar agreed, without consulting Gertrude. Had he done so, their remaining years in Bowling Green would have been decidedly different, for Gertrude remembered only too well what had happened when Judge Roup witnessed a reading and would certainly have tried to talk Edgar out of working with the committee.

The team that Blackburn would eventually form was made up of Edward Stone, Fred Reardon, Fred Cartwright, George Meredith, Joe Ford, and Hugh Beazley. A stenographer, Jonnie Massey Clay, whose father received one of Cayce's earliest readings, transcribed many of their proceedings. The experiences of this self-appointed investigating committee, which studied Edgar for the next year and a half, would be described by Blackburn as "sometimes amusing, sometimes exciting, and very often disturbing."

Naturally, the team of doctors were initially skeptical of their subject's alleged powers. As a result of a series of tests conducted by Stone and Ford, they all quickly became converts. During one of their early tests, a member of the committee chose a piece of paper at random from his safe deposit box, sealed it in an envelope, and placed it in his inside coat pocket. The coat was buttoned and the doctor put on an overcoat over the jacket. While in trance, Cayce reportedly read to them the contents of the document and named the signatures at the bottom.

This incident was particularly memorable because a priest from the local church, Father Hynes, happened to walk into Stone's office while this reading was taking place. Like practically everyone else in Bowling Green, he too had heard of Edgar Cayce's alleged powers and said he would challenge the sleeping man to tell him what he was carrying in the bundle under his arm. Hynes himself didn't know because it was unmarked and had just come in the mail. Hynes asked Stone to put the question to Cayce. The reply came, "Altar candles." The priest opened the package to find altar candles, crossed himself, and hastily retreated down the stairs.

Another test was conducted to see if Cayce was able to tell the sex of unborn children. Nine expectant mothers, all patients of local doctors, were used as subjects, and Cayce listed the gender of each of their children. All nine predictions were correct.

The team of doctors also experimented with Cayce's apparent ability to cure himself of his speech difficulties. In trance, Cayce was asked to explain how the circulation in his body was changed merely by a command or a suggestion from the person conducting the reading. Cayce reportedly lectured the team of doctors on the power of mind over body. As Cayce—in trance—would state in thousands of later readings: "Mind is the builder . . . the physical is the result." The Source, as Layne and now Blackburn had begun to refer to Cayce's "higher self," had the power of mind control and was the controlling factor in one of the fundamental laws of nature: that material conditions in the body can be a direct outgrowth of the thoughts of the individual. A person could, by establishing control over his or her own thoughts, heal or even feasibly harm him or herself. "Every thought is a deed," Cayce said in trance. "What is held in mind largely determines the content of the experience."

In seeking to understand this message, the committee experimented by giving Cayce different kinds of suggestions while he was in a trance state. They told him that on waking he would be given a drink of water and that it would act on him like a dose of mineral salt. Cayce later gagged upon drinking the glass of water given him. During another trance reading on this same topic, Ford, a dentist, gave Cayce a cane to hold, telling him that it was a snake. Upon waking, Edgar became excited and, grasping the cane, tried to break it in half. Ford immediately interceded—the cane was an old family heirloom.

For the first time during a trance reading, the Source itself addressed the committee directly, suggesting that they conduct an experiment that would demonstrate that "mind is the builder." In trance, Cayce suggested the committee choose a person they all knew and assumed to be healthy, then arrange to have that person convinced that he looked and acted sick. "For as the tree is bent, so does it grow," the Source told the group.

The committee acted on the Source's suggestion. They chose Dr. George Meredith's son, Claude, as their test subject. They then arranged to have five people likely to encounter Claude on a particular day tell him that he looked ill. According to the trance reading, Claude would not only start feeling sick, but he would literally become sick. The group chose Claude because he was not only known to be healthy, since he recently had had a checkup, but they were fairly certain of his movements each morning and were able to solicit the help of the various merchants and people he was sure to meet.

The first time he was reportedly told he didn't look well was during breakfast in Snyder's lunchroom in downtown Bowling Green. Several of the doctors were present to observe Claude's behavior. "How do you feel this morning?" Snyder reportedly asked Claude. "Fine," Claude replied. "Never felt better in my life. Give me a big plate of ham and eggs." Snyder gave him breakfast, but not before he questioned Claude a second and third time, pointing out that he looked "pale around the gills."

Claude next ran into the druggist who queried him in a similar way. Again he said he felt "fine." Like Snyder, the druggist also commented on his appearance, saying he looked piqued. Now Claude added that he did feel "a little achy between the shoulders."

Claude's next stop was to talk to a local beer distributor, where a man in the office had been tipped off to what had been described as a simple prank. When Fred Kubin asked how he was feeling, Claude said, "I feel like Hell." Kubin agreed, and Claude added: "I'm in awful shape." His shoulder ached, he had developed a pain in the small of his back, and his stomach was "heavy."

Kubin suggested he go home to bed. Later that day Claude was feeling poorly enough that he asked his father to examine him. Indeed, Claude was getting sick. He had an upset stomach, his circulation was poor, and he felt stiff and sore. He was coming down with the flu.

Fascinated by the results of this experiment, Edgar himself decided to do some experimentation. His receptionist at the State Street studio, a young woman who was also a trained musician, assisted him unawares. In response to a question Edgar posed to her, she gave Edgar the names of two people in Bowling Green who would not normally visit the studio. Edgar lay down as if going into trance, but instead concentrated for a period of thirty minutes as hard as he could on the two people, trying to mentally force them to come to him. Each of them allegedly arrived at the studio. The first man came the same day that Edgar concentrated on him, and the second arrived the following morning. Edgar's assistant, unaware of the experiment, was mystified and asked the first visitor why he had come. The man reportedly sat on the edge of Edgar's desk and admitted that he didn't know or didn't remember.

In the years ahead, Edgar conducted similar experiments, and also helped other people to develop their own powers of mental telepathy. The conclusion that he eventually came to was that everyone had the same ability to affect people's behavior as he did. They just didn't take the time to practice using it. The only difference was that Edgar seemed to have been born with the talent, a subject that would be discussed at length in later readings. However, just because someone was born or developed the talent on their own didn't make it right. Edgar cautioned everyone that mental telepathy was "dangerous business" and that trying to use "thought" as a means to control another individual was morally wrong. "The very thing you would control in another individual," he cautioned people, "will be the thing that will destroy you. It will become your Frankenstein."

The success of the experiments prompted the doctors to begin asking Edgar Cayce about their own patients. Among those requests was one by Dr. Stone, who inquired about the health of his mother. During the course of this reading Cayce was asked to describe the room in which the woman lay and some of the articles in it. Cayce proceeded to describe the color of the walls, the pictures displayed on them, and the position of the windows in the room. He then described the bed, told where the steel in the springs was manufactured, where the cotton in the mattress came from, where that cotton was grown, and who had manufactured the different parts of the bed. Stone couldn't slow the Source down.

Upon hearing such a detailed account of the patient's room, Stone and Blackburn adjourned to Stone's mother's house outside of Bowling Green to confirm the details. They concluded that Cayce had correctly named all the

labels on the manufactured goods, including the name of the steel manufacturer on the bed frame, which was visible only after they had dismantled
the bed.

Another patient that Cayce was asked to diagnose was from Tennessee.
She was told that the swelling in her abdomen was the result of a "lacera-
tion of the stomach." In the presence of Reardon, Blackburn, and another
physician, Cayce advised the patient to forget the admonitions of the doctors
treating her and to strictly adhere to the following suggestion, one of the
most unusual regimes he would ever offer: "Arise in the morning as soon as
you awake. Have a lemon handy, roll it, and cut it in half. Eat one half and
walk just as far from the house as you can be sure of getting back without
assistance. When returning, sprinkle a little salt on the other half lemon and
eat it, drinking all the water possible." In six weeks the woman reported to
the doctors that she had a normal appetite, the swelling had disappeared
from her abdomen, and she was able to walk a mile and a half without fatigue.

The committee's stenographer, Jonnie Clay, was as impressed as the physicians. In a letter written a few years after her experience with Cayce, Clay
described his psychic powers as the most "wonderful" thing and pointed
out that even these early readings contained references to the Bible or biblical concepts that were either ignored by the committee of physicians or
deemed unworthy of inclusion in their own reports. The Source had not yet
arrived at the point when many readings would begin and end with a prayer,
or patients would be admonished to treat their bodies as a "living temple,"
but biblical language—"thee" and "thou," and metaphors such as "fruit of
the tree"—were already creeping into the readings.

The committee was far more interested in the novelty of having their
medical questions answered than in who or what the possible sources of
Cayce's powers were. As they became convinced that Cayce truly had special
powers, they gave press interviews and arranged demonstrations in front of
fellow colleagues and interested parties, all of which generated much publicity. An experiment of particular note was conducted before the Psychology Club at Potter College, for which Cayce received a gold pocket watch. A
volunteer from the audience asked Cayce about a family business matter—
about the misappropriation of funds by someone in her father's employ. The
girl later reported that Cayce's reading proved to be correct and the employee admitted to embezzlement.

One public demonstration was requested by a Professor Lambert at the
Bowling Green Business College, who was interested in a murder that had
taken place in his hometown in Canada. The victim had lived with her sis-

ter in an elegant home. Police investigators didn't have a suspect or a motive. All the investigators had concluded, based on the available evidence, was that the woman was shot sometime in the afternoon when she was walking down the stairs to the first floor of her house.

The trance information that Lambert received said that one sister had killed the other. It also told the name, make, and serial number of the pistol used, its caliber, the fact that it was purchased in Roanoke, Virginia, and the number of empty chambers in it. Furthermore, it stated that the sister, after firing the weapon, threw the pistol out the window into a gutter along the roof, where the pistol slid down the drainpipe and could be found just at the point where the gutter entered the sewer.

Lambert sent the information to the chief of police in the Canadian town. By all accounts, Cayce's data proved to be so accurate that the chief of police in Bowling Green received warrants and extradition papers for both Cayce and Lambert. When the situation was explained to the Canadian official, he requested that a second reading be conducted to describe the motive for the crime. According to the reading, the victim had sabotaged her sister's relationship with a young suitor—she had hidden a love letter in which the man asked for the sister's hand in marriage. The sister found the letter many years later, long after the "love of her life" had given up hope and left to marry another woman. The Bowling Green police chief sent the report to Canada and the suspect was confronted with the story. After hearing a description of the reading, she reportedly confessed and was sent to prison.

An equally fascinating nonmedical reading—the first known case of Edgar demonstrating precognition—was done for a division superintendent of the Southern Railroad, to whom Edgar was introduced by the president of the school where he had studied photography in McMinnville, Tennessee. The railroad executive wrote to Cayce about a mysterious accident that had occurred on his division, asking if Cayce could tell him how it had happened. The reading was conducted and the answer was sent to the railroad office. Cayce's reading suggested that a particular person had been responsible and should be let go from the railroad. The executives were skeptical, however, and requested Cayce to give another reading on the same subject. In a letter from the vice president of the railroad, Cayce was asked how they could go about proving the information in the reading. In trance, Cayce said: "If the one [person] we have given that caused this trouble is allowed to remain in the service he will, before the first of December, be the direct cause of an accident which will mean the death of the one who refused this information. It will happen in Virginia and West Virginia."

There were two interesting things about this reading: the Source implied that, by taking certain measures, disaster could be avoided. In other words, the future was not preordained—it could be altered. The reading also suggested the existence of something like karma, a theme that would reappear in Cayce's reading more and more in later years: the man who refused the information provided would suffer for not acting on it.

Nine months after Edgar Cayce gave the initial reading for the railroad executive, news reached Bowling Green of a tragic train wreck involving the individuals named in the reading. The employee who had failed to throw the switch to change the tracks the first time repeated his mistake, this time causing another accident. The railroad executive who had requested the information and hadn't acted on it was in a private car on the same tracks. Cayce's prediction that it would occur in Virginia and West Virginia had come true, for the train smashed into the private car in one state and pushed it over the line into the next.

At around the same time of the railroad reading, Blackburn reported witnessing phenomena that has almost universally been dismissed as being a figment of his imagination, or at worst an outright lie. The phenomena, as described to Cayce by Blackburn, took place at the end of a reading that was being conducted for a patient suffering from infantile paralysis. As the reading progressed, Cayce began to speak too fast for Blackburn to write down what was being said. Blackburn allegedly stuck out his left hand and told Cayce to "Hold up, there. Not so fast." At the mention of the word "up," Cayce was purported to have "floated up from the couch" so that his chest pressed against Blackburn's extended hand. Shocked, Blackburn withdrew his hand, at which point Cayce fell back onto the couch.

At first glance, an account of Cayce "levitating" would appear to be nothing more than tabloid sensationalism, for at no time before or after this incident was Cayce ever reported to have risen into the air. And yet, all other reports by Blackburn and his committee are consistent with the generally accepted facts of Cayce's alleged psychic powers. An incident that occurred some years later, during a November 1933 reading, witnessed by thirty-five people, might provide a clue that could unravel this mystery.

During this reading, one of Cayce's friends leaned over to hand the conductor a list of questions. As he did so, his hand passed over the sleeping psychic's solar plexus. The instant that the hand had crossed his body, Cayce stopped talking and jerked up from the couch into an upright position. A witness described what she saw: "[It looked as if Cayce was] being propelled [upward] by an unseen lever or pulley, without unfolding his hands from his solar plexus or using them in any way to rise to his feet." Because of this experience, investigators learned that when anything passed directly over Cayce's body in the area of his head or stomach during a reading it had the effect of interrupting the reading, as if an unseen cord between Cayce and the Source had been severed, preventing any further connection. But it also could result in an involuntary contraction of Cayce's stomach muscles, the equivalent of him being punched in the solar plexus. Cayce's sudden movement upward when Blackburn put out his hand in the midst of the reading must have seemed like levitation to the startled doctor.

By this point in Edgar Cayce's career, reports of his amazing talents had begun to cross state borders. This was mostly the result of the work of Blackburn's committee, but also of efforts made by a new friend and admirer—Professor Joe Dickey, who was soon to become the president of Bowling Green Business University. Like Blackburn, Dickey witnessed and conducted numerous trance readings between the years 1905 and 1907, and along with other Cayce supporters, sent a veritable deluge of letters to important people asking that they witness for themselves the Cayce phenomenon.

Among the people that Edgar Cayce saw during this time were the inventors Thomas Edison and Nikola Tesla, who had been invited to Bowling Green Business School by Dickey as part of a university lecture series on modern scientific discoveries. Unfortunately, little is known about these meetings. No documentary evidence exists in the Edison or Tesla archives, and Cayce's date book and other records pertaining to the meetings were later destroyed in two separate fires at Cayce's Bowling Green photography studios. Additional correspondence known to have existed between Cayce, Edison, and Tesla was also later destroyed by a well-meaning but shortsighted volunteer at the Edgar Cayce archive in Virginia Beach.

However, while no diary or first-person correspondence now exists to describe the meetings, the original letters from Edison and Tesla would be reviewed by Cayce's longtime secretary, Gladys Davis, as well as Roswell Field, a Chicago reporter who sought biographical information about Cayce for a Hearst newspaper story in 1911. This evidence, along with the text of a recently unearthed speech Cayce delivered in Washington, D.C., and a brief passage in one of Cayce's memoirs, provides tantalizing clues as to what may have transpired.

The topic of interest to Edison—like Tesla—was the possible connections between electricity and psychic phenomena. Tesla's interest in the subject was legendary, for he himself claimed to have received inspiration from his "higher self," not unlike that received by Edgar Cayce. Through dreams and visions, Tesla received mental pictures of blueprints and other technical data, which included innovations he made on high-frequency electrical transmission and wireless communications. He viewed his role as an inventor as merely tapping into his own imagination and turning what he saw in visions into a physical reality. Tesla's one-time partner, Edison, did not ascribe his inventions to any such help from "above." And yet, the fact that Edison developed a keen interest in psychic phenomena and electricity is also well documented, as were his comments to associates concerning his intent to build a device to measure the electrical vibrations emanating from people engaged in psychic activity. Edison's interest in building such a device may well have been the result of his meeting with Cayce.

The fact that Cayce, in trance, addressed this same subject at length with two other inventors—Tim Brown, a Dayton engineer who helped to found Delco, and Mitchell Hastings, a pioneer of FM radio at NBC and later an electrical engineer at IBM—is evidence that the Source was not only capable of addressing this topic, but believed that it could provide an important avenue or bridge for raising the consciousness of inventors seeking to understand the relationship between science and spirituality, which according to the Source, were the same thing. "Electricity is at the heart of all life," Cayce, in trance, would frequently tell these inventors. "Electricity *is* life."

In one particularly fascinating exchange between Cayce and Hastings, the Source would describe the physical universe as consisting of mind, matter, and energy, which were all said to be various forms of electrical vibration. The Source stated unequivocally that every phenomenon was a manifestation of the vibrations emitted by these three elements, and that Hastings must understand that a vast range of frequencies existed on or about the earth that were as yet undetectable by modern scientific equipment. The origin of all electricity, or the "first great vibration," was God's creation of the universe, which was described as a cosmic blast that started everything in motion and created matter itself. On a smaller scale, man could manifest the same Divine power as a creator or co-creator of their personal universe. "That . . . [mind, matter, and energy] are inseparable I do not believe," the Source told Mitchell Hastings, "for energy is the mind seeking to find expression—the seeking is the energy, and that expressed is the matter." In keeping with this philosophy, Cayce, in trance, would tell both Hastings and Brown that devices could be made to measure "thought forms," much like meters were made to measure volts and amperage.

The meeting between Edison and Cayce presumably took place in one of the classrooms at Bowling Green Business School and was arranged through Joe Dickey. No doubt Dickey escorted Edison into the classroom, where Edison reportedly witnessed a reading and then attempted to record Cayce's voice using a prototype wire recorder. Edison was unable to record Cayce's voice because each time he placed the speaking tube over the psychic's mouth the reading would abruptly terminate.

At the time of this meeting, it was believed that Cayce's voice could not be recorded: that his trance voice somehow did not fall within the range of Edison's equipment. However, later tests revealed that this wasn't the case. A poor but authentic wire recording of Cayce giving a reading is still in existence. The problem with Edison's experiment was a result of the inventor's equipment interfering with the alleged connection between Cayce's sleeping body and the Source. Just as Blackburn had severed the connection between Cayce and the Source by passing his hand over him, so, too, had Edison or his assistant interfered each time the speaking tube was placed over Cayce's mouth. Later attempts to record Cayce's voice were successful because the device was not placed over Cayce's body.

All Cayce said about the meeting was that he and the "electrical wizard" had a difference of opinion regarding the nature of a man's soul. Edison was a firm believer that such a thing as a "soul" didn't exist, that it was purely a cultural ideal. Edison did, however, believe that much more research needed to be conducted on the subject. "When we see the entire world seeking, seeking, seeking, there must be something [to it]," Edison was quoted by Cayce as having told him. "I am convinced that when scientists go to work at studying God, just as they have undertaken to study how to make great conveniences for mankind, we will learn something about the soul—if there is one."

Given the subject of the Edison meeting, it is also interesting to note that Edgar Cayce, in trance, could actually discuss more than just the theoretical foundations of the alleged electrical link between mind, matter, and energy. In the 1920s, Cayce would provide blueprints for devices that were purported to prove the existence of a spectrum of vibrations as yet imperceptible to modern science, and in the 1930s, would help Mitchell Hastings patent electrical devices that are still used today. But there is ample evidence that even during the early Hopkinsville and Bowling Green years that Cayce—in trance—sought to make a scientific contribution along these same lines.

In 1910, Edgar Cayce would give a reading for Tom Baugh, an electrician who had moved to Kentucky from Virginia to establish a new power grid for the city of Hopkinsville and had already installed the first dial telephone system in that city. According to Baugh, when he requested help from Cayce, the electrician wasn't aware of the photographer's reputation as a psychic. He knew only what a friend had told him: that Cayce knew the answers to many questions and could help practically anyone who came to him. Baugh asked

for and obtained a reading that provided him with technical data and a
wiring diagram, which he used to redesign an existing steam power plant on
Coleman Street when it was bought by the Kentucky-Tennessee Light and
Power Company. The grid he built based on the advice in the reading—according
to Baugh—was far superior to that of systems being installed anywhere else in the country. The fact that this power plant and grid would not
need to be overhauled until 1942, and that parts of the original power grid
are still being used today, is evidence of Baugh's success.

11.

Final Days in
Bowling Green

Ironically, just as Edgar Cayce had reached a point in his career when he was poised to receive national attention for his trance readings, an untimely series of events caused him to close his photo studios and leave the spotlight. As was the case often in his career, the problems first began with his own declining health.

On January 1, 1906, Edgar spent the afternoon in a furniture factory making photographs for a client's mail-order catalog. It was a particularly cold day, with snow on the ground and no heat in the warehouse where Edgar was shooting photographs. It was 7 P.M. by the time he returned to his studio and went into his lab, where there also was no heat. He emerged from the lab a few minutes later, shivering, and sat down by the fire to warm himself. No sooner had Edgar sat than he slumped over unconscious, sliding to the floor.

Tom Barnes and Frank Porter, who were at the studio developing pictures, carried Edgar to the sofa and called Dr. McCraken, who had an office across the street. They also sent word to Blackburn and his committee. McCraken, who arrived first, attempted to pour whiskey down Edgar's throat. The photographer's jaws locked and his teeth clenched. In an effort to pry his jaws apart, McCraken broke Edgar's lower front teeth. The doctor then put a damp cloth in Edgar's mouth to keep him from chewing his tongue. By this time, however, he could not detect a pulse.

Other doctors soon began to arrive. Some were members of the Blackburn investigating group, others were not. Edgar was given an injection of morphine, one of strychnine, and finally one of nitroglycerin. They also wrapped him in hot towels and put hot stove plates and heated bricks on the bottoms of his feet in an effort to warm him up. But there was no sign of life. Edgar's face had become ashen, with charcoal-gray circles around his eyes. No one knew what else could be done for him. They covered him with a blanket and pronounced Edgar Cayce dead.

All of the doctors but McCraken had left by the time Blackburn himself arrived, wanting to know what had happened. Blackburn became angry, telling McCraken that nothing should have been done. "Even if he were well, the stuff you put in him would kill him," Blackburn said. He sat down by the sofa and began to talk to the unconscious Cayce. He suggested that Cayce wake up, that his blood circulate normally, that his pulse increase. Blackburn talked steadily for half an hour.

After twenty minutes, Edgar Cayce's muscles began to twitch. His pulse became detectable. Finally, with a groan, he woke up. Pain wracked his whole body. His mouth was full of blood. Two teeth were gone, and the bottoms of his feet were burned. Blackburn told him what had happened and asked what he thought they should do.

Edgar told him to put the question to him when he was in trance. Blackburn put him into trance and, after seeking advice from the Source, gave him the suggestion that the poisons in his body not be assimilated, that the burns be healed, and that normal conditions return to all parts of Edgar's body. Cayce responded as he had done when curing himself of his voice problems. The area around his arms where the hypodermic needles had been administered became discolored and swollen, as if the drugs were being held there. Blackburn injected a needle and withdrew the plunger. Most of the drugs came out. At the same time, however, Edgar's pulse dropped to such a degree that Blackburn could not detect a heartbeat. After an hour Edgar's pulse returned and his muscles began to twitch. Blackburn gave the suggestion for Cayce to wake up. He opened his eyes and stretched his arms. Most of the severe pain was gone, but he was still sore from head to foot. Blackburn bundled him up and walked him home.

"I'd better stay with you tonight," he said when they arrived at the Cayce home. Gertrude was stunned, angered, and frightened by what had hap-

pened. It was perhaps because of her that Blackburn agreed to spend the entire night at Edgar's side. Early the next morning, the Cayces and Blackburn
were awakened by the sound of the front doorbell. A messenger was delivering a large floral arrangement. The card, edged in black began, "with
deepest sympathy . . ." Edgar Cayce's obituary had appeared in that morning's paper.

Four months later, Edgar was again injured, this time at the hands of the
Blackburn committee. The incident occurred during what was billed as the
committee's "final experiment," in which physicians from the County Medical Society were invited to a guild hall by the E.Q.B. Literary Club to witness a reading. Though Gertrude opposed Edgar's participation in the
evening's activities, there was little she could do short of boycotting the event
altogether and sharing her displeasure at the prospect of having her husband
put on display once again. No doubt their conversation on the subject took
place in private—if indeed it took place at all—for Gertrude remained home
all evening, and Leslie, who had traveled from Hopkinsville for this event,
accompanied Edgar, the guest of honor. The only concession Gertrude seems
to have elicited was from Blackburn himself, who promised her that he
would take good care of her husband. "I want him brought back in as good
condition as he is now," she demanded. "Don't try any tricks with him."

Blackburn made the introductory remarks before an audience of twenty
or thirty of the state's most distinguished physicians. Eventually, Edgar was
invited onto center stage. There is no record that he was asked to say a single thing about himself. He was ushered over to a table that had been placed
on the stage and laid down. As a hushed silence fell over the room, Blackburn
guided Cayce into a trance and gave him the name of a patient to diagnose.
The patient was a black man who was waiting in the next room for his cue
to come inside and be examined by the committee. But the Source disappointed everyone by saying that he couldn't do anything for the man. Later,
critics of Cayce and the work would claim the reason was racism: that Cayce,
or the Source, didn't diagnose or treat black Americans. This was patently
false. Cayce provided numerous readings for blacks and other minorities.
The most probable reason that a diagnosis was not made, as evidenced by
many later readings, was that the Source had determined the patient to be
incurable, and he literally could "do nothing" to help him.

The demonstration continued when one of the doctors in the audience
asked Cayce to diagnose a patient he was treating at Potter College, located
just outside of Bowling Green. Blackburn gave the suggestion. This time the
information came through. Cayce stated that the young man was recuper-

ating from typhoid fever, that he had a pulse rate of 96, and that his temperature was 101¼. Cayce then recommended that the patient be placed on a new diet and said that his current treatment was not adequate to facilitate his recovery. As soon as Cayce had finished, three physicians were dispatched to Potter College to ascertain whether or not the information was accurate. Upon their return, the doctors reported that the information that had come through was absolutely correct. The patient was indeed recovering from typhoid fever and his blood pressure and temperature was what Cayce had said it was.

The subsequent diagnosis and report caused much commotion in the guild hall, prompting other doctors to come onto the stage and "test" to see if Cayce was truly in trance, or whether the performance was an elaborate hoax. Blackburn apparently didn't know what they had in mind or didn't react quickly enough to prevent them from their experimentation. It is also possible that Blackburn and his committee would have rather risked Cayce being injured than taint the proceedings by suggesting that doctors besides those on the committee would be prevented from personally examining him. Before Blackburn took action to shield Cayce, Dr. William Sadler, a visiting osteopath from Chicago, mounted the stage and drove a long surgical needle into Cayce's arm. When this didn't result in the reaction that the doctor expected, the needle was driven into the sole of his foot. Cayce still didn't react. In the meantime another doctor had thrust a hat pin through one of Cayce's cheeks while a third ran a penknife under the nail of his left forefinger, slowly lifting the nail away from the flesh. Still there was no indication of pain and blood did not flow. The doctors were mystified.

When Blackburn gave Edgar Cayce the suggestion to end the session and Cayce came out of his trance, he groaned loudly. Blood poured out of his cheek and onto the table. But however painful and humiliating the experience was for Edgar, he kept his anger to himself. The worst he said about his treatment at the hands of the medical association was a single comment in his memoirs. "In their enthusiasm and curiosity, the doctors had forgotten that I was someone like themselves," he wrote.

Leslie took Edgar home. Blackburn's sincere apologies were not enough to assuage Gertrude's anger or dull her husband's mental and physical pain. Although Blackburn and Cayce still called one another friends for the remaining three years the Cayces would live in Bowling Green, Edgar never again submitted himself to the committee for a reading, and the committee subsequently disbanded. And it was perhaps because of Gertrude's lingering resentment toward what had happened that Blackburn failed to conduct follow-up readings about how best to treat Edgar's wounds. The injuries that

Edgar sustained from the experimentation took months to heal, and the cuts under his nail left his finger disfigured for the rest of his life.

Had this been the last of the misfortunes visited upon Edgar and his family he might never have left Bowling Green. But three days before Christmas in 1906, while Edgar was still in the midst of recovering from the committee's last experiment, an arsonist set fire to the State Street studio, burning the building to the ground.

Neither Edgar, Gertrude, or John Blackburn revealed the name of the suspected arsonist, but there is ample evidence to suggest that the likely candidate was a member of Dr. David Amoss's Night Riders, the infamous group of hooded vigilante tobacco farmers who pillaged and burned many homes and properties in Christian County during this time. The presumed motive was revenge for Edgar allegedly having given readings for John T. Hanberry, a Christian County circuit judge who had organized a campaign to infiltrate the Night Riders. The truth about the fire may never be known, for Hanberry would later deny having received any readings, and Dr. Amoss never publicly acknowledged or revealed the details of his many terrorist acts.

Arson for insurance purposes, however, can be definitely ruled out as a motive for the fire, for the State Street studio, like the one on College Street, was doing brisk business. The State Street fire was also far more devastating to Cayce and his family than anyone outside their inner circle could have imagined. Insurance was paid for the loss of his photography equipment, but not for thousands of dollars' worth of paintings, prints, and watercolors that were on consignment from a New York art gallery. Had Edgar actually purchased the prints, his insurance policy would have covered the loss. Because the prints were on consignment, the photographer and his partners owed the New York gallery $8,000, which was equivalent to $80,000 in today's currency.

Joe Adcock declared bankruptcy. Edgar couldn't do the same because a lien would have been placed on The Hill. He had to pay the money back or risk his in-laws losing their home. The pressure was especially intense on twenty-seven-year-old Gertrude, for not only was her family house at risk of foreclosure, but she was six months pregnant. To help out, Gertrude's mother came from Hopkinsville, and she and the Cayce family moved together from the Vick house to a less expensive rental on the corner of Main Street and Park Avenue.

It was at the Main Street house that Gertrude gave birth on March 16, 1907 to a nine-and-a-half pound boy, whom they named Hugh Lynn, after both of Gertrude's brothers. Dr. Blackburn attended, Miss Daisy Dean was the nurse, and they were assisted by Gertrude's mother, Lizzie. Although the delivery went smoothly, the dark-haired Hugh Lynn cried incessantly. Edgar thought that the child would "scream itself to death" before a reading told them that the infant was not receiving enough nourishment from his mother's milk. They obtained a wet nurse and the problem was solved.

Hugh Lynn's crying, however, didn't detract from the joy Edgar felt at finding himself a father. Nearly twenty years later, he would reflect back on the experience in a letter to a young couple expecting the birth of their own first child. "I often feel no one knows how to appreciate . . . [having a child] until they have experienced such a thing themselves," Edgar wrote. "The expectancy of seeing a miracle enacted before your very eyes . . . [will cause the two of you to grow] bigger, better, and [be] drawn closer and closer to the Giver of Good and perfect gifts, and you will realize, too, the wonderful trust and responsibility that has been placed in your hands."

While Gertrude and her mother looked after the baby, Edgar moved his operation into his other photography studio and worked more hours than ever before. He barely took time out to give readings. And yet, in September of 1907, hardship would plague the family once again with another unexplained fire, this time at his College Street studio. It was not as devastating as the earlier fire, though indeed almost all of Edgar's film equipment and negatives were lost. The difference was that he had no goods on consignment and the insurance adjusters were generous. The only thing Edgar seriously regretted losing was the negative of a print that had won him first prize in a national Kodak photography contest. The award had been announced, but the negative had to be delivered to the judges before the money could be sent. Edgar never found the glass plate amidst the rubble.

No mention was made in correspondence or diaries as to what caused the second fire. All the historical record reveals is that Frank Potter, Edgar's partner at this time, decided to bail out of the photography business altogether. The Salters took out another loan against The Hill and bought out Potter's interest in the studio to keep the bank from foreclosing on the property. The studio was legally closed for the seven minutes it took for Potter to sign off and Dr. and Mrs. Thomas House to sign on as new partners.

Edgar put carpenters to work immediately and in two weeks they were back open for business. To save money, Gertrude and baby Hugh Lynn moved to The Hill while Edgar remained behind in Bowling Green, sleeping on a mattress in the studio. Dr. House temporarily moved to Bowling Green to help Edgar as the new manager of the studio. Besides assisting Edgar at the studio, he also began to conduct Edgar's trance sessions. These weren't, however, medical readings. They were almost exclusively on methods to help Edgar and the Salters out of their financial bind.

The first nonmedical reading Dr. House conducted was to find gold that had been long rumored to have been buried in the vicinity of The Hill during the Civil War. Cayce, in trance, began the reading by providing House with a description of soldiers coming to occupy Hopkinsville and its adjoining insane asylum. The activities of the two armies were followed as they gained and lost ground, then focused on the area, on the outskirts of town, where Confederate pillage was allegedly buried by a Confederate soldier. The reading went on to describe how the soldier who buried the treasure sent the details regarding its hiding place to his family at home, and how two of the soldier's family members came to Hopkinsville after the war and recovered it. According to the reading, only one got to keep it, because an argument turned into a fight and then a shooting.

Leslie, who paid a visit to Edgar in Bowling Green, also wanted to try his hand at having a reading to raise funds. A large reward had been offered for information leading to the apprehension of one or more people who had stolen several thousand dollars worth of bonds in western Pennsylvania. Cayce—in trance—provided a description of the main offender in the case, who turned out to be the wife of the man who had posted the reward. According to the reading, his wife had left with one of her husband's associates. Cayce allegedly identified the woman by name as well as by an unusual birthmark, which was not ordinarily visible. He also said that two of her toes had grown together on her left foot, the result of a burn she had received as a child.

Leslie wired the information to Pennsylvania. The woman's husband told him over the phone that the descriptive details were all correct, and that a reward would be forthcoming when the woman and her accomplice were apprehended. Further readings were conducted to determine where the thieves had gone. They were reportedly arrested later in Columbus, Ohio.

Although Leslie collected the reward, Edgar did not himself profit from the venture. Leslie put the money into a business syndicate that he and a few Hopkinsville associates had started. Their aim was to use psychic information to make money on the commodities market. Edgar agreed to help on the condition that a percentage of what was gained would be put toward alleviating his and Gertrude's substantial debt.

By previous arrangement, Leslie conducted readings in Bowling Green and wired the information to his partners in Hopkinsville, who traded on the Chicago commodities market. All of their earnings, except for the cost of a hotel room in Bowling Green for Leslie, was put back into the venture. The first week reportedly generated several hundred dollars. The second week was apparently profitable enough that the investors left their jobs in Hopkinsville and moved their operation to Chicago, where they would be closer to the trading floor. At this point the readings insisted that a man named "Leiter" would corner the wheat market and that the trading price would go to $1.19 and then break very suddenly, dropping down several points. Leslie's partners, who were certain that this couldn't be the case, failed to act accordingly and allegedly lost their syndicate's entire holdings.

In the midst of giving this series of commodities readings, Edgar's friend Joe Dickey from the business college came up with another scheme to make money. He pleaded with Edgar to take his talent to a place like New York, where Dickey was sure they could interest people who would pay off the studio's debt. Dickey wrote to a New York attorney and businessman named Paul Cooksey, who was a son of a third generation member of Bowling Green's First Christian Church. Dickey believed that Cooksey was capable of raising enormous capital through his various business associates. As his correspondence reveals, Cooksey was suitably impressed by what Dickey had to say, but wanted proof.

"I am in position to present the matter suggested to some of the big moneyed men," Cooksey wrote. "However, the proposition is hardly in tangible shape to present . . . The things you suggest that are possible with Mr. Cayce would strike a man as being beyond human powers, but if you will go somewhat into detail and let me have something a little more tangible to present, I will be in position to lay the matter before the parties you refer to . . . Let me hear from you at your convenience, and I will see what can be done at this end of the line." Dickey couldn't wait to move forward with Cooksey, so he and Cayce arranged for Dr. House to conduct a demonstration by eavesdropping on a typical day in the life of Paul Cooksey. During the experiment, however, House and Dickey got carried away and tried to see if they could actually influence or direct his movements.

The reading was done in the early morning. Cayce appeared to locate Cooksey easily and followed him as he walked to a cigar store where he went to buy cigarettes. At Dickey's instruction, the sleeping Cayce directed him to buy two cigars, had him light one, and put the other in his pocket. Later, when Cooksey arrived at his office building in lower Manhattan, Cayce again had him break his routine. "Normally he waits for the elevator," Cayce stated in trance. "This time we'll have him walk up the stairs so he'll remember it." Cayce went on to describe Cooksey as he walked up the steps whistling the show tune "Annie Laurie." Minutes later he was in his office, where another gentleman was waiting for him to discuss the development of a piece of real estate. Cayce, still in trance, remarked that there was a legal action concerning this property and that the case would be called into court that afternoon at three o'clock. Cayce then described how Cooksey examined the morning's mail after his meeting ended. There were three letters. The first he opened was a bill, the next a business letter, and the third was a personal letter from his girlfriend, which began "Dearest . . ." In the midst of reading the letter the telephone rang and he talked with a man by the name of Dolligan.

Dickey was excited by both the detail and ease with which Cayce responded to the questions put to him by House. He immediately wired a transcript to New York. Andrews replied to the wire within the hour: "Your reading as to myself was correct in the main," Cooksey wrote. The only part that Cayce seemed to have had wrong concerned the man named Dolligan, whose name, Cooksey said, was Downey. The rest of the information was so accurate, however, that Cooksey needed no other demonstration. He began speaking to his "money people."

More letters were exchanged. By January 20, 1908, Cooksey was ready to have Cayce, Dickey, and House come to New York. Now it was Edgar who was having second thoughts. It wasn't that he didn't desire the proceeds from a potential partnership, but he had concerns about using his ability to make money, which is all Cooksey and his associates seemed to be interested in doing. He also did not wish to leave Kentucky to become involved with relative strangers. It is quite conceivable that Gertrude—in light of the fiasco that resulted from the Blackburn committee's investigations—had put her foot down about giving readings for anyone outside of the family circle, and that this time, her husband heeded her advice.

Both Dickey and Cooksey were upset. "You're playing with high stakes, old soldier," Dickey wrote to Edgar. But Edgar was reticent to act in a way that was not in keeping with the "spirit" of the readings. "It [his psychic talent] isn't anything to be toyed with," Edgar later wrote a business associate.

When it looked like Edgar still wouldn't come to New York, Cooksey visited him in Hopkinsville, interviewed people whom he had helped, and then pleaded with him to come East, if only for a few days. Meeting Cooksey made Edgar all the more sure that he shouldn't go to New York. Gertrude concurred. Cooksey, however, wouldn't leave. He claimed to be upset, saying that Edgar had backed out of an agreement and owed Cooksey at least one reading. Finally, Edgar agreed to give one reading on the condition that Cooksey board a train for home and leave the Cayce family alone.

All that is known about the reading and what became of Cooksey comes from Leslie, who conducted that reading. According to him, the Source gave stock quotes that earned Cooksey approximately $20,000 on the market. From this sum he paid one of Edgar's outstanding bank loans.

Dickey made one more attempt to persuade Edgar that easy money could be made using his psychic gifts. He talked Edgar into giving a reading on the races at Latona. In the course of a test reading, Cayce was alleged to have correctly named six winners in seven races. The only race in which he hadn't called a winner was one that Cayce—in trance—had said was fixed and couldn't be called. Dickey was so excited by the success of the experiment that they took the train to Cincinnati and went to the races. Dickey put up the front money. This time the reading indicated that only four out of the seven races that day were not already fixed. Dickey bet and won in each instance.

Edgar's share of the take was enough to get him out of debt. But the price he paid was higher than he or Dickey could have imagined. The trance readings could be a Pandora's box for anyone who chose to ignore the advice, take the information lightly, or use it in ways that were not in accord with its "purposes" and "ideals." Two months after giving the Latona readings, Dickey went on a temporary two-year leave from his activities at the university to undergo psychiatric therapy. Edgar also suffered, but the price he paid was not apparent until a short time later when he tried to give a reading for Hugh Evans, Gertrude's brother, who had checked into a hospital in Texas with tuberculosis. Edgar was unable to go into trance.

Dr. House repeatedly attempted to guide Edgar into trance and obtain a reading, as did Lynn Evans, John Blackburn, and Al Layne. But no matter how hard they tried, Edgar either developed a migraine headache or fell asleep. He couldn't give a reading for Hugh Evans, nor could he help anyone else who came to him, no matter how genuine their need. The Source had become silent.

To Edgar, this was a clear message that he was being punished for putting his own and others' material concerns above the greater spiritual good that could come through the readings. Just as he had come to believe that he had earlier lost his voice by not following the directives of his childhood angel, he now believed that he had squandered "God's gifts" by putting them to the wrong use. And besides the obvious impact the Latona racetrack readings had had on his ability to go into trance, there was the more subtle impact that the readings had had on his and Gertrude's personal lives. "I realized that the attempt to use such information for speculative interests had brought a sudden, definite change in my whole being," Edgar wrote. "I realized that my likes and dislikes had changed. My associations that I sought were different." In other words, by using the readings for speculative purposes he was becoming more like the people requesting such readings.

Despondent, believing that he would never be able to give another reading, Edgar closed his Bowling Green studio, returned to The Hill, and sought consolation and refuge through Bible study. "I decided to leave it all [behind]" he later said, "quit messing with . . . [the trance readings], quit experimenting [altogether]."

12.

The Discovery
of Edgar Cayce

Edgar remained at The Hill for the next three months, where he mostly worked in the vegetable garden or sat on the veranda reading the Bible and praying for forgiveness for having lost sight of what he believed to be the greater good that must come from the readings. He considered himself to be a dismal failure, both as a husband and a father, and in what he perceived as his short-lived career as a "psychic diagnostician." In actuality, Edgar had taken a crucial step forward in understanding himself and the work. He had come away with a rudimentary knowledge of how his gift was to be used and how it could be squandered. And though Edgar did not know it at the time, a team of physicians from as far away as Los Angeles, Boston, and New York were soon to make Edgar Cayce the most celebrated psychic in the nation.

Had Edgar even the slightest knowledge of what was about to take place, his Bible study would have been more reflective. Instead of indulgently wallowing in self-pity and seeking only consolation and refuge, he might have sought guidance in how to better conduct himself and his business affairs. As it was, his self-loathing got on everyone's nerves: with Gertrude, Hugh Lynn, and Lizzie sharing one bedroom with Edgar, and Dr. and Mrs.

House and their child, Tommy, sharing another, relations became strained. Moreover, Hugh Evans's medical bills were draining the family's coffers, and with the increased cost of feeding the many people dining at The Hill— which also included Lynn Evans, Aunt Kate, and assorted farm laborers— there was barely enough money to buy two-year-old Hugh Lynn his first pair of shoes or treat Gertrude to a show at the Holland Opera House. Again, Gertrude began losing weight. Photos reveal a pale, shrunken woman, invariably dressed in black, her once waist-length hair cut short and no longer adorned with flowers.

As the weeks turned into months, Edgar increasingly despaired that he had accomplished nothing in his life, that he would never again be able to give readings, and that he would continually have to accept charity from his in-laws. To help earn his keep he offered to move the kitchen over to the house and join it to the main building. It was a prodigious undertaking, which required that the kitchen be removed from its foundation, logs placed underneath, and the building literally rolled across the yard to the main house. The only crisis they encountered was when Gertrude's Aunt Kate, in an effort to help roll the building across the yard, had her thumb smashed.

Having accomplished that task, Edgar decided to look for paid employment and sent letters to contacts he knew in Texas and Alabama. In early June of 1909, through one of his Bowling Green contacts, Edgar obtained work in Gadsden, Alabama, for a photographer named Harding. Edgar bid Gertrude and Hugh Lynn good-bye, promising to send for them as soon as he had become established.

All reports indicate that Edgar felt happier to be working in the photography business again, especially alongside Harding, whom he described as a young, pleasant man. Harding's parents, in whose home Edgar resided, were paid his highest honor when Edgar called them the most devout Christian family he had ever had the pleasure to know. In their company the healing process began.

Edgar didn't keep his previous life a secret from the Hardings. But he did present his former activities in the past tense, letting the Hardings and others know that he couldn't do it anymore. Edgar was so sure that he had lost his talents that he didn't attempt a single reading during the first month he stayed in Gadsden. As he later said of himself, this was a time when "he studied [him]self in silence, [for] days and weeks and months."

In Gadsden, Edgar was essentially doing the same thing he had done for Bowles when he first began as a roving photographer traveling from one school classroom to another. There were long lonely trips between towns. He often packed only necessary equipment on his back and set out on foot through the woods. He says he worked with two ambitions in mind: to heal his "body, mind, and soul" and "to have his own studio again."

In this prayerful, meditative state of mind, and focused on the good that might again come from using his talents to help people in genuine need, Edgar was again able to go into trance. He had just moved from Gadsden to Anniston, Alabama, where he had taken a higher paying job at the Russell Brothers Studio. The subject of his reading was a twenty-one-month-old child named Gordon Putnam, whose mother and father had known Edgar in Bowling Green, and with the help of Leslie, had tracked him down in Anniston. Leslie had told the parents that Edgar had lost his powers, but at their insistence, traveled with them to Alabama to see if something couldn't be done to help their son.

The reading took place on July 17. Leslie conducted. Although the actual words Cayce spoke were not saved, there are testimonials from the parents and their physician that provide definitive proof of the results. Gordon Putnam, so the letters state, had a serious motor coordination problem, which prevented him from being able to move his legs. Cayce prescribed osteopathic treatments to be conducted by a physician named Tom Posey, who implemented the treatments and was able to affect a cure. "To express my gratitude to you is impossible," the child's mother later wrote Edgar. "Anything I could say would fall far short of my real feelings toward you and I can only say from the depths of a mother's heart that I appreciate your assistance in the case of my little boy more than anything anyone could ever possibly say."

Dr. Posey concurred, saying that he had witnessed "wonders" done by Cayce. Posey was quite beside himself and urged fellow physicians to try him out. "I can't explain how he does it. I don't suppose Mr. Cayce himself can. The best way to substantiate what I have said . . . is to try him out on a case . . . and see for yourself just what he can do."

Dr. Posey began to refer all his patients in Anniston to Cayce. Among them was a blind woman suffering from glaucoma, who had two readings and was reportedly cured by the treatments recommended. It was also during this period that Cayce is believed to have done what may well have been the first reading on what was later to become known as "the work." Cayce was asked where the best location was for him to conduct trance readings and how he could best be of service to mankind. Details of the reading are scant, but it is known that Cayce—in trance—said that his contribution to God's work wasn't truly going to begin in Kentucky or Alabama, but in Dayton, Ohio, and that it would not reach its fruition until he was in Virginia Beach, Virginia.

Despite the curious references to Dayton and Virginia Beach in this one reading, the success of Cayce's Anniston trance sessions opened up many new channels with local doctors and their patients. Lynn Evans, who was now working for the Louisville and Nashville Railroad, traveled through Anniston regularly and conducted the first series of readings, while Leslie, who moved from Hopkinsville to Anniston to live with Edgar, conducted the later readings.

Edgar's year in Anniston was remembered best by Bessie Russell, the daughter of one of the two Russell brothers who owned the studio where Edgar worked. Both brothers, she said, found out about his psychic abilities, or as she described it, his "unusual qualities." According to her, he didn't talk about what he did, or charge a fee. "He seemed to consider them more of a burden than an asset," she later told reporters.

Edgar stayed in Anniston with the Russell Brothers until July 4, 1910, when he and his father moved to Jacksonville, Alabama, to open a branch studio for them. More readings were conducted here, the most notable one being for the superintendent of the school district, Andrew J. Hyde, who later became the postmaster at Nauvoo, Alabama, and who named his son, Cayce Hyde, after Edgar.

Hyde had been completely astonished by what he saw and heard during his own reading. In a letter he wrote to a local paper recommending Cayce, he called him "the world's wonder." He went on to say that he knew "beyond a shadow of doubt" that Cayce could diagnose physical illness and disease "as true as any doctor or the person who was sick." Unfortunately for Edgar, the return of his ability to give readings was too late to help his brother-in-law, Hugh Evans. A number of readings were conducted on his behalf, and Gertrude and her mother visited Texas to try to nurse him back to health, but tuberculosis soon would claim his life.

Edgar moved once again in 1910, attempting to find a location as desirable as Bowling Green. This time he moved from Jacksonville to Montgomery, Alabama, where he took a job with the Tressler Company of Nashville, a large studio syndicate operated by Sidney Pinney Tressler, one of the best-known and respected photographers in the southern United States. His eldest son, Herbert P. Tressler, had embarked upon an ambitious expansion program, targeting growing cities such as Montgomery and staffing his studios with competent photographers.

As Edgar's new address became known, many of the doctors who had consulted him in Bowling Green, Hopkinsville, Anniston, and Jacksonville, would once again come to him for help with their patients. Among them was Dr. Wesley Ketchum, a short, thickly built, well-groomed young Hop-

kinsville homeopath who requested that Edgar briefly return home to conduct readings for three of his patients. Enclosed with the letter from
Ketchum was a round-trip railroad ticket home.

Edgar considered Ketchum in a different category than Blackburn,
Layne, House, and the others. Not only was Ketchum better educated, but he
demonstrated remarkable courage in applying the recommended therapies
and treatments, despite the ridicule he often received from fellow physicians for having consulted Cayce. The reading that had most convinced
Ketchum of Cayce's legitimacy was one conducted five years earlier for
George Dalton, a wealthy building and railroad contractor and the owner of
Hopkinsville's only brickworks. Dalton—who weighed about 240 pounds—
had tried to jump a space of about four feet at a construction site where
steps had not yet been installed. He fell and broke his right leg both below
and above the knee. Most Hopkinsville doctors said that Dalton would never
walk again and that amputation would be necessary. But Ketchum—on
trance advice from Cayce—said that the knee could be healed.

In trance, Cayce had described the condition of Dalton's leg, instructed
Ketchum to bore a hole in the kneecap, then to nail the cap to the bone and
put Dalton in traction. Ketchum was initially taken aback. He had never
heard of such a treatment, nor had his colleagues. Surgeons used splints, but
inserting metal screws or nails into bone was a procedure, according to
Ketchum, that had never before been tried in Kentucky or anywhere else.

Ketchum's first step was to go to Forbes Blacksmith Shop and describe exactly what he wanted. The blacksmith made a nail to Cayce's specifications
that looked like a large iron roofing nail, with a flat, large, round head on the
top. Then Ketchum, assisted by another doctor and two nurses from St. Louis,
set about boring a hole in the knee and nailing the kneecap in place. The procedure became the talk of the town as fellow Hopkinsville physicians lam-
pooned Ketchum, whom they disparagingly called that "damned Yankee"
because he had been born and educated in Ohio.

A few weeks after performing the operation, Ketchum again found himself the center of attention when he decided to x-ray the leg. The problem
was getting Dalton to Ketchum's office, which had the only X-ray machine
in Hopkinsville. The X-ray machine was too large to transport to Dalton, and
Ketchum didn't want to risk transporting his patient in a wagon or car because Dalton's leg was wired to his bed with a special rig that facilitated traction. The problem was solved by having Dalton's brother and three others
carry the contractor and the bed down the stairs and along Seventh Street to
Ketchum's office. The parade of people along Seventh Street, amidst the
early morning traffic, brought store owners out of their shops and left pedes-

trians gawking from the sidewalks. It took two months for the bones to heal but George Dalton did walk again. The nail was still in his knee seventeen years later when he died.

Five years after the Dalton reading, and more than a year after Cayce had last seen Ketchum, the physician was again requesting Cayce's help. Edgar agreed, but still wary of involving himself in giving any readings that were not medically related, first obtained Ketchum's solemn promise that readings were to be given "for sick people only."

Ketchum agreed, and the readings were scheduled to begin in late August. Like many future readings that Cayce would give for Ketchum, the first trance session was held in Ketchum's spacious two-room suite on the upper floor of the Dalton Building at the corner of Virginia and Seventh Streets, where Cayce was laid out on a black, tufted leather couch.

The first reading Cayce provided to Ketchum was for a boy with an obstinate leg sore. The reading advised using "oil of smoke." Thinking this was a commercial preparation, Ketchum did not ask where the product might be found. A search of the local drugstores didn't turn it up, nor could it be found in pharmaceutical catalogs. A second reading was taken in which Ketchum asked where he could locate "oil of smoke." Cayce named a drugstore in Louisville, but when Ketchum wired the drugstore, the manager informed him they did not have "oil of smoke," and in fact, had never heard of it. A third reading was taken. This time Cayce described the back room of the Louisville drugstore, named a shelf, and said that behind a particular item on this shelf there was a bottle of "oil of smoke."

Ketchum wired the instructions to the manager of the drugstore. He received a brief reply: "Found it." The label was discolored and faded, and the company that had prepared it was no longer in business, but sure enough, the product was billed as "oil of smoke," which was a trade name used for oil that had been filtered through smoke from burning wood.

Ketchum also used Cayce to diagnose a problem of his own. For years he had been suffering from attacks of severe pain in his lower abdomen. The symptoms indicated an appendicitis, a diagnosis that was supported by two fellow doctors. Before having the operation, however, he wanted a reading. Cayce said that although he would someday have to undergo a very painful and difficult appendix operation, his present malady was the result of having wrenched his spine a few years earlier. The earlier injury, Cayce reported, had put undue pressure on his last dorsal vertebra. "As this was caused mechanically, it will require mechanical treatment or manipulation to relieve it," Cayce said. Ketchum followed the treatment and after nine sessions with an osteopath the pains vanished and he had no further trouble.

Years later, Ketchum did in fact have his appendix removed, and as Cayce had said in his earlier reading, it proved to be an extremely difficult operation.

Despite their early success in working together, Edgar didn't much care for Ketchum's company, and the two men traveled in completely separate social and religious circles. Besides his dedication to homeopathy, which consisted of dispensing medication to stimulate the body's own immune system, Ketchum's primary personal interest was in gaining social prominence and power, as evidenced by his almost pathological desire to be accepted into the Hopkinsville chapter of the Elk's Club. Ketchum himself later admitted that he resorted to blackmail to become a member, availing himself of personal information about committee members that he had obtained through Cayce in trance to further his cause.

Edgar hadn't the slightest interest in the Elk's Club, the Masons, the Odd Fellows, or any of the other popular social organizations in Hopkinsville. He also wasn't particularly concerned or interested in who Ketchum's patients were and what treatments they were receiving. He accepted the train ticket Ketchum sent him, gave the readings that were requested, asked few questions about them, and then headed directly to The Hill to see Gertrude and Hugh Lynn. This, and photographing Halley's Comet, were Edgar's only preoccupations during his first trip home from Montgomery, Alabama.

Edgar exhibited such lack of interest in Ketchum's activities that he wasn't particularly surprised or annoyed when Ketchum didn't call him for the rest of the summer. The reason was that he and one of his patients had attended a meeting of the National Society of Homeopathic Physicians, which was held at Cal Tech, in Pasadena, California. Here Ketchum presented a paper that he and an Ohio colleague had been working on for over a year. The subject of the paper was Edgar Cayce and his psychic abilities, and it triggered a nationwide sensation in the medical community. Edgar didn't hear about the paper until three months later, and by then, he and Ketchum were national celebrities.

Edgar would find out about his new status on Monday, October 10, 1910, when he returned to the Tressler studio after a photography assignment at a local school. Back at his office he found a reporter from one of the Montgomery newspapers waiting to interview him. "You're famous!" the reporter announced, showing him a day-old copy of the *New York Times*. The front page headline read: "Illiterate Man Becomes a Doctor When Hypnotized." Along with the full page article were three pictures: Edgar, his father, and Ketchum.

As Edgar read further, the source of the story became clear. Ketchum had presented a paper in Pasadena and then had given it to a Chicago physician who had in turn presented it to five hundred or more physicians who had been gathered at the Clinical Research Society's annual meeting, which had been held at Harvard University in September. The Associated Press had picked up the story, gone to Hopkinsville, and done their own research.

Edgar went on to read about how doctors throughout the country were taking a lively interest in the "strange power" that he had to diagnose difficult diseases while in a trance. The *New York Times* called the medical report a "sensation," generating hundreds of letters and telegrams to the medical society. The article went on to add that Dr. Ketchum was a reputable physician of high standing with a successful practice and was vouched for by other physicians in both Kentucky and Ohio.

Ketchum hadn't actually named Cayce in his speech. All he had said was that he had made the acquaintance of a young man in Hopkinsville who at the time was twenty-eight-years-old and who had the reputation of being a "freak." Reporters who had followed up on the story had easily obtained Edgar's name by asking people in town. Based on the speech and independent research of their own, they outlined Edgar's life since childhood, with observations and photographs that had been happily provided by Leslie.

The article described Cayce's "precocious" behavior as a child and his strange ability to learn the contents of books by sleeping on them. The article went on to tell of how the family had moved to the city, and how he eventually joined his father's insurance business. It further described how he had lost and regained his voice and begun to diagnose other people's illness. The Dietrich case was recounted in detail, though the family's name was not used.

"His language is usually of the best," Ketchum was quoted as saying. "His psychological terms and description of the nervous anatomy would do credit to any professor of nervous anatomy, and there is no faltering in his speech and all his statements are clear and concise. He handles the most complex 'jaw breakers' with as much ease as any Boston physician, which to me is quite wonderful, in view of the fact that while in his normal state he is an illiterate man, especially along the line of medicine, surgery, or pharmacy, of which he knows nothing."

Edgar felt insulted that he was being called an "illiterate." He also took offense at being labeled a "freak." Both terms were blatantly wrong, just as was Ketchum's exaggeration that he had used Edgar on approximately a hundred cases. Ten or twenty was closer to the truth. However, Edgar felt a certain excitement and gratification that nationally recognized doctors and other professionals believed there was substance to what Ketchum had said about him.

Ketchum told the *New York Times* that he had never known of any error in the readings except in two cases where father and son had the same name and resided in the same house. He simply described the wrong person. "Now this description [of Cayce], although rather short, is no myth, but a firm reality," Ketchum went on to report. "The regular profession scoff at anything reliable coming from this source, because the majority of them are in the rut and have never taken to anything not strictly orthodox."

Ketchum also provided a possible explanation, which he claimed to have obtained from Cayce while in a trance, and his statement has since become the most quoted explanation of Cayce's psychic talents. "[Edgar Cayce's] mind is amenable to suggestion, the same as all other subconscious minds, but in addition thereto it has the power to interpret to the objective mind of others what it acquires from the subconscious mind of other individuals . . . The subconscious mind forgets nothing. The conscious mind receives the impression from without and transfers all thoughts to the subconscious, where it remains even though the conscious be destroyed."

The lengthy article also contained a complete transcript of an actual reading for one of Ketchum's patients in Indiana. It was a typical reading, certain to make Ketchum's points, and of particular historical interest because it was the earliest reading to survive in its entirety, and the first ever to be published.

Impressed by Ketchum's account as presented in the *New York Times*, numerous other newspapers joined the bandwagon in doing stories on Cayce. They included the *Seattle Times*, the *Cincinnati Times-Star*, and the *St. Louis Dispatch*. And four days after the *New York Times* ran its story, the same paper would print a follow-up report based on their own subsequent investigations.

Upon seeing the fistful of clippings that the Montgomery reporter held in his hand, Edgar could well imagine what the situation was like at home. As Ketchum later confirmed by telephone, the city was literally deluged by reporters as well as by the sick seeking cures and the merely curious. The Hotel Latham was completely filled up and the overflow went to stay in a hotel in Evansville. People camped out on the steps of Leslie and Carrie's house and sat on the lawn waiting for Edgar to come home for a visit—as Leslie assured reporters that he would. A particularly brazen reporter had even gone inside the house and stolen pictures that they published in the *New York Times*. Leslie was conducting interviews in Edgar's stead. Thankfully, reporters hadn't realized that Edgar's wife and son were not with him in Montgomery but living in Hopkinsville, at The Hill.

Edgar received a telegram from Ketchum that same day. The Hopkinsville physician didn't apologize for having revealed the intimate details of Cayce's life to the press, but rather wanted Edgar to return to Hopkinsville and make a business of giving readings. Albert D. Noe, the manager and later owner of the Latham Hotel in Hopkinsville, had agreed to bankroll the partnership, and Leslie had expressed his desire to conduct the readings. All they wanted to know was what terms Edgar would accept for his services.

Ketchum said they would agree to any terms that were reasonable. However, what Ketchum had failed to mention in the telegram, but that would be revealed when Edgar returned to Hopkinsville two days later, was that patients were already standing in line in Ketchum's office to receive readings and that letters and money were arriving in large sacks from people throughout the country desiring Cayce's psychic help. In the first month alone, Ketchum received approximately ten thousand letters and over $2,000 in cash. And the letters, like the cash, continued to pour in.

Here, presented to Edgar, was public validation of his psychic gifts as well as an offer to return home to his family. As a business associate later said, he had the most important decision of his life to make. "He had to [finally] make up his mind about himself and the weird things that came out of him."

There was one thing, however, that Edgar had already made up his mind about. His psychic ability was not a trick or an ailment or the work of the Devil. It was a talent, a gift that the Lord had provided him. And as a gift from God, it had to be used. This more than anything else compelled him to go into partnership with Ketchum and Noe.

The fact that Edgar knew that Gertrude would not approve of the partnership did not interfere with his decision. In time—Edgar believed—Gertrude would come to realize that the business of giving psychic readings had to be accorded the same degree of professionalism as his photography business. He needed an established location where truly sick people would know where to find him, a reliable stenographer to take the readings down, and a conductor whom he could trust to represent his and the patient's best interests. Edgar also desired to be near his family—not only Gertrude and Hugh Lynn, but his mother and father and four sisters.

The next morning, after receiving Ketchum's telegram, Edgar sat in the lobby of the First National Bank of Montgomery and wrote to Ketchum on a piece of borrowed stationery with one of the bank's pens. He told Ketchum he would accept the proposition on the express condition that no one seeking trance counsel would be turned away because of financial hardship. The poor would be treated for free. In addition, Leslie would conduct all the readings. Half the income generated by the proposed partnership was to go to Edgar and his father. The other half would go to Ketchum and Noe, who would pay the partnership's overhead expenses, and in addition, finance a photography studio in Hopkinsville that would be owned and operated by Edgar and his family. By return telegram, pending a formal five-year contract, which was signed a day later, on October 12, Noe and Ketchum agreed to Edgar's terms.

Gertrude was pleased at the prospect of having Edgar back in Hopkinsville, but was rightfully distrustful of Ketchum, and dubious of any business in which Leslie was a partner. Edgar's father had proven himself to be unreliable, and his willingness to trade off Edgar's name and growing reputation was a matter of serious concern. She didn't have an opinion of Noe, other than the obvious. He was getting involved in the partnership to fill the rooms in his hotel, which did not necessarily go hand-in-hand with the business of healing people. Edgar assured her that everything would be fine. He also volunteered to let the Source itself make the ultimate decision if this partnership was a good idea or not.

A reading on "the work" was conducted on February 13, 1911, four months after a formal contract had been signed, and three months after the "psychic partnership" and the new Cayce photography studio was legally operating in the state of Kentucky. There is no mention in any of the subsequent letters and correspondence about why it took this long to ask advice on a subject that could be reasonably viewed as the partnership's primary directive or purpose for existence. The likely reason is that the "psychic partnership" was so deluged with requests for trance medical advice—the vast majority from desperate patients whose physicians had described their conditions as "incurable"—that conducting a nonmedical reading seemed like an indulgence.

Leslie conducted the reading, and Katherine Faxon, the partnership's stenographer, recorded the session. The overall thrust of the reading was positive: much good had already come from the proposed partnership. The message that came through, and one that the Source would articulate time and time again, was that the patients, or those who benefit from the readings, should supply the funds necessary for the survival of Edgar and his partners. In addition, the more credibility that the readings generated, and the more people who believed in the value of the information being given them, the more Edgar and his partners would gain materially from it.

Despite the esoteric language in which this message was presented—

using terms such as the "inner conscience," "ethereal body," and "subconscious mind"—it sounded like good old-fashioned business advice. And although offering material benefits was clearly a necessity in developing the practical business aspects of the partnership, the most important aspect of this reading was the suggestion that the ultimate purpose of "the work" was not to provide diagnostic insights to aid physicians or bring about miraculous cures, but to help people "open" their minds and accept the truth of the "ethereal" or "spiritual world." It is no doubt for this reason that the Source then offered an important clue to the future success or failure of the work. The reading ended with the statement: "The minute we gain credence and give credit to ourselves we lose it all."

The transcripts of this reading, reported to be the first fully documented trance session dedicated specifically to the work, were quite telling. Cayce— or the Source—responded to questions posed by Leslie in highly spiritual or esoteric terms, while Leslie persisted in talking dollars and cents and asking practical questions about who should pay for publicity, stationery, and other costs. It appears that the Source was trying to force Leslie and the others to view their partnership in a nonmaterial way, or at least to envision the work as it manifested itself in both material and nonmaterial dimensions, and to acknowledge that one dimension acts upon another. The language that Cayce used was difficult to understand, and it is doubtful that Leslie, Ketchum, Noe, or even Edgar himself comprehended its full meaning, let alone the potential consequence of ignoring its greater spiritual message.

13.

The Psychic
Partnership

Edgar, Leslie, Noe, and Ketchum chose to make their headquarters in a suite of rooms on the top floor of the Thompson Building at 702 East Main Street in downtown Hopkinsville, which they rented for $12 a month. It was a large redbrick building that was adjacent to Hopper Bookstore and one block from Ketchum's office on Seventh. A long-running joke that circulated in Hopkinsville at the time was that Edgar Cayce had finally moved up in the world since leaving Hopper Brothers: He had moved upstairs.

A sign reading CAYCE PHOTO STUDIO was posted outside on the street, pointing the way up a short flight of stairs. In the hallway at the top, another sign marked the entrance to Edgar's three-room photo studio, which was outfitted with the most modern photography equipment. There was a large-format Kodak camera on a tripod, plenty of freshly painted scenic backdrops, and new furniture on which clients could pose for portraits. A few yards farther down the hall from the entrance to the photo studio was posted a third sign, written in smaller letters. It read PSYCHIC DIAGNOSTICIAN, and the door beside it opened into a suite of offices that were connected through the back to the photo studio. It was in one of these rooms, on a tall couch that resembled a doctor's examination table, that Edgar gave the readings. Adjacent to the couch was a footstool where Leslie sat to conduct the readings and a small table and chair for the stenographer. Patients themselves were not normally invited into this office and didn't get to meet Edgar Cayce personally. Rather, patients who desired to come to Hopkinsville and be examined by a physician—as opposed to those whose requests were handled through the mail—would meet with Ketchum at his Seventh Street office and could, by appointment, receive the treatments or therapies recommended in the readings.

The concept of keeping Edgar physically removed from his patients was Ketchum's idea. This was not only for legal reasons stemming from the fact that Edgar was not a licensed physician nor was capable—in a conscious state—of dispensing medical advice, but also for purely practical reasons. Personal contact between Edgar and his patients was viewed as an unnecessary interference in Edgar's personal life and to the business of conducting daily trance sessions. By previous agreement between the partners, Edgar set aside approximately two hours a day—one in the early morning and one in the late afternoon—to enter a trance and answer medical-related questions that Ketchum wrote out and Leslie would put to him. In this way, readings could be scheduled in advance and need not be dedicated to one specific individual. One patient after another could be diagnosed, their condition and treatments discussed, along with any necessary reviews or follow-up recommendations for patients who had already sought trance counsel. It is not known how Cayce and his partners arrived at this particular arrangement, but it became a standard that would be applied until the later years of Edgar's life and one that was supported by the Source, who would say that more than two readings a day was detrimental to Edgar's health.

Despite the specific attention given to how and when readings were conducted, no agreement was made concerning how much patients were to be charged for Edgar's trance services. No doubt it was Edgar himself who resisted making such a provision as part of their partnership agreement, for he remained adamant that no one should be turned away because of their inability to pay for a reading. Much to the consternation of Ketchum and Noe, and perhaps even Leslie, Edgar had also demanded that all the unsolicited money that they received in the mail—which would grow to an estimated $7,000—be returned, which was a far more laborious task than anyone had expected since Edgar insisted on answering each accompanying letter personally.

Rather than specify a set amount to be charged for the trance readings, Edgar agreed to establish a $25 guideline for each reading. Further, Ketchum was given the discretion to charge what he liked for treatments he performed in conjunction with the readings. Noe would be expected, but not required, to give patients visiting Cayce a discount at his hotel and was contractually obligated to give Leslie and Edgar 10 percent of that income. And, as previously agreed to, all income generated by the readings would be split equally. Half would go to Edgar and Leslie, and the other half to Ketchum and Noe, who would pay for the expenses of running the office, which included secretarial and stenographic expenses.

Due to the unique nature of their proposed partnership, and before their formal five-year contract was signed, several prominent Hopkinsville judges, among them John T. Hanberry, were invited to witness a reading and give their honest opinion as to whether or not laws would be broken by conducting the business they had in mind. These consultants were asked to give an opinion on the legality of selling information from such a source and they responded that they knew of no law that prohibited it. In fact, Judge Hanberry, who had previously received his own readings when Edgar was living in Bowling Green, was so impressed by the demonstration that he later offered to purchase Cayce's contract from Noe and Ketchum.

In addition to the attorneys, the state medical authorities were asked for an opinion. They too witnessed a reading and replied that nothing could prevent such a practice unless a special law were enacted against it. And since such a law would have to name Cayce specifically, and since this in itself was unconstitutional, it appeared that nothing whatever could be done to stop them.

Having explored the legal ramifications of their partnership, Edgar, Leslie, Noe, and Ketchum met at the Latham Hotel to sign the documents. Edgar was handed five one hundred dollar bills to purchase photo equipment for his new studio. He had never seen a single bill that large before, let alone five. And this was just the beginning. The eventual cost of opening the new studio ran in the neighborhood of $5,000, and several more thousand dollars were spent furnishing and decorating the adjacent suite of offices where readings were given.

The partners all seemed to be in a good mood going into the venture and agreed to celebrate over a fine dinner on the day when the papers were drawn up and money was to change hands. Nothing unusual occurred that afternoon except for the appearance of an uninvited visitor at their hotel room door—someone who clearly wasn't from Hopkinsville. He had the dark features of an East Indian, was dressed in a conventional light-colored suit, and wore a turban.

Edgar later described the events that followed: "There was a knock on the door, when opened this figure came in, he introduced himself to each [of us]

and shook hands with all . . . Asked why he was there, [he] said he came to
see what they were going to do 'with Edgar.' [He] asked each their purpose
in the matter, and gave each a warning."

No two warnings were the same, but at the heart of each was the same
message that would come through in the first reading dedicated to the
work—that "greed" and "self-serving interests" could destroy the good that
could come from the partnership. The men were urged "not to lose sight of
the real value that such information could be in the spiritual life of individuals." In other words, there was a higher purpose to their partnership
than diagnosing disease for a profit. Having delivered his messages, the East
Indian promised to join the party for dinner and then left.

"Everyone thought that he was just a friend," Edgar later wrote. "But no
one seemed to know him. Just after he had gone one of the men said, 'I forgot to tell him where the dinner was to be,' and went to call him, but no one
was there and no one in the hotel remembered seeing him."

The East Indian did not join them for dinner and the partners didn't
think anything more about the curious incident. However—in years to
come—his reappearance in Cayce's life would make Edgar and Gertrude
wonder exactly who he was and why he had come. Like the fires that periodically destroyed the Cayce photography studios, his unexpected appearances in Edgar's life were too much of a coincidence to be ignored.

Edgar and his partners didn't know what to make of their curious visitor
that day at the Hotel Latham. They went ahead and signed the contract. No
legal document of its kind had ever before existed in Kentucky, or anywhere
else for that matter. Edgar was, in the eyes of the law, a psychic diagnostician—and a highly paid one at that.

Readings were begun in earnest the same day that the documents were
signed, and before the first week had ended, nine patients had received and
paid for readings. Mrs. Gussie Ellington, a patient from Chicago, Illinois,
who was dying of tuberculosis, received the first reading. Two months later,
when she requested and received a second reading, her physician reported
that her condition had measurably improved. The second reading was conducted for Robert B. Hall, a local businessman who was suffering from an inflammation of the mucous membranes in his nose and throat—for which he
had been unable to receive help from standard medical practitioners. He
was prescribed a unique diet, which included drinking large quantities of
pure water and the ingestion of various kinds of tree bark and juniper oil.
Hall's complete recovery after having followed this unusual treatment was
considered nothing short of phenomenal. Mrs. Eleanor Sledge, who received
the last reading of that first month, came to Ketchum complaining of mi-

graine headaches, which had plagued her for years, and for which she had despaired of ever finding a cure. Cayce—in trance—suggested that the problem was the result of a lesion that had grown on her spine, which could be removed through osteopathic manipulation. Her eventual cure—less than two months later—was again considered nothing short of remarkable.

Katherine Faxon, a court reporter, was the official stenographer for all these readings. Later she would be followed by Miss Addie P'Pool, who had worked for Cayce earlier. Miss P'Pool's memories of those early days would remain poignant until the end of her life. Her fondest recollection was of the very first reading that she recorded. At the end of the reading, Edgar took her out into the hall where they could be alone and asked if she thought what she had witnessed was a fake. "God is going to punish me if I'm doing something wrong," she remembered him telling her. She assured him that what she had witnessed was the work of the Lord, and that he should not worry.

A particularly memorable reading conducted in the early months of the partnership was for a Nashville businessman who came to the studio accompanied by two doctors and two or three elderly pharmacists. It was quite a complicated case. After a lengthy trance session, Cayce prescribed "balsam of sulfur" in combination with other drugs. The pharmacists were certain that there was no such thing as balsam of sulfur. Nor had Ketchum or the other doctor heard of it. Eventually the druggists went back to their pharmacies and opened their copies of the U.S. Dispensary. It wasn't listed. Then one of the druggists, E. G. Gaither, remembered that they had a much older copy of the dispensary in the attic. The book was brought out, and there they found balsam of sulfur. The book described exactly how to make it.

Another reading was for a patient who had been referred by a physician in Cleveland. Cayce was given only the name and address of the patient. A reading was taken, then forwarded on to the Cleveland physician. The doctor eventually wrote back and wanted another reading on the same patient. Cayce started to give the reading, but suddenly stopped. All Cayce said was: "He's gone." A week or ten days later Ketchum received a letter from the Cleveland doctor saying that his patient had taken a boat for Detroit and died on board at twenty minutes past eight, the very same hour that Cayce had stopped giving the reading in Hopkinsville.

A third case was that of a Cleveland woman who was suffering from "paralysis agitans," otherwise known as shaking palsy. The husband asked if Ketchum could bring Cayce to the house for a diagnosis. Ketchum told him there was no need. He could take care of it at his office. Cayce gave a reading that was so elaborate it took several pages to write it down. But in the end

Ketchum had a full diagnosis and treatment plan. He had several copies made of the reading and then paid a personal visit to the patient.

Ketchum remembered it being a beautiful sunny day when he arrived at the woman's large house in Cleveland. In Cayce's outline of the case, he had started out by saying that the patient was in a wheelchair. "She's as rigid as a piece of marble. She can look neither to the right nor the left. She has two trained nurses with white caps."

As soon as Ketchum got out of the carriage, he saw the patient sitting on the front porch in a wheelchair. On each side stood a trained nurse in a white cap, exactly as Cayce had described it. Ketchum chatted with the patient until her husband asked about the reading. The patient was wheeled into the house and Ketchum proceeded to review the case. But before he discussed the details, he told the husband and wife that he had a typewritten copy of what he was going to tell them in his pocket.

The patient's mind was quite lucid, but she could look only straight in front of her. Ketchum took out the reading and began by describing her history. It said that as a result of a "secret sin" she had delayed marriage until she was thirty-nine years old. She eventually did marry, and she and her husband had two children. It was then, just after the birth of the children, that the palsy set in. Ketchum went on to explain the prescribed treatment and how to administer it.

The patient remained quiet while the diagnosis was being read, but as soon as Ketchum had finished, she asked her husband to take the nurses into the next room so that she could be alone with the doctor. As soon as the door closed the woman expressed her astonishment that anyone could have known about her "secret sin." She told Ketchum, "I *did* have a secret sin from the age of eighteen until I was thirty-nine. I never told a single person in my life. Only I and my God have ever known of it."

That sin, in her own mind, was masturbation. It had no direct bearing, as far as Ketchum knew, on the palsy. But it did have an impact on her mental health. Believing that it was wrong, but doing it anyway, she had carried much guilt for many years. And discussing it now was part of the healing process. Cayce's knowledge of that "secret sin" convinced her of the validity of the rest of the reading. According to Ketchum, she saw to it that the treatment was followed and was reported to have lived normally for the rest of her life.

Another case was that of a mother who came to Ketchum about her teenage daughter who was suffering from an upset stomach. She had been away at school and was now home for the Christmas holidays. Ketchum had a full load of patients that would have required the woman and her daughter to sit a long time in his waiting room. Instead of keeping them, an appointment was set for nine o'clock the next morning. To speed up the process, that evening Ketchum gave Cayce the name and address of the girl and had him do a reading on her, although he had not yet even seen her. Cayce lay down and went into a trance. He was quiet for a number of minutes and then said: "The trouble with this body is right here, right here. There is new life developing here in this pelvis. As a result we have nausea, vomiting—well—otherwise known as morning sickness."

The next morning the mother brought her daughter into the office. Ketchum asked to speak to the girl alone. After her mother had left, Ketchum asked her to tell him about herself. Eventually she admitted that she hadn't menstruated for two months. Ketchum asked about the "lucky man." She told him that he was home for the holidays, and that he was a senior in college. After they had spoken for a while longer he told the girl that this was a delicate situation, but that she wasn't the first girl to have gotten pregnant outside of wedlock, and that the first thing they must do was to tell her mother, who Ketchum was sure would understand. He opened the door and explained the situation to the mother. "The scene I witnessed then," Ketchum said, "couldn't have been put on paper. It was really something."

Once the mother calmed down she asked Ketchum what they should do. Ketchum told them that General Lee had once made the statement that any fool general could lead an army into battle, but it took a very wise one to get the army out again. His advice was to contact the young man and have him come to Hopkinsville. "I wouldn't ask any man to marry a girl unless she is the only one in the world for him," Edgar said. "And if you feel the same way about him, the nice thing to do will be to slip off to another state [to] get married."

Readings like this one, and the delicate evenhanded manner in which Ketchum handled them, led many people to believe that Edgar and the doctor were perfectly suited to one another. Clearly Cayce, or the Source, responded well to Ketchum, offering more detailed information and insights than it had to Layne, Blackburn, or other doctors for whom readings had been conducted. But there was more to Ketchum's success than his "bedside" manner. For the first time in Edgar's career as a psychic, transcripts of the readings were being saved, compared, and studied in a routine and systematic way. Ketchum was not only learning how to best avail himself of Cayce's trance advice, but developing an actual rapport with the source of his information.

In the first few months of the partnership, Ketchum became aware of the Source as a distinct personality or being, with many human characteristics,

which included, at times, poor grammar and an almost childlike appreciation and wonder when visiting new places and examining new patients.
However "all-knowing" that the Source might be, it could also be short- or
long-winded, disliked what it considered inane or sloppy questions, and had
a highly developed sense of humor.

Examples were numerous. Asked once about how a person should overcome worrying, the Source simply said "Quit worrying!" Asked for advice for
a particular doctor in charge of an operation, Cayce said, "They wouldn't
take the advice if you gave it." A woman, wanting to know if wearing
glasses—as Cayce had recommended—was really necessary, was told: "The
body really needs glasses, else we wouldn't have said it!" To a man worried
about becoming bald, Cayce stated: "Don't worry too much about this . . .
Brains and hair don't grow very well together—at times anyway." When a
patient asked if a medication should be rubbed on the outside he was simply told: "You can't rub it on the inside."

Ketchum believed that because the Source sounded so "human" that it
was none other than Cayce's subconscious mind tapping into a vast database
of information. He believed that a heavenly presence didn't take over when
Cayce went into trance, but rather Cayce's spirit was free to communicate
with other spirits when he lost consciousness. Although subsequent readings
suggested that there was clearly much truth in this theory, Ketchum himself
later admitted that whatever happened was far more complicated than
"Cayce's spirit reaching out into the universe." This was, however, a good
starting point. As would be demonstrated on numerous occasions in the future, Cayce's higher self may indeed "retrieve" information, but there were
also many instances when a "heavenly presence" interceded or guided trance
sessions and would sometimes actually introduce itself to the conductor.

Ketchum also became certain that Cayce's subconscious mind could travel
to the physical location of the patient. There were so many references to the
actual surroundings of the individual for whom he was doing the reading
and details, such as weather conditions at a particular location, that no other
explanation seemed possible. During one reading, Cayce remarked on the
color of a patient's pajamas, and on another occasion, appeared to pause on
the way into another patient's house to mention that she had a particularly
beautiful tree in her yard. Remarks such as these naturally led Ketchum to
believe that Cayce wasn't just seeing the surroundings through the eyes of
the patient, but was acting as a disembodied mind having an out-of-body experience.

The fact that readings would end abruptly whenever anything was passed
over Cayce's body provided evidence to Ketchum that this disembodied mind

somehow remained connected to the physical Cayce by an invisible cord. Ketchum also came to believe that someone or something actually hovered over Cayce while he was in trance. Later, when Ketchum asked Cayce—in trance—about this phenomena, the Source confirmed such a conclusion by describing what it called the "etheric body" that rests above the "natural body" whose "connections" and "associations" must remain undisturbed for communication to take place.

An especially curious aspect of the readings was the effect that an individual could have on the information being given. Ketchum never came up with a theory to explain why in some cases information would be revealed when a particular person was in the room, or why the Source was silent when another person was present. This naturally would lead someone to think that the information had to do with that person, but this didn't appear to always be the case. In one example, a man telephoned to make an appointment for a friend. They came to the studio that evening and were given a reading. Leslie conducted. Cayce went into trance as usual, but did not give any information. The next evening this was tried again without results, as it was a third time. On the fourth attempt satisfactory information came through. This time, however, the friend was not present.

Ketchum was also interested in where Cayce's subconscious mind went to retrieve the information when the Source did come through. The destination was apparently determined by the type of questions that the conductor asked and the degree to which the subject was willing to accept the information given. And as Ketchum realized, the process of "communing" with another person's subconscious mind was not always easily accomplished. Cayce—in trance—would sometimes come right out and say that this information wasn't to be shared. At other times Cayce seemed to be able to peer at will right inside a person without interference, which suggested that individuals themselves could block Cayce's examination of their bodies. Ketchum felt sure that a patient's motivation was a key factor in the equation—both on a conscious and an unconscious level. The times when Ketchum got the best results from Cayce were when a person genuinely wanted help for the reasons that they had stated and when ultimately the person receiving the information had good intentions. A person saying one thing and thinking something different resulted in a miscommunication. Information that would hurt or harm someone would simply not be given.

Ketchum, like others who conducted or listened to readings, was also interested in knowing if other people could leave their bodies and go to different places. Cayce said they could and did. "Each and every soul leaves the body as it rests in sleep," he said in a later reading. "As to how this may be used constructively—this would be like answering how could one use one's voice for constructive purposes."

Like Ketchum, Edgar himself was slowly beginning to understand some of the dynamics involved in giving readings. He also began to take a keen interest in the medical side of the business. For the first time in his career he made a conscious effort to study the completed trance discourses. He seemed to genuinely want to know how the treatments he recommended worked. However, he was a long way from understanding them. There were often dense, detailed descriptions of organs and blood supplies that meant nothing to him. There were phrases like "over stimulation of the hepatic circulation," and "it's destroying the red corpuscles in the spleen" that seemed to him entirely like a foreign language. Ketchum helped to explain them to Edgar, but the information that came through was often no more intelligible to Edgar than some "tribal incantation." The one thing he did understand was how very complex human beings were and how interrelated all parts of the body appeared to be.

Reading the transcripts also helped Edgar become aware of the variety of ills that could afflict the human body, and how diet, for example, could affect coordination and spinal misalignments and interfere with a person's eyesight or sense of smell. Perhaps equally intriguing to Edgar was the myriad of different kinds of treatments recommended, which sometimes included the use of various electrical devices. The Source not only described how patients were to use these devices, but explained in detail how the devices themselves were to be manufactured. The most common of these devices was what is now known as a "Radiac," which consisted of two pieces of carbon steel separated by glass, surrounded by carbon and charcoal, and sealed in a copper container. To use the device, it had to be cooled in ice for thirty minutes and connected to positive and negative leads, which were then attached to the arms and legs of a patient.

Exactly how these devices were supposed to work was a mystery. Ketchum didn't know, nor did Edgar. Archie Higgins, the insurance salesman in the office next door, remembered how he used to laugh when he heard reports about some of the strange contraptions that were suggested in the readings, and how Edgar himself would sometimes laugh when Ketchum told him some of the things that he said in trance. Their humor, however, was short-lived, for despite the numerous instances that the Radiac and other treatments were recommended, most doctors were not letting their patients use them. In fact, as Edgar and Ketchum soon realized, their challenge was not so much obtaining helpful information from the Source as much as finding doctors willing to apply the treatments.

Edgar came to realize the extent of this problem when he began writing personal notes or letters for patients, which accompanied the readings. In the return mail he would receive dozens of requests from patients asking the names of doctors who would conduct the treatments as outlined. Many of the patients did indeed find relief and help from the readings, but the vast majority weren't being treated because their doctors at home wouldn't conduct the treatment that had been prescribed, and some even talked their patients out of trying the treatment elsewhere, too. In Hopkinsville, it was more possible to get cooperation from the various doctors, but most of the patients that were coming to Edgar and Ketchum were from out of town.

This realization was weighing heavily on Edgar's mind when he was visited by Frank Mohr, a successful businessman from Columbus, Ohio, who had heard about the psychic partnership from a man who had opened a coal mine on the basis of a Cayce reading, which stated that there was a vast underground deposit of coal in Nortonville, Kentucky. Mohr had become the new owner of that mine and was turning it into the highly successful Norton Coal Corporation. But Mohr, and his wife Ella, didn't call on Cayce for advice on where to look for more coal. Their interest was in helping their three-and-half-year-old niece, who suffered from polio. Physicians didn't hold out much hope for her recovery.

Although there are great discrepancies as to when this reading was conducted and the timing of Mohr's entrance into the Cayce story, there is reason to believe that he first requested a reading for his niece in December of 1910. All that can be said with any certainty is that Ketchum conducted the reading, since Leslie had broken his kneecap, and that Cayce diagnosed the illness and recommended treatments. The results were nothing short of phenomenal. Mohr was alleged to have been impressed to the point that he offered to buy Cayce's contract, or at the least, have their existing agreement expanded to include a hospital where an entire staff of doctors and nurses could be assembled who would become familiar with the specialized treatments recommended in the readings. This was, as far as can be determined, the first time there was any discussion of a hospital being built.

There is no evidence to suggest what Gertrude may or may not have thought about the proposition. Though it was clear that she was relieved to have her husband home, her life with Edgar ended when he walked out the door to go to the photo studio or give readings. At no time in their lives together, except perhaps in Bowling Green, did she play such a minor role in his career. It can only be presumed from comments that family friends later made, that her lack of involvement was a form of protest at his being involved in the partnership in the first place. The family's financial well-being didn't enter into the equation. As in Bowling Green, she still entertained the dream that their lives would somehow follow a more prescribed and orderly course should Edgar only give up "that thing he did." There was also the possibility that she was becoming increasingly ill, though no one, including herself, seemed to notice until much later.

Edgar himself loved the idea of expanding the partnership because it solved what he was beginning to view as the central problem of the work that he and his partners had embarked upon. Treatments would be carried out exactly as the readings suggested, whether that was through osteopathic manipulation, homeopathy, or surgery. Specialists could be brought in to examine the patients, as many readings also recommended. And Nortonville, which was only thirty miles from Hopkinsville, was viewed as an excellent location for a hospital because this was where the Illinois Central Railroad crossed the Louisville and Nashville tracks. Patients could easily make the journey from such distant locales as Chicago, Illinois, and Jacksonville, Florida.

Initially, Noe and Ketchum also liked the idea. Their only concern was that they should be adequately compensated for the work they had done in "developing" and "publicizing" Edgar's abilities, and that they would share in any profits generated by a hospital. Toward this end, they discussed revising the original contract and extending it by an additional five years. Their general understanding—agreed to in principle in a meeting between Noe and Mohr—stipulated that Noe and Ketchum would receive a share of all proceeds from the hospital in addition to the terms previously agreed upon between themselves and the two Cayces. Mohr would use his resources to build and outfit a hospital in Nortonville, along with an accompanying hotel to house visiting patients or their families. Based on their oral understanding, pending a formal written agreement and a separate document signed by Edgar stating that he would be available to give readings at the proposed hospital, Mohr hired architects and began building the hospital. By the middle of 1912, land had been surveyed and cleared in Nortonville and a team of laborers had poured the foundation. Land had also been purchased and cleared for the accompanying hotel.

Problems arose almost immediately. Noe and Ketchum kept coming up with one reason after another for not signing the new contract, giving Mohr the impression that they were stalling in an effort to exact a greater share of stock in the new corporation. The truth is difficult to determine from the exchange of letters and legal documents that passed between the prospective partners. Nor are the dates of the documents consistent with the later recollections of the principal parties. All that is certain is that Ketchum and Noe had decided to stall negotiations until a dollar value could be placed on the worth of their operation in Hopkinsville. Meanwhile, Mohr believed that he had acted in good faith by buying land and beginning the hospital construction.

In the midst of the discussions that ensued, Mohr was badly hurt in a mining accident. Stirling Lanier, Mohr's chief foreman, immediately sent for Edgar. Ketchum conducted an emergency reading, which recommended surgery and plenty of rest. But the reading also insisted that Mohr's spine had been seriously injured in the accident, and, if certain corrective measures were not taken, the spinal curvature would gradually produce uric acid poisoning, eventually causing an overload on his system, which would result in blindness. To Mohr and his doctors this sounded absurd. Ketchum, perhaps not wanting to look foolish to his peers, allegedly laughed along with Mohr's doctors at the suggestion that a curvature of the spine could cause blindness. Mohr didn't know whom to trust, for it looked to him that even Ketchum didn't put much faith in the reading. Either that or Ketchum was trying to manipulate the situation to drive a wedge between Mohr and Cayce.

Edgar seemed to be oblivious to the unpleasant politics and the growing rift between Mohr and his other two partners. He truly believed that the idea of building a hospital was the answer to many of his patients' problems and that this was where his psychic source was directing him. Whether or not the hospital would generate a greater income for the partners was not foremost on his mind. Edgar mistakenly supposed that Ketchum felt the same sense of altruism and didn't once consider the possibility that Ketchum might be trying to undermine his credibility with Mohr.

Two separate civil lawsuits resulted from the rift that grew between the prospective partners. Mohr sued Ketchum and Noe to release Edgar from his contract, and Ketchum and Noe filed a countersuit claiming that Edgar's and Mohr's written agreement was invalid because it breached the previous agreement they had with Edgar. The two cases were never heard in front of a judge because Mohr returned to his home in Columbus, Ohio, to recuperate. Construction on the hospital ceased. Its foundation, on a hillside in Nortonville, disappeared under a growth of thick brush, and to this day, it stands as a mute reminder of what could have been. Edgar was visibly hurt by the lack of trust exhibited by his partners and for the first time began to suspect that Ketchum hadn't been completely honest with him or Mohr.

The situation became all the more tense when another visitor appeared in the Cayce Studio. He was Roswell Field, a reporter for Hearst's *Chicago Examiner* and the brother of Eugene Field, the famous American poet and journalist. Field's visit to the studio was triggered by some of the things that Mohr had told him about Cayce before the accident. He wanted to write a series of newspaper articles for the Hearst newspapers, and discussed the possibilities of writing a book. Edgar was courteous to him and showed him around Hopkinsville. Field photographed him holding Hugh Lynn on his lap and took another picture of Edgar on his sofa with Leslie standing by him and a stenographer seated at a table. The pictures, along with Field's stories, were sent to all the Hearst newspapers.

In the articles that were printed, Field described Edgar Cayce as he found him in the office of the psychic diagnostician, killing time in what he described as "the most approved Kentucky fashion," which was lounging on his sofa. No mention was made that Edgar was reading the Bible when the photo was taken, and did, in fact, spend half an hour or more each day doing so. "His appearance was neither conspicuously encouraging nor disappointing," Field wrote. "His photograph, which is an admirable one, bears out the impression of a tall, slender young man, with good, honest eyes, sufficiently wide apart, a high forehead, and just the ordinary features. He admitted that he is thirty-three years of age, though he does not look over twenty-five."

Field had listened to the yarns, which were already becoming legends in Hopkinsville, and attended several readings. His reports captured the attention of Hearst himself, who invited Edgar to visit Chicago as his guest. Edgar went in early March of 1911, along with A. D. Noe and Leslie. During their ten-day trip, Edgar gave more readings and answered what he later described as "the most preposterous" questions he had ever heard. Noe and his father seemed unwilling to intervene in what clearly was an effort to sensationalize his story. Everyone he was introduced to through the Hearst people reportedly considered him to be a freak, even the bellboys at the LaSalle Hotel, who charged people five dollars to slip them into the crowded living room of the bridal suite where they could watch the "marvel of the age" as he talked and smoked and told stories. Hearst himself, who had allegedly arranged for the visit, never made an appearance.

Leslie, Edgar, and Noe were quartered with one or two people who acted as escorts or guards. They were told that arrangements were being made for the deans of Chicago's largest university to see a demonstration, but after three or four days the Cayce party was informed that the Hearst organization had been unable to make the right connections. Instead, three physicians were invited to examine Edgar and asked that he do a reading for them. One of these doctors, William Sadler, was reported to be none other than the physician who had previously assaulted Cayce with the hypodermic needle back in Bowling Green five years earlier.

Before the reading had even begun, these physicians refused to allow their names to be used in a story, whether the experiment was a success or not. They also had their own ideas on what constituted an experiment. They insisted that Edgar try to locate a missing woman and to unravel several other local mysteries that had been troubling them. At Edgar's behest, Leslie finally demanded that no readings of this kind be given, but that an actual patient needing assistance be used for the experiment. Edgar looked toward Noe for support but didn't find it. The reporters covering the story continued to insist that something more sensational than a physical reading be given. They said that Edgar at least owed it to them for all the newspaper notoriety they had given him. Early the next morning, at about 2 A.M., they finally agreed to conduct a reading for what had been presumed to have been one of Dr. Sadler's patients.

Immediately after the reading, once Cayce was conscious, one physician asked the other if the description that had been provided was a fair and accurate portrait of the patient. His reply was rather cryptic, neither saying the reading was correct or not. The third physician didn't wish to talk about the reading at all, but insisted that Cayce go back into trance and attempt information for a member of his family who was ill. Cayce did so, apparently with much success. But when the reporters asked the doctor to sign a statement, he absolutely refused.

The next morning, bold headlines on the second section of the *Chicago Examiner* read: "He Came, We Saw, But He Did Not Conquer." The accompanying article stated that Cayce claimed to be able to do many things and refused to do them, that the doctors had said there was nothing whatever in what was given, and that the stenographers had failed to write anything at all, saying it was such "gibberish" that it was not understandable to anyone and amounted to a lot of "bunk." The next afternoon's paper did print testimonials of people who claimed to have been helped by Cayce, but the damage had already been done.

Edgar naturally felt let down and was fearful of the direction that their partnership had taken. Ketchum and Noe didn't seem to have the best interest of Edgar or their patients in mind. They were far more interested in promoting themselves and the partnership than they were in helping people—which was precisely what they had been warned about in both the reading on the work and in their brief meeting with the East Indian.

14.

Under
Investigation

Just days after his return home from Chicago, Edgar became a father for the second time. Gertrude gave birth to another son on March 28, 1911, at 8:30 P.M. They named him Milton Porter, after Gertrude's two cousins.

Edgar was so preoccupied with Noe and Ketchum that he did not pay close enough attention to the situation at home. As had been the case with Hugh Lynn, the baby was not receiving enough nourishment from his mother's milk. But by the time a wet nurse was found, the already weakened child was ill with whooping cough and then colitis. Edgar didn't listen to Dr. Jackson's warnings about the severity of the case, and Gertrude didn't demand psychic help for Milton as Carrie had done for her son, Tommy. It was not until their son had reached a critical condition that Edgar gave a reading. Although no transcript of this reading is in existence, it apparently held out no hope for a recovery. Milton Porter's death certificate states that he died on May 17 at 11:15 A.M., one month and twenty days after his birth. The impact on the Cayce family could not have been greater.

Edgar naturally blamed himself for not giving a reading sooner. Hugh Lynn, who had just turned three years old, also blamed himself, the result of overhearing his mother say to her mother that she thought Milton had caught the sickness from Hugh Lynn, who had had whooping cough at the time of his brother's birth. As a way of doing penance, Hugh Lynn decided to run away from home. He got only as far as the crawl space under the front steps of the porch at The Hill, where Edgar later found him and where he and his son had their first father and son talk. He comforted Hugh Lynn by explaining that Jesus had taken Milton Porter, not Hugh Lynn.

Edgar was not able to console Gertrude as he had Hugh Lynn. She felt that she hadn't taken proper care of the child, and that Edgar had been too busy with reporters to address the family's needs at home. Distraught, Gertrude stopped eating and spent much of each day in bed. Eventually her health gave way. The early symptoms were at first considered merely a result of the delivery: she suffered from vaginal bleeding, irritation, and constant fatigue. Edgar believed that she was just overcoming the sorrow of losing the baby and would, with prayer and attention, regain her strength, as she had done after his return to Louisville. However, Edgar underestimated Gertrude's condition. By June 10, 1911, she was unable to do any work around the house at all, and by July she was throwing up blood.

Dr. Jackson told her she had pleurisy. His real fear, however, was that she had contracted tuberculosis from nursing her brother Hugh on a trip to Texas with her mother. In late July, Dr. Jackson confirmed that Gertrude had tuberculosis. Dr. Beazley, who had come in from Bowling Green, concurred. Edgar did not hesitate before volunteering psychic help. "I knew the conditions were rather desperate," Edgar later said. "I knew I had to give a reading."

This time the problem with doing a reading was not Edgar, but Gertrude. She didn't want one. In fact, she had been the only person in the immediate family who was opposed to ever having one. It wasn't that she didn't believe he could use his psychic powers to help her, for this had been proven to her in the case of her nephew Tommy. Gertrude was reluctant to ask for a reading because she still didn't like the business of his giving readings and didn't want their lives to revolve around them. Well-meaning but uninformed friends had also told her that Edgar would eventually become insane if he continued giving readings. And there were always suspicious people around Edgar with various get-rich-quick schemes, including, in her opinion, Ketchum and Noe. Her steadfast refusal to have a reading was her way of asserting what little control she did have over the situation.

Edgar wasn't about to sit back and see Gertrude die like Milton Porter had. In the quiet of their bedroom he prevailed upon her to put her concerns about the Ketchum and Noe partnership out of her mind and to have faith in the greater blessings that could come through the work if only she could give herself over to it. Gertrude finally agreed to try. In Edgar's mind, it was the most important reading that he would ever attempt, and he wanted it to be the best. The conditions in which he chose to have the reading conducted, and its eventual outcome, set a new standard for all later readings.

Knowing that the best and most productive readings were given in a prayerful atmosphere, Edgar assembled the family's loved ones into his office and asked practically everyone else he knew to pray for him and Gertrude too, specifically at the time the reading was to take place. Gertrude's mother, Lizzie, and Carrie House agreed to be at Edgar's side when he went into trance. Accompanying them was Dr. Kasey, the Methodist minister who had known Gertrude since birth, and Harry D. Smith, the minister from the First Christian Church who had married Edgar and Gertrude. Their congregations, like Edgar's friends, had all been notified as to when they should begin praying. Edgar had also invited a tuberculosis specialist from Louisville to join them for the reading, along with Dr. Sergeant, another specialist, and Louis Elgin, a druggist, in hopes that their collective expertise would contribute to the success of the reading. Ketchum officiated, while Leslie conducted.

The first reading was done on August 2, 1911. None of his previous readings were more detailed and thorough, nor could any of them be considered more successful. For forty-five minutes Cayce detailed the condition of virtually all of her major body organs and nervous system, starting at the top of her spine, moving to her lungs and diaphragm, and then on to her digestive track and colon. He outlined treatments that included osteopathic adjustments for her back, inhalation of spirits to relieve the congestion in her lungs, powerful drugs to help cleanse the blood and various organs, a diet high in iron supplements and raw vegetables, and laxatives, which were to be injected directly into her colon. When Cayce woke up the doctors were pacing up and down the room, shaking their heads. The Louisville specialist believed the trance lecture to be the "most remarkable" discourse he had ever heard on tuberculosis. "Your anatomy is fine . . . your diagnosis is excellent." His concern was the strange and unusual treatments.

From the specialist's perspective, the osteopathic adjustments were not harmful, nor were the laxatives. It was the unusual treatment to clean out the lungs that alarmed him. This treatment consisted of inhaling the fumes of apple brandy from a charred oak keg. Then there were the drugs. Cayce had recommended that she take a combination of heroin, eucalpyptol, terebene, and creosote, which were to be mixed into a liquid and placed in a pellet or capsule made from crystallized phosphates of soda. They were to prepare only enough medication for three days, for the reading said that the compound would begin to disintegrate after that time.

The various doctors argued among themselves. All the while, Edgar and his family looked on silently. After all the astonishing cures and help he had given over the years, even Ketchum seemed to be at a loss. As Ketchum later wrote of the incident, he felt "sick in his soul, in his heart, and in his body" because he didn't see how Gertrude, in her current condition, would survive the combination of drugs and treatments. And yet the Source had said that she would live if the recommendations were followed.

Edgar declared that he was going to act upon the reading immediately. Since Sergeant and Jackson refused to sign the prescription for the drugs, he asked Ketchum to do so. And fortunately, Elgin, the pharmacist, agreed to fill the various prescriptions "even if it means going to jail." Gertrude was too weak to resist or care. She could barely raise her head from the pillow.

After taking the first capsule, Gertrude stopped hemorrhaging. The fumes of the apple brandy in the charred oak keg reduced the congestion in her lungs. Within a few days her fever broke and within two weeks she was decidedly on the mend. But it wasn't just the medication or therapy. Gertrude truly desired to get well and had summoned her strength and courage to come to terms with the readings and her husband's unusual career. Perhaps Gertrude could now sympathize with those who were ill and their families, and the enormous gift Edgar's work could be to them. And perhaps she also understood, more fully, the sense of responsibility Edgar felt in making himself available to those who needed his help.

Although Gertrude sometimes had relapses, she made great strides forward. Gradually she gained strength and within several months she was back on her feet. Ironically, it was in the midst of Gertrude's recovery—in what might be viewed as Ketchum and Cayce's most spectacular success— that the year-old partnership would come under the most intense scrutiny and criticism by the medical profession.

In November of 1911, while Gertrude was still in bed recovering from tuberculosis, Ketchum learned that he was being investigated by the Christian County Medical Society, and that a resolution had been passed to demand that the governor and the attorney general revoke Ketchum's medical license. Dr. Frank Stites, a fellow physician and neighbor, told Ketchum exactly what the medical society was up to: "Here you've got all this publicity, and the town's filled up, and we know it's all a fake, so now we're going to do something about it."

In due course, Ketchum received a notice that another meeting to discuss suspending his license was to be held at the courthouse. Ketchum wasn't sure what he should do about it. He knew that there would be upward of forty-five doctors in the county attending. He could bring in eyewitnesses and patients he had helped, along with affidavits. There were plenty to be had. However, he had another idea. On the day of the meeting he went to the First National Bank and withdrew a thousand dollars in cash from his account, separating it into two packs of five hundred dollars each. Ketchum left the bank with the money in his pockets and then walked to the courthouse where the doctors were assembling. He entered the meeting room and took a seat in the back. Many more doctors were there than he had anticipated.

The meeting was called to order by the medical society secretary, who read the names of the committee who had been chosen to go to Frankfort to see the governor and attorney general about revoking Ketchum's license. Ketchum was then invited to address the group. He slowly walked to the front of the room, put the cash on top of the table where everyone could see it, and delivered a short speech, which he had previously prepared.

"I'm sorry to have brought this on the doctors of Christian County," Ketchum said. "But you were born and raised here . . . [and] I came here . . . on the encouragement of quite a number of your top citizens—in particular Professor Dietrich . . . And when he told me about this boy Cayce all I did was investigate him—and that's all I'm still doing now . . . If you gentlemen want to get the real meat of the bull . . . I want your help. Of course, if you're just going to kick me out of the profession, that's different. But I have a suggestion to offer you . . . I'd like you to appoint six men . . . to choose one of his most complex cases, then have Cayce lie down and go to sleep and diagnose each of the six cases . . . If the diagnoses are not absolutely correct . . . I will turn . . . this money over to any charity you name in Christian County."

There was silence after Ketchum had finished speaking. Then someone in the back of the room made a motion that there be further investigation before their committee visited the attorney general. Ketchum heard nothing more from the medical society. But he did eventually speak with the attorney general. The occasion was at a meeting of the Bar Association of western Kentucky, northern Tennessee, and southern Indiana, which was held at the Hotel Latham later that same year. Cayce had been invited to put on a demonstration. There is no mention in the records who made the request, but in all likelihood it was Ketchum, for he conducted the reading, and with Edgar's help, put on a demonstration of his own. After Cayce had gone into trance, Ketchum asked the assembled attorneys to write out questions, which he would attempt to have the psychic answer. Approximately eighteen lawyers obliged. Cayce—in trance—repeated each of the questions after they were read and then answered them. In certain cases he went into full detail. Other times he would just say yes or no.

The attorney general was the guest of honor at the event and after it ended one of the local prosecutors introduced Ketchum to him. The attorney general, who had heard about the trouble that Ketchum had had with the local doctors, looked at Ketchum for a moment and then said: "Well, I'll tell you. It's not far from *here* to over *there*. I think this fellow falls through." This was all the attorney general said, and all that Ketchum believed he needed to hear him say. "[In] some way and somehow," Ketchum said, "he does fall into another sphere about which we know nothing."

At around the same time that Ketchum was under investigation, a far more thorough investigation was being conducted by Dr. Hugo Münsterberg, the dean of psychology at Harvard University, former president of the American Psychological Association, and a friend and associate of William James. He had heard Ketchum's paper read at Harvard and had followed some of the later press accounts. Now, in mid-December of 1911, he paid a surprise visit to Hopkinsville. There was no question what his intentions were, for he told his students and fellow faculty members at Harvard before he left that the reason for his trip was "to expose Cayce to the world."

Edgar was cordial, despite his initial shock at the distinguished professor's unexpected appearance at the door of his house. Münsterberg stood well over six feet tall and weighed about 250 pounds. He had an abrupt manner and, with his thick German accent and penetrating gaze, could be quite intimidating.

When Münsterberg came for his week-long visit, Edgar and Gertrude were living at Gertrude's mother's cottage on the Russellville Road, adjacent to The Hill. Münsterberg knocked on the door, introduced himself to Edgar, and then immediately asked to see the cabinet, lights, crystal ball, or any of the "modus operandi" that were the trademark of psychics such as Madame Blavatsky, whose practices had recently come under intense scrutiny in the New York press. Edgar didn't know what Münsterberg was talking about. He told the professor that he could go into trance whether he was lying on the floor in the living room, outside in the yard, or in the middle of the road. He also informed him that many of his readings were recorded by a stenographer and that typed transcripts were available for inspection. Edgar took out his last reading for Gertrude, which he gave Münsterberg to read.

Edgar agreed to meet Münsterberg at the studio the next day. When Edgar arrived in the morning, Leslie, the stenographer, and Ketchum were already there. Edgar had just finished telling them about Münsterberg's unannounced visit to his home the afternoon before when the professor arrived. He took a seat in one of the large rocking chairs and began putting questions to Edgar and Ketchum. The partners answered the questions and showed him more transcripts of readings as well as letters from patients.

Eventually, Edgar's morning appointment arrived at the office. August Boehme had come from his home in Newport, Kentucky, and hadn't told Ketchum or anyone at the office the reason for the reading he was requesting. Edgar and Boehme chatted for only a few moments before Edgar lay down on the couch, put himself into trance, and proceeded to give a reading. Leslie stood beside the couch and Ketchum and Boehme sat in chairs while Münsterberg chose to sit at the door where he could best view the proceedings.

Cayce gave a typical reading. He reported on Boehme's body from head to toe, pointing out problem areas and making suggestions for treating them. According to the reading, he was suffering from a complicated stomach disorder, which resulted in chronic malnutrition. When Cayce came out of the trance, Münsterberg resumed questioning both Edgar and Ketchum, and now Boehme. He asked Boehme about how much Edgar knew of his condition before the reading. "Nothing whatever," Boehme answered. "I never saw him before in my whole life. I only read something about him in the paper—I've been a sufferer for a long time with no results, so I came to see him, only arrived this morning." Münsterberg asked Boehme if he was convinced by the reading. "I certainly am!" Boehme announced.

Apparently so was Münsterberg, for he spent the next two days interviewing more of Ketchum's patients. Among his interviews were the Dietrich family and Carrie House. At the end of his visit, Münsterberg admitted to Edgar that he had no explanation for what he had seen and heard, but he had to conclude that Edgar was the real thing. He also urged Edgar to continue. "If you never do another case other than the little Dietrich child, your life has not been in vain," he said. "I believe you will go far."

Münsterberg told Edgar that he would hear from him again, but Edgar never did. Although the professor did not take the trouble to write a case study of Edgar Cayce for one of the medical journals or deliver a paper on the subject, he was not ashamed or embarrassed to describe his experiences in Hopkinsville to his colleagues and students at Harvard, among them, the distinguished Dr. William McDougal, who would later conduct a study of the readings himself. To them, Münsterberg admitted that he had failed to expose Cayce as a fraud and, after spending a week with him and conducting studies of three of the patients who had received readings, had become convinced of his legitimacy. He said that Cayce had "an unusual power" but did not elaborate further.

With the praise that Münsterberg gave also came some advice, which he shared with Cayce in private. Münsterberg thought that Cayce was "running with the wrong bunch." He was referring to Noe and Ketchum and perhaps even Edgar's father, Leslie. Münsterberg urged Edgar to continue "listening to the voice," as he referred to the Source, but to reconsider the company he kept.

Gertrude was not surprised to hear Münsterberg say this because she was convinced of the same thing. She had not trusted Ketchum from the start, especially not since Leslie had broken his kneecap and Ketchum himself had begun conducting the readings. Many times Ketchum had dispensed with the stenographer altogether. He told Edgar that he took notes and then would dictate his own version of what had been said. Gertrude also had begun to suspect Ketchum of either extorting money from various patients or using the readings to profit personally. Nearly everyone in town knew that Ketchum had bought one of Hopkinsville's first cars, a two cylinder Brush roadster. It was also common knowledge that Ketchum had purchased a stud farm on the outskirts of town where he kept a stable of racehorses. And perhaps most damning in a community like Hopkinsville, Ketchum was rumored to be financially supporting Miss Katy deTuncq, a French teacher at the Bethel Female College, with whom he was having an extramarital affair.

His suspicions raised, Edgar decided to check up on Ketchum. He wrote a letter to a patient who had allegedly received a reading on one of the days the stenographer had been dismissed. He asked her if the readings had been beneficial to her. The woman said that she had applied for a reading, but had never received one.

Edgar confronted Ketchum with the letter. Ketchum told Edgar that he had had to change some of their rules because they needed the money to build a hospital—that with Mohr gone, it was up to him and Noe. And they couldn't get it built getting $25 for readings, not to mention all their charity cases. Under pressure, Ketchum admitted taking readings on the horse races and other forms of gambling. He referred to it as "getting a few tips." As far as Edgar was concerned, the partnership was finished. Ketchum himself must have realized it, for he left town before the partnership was officially disbanded. Edgar never saw him again.

By no small coincidence, Ketchum left for Boston, where he took a refresher course at Harvard Medical School and delivered another paper on Cayce. Attempts he made to strike up a relationship with Münsterberg proved futile, for Münsterberg apparently would have nothing to do with him. Ketchum's girlfriend, Miss deTuncq, left Hopkinsville about the same time as Ketchum. The two of them later traveled to Hawaii, where Ketchum married Miss deTuncq, after divorcing his wife.

As Edgar had done before, and would do again, he turned his back on an unpleasant situation and moved to a city where no one would know him. In January 1912, Edgar literally walked away from the studio, leaving the photo equipment, negatives, and files of readings behind, and moved to Alabama.

Leslie, on his own and on Edgar's behalf, would later sue Noe and Ketchum for breach of contract and back rents at the studio totaling some $28,000. The suit was tried before J. T. Hanberry of the Christian County Circuit Court, the same judge who had witnessed a reading when the partnership was being formed, and who had later offered to buy Noe and Ketchum's contract with Cayce from them. Although his presence as judge in this case was clearly a conflict of interest, he presided over the trial and ruled from the bench that the contract as originally drawn up was illegal. The case was summarily dismissed, and the two Cayces were asked to pay legal fees and make a small settlement. Leslie blamed himself for the chain of events that took the parties to court, doggedly insisting that the partnership would have survived and "things would have been all right" had he not broken his kneecap.

At Leslie's request, Edgar would briefly return to Hopkinsville from his new home in Alabama to be present when the ruling was handed down in March of 1913. It was a deeply unpleasant experience for him. In a letter he would later write to a business associate, Edgar described sitting in the courtroom with his father and being overcome with anger by what he believed was a great miscarriage of justice. He also described doing something that he had never done before, nor would do again, and which he would sincerely regret later. "Something within me at this time made me rise and ask the judge if I might speak without the judge ruling [me] . . . in contempt of court," Edgar wrote. "He said I might speak. That same something [within me] said, 'For the lie you have this day enacted, the worms of your body will eat you up while you are yet alive!'"

According to Edgar Cayce, what he had "willed," was indeed what later happened. Hookworms, or some form of intestinal worm infestation, brought on anemia and eventually killed Hanberry. "Possibly it was only a coincidence," Edgar told his friend. "Possibly it was playing with fire." Edgar left Hopkinsville promising himself never to let his anger get the best of him again.

15.

Little City
on a Big River

Edgar Cayce liked to say that he moved to the river city of Selma, Alabama, for the simple reason that "it was a good distance from anyone who knew what I did." This may well have been true. However, it was also true that the H. P. Tressler Company, which hired him to open a photography studio in that city in early January 1912, had strategically chosen Selma because it was the fastest growing city in the entire state. Its double-width streets hummed with traffic going to and from the jetty, where row upon row of riverboat steamers docked to unload their cargo into the wholesale cotton warehouses and rolling mills along Broad Street. And yet, despite the hectic pace of life in a city suffering growing pains, its population of nearly twenty thousand still enjoyed the gracious antebellum custom of shutting down all day Thursday so that visitors and residents alike could "cool their feet" in the meandering currents of the Alabama River.

There is little doubt that Gertrude, still recovering from tuberculosis at home in Hopkinsville, feared that the fast life of a city like Selma might have the same effect on her husband that Louisville previously had. This was not to be the case. Upon arrival, Edgar immediately set about preparing a home where he, Gertrude, and Hugh Lynn could be together. He consciously saved his money, avoiding the temptations of gambling and other riverboat entertainment, and except for his work at the First Christian Church on Selma Avenue, dedicated himself to the day—a year and three months later—when the family would be reunited. "I can hardly wait until you're strong enough to travel," Edgar wrote home in a postcard when he first arrived. "You'll love it here, and prospects are wonderful."

Headquarters for the Selma office of the H. P. Tressler Company was at 21½ Broad Street, located in the heart of the business district over Cawthon-Coleman's drugstore. Edgar selected this spot because of its large skylight, its central location to pedestrian traffic coming up from the river, and because his two competitors in the photography business, the King Brothers and J. N. Smith, had already established businesses in the more exclusive tree-lined residential district to the north.

What the location may have lacked in charm was made up for in space— fourteen hundred square feet. The stairs from the ground floor led directly up to the reception room, which Edgar would furnish with a large rolltop desk, plush easy chairs, tables, and showcases full of photos, along with a portrait camera and backdrops. Immediately adjacent to the reception room was a large developing and printing room, and a third room that was used for equipment storage.

The apartment he rented for his family was on the third floor, just above the studio. He could access the apartment through a back stairway just off the reception room. At the top of the stairs, off a long hallway, was a small bedroom where Hugh Lynn eventually slept, a larger master bedroom for Edgar and Gertrude, a dining room that doubled as a living room, and a small kitchen, which looked out over the Alabama River. The apartment's only drawback was its proximity to the wholesale grocery outlet next door. Because of the large volume of food being stored in the outlet, there was a constant infestation of rats, which would eat through the walls into the Cayce kitchen to escape the army of cats that the grocery outlet kept to protect their produce.

Along the walls of the staircase leading up from the street below, Edgar hung many of his best-framed photographs. It was the display outside, however, that captured customers' attention. Mounted beside the door was a large wind-up eight-day clock with only one hand. Edgar would put photos of people whose portraits he had recently done around the face of the clock. When the clock wound to a stop, the person whose picture the hand was pointing to received his or her photo-finishing work for free.

By all accounts, the lion's share of Edgar's early customers were from the First Christian Church on the corner of Selma Avenue and Franklin Street, which he had joined on January 12, 1912, the day after he had arrived. The congregation of this church, which numbered close to five hundred, quickly grew to unabashedly adore Edgar. It was within just a short time of joining the church that he was made a deacon, assigned a Bible study class to teach, and was put in charge of the Christian Endeavor program. Fellow deacons would later remark upon Edgar's gentle nature, the small acts of kindness he showed to whomever he met, and his vast knowledge of the Bible. At no church before or after was Edgar welcomed with such open arms, nor did he form so many deep and lasting friendships.

Church records provide ample evidence that he hosted what was arguably the most remarkable Bible study class that had ever been assembled in a Selma church. Edgar's "Class No. 7," named for the number on the room where the class met, included Catholics, Presbyterians, Baptists, Methodists, and Episcopalians, along with students from the Christian Church. The class was so popular that they published a magazine that Edgar wrote and edited called the *Sevenette*.

Equally popular was the Christian Endeavor program that he organized. This became such a hit among local teenagers that it would receive a national award, which would be presented in Birmingham, for having the most active participants or "junior experts" ever credited to a single chapter in the history of the movement. Members of that class would go on to become missionaries in Mexico, Japan, and India.

Although the official Christian Endeavor meetings and Bible study took place at the church, the unofficial gathering place was the reception room at Edgar's studio. Among those who were regulars were Alfred and Roger Butler, Harry Bredin, Charlie Le Noir, and Alec Cawthon. Edgar entertained the group with discussions of current affairs, and as he had done in Bowling Green, card games of his own invention. Among them was a game Edgar invented called DrinX, which involved fifty-nine cards representing nonalcoholic beverages and one trump card. The object of the game was to collect all the cards in a particular suit, represented by different types of fruit juices, soda, and ginger-ale, or play a trump card, called a Mixed Drink, which permitted a player to collect cards in different suits. Popular as the game became in Selma, it didn't catch on as did his first game, The Pit, though this time Edgar, in 1913, would take the trouble to consult a lawyer to have it copyrighted.

In addition to the Sunday school and Christian Endeavor groups, Edgar sometimes participated in activities organized by the First Christian Church ladies auxiliary, known as the Helping Hands. A particularly fun photograph taken at a Helping Hands meeting shows Edgar posing provocatively in a dress and bonnet—his costume for a play staged to raise funds for the church. As in other photographs of Edgar taken during this time, there is a level of humor and animation in his face that had been absent during his years in Hopkinsville working with Ketchum and Noe. His letters home were equally full of energy and love of life. In one note to Gertrude he went so far as to try his hand at poetry:

I asked the roses as they grew
Richer and lovelier in their hue
What made their buds so rich and bright
They answered: Looking Toward The Light

In another letter home, Edgar shared the details of the first known trance reading given since the demise of the Ketchum partnership, which was given in Selma in April of 1912. The reading took place toward the end of a week when a long series of rainstorms had temporarily shut his business down. He hadn't had a customer in over two weeks. In the midst of saying his daily prayers, he heard someone coming up the steps to the studio. There soon appeared a short, elderly lady, all wet and bedraggled. The bonnet she was wearing stuck to the side of her face. As she pulled it off and brushed her hair back, she asked if he made enlargements. Edgar said that he did. The woman fumbled in her dress and brought out a small tintype, saying that this was a picture of her son in Alaska. She wanted to have the best picture that could possibly be made from it. The only way she could pay him for it, however, was if he would be willing to cash an out-of-state check. "This is from my boy. I have been to everyone in town, but nobody will cash it."

Edgar took the check and asked her to wait for him to see if anything could be done. He went to the City National Bank of Selma a few blocks away. The bank president, H. C. Armstrong, told Edgar that the check had been to his bank three times already that day. He had no reason to think that the check was bad, but couldn't be certain because he didn't know the woman. Edgar talked Armstrong into cashing the check anyway. "Let's together help this woman out," Edgar said.

Edgar remembers how delighted the woman was when he gave her the money. Out of that money she paid Edgar for the picture, and he, in turn, was able to the pay the rent on his studio that month. In the course of their discussions, the woman told him of her daughter who was suffering from infantile paralysis and had a crooked leg and foot. Edgar then told her of some experiences he had had in the years before coming to Selma. She asked him to give her little girl a reading.

A few days later the woman brought her daughter into the studio. Alfred Butler, from Edgar's Sunday school class, agreed to conduct the reading, and Harriet McSwain, a friend of Butler's and the bank president's secretary, took notes. Edgar had also obtained the help of Dr. Samuel Gay, a former army surgeon who agreed to study the reading and give his opinion of the diagnosis and recommended treatment. This reading, like many others from the early years, is no longer in existence, but by all accounts the child's leg and foot were healed completely when the treatment suggested was carried out. From that moment on, and for as long as Edgar lived in Selma, hardly a week went by when at least one member of that child's family did not visit the studio, bringing with them a token offering of thanks.

The next reading Edgar gave was for Dr. Samuel Gay's father. He had asked for a reading on an open sore on the side of his face that had been diagnosed as cancer. A suggestion was given for injections of a compound or serum made from the skin of rabbits, a treatment that the Source routinely recommended for skin cancer, and which later proved effective in hundreds of similar cases—though its preparation and combination in many instances were altered for individual use. In this particular case, the open sore healed and reportedly never gave Dr. Gay's father any more trouble.

Alf Butler, who had conducted both of these readings, then requested a reading for his sister, Flora Butler, who had quite suddenly exhibited severe psychiatric problems and who was now being hospitalized in an asylum in Tuscaloosa, Alabama. The subsequent reading surprised everyone connected with the case. It specifically stated that her behavior was being caused by a double-impacted wisdom tooth and that removal of the tooth would result in her complete recovery. Alf and his brother, Roger, made a hurried trip to Tuscaloosa, where Flora's jaw was x-rayed in the presence of the girl's aunt, who was a physician. The tooth was located and removed and a few months later Flora was able to return to school, by all accounts completely healthy.

Flora Butler's case attracted a great deal of attention and was written up in the *Selma Times-Journal* as well as other newspapers. Eventually this caught the attention of Sir Arthur Conan Doyle, who had already heard favorable reports of Edgar since Elbert Hubbard had met the psychic in Bowling Green. Doyle and Edgar would later exchange a number of letters on Flora Butler's reading during one of Doyle's well-publicized American speaking tours.

This reading was not, however, the last one Edgar gave for one of Alf and Roger's sisters. Four years later, Mary Butler was on a trip to Baldwin County, Alabama. Her brothers became concerned because they hadn't heard from her. They asked him to give them a reading to find out if she was safe. Edgar went into trance and said that they shouldn't worry, for she had been delayed on her trip, and a letter stating as much would arrive at the family's home the next day. Mary's letter arrived as promised, and along with it, the lifelong devotion of a family who sought readings and sang his praises for three generations to come.

The Butler family would also receive what was deemed at the time to be the strangest and most preposterous medical reading to date. In March 1917, Alf requested a reading for his father, Alfred Berry Butler, who was suffering from a condition about which Cayce was given no previous information. The subsequent reading diagnosed cancer of the bladder, stomach, and kidneys, and held out little hope for recovery. The only cure, Cayce said, was an organ transplant, performed by the Mayo Brothers at their clinic in Minnesota. This, in itself, was a remarkable recommendation, considering the fact that organ transplants wouldn't be done until 1954—over thirty-five years later. Cayce went on to suggest that the diseased organs could be transplanted from a living animal, a procedure that wasn't attempted until 1964. Despite the success of Cayce's earlier reading for Flora and Mary Butler, Alf and Roger were unable to convince their mother that such an operation was medically sound, and the recommendations were not carried out. Alfred Berry Butler died within sixty days.

The reading that Edgar Cayce conducted during this time that had the most lasting impact on his career wasn't conducted in Alabama, but back in Kentucky. It was given at the request of the DeLaney family of Lexington, who, like so many others, had heard of Edgar through Charles and Minnie Dietrich. Although Edgar himself and previous biographers have said that this reading occurred much earlier in his career, evidence suggests that it was conducted in December 1913, when thirty-six-year-old Cayce was already well established as an Alabama photographer.

Amanda Fay DeLaney, the wife of the wealthy owner of the Kentucky Lumber Company, had been crippled in an automobile accident and was anxious to have Edgar visit her home. After they had exchanged letters, Edgar agreed to go to Lexington to conduct a reading. Prior to his departure, she asked Edgar to bring a physician with him to take down the suggestions and facilitate treatments.

Unable to find a physician in Selma to accompany him to Lexington, Edgar wired John Blackburn in Bowling Green, who agreed to conduct the reading. However, when Edgar arrived by train in Bowling Green to meet Blackburn, the physician was unable to go due to an emergency operation he had to perform. Edgar sent a telegram to the DeLaney family and went on to Lexington alone. He was relieved to learn when he arrived at the station that William DeLaney, Amanda's husband, had arranged for a physician along with a stenographer and a person to conduct the reading.

The DeLaney family lived in an exclusive housing complex in Lexington called Hampton Court. A carriage, which was waiting at the station, took Edgar to their large house. When Edgar arrived and was shown into the living room, Mrs. DeLaney was wheeled in on a stretcher to meet him. The mere sight of her evidenced her serious condition. Her body was so swollen that she could barely move her hands or feet. She could not feed herself or even comb her hair. Doctors described her condition as a severe case of arthritis that was the result of injuries she received nearly a decade before. Her skin was apparently sensitive to the degree that she could not bear to be touched by bed sheets. Unable to move because of the pain, she had put on a considerable amount of weight. At only five foot five, she weighed two hundred pounds or more.

Edgar described her as being in the most "pitiful" condition of anyone he had ever seen. Although the case seemed hopeless, he was still willing to try. He told the DeLaneys and their physician about his experiences throughout the years and described in detail how the readings had helped Gertrude survive tuberculosis. Gertrude's condition was of special interest to them since they had lost many friends and relatives to the disease.

Mr. DeLaney declined to conduct the reading himself on the grounds that the Roman Catholic Church forbade the "calling up of spirits." He instead had arranged for a Jewish neighbor to conduct the reading—a handsome young college student named Dave Kahn. Edgar handed Dave the small black book, which contained the suggestions that were to be put to him, and instructed him on how to ask the questions at the proper time.

Edgar first tried to lie down on the couch but discovered that it was too short and opted for a place on the floor. Then, in trance, he proceeded to go over Mrs. DeLaney's body like a doctor, giving blood pressure, blood count, and other physiological and medical details. He also stated that the family had lived in Fort Thomas, Kentucky, which was where Mrs. DeLaney had been in a horse-and-buggy accident. She had jumped out of the carriage and hit the base of her spine on its step. He said that six or seven years later she had been in an automobile accident and that this second accident had compounded or "brought out" the original injury. This combination of conditions resulted in her almost complete paralysis.

During the course of the reading, the Source suggested that an osteopath be called in to treat her and recommended a physician who had just arrived in Lexington. Cayce then proceeded to give several medicines and mixtures, which were to be taken internally. When Edgar awoke, he asked what had been given. "Everything, including the kitchen sink," Mr. DeLaney said with obvious delight. "You gave something for every square inch of her body." Dave Kahn was dispatched with the prescriptions to one of Lexington's leading pharmacies to get them filled as prescribed. Edgar stayed with the DeLaney family for the rest of the afternoon before returning home.

It would be another six months before he would have a chance to make a return visit, at which time he would give a follow-up reading. She was slowly getting well though a strange rash had broken out all over her body. The follow-up reading said that an important ingredient—black sulfur—had been left out of the medicine. The lack of this mineral had caused the rash. About a month later Edgar received a wire asking that he return to Lexington. He was quite moved by what he saw when he arrived. The same woman who had once looked so hopeless was sitting comfortably in a chair. She asked the nurse to loosen her hair and to give her the comb and brush. She had done her own hair, she told Edgar, and had also begun to feed herself for the first time in three years. "It has been five years since I even attempted to raise my hands high enough to do up my own hair," she told him. Her feet and lower limbs seemed much better, and her swelling had decreased. Eight or nine months later she would invite Edgar to Lexington once again, this time to see her walk across the room at her own birthday party. Later, she was driving her own car.

The sessions with the DeLaney family, like other readings he gave during his early years in Selma, did much to build Edgar's confidence. But it was important for another reason. Through the DeLaneys, Edgar had begun to develop a relationship with the twenty-one-year-old Dave Kahn. The handsome and inquisitive young man quickly became enamored of Edgar, finding him, as he later said, "full of pep and promise." In the years ahead it would be Kahn more than anyone else who would bring people into the work, and nearly one-third of the readings Edgar would subsequently give can be traced to Kahn or one of his acquaintances. Like Alfred Butler, Kahn would become Edgar's frequent traveling companion, good friend, and confidant.

Edgar got to know Dave and his family better with each successive trip he made to Lexington. Eventually, he would become a regular guest in their large yellow-brick home next door to the DeLaney house. Edgar would sit next to the fireplace in the library and entertain Dave and his eight brothers and sisters with stories, or simply try to field Dave's seemingly endless questions.

Edgar distinctly remembered his first evening at the Kahn house because it was the first time he had ever been in a Jewish home. He paid special attention because it had been given in an earlier reading when he was in partnership with Ketchum that one of the people who would make a significant contribution to the work would be Jewish. Ever since then, Edgar had been on the lookout, wondering who that person would be.

Edgar discussed and recounted many of his early experiences, well into the night. Dave's mother, Fannie, whom Edgar knew simply as Mother Kahn, a tall handsome woman, seemed to feel a special affinity for him. Together they discussed their particular outlooks on life and their various experiences. Mother Kahn was supportive of Edgar and what he stood for primarily because she herself had a psychic bent.

Fannie's husband, Solomon, who was a trained Biblical scholar and student of the Talmud, initially had grave reservations about Dave's growing interest in Cayce. He reminded his son how Saul, when about to go into battle, called up the spirit of Samuel through the witch of Endor and then had to pay the price for disturbing the dead. Edgar explained that he was not calling up ghosts of the departed, as had Saul. He was linking to a higher consciousness. This explanation apparently satisfied Solomon, and he ultimately gave Dave his blessing when his son asked if he could conduct one of Edgar's readings.

The first reading that Dave conducted was for his brother, Leon, who suffered from epilepsy. Help was promised, provided they could get the whole-hearted cooperation of a doctor who could give the very difficult treatments that were suggested. Fanny was greatly impressed by the reading, but they didn't find anyone who would carry out the treatments, and Leon died. The mistake the family made with Leon was not repeated when Edgar did a reading for Dave's sister, Eleanor, who became seriously ill with scarlet fever. This time the family saw to it that the readings were carried out to the letter, and Eleanor recovered.

Edgar did many other readings for the Kahn family throughout 1914 and 1915. One interesting reading was aimed at improving the Kahn family's grocery business. In a letter to Edgar in Selma, Dave posed the simple question, "How do we [the Kahn family] improve business?" The subsequent reading might be considered the first of nearly eight hundred business readings that Cayce would do over the next three decades.

Edgar sent back a detailed report of the reading. In all likelihood, the reading was conducted by Lynn Evans, who was able to visit Edgar in Selma frequently since his job with the railroad had transferred him to nearby Anniston. The reading stated that the schools and universities in central Kentucky—which had to feed anywhere from 150 to 200 students a day—bought their canned goods in one-, two-, or three-pound cans. This meant that many cans had to be opened by hand each day as there were no mechanical can openers yet on the market. This was costly in time and effort. The reading said that Dave should go to Chicago and buy one-gallon cans of the same product. They had never heard of gallon-sized cans being available, but since the information came from Cayce, Solomon believed they should follow it up at once.

The family sent Dave to Chicago. He visited the company named in the reading, explained who he was, and told them about his family's large grocery operation. He not only bought the one-gallon cans, he also made arrangements to become the company's representative in Lexington. A few weeks later a full freight car loaded with canned goods arrived. Almost overnight the Kahn chain became the purveyor of foods to major institutions in the Lexington area.

The success of this reading prompted Dave to ask another type of question: whether or not he should pursue his father's grocery business as a long-term career. The answer to that question spawned yet another kind of reading: those devoted to career guidance. These readings became known as mental and spiritual readings, and Cayce would deliver four hundred of these in the ensuing years. Dave Kahn conducted and received the first.

In this reading, Cayce suggested that there would be "a mighty change" in the country, and that as conditions developed, Dave Kahn would be forced to leave home. Subsequently, Kahn would find his life's work in an area in which he had not been trained. Furthermore, Cayce said, Kahn's family would be very much averse to the choices that he would make. Cayce said that he would also have to "leave the flock" and go into uniform. The reading said that Kahn would be in uniform for some time, and that he would "go in honor," and "return in honor."

Initially, the reading seemed ridiculous, for none of the Kahns had ever worn a uniform. Dave didn't come from a family that raised policemen or firemen. The family's assumption was that Dave, being the eldest, would remain in Lexington and inherit his father's grocery business. Dave Kahn set the reading aside, unable at the time to comprehend that Cayce had made the first of many references to the war that would send a generation of American boys to the battle fields of Europe.

16.

Trial by Fire

Hugh Lynn didn't want to leave The Hill to move to Alabama. He was having more fun in Hopkinsville than he had ever had. He, Tommy House, and their cousin Gray Salter shared the same room at The Hill and had turned the house and its adjoining property into their private playground. It was all Gertrude and her aunts could do to keep them contained. They had a "rat pack" that rivaled the pests that constantly tried to eat their way into the Cayce apartment back in Selma.

The oldest boy, Gray Salter, led the pack. Gray's mother had died and Aunt Kate was raising him as her own. He, like the other boys, could be quite a handful, but Aunt Kate was a good match. A story that is sometimes told about these boys—though it occurred a few summers later—was when Kate had caught Gray smoking. Gray took off with Tommy and Hugh Lynn eagerly trailing behind him, outrunning Kate and eventually finding what he considered to be a safe refuge in a cherry tree. Kate brought a switch, a chair, and the evening paper to the foot of the tree and settled down to wait for him to come down. Gertrude, who came out to watch, asked Kate how long she intended to stay out there. "As long as my heart beats," Kate replied.

Eventually Gray did come down and took his licking, but not before he pointed out that Gertrude—among others in the house—also smoked. She just did so in the privacy of her room. The licking led to an argument between the boys about who could take the most licking. They ended up in a fistfight, which ultimately served to cement their long and steadfast friendships.

Hugh Lynn was sad when they had to go. But Selma would not turn out to be the disaster he thought it would be, for the years before the declaration of war were some of the happiest in the lives of the entire Cayce family. Having Gertrude and Hugh Lynn at his side in Selma, and with Gertrude now firmly in support of his trance readings, gave Edgar a new confidence in his career both as a photographer and as a psychic. The photography business was doing so well that Edgar was not only able to buy out Tressler's interest in his studio, but he was able to help his father get settled in another Cayce studio in nearby Marion, Alabama, where Edgar had obtained contracts for annuals and school albums. Although Leslie remained a poor manager, he did become a competent photographer.

It was now Gertrude who was spreading the news of Edgar's readings and who was his most outspoken defender and champion. Despite the fact that she still had to depend upon her apple brandy keg to help keep her lungs clear, and did, in fact, keep the keg near her bedside for the next three decades, she recognized that she was living proof of the good that came from the readings. During her early days in Selma, she became his guide and mentor and began to share, for the first time, in the wonder and curiosity of his psychic work. Despite claims to the latter, she also began to conduct readings. And in addition to being Edgar's chief photographic model, she became the studio's business manager, a job that involved making the appointments, handling collections, keeping the books, doing the banking, and directing the efforts of their sole employee.

Edgar was becoming an even better photographer, and for the first time was learning how to comfortably juggle his obligations as a father and photographer and his life as a psychic. Through sheer talent and a bit of good luck he landed an account with the Southern Railroad to shoot all of the photos in their publications and promotional materials. Also, with encouragement from the Kahn family, he was able to get contracts to shoot photo layouts for various grocery products. Among those contracts was one with the Mellin's Baby Food Company. Hugh Lynn became the Mellin's very robust poster child. During this time, Edgar began to put on pounds, most of which settled in his tummy, requiring his pants to be let out. Gertrude also gained weight, though on her it was quite becoming. And now, with Hugh Lynn getting older, the family was able to enjoy life in Selma as they had never done in Bowling Green. From postcards and family photos it is clear that they spent time fishing in the Alabama River, going on picnics to Elkdale Park, attending Masonic parades, and as always, participating in church activities.

Dr. Paul Allen, a dentist in Selma, and a former member of Edgar's Bible study class, tells one story that demonstrates Edgar's creativity in his work. Edgar wanted to take a group photo of all the members of the First Christian Church. To do so, without resorting to a wide-angle lens, which tends to distort portions of the image, Edgar devised a novel tripod and shutter system that allowed his camera to be swiveled from left to right in such a way that all the members of the congregation could appear in the same photo. Paul Allen and other younger members of the congregation availed themselves of the opportunity to appear twice in the same photo. They stood on the left when Edgar released the shutter, then ran around behind the congregation and stood on the right side when the camera finally came to a stop. The movement of the camera also gave Edgar time to get to the edge of the group in time to show up in the photo, too.

Although the family was very happy for these years in Alabama, their life was not without its frightening moments. The first was an accident that nearly caused Hugh Lynn to lose his eyesight.

Hugh Lynn, then a healthy and inquisitive six-year-old, loved to play with animals, which is why he was determined to be in the studio one cold day in January 1914. A family had brought in a box of squirrels, which they wished to have photographed. Since the squirrels could not be counted on to sit still, Edgar had to use flash powder to shorten the time of exposure necessary. When he was done, he thoughtlessly left the box of flash powder on the camera stand. The next morning, as a cleaning lady was working in the studio, she knocked the closed box onto the floor. Hugh Lynn, finding the box, carried it into the family's upstairs apartment and decided to play a trick on the cleaning lady. He set some of the powder out on the stairs. As the cleaning lady approached, he tried to light a match. The match head, breaking off, fell into the entire box of powder which exploded in Hugh Lynn's face. The flames burned his hair and face and went right up his nostrils.

Edgar and Gertrude, hearing the explosion and Hugh Lynn's screams, rushed out of their bedroom to see the horrible scene that awaited them at the top of the stairs. Hugh Lynn was writhing in agony. Edgar swept the child into his arms and carried him, kicking and screaming, down the street. Gertrude followed close behind. They arrived moments later at the office of a local eye specialist, Dr. Eugene Callaway. Callaway reportedly looked at

Hugh Lynn and shook his head helplessly, not knowing what to do. Dr. Gay, the family physician, who arrived next, undertook to do what he could for the damaged skin. But he too had no idea how to best treat Hugh Lynn's eyes. Doctors began to gather in Callaway's office, each dispensing advice but unable to help.

Eventually all the doctors agreed that the vision in Hugh Lynn's right eye was gone completely, and perhaps that of his left was gone, too. The specialist advised Edgar and Gertrude that they were going to have to remove Hugh Lynn's right eye. Upon hearing this, Hugh Lynn, who had still been crying loudly despite the treatments he was receiving and attempts by his Sunday school teacher to soothe him, suddenly became quiet. He raised himself up on one elbow and told the doctor not to take out his eye. "My daddy, when he's asleep," he said, "is the best doctor in the world. He'll tell you what to do."

Edgar and Gertrude had been so caught up in the emergency that they had not yet had a chance to think of getting a reading. This bold statement by Hugh Lynn brought them back down to earth and they immediately returned with Hugh Lynn to the studio to conduct a reading. This may have been the first reading that Gertrude ever conducted, although it is difficult to say for certain since the original reading is gone and not all the accounts of what went on are the same.

Many of the people from their church, including Alf and Roger Butler, and the pastor, Reverend D. P. Taylor, had been congregating at the studio and were there to join Edgar and Gertrude in prayer before Edgar went into trance. Reflecting back on how he felt at that moment, Edgar said that there was energy in the room like never before. He said it was like "electricity."

The reading stated that Hugh Lynn's sight had not been completely destroyed and suggested that the solution that doctors had already put on his eyes was correct, except that tannic acid had to be added to it. The reading also specified times for changing the dressings, saying that after two weeks the mass of burned flesh and poisons would drop off, leaving the eyes healthy. Upon reviewing the contents of the reading, the specialist talked with the other doctors. They all agreed that the tannic acid recommended was too strong for use on the eyes. Edgar and Gertrude pointed out the obvious. If they believed that the child's sight was gone, then there was no reason to worry about tannic acid injuring them further. This was a difficult argument to counter, so they immediately set about treating Hugh Lynn as recommended.

Whether it was Hugh Lynn's faith in his father or the actual effects of the new solution, it seemed to have a calming effect on Hugh Lynn, who stopped sobbing almost immediately after the solution was administered. For the next two weeks Hugh Lynn lay in bed in a darkened room, his bandaged eyes constantly bathed in the solution. At the end of this period, as predicted, the white mass of burned flesh came loose and fell away, revealing his two brown eyes. He looked with a smile at his mother and father. "I can see!" he announced.

In the months to come Edgar and Gertrude took every precaution they could to protect their son's vision. They watched him carefully and did follow-up readings to ensure that nothing was going wrong. Not a single scar was evident and although Hugh Lynn was to suffer from myopia from his teen years on, it was nothing that diet, exercises, and eye glasses—all recommended in readings in the years to come—couldn't solve.

Later that year, on March 8, 1914, Edgar had to do a reading on himself. While out shooting some photographs in a nearby town, he had had an attack of cramps and nausea. Dr. Gay diagnosed the case as appendicitis. But rather than operate, he treated Edgar with drugs. For a few days his condition improved and he was able to go back to work. He decided, however, that for good measure, he would do a reading on himself. The reading stated that although the X rays indicated that the condition was stable, in fact an operation was in order and should be performed immediately. It further stated that the operation would be difficult since his appendix was twisted around his intestines. The reading also suggested that, at the same time the operation was performed, surgeons treat a clot or stricture that would be found in the same area—a result of the improper healing of the wound to his testicle that he had suffered as a child.

Edgar Cayce went into the hospital that same night and the doctors performed the operation the next morning. As predicted, the operation was a difficult one because his appendix was twisted around his intestines. In fact, doctors reported that "they had never seen such a difficult case." Given the extreme difficulty they encountered, the doctors were not able to treat the clot and that condition would periodically cause him trouble for the rest of his life.

About this same time, Hugh Lynn, who had started school, was being teased by some of the older boys. They were calling his father all kinds of names and telling Hugh Lynn that he was the son of a freak. They would say such things as, "How's that freak father of yours getting along, Cayce?" Uncertain of what he should do, he asked Edgar for advice. "Just don't pay any attention to them," Edgar said. "Just laugh with them. That doesn't hurt me and it doesn't hurt you." The time came, however, when Hugh Lynn was big enough not only to fight the older boys, but to win. "I'd fight every time,"

Hugh Lynn later said. "They'd do it again and I'd fight them again. And they got tired because they knew I'd fight. The more I fought the better I got."

Hugh Lynn eventually made an impression on some of the bigger boys. He developed a reputation as a fighter and frequently came home with torn clothes and bruises on his face and neck. Edgar felt bad about the situation, but knew from his own childhood experiences that it was better for Hugh Lynn to come to terms with his classmates early on. Despite the fighting, or perhaps because of it, Hugh Lynn became withdrawn and introspective. His true personality emerged only when he was by himself, playing in the shallows of the river or climbing the tall magnolia trees that grew beside the large redbrick homes in Selma's residential district.

Once, Hugh Lynn played hooky from school, going down the river for a swim instead. The moment he got home, his father knew where he had been and what he had been doing. As Hugh Lynn later reported, his father knew the exact spot he had left his clothes and the exact spot he had gone into the water. "[At that moment] I knew that I couldn't fool my father," Hugh Lynn said. "He could read my mind."

Another curious phenomenon involving Edgar would occur around the same time. Dr. Gay had introduced him to some of the people at the new Baptist Hospital where he had had his appendix taken out. Because of Edgar's ability as a photographer, some of the doctors thought that he would make an excellent X-ray technician. Edgar gave the machine a try. The results confounded everyone who studied them. Whenever Edgar operated the machine he got a double exposure, or the picture of two bodies on one negative. Other people operating the machine didn't seem to have this problem, and this phenomenon was never adequately explained.

In the spring of 1915, Edgar lost his voice again. Gertrude, who was visiting Lynn Evans in Anniston, was unavailable to conduct the reading, so Edgar obtained the help of one of the specialists who had treated Hugh Lynn. As instructed, the doctor gave Edgar the suggestion to go into trance. However, the conductor didn't give Edgar's address where the reading was being conducted. He gave the address of the second floor across the street from Edgar's studio. Subsequently, he did a reading for a man at 22½ Broad Street, not 21½. The room that was described by Cayce in trance didn't match that of the photo studio at all and it went on to describe a man in the process of embezzling funds from his employer. The mystery of the reading was not solved until later that day, when Edgar and the physician walked across the street and found an apartment that matched the description in the reading. Inside was an accountant pouring over company books. No mention has been made in Cayce's notes as to whether or not they reported the embezzler, or whether the embezzler knew that his neighbors had discovered his crime.

Inexplicably, it took several months before Edgar was able to regain full use of his voice. During that time, a fire broke out in his studio. As had occurred in the two Bowling Green fires, many precious negatives and personal belongings were lost and they were forced to temporarily relocate. Although the Selma fire held up his photography business, he was doing more readings now than he had since the demise of his partnership with Ketchum.

By far the most unusual reading during this period was for Edwin Williamson, the general agent for the Southern Railroad in Selma, who was interested in a writing career in Hollywood. He had sold some stories and articles to magazines and thought that a reading might help him develop plots. He asked Cayce to give a reading that would outline a good plot for a motion picture. Edgar decided to give it a try, thinking that it would be a fun experiment. Hugh Lynn and the Williamson children, Ethyl and Malcolm, also thought it would be fun, for their favorite pastime was to play "motion pictures." The Williamson children were always the stars and Hugh Lynn the director and cameraman. Edgar was now to enter their game as screenwriter.

Unbeknownst to the Cayces, however, there was more to the request than Williamson let on. Without the Cayces' permission or knowledge, on December 13, 1916, Williamson had written to Carl Laemmle, the head of Universal Pictures. He had described himself as the "spiritual advisor, or spiritual business manager" of Edgar Cayce, the "great psychic." He described how his friend was able to go to sleep, and in that state, diagnose many diseases, find lost articles, and perform other amazing feats. "If you are interested, and will write me, name a date and the hour, allowing for the difference in time, stating the name of the party who you have in mind to take the lead in a photoplay and tell me the street and the house number where the party will be," Williamson wrote. "I think I can surprise you."

Laemmle was intrigued by the promotional possibilities of having a psychic develop a script and called in his publicity director, Nat Rothstein, who decided that the right actress for the photoplay would be Miss Violet Mesereau, a performer whom Universal Studios believed to be poised for stardom. Accordingly, the Universal publicity staff arranged for a party at Churchill's, a New York nightclub. Newspapermen were invited to attend, along with Dr. William E. Young, a reported authority on the subject of hypnotism and mental telepathy, who would give a brief lecture on the powers of mental suggestion as part of the performance. Eustace Hall, a screenwriter currently writing a movie serial for Universal, was the master of ceremonies.

On the night of the event, February 8, 1917, all the tables except one were pushed away from the center of the room. Miss Mesereau placed a single sheet of paper facedown on the middle of the table. On this paper, unseen by anyone else, she had written a few lines outlining the type of story she wanted to use in her next film. The lecture by Dr. Young was then given, followed by dancing.

While guests enjoyed themselves in New York, Edgar Cayce, back in Alabama, was giving a reading. Its contents, amounting to approximately 450 words, was then wired to Churchill's. The title, presumably tacked onto the reading by Williamson, was "Through the Subliminal." Although the text of the reading is lost, the reports from the newspapermen were as favorable as their reports on Miss Violet Mesereau's dancing. One account read: "His psychic self, traveling more than twelve hundred miles on a space-annihilating train of thought . . . the first psycho-scenario writer of record transmitted from Selma, Alabama, to New York, a five-reel scenario for Miss Violet Mesereau."

The film never got made and the screenplay reportedly became the property of legendary producer Thomas Ince. However, Universal Studios obtained so much good press as a result of the stunt that they paid for Williamson and his family to come to Hollywood, where he tried his own hand at screenwriting. He eventually sold two screenplays and was able to get his daughter a brief cinema career under the name Ethylyn Clair. His son became the popular radio character "Uncle Mal." Before leaving for Hollywood, however, Williamson asked one more favor of Edgar. He wanted him to try using a Ouija board and pestered him until he finally agreed.

Edgar enlisted the help of Gertrude. Together, they sat down at a table and put their hands on the pointer. Hugh Lynn, who sat beside them, was impressed. "I never saw a piece of wood cavort like that thing did. It was exactly like there was a line of [unseen] people standing up and they could have only three seconds or three minutes to give their little speech and the next one would come on."

The first message to come through was from a boy who had been in Edgar's Sunday school class and had gone into the army where he had died. He had given Edgar payment on some insurance, which Edgar had forgotten about and put in an envelope in a desk drawer—which was where it was later found. Another message came through from someone saying that he wanted Edgar to go and talk to his brother because his brother was going to soon die of a heart attack and he wanted Edgar to prepare him.

The most astonishing message was from a teenager who said he had drowned in a pond in Ohio. His family had thought that he had run away.

According to the message, he had gone swimming at another farm, hit his head on a submerged stump, and died. He said his body was caught in barbed wire under the water and was still there. He wanted them to discover the body so that they knew he had not run away from home. Williamson later wrote to the family, who wrote him back saying that they had retrieved the body.

Hugh Lynn never again saw his father put his hands on a Ouija board. Like the practice of automatic writing or drug-induced hallucinogenic states, Edgar believed that more harm than good would result. "A lot of good stuff has come through Ouija boards and automatic writing," Edgar later said. "But a lot of people have gotten disturbed through it, too. The balance is on the negative side."

Another reading from this period is particularly touching. It was given for a pregnant Hopkinsville woman, Eddie Jones Smithson, a relative of Cayce's, whose family had little confidence in the readings, but who were desperate for any help they could get. Mrs. Smithson had a dream that incited her to ask her younger sister to write for a reading. Cayce gave the reading upon receipt of the wire. It said that there was little hope for Mrs. Smithson's recovery, but there could be drugs given to keep up her strength and vitality until her baby was born. The reading said that although the mother would die, her child, a baby girl, could be assured good health. The reading was sent to the sister, who had a physician prepare the compound that Cayce had recommended. Mrs. Smithson reportedly lived for forty days, dying a few hours after her child, a little girl, was born.

A few years later, when Cayce was in Hopkinsville, he would sit down in a barber shop, and a child, who had been playing around the room, gave him a strange look and then came over and climbed onto his lap. She put her arms around his neck. The barber who was shaving the girl's father told him somebody was talking to his little girl. The father got up, asking the barber who the man was. When he told him it was Edgar Cayce, the father went over to him, and introduced himself as the husband of the late Eddie Smithson. He expressed his amazement that his daughter—who had never laid eyes on Cayce before and who rarely approached strangers—seemed to be so familiar with him. Edgar didn't know how this could be possible, but acknowledged, as did the man, that "God worked in mysterious ways."

17.

At Home
and Abroad

As hostilities in Europe began to escalate, it soon became apparent to Dave Kahn that the reading he received indicating that he would go into uniform had not meant a police or fireman's uniform at all, but that of the United States Army. Feeling sure that the military was in his future, he sought and received a commission rather than take his luck with the draft. He obtained what amounted to an "honorary" commission as a second lieutenant in the army. By the beginning of April 1917, he was in New York City recruiting in front of the New York Public Library at Forty-second Street and Fifth Avenue.

Around this time, Edgar received a wire from Kahn requesting a reading for problems he was having with his voice, the result of his Fifth Avenue recruiting activities. The reading that was requested and obtained was different from many others because it had a twofold purpose. Kahn really did want help for his voice, but he also sought to prove to skeptical friends he had met at the Hotel Girard that Cayce was "the real thing." Although the actual wording of Kahn's wire may have varied in some minor way, it stated, in essence: "Please tell me why I am in New York. Advise as to my physical condition and what I should do next."

Because of impending entry of the United States into the war, all honorary commissions had been canceled until further notice. The wording of Cayce's reply to his message, again in essence, read as follows: "You are in New York in regard to final commission in U.S. Army. Pull will get you nothing. Apply to army post nearest you in New York as training camps will open May 15. You will be accepted. As to physical condition you have lost voice by exposure to weather. This is prescription: cherry bark from north side of cherry tree, taken three times a day." Kahn obtained the cherry bark and took it to a druggist, who ground it up in a solution he could gargle. His condition improved dramatically and his cough was gone three days later. More important to his friends, who had seen the original telegram, was the fact that Cayce had diagnosed his condition from nearly a thousand miles away.

Kahn followed Cayce's other instructions as well. He went to Governor's Island in New York harbor, the main army post in the area, and talked with the commanding officer. Kahn told him that he had been instructed to come to see him about a commission in the army, which was in connection with the training camp that was to open on May 15. The commanding officer flushed with sudden anger, demanded to know where Kahn had obtained the information, and was annoyed that Kahn knew the exact date. No one but the top officials had this privileged information because it had not yet been released. "In a more security-minded age, I might have spent the next few days undergoing interrogations and possible arrest," Kahn later said. "Moreover, I could hardly tell the commanding officer the real truth without probably compromising myself as possible army officer material."

Kahn told him he had learned the information from other army personnel with whom he had been associated while recruiting in New York. The answer apparently satisfied the officer. After conducting a background check, he agreed to accept Kahn as the first candidate for officers' training at Camp Plattsburg, New York, and then later at Fort Benjamin Harrison in Indianapolis, Indiana. By early the next year Kahn was commissioned as a second lieutenant in the United States Army and then later assigned to the officers' staff at Fort Worth, Texas. Meanwhile, during the training period, Kahn continued to seek guidance from Cayce, who had told him that he would do well at this camp and would "get ahead in the military swiftly."

Kahn received a particularly interesting reading over the telephone on the Fort Worth parade grounds. Dave was finally being shipped overseas and wanted to see his family one last time before he went. He said to Cayce, "I have two questions. Please listen to me very intently. I want to know if I will be able to get a leave of absence to go home to my family and if so, can

I stay two or three weeks when I get there? If I cannot go, I want to know why. I'd like to know what is going to happen to me in the next six weeks."

Kahn waited by the phone as Gertrude guided Edgar into trance. In trance, Cayce said that Kahn could go home for three weeks if he wanted to because he wasn't leaving Texas right away. "There'll be an order very soon directing troops who are now on the Mexican border to report to your division to be inducted into the national army," Cayce said. In addition, the general in charge of Kahn's company would not be going with the division when the unit was shipped overseas, which would not happen for at least three months anyway. At that time, according to Cayce, Kahn would be given the opportunity to go with the general to Virginia as his aide, or to go with the division under a new general. Cayce advised him to go with the division. The reading further added a reminder of something that had been said in a previous reading. "You will go with honor, and you'll return with honor. You'll have many narrow escapes but you'll never have an accident. You will come back in good health. You will move with the division and you will be successful."

Kahn put the information to use immediately. At breakfast the following morning he told his commanding general that he would like to make a prophecy. Kahn told him that he would not be leaving for the European front at the end of the week. He said he would not leave for at least three months. He further said that he thought there would be a large contingent of soldiers brought up from the border who would be inducted from the National Guard into the regular army and that they would train them for overseas duty. Furthermore, he said: "But when we do go overseas, sir, you are not going with the division. I think you are going to have a continued training program to carry out."

The general listened politely, and then showed Kahn an order he received from Washington that was stamped with the seal of the adjutant general and countersigned by the secretary of war. These were the official orders sending the division abroad. The general informed him that this effectively ruled out any of the predictions he had just been making. Kahn said that he would stand by his original prediction, no matter how unlikely it sounded. He urged the general to remember what he had said. "If you want to know the full facts, I'll tell you."

Twenty-four hours later a message came with instructions to unpack the equipment from the trains that had been scheduled to take Kahn's company to the East Coast. Kahn was granted his three-week leave and more recruits eventually arrived from the Mexican border. Then three months later, shortly before the division was to leave for Europe, the general sent for Kahn.

He wanted to know how he knew what was going to happen. Kahn told him about Cayce, singing his praises. He then added what Cayce had told him about the two opportunities that would be presented to him. The general confirmed that going with him to Virginia was one of Kahn's options. Kahn told him that he would go with his division to Europe under the new general, as Cayce had said he should.

During the years of the war, Edgar Cayce would exchange many letters with Dave Kahn. The most difficult letter that Edgar had to write to him was a letter of condolence. Solomon Kahn had died suddenly in December of 1918. Although the war had officially ended, Dave was still unable to return to America to attend his father's funeral or to help sort out his father's business affairs. The Kahn grocery business, which had been booming prior to the war, was in deep debt by the time demobilization took place.

There were many other letters of condolence that Edgar had to write throughout these years to console the families of members of his original Bible study and Christian Endeavor classes who had been killed in the war. But Edgar also had the more pleasant task of doing readings for his friends abroad or their families back home. As his students spread out across Europe, he was given the chance to do readings where the subject was not only hundreds of miles away, but thousands of miles. One of the first readings of this kind was for the wife of the American consul general stationed in Italy.

The reading was apparently quite successful because the Cayces soon received many more requests from Italy. One request was from a wealthy woman who owned a villa in Palermo. It took Cayce no longer to find her in Italy than if she had been in the same room with him in Alabama. There was a slight problem however. Cayce reportedly gave the reading in Italian. The stenographer who had been hired to transcribe the reading was unable to understand it. They quickly put a stop to the reading and sent Hugh Lynn to look for someone in Selma who could speak Italian. He eventually found a fruit vendor who sat in on the next reading and translated the best he could. The translator was both astonished and impressed: first that a local photographer had been contacted by Italian royalty, and secondly, that Cayce's Italian was like that of a native. The vendor had not been able to understand all of the words simply because he wasn't familiar with the Sicilian dialect. This problem was later solved when Gertrude discovered that she could specify that Edgar give the reading in English instead of Italian.

With each new letter that arrived from Europe, Edgar felt closer and closer to the battlefront. One letter in particular captured his imagination. It was from Robert Ladd, a member of his Bible class, who had found himself driving an ammunition truck. Moving up to the front one night through an enemy artillery attack, he became more and more frightened. To bolster his courage he began to sing, as loudly as he could, his Bible study class's favorite hymn, "I Love to Tell the Story."

Then, a truly remarkable thing happened. As bombs detonated on either side of them, soldiers from his platoon took up the song. Infantry troops moving up along both sides of him adopted the hymn as a marching song. When the attack had ceased and the air was suddenly quiet again, they were all still singing the hymn. The ammunition truck made it through the attack and on to its destination.

Edgar continued to receive many more wartime requests for readings. Possibly as a result of the growing number of requests in general, and, more specifically, the correspondence with the American consul general in Italy, Edgar received two mysterious summonses to visit Washington, D.C. All Edgar Cayce would say about these trips was that they were "top secret." In his memoirs he recalled, "I was called to Washington to give information for one high in authority. This, I am sure, must have been at least interesting, as I was called a year or so later for the same purpose."

Exactly who requested these readings and what prompted the visits, is still a mystery. The most generally accepted theory is that Cayce's mail to the consul general in Italy and to Dave Kahn had been intercepted, and that Cayce had been investigated as a result. Reports by the U.S. Department of Military Intelligence, which have never before been released until now, confirm that indeed an investigation took place. And perhaps because of this investigation, Cayce was then invited to Washington to give readings on war strategy. Cayce himself may never have known who the real recipients of these readings were because his only knowledge of what he said in trance would be told him by the conductor or other witnesses if they chose to tell him. All he may have known about these readings was that he was summoned to Washington, D.C., then guided into a trance.

Another reason to believe that some form of a secret and continuing relationship existed between himself and government agents is that on May 30, 1944, when Cayce was suffering from the illness that would claim his life seven months later, an unnamed government agent had a private meeting with him in Virginia Beach, at which time a reading—not part of the official Cayce archive—was either conducted or discussed. Though the Cayce family never revealed the purpose of this meeting, a secretary in Cayce's office later reported putting a call through to Edgar from the office of Harry Truman, then a United States senator. This suggests—at the very least—that someone, or some government agency, kept tabs on Cayce throughout his later career.

Harmon Bro, one of Cayce's biographers, and the secretary who intercepted the call from Harry Truman's office—has claimed that the two readings Cayce gave in Washington, D.C., were conducted in late 1917 or early
1918 on behalf of President Woodrow Wilson during his efforts to create the
League of Nations. Bro's source, like that of another Cayce scholar, Howard
Church, were conversations that Bro had had with Gladys Davis, Cayce's
then longtime stenographer and confidant. In interviews and in print, Bro
would say that "the Cayce family was sworn to secrecy." This may well have
been true, although no such claims were made by Gladys Davis to her biographer.

The only other first-person testimony concerning trance readings for
President Wilson comes from Dave Kahn in an oral history interview that
was conducted by Hugh Lynn Cayce twenty years after Edgar's death. In
these interviews, Kahn specifically says that Cayce gave readings for Wilson,
though Kahn himself was not present when the readings took place and
was unable to specifically say how or when these readings were given. Kahn
also said that Cayce's readings did not relate to war strategy or the formation
of the League of Nations, but were medical readings conducted when
Woodrow Wilson returned to the United States and suffered the September
1919 stroke that paralyzed the left side of his body and made him an invalid
in the closing months of struggle over the Congressional ratification of the
League of Nations.

However easy it might be to dismiss Kahn and Bro's claims as mere speculation, there is much evidence connecting Cayce to President Wilson, much
of it involving Edgar's well-documented friendship with Major Alfred M.
Wilson and his brother, Major Edwin G. Wilson, from Franklin, Pennsylvania, both first cousins of the president, whom Cayce came to know through
one of his Selma Bible students, and who would receive and conduct numerous readings after the war. Their confidence in Cayce was unshakable,
as evidenced by numerous letters in the Cayce archive.

A second potential connection between Edgar and the president was
through Cayce's friendship with Colonel Will Starling, the star pitcher on the
Hopkinsville Moguls, who became a member of the secret service detail assigned to protect the president during the war years. Reporters have described the deep personal relationship between Starling and the president
and observed that during many a cold day in Rock Creek Park, Starling
chaperoned Wilson while he courted his soon-to-be second wife, Edith
Bolling Galt. Like the president's cousins Alfred and Edwin, Starling would
also receive readings from Cayce and become quite an outspoken champion
of his abilities.

Apart from these connections, there is the fact that Cayce—in trance—frequently discussed the formation of the League of Nations and how crucial it was that the president gain the support and confidence of the American people in his endeavor to ratify the peace treaty. In these readings, poetic in their delivery and prophetic in their message, Cayce clearly suggested future problems and another "great war" that might come as a result of the failure by the United States to support the president.

In readings conducted in 1917 at the request of the two Butler brothers and other members of his Bible class, Cayce stressed the importance that the peace treaty conference be conducted in the spirit of "compassion and brotherly love." In a later reading, Cayce would assert that the "spirit of Christ" was actually at the table during the Versailles peace treaty conferences where the league was proposed. Another reading stated that the people of the United States must turn to the "spirit" of that which was "in the directing of those influences in the peace at Versailles, that which has been so demeaned by others." Cayce would also foretell eventual problems if the treaty was not supported by the American people, saying: "I am my brother's keeper . . . The blood of my brother will cry out from the ground if we heed not the warnings that were given [to ratify the League of Nations agreement]!" Thus, to Cayce, the president's efforts in Paris could be viewed as a "divine mission" that ended in failure.

Despite the question of whether or not Cayce actually conducted readings on the League of Nations for the president as he did for his Bible students, it is clear that he gave hundreds of prophetic and life-saving readings between 1917 and 1920. As Gertrude later described the period, "It was as if readings just tumbled out of him." In a letter to Dave Kahn, Cayce described himself as being as busy "as a one-legged man in a kicking match."

A most unusual reading, if indeed it could be considered a reading at all, came soon after the birth of his and Gertrude's third child, Edgar Evans, born on February 9, 1918. Nothing unusual happened during the delivery and the child was a normal, healthy boy. It was Edgar, not Gertrude, who let himself get run down, again losing his voice. Gertrude conducted the standard reading to restore his voice. The session lasted approximately thirty minutes and turned out to be the first time in which Cayce remembered all that transpired while the reading took place.

During the reading, Edgar recalled seeing all the graveyards of the world spread out before him. As he looked toward India, a voice spoke to him, saying that he would know a man's religion by the manner in which "his body had been disposed of." The scene then changed to France, and Edgar saw the graves of three boys who had been in his Bible class. In front of these graves there appeared the boys themselves. Each of them told Edgar how they met their death. One had been killed by machine-gun fire, another in the bursting of a shell, and the third in heavy artillery fire. Two gave Edgar messages to tell their loved ones at home. They appeared much in the same way and manner as they did the day each had said good-bye to Edgar in Selma. The scene changed again as Edgar had the distinct impression that the dead were yet alive in some other plane of existence. He began to wonder if he could see his own dead son, Milton Porter. Instantaneously, Edgar said, it was "as if a canopy was raised, [and] tier on tier of babies appeared." In the third or fourth row from the top, to the side, he recognized his own child. Milton Porter knew his father, as Edgar knew him. He smiled in recognition, but no word of any kind passed between them.

Again, the scene changed and there appeared a friend of the family who was being buried in the local cemetery at the same time that Cayce had gone into trance. He had known her well because she had sold him the many flowers that his church class had distributed to hospitals. She talked with Edgar about the changes that men call "death," saying that it was really "birth." She also spoke of the effect that a gift of flowers had upon individuals, and how they should be given in life rather than at funerals or death, because they meant so little to those who had passed from the material to the spiritual plane. Then she said, "But to be material for the moment, some months ago someone left $2.50 with you for me. You are not aware of this having been done and will find it in a drawer of your desk marked with the date it was paid, August 8, and there are two paper dollars and a fifty-cent piece. See that my daughter receives this, for she will need it."

The scene changed once again with the appearance of Alfred D. Butler, the dead father of Alfred and Roger. He spoke of his son, Alfred, saying that he would no doubt return to his place in the local bank after the war but advising that he should rather accept an offer to be a manager of a motion picture theater. Then he spoke concerning the affairs of the First Christian Church in Selma.

By the time Edgar awoke, his voice had returned to normal. Gertrude reported to him that he had not said a word during the whole thirty minutes he had been under. Edgar told her immediately about the experience. He then went to look in the drawer for the money that the flower vendor had said would be there. The drawer did indeed contain the money—it had been received on the eighth of August by their studio assistant. Thus, it came as no surprise to Edgar the next day when he went to the bank and was waited upon by Alfred Butler Jr., who had returned home from the war and resumed his job at the bank.

Edgar asked when Butler had returned to Selma and was told that he had arrived home the night before. Edgar then asked him if he expected to remain at the bank, and when he was told that he most probably would, Edgar told him about his reading of the day before and about Alfred senior's advice that he take a job with the theater. Alfred was taken aback, telling Edgar that on his way home from Washington he had stopped in Atlanta where a friend asked him to take over the management of a motion picture theater. He had declined the offer. Upon hearing about Edgar's dream, he changed his mind and wired his friend to accept the position.

Edgar continued to give readings at an ever-increasing pace. The only difference now was that the Source began providing information and answering questions that hadn't yet been requested. During one particular session in March, for example, the Source diagnosed the condition of eight different people in addition to the information that was requested for the individual whose reading had been scheduled that day. The requests for all eight of these readings were already in the mail, but had not yet reached the Cayces.

Also in the mail was a letter from Dave Kahn saying that he was returning home from France and wanted to meet with Edgar in Lexington to discuss forming a "psychic partnership." Kahn had not yet been released from the army, but was on leave until European demobilization was completed. The brash young Captain, was, he said, "bursting with ideas."

PART FOUR

Riches from the Earth

18.

❀

Lucky Boy

Like so many of those who had held positions of leadership in the "war to end all wars," Dave Kahn had returned from Europe flush with excitement and confident in the expanding role American industry and technology would play in the new world order. That Kahn had a part to play in that new world order was not a question. He had only to decide how to use his leadership skills in the private sector—and his expectations went far beyond the chain of Kentucky grocery stores his father had operated in Lexington. The deep financial debt in which he and his family found themselves was merely one challenge to overcome as he climbed the ranks of American industry. He didn't wish to run any single business, but to become a broker who helped to make others' dreams come true. He believed that Edgar's vision of building a hospital—where patients could receive treatments recommended in the readings without having to be at the mercy of skeptical doctors and nurses—was not only possible, but within their reach if Edgar could only expand his horizons beyond the narrow scope of his photography business.

Although Edgar was still fearful of entering into another partnership and making a "business" out of the trance readings, he agreed to meet with

Kahn in Lexington in April 1919 to discuss a number of potential joint ventures: from using psychic advice to develop a new technology that could be patented to business consulting, with Edgar providing trance insights to corporate leaders as he had once successfully done for Dave's father. There had been no ill side effects during their earlier "business reading," and Kahn supposed the same would be true now.

It was not until the end of his five-day stay in Lexington that Edgar mentioned an unusual request for a reading that he had received a month earlier from the editor of the *Cleburne Morning Review*, in Cleburne, Texas, a man named Day Matt Thrash—or D.M. for short. Thrash had read about Cayce in the *New York Times* and wondered, among other things, if it were possible for him to use his psychic powers to locate oil underground. A subsequent letter contained a detailed map and other technical and logistical information that pertained to the Sam Davis Petroleum Company's undertaking in Texas, of which Thrash and his partners were principal stockholders.

Edgar had initially dismissed Thrash's request for the same reason he had stopped giving racetrack readings. Experience had taught him that readings of this kind ultimately didn't generate much long-term good, and could actually be quite harmful to himself and to those who obtained them. To Dave Kahn, however, the prospect of applying trance information to search for oil was not in the same category as exploiting it to gamble on horse races or locate lost treasure. Using psychic power to gamble at the racetrack or poker tables amounted to taking an unfair advantage over others. The same could be said for using psychic power to locate buried treasure. Hidden gold or other valuables didn't necessarily belong to the person or people who went seeking it. Petroleum, on the other hand, belonged to the people who owned the land it could be found on. Kahn didn't see anything wrong with the notion of helping people—for a fee—to locate it, just as Edgar's grandfather had used his talents to help farmers find water.

Kahn's argument convinced Edgar to give a test oil reading for Thrash and his partners. The information Thrash sought concerned an abandoned well located in Desdemona, an oil-boom town outside of the crossroads village of Comyn, in Comanche County, Texas. Thrash and his partners had poured an estimated $21,000 into drilling the well to a depth of 3,500 feet and found nothing, though adjacent property drilled by other companies had made Desdemona the oil capital of north central Texas.

Cayce—in trance—said that the well wasn't a "dry hole," but that it had been prematurely abandoned. All that was necessary for the partners to obtain oil was to clear equipment and other debris blocking the drill shaft, then "plug" the hole with cement at the three thousand foot mark, and "shoot" it with a quantity of nitroglycerin. The reading described the geological rock and sand formations in which the well had been drilled, specified the flow of the oil that could be pumped out of it, and the number of quarts of nitro that would be required to reach it. Intrigued by such a specific and detailed reading, Kahn sent the information to Texas to see what Thrash and his partners could do with it.

Like Edgar, Kahn knew that the Texas oil fields were making many people overnight millionaires, and the demand for oil was only growing. The number of automobiles in the United States had risen from a few thousand at the turn of the century to over two million during the war years. Having spent a considerable amount of the war supplying the soldiers in the field, Kahn also knew that U.S. troops could credit their victory largely to the oil that got them to Europe and that was now powering U.S. industry. Mineral rights on oil properties could not only generate enough income for Edgar to realize his dream of building a hospital, but help Kahn pay off the tens of thousands of dollars of debt that he had inherited as a result of his father's sudden death.

Edgar's and Kahn's interest became unabashed enthusiasm when they received news from Thrash and his partners that Cayce had provided a perfect geological description of Desdemona's oil-bearing rock and sand formations and a detailed report on the condition of their well before it had been abandoned. Although it would be months before the Sam Davis Company could raise the money to rebuild the derrick and mount the drilling operation necessary to free their well of obstructions, Thrash and his supervising driller, Martin C. Sanders, had every reason to believe in Cayce's prediction. In subsequent correspondence with Cayce and Kahn, Thrash and his other investors discussed the possibility of forming a partnership to "bring in the well."

Intrigued, Kahn proposed that he and Edgar make a preliminary trip to Texas to meet with Thrash and see the Desdemona well for themselves. The timing looked good for all concerned. Kahn was on temporary leave from the Army Reserves and could travel at no personal cost to himself. Edgar was also free to travel. His assistant at the studio, a young man named J. B. Williams, could handle daily operations during the proposed ten-day trip, and Edgar could get a reduced fare train passage from his brother-in-law, Lynn Evans, now an executive with the Louisville and Nashville Railroad. Since the visit would be short and Dave Kahn would accompany Edgar, Gertrude gave her blessing to their endeavor.

Their bags packed, Edgar and Kahn set out by train from Alabama in early July of 1919. Their ultimate destination was Cleburne, a thriving industrial city of twenty thousand people just west of Dallas, where the Gulf, Colorado, and Santa Fe Railroads arrived from Galveston and Fort Worth. Upon arrival, Edgar and Kahn were met by Thrash—described as being a giant of a man—along with three other men: Martin Sanders, an experienced oil driller and land speculator; Sam Davis, a rich land owner and cattle rancher who was the principal investor in the Desdemona well; and Brown Douglas, president of the American Dry Goods Company. Thrash and his partners represented Cleburne's elite. They published Cleburne's two daily newspapers, had substantial investments in the city's privately owned transportation and utility company, owned cattle ranches and dry goods stores, and had a major interest in one of Cleburne's largest banks.

Thrash and his partners treated their out-of-town guests like visiting royalty. They were escorted from the station on one of the newly installed streetcars and shown to the Cleburne House, a Victorian three-story brick hotel on the town square in the heart of the downtown business district. Later, they dined at the hotel's restaurant and were taken sightseeing in a Chaparral touring car. Edgar and Kahn must surely have been impressed— the luxurious hotel, the city's three train stations, and its manufacturing plants were far more modern than they could have expected in a part of Texas where less than a generation earlier lawmen had hunted Jessie James, and members of the notorious "Wild Bunch" rode the Chisholm Trail. No doubt they were equally impressed with Thrash himself—an accomplished writer, a local historian, and a well-read student of astrology and spiritualism.

The highlight of their first Texas trip was their overnight excursion to Comyn, in Comanche County, Texas, where Edgar and Kahn traveled by train before boarding a buckboard wagon that took them on to Desdemona, or "Hog Town," as drillers called the small inland village of oil rigs located about one mile outside of town. Desdemona was near the boundaries of Comanche, Eastland, and Erath Counties, in a region of rolling hills and scrub mesquite, elm, and oak. Outside of town, in Desdemona, stood rows of cable-tool drilling rigs, eighty-four-foot wooden derricks, pump jacks, and ox-drawn freight wagons—all operated by a small army of roughnecks, roustabouts, and tool dressers. An ever-present cloud of smoke and steam from the engines powering the rigs filled the air.

Thrash and his partners recounted the short and very lively history of Desdemona for Edgar and Kahn. The oil business was first developed by the village barber, J. W. Carruth, who prospected throughout the area but did not ultimately discover any oil. That honor went to L. H. Cullum, a dedicated oilman who took over the leases and struck "black gold" at the Joe Duke #1 well on September 1, 1918. The Duke well caught fire almost immediately, sending up flames that lit the night sky for the three days before they could be extinguished. Pumping wasn't necessary to bring this well and the others into production. More than three thousand barrels a day poured out of Joe Duke #1. By 1919, the twenty or more wells in Desdemona had produced over seven million barrels of oil, and the boom was on. And yet, almost half of Desdemona's oil never reached refineries during the first year of production: pipelines weren't adequate to meet the demands placed upon them and the poor condition of the dirt roads and unavailability of trucks made it difficult to haul the oil. And oil spills were common: just eight months before Edgar Cayce's arrival, visitors to the field were greeted by a three-mile river of "lost" oil. Often, a well spewing natural gas was allowed to flow for weeks in the hope that it might eventually spout oil, and gushers were allowed to flow until the pressure subsided enough to lay pipes to a collection tank.

Unlike the oil-producing fields in Ranger, Texas, and the legendary Spindletop, where most of the leases were in the hands of one large company, the oil property in Desdemona was owned by independents, small business syndicates like the Sam Davis Company, consisting of less than a dozen investors who bought and sold small, short-term leases at extraordinarily high prices. In one case, drilling rights were leased on a property that was one one-hundredth of an acre. Leases were now at an all-time high, making the Sam Davis holdings some of the most valuable property in Texas. The price per barrel for oil was also at an all time high. Never before in Texas's history could oil speculators realize such great profits.

As Edgar and his party drove through the pasture land and peanut fields outside of Comyn, the sight of Desdemona must have seemed unreal. For three miles north of town, one mile east, and two miles west, there was a vast city of giant derricks, pumping stations, and collection tanks. And yet, all that Edgar and Kahn saw when they arrived at the Sam Davis well was a wooden stake marking the location of a ten-inch round drill hole—now plugged with mud and capped with cement. On that spot, one year earlier, stood a giant sixty-foot wooden derrick supporting a cable rig that had lifted and dropped a length of heavy steel pole to "punch" the hole. Had the Sam Davis partners used more modern rotary technology, which later permitted crews to drill two hundred or more feet in a single day, they might have accomplished in two weeks what had taken them four months.

The other highlight of the trip was a demonstration that Cayce did for Joseph P. Long, an executive at the Home National Bank of Cleburne, who requested an oil reading for the Cleburne-based Lucky Boy Oil Company. The reading for Long concerned the Lucky Boy #2 well in Desdemona, which, like the Sam Davis well, had been considered "hopeless." Drillers had gone down 3,500 feet and found nothing. Cayce—in trance—told the Lucky Boy partners that they had gone down too deep. He advised them to come back to the 3,000-foot mark, plug the hole, and shoot it with a hundred and fifty quarts of nitroglycerin, which he said would result in a daily production of 600 barrels of oil.

Despite the fact that the veracity of Edgar Cayce's oil readings hadn't yet been tested, the trance information about the geology of the Desdemona field and the condition of the Lucky Boy and Sam Davis wells more than convinced the drillers that Cayce had powers beyond anything they had ever encountered. Kahn had also become convinced of the legitimacy of the oil readings and upon returning from Texas proposed that he try to raise the funds necessary to buy into the Thrash partnership and expand that company's interests beyond their single well. "The gushing promise of Texas oil," Kahn later wrote, "appeared to hold the answers to all [our] needs."

Kahn's first decision upon returning to Alabama was to retain his commission in the Army Reserves. By remaining in uniform he could not only avail himself of the stature and travel advantages accorded his rank as a first lieutenant, but he was legally shielded from the many creditors who had claims against Kahn family business holdings. Using military connections he had established with General Pershing, the army's chief-of-staff, he obtained a year-long assignment to tour Texas and other Southern states and report to his superiors on the burgeoning oil business.

Kahn also enlisted the participation of Edwin Wilson, with whom he had served in Europe. The "Major," as Kahn called Wilson, was about to give up his commission and was searching for a position in the private sector commensurate to his previous rank in the military. Although Wilson himself had only limited experience in the oil business, his younger brother Alf, a graduate of Princeton and West Point, had been an executive for Sigma Oil before that company was bought by Standard Oil. And the Wilson brothers were cousins of Woodrow Wilson, then the president of the United States, a fact that would not be lost on the status-conscious Thrash and city fathers in Cleburne.

What Major Edwin Wilson knew about Edgar Cayce before their shared interest in oil speculation is a matter of debate. Through Kahn they had met on at least two separate occasions, during which Cayce demonstrated his ability to give medical and business readings. Major Wilson himself had received readings during the war years, and, according to Harmon Bro, Major

Wilson may have provided Cayce with a contact to the oval office. All that is known for certain is that Kahn, accompanied by Edgar, met with Major Wilson in a veteran's hospital in Virginia in September of 1919. Later that same month, when Wilson was decommissioned, he traveled to Texas on Kahn's behalf, where he examined the Sam Davis Company's business records and lease agreements and negotiated the terms of a new partnership.

Existing correspondence makes it difficult to determine the degree to which Edgar was involved in Kahn's negotiations to buy into the Sam Davis partnership. He had clearly met with the principals and gave them numerous readings during the latter part of 1919, but despite published reports to the contrary, Edgar Cayce never had a legal relationship with the Sam Davis Company, nor did he invest his own money into the partnership. It was Kahn who eventually raised the money to buy into the partnership in January of 1920, and who, with Major Wilson's help and the support of Kahn's investors, became its managing director. There is no doubt, however, that this was done with Edgar's blessing and with the understanding that through Kahn the partners would receive as many readings as they needed to "bring in" their well.

Edgar's reluctance to become a contractual participant in Kahn's endeavors may have come from Gertrude. She didn't want Edgar becoming involved in activities that would not only draw him away from home, but would align him with partners whose interest was purely financial. However, Gertrude must also have viewed Kahn's role in her husband's career as an improvement over what had happened with Leslie who, by default and negligence, contributed to the demise of the Ketchum and Noe partnership. The fact that Edgar needed a person with good financial skills in his life worked in Kahn's favor. Although Gertrude was not a great fan of Dave Kahn's—she had in all likelihood met him on only two occasions prior to Edgar's first trip to Texas—she was aware of Edgar's earlier reading indicating that a Jew would promote the work more than anyone else.

Gertrude may not have been the only source of Cayce's reluctance. There is reason to believe that the readings themselves told Edgar not to become a partner in the Sam Davis Company. According to published accounts, the readings focused only on Kahn's role in the prospective partnership—not Cayce's. Nor was Cayce giving readings exclusively to the Sam Davis partnership. Besides those he gave to the Lucky Boy partners, Cayce gave numerous oil and mineral rights readings for an assortment of investors with whom he had no business relationship. And despite offers to become financial partners in other investment groups, there is no record of Cayce asking or receiving profit from his participation in any of them.

Readings that Edgar Cayce gave to speculators during this period included several provided for Henry Orman, manager of the Normandy Oil Company of Bowling Green, which controlled tracts of land in Kentucky and Tennessee. In November and December, Edgar obliged Orman with readings that stated authoritatively that oil could be found on the Normandy Oil properties. Orman subsequently reported acting on the trance advice and hitting a gusher, with "oil shooting more than a hundred feet above the derrick." Another reading was conducted for Frank Williams, a Nashville businessman who had been recommended by the father of a man Cayce had done a medical reading for in Michigan. This time the request was not to locate oil, but phosphate. Again, Cayce—in trance—provided specific geological descriptions and details as to where and how to find deposits on the Williamses' property. He also provided a chemical analysis of the type and grade of phosphate that would be discovered. A geologist's report accorded exactly with the chemical composition and tonnage of phosphate that was later mined.

Throughout the latter months of 1919, Kahn continued to request and receive readings for the Sam Davis partnership. These readings were not saved, but it is clear from the existing correspondence that Cayce—in trance—recommended that Kahn join the partnership and suggested that a great deal of money could be made as a result. The only specific thing that is known about these readings was details regarding the type and length of oil leases that Kahn and the Sam Davis partners were to obtain.

According to Kahn, the readings specifically said to obtain leases that were to last for ninety-nine years. The significance of this recommendation appears to have been lost on both Cayce and Kahn, for although the question of ninety-nine–year leases was discussed at length at various points during the formation of the oil partnerships, the Sam Davis Company did not obtain ninety-nine–year leases, nor is there any record of Kahn having tried to obtain them. As would frequently be the case in the months to come, Kahn and his partners did not act upon the trance advice in its entirety. Instead, they extracted from the readings only the recommendations that were generally considered to be the most worthy or cost-effective—a practice that ultimately proved as unsuccessful a means for prospecting for petroleum as it was for administering medical treatments.

Despite the fact that Kahn didn't actually obtain ninety-nine–year leases, this was a topic of discussion when Cayce and Kahn met with a Lexington attorney to discuss the legal formalities of the proposed patnership. The attorney, who was a member of both the Lexington, Kentucky, and Fort Worth, Texas, bar associations, declared that ninety-nine–year leases as suggested in their reading were impossible to obtain, and that he, not Cayce, should be the ultimate authority on this subject.

The attorney stood firm on this point. At Kahn's suggestion, Cayce did another reading, this time in the attorney's office. The reading directed the lawyer to go to Frankfort, the capital of Kentucky, and look in the archives for the statutes of the state of Texas. Cayce then went on to give the page number on which the correct information about oil leases was to be found. This infuriated the attorney. To prove Cayce wrong "once and for all," he traveled to Frankfort and looked in the archives. He called Kahn from Frankfort. Obviously shaken, he admitted that Cayce had correctly cited the page number on which the fact bearing out the reading was found.

By November of 1919, Kahn and Edgar had received more correspondence from the city fathers of Cleburne. Joseph Long and the Lucky Boy partners had shot their Desdemona well with fifty quarts of nitro. Although traces of oil and gas showed immediately, they didn't hit the gusher that was hoped for. Another reading was requested. Again, the Source said they would find oil at the exact depth specified in the first reading conducted in Cleburne. The reading advised to "clean out the hole" and shoot with an additional one hundred quarts of nitro, as had been previously indicated.

Long now did exactly what he had been advised. The hole was plugged at 2,980 feet and shot with one hundred quarts of nitro. The result was nothing less than spectacular: a geyser of crude oil. Cayce had not only named the exact depth in which they would strike oil, but the precise daily production—six hundred barrels—that the partners pumped out of the well.

Kahn couldn't contain himself and immediately made plans for his and Edgar Cayce's triumphant return to Desdemona in January of 1920. "No one in the world can stop us now," he grandly announced.

19.

Desdemona

The front-page headlines of Cayce's success with the Lucky Boy well in Desdemona, the detailed reports of his endeavors in Kentucky and Tennessee, and the participation of the president's cousin provided all that Dave Kahn needed to buy into and then become the new managing director and vice president of the Sam Davis Oil Company. Exactly how much cash Kahn personally brought to the partnership and the dollar value given to the existing Desdemona lease agreement are not known, but it is reasonable to believe that Kahn and his investors provided the lion's share of cash, while Thrash, Davis, and Brown delivered the pre-existing Desdemona lease.

Certain that success was near at hand, the partnership invested in the most sophisticated rotary equipment then available. Kahn, accompanied by Edgar and Major Wilson, traveled to Ardmore, Oklahoma, where they bought a giant steam-driven motor, a steel drill head, several thousand feet of pipe in thirty-foot lengths, and enough explosives to drill twenty wells. Although Kahn didn't anticipate the Desdemona well would require such a substantial investment in heavy equipment, he acted with the assumption that once they had "cleaned out" and drilled the original well, they would move on to other locations. Profits from their first well would pay for leases on other property until the company could sustain itself.

Equally important to the success of their operation was finding a veteran driller who knew how to use the equipment. According to Kahn, a trance reading—now lost—told them to go to Strawn, a small Texas cow town, where they would find Cecil Ringle, a contract driller who was, at that moment, on his way to Desdemona looking for day work. The reading came complete with the name of the hotel and the room number where Ringle and his family would be found.

Ringle could not have been more surprised to find two army officers and a professional psychic knocking on his door. That Edgar and Kahn—or anyone else—had found him seemed incomprehensible. He and his family hadn't planned to be in Strawn at all and had arrived only two days earlier, to rest up after a long trek from Illinois, where he had been drilling the year before. Cecil's wife, Leona May, had written letters informing family and friends that they were stopping over in Strawn, but the letters hadn't been sent yet.

Had Kahn given Ringle a moment to stop and consider who these people were and how they had found him, he might have sent them on their way. But as soon as Leona May opened the door, Kahn marched inside, selling himself as he sold Edgar. A demonstration reading and the promise of profit participation was all it took to secure the entire family's services, which included not just Cecil and his father, A. A. Ringle, also an experienced driller, but also Cecil's son, Cecil Jr., who would serve as the chief "tool dresser," and Leona May, who would be their cook.

Together with their newly purchased equipment, the Ringles and the Kahn party boarded a train for Comyn and then traveled by mule-driven buckboard on to Desdemona. Though they had planned to arrive in late January of 1920, it wasn't until February that the crew established camp and another month before they built a derrick suitable for their as yet untested equipment. Having already experienced life in Desdemona, Thrash and the other Cleburne partners had the good sense to remain at home—which is where Edgar, in hindsight, later declared he should have been.

"Ragtown," where the Kahn party made camp, consisted of a quarter mile of flimsy metal shacks and tents for the workers and a giant mess hall catering to the two hundred or more drillers who called the place their home. Nearby, in Comyn, was the saloon and brothel. Like the other prospectors, Edgar slept on a cot, used an outhouse, and soaked his oil-stained clothes in soapy vats. Along with Kahn, the Ringles, and the assortment of other men needed to drill the well, Edgar spent his daylight hours toiling at the construction site, building the rig and then chopping firewood to fuel the steam engine. At sunset, however, when many in Desdemona began drinking and gambling, he would read his Bible or take long walks along Hog Creek. Edgar's only trips into Comyn were to purchase supplies, get his hair cut, or accompany Kahn to the dance hall. Out of deference to Gertrude, Edgar abstained from dancing.

Besides the rugged living conditions that Edgar encountered, he also became aware of how dangerous and violent the oil boomtowns of Texas could be. A story about Desdemona was told around this time by a Comyn undertaker who was returning home after picking up the body of a man who had fallen off a derrick. On his way back he was stopped by a man who waved him over to the side of the road. He discovered that a woman and baby had been accidentally shot by two drunks, and the men had been subsequently hung and were swinging from a nearby tree. The undertaker returned to Comyn with a full load.

Try as he might to keep himself from becoming embroiled in the depraved lifestyles of many of the men he encountered, it was next to impossible for Edgar not to become part of the life in Desdemona and the people on whom the partnership depended. In Ragtown, he and Kahn had to contend with a population that was as diverse as any that they had ever known. There were the workmen necessary to build the rigs, drill the wells, erect the storage tanks, lay the pipelines, and supervise the drilling. There were also promoters, lease brokers, boardinghouse keepers, clerks, waiters, dishwashers, bank tellers, saloon keepers, bootleggers, gamblers, prostitutes, and pimps and—as Edgar himself admitted—a large assortment of outright criminals, thieves, holdup men, and narcotics pushers. Like the oily black tar that collected on Edgar's clothes and leaked from the ground, these people were all part of Edgar's daily life in Ragtown.

The fact that Edgar had a reputation as a psychic and not as a trained geologist or driller was not held against him. In fact, it was viewed in a positive light, for he wasn't as much an anomaly in Desdemona as one might suppose. The Texas boomtowns gave rise to an entire class of people known as "oil smellers" or "oil witches." Many of them used the fork of a tree branch to search for oil, as a dowser would. But many others claimed they could psychically look down into the earth and see dark pools of bubbling oil waiting to be pumped to the surface. The most prominent of these was an East Texas minister who was alleged to have X-ray eyes that could look several thousand feet down into the earth.

An incident confirming Edgar's status as a psychic occurred one day when a Texan, complete with spurs and a six-shooter, approached him on the street. He asked Edgar if he was the man who was supposed to know everything. The cowboy, however, wasn't interested in obtaining an oil or medical reading. He wanted Edgar to tell him when it was going to rain, a question currently on the minds of Comyn cattlemen—a long drought had reduced Hog Creek to a trickle. Without thinking, Edgar looked up at the cloudless sky and said, "Four o'clock on Friday." Edgar later confided to Kahn that he hadn't known why he said what he did. "The information just popped out," he said. But as predicted, a heavy downpour arrived precisely at 4 P.M. that Friday.

Edgar's reputation as a psychic was, perhaps, at the root of many of the problems that he and Kahn would encounter in Desdemona. Belief in Cayce's ability meant that everyone in Desdemona expected that the Sam Davis Company would eventually find oil. While for some this meant a windfall of profits, for others it meant the triumph of a competition. There were many in Desdemona who had a vested interest in seeing the Sam Davis operation fail, at which point their leases could be picked up by others. Though Edgar and Kahn had implicit trust in the Ringles, they didn't know if the other laborers working their well weren't also in the employ of potential competitors. Like hundreds of other oil-driven boomtowns, Desdemona was the setting for numerous scandals, as investors were swindled out of their holdings by con men. The most common tricks were for drillers to misrepresent the depth of the well being mined, to "spike" one well with drill samples from another, to purposely sabotage a promising drilling operation by breaking off a set of tools in the well, or to "slant hole" drill, so that while the derrick was standing on one piece of property, the drilled hole reached into another. The fact that Edgar and Kahn were acknowledged greenhorns made them all the more susceptible to unfamiliar tactics.

The Sam Davis partnership experienced an unusually large number of expensive delays. Equipment and parts brought in from Oklahoma went missing. The connecting cables from the motor to the rotary drill broke and had to be replaced. And when the derrick was finally built and their rig was operational, no sooner had they begun to drill than the pipes that supplied the drilling water were broken off and new pipes had to be laid. But the most devastating delay occurred when their drill head encountered the blockage described in the initial reading for Thrash.

Toward the end of their first month of drilling, when they had reached approximately 2,500 feet into the ground, the team hit an obstruction. Kahn's new rotary drill bit couldn't cut through it, water pumps couldn't wash it out, nor could Ringle catch hold of the debris with a grappling hook. A subsequent reading revealed that saboteurs had dumped a load of scrap iron into the shaft. The reading also indicated that an electromagnet would have to be used to pull the debris out and directed Ringle to a Cleburne electrician who could build an electromagnet and provide a generator to power it. The equipment was hauled to the site, where Ringle successfully fished from the hole several lengths of chain, barrels of nuts and bolts, and the upturned head of a twisted drill bit.

Further readings warned about forthcoming attempts to sabotage their operation. In one instance, what might have been a costly delay was averted when a reading stated that a driller disguised as a tramp, dispatched by the competing oil company that stood to inherit the Sam Davis lease, would be arriving in Comyn by train. Cecil Ringle confronted such a man with a loaded .45 and promptly escorted him out of town.

Edgar shared few details of his experiences in Desdemona on his return home at the end of March 1920. Gertrude, however, would surely have seen the many telegrams that arrived from Thrash in Cleburne, and then from Kahn, who was fulfilling his military duties in Atlanta. They requested more readings and urged Edgar to return to help them straighten out the problems. With his hands full at the photo studio, Edgar was unable to return until July, at which point Hugh Lynn—on summer vacation—accompanied his father to Comyn, where they met with Dave Kahn.

Like many thirteen-year-old boys, Hugh Lynn considered himself and his friends back home to be a tough lot—well experienced in the ways of the world. His opinion of himself changed quickly upon his arrival at the Comyn train station. Rain the night before had turned the road from the depot into a river of sticky black mush. Hugh Lynn—his hair cut in bangs and wearing the short pants and white sport shoes that his mother had purchased for his trip—stepped off the train into foot-deep mud. This was much to the amusement of a group of boys his own age who were there at the station, each in their high boots, ten-gallon hats, and, like their fathers, carrying guns.

Leona Ringle took Hugh Lynn under her wing. After getting him properly outfitted in hand-me-downs from Cecil Jr., she began to teach him the rudiments of being a cowboy. Hugh Lynn also started making friends with several older boys. The second night he was there, one of them, a young man called "Bud," tapped on his window and asked him if he wanted to go swimming. He was whispering and rather secretive. Hugh Lynn soon found out why: he was being invited to swim in one of the giant tanks that supplied Desdemona's drinking and drilling water. Together they sneaked out of the camp and went "skinny dipping" at the "tank farm." Afterward, Bud offered

Hugh Lynn a smoke and they launched into some stories that Hugh Lynn later recalled were "an education in themselves."

In the days to come, Hugh Lynn met the kinds of people he had only read about in westerns: gun-toting cattlemen and cowgirls who used language as colorful as the Indian ponies they rode. Most important, however, Hugh Lynn came to view his father in an entirely new light. Edgar was no longer a dowdy and conservative Alabama Sunday school teacher, but a seasoned Texas oilman, complete with high boots and a ten-gallon hat, who worked on the rigs, dug trenches, rode on horseback, and told stories around the campfire. There was still time out for prayer and reading the Bible, but just as often he saw his father knee-deep in mud from the oil rigs or riding over the high desert on the backs of barely broken horses. At night, he and his father played games with the other men. Their favorite was a type of poker called Texas Pitch, or High, Low, Jick, Jack, Julie, and Game. Edgar won repeatedly. Joe Rush—one of the oil drillers—was constantly complaining about the "Cayce touch," and accused Edgar of reading his mind. More than once he offered to back Edgar in any gambling venture he might want to take on. Edgar always replied that the oil business was enough of a gamble for him.

Once the shaft was cleared and drilling had resumed, the Desdemona operation called for much less physical labor, so Edgar and Dave, accompanied by Hugh Lynn, used their downtime to scout for more oil property. In July, they took a trip to inspect prospective leases on the Hofstiter ranch near San Antonio, Texas. The three rode on horseback through field after field of cattle and herds of goats. Upon returning, they spent the night at a ranch house where the western writer Zane Grey allegedly got the inspiration for his book *Riders of the Purple Sage*. That same night, Edgar gave a reading that Dave Kahn conducted, asking questions about the land over which they had just ridden. There was oil on the land, Cayce said in trance, but not enough to make drilling worthwhile.

Back at Desdemona they were met with bad news. A cable had broken and an entire set of drilling tools was at the bottom of the hole. Fishing for them could be as time-consuming and costly an operation as clearing the scrap iron out of the shaft had been. Cayce—in trance—didn't reveal much in the way of how the "accident" had been caused or how to speed the operation of its removal. Everyone was feeling tense. Hugh Lynn was sure that one of the drillers suspected of being in league with the competition was about to get shot. But before that happened, Ringle succeeded in extracting the tools with his grappling hook.

In letters home, Hugh Lynn reported this incident and others: "There is

nothing wrong with Dad," he wrote his mother. "But I think there is something wrong with everybody else. They all want to drill wells and make lots
of money. They think everybody [else] is crooked. They are afraid of Dad because they think he can go to sleep and tell Dave and the others where the
oil is coming in. I think somebody or some people are trying to keep the well
from being drilled. It's all a mess." Hugh Lynn also voiced his concerns to
his father. But Edgar apparently didn't listen. He was convinced that the
men were "rough on the outside, but all right underneath," and said that as
soon as they got the money everything would be all right, and they would
get to build a hospital. The oil was there. All they had to do was drill down
to it.

The legitimacy of Hugh Lynn's concerns became clear when he overheard a trance session during which the person conducting the reading—
presumed to have been Thrash himself—told Cayce that when he awakened
he would agree with him on "certain matters of policy." In other words, he
was planting a posthypnotic suggestion in Cayce's mind to take a certain position about the company and to forget that he had been told to do so. Kahn
was in Atlanta when this reading took place, therefore only Edgar and the
conductor were in the room. Hugh Lynn said nothing about the matter to his
father, fearing retaliation, but he told his mother immediately upon returning to Selma with his father in August.

The situation didn't improve. In September 1920, when the well still
hadn't come in, Edgar and Kahn made yet another trip to Desdemona. By this
time, suspicion had shifted to Kahn, whom Thrash accused of siphoning
company funds to pay his substantial debts back in Lexington. Thrash also
suggested that Kahn was not being entirely honest about the readings he was
conducting on behalf of the partnership, that, in fact, Kahn was trying to
delay the operation in Desdemona until the lease expired so he could form
his own company and drill the well himself. Although Kahn's disillusionment
with the partnership had indeed grown to the point where he had already
made plans to open his own oil-prospecting company with Edgar, such an enterprise would not have interfered with operations in Desdemona. Kahn had
everything to gain and nothing to lose by seeing their well come in.

In the heat of the moment, Thrash and a party of laborers questioned
Edgar about Kahn. Edgar rose to his friend's defense, saying that he had no
reason to believe that Kahn wasn't being entirely forthcoming about the
trance readings and assured them that Kahn wasn't taking money out of
the company. This apparently didn't satisfy the partners or the drillers themselves, who demanded a reading to clarify Kahn's role in the endeavor.

All concerned were present on the night the reading took place. Edgar lay down on his back on the floor, but before he could say anything and before Kahn could give him a suggestion, Edgar fell into a deep sleep, so deep he was unable to answer any questions. Kahn told the others that this was sometimes the case with Edgar and urged the men to come back the next day, when they would try again. What he didn't let on about was his concern that Edgar hadn't been able to go into trance because of stress—that he was "escaping" from the "animosities" and "selfish interests" that encircled him. There was greed on all sides, Kahn later admitted, including his own. Edgar and Kahn were "too eager and too hungry," as Kahn later said, to realize that they had moved into an alien world of "violence, greed, deceit, and sabotage." After the others had left, Kahn was unable to wake Edgar up. He waited beside the cot for the rest of the night. At sunrise the next morning, Edgar awoke.

The Sam Davis crew spent the whole day feeling considerable uncertainty and uneasiness. As requested, the men returned to witness Edgar's reading that night, and this time, Cayce was able to go into a trance. According to Kahn, the reading said he was not to blame for the mismanagement of company funds, and a later reading stated, quite bluntly, that it wasn't mismanagement of funds or drilling techniques that were at the root of their problems, but that certain unspecified "grasping, selfish, turbulent minds must be kept from the venture." The fact that Kahn was exculpated, however, did little to ease the tension between him and the rest of the company. Not long after the reading, Cecil Ringle accused Kahn of having developed an inappropriate affection for Leona May. Ringle got so infuriated that he pulled a gun on Kahn. Edgar interceded, and although no shots were fired, the relationship between the men could not be repaired.

Thrash also contributed to the ultimate demise of the partnership, most evidently in his fraudulent treatment and eventual dismissal of Cecil Ringle. This final blow to the company was dealt not long after Edgar and Kahn had left to form their own petroleum company, when drilling in Desdemona had finally reached the depth that readings had indicated oil would be found. Ringle reported sampling "the prettiest sand and green oil" he had ever seen and spent much of one day and long into the night pumping oil before shutting the rig down, certain that their well would "come in" the next morning.

Meanwhile, Thrash—or one of his partners—paid a visit to Leona Ringle, who had become concerned when Cecil failed to show up for supper. Leona was told not to worry—Cecil had his hands full at the drill site and would be home shortly. Leona was also told that Thrash needed to borrow her husband's drilling contract, as no other copy was available at that moment and Cecil had to be paid the next morning. Leona unthinkingly obliged. The contract was brought back to Cleburne, where, according to Cecil Ringle, the first page was rewritten, cutting the Ringles out of any future percentage of profits in lieu of day-rate pay. The new first page was attached to the old second page containing the signatures, and the contract returned to Leona before Cecil returned home.

The next morning Cecil was paid for his services and summarily dismissed. Angry, he threatened to shoot Thrash and might actually have taken justice into his own hands had Leona not begged him to put away his gun. Ultimately, Ringle believed that he had no option but to leave town, for in a city like Cleburne, the law didn't look kindly on a day-rate driller accusing the city fathers of fraud. Thus ended Edgar and Dave Kahn's first oil partnership. They had nothing to show for their year-long endeavor. But the "gushing promise of Texas gold," as Edgar later said, "still ran high."

20.

Luling and
Edgar B. Davis

The decision to incorporate the Edgar Cayce Petroleum Company was made before Edgar and Kahn left Desdemona. There were to be four principal partners: Edgar Cayce, who would give readings; Dave Kahn, who would conduct the readings and determine drilling sites; Major Wilson, who would handle lease agreements; and Martin Sanders, who contributed several thousand dollars to draw up the partnership agreements. The incorporation papers were signed at the Home National Bank in Cleburne on September 20, 1920, and although it was unclear how the company would raise the necessary capital to finance its operations, a reading conducted in Cleburne recommended they drill in the area of Luling, a dusty and impoverished small town forty-four miles south of Austin.

Unlike previous readings requesting information on potential drilling sites, the Luling reading did not name local landmarks, provide detailed geological descriptions of the area, or name the property owners whose land they were to lease. All the initial reading said was that Edgar and Kahn should go to Lockhart, in Caldwell County, where they would meet a man on the steps of the county courthouse. He would then tell them where to look for oil in Luling.

Edgar and Kahn were accompanied on their trip to Lockhart by one of the Desdemona drillers, a Texan named Joe Rush, who hadn't been surprised that the reading named Luling: his previous employer, Morris Rayor, had been sent to prospect in that area under equally unusual circumstances. An avowed spiritualist and a principal in a petroleum company based in Detroit, Rayor had drilled in Luling for almost a decade, believing that the "spirits of the dead" communicating through a Detroit medium had directed him there. Rayor was once known to have brought his medium to Luling to hold seances. He never made a big strike and gave up his holdings the year before Edgar and Kahn arrived, but the legend that spirits of the departed had selected Luling as the site for a major find persisted.

At the time Edgar and Kahn arrived in town, Luling was little more than a cluster of false-fronted stores and one-story homes along the railroad tracks, surrounded by an assortment of unpainted farmhouses occupied by impoverished cattlemen and cotton growers.

The three men had no trouble finding the courthouse. As the reading predicted, there on the steps they met an elderly man carrying a cane. Kahn went up to him and introduced himself, and then said, "I'm here investigating any possible oil leases in this area." The old man's answer was, "Well, you couldn't have picked a better man." He explained that he was a county judge who had lived in the area for many years and knew its geography as well as its archives and records. He was certain that oil could be found on a site a few miles outside of town, in neighboring Gonzales County. He told them to go into the building across the street. Down the hall they would find the office of the state geologist.

The geologist told them what he could about the site that the judge had recommended. Although the land was primarily owned by impoverished black farmers, it was controlled by a white woman, Minnie Phillips, who was known to play a protective role in the black community. Unless she gave her approval, the farmers wouldn't do business with Edgar and Kahn. And Minnie Phillips, the geologist added, was known to greet strangers with the barrel of her shotgun.

Edgar and his party got into Joe Rush's Marmon automobile and drove out to the Phillips ranch, which turned out to be little more than a ramshackle farmhouse with a dirt floor. Just as they had been warned, they were greeted by the barrel of a shotgun. Through a crack in the door, they heard a woman say: "Be you oil men . . . I'll kill you." Kahn told her that he was an army man, gave her their names, and explained they were there from Kentucky. Upon hearing mention of Kentucky, Minnie Phillips opened the door a little wider, peered out at Kahn, and demanded to know exactly what part of Kentucky he was from. When he replied that he came from Lexington, the door opened wider—enough to reveal an aging barefoot woman dressed in rags. Her hair was gray and lines in her face spoke of the strain of poverty and exposure to the elements. She was still holding her shotgun, although now she pointed it away from them. She asked if Kahn knew a man named Phillips in Lexington. Kahn responded yes, and proceeded to describe his Lexington druggist, from whom Kahn had obtained prescriptions for his neighbor, Mrs. DeLaney, when Edgar had done that first reading for her. Minnie Phillips told Kahn that the description he gave was the right one. "He's my brother!" she announced.

To Kahn it seemed as if meeting the man on the courthouse steps and coming out to the Phillips ranch had all been preordained. He felt as if they were actors in a play, except that they hadn't seen the script. What happened next only served to further suggest that it was all part of a larger plan.

Kahn asked Phillips to send a telegram to her brother in Lexington and ask for a character reference. He also said that they were hungry from a long drive and asked if there was anywhere around that they could get something to eat. To this she replied, "I don't have no money and I don't have no food." Kahn gave her some money and suggested that Joe Rush drive her into town to buy groceries on the way to the telegraph office. She agreed, and her brother later responded to the telegram with a favorable report.

Upon her return from the village, Kahn queried her about her own health. She replied that she had not been in good health for a long time. Her son had developed tuberculosis and she had brought him to Texas where it was dry enough to cure his condition. "But now he is in Kansas City and I am here protecting these poor colored people from the oil swindlers," she added. Kahn then told her frankly that they were there to find oil. He described how Edgar could go into trance and how the readings told them that they would find oil in this area.

"There's a lot of oil around here," she said. "And they don't have to drill more than a hundred feet to get it." According to her, there was so much oil coming up from the ground that on rainy days the cattle wouldn't drink the water because it was covered by a thin layer of petroleum. There were spots near the San Marcos River, she said, where a kitchen match could ignite natural gas escaping from cracks in the earth.

Kahn said he wanted to talk about the oil but that first, his associate could give her a reading about the state of her health. Kahn laid newspapers over the dirt floor, and Edgar stretched out on his back. Cayce proceeded to give a detailed reading in which he described a circulation problem in the nerve fibers in her neck, shoulders, and face. All the while, the old woman watched Cayce intently. When the reading came to an end, she began to cry. "I never saw anything like this in my whole life," she told them. She said he had described exactly what was wrong with her, and that his reading was the most wonderful thing that had ever happened to her.

It was not long before she was again talking about oil in the ground. She said she was holding it for the blacks. Edgar said that maybe he could help by taking a reading to determine how much oil there was and how to handle it. Another reading was conducted. This time Cayce told of a fabulous "sea of oil" trapped in a giant salt dome directly under them. Nearby, he said, was a dead tree, with two prongs of the trunk sticking up against the Texas sky. He told them that about thirty feet from this tree they would find oil only three hundred feet down. It was supposed to be the richest oil deposit in that part of Texas.

Through Phillips, Edgar and Kahn were able to obtain a fourteen-month lease to drill on five thousand acres. It was a standard oil agreement for which they had to pay a dollar per acre per year and would forfeit their lease along with a $1,000 bond should they fail to break ground within the first six months. Cayce Petroleum would pay all the expenses of drilling. A portion of the profits would be theirs, the rest would go to Phillips and the black community of Luling.

Edgar and Kahn left Luling with the intention of mounting a drilling expedition not unlike the one they had begun in Desdemona. But despite published accounts to the contrary, Cayce Petroleum couldn't raise enough money to break ground in Luling. All they accomplished within the first six months was to deliver a load of timber to build a derrick. And although Edgar and Kahn eventually had to give up their leases, there was a curious twist in what later came to pass in Luling. The same year that Edgar and Kahn gave up their leases, an oil prospector named Edgar B. Davis—whose personal story is almost as remarkable as Cayce's—began drilling on property adjacent to the Phillips ranch.

Like Cayce, Edgar B. Davis was over six feet tall, though considerably heavier than Edgar. Also like Cayce, Davis was extremely polite, well-mannered, an ardent Christian, and a believer in the power of prayer—qualities that were not commonly found among oil wildcatters. Prior to his arrival in Texas, Davis had made and lost two fortunes in the rubber business, suffered a nervous breakdown, and had a mystical experience in which the voice of God directed him to invest his life savings into prospecting for oil in Luling.

There is no record of him meeting Edgar Cayce in Texas, but it is clear from correspondence and the recollections of Luling residents that communication in some form—if not a personal meeting—took place. Dave Kahn reported handing over to Davis the readings and other files on the Edgar Cayce Petroleum interests in Caldwell County and claimed that Davis— acting on the Cayce readings—began drilling on land formerly leased by Cayce Petroleum. The truth is difficult to ferret out from the existing lease agreements, but there is no question that Davis knew about Edgar Cayce's in- terests in Luling and that Davis prospected for oil on land mentioned in the readings.

In the latter part of 1921 and early 1922, Davis lost a substantial fortune in six dry wells. Broke, he turned for financing to Frank Seiberling, of Akron, Ohio, with whom Davis had once served on the board of the U.S. Rubber Company. Despite frequent setbacks, he continued drilling, and on August 9, 1922, long after Cayce Petroleum had forfeited their Luling holdings, Davis's first well came in. It was not the "gusher" as it was later described in the newspapers, but the hole had "legs," as oilmen call it, and consis- tently produced more than a hundred barrels a day for over a decade. It is still an active well today.

Davis drilled his next well within a hundred yards of the first. This well, which reportedly was drilled into a salt dome not unlike the one described in the Cayce readings, came in much bigger. A major petroleum company agreed to lay a pipeline to the field and to pay Davis half a million dollars in advance for one million barrels, and another company bought $100,000 worth of oil in advance of future production. Using this money to fund fur- ther exploration, Davis "punched out" sixteen more wells in Luling, which he later sold for twelve million dollars.

Davis called Luling and the other places he prospected "faith locations," and openly said that God had directed him to them. In one instance, Davis allegedly received a message from God to go to a particular field, pull a rag- weed out of the ground, then drill in the hole where the roots had been. The result was a geyser of oil. Another time, he was out for an evening drive when he ordered his chauffeur to pull off to the side of the road. Davis got out of the car, walked across a field, and thrust a stick into the ground to mark the spot where he would drill his next well. Again, he discovered oil, so much, in fact, that the well ran wild for an entire week, leaving a shoulder- deep pool of oil in a nearby valley.

Kahn, who had read about the fabulous strikes in the newspaper, later wrote Davis a letter asking for a share of the fortune, based on the fact that they had provided him with Cayce's readings, and suggesting that the leases to the land had originally been obtained by Cayce Petroleum. Davis wrote back saying that he had made other commitments with his money. A substantial portion of his considerable fortune was given to the people of Lul-ing, both blacks and whites.

This was not, however, the last contact Edgar Cayce would have with Edgar B. Davis. In the late 1930s, Davis would become a commanding fig-ure in an attempt to bring about a gigantic merger of rubber companies. In the process, Davis and his longtime friend and partner, Frank Seiberling, had a falling out. Just as had occurred in Cayce's attempts to locate oil in Desde-mona, Davis's proposed merger became bogged down in a complicated web of divided interests.

Edgar Cayce was asked for trance advice because Davis was a deep be-liever in psychic power, and Seiberling himself may have been predisposed to accept Cayce's advice since his daughter and son had received medical readings from Cayce. The subsequent readings for Davis and Seiberling sug-gested that the two men had strong psychic powers, and that much good could come from a partnership between them. However, the reading also in-dicated that both men were hardheaded, and that "cooperation" and a de-sire for the common good was essential for their own financial well-being and the continued success of their companies. Together, Davis and Seiberling had and could accomplish much good. Apart, they would fail.

"The law of the Lord is as the two-edged sword," Cayce—in trance—said in the 1937 reading for Seiberling. "Unless good is done to all, good cannot grow out of same. For what ye sow, ye reap!"

Neither man followed Cayce's advice to look after his partner's interests. A settlement was reached, but only through the courts. The two men never worked together again. Edgar B. Davis and Frank Seiberling, at one time two of the richest men in America, lost their fortunes.

21.

❖

Harry Houdini
and Cayce Petroleum

Lack of adequate financing had plagued Cayce Petroleum since the company's inception in September 1920. They had enough money to lease property, but not enough to drill. It was for this reason that Edgar and Kahn embarked on what became a year-long, five-thousand-mile journey to sell shares in their new company. "The lust for oil [and the money to drill for it]" Kahn said, "had become an obsession that could not be denied."

Birmingham was chosen for their first stop because Edgar had two good contacts in that city: William K. Schanz, a court reporter who had once been the Alabama state treasurer of Christian Endeavor, and Dr. Percy Woodall, the osteopath who had been used by Al Layne's classmates to "expose" Cayce as a fraud. The eighteen-day Birmingham trip was a great success, largely owing to a reading Cayce gave for Miss Estelle Bealle, whose brother was an editor at the city's largest newspaper, the *Birmingham News*. The result was a series of favorable articles, followed by requests for more readings than Edgar could accommodate.

Edgar and Kahn's next trip, to Nashville, wasn't on their itinerary. They were on a train heading to Hopkinsville to meet investors when Edgar got a cinder caught in his eye. The eye quickly became inflamed. Kahn suggested they get off at Nashville, the next stop, to find a doctor, which they did. Kahn got out the classified phone book and happened to notice that one of the doctors listed was a physician named Edward B. Cayce. Kahn reached him on the phone and told him of their situation. He agreed to examine Edgar.

Some published accounts of Edgar's visit to Nashville mistakenly claim that Dr. E. B. Cayce wasn't any relation to Edgar, when in fact he was a cousin of Edgar's grandfather, Thomas Jefferson Cayce. The degree to which he knew of Edgar's previous medical readings in Hopkinsville is not clear, but he was reported to be so enthralled by the stories that Kahn told him that after he treated Edgar's inflamed eye, he asked Edgar and Kahn if they would delay their already interrupted journey long enough to have lunch with him at the Union League Club.

That afternoon Dr. Cayce introduced Edgar and Kahn to four prominent Nashville businessmen: a banker, a real estate tycoon, the president of a railroad, and the owner of Nashville's leading newspaper. Edgar, who didn't normally like to talk about himself in front of an audience, was feeling unusually gregarious, and Kahn was only too happy to fill in any missing details. Subsequently, they remained in Nashville for two weeks as Dr. Cayce's guests, during which time Edgar gave many readings for Dr. Cayce's patients and friends.

A particularly dramatic episode occurred as a group of doctors was witnessing a reading for a local rabbi. The session was interrupted by an emergency call from Birmingham, where a young woman, distraught over her failing relationship with a newspaperman, had swallowed poison and was critically ill. The Nashville doctors were suddenly much more interested in the phone call than in the reading for the rabbi. It was quickly decided that at the end of the reading in progress, they would ask Cayce about the girl in Birmingham. Cayce proceeded to describe the poison she had taken as bichloride of mercury. He then gave the antidote, strychnine, which was itself an extremely toxic liquid. Cayce stated in the reading that she would not survive unless the treatment was administered exactly as recommended.

In front of the Nashville group, Kahn telephoned the new information to Birmingham. The Nashville doctors heard him confirm on the phone that the girl *had* taken bichloride of mercury. Although Cayce's reading warned that the antidote had to be administered exactly as described, as would later become apparent, the doctors in Birmingham refused to give their patient another poison as a countermeasure. The girl died three days later.

During another reading, eight physicians watched Cayce go into a trance while the patient, whom Edgar had not met, was held in another room. Before Cayce had even finished, the incredulous doctors were marveling at how accurate the reading was. One of the doctors—convinced that Cayce was reading their minds—reportedly exclaimed: "Tell me something about the patient I *don't* know."

Cayce—still in trance—obliged. According to one account, the Source, without being asked, told the skeptical doctor to go back into the other room and look at a rash that had just developed between the patient's toes. Without a word, the doctor left the room to examine the patient. He returned a few minutes later and reported that the patient did indeed have a rash between his toes. "It was not there when I examined him three or four days ago," the doctor reportedly told Kahn.

Another interesting episode in Nashville grew out of a reading Cayce gave for a young girl. The supervising physician contested the diagnosis. Cayce was put back into trance and asked why the patient's doctor had made a different diagnosis. Cayce's reply was almost indignant, implying that the doctor hadn't examined his patient carefully enough. "He won't agree also that there's a scar on the bottom of the girl's foot because he's never seen it, but if he examined under the big toe, he'll find it there. It was caused by stepping on a hot cinder when she was a little girl and the scar is still there. She knows it but he doesn't." As Kahn later pointed out, this odd and insignificant physical detail—which was later confirmed by examination and by the young lady herself—proved to win the doctor over.

Edgar might have remained in Nashville for the Christmas holiday had he not received an urgent telegram summoning him to Washington, D.C. There is no record of what was said in the telegram, who paid for the trip, or exactly when and how Edgar got to the city. All that Edgar later said was that Kahn left Nashville for New York to talk to potential investors in Cayce Petroleum while Edgar was called to Washington "to do some special work" for an unnamed government official on an undisclosed subject.

Although the record is not clear, there is reason to believe that this was when Cayce was asked to give medical readings for President Wilson, who had suffered a stroke while campaigning for the ratification of the ill-fated League of Nations and was confined to a wheelchair. By late November or early December of 1920, when the readings were presumed to have been conducted, Dr. Cary Travers Grayson, the president's physician, had given up all hope for Wilson's recovery.

In the oral history interview conducted by Hugh Lynn Cayce after his father's death, Kahn didn't specify when the first reading took place. "I believe . . . [Cayce gave a reading for the president] during the time that he was in the wheelchair and incapacitated, and Mrs. Wilson was looking after his affairs," Kahn said. "My recollection was that Colonel Starling arranged this reading, as he was a lifelong friend of Edgar Cayce, both having been born in Hopkinsville, Kentucky, and I did not see the reading given, but as I understand, it described the president's condition and foretold that his time was limited and that he would not get well."

Besides Kahn's recollections, circumstantial evidence suggests that it was indeed the president for whom Cayce gave readings. Alf Wilson, the president's cousin, was known to have been in Washington, D.C., at the same time as Cayce, and early the next year accompanied him to New York where they joined Dave Kahn. Alf also became Edgar's constant companion for the next five months, during which time Alf conducted a number of private readings for which there are no transcripts. Given the availability of Alf to conduct readings, and Will Starling to act as go-between or messenger to the president or his physicians, the mechanism would have been in place.

There has also been much mystery regarding President's Wilson's activities during this same time period. By almost all accounts, the president's duties were being conducted entirely by his wife, the president's secretary, Joseph Tumulty, and various cabinet members. The president himself had retreated into his private quarters and with rare exception saw no one but his physicians and family. There was such secrecy regarding the activities taking place on Pennsylvania Avenue that rumors circulated among Washington insiders that the president might be dead or completely incapacitated. The truth of Cayce's visit may never be known. Having failed in his effort to have the League of Nations ratified, Woodrow Wilson was a mere shadow of his former self. He died in relative seclusion in February 1924.

The only other event of interest during Edgar's trip to Washington was his receiving an invitation to attend a party in Manhattan in January of 1921. Edgar described the affair as a "stag" dinner: fifteen men sitting around a table eating a sumptuous meal and drinking large amounts of liquor. During the party, an incident occurred that resulted in a new nickname for Edgar.

The man seated to Edgar's right reportedly showed surprise at learning that Edgar was from Selma and asked if he knew Alec Cawthon. "Yes," Edgar replied. "He's a very good friend of mine." This was not the response Edgar's dinner companion wanted to hear. "That son of a bitch killed my brother!" the man announced. The "murder," as it was related to Edgar at the stag party, had taken place in the Cawthon-Coleman drugstore, in the same building that housed the Cayce photo studio. The brother of Edgar's dinner companion was a traveling salesman who got drunk and picked a fight with Cawthon over the price of an ice-cream soda. There were no witnesses to the brawl that resulted in the salesman's death, but a jury later absolved Cawthon of blame. At the stag party, Edgar was asked to go into trance to judge whether or not Cawthon should have been found guilty. Edgar declined the request on the grounds that everyone at the table, including the man sitting beside him, was drunk. Not long after the dinner party ended, Kahn began referring to Edgar as "Judge," and the name stuck—Kahn and several others referred to him that way for the rest of his life.

Edgar attended many other interesting meetings and parties during his five-month stay at the McAlpin Hotel on Thirty-fourth Street and Broadway, the most notable of these being a series of demonstrations that Edgar gave in late January or early February of 1921 for Dr. William McDougal, chair of the psychology department at Harvard University. McDougal was joined by his associates, Hereward Carrington, a noted writer [and later president of the American Psychic Institute in New York], and Carrington's friend, master-magician Harry Houdini, who were invited to the McAlpin Hotel to sit in on readings.

Edgar had come to McDougal's attention through the physician's predecessor at Harvard, Hugo Münsterberg, who had investigated Edgar in Hopkinsville in 1912. This was the first time McDougal met Edgar in person, though he had already been following Cayce's career and would, a few years later, conduct his own investigation with a colleague, J. B. Rhine, when the two were teaching at Duke University in the 1930s. Houdini had come to know McDougal through Carrington and through Arthur Conan Doyle, whom Houdini had just visited in England. Although all three—Houdini, McDougal, and Carrington—were just getting to know one another in 1921, over the next four years they would launch some of the most intensive and well-publicized investigations of spirit mediums ever conducted.

Unfortunately, no records of the McAlpin readings are in existence. Kahn was not present, for he had returned to Cleburne to formally end his partnership with the Sam Davis Company and to report to Joseph Long and other investors about the fund-raising efforts on behalf of Cayce Petroleum. The McAlpin readings for McDougal, Carrington, and Houdini are presumed to have been conducted by Gordon K. Nicodemus, an executive with a securities brokerage firm that Kahn engaged to raise funds for Cayce Petroleum. Alf Wilson, who had by this time purchased shares in Cayce Petroleum, and with whom Edgar spent most of his time in New York, is believed to have been the stenographer for these readings.

McDougal—already inclined to believe in the veracity of Cayce's alleged powers—later reported being "quite impressed" and "mystified" by how

Cayce was able to do what he did. Cayce didn't conjure "spirits of the dead" or manifest strange phenomena common to the many spiritualists with whom McDougal had attended seances. Cayce merely closed his eyes and provided one medical diagnosis after another. "I just don't know what it is," McDougal told Edgar. "Just when I think I know what it is, the next experience convinces me that I don't know."

Much the same sentiments were expressed by Hereward Carrington, who also came to believe in Cayce. Although he was initially skeptical of all mediums, he described how impressed and mystified he was by the Cayce phenomena. "My belief in Mr. Cayce's sincerity and in the integrity of his purpose is absolute . . . As a scientist, I would find that all diagnoses and prescriptions purported to come from Mr. Cayce do not in fact come from him, but come from some higher intelligence manifesting itself through him. I am not prepared to say what that higher intelligence is . . . [but] certainly the conscious mind of a man, uneducated in medicine, could not produce even the technical terms which come through Mr. Cayce."

The impact that the meeting had on the fifty-year-old Houdini is a matter of conjecture. All that the record indicates is that Edgar came to know Houdini "personally" during his stay in New York and attended, as Houdini's guest, the heavyweight championship fight between Jack Dempsey and the French military hero Georges Carpenier. Evidence also suggests that Houdini may have invited Edgar, along with McDougal and Carrington, to his luxurious Harlem town house. Like other guests, Edgar would have been shown into a long room crowded with tapestry-covered, gilt-edged furniture, packed floor to ceiling with the magician's many mementos from his years touring the world. Edgar would have seen the jewel-encrusted cup given Houdini by Grand Duke Sergei of Russia, the ebony-and-gold wand from the king of Belgium, and the lifelike bronze bust of Houdini himself, commissioned in England, which sat on a pedestal. Houdini would also have shown his guests upstairs to his world-class library, where playbills, engravings, photographs, and thousands of dollars in books were wedged into every available nook and cranny.

In public and in private, Houdini remained strangely silent about his meeting with Cayce. Houdini didn't expose him as a fraud—as he had done to hundreds of others—but neither did he invest in the Cayce Petroleum Company or publicly acknowledge Edgar to be "the real thing." Like McDougal and Carrington, he wasn't the least interested in oil wells. He also had a reputation to maintain as a "debunker" of fraudulent mediums. However, the magician's activities in the months immediately following the McAlpin demonstrations suggest that Houdini may have become convinced—at least temporarily—that there could be genuine communication with the spirit world.

Prior to the McAlpin reading, Houdini had just returned from an extended trip to England, where he had exposed, by his count, the fraudulent practices of upward of a hundred self-described mediums and spiritualists who—through sleight of hand, ventriloquism, and other tricks and illusions typical of the carnival circuit—conjured up ghostly hands who rapped out messages on typewriters, rang bells, and levitated tables and other objects. His most famous investigation in England was that of the celebrated French medium Eva Carriere, who had convinced Conan Doyle beyond any shadow of doubt that she had a direct line to the "spirits of the dead."

Carriere's specialty was to produce a bubbling white foam called ectoplasm, which purportedly dripped from her mouth, ears, and nose when she conjured spirits in a seance. Houdini convincingly argued that this was mere trickery. Ectoplasm, he said, was nothing more than a dry mixture of soap, gelatin, and egg white, which she slipped into her mouth or regurgitated from her stomach. Houdini himself had met a regurgitator who could "manifest" a snake and a frog in his mouth by doing much the same thing.

But Houdini would not have so easily been able to dismiss Cayce or ignore the Christian messages that came through him. The fact that Cayce didn't require a darkened room, a crystal ball, or step into an enclosed "spirit cabinet" in order to produce psychic phenomena presented a challenge unlike anything Houdini had encountered in England. As Houdini was aware, Edgar could go into trance at any location of the conductor's choosing and didn't have to be told the subject's name until he was already in trance. When Houdini wrote his famous exposé, *A Magician Among the Spirits,* he steered clear of discussing mediums who, like Cayce, *didn't* lift tables, produce ectoplasm, or rap out spirit messages.

There is one other reason to believe that meeting Cayce had an impact on the magician. Around the time of the McAlpin demonstration, Houdini surprised and confounded his friends by dropping plans to make a film version of his favorite book, *The Count of Monte Cristo.* Instead he wrote an original screenplay for a movie to be called *The Man From Beyond.* Filming began in the spring of 1921, and the feature, staring Houdini himself, was released the following year. For a practicing Jew who purportedly hadn't met a medium he couldn't expose, his choice of subject matter and presentation raised many curious questions. The movie opened, surprisingly enough, with a picture from a page of the New Testament, highlighted with a prophecy from the Book of John: "Marvel not at this: for the hour is coming, in which all that are in the graves shall hear his voice."

In tone and substance, such a quotation could have been lifted directly out of a Cayce reading. The movie's plot unfolds around Howard Hillary, an Arctic explorer—played by Houdini—whose body was discovered inside a wall of Arctic Ice, where it had been frozen for an entire century. Hillary is thawed out and brought back to life. He falls in love with a woman he believes to be the reincarnation of his long-lost lover and must convince her that they were meant to be together. There is no doubt of the message: Christian mysticism and the immortality of the soul—subjects that would engage Edgar Cayce for the rest of his life.

Houdini eventually gave up the movie business and, apart from creating his own illusions, returned to what became his overriding obsession in his later years: exposing fraudulent mediums. But despite having many opportunities through his friendship with McDougal and others, he never investigated Cayce further. And despite the countless mediums he investigated and publicly exposed, Houdini sought, on several occasions, to make contact with the spirit world up until his death in 1926, including his much publicized pact with his wife, Bess, to try and contact her after he died. Although there has been much controversy regarding the breaking of the mysterious "Houdini Code," it was none other than Arthur Ford—Edgar Cayce's supporter and friend and a medium with as large a following as Cayce's during his lifetime—who succeeded in convincing Bess that Harry had indeed contacted her from the "other side."

However much or little Edgar had impressed Houdini, he did impress potential investors in the Cayce Petroleum Company. By some estimates, Edgar Cayce gave more than a hundred readings while in New York. Nicodemus helped to raise approximately $100,000 in promissory notes, and an additional $50,000 in cash from a pool of investors that included Edgar's uncle Clint Cayce, Gertrude's uncle Hiram Salter, Dr. Al Layne, the Butler family of Selma, and Cleburne bankers J. T. McConnell and Joseph Long.

Although Cayce Petroleum had, by this time, lost its leases in Luling, the readings directed them to a spot ninety miles northwest, in San Saba County, where Big Rocky Pasture joined Little Rocky Pasture. Correspondence no longer exists to explain how Cayce Petroleum obtained leases on this land, but it is clear from the resulting contract, signed on May 18, 1921, that Cayce Petroleum made an agreement not unlike the one Kahn had made in Desdemona a year and a half earlier. Cayce Petroleum put up the cash, and William Barrow, a Texas financier who held the mineral rights, became a major stockholder and an officer of the Cayce company. Together, they would drill Cayce Petroleum's first well, which would henceforth be known as Rocky Pasture #1.

22.

❂

Rocky Pasture

News of Edgar Cayce's desire to return to Texas in the Spring of 1921 was not warmly received at home for several reasons. Income from the photo studio, which had covered household expenses during his long absence, was now in short supply, due to the fact that Leslie had thrown his back out and was laid up in bed, leaving J. B. Williams to shoulder the lion's share of photographic responsibilities—a job for which he was paid. Gertrude helped out when she could, most notably tinting photographs, but she had her hands full with fourteen-year-old Hugh Lynn and three-year-old Edgar Evans. In letters home, Edgar assured Gertrude that the revenue he anticipated receiving from Cayce Petroleum would meet all the family's needs and promised to send Gertrude $100 a month for household expenses. But dollars alone couldn't make up for the fact that Edgar had only visited the family twice during the last year and a half, and on those occasions had stayed home barely long enough to unpack his bags. However strained Edgar and Gertrude's marital relations were at this point, and would be in the future, she nevertheless did not interfere in her husband's activities and supported him unconditionally.

In a curious reversal of roles from their earlier experience in Desdemona, it was now Edgar Cayce, not Dave Kahn, who made the decisions in their new petroleum venture. Kahn visited Cleburne with Edgar in May 1921, where they attended a meeting of the board of directors, but over time Kahn's role in the company became greatly diminished. That same year he stepped down from the company as trustee and secretary. Joseph Long became vice president and J. T. McConnell was made secretary and treasurer. The reason, perhaps, had less to do with a desire on Kahn's part to assume the duties he had previously held, but because Nicodemus and others instrumental in the company's fund-raising efforts were actively seeking to maintain the spirit of "cooperation and goodwill" they believed was necessary for the Source to properly guide the partnership during their drilling operations at Rocky Pasture. Kahn was a one-man team—good at giving orders and good at taking orders—but unwilling or incapable of addressing the collective interests of all concerned. As had been proven in Desdemona, the partners were going to have to work and act together in mutual harmony. Nicodemus took over Kahn's previous role as conductor of the readings, and Fay Autry, the teenage daughter of a Cayce Petroleum shareholder, became his stenographer and secretary.

The driller put in charge of the Rocky Pasture drill operation was Riley Hurst. He came highly recommended as an oilman and had already formed relationships with Barrow and the San Saba property owners. Together with Martin Sanders, Hurst set about purchasing rotary drill equipment and established a base of operations in an outbuilding owned by a local rancher, Charles Moore. Both Charles and his mother, Julia, whom Edgar affectionately called Grandma Moore, lived on the property, shared meals with the Cayce Petroleum crew, and established a friendship with Edgar that went far beyond their interest in discovering oil.

Preliminary work began in Rocky Pasture in March 1921, although they did not raise the financing to begin drilling until two months later when the formal agreements were signed. The readings on this property were extensive in both the number of questions asked, the guidance and advice offered, and the detailed descriptions given of the various rock geological formations that would be encountered as they drilled. By the time Edgar arrived in late April, the exact location had been selected and much of the equipment was on the site already or soon to arrive by train. Edgar was pleased at both the locale and the men that Hurst had assembled. Not long after Edgar's arrival, the derrick was erected. Edgar himself helped to dig the collection pits and embankments in which to hold the oil should they hit a geyser. He also laid water lines, a project made easier by the fact that the well was conveniently situated between two rivers.

Edgar enjoyed his time at the Moore farm and the adjoining property very much. In addition to being a rich oil-prospecting area, the land offered all of the wilderness and wonder that he had come to appreciate about Texas. The primitive outdoors life on the plains, free of boomtown saloons and brothels, provided Edgar with an escape from the problems and antagonisms that he believed had undermined their work in Desdemona. His favorite activity, when not engaged in constructing the rig or reading his Bible, was eating Grandma Moore's chicken-fried steak and potato pie, and fishing for bass on a large nearby lake.

According to the readings, the first showing of oil would be in a water well that they would reach at approximately 1,000 feet. A larger amount of oil would be hit at 2,600 feet. The readings further said that their well would produce 5,000 barrels each day, for a total of 40,000 barrels in the first eight days. Before they had drilled even their first 250 feet, however, problems began to develop. The bore samplings being taken didn't match the geological descriptions given in the readings. Edgar began to question himself and his psychic abilities, thinking perhaps that he had burned himself out doing oil readings. Otherwise, one or more of the drillers were not following directions precisely, or couldn't be trusted. They may have been drilling at one depth and reporting that they were at another.

But drilling continued, and as anticipated, at approximately 1,000 feet, the Cayce team reached a pool of water that contained traces of oil. Before they could dig farther, however, the team was beset by more problems. A set of tools disappeared from the drilling site. No sooner had they been replaced than the second set was stolen. Had this been Desdemona, where they were surrounded by competitors, it would have been easy to point the finger at outsiders. But here, where they were alone on the vast plains of central Texas, the culprit was suspected to be among them. Later that same month, one of their own men was discovered to have dropped a tombstone into the drill hole.

Due to the unexpected delays while equipment was replaced or being modified, and due to a pressing need for more cash, Edgar went back on the road. At the end of May and beginning of June of 1921 he traveled with Gordon Nicodemus, Fay Autry, Alf Butler, and Major Wilson on a whirlwind trip to Fort Worth, Atlanta, Denver, Little Rock, and then New York. Throughout his trip Edgar expected a wire from Riley Hurst back in Texas, indicating that their problems had been solved and that the well had come in. But the well didn't come in, and there was no immediate sign that it would. On June 19, drilling had reached 1,626 feet. During the next three months they were able to drill only another twenty-four feet due to unanticipated financial problems. Cayce Petroleum's New York partners were reluctant to make good on their promissory notes without a geologist's positive proof of oil. Unable to provide the proof, Cayce Petroleum had to sell an additional fifty thousand shares at a reduced price in order to keep drilling.

Upon his return to Rocky Pasture in December, Edgar received his first sign of hope that their problems were behind them. Hurst announced that they had reached the oil-bearing sands. As indicated in the readings, a mixture of water and oil came gushing over the derrick, raining down upon them. Everyone believed they were within feet of making a significant strike. But that night, before their clothes had even dried, one of the crew members dislodged a coupling, sending their third string of tools to the bottom of the well. Another month would pass before drilling could resume. By the beginning of March 1922, Edgar had become convinced that Hurst or some members of his crew didn't want the oil to be found.

Troubled by Edgar's infrequent letters home and the long delays in Texas, Gertrude sent Thomas House to Rocky Pasture to investigate. Her concerns had been growing only since Edgar's departure. She had not been receiving the $100 per month that had been promised for household expenses, and to date, she had received only $360 in sporadic installments of $30 to $75 checks. Now, she had stopped receiving any money at all. The squire's management of the photo studio was also less profitable than expected. Perhaps as a result of his back injuries, or his ongoing problems associated with venereal disease, Leslie rarely left his bed. His skill in managing the business had never proven to be very good in any case, and J. B. Williams now had to take over all of Leslie's duties at the studio. Gertrude also had to contend with unpleasant rumors at church and among her small circle of friends. The fact that Edgar had been gone from his home and family for over two years had naturally led to speculation in Hopkinsville that Edgar had foolishly given up a profitable and established photo studio in pursuit of a quixotic adventure in the wilds of west Texas. A second, potentially more damaging kind of rumor may also have already begun: the real reason Edgar did not come home was that there was another woman in Edgar's life—Fay Autry.

Fay Autry was indeed another woman in Edgar's life, but it is highly unlikely that she presented a threat to Edgar's affections for Gertrude as Margaret in Louisville had. Born and raised in Meridian, Texas, Autry was eighteen when Cayce Petroleum hired her to become the company stenographer. Though skilled as a secretary, she was most remembered by those who knew her as an outdoors woman and was said to be more at home roping cattle and riding the range than taking dictation. During the more than three years working with Cayce Petroleum, she recorded upward of two hundred readings and traveled more than one thousand miles from her home in Meridian to Birmingham, Alabama.

There is little evidence to suggest that Edgar's relationship with Autry was anything but professional. The reason that she accompanied him on business trips was no mystery—everyone who worked with Edgar knew the challenge of finding a capable stenographer who could step in at a moment's notice to record the strange utterances of the man in trance. The Cayce files are filled with cases of secretaries who bolted from their chairs just as a reading got underway, or who were so stunned by what they were witnessing that they could not focus on their task. Autry not only did her work under conditions that would have tested the finest of stenographers, but she produced transcripts that have withstood intense scrutiny.

Edgar Cayce was also never alone with Autry. In Texas, and later in Birmingham, they were accompanied by Alf Butler, Edgar's devoted Bible student, and Major Wilson, who considered Edgar a model of integrity. Edgar's uncle Clint Cayce—another investor in the oil ventures—spent weeks at a time with Edgar and Autry, as did Dr. Thomas House, who invariably had Gertrude's best interests in mind. None of these people ever intimated that Edgar was anything but circumspect in his relationships with other women.

However, a rumor did get started, along with veiled references by a family friend, Lillian Hale, to an undisclosed "burden" that Gertrude had to carry during her marriage, all of which likely contributed to Gertrude's decision to ask Thomas House to visit Texas. Like Hugh Lynn before him, House enjoyed his two-week trip greatly. But trouble arose toward the end of his visit, when he was injured in an accident on the oil rig. House, who apparently wasn't aware of the dangers of working on the oil rigs, was standing next to the drilling platform, lighting his pipe. The spark from his match ignited the natural gas leaking from the drill hole, creating a giant fireball of burning gas. The explosion blew House, along with the other men, right off the platform. Besides burns to his neck and face, House lost the handlebar mustache of which he had long been proud.

It was perhaps because of this accident that Edgar returned to Alabama in the summer of 1922. The details of Edgar's activities are sketchy, but it is clear that he accompanied House to Hopkinsville before he left for Selma alone. All that is known for certain is that Gertrude, the boys, and Thomas House were in Hopkinsville, Kentucky, that summer, where they would remain for the next year, while Edgar spent the last few days of June, all of July, and part of August in Selma before returning to Rocky Pasture with Alf Butler.

No explanation for the family's separation has been given. Although it is entirely possible it had something to do with Fay Autry, it is more than likely that Edgar was preoccupied with trying to save the Cayce Art Company from financial ruin—Gertrude herself cited financial hardship as the reason that she and the boys remained in Hopkinsville, where Hugh Lynn would complete his sophomore year. Edgar also may have had his hands full in the aftermath of a fire of undisclosed origin that gutted the Selma studio around this time. Edgar apparently saved his equipment, but lost much personal property and possessions, including the family china, which a well-meaning but unthinking photography assistant had tossed out the window. The fire may well explain the family's absence from Selma, not only for the summer, but for the entire next year.

Despite Thomas House's short and ultimately unhappy visit to Texas, he did stay long enough to describe what he had seen to Gertrude. No mention of Autry is made in his report, but he did note that the trouble that Cayce Petroleum had finding oil seemed to be coming from members of Edgar's crew who appeared to have conspired with outsiders to see that their well didn't come in until the company's leases had expired.

Despite the fact that Edgar himself was operating his own company and had presumably hired people whom the readings said he could trust, it seemed as if what was happening at Rocky Pasture was merely a replay of their experience in Desdemona. The mere fact that Edgar had already earned a reputation for knowing where to find oil greatly increased the chances that other companies were not only aware of his decision to drill in Rocky Pasture, but had sent spies to monitor their progress. By the summer of 1922, another company had begun drilling on an adjacent tract of land and had, in fact, sunk a well that was technically on Cayce Petroleum property. There is also evidence to suggest that Riley Hurst was concerned that readings conducted during Edgar's trips to New York were being opened and read before Hurst received them. Concern that their competitors were spying on their operation may have been the reason that Cayce Petroleum later reorganized and put its holdings in such companies as Big Five Petroleum and the Miami Land Development Company, whose names hid the fact of Edgar's participation in them.

Cayce himself—in trance—was unusually silent on the subject. Readings urged the partnership to "act in accord," but didn't name the people who were preventing them from reaching their goals. The reason for their failure, according to the readings, was their lack of a common ideal, a subject discussed at length by Curtis Willmott, an Oklahoma rancher and oilman who would later bring his own crew and equipment to drill in Rocky Pasture.

In letters to Edgar, it is clear that Willmott, perhaps more than anyone

connected to Cayce's oil ventures, understood that a spiritual "accord" between the participants was necessary if success was to be realized on a material level. "All hands," he told Edgar, "have to be pulling together with a
common purpose." Moreover, their common purpose couldn't be the desire
for riches, but "God's purpose," or the "First Purpose." As Edgar himself
later acknowledged: "There are cosmic or . . . [Divine] laws just as we have
a penal law. [Treasure hunters must give up the idea of finding great wealth
until] each one has come to the consciousness of making himself right with
the Creative Forces"—a provision repeated many more times in the readings
in years to come. The moment the "material" side of life takes over from the
spiritual," the same source admonished, "conditions are materially turned,"
and the seekers will lose, and literally become the enemy of one another.

Edgar may have understood this principle in the abstract, but Willmott
believed it in a literal sense. Willmott never doubted that oil would be found
exactly where Cayce had said it would be, but he was convinced that it
couldn't be brought to the surface without God's blessing on their joint endeavor. Failure to commit to the "First Purpose," he believed, created material impediments as real as a logging chain or tombstone blocking the
drill hole.

Three years would pass before Edgar Cayce explored this subject in
greater depth, and another decade would elapse before Edgar himself understood that he hadn't yet begun to grasp the greater message coming
through in the readings: that certain cosmic or Divine laws influenced not
only man's physical health, but also his ability to obtain material blessings.
However much Edgar believed he had reached the proper "accord" described
in the readings, the truth was self-evident. Dave Kahn, who was still heavily influencing Edgar's decision-making process, never stopped fashioning
get-rich-quick schemes. And Edgar himself confessed, their search for oil in
Rocky Pasture had become an "obsession" beyond his desire to build a hospital. This was perhaps why Kahn had originally been urged to obtain
ninety-nine-year leases: it might take that long for the partners to truly
reach the "accord" necessary for their success.

By the end of the summer of 1922, the San Saba leases expired, and
Rocky Pasture #1, having, as Edgar said, "been expertly sabotaged a dozen
times," had not come in. The company's funds ran out and the Rocky Pasture project had to be abandoned.

"The oil was there," Edgar later confessed in a letter to a trusted friend.
"I just wasn't equal to handling the men who were associated with it."

23.

Birmingham
and Dayton

Prior to his departure from Rocky Pasture, Edgar Cayce received a letter from Frank Mohr, the mine owner who had begun building a hospital in Nortonville, Kentucky, when Edgar was in partnership with Ketchum. In the decade that had elapsed since Edgar last communicated with him, Mohr had slowly gone blind, just as Cayce's readings had predicted. Doctors insisted that Mohr undergo an operation to remove both eyes as a means of saving his life. He then had remembered Edgar's reading, which said that if he went blind, he would have to undergo hydrotherapy treatments to reverse the damage. Having once doubted the contents of the reading, Mohr undertook the recommended treatments in earnest. In a letter in June he reported to Edgar of having undergone several hundred treatments and having his sight completely restored. He praised and thanked Edgar for the reading and, most important, expressed his renewed desire to build the hospital.

Thrilled and encouraged by the news, Edgar invited Mohr to come to Texas in the late summer of 1922. They spent several days in Rocky Pasture before Edgar accompanied him to his home in Columbus. Although Edgar was as eager to build a hospital as Mohr, there was one major obstacle: Mohr had lost his wealth. During his long illness, he had to give up virtually all of his extensive mineral holdings and sell off his assets to support his family and pay medical bills. He wanted to help Edgar get started, but the only assistance he could provide was thirty-five years of business experience, not cash.

A short time after arriving in Columbus, Edgar received a wire from Dave Kahn, who was in Denver, Colorado. In the months that had elapsed since Kahn left Cayce Petroleum, he had gone to Denver to work for a prominent lawyer, B. D. Townsend, who also was involved in the oil business. Through Townsend, Kahn met some of the most influential citizens of Denver, including Frederick Gilmer Bonfils, the owner and publisher of the *Denver Post*. Bonfils, having heard all about Edgar from Kahn, wanted to witness a reading and agreed to pay Edgar's travel expenses. Edgar and Mohr packed their bags again and boarded the train to Denver.

The first reading that Edgar gave was for Bonfils himself and was conducted on a couch in his private office. Bonfils was very excited about what he heard. As Cayce, in trance, went over his body, describing the condition of each part, Bonfils placed his hand on that area of his body. When the reading was over, Bonfils exclaimed, "This is the finest thing I have ever seen!"

Cayce then gave another reading, this time in a hotel room. Bonfils had assembled a team of doctors who had selected a patient to be given a physical diagnosis. Bonfils and the others were astonished by the intricacy and accuracy of Cayce's medical knowledge, and Bonfils immediately offered to hire Cayce to give readings at a reported sum of $1,000 a day. Townsend would be general counselor, Kahn the general manager, and Bonfils would direct the operation.

There were several "catches," however, to the agreement. Bonfils would be in charge of publicity, and Edgar Cayce would have to adopt a new "persona," which would require him to dress in a white silk costume with a turban. He would be chauffeured around Denver in a specially made Cadillac or Packard limousine with its curtains drawn and have footmen at his service. Bonfils would make two appointments a day, one of which would be reserved exclusively for him. During readings, Cayce's face would be hidden behind a veil. At all times he would be accompanied by bodyguards and could never be seen alone.

Edgar was indignant. "There's [only] one thing I can tell you," he said. "I'm not a showman . . . [nor am I] going to be portrayed as one. And I'm not wearing any turban because I am not what the turban says it is . . . I'm a country boy from [the] Kentucky hills. I can give you a reading like you saw today and that's the way it has to be kept."

Despite their failure to reach an agreement, the publisher had him conduct several readings for family members, which proved successful. But however pleased the publisher was with the outcome, he either didn't feel that it was necessary to pay for the readings, or Edgar didn't accept his money. Edgar and Mohr were left stranded in Denver. To compound what had now become a desperate financial situation, Leslie arrived unexpectedly from Alabama by train. He, too, was broke, but had scraped together the money to come to Denver when he misunderstood a wire Edgar had sent him requesting that Leslie send them money for train tickets back to Selma.

Just as the Cayce party appeared to be in desperate straits, a telegram arrived for Edgar from the secretary of a woman's club in Birmingham, Alabama, who wanted to know how much Edgar would charge to deliver a lecture. Edgar replied immediately and, risking their poor opinion of him, stated the price as three railroad tickets, two from Denver to Birmingham for Edgar and Frank Mohr, and one back to Selma for Leslie. Edgar was both surprised and pleased by the invitation, for until that time he had never been invited to give a paid public speaking engagement.

Edgar and Mohr arrived in Birmingham on the cool fall afternoon of September 13, 1922. Having spent a few weeks in that city two years earlier with Dave Kahn, Edgar had already developed a reputation. And now, with Frank Mohr available to conduct readings and to help get the word out, physician Percy Woodall to consult on treatments, and court reporter William K. Schanz to coordinate stenographers, Edgar was more prepared than ever to find people to pay for his trance sessions. While he expected to stay only a few days, the demand for his readings and lectures was so great that he hired Fay Autry to join them to act as his secretary and stenographer. She arrived in November, and by January, Edgar was still giving readings. Edgar's old friend from Selma, Alf Butler, who had joined Cayce Petroleum back in May 1921, and was now living in Birmingham, occasionally sat in or conducted readings himself.

The success of Edgar's lectures and subsequent readings in Birmingham were unprecedented. During his four months living on the tenth floor of the Tutweiler Hotel, Edgar gave 240 documented readings—more readings per month than he had had ever given before. For the first time in his life, Edgar's sole income was derived from giving readings and talking about them.

The first reading he gave was for a two-year-old Dayton boy named William Darling who was dying of cancer. William had gone with his parents to Denver when he fell ill and was diagnosed as having lymphosarcoma. The doctors gave them no hope. It was on the train home, via Chicago, that they met Dave Kahn, who told them about Edgar's readings. The mother and child continued home to Dayton, while the father, accompanied by Kahn, headed for Birmingham to meet Edgar. The subsequent reading stated that the cause of his cancer was a combination of factors, which included the way the umbilical cord healed just after the child's birth: a powerful drug used to dilate the mother's uterus during labor had been trapped in the child's system. Among other treatments, Cayce recommended injections of atropine, which proved to be highly effective. The child immediately began to recover.

Other Birmingham readings were conducted for a man who came to Edgar with severe tooth decay, a young woman with a blood condition, a businessman who had suffered a nervous breakdown, and an older woman with arthritis. In a particularly dramatic case, Edgar was asked to do an emergency reading for one of Woodall's patients who was suffering from a blocked Eustachian tube. Cayce recommended a remarkable and highly effective procedure he called "finger surgery," which amounted to a doctor using his own fingers to reach up inside a patient's mouth and manipulate the Eustachian tube through the soft membranes separating it from the mouth cavity. Dramatic readings such as these were in no small part the reason that people stood in line at the Tutweiler Hotel to see Edgar. As Schanz later described it: "At most of these readings the room . . . was full of spectators, and at nearly every one there was from one to three doctors."

A particularly humorous incident occurred when Frank Mohr, Alf Butler, and Edgar were attending a magic show. A stranger sitting next to them asked Edgar if he knew how the magician was able to perform a particular trick. "No I don't," Edgar replied. The stranger, not realizing that he was speaking to Edgar Cayce, then said, "There's a lot of things we don't understand—but I think I know how this fellow, [Cayce] up here at the Tutweiler does his tricks." Alf Butler asked the stranger how he thought Cayce did it. He answered: "[Cayce] has his appointments a long time ahead and he has somebody who finds out everything about the patients. He's a pretty smart fellow, from what I heard, and then he just tells it back to them." It was at this point that Alf Butler and the others introduced themselves and invited the stranger to attend a reading at the Tutweiler. He later became one of Edgar's greatest supporters in Birmingham, and in the 1930s formed a study group dedicated to the readings.

The people of Birmingham couldn't seem to get enough. Edgar even passed the test of an attorney sent by the authorities to spy on him. The attorney had a reading done for himself and his wife and concluded that there was no "hocus-pocus" going on. Moreover, Cayce's enthusiastic supporters pledged over $50,000 to build a hospital that would keep Edgar in their city for the rest of his career. By January 1923, plans were being made for Gertrude and the children to move to Birmingham.

Before Gertrude was able to come from Hopkinsville, however, two problems developed. The first was relatively minor and stemmed from the fact that city authorities were asking Edgar to obtain a medical license. A committee of doctors successfully overcame this obstacle by claiming that Cayce didn't need a medical license because he wasn't practicing medicine—only giving advice. The second problem was considerably more difficult to reconcile, the result of a reading Cayce gave to determine the proper site on which to build the hospital. The reading flatly stated that Birmingham was not the location to build the hospital because it was too commercial. Nor did it fit a requirement previously stated in a reading: the Source indicated that Edgar Cayce must conduct his trance readings in close proximity to a large body of water. Edgar himself—to one degree or another—had already been aware of this, but still hadn't given the "environment" in which he gave readings much thought. Now, in Birmingham, he was forced to confront this issue directly.

The readings again suggested that a small town called Virginia Beach, on the coast of Virginia, was the best location for Edgar Cayce to conduct his trance readings. This did not come entirely as a surprise to Edgar, for this location had been suggested in previous readings—now lost—that had been conducted in Anniston, Alabama, in 1910, and then in Hopkinsville in 1911. The previous readings had made sufficient impact that Lynn Evans—who, because of his job with the Louisville and Nashville Railroad could travel freely by train—had visited Norfolk and nearby Virginia Beach. Lynn was later followed by Hiram Salter, Gertrude's uncle, who vacationed in Virginia Beach in 1915. They reported that although Virginia Beach met the requirement of being near a large body of water, it was nothing more than a sleepy fishing village, certainly not a place to build a hospital dedicated to the healing arts of a psychic. The impact that the new reading had on his support group was not unexpected. Judge Robert Benson Evins and the other influential supporters who had pledged financing, were understanding of Edgar's dilemma but unwilling to raise money for an institution that would be hundreds of miles away.

In letters home, Edgar lamented what he considered yet another failure in Birmingham. But although he still hadn't raised any money to build a hospital, his dream was very much alive. He was still desperate for the oil to come in, if indeed it ever would, to finance his dream, but in the meantime decided he would have to continue to broaden the scope of his endeavors. Determined to act in accordance with the readings, Edgar and Frank Mohr left

Birmingham to give more readings and lectures and to sell additional shares of Cayce Petroleum. In late January, Edgar headed for Atlanta, where a snowstorm virtually shut down the city. Exhausted and unsure what to do next, Edgar decided to take a long and badly needed rest, first going to Selma, and then stopping off in Hopkinsville before leaving on yet another search for more financing for his oil ventures.

There is no record of what transpired when Edgar finally did get to see his wife and children at The Hill. No doubt Gertrude tried to convince him to stay in Selma, and at the very least, to devote himself to the photo studio in addition to giving readings on his petroleum endeavors. As Hugh Lynn reported, relations between his parents were strained. During their twenty-nine years together, they had overcome many challenges, and Gertrude had made more than her share of concessions. To her mind, Edgar was behaving like a traveling salesman or, at the least, living the life of one. But Edgar, headstrong and still convinced that he was on the "road to riches," didn't waiver from his present course. If anything, his four months in Birmingham convinced him that God intended him to give readings full time. Any other type of work, whether it be photography or not, would have to take a back seat.

By mid-March, Edgar was back on the road, first to Cleburne, and then to Meridian, Texas, where he stayed with J. T. McConnell, the secretary-treasurer of Cayce Petroleum. He and McConnell were now in discussions with William K. Rice, known simply as "Tex Rice," whom Edgar described as "a high-pressure salesman." Rice had received a physical reading done the previous December in Birmingham, and in subsequent discussions, discovered that Edgar still controlled leases on twenty-five thousand acres of land where readings claimed oil would be found. He was interested in "floating an oil proposition" in Texas for his own Penn-Tenn Company and wanted to include the Cayce Petroleum leases in his proposition. In exchange for cash and shares in the Penn-Tenn Company, Edgar transferred his holdings out of Cayce Petroleum and into Penn-Tenn. Dave Kahn also invested, as did his employer, B. D. Townsend.

For the moment, it was Tex Rice's job to seek investors. Kahn would run the "home office," and Cayce would recruit investors and give readings on individual oil fields when the time came. The series of readings conducted for Penn-Tenn reveal some amusing ways that the Source communicated information through Cayce. In one reading the Source said: "As to the affairs and physical forces of Dave Kahn, well, he is right smart up in the air at the present. It will be better for him, though, when he lights [down]. He will have some better judgment of handling affairs." And when Kahn, as ambitious as ever, asked if he should attempt to also handle another line of business, Cayce—in trance—replied, "And get himself in trouble. If he wishes to, let him try it. He cannot serve two masters!" Another reading revealed how often the Source's approach to business was compatible with good business sense. Kahn wanted to know if they should launch a newspaper campaign in an attempt to find more investors. Cayce—in trance—replied: "Not just yet. Actual operations must be effective before newspaper operations would reach any condition worthy of the outlay."

Cayce's response in a subsequent reading also nicely demonstrated not only his sense of humor and awareness of contemporary issues, but the necessity of the conductor to be very specific in how he spoke to the Source. After asking several other questions about the affairs of the Penn-Tenn Company, Kahn asked what the company could sell through mail order that would reap substantial returns. Cayce—in trance—replied, "Stills [to make liquor] would be the best thing."

This wasn't the only time Cayce's trance readings dealt with the subject of alcohol. The Source also had something to say about Prohibition, which, at this point, had been in effect for three years. While the Source generally recommended moderation in all things and viewed alcoholism as dangerous to one's health, it didn't view Prohibition as the solution. When asked if Prohibition would prevent people from drinking, the response came: "No one may ever legislate goodness into the heart or the soul of anyone . . . [Prohibition] has already lost in America, and only waits the decisions of those as to whether . . . [Americans] will . . . [be] law abiding or . . . law breaking."

Although the rate at which Edgar Cayce gave readings had dropped off considerably from what he had done in Birmingham, there were many notable trance sessions in Meridian beyond those given for Penn-Tenn, including one for McConnell's mother-in-law, a seventy-one-year-old retired nurse who was always complaining of being cold. In trance, Cayce recommended she use a device not unlike those Cayce had recommended Ketchum's patients use. McConnell's mother-in-law was told how to make the appliance using copper wires attached to steel rods immersed in ice-cold water, which she was to attach to her ankles and wrists for an hour or two at a time whenever she felt cold. Based on specifications in the readings, she went ahead and made the first prototype. McConnell's mother-in-law became a convert to Cayce after her first treatment with the device and reportedly once got so "warm" using it that she hopped out of bed and quickly tried to unhook herself from it. Her son, a doctor, said to her: "That's just pure imagination," to which she responded, "Then just please God give me some more imagination!"

In May 1923, Edgar and Tex Rice traveled to Chicago and Pittsburgh. At each stop, Edgar continued giving lectures and physical readings, hoping to raise money for either Penn-Tenn or the hospital. Next they went on to Altoona, Pennsylvania, where they were met by Dave Kahn before traveling on to New York. The reason was that fund-raising was not going as well as expected. According to the readings, Rice wasn't conscientious enough in following up leads. Readings also revealed that Rice was struggling with hypertension and kidney problems, brought on by heavy drinking and marital discord, and indicated that he should not undertake much on behalf of their business enterprise until his personal affairs had improved. In the meantime, B. D. Townsend, Kahn's employer, was also not following through on his part of the bargain, which involved selling shares of the company on the stock market. It is not surprising that in one reading the Source commented that for Edgar Cayce, there was "a good deal of sadness . . . right now."

In June, the search for new investors and a desire to meet the now three-year-old William Darling Jr.—the child who had been diagnosed with cancer—took Edgar to Dayton, which was also the home of Tim Brown, a friend of the Darling family, and an inventor and auto-parts manufacturer who had received readings back in Birmingham. Edgar must also have been aware of the special significance of that city—back in Anniston, in 1910, the Source had said that Dayton was where the work would begin.

At the height of his illness, William Alfred Darling Jr., whom Edgar had diagnosed nine months earlier, had over a hundred cancerous nodules. Cayce had continued giving readings for him, and although his previous recommendations had not always been followed to the letter, the parents and their osteopath, Dr. Gravett, had become more proficient and successful at implementing the recommended treatments. By the time Edgar arranged a personal meeting in Dayton with the young boy and his mother, the child had only three walnut-size nodules left on his body: one beside each eye and one on his left wrist. In a fifth reading for the child, given in Dayton, Cayce stated that while the condition appeared to be almost eliminated, the parents and their physician had to be careful. If the treatments were not kept up, the disease would return.

Edgar, still waiting for more developments with Penn-Tenn, spent over a month and a half in Dayton, staying at the Phillips Hotel, where he conducted mostly physical readings. While he did not receive an hourly fee for his trance sessions, the donations that came in were adequate to cover his hotel and food bill and that of his stenographer, Fay Autry, who joined him in Dayton as she had in Birmingham. Frank Mohr had returned home to Columbus, and the vast majority of readings were conducted by William

Darling's godfather, Linden Shroyer, an accountant who had been living with the Darlings during their ordeal. A short, slight, bespectacled man with dark hair neatly parted down the middle and a quiet demeanor, Shroyer didn't know what to think of the stranger from Alabama. But each trance session made him more convinced that Edgar was indeed legitimate and that the true wealth of his "gift" was as yet untapped. The tragic irony was that the patient whom Cayce was closest to, William Jr., was also the only patient diagnosed in Dayton who would die.

In early June, the young Darling boy was playing around a swimming pool and fell, striking one of his remaining cancerous nodules. The nodule quickly grew to the size of an orange. Cayce immediately gave another reading, stating a new kind of osteopathic procedure would have to be undertaken, which, if handled properly, would actually speed his recovery. Unfortunately, the treatments were not conducted in a timely or effective manner, nor were the child's activities properly monitored. As later became clear, the child's parents had been fighting, and his father, Alfred Darling, had gone on a long drinking binge. The child suffered a second fall, again bruising one of the cancerous growths. Dr. Gravett, who was away at a medical convention, appointed an osteopath who wasn't well trained in the new procedure. Although the cancer had been virtually eradicated, the child's condition quickly grew worse and within a matter of days, he was dead.

It was with great sadness that Cayce conducted his first postmortem reading, confirming what Shroyer and Dr. Gravett already suspected: the osteopathic treatments had not been carried out properly and the poisons from the broken bump had been allowed to spread throughout the child's body.

24.

Divine Law

For Shroyer as well as Edgar, the tragedy again highlighted the need for a hospital where patients like the three-year-old Darling child could receive constant attention and care. By this time the subject of building a hospital had also come to the attention of Shroyer's employer, Arthur Lammers, a middle-aged business tycoon who had made his fortune in Chicago and who now owned a large printing and photo-engraving company in Dayton that published a Baptist newspaper. At Lammers's request, Cayce gave the first in a series of readings—not only on investment opportunities for the Penn-Tenn Company, which Lammers was interested in buying into—but on how best to use Cayce's "psychic powers" and establish an institution or foundation to study them. Although the amount of time Cayce would personally spend with Lammers was quite short and the readings conducted at his request numbered less than ten, their short partnership forever altered the scope and substance of the work.

However reluctant Edgar was to probe the Source with questions beyond the scope of his medical and business interests, he was flattered by the way Arthur and his wife, Zelda, embraced him and his ideals, and intrigued by their knowledge of Eastern philosophy and metaphysics. They not only read

and studied the books and teachings of Madame Blavatsky and other
Theosophists, they held seances in their own home—a sprawling Victorian
mansion with stained-glass windows, a giant pipe organ, and an extensive library of esoteric books and manuscripts on such subjects as medieval alchemy,
yoga, and astrology. It is believed that Edgar attended at least one seance at
the Lammers home, although no record of what transpired remains.

A short, clean-shaven man with a square face and the well-muscled build
of a heavyweight prize fighter, Lammers wanted answers to life's most important questions: the purpose of man's existence on earth and what to expect after death. And like Ketchum before him, Lammers also wanted to
know about the source of Edgar's information, and what exactly happened
when Edgar went into trance. Lammers put these and other questions to
Cayce in two trance sessions held in June 1923 at the Phillips Hotel. More
readings in this series, all of which were conducted by Shroyer, took place in
early October and November, and the last reading of this series was done on
Valentine's Day, 1924.

The first question put to Cayce dealt with his ability to obtain and communicate psychic information. As Cayce had previously said in a reading
for Ketchum, the "state" in which he gave psychic information was under
"subjugation" of the "subconscious mind." The human body was described
as a "trinity," composed of the physical body, the mental or conscious mind,
and the spirit, which was described as the subconscious or "mind of the soul
force." The spirit, the Source said, could not be "seen" or revealed unless the
physical and mental mind were subjugated. In other words, when Edgar
Cayce went into a trance state, his physical body and conscious mind did not
interfere with his subconscious mind or "soul forces."

As a natural extension of this question, Lammers asked exactly what the
"soul" was, and whether it ever dies. The Source replied that the soul was
"that which the Maker gave to every entity or individual in the beginning,
and which is seeking the home again or place of the Maker . . . [The soul]
may be banished from the Maker, [but] not [by] death." He went on to say
that the subconscious mind was only one attribute of the soul, and that there
were other influences or Divine laws that governed or directed the soul in
its path back to the Maker.

Asked what kinds of questions should be put to Cayce while in trance, the
Source answered: "Only those that are in accord with spiritual and soul
forces and laws." According to the Source, the proper questions should consist of those that lead to relief from pain or suffering as long as they are not
at the expense or detriment of another individual.

The Source was then queried as to whether the information given while in trance was always correct. The response provided an interesting insight to the frequent references the Source had made over the years to the concept that "mind is the builder," and also had a direct bearing on the Texas readings. The Source said: "Edgar Cayce is in the state of being guided by the individual who makes the suggestions, and so long as the suggestions are in accord and the mind of the individual is kept in accord [the information will be correct]." In other words, the Source was saying that what was held in the mind of the person conducting the reading and the person requesting the help or information would largely determine the result. The Source illustrated this same point by comparing the effects of the inquirer on the reading to the effects that water can have on a partially submerged object: "Any object . . . projected into water appears bent, just so with the reflection from suggestions to the subconscious [mind]."

The Source further said that the intent of those making the inquiry didn't just affect the quality of the reading, it sometimes determined whether any information came through at all. This explained why the Source sometimes ended a reading by saying, "We are through," just as a session was getting started. Cayce—in trance—said: "[The correct information was] being deflected . . . by question or environment as to cause the distress to the connection between the conscious and the subconscious."

As it was revealed later in this same series of readings, the Source was directed by "God's laws," or "Divine Laws," which could neither be ignored or put aside. While a person breaking man's laws only suffers the consequence if she or he gets caught, when breaking God's laws, he or she always gets caught. Cayce—in trance—had to be asked the right question for the right reason.

Perhaps the most important of the laws cited was the "law of love," which the Source said "no man should cast aside." Put most simply, the Source said: "Love is Law, Law is Love. God is Love. Love is God." This amounted to the same thing as "the gift of giving" without "hope of reward or pay," or serving others.

In answer to the question of whether or not the readings should be used for purposes other than for assistance of curing human ills, the Source highlighted how they had to adhere to the "law of love." The Source said that all information obtained psychically should *not* be used for selfish purposes, but "may be, should be, used and given to the world." The Source suggested that people should seek an understanding of that Divine law of love in their lives and act accordingly. "The use of psychic force by any individual is only using of that spiritual law that makes one free, but not freedom to take advantage," the Source said.

Another reading stressed the importance of understanding that God is the creator and law-giver, not man: "Remember first that all force that is granted . . . comes from the all-giving force of the God of the Universe and not from the self . . . for by taking that [force], no one can change any law. Only by the compliance of that law may it be made or diverted to their individual use of self . . . [through man's power of free will] for with the [free] will man may either adhere [to] or contradict the Divine law."

Further practical questions were posed to Cayce regarding how to conduct future readings. The Source said that only one person at a time should put questions to him in a trance state, and that for best results, the person should have a certain polarity. "The body," Cayce said, in trance, "is made of both the opposite, or positive and negative poles. The body is not complete without the whole or both . . . [The ideal condition exists when there is] the perfect union in all forces, whether of the physical, mental, material, soul, or spirit [each with both positive and negative polarity].

Linden Shroyer was clearly following Cayce's train of thought. He next asked the Source *who* would be the best person to conduct the readings. The Source replied that the sex of the conductor didn't make any difference, just the polarity and intent of the conductor. Edgar was described as being positive. Hence, it was best that a person who was negatively charged put the questions to him.

Information continued to pour out of Cayce. Like Ketchum before him, Lammers wanted to know if it was possible for anyone other than Edgar Cayce to accomplish the kind of psychic work he was doing. The answer was an unequivocal yes. "All can do it," the response came. The determining factor was the degree of "development" on the part of the individual in question. "As to the degree of the development, only the law of concentration through subjugation [is] brought out into play and [one] only need[s] the opportunity of [his] self-expression."

Lammers also asked if it was possible for Edgar Cayce to communicate with people who had passed into the spirit world. The response was affirmative. In the first known reading to make clear reference to what happens when a person dies, the Source said: "The spirit of all that have passed from the physical plane remain about the plane until their development carries them onward or are returned for their development here . . . There are thousands about us here at present."

When asked how Edgar Cayce should use his psychic talents to do the most good, the Source gave another astonishing response. It is difficult to determine how much the answer was understood by Lammers or the others, but it was clear in retrospect that the Source was introducing what would become the most discussed aspect of the Dayton readings: soul development "through reincarnation." "[Edgar Cayce is able to give trance advice] under the laws of the governing force as . . . given to this individual [through] eight generations [of soul development]," the Source said. Finally, Cayce was asked if the time was right to start an institution through which all future readings would be conducted. "Very good," the reply came. "The time is nigh!"

How much or how little Edgar Cayce understood the implications of the Lammers readings is not clear, but there is no doubt that he came to realize his psychic abilities could be used for much more than locating underground oil reserves or giving physical readings. Lammers had urged Edgar to expand his horizons beyond even what could be accomplished in a hospital—to understanding the mysteries of life itself. The fact that Edgar truly considered taking the plunge is apparent in his decision, upon his return to Alabama later that year, to set aside a dedicated place to conduct his trance readings and to hire a permanent stenographer to transcribe them. His return home, however, was not the joyous event he had long anticipated it would be.

Before returning to Alabama, Edgar made yet another trip to Texas to try and build financial support for the Penn-Tenn Company. Lammers—whom Edgar believed to have "very deep pockets"—was considering making a substantial investment in the company, as was Tim Brown, the auto-parts manufacturer, and Alfred Darling, father of the late William Jr. Their interest and enthusiasm took Edgar back to Meridian, Texas, where Penn-Tenn's banker, J. T. McConnell, was in the midst of obtaining more leases based on anticipated income from Tex Rice's fund-raising efforts.

Edgar's trip to Texas was short and discouraging. Kahn and B. D. Townsend's contacts had failed to raise any money. And then Edgar received news that Tex Rice had been arrested for fraud in a scheme to swindle investors in a phony land-development deal. Prosecutors sought—and ultimately obtained—an indictment against Rice for grand larceny. Edgar and the Penn-Tenn Company were shielded from prosecution because Rice was an independent operator and the property he had used to defraud investors was not part of Penn-Tenn's holdings. Regardless of the fact that Penn-Tenn had not been named in the indictment, Edgar—like McConnell—was appalled by Rice's behavior, and couldn't in good faith accept financing from anyone until the entire matter was resolved. Edgar also felt personally responsible, realizing that he had been the one who had introduced Tex Rice to his circle of friends. And it was Edgar's participation in Penn-Tenn that Rice had based his fund-raising efforts on in the first place. Edgar later referred to Rice as "the most notorious character [with whom he had ever done business]." Gertrude's overriding concern that Edgar attracted gamblers and other people looking for the "easy money" had again proven to be true.

Although earlier readings had revealed Tex Rice's personal difficulties, Edgar couldn't fathom why the Source hadn't warned him that Rice was a criminal. In retrospect, Edgar eventually came to the conclusion that the "failure" of the readings to predict someone's behavior was not a result of any lack of insight or "development" on the part of the Source, but a matter of the inexorable influence of an individual's free will. Free will—described in the Lammers readings as the supreme Gift from God to man—ultimately determined an individual's fate. No one, not even God, could conclusively predict events shaped by the free will of an individual, or the collective will of groups of individuals.

As a result of his experience with Tex Rice, and feeling strained and unnerved by delays, empty promises, and the constant parade of potential investors who expressed an interest but didn't put up any money, Edgar finally gave up on the Penn-Tenn Company. Although it is popularly thought that he never again worked in the oil business, Edgar later gave about eighty other readings on potential drilling sites in Alabama, Arizona, Florida, Louisiana, Tennessee, and Wyoming. Many of these readings were for people with whom, like Curtis Willmott and Byron Wyrick, he was later in partnership. The only difference was that he would never again devote himself solely to the oil business.

Feeling destitute and embarrassed, he returned home—this time, he believed, for good. He wired Gertrude in Hopkinsville for her and the children to join him in Selma. It was a short but heartfelt message: "I'm home to stay. Please come back."

Forty-six-year-old Edgar Cayce had, it seemed, nothing to show for the last four years except more lines in his face, hair that had gone prematurely gray, and an extra forty pounds, which showed around his waistline. Edgar Evans had been just a little over one year old and Hugh Lynn had been just twelve when Edgar had set out for Cleburne. Now Edgar Evans was ready for kindergarten and Hugh Lynn was going into his junior year in high school, dating girls, and thinking about college. Edgar's photography business had barely managed to keep its doors open in his absence. And Gertrude—whose hair had also gone prematurely gray—felt hurt and abandoned. Throughout that time she had naturally questioned why he hadn't come home much sooner, instead leaving her and the boys to fend for themselves and rely on handouts from relatives to survive. The answer was hard for her and anyone else to understand. Edgar did not want to come home empty-handed and in worse shape than he had started. At each stop along the road home he genuinely believed he would be returning a rich and prosperous man.

For now, his dreams of doing readings and, at minimum supporting his family, or at best building a hospital—without having to ask others for payment or donations—were dashed. But the hundreds of physical readings he had given in Birmingham, Nashville, Cleburne, Hopkinsville—and the latest readings he had given Lammers in Dayton—had at least convinced him that the hours he spent in trance were worthwhile, and that it was his Christian duty and vocation to use the gift that God had given him to help others. He had a mission in life that could not be ignored or denied. And toward this end he had decided not to let anything else—photography, the oil business, or his family's lack of income—interfere with him giving readings. "As I studied over the happenings of the years I had been away, I realized there must indeed be a change in my outlook on life," Cayce said. "The work [must come] first . . . self second."

PART FIVE

I asked the roses as they grew
Richer and lovelier in their
  hue
What made their tints so rich
and bright.
They answered—
Looking toward the Light

Venture Inward

25.

Miss Gladys
and Mr. Cayce

Upon his return home, Edgar immediately dedicated a room in his studio to house transcripts of the readings he had already given, and where he intended to give more. The location he chose for this "spook room," as Edgar called it, was the former storeroom of the Cayce Art Company. He wanted to decorate it with furniture that his friends gave him, along with photographs and personal possessions. He realized, perhaps only intuitively, that having mementos from friends was important to the readings themselves. To a close associate he wrote, "I want the place to be so personal that when I go in my best friends will speak to me."

Gertrude's reaction to Edgar's turning a portion of the studio over to the work is not known. No doubt she was happy to have him home after years of constant travel, and if this meant setting some space aside for him to conduct readings, she was quite willing to oblige him. Not wanting to waste any time, Edgar also immediately sent his new address to everyone on his ever-increasing mailing list.

Edgar also needed to find a stenographer whom he could train to transcribe the readings. Fay Autry, the secretary who had been hired by Cayce Petroleum, was now married and living in Houston, and finding another secretary who could properly transcribe the readings in a manner that made sense turned out to be as difficult as finding investors for his oil company. In trance, Cayce sometimes spoke rapidly, often using conjunctions, prepositions, and relative pronouns so profusely that normal rules of punctuation could no longer be applied. Being without a stenographer suited to the task made the Cayce readings less valuable, at times completely useless. Edgar interviewed and tested more than twelve secretaries before he found one who could do the job. Her name was Gladys Davis, and other than Edgar himself, she would become the single most important part of the work—the person who, more than anyone else, elevated it to a professional level.

That year, 1923, Gladys Davis had turned eighteen years old, just two years older than Hugh Lynn. Tall and blond, with broad shoulders, delicate features, and blue eyes, she was the eldest daughter of a peanut farmer from Alabama whose joy and passion in life was having get-togethers with plenty of family and friends gathered to eat, sing, and listen to him play his fiddle. Her family was also related to Jefferson Davis, president of the Confederacy—grandfather Zedoc Hookey Davis, affectionately called "Hook," had been his cousin. Dorothy Gladys Davis was the eldest of five children and had two brothers and two sisters: Lucile, Boyd, Burt, and, Gladys's favorite, Mary Frances, whose nickname was Tiny, and who married at the age of fourteen.

Gladys was far more capable and independent than her other siblings, so much so that for more than five years after her father passed away in 1924, she became the sole source of financial support for the family. Since her early teens, it had been a forgone conclusion that Gladys would became a school-teacher. But after attending Selma High School for one year, she took a liking to a recent invention that was just then appearing in Selma—the typewriter. She enrolled at Central City Business College to learn how to use one.

Gladys went to work at age fifteen, the same year she graduated from business college. Her first job was at the Cawthon-Coleman Drug Store, where, thanks to the office manager, she learned to punctuate. As it happened, the drugstore was located beneath the Cayce Art Studio, and although it would be another two years before she would get to know the Cayce family personally, she remembered seeing them go up and down the stairs to their home and studio. She remembered how Edgar had once come into the drugstore after what must have been one of his visits to Texas and said "Good morning, Miss Gladys," though they had never been introduced and she didn't know how he knew her name. The manager jokingly told Edgar to stop flirting with his secretary by calling her "Miss Gladys." Edgar ignored him. From that moment on, and for many years to come, he would invariably call her "Miss Gladys," and she would call him "Mr. Cayce."

Gladys's tenure at the drugstore was short—she had been substituting for the regular stenographer while she was on vacation—and the next job she took was as a stenographer at Tissier's Retail and Wholesale Hardware Store, earning seventy-five dollars a month. As she later said of the experience, she was hoping there would be more to life than lists of coal buckets, hammers, nails, nuts, bolts, plows, and cultivators. Although she didn't know it at the time, her hopes would be realized when the opportunity came to type up one of the Cayce readings.

The request came through Miss Willie Graham, the manager of the china department at Tissier's, who sometimes recruited Gladys to help demonstrate chinaware for guests at the Prince Albert Hotel. In late August of 1923, just after Edgar's return to Selma, Graham asked Gladys if she would be willing to take down a clairvoyant "reading" to be given by Mr. Cayce that afternoon. The trance session was to be conducted on behalf of her three-year-old nephew, Virgil Graham, who was suffering from a nervous disorder.

Despite Edgar's long absence from Selma and the extended holiday Gertrude and the boys had taken in Hopkinsville, the Cayce family was not entirely unfamiliar to the Davis family, for their paths had crossed many times since Gladys and her siblings had attended high school in Selma. Hugh Lynn Cayce was a friend of Gladys's sister Tiny when he was in seventh grade at the Dallas Academy. He often walked Tiny home after school, exchanging books and comparing homework assignments with her, and sometimes took her to Cawthon's drugstore for sodas.

In addition to Hugh Lynn, Tiny had come to know Edgar through her membership in Christian Endeavor. She and the rest of the Selma branch of Christian Endeavor had gone with Edgar to Birmingham when he was honored for his outstanding work with the young people. Despite the acquaintance between the two families, Gladys was confused about which member of the Cayce clan did the psychic readings. She had assumed that the older Cayce, the "dapper man" with the mustache whom she had seen on occasion and who had not long ago taken her photograph, was the person Miss Willie Graham had referred to. Gladys's friend Ruth de Bardeleben, who worked in the stationery department at Tissier's, set her straight. It was the son, Edgar, the tall man who had taught Sunday school at the First Christian Church, the man who had just returned from exciting adventures in the oil fields of Texas, and the man who called her "Miss Gladys," who did the psychic readings. Ruth was excited, telling Gladys she had heard that people who followed what Mr. Cayce said in trance were cured of whatever ailed them.

The reading for Virgil Graham was set for August 30, 1923—not much more than a week after Edgar's arrival home. As arranged, Gladys joined Miss Graham after lunch and climbed the steps to the photo studio. Gladys was not the only stenographer who had come. Among the ten or more others being considered for the position was Gladys's friend Maud Doughty and another woman whom Gladys did not recognize. Gladys glanced around the room and spotted Edgar, who smiled at her. He quietly got up and moved a small table over to where she was seated. He then went to a long couch and sat down. Next to him sat the elder Cayce, Leslie.

Edgar briefly explained what was about to happen and told the girls it was better to be accurate than to try to make sense out of what was said. Then he lay down while Gladys and the other stenographers sat quietly watching. It seemed to Gladys that he was going to take a nap, right there in front of everyone. As usual, Edgar closed his eyes, loosened his tie, and proceeded to "relax." Leslie settled down next to him. After a few minutes of silence, Edgar's eyelids fluttered and Leslie spoke a few words to his son, ending with instructions to find the body of Miss Graham's nephew. Edgar Cayce then proceeded to describe the boy's body in detail.

Gladys followed the reading carefully, although some of the language was quite unfamiliar, and she became more baffled with every passing moment. During his diagnosis, Edgar used highly unusual phrases, such as "cerebrospinal system" and "perineurial and secondary cardiac [centers]," and then recommended that the child be treated with an electrical device known as the "Abrams oscilloclast," which was to be attached to the patient's "wrist and seventh dorsal."

No matter how foreign the words were to her, Gladys kept writing—she was determined to get it all down. Although the atmosphere was quite businesslike during the trance session, later she realized how truly unusual the experience was. Cayce had not only diagnosed a child's nervous condition in his sleep, but he had prescribed the use of a device manufactured by a person whom most of the medical profession considered a "quack."

That "quack" was Dr. Abrams, a once eminent physician who had studied in London, Paris, Berlin, and Vienna before becoming professor of pathology at a clinic in San Francisco, which eventually became part of the Stanford University Medical School. In 1912, Abrams shocked the medical profession by announcing that the proper manipulation of certain nerve centers in the body could relieve an assortment of ailments generally considered curable only by the knife. Abrams's claims, in effect, supported much of what showed up in Cayce's readings. He caused another furor when he contended that he could manipulate the sex of an unborn child through the use of electrical vibrations on a pregnant woman, and that he could tell whether or not a person was lying by charting a person's "vibrational" level. Abrams, a millionaire many times over because of various electronic devices that he had patented and sold, was completely dismissed by his professional colleagues and died not knowing that a device based on his idea, the "lie detector," would someday be used by nearly every police department in the country. As Gladys later learned, the fact that Abrams, not to mention Cayce, was dismissed as a "crackpot," was probably why Virgil Graham was not given the treatments that Cayce had recommended.

Gladys Davis was the only stenographer present that afternoon who was able to adequately take down what Cayce said. One of the other stenographers admitted to Gladys that she was certain she wouldn't get the job because she was "too shocked" by what went on to take down a single word. Like the others, Gladys typed up two copies of the reading and was asked to give them to Miss Graham, although she hoped that Mr. Cayce would also get to see a copy, and maybe even offer her the job. As Gladys later said, she somehow knew he would. Still, she was pleased and excited when Miss Graham approached her and said that Mr. Cayce wanted to speak to her.

Gladys arrived at the appointed time, and when she entered the studio, Edgar came out of his darkroom drying his brown-stained hands on a towel. Gladys later described the feeling she experienced in his presence as "a lovely sense of renewing an old friendship." Edgar told her that he liked the way she handled the job of taking down the reading and that they needed a full-time secretary. He couldn't describe exactly what the duties would be because he didn't know. But she would probably have to travel. He thought there might be trips to New York and other places. Gladys accepted the job and almost immediately got a glimpse of what the future would hold when Edgar looked at her steadily, with a sparkle in his blue-gray eyes, and said softly, as if reading her mind, "No more nuts and bolts." On September 10, Gladys Davis began what would become her life's work.

Just one week later, on September 17, Arthur Lammers arrived in Selma. Although he had not been impressed with how Tex Rice and Dave Kahn had been handling the stock sales, or with the participation of Alfred Darling, whom he knew to be an alcoholic, he had become increasingly inspired by Cayce's work and wanted to form a partnership. The news that Rice was out of the proposition, and that another of Edgar's contacts, Abraham Rosenberg, was interested in replacing Kahn and Townsend in handling the stock sales, prompted Lammers to come to Selma. He proposed the formation of the Cayce Institute for Psychic Research, funded by himself and others and headed by Edgar Cayce, under whose auspices not only the oil ventures would be operated, but a hospital and publishing company. Lammers stayed a few days, discussing his ideas with Edgar and sitting in on a number of physical readings. Then on September 20, Lammers went to meet with J. T. McConnell and others in Meridian, Texas, before returning to Dayton. Edgar, despite his claim to Gertrude that he was "home for good," went with him.

Lammers's plan gradually developed into the formation of what he called the "Plan of Protected Investment Co." The partners in this endeavor were to be Edgar Cayce, Arthur Lammers, Linden Shroyer, and two others brought in by J. T. McConnell: Madison Byron Wyrick, a middle-aged executive with Western Union in Chicago, and George Klingensmith, a twenty-five-year-old construction engineer from Pennsylvania. Together they would issue ten thousand shares of preferred stock in the new company at $100 per share. The capital would be used to create an endowment for the building of the hospital and a study center, as well as to cover their initial operating expenses. An additional thirty thousand shares of common stock would be issued, twenty thousand of which would go to buy oil leases held by Cayce Petroleum and Penn-Tenn, and then another ten thousand shares designated for what would be called the Cayce Institute for Psychic Research.

In the midst of Edgar's negotiations, Gertrude took charge of training Gladys Davis. First, she asked Gladys to begin the job of collecting and organizing Edgar's readings, and for the next three weeks, helped Gladys practice her transcription skills by dictating from the five or six hundred readings on file. This provided Gladys with ample preparation for the real thing, as it gave her a chance to become familiar with the peculiarities of Edgar's language in trance. Their time together also gave Gladys a chance to get to know Gertrude.

By all accounts, Gladys's initial relationship with Gertrude was strained. The most obvious reason was that Edgar had hired a full-time stenographer when the newly revived Cayce Art Company was barely making enough money to put food on the family table. The fact that Edgar had hired her and then promptly left for Texas did not help matters. There were also, perhaps, more subtle reasons for their strained relations. Gertrude, by nature, was quiet and reserved and was not much interested in life outside of her house, whether it was church socials or garden parties. Gladys, in contrast, was an extrovert. She enjoyed meeting others and talking to everyone involved in Edgar's life, whether it was Texas oilmen, church elders, or Edgar's coterie of Christian Endeavor students. Gertrude, who was now forty-three, had never fully recovered from her three pregnancies and her tuberculosis, which had nearly killed her. She was also beginning to show the first signs of menopause, which may have been prematurely brought on by her poor health. At the age of eighteen, Gladys was young and vibrant, and quite good-looking.

Despite all of this, Gertrude and Gladys did ultimately develop a strong rapport, and their relationship grew to be one that they both treasured. The two of them got to know each other quickly, sharing the stories of their lives, their trials, and their triumphs, with Gertrude taking a motherly interest in Gladys, and Gladys acting as the daughter Gertrude and Edgar had never had. And when the two of them got down to work, Gladys proved her worth immediately. Young and beautiful though she was, she was much more business-minded than any of the Cayces and established procedures that would make the most of the readings. Her plan was to take down the readings in shorthand and later type them up. She also developed a system in which two copies would be made—one for the client and one for the files. It was Gladys's penchant for saving "one for the record" and compiling background material for each trance session that ultimately resulted in the collection of over fourteen thousand readings, and the thousands of letters and other documents, all of which she indexed and cross-referenced, making them that much more useful and valuable to the many doctors and others who subsequently studied them.

Gladys hadn't been at her job three weeks when a letter from Edgar arrived for Gertrude, informing her that he had stopped off in St. Louis—but hadn't the time to write—and was now in Chicago, not Dayton, where he said he would be. He had been on another fund-raising tour, giving readings, talks, and lectures. Edgar told her that he thought he had raised a half million dollars toward the hospital through Lammers and his associates and another $250,000 for drilling more oil wells, and wanted to know if Gertrude would be willing to join him in Dayton. He asked if she could arrange for Hugh Lynn to stay with family friends in Selma to finish out the first half of his junior year, and then join them over the Christmas holidays. He also wanted Gertrude to ask Gladys if she "wanted to be connected to the work all the time," and whether she would come too. Perhaps anticipating the weariness that Gertrude must have felt at receiving this letter, he added, in closing, "Love me, love me [a] whole heap, for I do love you, Gertrude . . . Kiss boys for me. Always, your Edgar."

There was much more Edgar Cayce could have said in this letter, things about which he chose to remain silent. For now, in addition to continuing the type of readings conducted in Dayton on the work, Lammers intended to explore a subject that had only been hinted at before: the possible influence that the stars and planets have on human behavior.

Ruled by Jupiter

The concept of astrology was not entirely new to Edgar and Gertrude. Despite at times feigning ignorance of such a distinctly "nontraditional" Christian subject, they both knew more about astrology than they had previously been willing to admit. Astrology had been the subject of a reading conducted four and a half years earlier, before the oil years, when Edgar was working full-time as a photographer in Selma.

This earlier astrological reading had come about as an indirect result of a request made by the same D. M. Thrash who had piqued Edgar's interest in doing oil readings. In 1919, Thrash wrote Edgar asking for his birth date in order to have his horoscope cast. Early the next year, Edgar and Gertrude received several communications from astrologers telling them that on a particular date—March 19, 1919—Cayce would be able to give a reading of "more interest to mankind" than any other reading he would be able to give during that year. Although Edgar did give a reading on that date, with Gertrude conducting and two trusted friends to witness the reading and take notes, the startling contents of that reading were not revealed to Thrash or to anyone else until Edgar met with Lammers in Dayton. The reason is not hard to understand. Astrology, like the principle of reincarnation, was a subject that challenged Edgar and Gertrude's deep-seated Christian beliefs. To discuss it openly would have opened doors that could not easily be closed.

As Lammers later discovered, the first question put to Cayce in trance on March 19, 1919, was much like the one Ketchum had put to him back in Hopkinsville in 1909: " . . . You will tell us how the psychic work is accomplished through this body . . . " Cayce, in trance, once again stated that "in this [trance] state the conscious mind is under subjugation of the subconscious mind or soul mind . . . It obtains its information from . . . other subconscious minds . . . or minds that have passed into the Beyond . . . What is known to one subconscious mind or soul is known to another, whether conscious of the fact or not."

The consistency between this response and the one given to Dr. Ketchum nine years earlier must have been reassuring to both Edgar and Gertrude. However, Gertrude's next question took them into an entirely new area of investigation. Given that an astrologer had indicated that this day would be an important one, and perhaps intending to put the question of astrology to rest once and for all, Gertrude asked if the planets have anything to do with the ruling of the destiny of men. Cayce replied: "They do."

Edgar then went on to expand upon the subject: "In the beginning, as our own planet, Earth, was set in motion, the placing of other planets began the ruling of the destiny of all matter as created, just as the division of waters was and is ruled by the moon in its path about the Earth . . . The strongest power in the destiny of man is the sun . . . then the closer planets . . . at the time of the birth of the individual." Here, and for the first of many, many times, Cayce—in trance—admonished: "But let it be understood here, [that] no action of any planet or any of the phases of the sun, moon, or any of the heavenly bodies surpass the rule of man's individual willpower."

Cayce then went on to provide an example of astrological influences by elucidating Edgar's own chart. "As in this body here [Edgar Cayce] born March 18, 1877, three minutes past three o'clock, with the sun descending, on the wane, the moon in the opposite side of the Earth—[the] old moon— Uranus at its zenith, hence the body is 'ultra' in its actions . . . Hence [there is] no middle ground for this body: [he is] very good or very bad, very religious or very wicked, very rich or always losing, very much in love or hate, very much given to good works or always doing wrong . . . As to the forces of this body [Edgar Cayce], the 'psychical' is obtained through action of Uranus and of Neptune, always it has been to this body and always will . . . just saved financially and spiritually by the action of great amount of water . . . This body will either be very rich or very poor."

Now, over four years after this previously undisclosed reading, enough time had elapsed that Edgar was willing to reexamine with Lammers its main subject. That Edgar was in the company of people who were truly supportive, as well as being ardent believers in astrology, no doubt made it all the more palatable. And ultimately, it was none other than the great Evangeline Adams—the most respected and famous astrologer of the 1920s—who personally reassured Edgar of the potential worth of the reading.

The brief meeting with Adams took place at Lammers's behest on a short trip he and Edgar made to New York City. By all accounts, Adams was not what Edgar had expected in an astrologer. The gracious and dignified doyenne of New York society lived in a beautiful and elegantly decorated Manhattan town house, the legacy of her illustrious family, who had given the world two signers of the Declaration of Independence and two presidents of the United States. Adams had studied astrology at Boston University, and her clients included opera singer Enrico Caruso; King Edward VII of Great Britain; prizefighter Jack Dempsey; Seymour Cromwell, president of the New York Stock Exchange; and screen star Gloria Swanson.

To Edgar and others who found their way into her book-lined study, the middle-aged Adams, with wire-rim glasses and a conservative black dress, appeared quite scholarly, almost professorial. Adams no doubt told Edgar some of the illustrious history of astrology, naming King Solomon, Plato, and Napoleon as practitioners, and showing Edgar the circular charts on which horoscope calculations were made. She then obtained the date, time, and place of Edgar's birth, and retreated to her study, where, for the next forty minutes she consulted the tools of her trade: a globe on which to pinpoint the latitude and longitude of Christian County, Kentucky, and a thick, leather-bound volume called an ephemeris, which she used to calculate the position of stars and other celestial bodies at the time of his birth. Using this information, she proceeded to draw a circular chart showing the position of the planets at 3 P.M. on March 18, 1877.

Edgar reported being quite impressed by the horoscope she gave him, for it was similar to that of the previous reading he had given on himself on March 19, 1919. And as Edgar later reported, much of what she said would later "prove to be true." There was only one thing about the horoscope that he found disturbing. "Resign yourself never to achieve [complete] success or to be [materially] happy," she told him.

Exactly when Lammers first broached the subject of astrological readings with Edgar is not clear. All that is known for certain is that on October 11, 1923, within just three days of Edgar's return to Dayton, he gave his first tailor-made "horoscope" reading for Lammers. Linden Shroyer conducted the reading at the Phillips Hotel, just as he had during Edgar's visit in June. Shroyer's exact words were not recorded, but it can be assumed that he asked about the astrological influences that acted upon Arthur Lammers.

The Source didn't hesitate in answering the questions. In trance, Cayce described Lammers as "one of strong body, yet gross with the force of a secular nature," one of "strong will and self-reliant," and "one whose destiny lies in success nearer the middle portion of his life on this plane." Cayce went on to say that Lammers was "ruled by Jupiter" with "Venus in the eleventh House," and that he was well "balanced" to deal with individuals whose birthday comes in March—as did Edgar Cayce's.

This latest reading again supported the concept that the stars and planets influenced human behavior. To Lammers, already a great believer in astrology, this would have come as no surprise. For many other people around Edgar, however, the concept of astrology would have been difficult, if not impossible, to grasp and accept. But according to the Source, the study of astrology had been around a very long time. When asked who were the first people in the world to use astrology, Cayce responded: "Many, many thousands of years ago. The first record [is] that recorded in Job, who lived before Moses . . . "

In another reading for Lammers, the Source challenged skeptics who would dismiss the notion of astrology by posing a question: "Astronomy is considered a science and astrology [is thought to be] foolishness. [But] who is correct? One holds that because of the position of the earth, the sun, the planets—they are balanced one with another in some manner, some form— yet that they have nothing to do with man's life or . . . the emotions of the 'physical being' in the earth. Then why and how do the effects of the sun . . . influence [life on earth] and not affect [man and] man's emotions?" In yet another session, for a twenty-year-old woman who came to Cayce for a physical reading, the Source stated that not only do the planets affect an individual's emotions, but that the moon affects the physical body: "The sympathetic nervous system has much to do with the changes of the lunar conditions."

However basic Cayce's pronouncements might have appeared to Lammers, the information about astrology that ultimately came through Cayce was a great deal more complex than even Evangeline Adams could have anticipated. As would later become apparent, not only did the power of a person's free will play the most prominent role in determining how their life unfolded, it was next to impossible for anyone without the gifts that Cayce possessed to accurately describe an individual's personality traits, tendencies, talents, weaknesses, and future challenges based solely upon his or her birth

date and hour of delivery. There were, at the least, other complicating factors to be considered. For example, in many astrological readings that Cayce
was later to give, the Source suggested that the "soul" of a newborn sometimes arrived into the body at a time different from the physical birth of the
child. In some instances, that arrival was considerably earlier than the birth,
other times it was much later. In a reading done for an eighteen-year-old student, Cayce said: "There was . . . thirty to thirty-five minutes difference in
birth physical and birth spiritual." Another reading, given for a college student, highlighted the difficulties that such a difference could produce: "The
spiritual and physical birth varied [a] little, there was the physical under one
sign and the spiritual under another. Hence the doubts that often arise, from
an astrological view."

In most horoscope readings, Cayce emphasized the specific influence that
various planets exerted on the individual. The role of the constellations,
however, such as Cancer, Leo, or Virgo, was considered relatively insignificant. Thus the Cayce readings suggested that the signs of the zodiac do not
play as fundamental a role in one's astrological influences as generally believed, in sharp contrast to the popular approach, which says that the "sign"
a person is born under is the main determining factor in shaping an individual's personality.

In a reading given for a thirty-three-year-old salesman, Cayce explicitly
stated: "As to those influences of the constellations . . . in the life of this entity, these are merely the 'wavering' influences in the life, and not those directing forces ever present in the inner soul of this entity. These we find in
opposition to much that is at present taught or given in the earth plane."

Yet another complication that arises in the readings for students of astrology was revealed in comments that Cayce made suggesting that there
were flaws in the Egyptian system of astrology, which is most prevalently
used. The "tropical" or Egyptian system of astrology, which was most commonly used by astrologers such as Evangeline Adams, is almost thirty degrees different from the "sidereal" or Persian system advocated by Cayce,
which then, as now, was the less popular means of casting astrological charts.

To further complicate matters for astrology students, Cayce asserted that
the influence of the planets was not necessarily what was popularly understood by most astrologers. As in standard astrology, Mars was associated by
Cayce with high energy and anger, but the Source consistently emphasized
the planet's "internal" influence rather than the "external" behavior by
which it is popularly understood by most astrologers. For an eight-year-old
girl born in Norfolk, Virginia, the Source warned: "Be angry but sin not." In
a reading for a thirty-nine-year-old housewife, also under the Mars influ-

ence, Cayce stated: "Righteous anger is a virtue. He that has no temper is very weak. But he who controls not his temper is much worse." Here, as elsewhere in the astrological readings, constructive growth through control of the human will was being highlighted.

Perhaps the greatest anomaly in Cayce's astrological information was his view of the influence of the planet Saturn. The ringed planet has historically represented a love of tradition and an opposition to change. In contrast, the key words that Cayce related to Saturn were "sudden" or "violent" change. "In Saturn we find the sudden or violent changes—those influences and environs that do not grow, as it were, but are sudden by that of change of circumstances materially, or by activities . . . of others." While most people might look upon Saturn as a negative or malevolent influence, Cayce went on to encourage his subject in the same reading by adding: "These are testing periods of thy endurance, of thy patience, of thy love of truth, harmony, and the spirit that faileth not." Again, constructive growth through control of the human will was the defining factor.

Uranus, in traditional astrology, has been described as the planet of insight, mysticism, originality, and change. The readings support the mystical aspect, but distinguish this from spirituality and suggest its influence is one of extremes: "[At] times very beautiful in character—at other [times] very ugly." In another reading he said: "The entity . . . finds periods when it is . . . to the mountaintops and again at the depths of despair." In a third, Cayce said: "There will also be periods when . . . the entity would be called lucky at any game of chance, yet there will be also periods when . . . it would be practically impossible for the entity to gain through games of chance."

Like Uranus, Neptune—which is linked to water—was also related to mysticism. "From Neptune we find that being close to waters . . . is very well . . . and this also gives those abilities of the mystic." This theme was repeated in a second reading for an individual purported to be under the influence of Neptune, for whom Cayce said: "Dwelling near large bodies of water . . . will be the natural elements for the development giving rise to . . . mystic abilities." Given this mystical connection evident in Uranus and Neptune, it is not surprising that these two planets figured prominently in Edgar's own 1919 horoscope reading.

Pluto was not actually discovered until 1930, seven years after Cayce did his first horoscope reading. But prior to its discovery and subsequent naming, Cayce made reference to a planet that he called Septimus, which was clearly a reference to Pluto, whose influence astrologers have not been able to agree upon. In a reading that Cayce gave for a Jewish businessman, he suggested that Septimus had an adverse or challenging influence, but was ultimately for constructive growth: "These make for that influence as has been of sudden changes in . . . relationships as respecting those of kinship and . . . physical or business relations. Yet these adversities may be used or applied in the experience of the entity as stepping-stones for soul's development."

The readings Edgar began with Lammers, like hundreds of others that would later become known as "life readings," suggested the very complex nature and difficulty of charting astrological influences. But the greatest challenges, and the most significant revelations were still to come. Cayce's astrological readings, like those of regular astrologers, discussed the influence planets have on human beings. However, no professional astrologers—not even Evangeline Adams—discussed *why* they have an influence. The answer that the Source gave was perhaps the strangest and most difficult aspect of any of the readings and would have shocked even the most veteran of astrologers.

In the fourth Cayce reading on astrology, conducted by Shroyer, the Source stated that the "influence as is given by many of those [professional astrologers] in . . . the earth plane is defective [in that] many of the forces of each [planet] are felt more through the experience by the entity's 'sojourn' upon those planets." Cayce would again make reference to this in a later reading for a thirty-year-old secretary: "It should be understood . . . that the sojourning of the soul in that 'environ,' rather than the position [of the planet] makes for the greater influence in the experience of an entity or body in any given plane . . . As we have indicated, it is not so much that an entity is influenced because the Moon is in Aquarius . . . but rather because those positions in the heavens are from the entity having been in that sojourn as a soul . . . not as a physical body as known in the Earth, but as a body adaptable to the environs of Jupiter: for there's life there—not as known in Earth!"

By these and other life readings, the Source appeared to be suggesting that the soul of an individual could actually "reside" on another planet and, as Cayce later elucidated, "in other dimensions." This additional information helped to clarify some of what the Source had said in the first readings for Lammers, back in October. In response to the question of whether or not the soul ever dies, Cayce said: "May be banished from the Maker, [but] not [by] death." The next question for the Source was what it meant by banishment of a soul from its Maker, and why an "entity" or individual might chose to be "banished." The Source answered: "out his own salvation . . . the entity or individual banished itself, or its soul [from Earth to Saturn]."

The message coming through Cayce suggested that the planet Saturn was a place not unlike the Roman Catholic vision of purgatory. In these and

The only available photographs of Thomas Jefferson and Sarah Cayce, Edgar's grandparents, circa 1865. Edgar worshipped his grandfather, who also had "the gift of second sight," and his grandmother taught him not to be afraid of his special talent.

Edgar's parents, Leslie B. and Carrie Elizabeth Cayce. Although some members of Edgar's extended family believed he had "the Devil in Him," his parents never discouraged him from developing his psychic abilities.

Edgar Cayce and other students at the Beverly Academy, not far from Cayce's child-hood home in Hopkinsville, Kentucky. Edgar had been considered "strange" by classmates at a school he'd attended earlier, but students at this Academy, consisting mostly of members of his extended family, were kinder. His formal education ended here, in the eighth grade.

Gertrude Evans and her cousin, Edith Estella Smith (wearing glasses). Edgar was immediately struck by the fifteen-year-old's beauty when he met her; the two fell in love during his many visits to her family home, known as The Hill.

A youthful Cayce, with Smith cousins on either side of him, and Gertrude Evans's brothers behind him.

Gertrude and Edgar as newlyweds. The couple was married on June 17, 1903, after a long and sometimes turbulent engagement. "She didn't give up on him when he would have preferred that she do so, and when she had every reason to want to," said one family friend.

A self-portrait of Edgar, done at the Russell Brothers studio in Anniston, Alabama, which he sent as a photo postcard to Gertrude when his work there kept them apart. Despite his lack of formal education, Edgar became an expert photographer. The price list is from Cayce's own studio, which he later opened in Selma, Alabama.

1916 ?
(over)

HANG THIS UP
PRICE LIST

FINISHING KODAK PICTURES

Developing any size roll 10c

Developing Film Packs.................. 15c

PRINTING

Any size up to 2 1-4 by 4 1-4......3c each

2 1-4 by 4 1-4 up to 4 1-4 by 6 1-2, 4c each

Post Cards........................ 5c each

Enlargements....................25c up

Best Results Obtained By
Practical Workmen

"LET US FINISH YOUR SNAPS"

CAYCE
ART COMPANY

21 1-2 Broad St.   Selma, Alabama

Dr. Wesley H. Ketchum, a homeopath from Hopkinsville, was never intimidated by the daring medical recommendations set forth in Cayce's readings. Although the "psychic partnership" Cayce formed with Ketchum ended badly, the doctor is generally credited with being the first person to bring public validation to Cayce's work.

Edgar with the Bible study class from Selma's First Christian Church. Edgar (center) was a passionate student of religion, and although he joined many different church groups, none welcomed him with such open arms, or gave him so many lasting friendships, as the church in Selma. Alfred Butler is seated next to Cayce, on the right.

Although a trance reading said a Jewish man would figure prominently in his life, Edgar didn't grasp its meaning until he was introduced to David Kahn, who became a lifelong friend and business partner. Here, Lieutenant Kahn is pictured shortly before being shipped overseas to fight in the First World War.

Perhaps the most exciting—and most frustrating—adventure Cayce ever embarked upon was his decade-long, on-again, off-again attempt to prospect for oil in Texas. Here he is pictured with partners after their well had been sabotaged by a rival company.

Edgar Evans, Gertrude, Edgar, and Hugh Lynn, in 1922. Edgar was spending a great deal of time on the road, but this photograph, taken by Edgar's father, captured him during a rare visit at home in Selma.

Apart from Edgar himself, no one contributed more to the seriousness and professionalism of Cayce's work than Gladys Davis. Hired as his secretary in 1923, Gladys stayed with Cayce for the rest of his life, and in later readings was revealed to be Edgar's "soul mate."

Already a prosperous pair of Wall Street stockbrokers when Dave Kahn introduced them to Edgar, Morton and Edwin Blumenthal grew even wealthier through their association with Cayce, and provided the financial backing for the Cayce Hospital and Atlantic University. Beyond their leadership and corporate abilities, they also brought a genuine enthusiasm to the work and had a "burning desire to understand the secrets of the universe."

The dream that consumed most of Edgar's adult life—to build a place where physicians trained in the medical practices suggested by his readings could treat the ill—was finally realized in the construction of the Cayce Hospital in Virginia Beach in 1928.

Dr. Thomas House, seen here in his hospital office, was the chief resident, and related to Cayce by marriage.

Edgar in the office of his Arctic Crescent home in Virginia Beach, where he spent the last years of his life. Cayce transformed what was a dilapidated old house into a place suitable to receive his many visitors and to host the annual Congress of the A.R.E.

Edgar, Gertrude, and Gladys, outside the Cayce home in Virginia Beach, in 1940. Despite a rocky beginning to their relationship, Gladys and Gertrude ultimately formed a strong bond, and both were a great source of strength to Edgar.

Cayce loved fishing and had ample opportunity to do so in the lake near his Arctic Crescent home. Here he is seen with a floating tree he rigged up himself, which he could move to keep himself in shade all afternoon. Apart from tending his garden, fishing was his favorite pastime during his final years in Virginia Beach.

other astrological readings, the greater truth suggested by the trance information was made clear. The purpose of an individual's sojourn on various planets, including Earth, was a means to an end: to prepare an individual, through "soul development," to meet the Creator.

Edgar and others naturally desired to know how "sojourns" on different planets affected man. A later reading would provide an important insight, which would later be discussed at length: "Each planetary influence vibrates at a different rate . . . An entity entering that influence enters that vibration, not necessary that he change[s], but it is by the grace of God that he may." In a second reading, Cayce described this influence in another way: "The shadows of those things from the sojourns of this entity in Mercury [influence] the very relationships and activity of the entity . . . Just as the entity's attending this or that . . . place of learning, would make for a parlance peculiar unto itself. Even though individuals may study the same line of thought, one attending Harvard, another Yale, another . . . the University of Arizona, they each would carry with them the vibrations created by their very activity in those environs."

In another reading, Cayce explained how these sojourns could bring about variations in people, despite their common family, heritage, or the environment in which they lived: "The sojourn of a soul in its environ about the Earth, or in this solar system, gives the factors that are often found in individuals . . . that are of the same parentage, in the same environ. Yet one might be a genius and the other a fool." Vibration, Cayce would point out later, determines the "environment" that exists on another planet or in another dimension, in much the same way as it governs color, sound, and the "substance" of matter on Earth. "For it is not strange that music, color, vibration are all a part of the planets, just as the planets are a part and a pattern of the whole universe."

According to Cayce, ultimately, an individual's task was to use his or her free will to return to God, the Father. "First there is the spirit, then soul . . . then mind with its various modifications and with its various incentives, with its various ramifications . . . and the will, the balance in the forces that may make all or lose all [Man must pass] through all the stages of development until the will is lost in Him and he becomes one with the Father." As Edgar well knew, this, in a large sense, was the same message as put forth in the Lord's Prayer, that "Thy will be done."

27.

A Monk in His
Third Appearance

Accepting astrology as an influence on human behavior was a formidable challenge for Edgar and Gertrude. But what came next would test them more than anything they had previously encountered, for at the end of Lammers's first life reading came a brief, matter-of-fact statement that added yet another dimension to their understanding of man's place in the universe. According to the Source, this was Lammers's "third appearance on this plane. He was once a monk."

It is not hard to imagine that this simple statement caught everyone in the room off guard, for Lammers had never been a monk. This was, as both Edgar and Lammers knew, a clear reference to reincarnation, a belief that was even further removed from accepted Christian theology than astrology. Nearly a week elapsed before they asked the Source for an explanation, perhaps because Edgar was nervous about what they would learn. When they finally did ask more questions, the Source confirmed that Lammers had appeared "upon this [earthly] plane" three times, and that previously he had appeared as a monk. The Source went on to say: "In this [incarnation] we see glimpses in the life itself of the entity as was shown in the monk . . . The body [is] only the vehicle ever of that spirit and soul . . . through all times and ever remains the same."

Two days after giving this interpretation, the Source again introduced the topic of reincarnation in a physical reading Cayce gave for himself. "The soul forces of . . . [Edgar Cayce] are developed beyond those . . . of the normal bodies with which this body may meet. Hence the insight of the real soul or elemental forces of every question that may be presented to this body through manifestations of other minds or souls. For this soul has seen its seventh manifestation upon this physical or earth plane."

In retrospect, it is hard to imagine that Lammers would not have immediately gone back to question the Source about this latest pronouncement. And it is a cause for wonder: given the estimated two thousand readings Cayce had given since leaving Hopkinsville, why had it taken twenty-odd years for the Source to have addressed this subject. Though the Source had hinted at the existence of reincarnation in readings conducted in 1911 and 1922, the references were sufficiently vague that they were overlooked. Nor would the subject have been embraced by Cayce himself, for the concept of reincarnation had always seemed to him to be, as Edgar's Aunt Lulu would surely have agreed, "the work of the Devil." The latest readings, however, could not be ignored. The reason the Source was now making such reference was likely the same reason for the astrological information coming through Cayce: Lammers was not only a believer in astrology, but also in reincarnation.

Despite Edgar's obvious reticence in pursuing this topic, the Source was not about to let it go. Four days after the Source noted that Edgar Cayce's soul had seen its "seventh manifestation," a physical reading was conducted for Penn-Tenn partner George Klingensmith, in which the Source said that Klingensmith's "soul and spirit developed beyond the normal . . . for [he] has been four times upon this earth plane."

Again, Edgar managed to ignore this statement. But the Source was apparently determined to get their attention. Shortly after this reading, in one that Edgar, Lammers, Klingensmith, and Shroyer had requested to seek business advice, the Source admonished them to make a success of the work they were doing because all four of them had previously worked together for "destructive purposes." Edgar was clearly still reluctant to probe for a further explanation of this statement, but two weeks later, he would allow Linden Shroyer to ask the next logical question: "Give the name and profession . . . of each of the appearances on this plane of each of these four individuals." The response was not one of those readings cut short with, "we are through," but rather suggested that this kind of direct query about past lives was exactly what the Source had long been waiting to be asked.

The reading stated that Shroyer had lived in the golden age of the Norsemen, and before that in the Persian army. Klingensmith's previous incarnation was at the time of Louis XV, and before that during the Grecian wars, when he was killed by Alexander the Great. Lammers had been Hector during the Trojan wars, and then a monk in Spain. The list of Edgar Cayce's incarnations was the most lengthy, and included a soldier in the vicinity of Dayton, Ohio, and a settler in Jamestown, Virginia. Before that he was in France at the time of Richelieu. Previous to that he was a chemist in Greece studying under Aristotle, and then, going backward in time, lived in the "plains country" of Arabia, where the Source said that his human remains could still be found in a cave $7\frac{1}{4}$ miles from a city called Shushtar. Perhaps Edgar's most impressive incarnation described in this reading was his second, in Egypt, when he was reported to be the high priest Ra Ta, who—according to the Source—was cast out of the Pharaoh's court. Finally, in his first incarnation, the Source harkened back to the creation of man: "when the morning stars sang together and the 'sons of God' came together and spread the news of the glory of the coming [of man]."

It is not known if Edgar leaked news of the life readings to Gertrude and Gladys at this point. Based upon circumstantial evidence, it is unlikely, for his notes and letters home urging them to come to Dayton were unusually terse. Perhaps Edgar himself didn't fully grasp the significance of what was coming through him, or more likely, the subject was too volatile to discuss in a letter. As he knew from the astrological readings, small doors could open into large rooms. However, regardless of what he chose to tell Gertrude and Gladys at this point, the impact that the readings had on him was dramatic, for he had lost all interest in returning to Selma and the life he had led there. Except for short visits back to see friends over the years, he would never return to Alabama, and all business matters concerning the studio would be turned over to his assistant, J. B. Williams, who eventually took over the studio altogether.

On November 14, 1923, at around noon, Gertrude, Gladys, and Edgar Evans arrived by train in Cincinnati. Edgar met them at the station and accompanied them to the Phillips Hotel in Dayton, where they would stay until their furniture arrived and they could move into a small efficiency apartment on East Fifth Street. Eager to have his "team" get started, readings were resumed the very day of their arrival, when Gladys recorded a 3:30 P.M. physical reading. Gertrude, perhaps wanting to show support for Edgar or help Gladys get established, sat in on the reading, which Linden Shroyer conducted.

Astrology was not mentioned in this reading, but the subject was undoubtedly raised that same afternoon when Gertrude and Gladys began to review the transcripts of the last month of Edgar's work in Dayton. To Edgar's surprise, their response was not entirely negative, although they too would be in no hurry to request readings of this kind for themselves. Hugh Lynn was not asked for his input because he hadn't accompanied them to Dayton. He had stayed behind to complete the first school term of his junior year in Selma and was living with a classmate, David Pierson, whose father knew the Cayces from church. By previous arrangement, Hugh Lynn would join the rest of his family in Dayton during the Christmas holiday.

Five-year-old Edgar Evans was the first member of the Cayce family to receive a life reading, which was conducted on November 19. Edgar himself, of course, had received information regarding his own astrological influences and previous incarnations, but a dedicated life reading—one whose single purpose was to define and describe a person's present incarnation in relation to previous lives—had never been conducted. Perhaps, even then, Edgar secretly feared what the readings might reveal.

The information that came through was typical of the previous readings in that it outlined various planetary influences and previous incarnations. The reading suggested that Edgar Evans would seem "strange to others" because of his innate knowledge or grasp of mechanics and chemistry. Four previous incarnations were mentioned, including ones in Germany and India, but specifics were not given. The Source went on to give parental advice and warnings as to various illnesses or injuries to watch out for, based on astrological influences, and specific dates during which the child would be prone to have a "fire"-related accident. There was nothing extraordinary about the reading except a brief and rather curious reference that "there were only two other souls upon this earth plane sent [at the moment Edgar Evans's soul incarnated.]" The suggestion was that Edgar Evans was unique in some, as yet, undisclosed way. The reading ended with the mysterious statement: "one in whom the many, in many spheres, will dread . . . [his] coming." Edgar and Gertrude, at this point, chose not to probe the Source on what aspect of Edgar Evans's previous lives "the many" might have to fear, or where he had been and what he had done on Earth—or on any other plane—before arriving in the Cayce household.

Gladys was the next person to subject herself to a life reading, obtaining the first of fifty-five such readings she would receive over her lifetime. She remembered how shaken she was by what came through—she was not only present when the reading was conducted, she had to record it herself. Not since the day she transcribed her very first reading in Selma had she felt so nervous. Gladys watched tensely as Edgar loosened his tie and lay down on the couch. Linden Shroyer conducted.

First, the Source provided Gladys with a description of various planetary influences, foremost among them that of Venus, Mercury, and Mars. He then gave a long list of Gladys's gifts and virtues, including this description: "One in whom there will be, in the future, little of the earthly ills for itself, though one that will lend much to the assistance in the earthly ills of others." He also said: "One who, with others, will draw much of the more beautiful things of the earth plane about them, and one to whom all obstacles become the stepping-stones for higher development in this present earth plane."

Unlike previous readings, which had provided a few single sentences regarding past lives, Gladys was given three paragraphs on each of her former incarnations. Her past lives numbered four and included a stint in the court of Louis the XV, when she was a member of the royal family and had been seduced by the Duke of York, bearing him a child. Before that she had incarnations in Persia, Egypt, and at one time lived in the house of the ruler of a place called "Alta," which existed—according to the Source—"ten thousand years before the Prince of Peace came."

The information revealed in this reading brought to light the importance of past-life experiences in contributing to the emotional responses, the trusts and the distrusts, likes and dislikes of the current incarnation. For instance, in reference to Gladys's life among the French royalty, the Source said: "The first change came in the seventeenth year of the life . . . with the meeting and betrothal of this individual to that of the Duke of York [which] brought to the individual that in the inmost soul of the distrust of . . . the opposite sex, and the body then became an inmate of the confined walls, where the rest of [her] life was spent, and only lived to the age in years then of thirty." About her time in Persia, the Source added: "[Gladys] was taken by the invading forces . . . and in this [she now has] the aversion to those cutting instruments, for in that manner the bodily destruction came."

Gladys was quite stunned by the reading. As strange as it seemed, the Source had said things she intuitively knew to be true. She did have a fear of being cut, and in fact had been afraid of knives since she was a small child. Her little brother had discovered this fear and taunted her with sharp instruments, chasing her all over the house with them. She couldn't bear to use even a kitchen knife, and if she did, she invariably cut herself. Gladys also, it would be revealed, had a fear of men.

The trance information that the Source provided Gladys set the pace for all future life readings in their scope of detail and length. Given that Linden Shroyer was present for all of these, it was not surprising that he requested and received a life reading on the same day that Gladys received hers. Linden's reading revealed something of the process that Cayce underwent when obtaining past-life information. Cayce—in trance—actually counted back in time, almost as if he were speaking aloud while flipping through the pages of a history book. This time he added a comment: "Awful day for those born in July 1915"—a reference to a flu epidemic that swept the country that month.

The Source stated that Shroyer's present incarnation was his fifth, and went on to detail each appearance. Failure to exercise his free will was highlighted as Shroyer's greatest challenge, often leaving him in the position, the Source said, of a human "pincushion." Cayce ended this reading with more advice, as had been given in the reading for Edgar Evans: "Keep the will force in the way that will lead to the Faith of the fathers."

Edgar would continue to give one or two physical readings a day. And while Edgar and Gertrude had still not done their own life readings, Shroyer and others were already stepping up for more. A reading given for George Klingensmith revealed that he was "one whose moral forces are beyond reproach." An incarnation during the reign of Louis XV—which was, coincidentally, at the same time as Gladys Davis's—and his life during the Trojan wars, were described in minute detail. Knowing that he had lived other lives too, Klingensmith must have been disappointed to have the reading suddenly end with "We are through for the present." In closing, however, the Source indicated that Klingensmith indeed had other incarnations that were perhaps equally or more relevant to his current life situation, but that these, the Source said, could not be disclosed: "[We] are forbidden here to give more at present." The Source clearly stated that there was actually much more that could be told to Klingensmith, but as Edgar himself would soon learn, the determining factor for when the information would be disclosed lay not only with the Source, but with the recipient of the life reading. In other words, "When the student is ready, the lesson will be taught."

Finally, on December 5, 1923, Gertrude summoned the courage to request her own life reading. During this—her fifth documented reading—the Source said that Gertrude's "soul" had waited several hours after her birth to enter her physical body. Though her mother had technically given birth in the early morning, Gertrude's soul was alleged not to have entered her body until late afternoon. Edgar apparently found this point quite humorous and later chided Gertrude by saying that she had waited until the last possible moment to incarnate because she knew "what a hard time she had ahead of her."

At age forty-three, Gertrude must have been pleased to hear the Source's next statement, that "the greater force in this life, and the greater understanding, will come in the later days upon this plane." However, any joy she received at being given this information would have been dulled by the remark that followed. "There will be three good years . . . [possibly] four, [when] . . . the greater blessings will be upon this life in this present plane." The Source went on to spend a disproportionately large amount of time explaining astrological influences upon her, and then briefly listed three previous lives. Her most recent incarnation was in the French courts, when Charles II lived in exile, and Louis XIV was still a child. As revealed in a follow-up reading, her name had been Lurline, and she was involved in many court-related intrigues as a royal courtesan. Before that, Gertrude lived in ancient Greece, and prior to that, "in the land of the Nomads in the [Egyptian] hill country" during the reign of the first pharaohs. In a follow-up reading these "nomads in the hill country" were said to be Bedouins, and she was described as a beautiful dancer.

Gertrude was no doubt as surprised and mystified by her life reading as Gladys had been. The thought that she, a Kentucky-born housewife, had once been a courtesan in the French courts was a difficult concept to accept. But there was at least one element of the information that caught her attention. Lurline was the same name she had given to her most cherished childhood doll. Gertrude also responded to the notion that she had been a dancer, for as a youth she spent her free time "dancing" in the woods, imagining herself performing before large audiences, though in fact she had never been to a dance or seen a stage performance other than those pictured in books.

Having now given more than twelve life readings, it would seem only natural that Edgar himself should receive one. He still resisted, perhaps because he was frightened of what he might hear. Given the strange events of his childhood—in which he was visited by an angel—and his own growing realization that he was somehow "selected" to be a messenger or communicator of powers beyond those of normal men, it wouldn't have come as any great surprise to learn that he had been Moses or one of the biblical prophets. His life until this point had been enough of a challenge. The prospect of being told that he could be some kind of modern-day Messiah would present unimagined difficulties. As the Source itself had said in an early reading, "He is thought [by others to be] crazy enough anyway!" In light of Edgar's fears, it came as no surprise that the next life reading was conducted for Hugh Lynn, who wasn't present to protest.

After a standard preamble, the Source said that Hugh Lynn possessed a powerful will or self-determination that would "bring much physical and financial success." The Source described him as "one with the affliction of Saturn, under conjunction of Mercury and Mars, [which] has the affliction in fire and firearms to the detriment of the body." Further, it stated that Hugh Lynn was "well balanced in body and mind," and was "one whose life-love will enter after years of maturity." The Source suggested that he had a deep love of nature and the outdoors, a mathematical mind, an inclination to defend "personal principles at any cost." Vocational advice was also given: "[Hugh Lynn is] one whose greater forte will lie in that of [a] writer, composer, historian, or compiler of data."

According to the list of six incarnations that the Source provided, Hugh Lynn had made an appearance in England, where he was a monk during the days of Alfred the Great. His name, Olaf Ericson, the Source said, could be found in records made by him at that time. Hugh Lynn had also been a knight in the Crusades, the leader of an invading force who carried the banner of "Him who was the giver of perfect gifts." Far more significant to Edgar—who already feared what the Source might reveal about his own incarnations—was information about Hugh Lynn's coming "in the days when the Prince of Peace walked by the seashore, [when he] answered the call, and was one of those followers . . . who brought his brother to the Master." His name was Andrew, one of Christ's disciples. The Source went on to describe an incarnation in Egypt and said that his physical remains could still be found in the north corner of one of the great pyramids. His earliest incarnation placed Hugh Lynn on earth during the same period as the one described in his father's physical reading: "when the forces of the Universe came together, when there was upon the waters the sound of the coming together . . . when the morning stars sang . . . and over the face of the waters there was the voice of the glory of the coming of the plane for man's dwelling."

As can be imagined, Edgar and Gertrude were both mystified and gratified by the reading. On one hand, they couldn't help but feel honored to have a son who, as the reading boldly stated, had "walked by the seashore" with the Master. The puzzle, of course, was what he and Gertrude and the others should do with the information. Unsure exactly what to do, or even whether to believe this startling new information, the decision was made to do nothing. No further questions about Hugh Lynn's past lives were asked, nor was the Source queried about the most perplexing question of all: why a soul who had helped found the Christian church had been reborn two thousand years later in Bowling Green, Kentucky, as the son of a struggling photographer and his twenty-seven-year-old housewife.

Edgar would do four more life readings before the Christmas holidays. By this time, the lives of Edgar, his family, and Gladys, had undergone a remarkable change, due not just to the new type of readings, but to the family's lack of income. Instead of receiving a December check from J. B. Williams, who had taken over the Selma studio, Edgar received hundreds of dollars in bills, for business and tax debts Leslie had failed to pay on the Cayce Art Company while Edgar was in Texas. And although Edgar had given thirty-four medical readings since coming to Dayton, the vast majority had been for friends and family of the people around him, for which he was not compensated. Nor had Edgar received compensation for giving life readings. Though Lammers had pledged to support him, he hadn't received a single check. As Edgar told his family back in Hopkinsville, Christmas, this year, was going to be "very thin."

The little money that the Cayce family had saved up to that point had gone to move Gertrude, Gladys, Edgar Evans, and their belongings to Dayton. Edgar and Gertrude's resources were so meager that Gladys hadn't been paid since before her arrival. Gertrude had been forced to use the last remaining gold coin from her dowry to raise cash to pay the train fare to bring Hugh Lynn home on Christmas Eve.

Until this time, Edgar and Gertrude had tried to shield Hugh Lynn from their growing financial concerns, but the desperation of their situation became apparent when Hugh Lynn arrived at the station. He had already begun to suspect from their letters that the family had depleted its resources and that Edgar's great benefactor, Arthur Lammers, had not come through with his promised support. Now, at the train station, in the midst of a snowstorm that had raged through the night and brought traffic to a halt, only Edgar was at the depot to meet Hugh Lynn. The rest of the family, as Hugh Lynn later learned, wasn't at the station to meet him because they had no winter coats. Neither did his father. When Hugh Lynn gave Edgar a great hug at the station, he heard the crackle of paper under his father's thin cotton jacket. To buffer himself against the freezing temperatures, Edgar had stuffed newspaper in his sleeves and under his coat, as John Latham had taught him to do back in Hopkinsville. Hugh Lynn thought his father looked gaunt and tired.

Edgar did his best to avoid his son's questions for the sole reason that he didn't want to burden Hugh Lynn with something he was powerless to do anything about. But Hugh Lynn soon learned the extent of the family's predicament. Although Edgar himself didn't know it yet, Lammers Photo Products had lost its largest account, the National Cash Register Company of Dayton, due to a disagreement between Lammers and the son of NCR's founder, Fred Patterson. The Lammers's company, which was already overextended by its acquisition of other smaller printing companies, had gone into a financial tailspin resulting in a costly lawsuit. Edgar himself only suspected the depth of Lammers's financial problems when he received a letter from Joseph Long in Texas saying that one of Lammers's checks had been returned for insufficient funds.

"Muddie," as Hugh Lynn still affectionately called his mother, had done her best to make the most of what she had on hand for the Christmas holidays. Upon Hugh Lynn's arrival, she prepared a sparse but delicious dinner. There was one chicken for the five of them to share. Hugh Lynn remembered the chicken being small enough that he could cup one of his hands around the entire bird. Yet, despite the meager portions being doled out by his father, Edgar, Gertrude, and Gladys were in high spirits.

"Excitement" was in the air, Hugh Lynn later reported, and the reason became clear when Gladys and the others began discussing the new kind of readings that the Source was giving, which she considered the most extraordinary "Christmas presents" that any of them could have received. Although no one—including Edgar himself—was entirely convinced of the truth of the information that was coming through, all were convinced that some major breakthrough had been made, and that the work would never again be confined to simply giving physical diagnoses and business-related readings. It was then—while the dinner dishes were being cleared—that Hugh Lynn was given his Christmas present: the life reading that had been conducted on his behalf on December 10.

At first, Hugh Lynn was confused, for he had never heard the word "reincarnation" before. Nor did he understand the purported connection between the movement of the planets and human behavior. As he studied his own life reading and came to the part about Andrew, the disciple of Christ, Hugh Lynn's confusion became disbelief, then anger, and finally, outright disgust. He didn't just intellectually disagree with his own life reading, he had a visceral aversion to reading it. By the end of the evening, when the family traditionally decorated the tree and left for evening vespers, Hugh Lynn couldn't contain himself long enough to sit in any one place for more than a few minutes. He demanded that no further readings of this kind be conducted and that no one in the family mention that they had ever been done. As he himself later reported, he felt as if his world "was crashing down around him."

28.

Karmic Debt and
the First Cause

Despite Hugh Lynn's initial reaction to his Christmas present, and the fact that he kept the details of his own life reading a secret for many years, he would later make penetrating studies of these new readings and ultimately embrace them more than Edgar, Gertrude, Gladys, or any of the others. In a 1949 letter addressed to the general membership of the A.R.E.— the Association for Research and Enlightenment, the institution most responsible for carrying on his father's legacy—Hugh Lynn pointed out what he came to believe made Edgar Cayce's life readings unique and valuable in the larger context of spiritualist writings and research on the subject.

"[Reincarnation] had been here in the form of Eastern teachings, Theosophy, and the Rosicrucians [for thousands of years]," Hugh Lynn wrote. "But what was different about Dad's material was the practical application of it for the individual. It wasn't just theoretical . . . There was a [deep and abiding] relationship between one life and another, and the talents and the abilities and the faults and all the emotional factors of one's life . . . were connected directly to this concept of rebirth . . . The readings made it a very personal and practical thing."

As Hugh Lynn made evident in this open letter to the A.R.E., he and his family had made much progress in their understanding of the concepts first presented in the life readings in 1923. In fact, ten years after receiving his first life reading, Hugh Lynn requested a series of readings, which became the most lengthy and comprehensive discourse the Source gave on the topic. There was one question asked during this series that seemed most pressing to Hugh Lynn: why is reincarnation necessary at all? The Source answered at some length:

"Man's consciousness . . . is gained through [what] he, man, does about the knowledge of [what] he is, in relation to that from which he came and toward which he is going," the Source said. "Hence, in man's analysis and understanding of himself, it is as well to know from whence he came as to know whither he is going."

The Source also made it clear that the knowledge gained through life readings is not the same as specific memories from previous incarnations. According to the Source, our forgetfulness of our previous lives is by design, not only for the purpose of maintaining "free will" but for our own protection, because the conscious memories from earlier incarnations could potentially become a great burden. The "memory" that a person takes with him into a subsequent incarnation is more in the form of a lesson that has been learned, or remains to be learned. Unless that "lesson" makes for a better person, it has no lasting value. This is what the Source referred to as "karma," or the impact that one incarnation has on another.

As Hugh Lynn sought to communicate to those who studied the life readings, karma was simply subconscious memory, and not a matter of Divine punishment as popularly understood by many believers in reincarnation. "It [is simply] cause and effect . . . simply internal memory," Hugh Lynn said. "People always thought you had karma with somebody [but] karma doesn't exist between people . . . You don't have karma *with* other people. You have a memory about [the experience]. But [their memory] may be quite different from yours. They may have gotten over it . . . and made it into a good relationship."

The point that the Source repeatedly stressed was that karma, and man's knowledge of it, has a purpose. "To find that ye only lived, died, and were buried under the cherry tree in Grandmother's garden does not make thee one whit [a] better neighbor, citizen, mother, or father!" the Source said. "But to know that ye spoke unkindly and suffered for it, and in the present may correct it by being righteous—that is worthwhile!"

Implicit throughout all of the life readings was the understanding that a soul, through its God-given capacity of "free will," literally chooses the conditions or environment that it is born into. In other words, a soul chooses how to make peace, or free itself of its "karmic debt." And just as an individual soul "chooses" the time and place to re-enter the earthly plane, specific choices are made regarding family, genetics, physical attributes, and personality. The Source compared bloodlines and family to a "river" through which an entity travels as it selects the approximate conditions or challenges to be faced. The concept of family genealogy as a kind of cosmic river held great personal attraction to Edgar himself, for his favorite passage in the Bible was in Psalm 46, which reads, in part: "There is a river, the streams whereof shall make glad the city of God."

To Hugh Lynn, like Edgar, the central message being communicated was that life has purpose and direction, and that reincarnation could only be understood in the context of where man came from and where he is going—*from* the "First Cause" or God, and *back* to God. The primary object of all human experience, the Source said, was to become a worthy companion to God. The great world around us is a matter of our own creation, and it allows us to see where we stand in our journey back to God.

Again, the Source stressed the concept of mind as the builder, referring to the good that can come from focusing on God and God's creation, and the harm that results from a preoccupation with earthly evils such as violence, carnal desire, and materialism. This would be especially true, the Source added, for children and young adults, whose natural tendency to see God in the world can easily be subverted by materialism and consumerism, which for many are the customary rites of passage into adulthood. "The mind is the builder ever, whether in the spirit or in the flesh," the Source said. "If one's mind is filled with those things that bespeak of the spirit, then one becomes spiritual-minded . . . Envy, strife, selfishness, greediness, avarice, are the children of man! Long-suffering, kindness, brotherly love, good deeds, are the children of the spirit."

Furthermore, the Source suggested that the only sure method of stepping off the seemingly interminable wheel of birth and rebirth was to follow the example of Jesus Christ, who, according to the Source, was the first person to make the transition back to God, the "Creator." In this context, the Source highlighted the Biblical teaching that Christ died on the cross to save mankind. He lived and died—the Source said—to provide a living example of man's route back to God. "He is the way, that light ever ready," the Source said. The route back, the Source said, involves making one's will the same as the will of the Father, as Jesus did on the cross. Although He had the power to save Himself, He showed His faith by leaving His fate in God's hands. It is in connection to this concept that Cayce would quote Jesus as teaching: "If ye would have life, give life"—a more specific version of "you

reap what you sow," and "what we do unto others, we truly do unto ourselves."

As difficult as it was for Edgar to accept the notion of reincarnation, he
knew from his years of Bible study that it answered many theological questions, not the least of which was the often-quoted passages about being
"born again." After making his own study of reincarnation and the Bible,
Edgar finally concluded that it contained several specific references to the
subject of karma and past lives. One such example was in the Gospel of
John, when the disciples asked Christ about a man who had been born blind.
The disciples wanted to know whether the blindness had been brought on
by the man himself, or his parents. As Edgar pointed out in a lecture he
later gave, "It wouldn't have been possible for the man to have sinned in this
life [and] be *born* blind. They [the disciples] must have believed that the man
lived before, else they wouldn't have asked such a question." Another reference Edgar cited was in the Gospel of Matthew, when Jesus, Peter, James,
and John came down from the Mount of Transfiguration, where they had
seen Moses and Elijah. Peter and John, questioning an earlier prophecy
about the coming Messiah, asked why the scribes had said that Elijah must
come first. Jesus replied: "Elijah is come already, and they knew him not . . .
Then the disciples understood that He spake unto them of John the Baptist."
The Source later supported Edgar's interpretation of this passage in a reading given to a forty-six-year-old housewife from Akron, Ohio, by making specific reference to John the Baptist's previous life as Elijah.

A logical question that came to Edgar's mind was why the subject of
reincarnation did not appear in Christian theology. The Source answered this
question in a reading given about Gnosticism, a doctrine practiced by an
early sect of the Christian church. In this reading the Source said that reincarnation was a commonly accepted belief until early church leaders began
to develop "set rules," which were, according to the Source, "attempts to take
shortcuts." The concept of personal responsibility disturbed the Christian fathers because of the degree of culpability it placed on an individual. If man
himself had chosen the circumstances of his life, he couldn't claim to be the
victim of bad luck, since it was his own actions, thoughts, and attitudes—as
developed in previous incarnations—that were holding him back. But this
change in church doctrine was, the Source implies, shortsighted. This same
reading pointed out, "There are [no shortcuts] in Christianity!"

As Hugh Lynn, like Edgar, would become intimately aware, the vast majority of life readings and their accompanying physical readings suggested
that karma was at the root of the challenges a person faced. In a reading conducted in 1944 for a twelve-year-old child suffering from asthma, the Source

said: "one doesn't press the life out of others without at times seeming to have same pressed out of self."

Perhaps the most interesting example of karmic debt belonged to a woman who came to Cayce suffering from gonorrhea. In her life reading, the Source said she had once been a prostitute in Yokohama, and that in her present incarnation she had been infected by the same strain of venereal disease she had knowingly passed on to countless sailors a century and a half earlier.

Emotional disturbances were also explained by karma, as evidenced by a reading Cayce gave for an eighteen-year-old girl who had an unusual fear of darkness. The Source said: "The experiences in the dungeon in which thou wert plunged [creates this fear]."

Often, in cases of karmic conditions, the Source recommended developing one's faith both in one's self and in God, before embarking on any physical treatment. In a reading for a forty-seven-year-old woman suffering from glaucoma, the Source said: "Hence the general health has much to do with the condition [but] karma has much more . . . Thy opportunities and purposes, as with each soul, are only . . . opportunities for thee. Use them to the glory of God and not to the willful disobedience in any manner."

In another reading, given for a thirty-seven-year-old New Jersey housewife suffering from arthritis and constipation, the Source advised that before medicines should be given, "first there must be a change in the mental attitude of the body. There must be eradicated that of any judgment or of condemnation on the part of self as respecting self or any associated with the body."

Ridiculing another person's life situation was not only seen as wrong by the Source, but as a source of bad karma and poor health in future incarnations. The readings revealed situations in which a person faced challenges he had ridiculed in others in a past life. In a reading for a seventeen-year-old student, the Source said: "Oft did the entity laugh at those less nimble of activity, owing to their heaviness in body. Hence do we find the entity not only meeting same in the present from a physical angle—obesity—but there are the necessities of it being worked out by diet as well as outdoor activity." In another instance, a young man who felt challenged by his homosexuality sought a physical reading he believed might explain his current life situation. The origins of his "challenge" showed up in a life reading. He had been a political cartoonist in an earlier French incarnation and had made fun of prominent people known or suspected to be homosexual.

The question naturally arose in regard to these readings whether all serious ailments or afflictions were the result of past-life experiences. In answer to this question, the Source repeatedly stated that very little happens by chance, whether physical conditions or associations with others: "It is never by chance but as with all things in this material world, there are causes and effects," the Source told a fifty-year-old man from Durham, North Carolina. "To be sure, at times there may be what might be called accidents. But these too, in a causation world, have their cause and effect."

However, the Source did acknowledge that occasionally, "accidents happen in creation, as well as in individuals' lives! Peculiar statement here, but true!" An example of such a nonkarmic accident was that of a nurse who apparently hadn't washed her hands properly before handling an infant who later developed hearing-related problems. The Source said, "a sad condition, and not a result of karma, but an accident." Another example was that of a nurse who accidentally dropped a child who subsequently developed spinal injuries.

Even when the Source said there was no previous karma involved in a particular life situation, cause and effect still applied. This was the case for a schoolteacher who asked whether or not she should undergo surgery. The Source said: "Unless something is done about the [current] conditions [your physical problems] may occur again! It is not the paying for karmic debts of other experiences . . . as the lack of conformity to the laws as pertaining to health." Frustrating as it must have been for this schoolteacher to be told that the ultimate responsibility for her life situation was hers, the Source described a means by which an individual might overcome her challenges through the act of "forgiveness." This, in a larger sense, was what Cayce believed Christ had accomplished in his life on earth.

Another reading made the point more directly: "Karmic influences must ever be met, but He has prepared the way that takes them upon Himself . . . as ye trust in Him . . . for karmic forces are [such that] what is meted must be met." Here, the Source seemed to be saying that although there is no way for a person to avoid his karmic debts, one can meet life's challenges by viewing them as stepping-stones to greater spiritual growth, and by forgiving the mistakes of others. According to the Source, it was only to the degree that a person forgives others their mistakes, that his own would be forgiven. "It is only as ye forgive [that] the Christ is able to forgive thee," the Source said in a reading in 1944. "Forgive, *if* ye would be forgiven."

Hugh Lynn, like his father, eventually came to believe that it is only in the context of karma that Jesus' healing powers could best be understood, for in the karmic sense, Jesus truly did heal people of their illnesses by "forgiving their sins," particularly those people born with whatever condition they suffered from. And almost the very last words Christ uttered on the cross—"Forgive them, Lord, for they know not what they do"—takes on a new meaning, especially in the light of the biblical teaching that says, "He is the way." To Edgar and other students of the life readings, the message was clear: people reap what they sow. If a person is judgmental and hateful, he will reap judgment and hate. If he acts with forgiveness and patience, his life will be filled with forgiveness and patience.

Although the focus in many of the readings was on what might be termed "bad karma," the Source devoted a greater number of readings to what might be called "good karma," or talents, abilities, and attitudes that were earned as a result of having successfully met challenges in previous life experiences. A good person would be given "greater responsibilities," which came in the form of wealth, station in life, good health, physique, or highly developed abilities and talents. The Source described these earthly blessings as "responsibilities" because they too were karmic and had to be used in a manner that was in keeping with the "First Cause" or Divine purpose.

This subject was addressed in a reading for a thirty-eight-year-old business executive, to whom the Source said: "Ye may find—as this world's goods increase in thy hands . . . they will not and do not become burdens to thy conscience nor separate thee from thy home or thy fellow man. But rather is the opportunity to serve thy Maker. Ye have earned that right for much of this world's goods."

In a reading for a thirty-year-old secretary, the Source said: "[You] have earned [harmonious companionship] for ye have practiced peace first within self, and the ability to make peace with others." In this same reading, however, the Source stressed the need for this individual not to take her blessings for granted. "[Be careful not to] talk too much! And these [present blessings] will ever stand the entity in good stead, to attain, to gain whatever may be the desire or the [soul's] purpose [Adopt the attitude] of 'live and let live,' and of helping the other fellow, [and] ye will keep those [previous life] experiences inviolate, and there will be harmony in this [present] experience."

As Edgar's own life reading would later reveal to him, his most special blessing—his ability to communicate on a psychic level—was a direct result of his "soul development" in previous lifetimes. The one incarnation in which he made the most development in this regard was a lifetime in which he had been wounded, and through his power of self-will, put aside his "carnal mind" to heal his own body. However, as this same reading revealed, his present situation was determined by more than his personal karma. By virtue of his special task in life, Edgar, like many others who obtained life readings for themselves, drew to himself people and groups of people with whom he had previously associated in prior incarnations. According to the Source, groups of people could incarnate together to work out individual

karma or complete some long-term "good" that had been started in previous incarnations. As Edgar gradually became aware while conducting the
first series of life readings, the people in close contact with him invariably
knew one another in Egypt many thousands of years earlier, which was
where the work had truly begun.

Not everyone in Edgar's life was with him in other "group" incarnations.
In many instances people were drawn to him because of "personal" karma
that needed to be worked out. A woman whom Edgar had treated poorly in
a previous incarnation was saved from certain death by a reading he provided. In this case, as in many others, Dave Kahn acted as a kind intermediary through which someone who might otherwise not have crossed Edgar's
path sought and received help. And Edgar, in doing these readings, was able
to erase bad karma resulting from his poor treatment of these individuals in
previous life experiences.

It is interesting to note, in this regard, that Dave Kahn, according to his
own life readings, did not participate in the work in Edgar's earlier incarnations and had not played the sort of role that Gertrude, Gladys, and others had in Cayce's "river of life." The "karmic" purpose of Dave Kahn's
participation in Edgar's current life seems to have been as an agent through
whom Edgar, on a personal level, was able to right injustices he had committed in previous incarnations. Kahn had played just such a role in Desdemona and Luling, where he had acted as the contact point through which the
various oilmen sought or received Cayce's help.

It is ironic—given the fact that recipients of physical readings as far back
as Hopkinsville and Bowling Green were admonished to "look within themselves" for the source of their life challenges, or to "make peace with God"
and "study the scriptures" if they wished to become physically well—that
another full decade elapsed before Edgar Cayce himself became personally
convinced of the message being put forth in the Dayton life readings. To a
young college student who asked Cayce—in trance—what would convince
him of reincarnation, the Source replied quite simply: "An experience." It
was just such an "experience" that ultimately convinced Edgar.

In the course of conducting life and physical readings for Cayce Jones, the
infant son of Edgar's best friends in Selma, the Source not only provided answers to questions regarding the subject's physical and mental well-being,
but had this to say to Edgar on a personal level: "Here you may have proof
[of reincarnation] Let your mother see the child, she will recognize him as
he will her."

The reference was to Thomas Cayce, Edgar's late younger brother, who
one of the life readings stated had been reincarnated as Cayce Jones, and who

would, in the present incarnation, allegedly manifest great psychic abilities. As Edgar remembered, ten-day-old Thomas Cayce had died in his mother's arms, and this had been a source of much grief for which Edgar and his mother had sought solace in prayer. In the reading for Jones, the Source suggested that if Carrie Cayce was introduced to the child, she would recognize him as her own from his previous incarnation. Unfortunately, Edgar didn't act upon the information in 1925 when Cayce Jones's life reading was given. A few months later Carrie died, and Edgar regretted not having put mother and "son" together to see what might happen.

But then, in 1927, Edgar visited Selma and spent an afternoon with the Jones family. On the way to their house from the train station, Cayce Jones's mother, Alva, and her husband, Lamar, told Edgar about their "very peculiar child," now 2½ years old. According to Alva, her son—who had been named after Edgar—was claiming that he was not a member of their family. "He insists he does not belong to us, [and] is only visiting us until his folks come for him," she told Edgar. "He will have nothing to do with strangers, calls us by our names, Mr. Jones and Mrs. Jones, and his sisters and brothers by their name."

When Edgar arrived at the Jones's home, he was introduced to young Cayce Jones. Edgar described the child as "lovely" and "normal in every way" and was surprised when the young boy would not greet or come near him. He merely watched Edgar intently from a distance, saying nothing. All of a sudden he then rushed over to embrace Edgar. The child's face became radiant. "Brother!" he announced. At once, the child began to beg Edgar to take him home, pleading with Edgar that he belonged in the Cayce family, not with the Joneses. Little Cayce Jones was so distraught at the prospect of not leaving with him that Edgar had to wait until the child was asleep before he could leave the Joneses' house.

Edgar did not see Cayce Jones for the next eight years, thinking that were he to do so, there might be serious repercussions to the child's relationship with his parents. Then, when he did return, Alva Jones related a curious phenomenon that was creating a great strain on their family life. She told Edgar that her ten-year-old child would not go alone into the house that they had recently moved into, nor would he enter his bedroom or their bathroom unless accompanied by a parent. This proved to be quite a problem, for one of the parents had to constantly accompany the ten-year-old. When Alva asked her son what the problem was, he reportedly replied: "You would not understand."

Lamar and Alva Jones asked Edgar to look into the matter and talk to their son. Edgar obliged. It soon became apparent to him that the ten-year-old child had begun to manifest the psychic abilities foretold in his first life reading. Cayce Jones told Edgar what he was reluctant to tell his parents: that he believed that the ghost of someone who had died in the house had re-mained behind to haunt its present occupants. Cayce Jones was "picking up" psychic vibrations, and it disturbed him to be in the house alone. In dis-cussions with Edgar about the "ghost," the problem was solved. The child had only to take a living thing into the room with him, such as a caged bird or potted plant, to offset the vibrations of the ghostly presence. As Edgar later reported in a letter to a friend, the child confirmed what both he and the child knew in their hearts to be true. "[A bird or a flower has] life, and Life is God. And when He is . . . [present] nothing can harm."

Helping the young boy overcome his fear of the house, however, was a great deal easier than convincing the child to remain with the Jones family. When Edgar was about to leave the Joneses' house to return to his own home, the young boy appeared at the door with his belongings packed in a suitcase. He demanded to be taken "home." As Edgar later said of the incident, "this wasn't proof [of reincarnation] to anyone [in a scientific way], but [it was] mighty meaningful to me!"

29.

History and
Hardships

Although the number of trance sessions Edgar Cayce had given had more than doubled since Gertrude and Gladys's arrival in Dayton in October 1923, Arthur Lammers hadn't requested a single reading for himself or his company, and all communications with him were now being routed through Linden Shroyer, his personal secretary. Nevertheless, Edgar still believed that Lammers would provide the financial support he had repeatedly promised. However, by January 1924, the Lammers Printing and Engraving Company had all but closed its doors. And in the midst of the related legal proceedings, Lammers and one of his partners had a disagreement over how to reorganize and streamline the Dayton Photo Products Company. In the months to come, Dayton Photo Products and Lammers Printing went into bankruptcy. The company's creditors foreclosed on Lammers's Bryn Mawr mansion and repossessed his automobiles. There wasn't even enough money to print a proposed book based on the series of readings that Edgar had conducted in Dayton.

In the last reported meeting Edgar had with Lammers, in December 1923, the businessman was still pretending that his situation wasn't as desperate as everyone believed it to be. Lammers arrived late to the meeting and was unhappy to discover that Linden Shroyer and Byron Wyrick had begun negotiating with another printer to publish Edgar's book. Lammers objected strenuously to letting anyone other than himself publish the book, and in the ensuing delay, the project as originally envisioned was abandoned. Looking back on those early months of the new year, Hugh Lynn remembered that he could see the "hurt look in [his] Dad's eyes when he talked about people [who had disappointed him]." But about money his father simply said: "It will come."

The truth of the matter, however, was that the family was flat broke, and they, along with Gladys Davis, were now stranded in a city of strangers during what was described as one of the coldest winters in Dayton's history. Besides Lammers and Shroyer, the Cayces knew practically no one except auto-parts manufacturer Tim Brown, who had left on an extended trip to Los Angeles and was not anticipated home for at least a month. And having no established ties to a Dayton church congregation, the family was either unwilling or unable to ask for charity. The only income the family received was from medical readings, which were being conducted on an average of one per day. They would have liked to give more readings, but no one besides their small circle of supporters at the Phillips Hotel knew who they were or what Edgar did. Having devoted the lion's share of his trance time to life readings, he hadn't developed contacts with the medical community or established the base of support that he had had in Birmingham and Nashville.

Income from doing a daily physical reading—billed at a rate of five dollars per session—barely put food on the table, let alone paid the rent at the Phillips Hotel, where the readings were being given, or for their two-room flat on East Fifth Street. The only reason Edgar kept the room at the hotel was because he couldn't pay his account and was afraid if he moved out completely, he would be arrested for nonpayment of rent. A brief comment that Edgar made in a letter to Byron Wyrick, in Chicago, that they were "still eating—sometimes," was not the joke it appeared to be, for physical readings being conducted for Gertrude repeatedly warned of complications due to vitamin and mineral deficiencies in her diet. Besides giving readings and playing long card games around a makeshift table in the kitchen, the family's only diversion was trips to the nearby Miami River, where Hugh Lynn and Edgar Evans, bundled up in several layers of clothing, chased a flattened tin can across a patch of ice under the Dayton View Bridge. They called the game "ice-polo."

In the midst of this abject poverty, Edgar gave some of the most inspired and provocative readings of his career. The most notable was the life reading he finally gave himself. Encouraged by Linden Shroyer and inspired by

Gladys's "bravery," he finally submitted on February 9. Due to the sheer amount of information that the Source had to provide, the reading was continued over a period of seven days. Gertrude, perhaps apprehensive about what the Source might say, or simply preoccupied with taking care of the children, remained at home.

The introductory statements to Edgar's reading were similar to those made by the Source for dozens of life readings over the years. The Source said it would give only the information that would be vital to Edgar at the time and also indicated that it treated Edgar with the same neutrality accorded other recipients of life readings. Though Shroyer and others no doubt put Edgar on a pedestal, the Source clearly stated the challenges that he confronted were those of an ordinary man. "[He is] one who finds much in the scope or sphere of intrigue in secret love affairs, one given often to the conditions that have to do with the affairs of the heart, and of those relations that have to do with sex."

It is interesting to speculate what Gertrude may have thought about this comment, for she of all people knew that what her husband may have lacked in good looks was more than compensated for by his gentle manner and personal charisma—as evidenced by the interest shown in Edgar by Margaret, the rich heiress in Louisville. Regardless of how innocent Edgar's intentions had been at the time, Margaret had created an intrigue that had threatened to end Gertrude and Edgar's engagement. However, Gertrude, like Edgar himself, was also aware that the Source was merely stating "inclinations," and had, in fact, prefaced its remarks by stating that such inclinations were without reference to Edgar's considerable personal force of free will. Edgar could be accused of many things, such as mismanaging money, but he was not a philanderer. He had learned to control the temptations put before him.

The Source then balanced Edgar's potentially bad inclinations with his positive ones. "[He is] one that finds the greater strength in spiritual forces and developing, one given to make manifest in the present plane much of the forces of psychic and occult forces, reaching the greater height of developing in such plane . . . one that will bring, through such manifestations, joy, peace, and quiet to the masses and multitudes through individual efforts."

The Source went on to describe upcoming astrological influences, some beneficial and others of danger to Edgar and then added the following reminder: "There have been many conditions that have been hindered by the effect of the will, and others that have been assisted. Keep the will in that of the spiritual development . . . that all work in present plane will be judged [by] the individual's manifestation of spiritual forces in and through the individual action in and before [all] men." Here, the Source appeared to be saying that the good that came through him would be judged less on the "material manifestation" of that good, than on Edgar's personal behavior, or how he comported himself during his present incarnation.

The next part of this reading, dedicated to vocation, appeared to be offering Edgar a choice of possible careers and suggested that he could do virtually anything that he willed, but that his work in the field of psychic research would be best. "As to the vocation, this in the present plane may be directed in any channel through will," the Source said. "The better condition . . . would be toward those of psychic and occult, or teaching or developing along the lines of such plane to give the manifestation of such forces to the populace."

The remainder of the reading described Edgar's previous incarnations. Cayce was currently in his eighth life on earth, and the Source went through his past lives in reverse order. In keeping with the information provided in the reading given in November, the new reading described his seventh incarnation, a British soldier named John Bainbridge, who was born in Cornwall, England, and received military training in Canada. His life as John Bainbridge ended when he drowned in the river during a battle near Dayton. From this incarnation, Edgar had developed "the ability to take cognizance of detail, especially in following instructions as given from other minds or sources of information."

The Source said nothing about Edgar's sixth incarnation, which the November reading had placed in Jamestown, Virginia. The Source merely jumped further back in time to describe an incarnation of short duration in the French courts, from which came Edgar's urges for "intense defense of those principles deemed to be right." In the earlier November reading this fifth incarnation was described as occurring during "the rule of Richelieu." The fact that the Source, in previous readings, had told both Gertrude and Gladys that they too had lived in France around this time suggested that the three had somehow been connected during this period. But as Edgar would soon discover, the Source was reluctant to expand on exactly what had happened. Either the Source did not deem this information to be necessary, or as Edgar himself later concluded, didn't think Cayce was prepared to hear what the Source had to say.

The Source continued with Cayce's fourth incarnation as Xenon, one of the defenders of Troy. In addition to citing his skills as a warrior, the Source said that Xenon had been a chemist, a sculptor, and an artisan, and from this incarnation Edgar had developed a great love of beauty and art. As the Source said in a later reading, Lammers, Shroyer, and Klingensmith had also been in Troy at the same time, and that all four of them were written about in Homer's *Iliad*. As Edgar would later confirm during a trip to the Dayton Public Library, Homer had described Xenon as one of the men who sat atop the battlements when Helen of Troy came to review the Greek army camped outside the city wall.

In his third incarnation, Edgar lived in the area of Persia now known as Iran, under the name Uhjltd (pronounced You-ult). Uhjltd was described as one of "power, prestige, [and] royalty," who at one time led many raids on surrounding tribes. His most notable leadership skills were said to have oc-curred during a war on a Persian ruler named Croesus. During an escape, he became badly injured, and in the process of trying to heal himself, had learned the "psychic force," which had now become his life's focus. Later readings would reveal that at this juncture, Edgar, as Uhjltd, decided to build a great city in the desert in which peace would reign and the people would thrive. He succeeded in realizing this dream, and "his" city became a great center of commerce. Later, however, he and his wife were kidnapped and killed by the Greeks, and the city's peace was overcome with strife. The Source commented that "there are many upon this earth's plane, and in dif-ferent locations, who were associated with this entity at that time."

The Source then described Edgar's second incarnation, in Egypt during the dynasty of the Rameses, when Hugh Lynn was said to have been a Pharaoh, and Edgar, as Ra Ta, was the high priest. "[The work] was cut short [by Edgar] allowing . . . physical forces and desires to enter in, and the taking of . . . Gertrude Cayce [as Edgar Cayce's lover]." As a result of what the Source characterized as an inappropriate liaison between Edgar and Gertrude, the Pharaoh banished them from Egypt, which not only "brought destructive elements to [Edgar's physical] body," but brought about hardship among the people he had served. As the Source pointed out in what might be considered the most ominous passage in the reading, "the karma of each must be met, Edgar and Gertrude, and in this plane overcome if each would enter [into companionship with God]." According to Gladys's life reading, she had also lived in Egypt during this era, although for only a short period of time. Her relationship to Edgar and Gertrude—and the karma associated with it—was a subject the Source would not elaborate upon.

As in the November reading, Edgar's first incarnation on earth was de-scribed in poetic terms, making it impossible to name a specific place or time. However, the Source suggested that it was the time when man first walked the planet: "We find in the beginning, when the . . . forces set in mo-tion that brought about . . . Earth . . . and when the morning stars sang together, and the whispering winds brought the news of [the] coming of man's indwelling . . . this entity came into being."

The reading also described some upcoming changes in Edgar's present life and added that "in this sphere or plane, we find there are many that come under the influence of the . . . personality . . . and for many years after this return to the other spheres [will] this influence [be] felt in the earth's plane." Edgar's reading ended, like so many others, with words of advice and inspiration: "Take this thou hast in hand and make and mold it into the present plane's development, that thyself and others may know that God . . . demands of His creatures . . . the knowledge of self, that they may better serve their fellows . . . bringing to others the knowledge of Him."

There was one final remark made by the Source, which suggested that there were still many undisclosed details about Edgar's past lives. "There are many other influences as have been shed abroad in the earth's plane from the entity's sojourn there," the source said. "These [that have been given] are [those] that all may know and understand."

Edgar was put immediately at ease, feeling that he shouldn't have feared what the reading would have to reveal.

The next member of the family to have his past incarnations revealed was Leslie Cayce, who was in Hopkinsville when his reading was conducted. Perhaps because Leslie had not requested this reading and wasn't present to put questions to the Source himself, the session was considerably shorter than Edgar's. His reading made reference to the negative influences "in that of Cancer . . . Mars, and Uranus" which brought many sudden changes to the "structural conditions of the physical body." Apparently this was referring to the fact that over the years almost every bone in Leslie's body had been broken at least once. The reading also pointed out that certain astrological influences "brought and does bring [much heartache] and has brought many of the earthly ills and material cares and worry." The following advice was then given: "Exercise will that these may be used in development and not meted against that karma that is made in each entity's [latest] sojourn."

Only three of Leslie's incarnations were described, one of whom lived at the time of Alfred the Great and who presumably had some relationship to Hugh Lynn, who also lived then as a monk. Apparently, Leslie was in the court of England, and as a result of that incarnation he manifested an uncommon understanding of written law. The Source went on to say that Leslie would become a lawyer in his next incarnation. In the incarnation before England, he was a Gaul who lost his life "in the hold of the trade ships." He was a slave rower for Hannibal's forces and died at the hands of his black slave driver. A later reading described this incarnation as the deep-rooted cause of his racist behavior.

As with Edgar's reading, the information now coming through highlighted the need for all of them—Edgar, Gertrude, Gladys, and Hugh Lynn—to head off to the Dayton Public Library to gain a better understanding of world history and geography. The fact that the readings—thus far—hadn't contradicted the known facts of textbook history made their research into the story of their past lives all the more rewarding. Nor would their readings be definitively contradicted by later scholarly research. In fact, the more the readings were studied, the more accurate they appeared to be.

In the years ahead, archival records and other circumstantial evidence would be found to support the life readings of more than 250 individuals, ranging from people said to have been Bavarian nobility to otherwise unremarkable housewives and carpenters. Among those people whose life readings were studied in depth was a Virginia music teacher identified in a previous incarnation as a rank-and-file Civil War veteran and Kentucky farmer. Documentation of his previous incarnation was found in Confederate Army records at the Richmond Library, in membership rolls at a Masonic Temple, and finally, on a grave marker at the edge of a Kentucky cornfield.

30.

Love and Marriage

It was in a vein of historical self-discovery that the life readings continued at an ever-increasing pace. The fact that the Source had piqued Edgar, Gertrude, and Gladys's interest in their past personal relationships made what they would hear next all the more disturbing.

On May 31, 1924, Gladys decided to have a second life reading. Several months had passed since Edgar had given the first life readings for his own family, and the possible connections between their previous incarnations had been discussed often. And yet, the most perplexing mystery still remained: how an eighteen-year-old girl arriving late into Edgar and Gertrude's life had become such an important catalyst to the process of giving deeper, more meaningful life readings.

The first incarnation the Source elaborated on in Gladys's follow-up reading was her French incarnation as the second daughter of Louis XIV. At age seventeen, she was reportedly seduced by the philandering Duke of York, who later became King James II of England. Gladys became pregnant and gave birth to none other than Edgar Cayce in his fifth incarnation. Here, the story becomes tragic. Gladys's mother, the queen, reportedly lost favor with King Louis who banished her and her daughter and grandchild from court.

"This brings [Gladys Davis] a great distrust of all men," the Source said. "The love does not cease in the heart but all is centered in the offspring of that love [Edgar Cayce] The monarch [wreaks] vengeance . . . on the [queen] mother . . . Hence, [the child] Edgar Cayce, is left in the care [and protection] of those whom . . . Gladys Davis felt were the closest friends in the household of the king . . . The offspring, Edgar, [is discovered and killed by the king] and [Gladys Davis] gradually gives way to [a broken heart] and [dies]."

Thus, according to this reading, Gladys had once been Edgar's mother and, losing him at a very young age, she died of a broken heart. This reading went on to recommend that Gladys "should find [her] rest in heart, soul, and mind in the life of that individual . . . Edgar Cayce . . . The affection which was lost in that plane should be manifest in this present [incarnation] for Gladys Davis [will] only find its rest in this earth's plane with that entity Edgar Cayce."

A crucial piece of the incarnation puzzle that had been laid at their feet over the last several months had now been revealed. And based on this reading, Gladys's entry into the lives of the Cayces was far more than a coincidence. It explained why she had stayed with Edgar in Dayton despite the obvious reasons she had for returning home. The fact that she hadn't received a paycheck and that she had to share a bedroom with two adolescent boys were minor problems compared to the uncertain future she faced by remaining with the Cayce family. The reading also explained why Gladys seemed to be the only stenographer in Edgar's life who could record his trance discourses with the seeming familiarity of a mother listening to her son.

Upon waking from his latest trance session, Edgar must have been just as intrigued as Gladys, for they immediately decided to learn about other connections, or perhaps wanted to test how well his and her readings could match up. Edgar went back into trance that same day to ask the Source about *his* French incarnation and his relationship to Gladys.

The Source said: "The entity [Edgar Cayce] was of tender years . . . born of [Gladys Davis] the beloved of the court, and of the ruler's son of the territory just across the waters [England]. And the change necessary in court proceedings prevented the culmination of this ruler's recognizing the earthly fatherhood of [Edgar Cayce]. The great trials came to the entity . . . when the separation was effected between mother and son, [and] the young life was gradually taken out on account of the jealousy arising in the court. For the king became fully aware of the lad's appearance, and the possibility of [him] becoming the ruler forced others to play the traitor to the mother, who loved the entity so well."

The next part of the reading must have really given them something to think about. "The lives of each have ever been bound in the other's life, and the conditions as exist are only the outgrowth of endeavor in earth plane . . . The outward manifestations of the inward desires of the heart and soul . . . find in each the answering chord in the other's affection that will never, never, never be found in any other. For since in the first meetings . . . in Persia, when this entity [Edgar Cayce], then the warrior in Uhjltd, found and became enamored with the beauty [Gladys Davis] and found the developing of the psychic through the suffering that both endured, and through which this entity, then the helpmate and companion of the king's daughter, 'lost its head.' Through the treachery of others, we find the same enacted in this French court."

The reading suggested that Edgar, in his Persian incarnation, had been with Gladys in other incarnations also, and that they were together when Edgar, as revealed in his last life reading, developed his psychic ability. He had apparently not only healed the wounds that he himself had suffered, but possibly those of Gladys too. The reading went on to advise: "Be faithful one to the other, irrespective of earthly conditions, [for] these two have ever been together . . . Be thou faithful unto the end and receive that crown that is ever for the faithful in heart, soul, and body. Be kind, affectionate, loving, ever giving, ever preferring the other."

By "ever preferring the other," the Source appeared to be saying that they, by necessity, must always put the other first, ahead of themselves. The statement that these two had "ever [always] been together" obviously prompted both wonder and curiosity—just two days later another reading on this subject was conducted. The first question asked was about the specific nature of previous connections between Gladys and Edgar. If the concepts of reincarnation and astrology were already too much to deal with, the Source's answer may have been more than they had bargained for.

"[Edgar Cayce and Gladys Davis] have had many experiences together, and their soul and spirit are well knit and must of necessity present each that they may be one. For we find in the beginning that . . . these two—which we shall speak of as 'they' until separated—were as one in mind, soul, spirit, body, and in the first earth's plane as the voice over many waters, when the glory of the Father's giving of the earth's indwelling of man was both male and female in one. In flesh form in earth's plane we find . . . both were confined in the body of the female [in their first incarnation]: for this being the stronger . . . form. Yet with the experiences as have been brought in that plane and period, we find then the separation of the body. For the desire of the flesh being to give of self in bodily form to the other, it brought the separating of the spirit and soul from the carnal forces when next brought to earth's plane . . . Hence . . . the separation . . . yet bound together in physical affections one for the other."

The Source went on to expound on their Egyptian incarnations when Gladys was the offspring of the controversial union of Edgar, the high priest known as Ra Ta, and Gertrude, who was said to be the favorite dancer of Pharaoh Hugh Lynn. Gladys was said to have died very young when she was taken away from her parents by the jealous Pharaoh. The reading also further clarified Edgar's Persian incarnation as Uhjltd, and Gladys's as Ilya, who became his wife. Both Uhjltd and Ilya were kidnapped and killed by the Greeks. As if to suggest "proof" of that experience, the Source went on to describe marks that they would find on their bodies "designating these conditions" through which they lost their lives. "On the female body [Gladys Davis], just below the left breast, to the side and on the edge of the breast itself, the mark, and an answering one on the body of the male [Edgar Cayce]."

There was still more the Source had to give. "At present we find they are again together . . . each paying out [their karma] that which has been gained or merited . . . They are again united in soul and in spirit . . . and through the joy and the pleasure of selfless service they may again know the meaning of . . . those joys . . . that bring . . . peace, and again [the] uniting of body, soul, and spirit in the next [incarnation]. Remain faithful, therefore, unto the end: gaining those joys through daily acts of selflessness for and with others, remembering that . . . they—and all souls—become knit one with the other."

Gladys may already have begun to suspect some strong previous relationship with Edgar Cayce. But this new information presented a challenge the likes of which neither she nor Edgar could begin to comprehend. Nineteen-year-old Gladys Davis was being told something that might otherwise have been a romantic dream come true: that her female soul had once been a single entity with another male soul in some distant realm or dimension, that soul mates through time did exist, and that she had found her soul mate. The nightmare was the fact that her soul mate, whose life was irrevocably tied to her own through time and space, was a happily married man twenty-seven years her senior—wedded to a woman whose friendship she had come to cherish—and who, according to the Source, had to remain married because of the karma that he and his wife had created in Egypt with Hugh Lynn. In other words, Edgar and Gertrude were meant to be together in their present incarnation, and Gladys and Edgar would have to wait until their next incarnation to be reunited.

Of Edgar's need to remain faithful to Gertrude there could be no question, for the Source had described this karmic debt in Edgar's first life reading. "In the plane before this . . . in the court and rule of the second Pharaoh, Hugh Lynn Cayce, or Rameses . . . the high priest [Edgar Cayce] gave the religious element and force in the age . . . yet was cut short [by giving into temptation] and taking [Gertrude] and leaving the shores of this country [which resulted in Gladys's death]," the Source said. "That same entity that was taken is at present in this earth's plane, the companion and mate as should be in the present sphere, Gertrude Cayce."

The mixed blessing of both knowing her soul mate but being unable to enter into a full marital relationship with him was a subject that Gladys— at this point, and for years to come—declined to discuss with anyone besides Edgar and Gertrude. And yet, the stress that came as a result of that knowledge could neither be concealed nor dismissed then or in the years to come. In one physical reading after another, the Source recommended that Gladys undertake exercises, meditation, and therapy to combat depression and physical problems stemming from mental stress and sexual repression.

Edgar too felt the burden of knowing Gladys was his soul mate. Emotionally, he may have loved her as a wife, but he could only treat her as a daughter, at best, and in her role as his secretary. This knowledge also created stress in his marriage to Gertrude. He had a wife "in the flesh," whom he clearly loved and with whom he had deep-rooted connections, and, now, in his young secretary, a wife "in the spirit" who ultimately would be his mate into eternity. How long it took Edgar to discuss this subject with Gertrude is unclear. The conversation, wherever it took place, must have been both awkward and uncomfortable. Any strain that might already have been felt between Gertrude and Gladys would have been exacerbated by this revelation, whether they truly believed it or not.

This much was clear to them: the present circumstances that Edgar, Gertrude, and Gladys found themselves in was karmic, and how each of them chose to handle it would determine their future challenges or blessings to come. In subsequent readings, Gladys and Edgar repeatedly sought trance advice as to how to deal with this awkward and potentially volatile situation, and occasionally sought "report cards" on how well they were doing.

In one of these readings, the Source said: "For the best development each must give of the other self in no uncertain terms if the best would come . . . for they are knit in one and their completeness will only be found in the other." Asked what their relationships should be with each other's family, the Source replied: "Ever in that same loving relation as one holds for the other, for in fact they are one and their relation to each other's family ties should be the same . . . Patience endureth all things, yet if we have not the love that is found between these in their relations, we become as a sound or as a tinkling of the vibration without the answering chord."

In keeping with the concept of an answering "chord," the Source repeatedly encouraged Edgar and Gladys to foster and hold to the deep innate love and harmony that would naturally manifest itself between them. The Source went as far as to suggest that a physical union, if handled discreetly, would not be inappropriate if they so desired, and would enhance their "unity." Based on the questions posed in subsequent readings and information that Gladys herself later confided to Jeanette Thomas, the archivist who carried on Gladys Davis's work with the readings, Edgar and Gladys made a conscious decision to abstain from any carnal experience. This was corroborated by a medical examination performed on Gladys shortly after Edgar's death, when Gladys was about to undergo treatment for uterine cancer. Her personal physician's report indicated that Gladys Davis, at age fifty-five, was still a virgin.

Their choice was not an easy one, made all the more difficult because anyone who knew of their true connection would naturally have questioned the nature of their close personal relationship. And even those who didn't study the readings sometimes reached their own conclusions about what they perceived as a young, pretty, unmarried secretary living with and working for a charismatic psychic. The fact that Gladys didn't date or was otherwise unavailable to the local male population, only magnified their suspicions.

Foreseeing the challenges that were to come, Gladys and Edgar also asked the Source how they should relate to each other in public. The reply came: "As has been given, walking circumspectly before men, let the good be not evil spoken of, not as servants, but as one that rendereth good unto all, only keeping each in that relation that makes for the best all in all to the other, for the higher forces . . . direct their relations . . . and only the 'will' of either being the destructive element entering in."

If Gladys had been considering bailing out on the Cayces in Dayton and returning home to Alabama, she now had a most compelling reason to stay. Edgar Cayce's work—the work—that had begun thousands of years before, was also her own.

31.

Blessings to Come

That Gladys Davis and the Cayce family managed to overcome the challenges of their early Dayton years was perhaps the most remarkable accomplishment of their life together. At no time before or since did Edgar and Gertrude have more reason to pack their bags and return to The Hill. Never was there more reason to give up doing the kind of readings that would render them pariahs to the Christian fellowships they loved and that had long sustained them. And yet, they stayed together, putting aside their own personal needs for the greater good that could come from the work. Even Hugh Lynn, who still harbored a resentment toward his father for the decision he made to remain in Dayton, and who secretly feared what more the Source would say about his own karmic relationships, spent his spare time studying the history books that gave relevance to the life readings that kept them there.

Edgar had told Hugh Lynn, upon his arrival in Dayton, that "the money will come," though he was not specific about how soon they could expect it. Like an answer to a prayer, their family was indeed provided for. Byron Wyrick, in Chicago, sent a check for fifty dollars, which permitted Edgar and Linden Shroyer to check out of the Phillips Hotel. Then Curtis Willmott, an oilman and friend Edgar knew in Oklahoma, sent a $100 advance against future profits he hoped to obtain by drilling in Rocky Pasture. Using this money, Edgar was able to pay the back rent owed on the family's East Fifth Street apartment and relocate into a three-bedroom duplex on Grafton Avenue, where Gladys wouldn't have to share a bedroom with Edgar Evans and Hugh Lynn. Despite the Cayce's move farther out of the city to what was a considerably less desirable neighborhood, an increasing number of people made the long trek to Grafton Avenue to have physical readings. Money, of course, was still the family's chief concern, but as Gladys later reported, the "divine hand of providence" was constantly with them.

An incident that reminded the Cayces that they would be cared for occurred on an afternoon when they were in the midst of discussing how they were going to pay for groceries that day. According to Gladys, they had thirteen cents between them. In the middle of deciding who would eat the single bowl of soup left in the kitchen, there was a knock on the door. A complete stranger stood in the doorway and requested a reading for his sister, for which he paid $25 in advance. A few hours later, Edgar opened the afternoon mail to find another $25, this time from someone in Chicago, whom he also hadn't met. "Angels in disguise!" Edgar declared.

Yet another "angel" who came to their rescue was Tim Brown, the auto-parts manufacturer Edgar had met on his first trip to Dayton. While visiting Los Angeles, Brown met with film producers to discuss the possibility of Edgar using his psychic abilities to write screenplays for a production company called Famous Players Lasky, which would later become known as Paramount Pictures. Given Edgar's previous success in 1917 writing the scenario for actress Violet Mesereau, which had ultimately become the property of pioneer film producer Thomas Ince, Brown believed the Cayces could generate a considerable income for themselves in the motion-picture business. The Source agreed, and over a four-month period in early 1924, Edgar conducted a series of twelve readings that resulted in treatments for two separate feature-length scripts that Brown sent to Hollywood.

The first screen treatment, titled *Why?* illustrated some of the new concepts that were coming through the life readings. The seven-page outline was given in five readings, which were done over the span of nine days, beginning on January 3, 1924. The scenario depicted a young handyman named Abe, who worked for a wealthy New York family. While delivering a load of firewood, he becomes engaged in a conversation with a dinner guest who has some experience with hypnosis. Deemed to be a suitable candidate for their experiments, Abe agrees to be put into trance. Much to the surprise and delight of the wealthy New Yorkers, Abe—in trance—is revealed to have many psychic abilities, including the power to compose and play heavenly music and answer questions regarding fate and the destiny of man. The rest of the story parallels Edgar's own experiences, telling of the dilemmas, lessons, and gifts that came out of this new and unusual knowledge and its subsequent impact on the household.

A few months after giving readings on this screen treatment, Brown requested that they do another scenario for Gloria Swanson, who was reportedly having trouble finding a story that suited her. In a series of seven readings, beginning on April 23, 1924, Edgar delivered what amounted to a twenty-page screenplay. Like the earlier scenario, this one also made use of information from the life readings. Only this screenplay, titled *Bride of the Inca,* was far grander in scope and told of an all-consuming greed for Peruvian gold and how it changed the lives of a young archaeologist and his party of New York socialites as they searched for treasure high in the Andes.

Alf Butler, who was now working as a film distributor in Birmingham, gave Cayce much encouragement, as did Brown. "You know it has always been my idea that your scenarios ought to get over swimmingly," Butler wrote Edgar. "Once you break the ice . . . all our worries . . . will be over. Perhaps you may recall how Jack London wrote his heart out without selling a thing till way late; then [he] could scarcely write fast enough to supply the demand. It's the same with what you will be able to turn out. And you will have the additional advantage of producing the greatest diversification of plots and themes that have ever come down the pike. Your stories would never get in a rut [because you] have more . . . ideas than any dozen authors combined."

However enthusiastic Brown and Butler were, these two screenplays, and one other, completed in 1932, were eventually rejected in Hollywood as not being "fully developed" and "not very interesting." And yet, Edgar's movie career had its benefits, for film producer Harry Goetz, like Gloria Swanson and other Hollywood notables, became lifelong admirers and financial supporters of Edgar, and at various points in the future discussed filming Edgar's own life story.

Tim Brown continued to spin out ideas he thought could translate Edgar's psychic talent into hard cash. His next plan was for Edgar to give readings on electrical devices that could be patented, produced, and sold on the open market. Brown began by asking the Source for information on something he believed would revolutionize electronic communications: an instrument that would suppress the "noise" or "static" that accompanied radio communication.

The subsequent readings, which began on May 26, 1924, resulted in detailed information on how to design and build radio tubes or "static eliminators," which when built, consisted of various types of synthetic disks around a copper filament housed inside a radio tube. The detail presented in the readings for these instruments was astonishing: the name and location of a company in Pittsburgh and a university laboratory that were capable of producing the tubes, the precise dimensions—down to thousandths of an inch—of their various elements, and a description of the actual chemical components of the materials that the discs were to be made from. Accompanying these detailed descriptions were fascinating discourses on the nature of radio communication.

"All force is created by vibration," Cayce said in trance on July 3, 1924, echoing the message previously given to Thomas Edison. "All vibration becomes electrical in its action and its effect . . . It either enlivens, bring[s] greater vibration, or . . . becomes deadened or destructive to one or the other of the vibrations thus met. That law governing . . . the vibrations in transmission of [radio] messages . . . is the relativity of vibration as set in motion in any one particular place and other vibrations attuned to that same vibration . . . created by the one [and] magnified in the other."

The Source recommended that prototypes of two kinds of static eliminators be built, which would work in tandem with one another. They corrected for changes in electrical vibrations resulting from the passage of electromagnetic waves through heat and light, which current radio communications devices didn't account for. Cayce's tubes stabilized the vibrational level of the signals filtering them through heat-treated, color-coded discs.

The static eliminator readings continued through September. Against the advice given in the readings, Brown attempted to build the prototypes himself, choosing not to use either the Pittsburgh company or the university lab. Building the tubes himself took considerable time, and he couldn't ultimately match his prototypes to the exacting specifications in the readings. Frustrated, Brown eventually gave up and moved on to other projects. However, years later, Mitchell Hastings, an electrical engineer, IBM consultant, and personal friend of the Cayce family, would continue experimenting with Cayce's static eliminators, and ultimately reported succeeding where Brown had failed. By this time, changes in basic radio design, from cathode tubes to solid-state circuitry had made Cayce's invention obsolete.

Other innovative technical designs suggested in readings would, however, be manufactured in Cayce's lifetime, although Edgar himself was never able to take credit for having invented or marketed them. The most out-

standing example was a fog light, whose basic color-filtration system was laid
out in a reading on December 7, 1925, and was further expanded upon four
months later. In these readings Cayce detailed a high-intensity filtration
system that penetrated dense fog and could be used to assist pilots or navi-
gators on oceangoing ships. Such lights would become state of the art by
1929 and now are in use at every international airport in the world.

Another innovation discussed in the readings was a textile that would
later become known as Plexiglas, which the Source referred to as "mal-
leable" or "elastic" glass. A reading in 1926 described it as a material made
from organic substances altered by the use of chemicals and resulting in "a
piece [or] strip of 'glass' [that could be] bent . . . after becoming crystallized
[but still retain its shape]." Celluloid, of course, had been around since the
turn of the century, but "elastic glass"—as described in the readings—
wouldn't become manufactured or marketed until the 1940s, two decades
after Cayce had first given readings on this subject.

Tim Brown would make attempts to explore these revolutionary concepts, but ultimately he was unable to do anything constructive with them.
However, the scientific concepts put forth in these readings engaged him to
such a degree that he developed a deeper appreciation for the Cayces and
their work. Subsequently, he would do whatever he could to relieve them of
the enormous financial strain they were under in Dayton. Toward this end,
Brown would be instrumental in placing Hugh Lynn in the Moraine Park
School, an advanced "experiment in education" set up by wealthy Dayton in-
dustrialists for their children.

Hugh Lynn's acceptance at the Moraine Park School, on a full scholarship, was a great relief to Edgar and Gertrude. Not only was it considered to
be one of the finest schools in the state, it was an institution that taught traditional Christian values above all else. Reading and writing and arithmetic
were important, but considered secondary to matters of character. Hugh
Lynn thrived in the "hothouse" atmosphere created at the school and got
along extremely well with the other students, despite the fact that he had
grown up in a rural environment and his schoolmates came from vastly different economic and cultural backgrounds. While Edgar's father was worried
about clothing his son for school, some of Hugh Lynn's friends had personal
bodyguards. His closest friends included Dick Funkhouse, whose father was
president of Delco, the two Patterson boys, whose father owned National
Cash Register, and Gene Kettering, whose father invented the self-starter for
the automobile. Through their association at the school, the Cayces also
came to know Orville Wright, who was a judge in the debating club in which
Hugh Lynn became active.

Life was getting easier. As the weather warmed up, Edgar began taking long walks through Forest Park or shorter ones he accompanied Gertrude on, around Five Oaks Park or across the river to what is now called Island Park. Sometimes they would go on picnics with Linden and Violet Shroyer, and their son, Donald, or with visitors such as Carrie and Tommy House or Gertrude's mother, Lizzie. In the afternoons, the family would sometimes play croquet or join others in lawn bowling. Edgar was good at any kind of lawn game, especially ten-pin bowling, also known as duck pins. Hugh Lynn said he never saw his father lose. Most of the family trips were on foot or by streetcar. A frequent destination was the Grotto, which was an old stone quarry that had formed a natural swimming pool. They also visited the Forest Park Zoo, which featured a large monkey house and many wild deer.

Now that the family was becoming better established in Dayton, discussions once again turned to forming a Cayce Institute, where the readings could be conducted and studied on a more formal basis and Edgar would receive a steady income. Just how far Edgar had come in his own personal vision and what he saw as his new vocation was everywhere evident in his correspondence.

In a letter dated June 3, 1924, to a physician who expressed interest in the concept of helping to build the Cayce Institute, Edgar wrote: "The work for others [has grown to such a degree] that I feel that my entire time should be devoted to it." To his cousin Fannie Cayce, he wrote, "In my younger days it was my desire to be a minister. I believe now that I am not only finding in this . . . a work of the ministry to the spiritual but also that which leads to the upbuilding of the spiritual through the building up of the physical." In a reply letter, Fannie said that she thought Edgar should take a vacation and pay them a visit and believed that he shouldn't spend all of his time chasing the "almighty dollar." Edgar replied: "I have not spent my life in trying to accumulate but rather have I been attempting to give myself in service to humanity, and I am in hopes and believe I am building for myself, and for the generations to come, the foundation for a more perfect knowledge of the Laws of Heaven and of God as relating to humanity. I do not mean to infer from this that I am trying to establish some new kind of religion but a more perfect understanding of how to live rather than [only] profess Christ's principles."

Despite the fact that Edgar didn't know where the institute would finally be located or how it would be financed, he was more impatient than ever to establish a more stable base of operations. As he said to George Klingensmith, he did not want to be "forever dingdonging everyone for a few shekels to get along." Knowing for certain that Lammers would not be playing a part in future endeavors and frustrated at the lack of success in his oil endeavors, Edgar now went searching for a business manager.

Linden Shroyer's name came up as a possible manager, but Edgar's relationship with him had diminished as Shroyer's need to earn a steady income sent him away from Dayton in search of employment. After a few months away from the Cayces, and still out looking for a paying job, he moved with his family to Florida to help Lammers develop a real estate project. As the readings conducted for him suggested, the decision was not a wise one, and his new business arrangement with Lammers, like his previous one, failed miserably. Lammers once again reneged on his promises and left him stranded in Florida. The last two readings Shroyer conducted in Dayton were held on June 20, 1924. From then on, and for many years to come, Gertrude would become the official conductor.

The strong relationship that Edgar had developed with Byron Wyrick also made him a possible candidate for the position of manager. But due to his busy schedule, running between a full-time job in Chicago and the oil business in Texas, Wyrick rarely came to Dayton, and unless Edgar and his family moved to Chicago, which the readings indicated was not a suitable location to establish an institute, Wyrick wasn't in a position to be a full-time business manager.

Another possible manager was George Klingensmith. Although his heart was in the right place, his youth and lack of business experience made him a poor candidate. Despite his own frequent reports that he had raised as much as $20,000 for various oil ventures or was near closing a deal for an institute devoted to Cayce, he was ultimately unable to raise a single dollar.

Given Frank Mohr and Dave Kahn's continuing interest, they too were considered for the job. But Edgar was reluctant to offer it to either of them because both had demonstrated from previous experience that they were unable to cooperate with the people Edgar most depended upon. After those successful months in Birmingham, Mohr—like Kahn before him—had grown accustomed to being in charge and was having difficulty adjusting to sharing the responsibility with Gladys and Gertrude.

It was the Source who helped Edgar Cayce narrow his search for a business manager. In a reading on August 13, 1924, the Source named several people suited to be his manager, including Morton Blumenthal, a twenty-nine-year-old Jewish stockbroker from New York, and a friend of Dave Kahn's. Despite the fact that Edgar had never met Blumenthal, he appeared to have all the right credentials. According to Kahn, he was young, well educated, much admired in the financial community, and, like Lammers "had a burning desire to understand the secrets of the universe."

32.

The Blumenthal
Brothers

There were many people Edgar Cayce loved and admired throughout his career. John Blackburn had been Edgar's mentor through many difficult years in Bowling Green and had a physician's devotion to the art of healing. David Kahn was a natural-born salesman whom Edgar loved like a younger brother. Lamar Jones was a fishing buddy and could make Edgar laugh until tears came to his eyes. And Tim Brown could spin out ideas faster than a stenographer could record them. But more than anyone else in Cayce's life, Morton Harry Blumenthal combined the leadership skills and grand vision of a corporate executive with a deep passion for truth and the courage to stand by his convictions. As Edgar later said, he never admired another man as much as he did Morton. And Morton, in turn, never gave more of his time and resources to someone outside his own family than he did to Edgar Cayce.

Dave Kahn made initial contact with the Blumenthals. On June 15, 1924, he met Morton at the Plaza Hotel, where they discussed a business partnership for the development of a furniture company. Kahn rarely discussed any topic at length without mentioning Cayce, and Edgar's name as well as the subject of psychic phenomena and trance readings soon came up in conversation. Blumenthal expressed mild interest in Cayce, but also cited the fre-

quency with which mediums were being exposed as frauds. Certain that
Blumenthal could be convinced of Cayce's genuine psychic powers, Kahn
challenged the young stockbroker to obtain a physical reading for his girlfriend, Miriam Miller, a chorus girl on Broadway. Kahn himself agreed to
pay for the reading if Morton and his girlfriend weren't completely satisfied.
They shook hands and called Dayton from the Plaza Hotel that same night.

Miriam Miller's reading was conducted the next day, and Gladys's transcript of the session arrived by post at Blumenthal's office on Broadway a day
later. Morton and Miriam got together that night and read it over at Morton's permanent suite at the Hotel Cambridge, where Morton lived with his
mother, Freda Blumenthal. The reading said that Miller was suffering from
fatigue, which was preventing her from realizing her ambitions on the stage.
The diagnosis was anemia, and the recommendations suggested she supplement her diet with nuts and vegetables, as well as stimulate her respiratory
system by inhaling the fumes of apple brandy from a wooden container. A
few weeks later, Blumenthal, like Miller, had to admit to Kahn that the diagnosis of anemia was correct, and the treatment was a great success. At
Miller's request, three more readings were eventually conducted on her behalf, one of which was a life reading that revealed a long and complicated
relationship between her and Morton in their previous incarnations.

Intrigued, Morton wrote a letter to Edgar thanking him for the first
physical reading. "You would be highly gratified if you knew how your
reading helped her," Morton said. "I studied the darn thing for hours preparing to explain it to her and then when she read it over she said, 'Why yes, I
know exactly what it means. I have it in me [to be a great actress], if only I
have the opportunity to show it [on stage]. It says I will get that opportunity
if I continue to do my best. It says a lot of other things too—and I understand, Morton, you don't need to explain!' . . . Miriam no longer sits in the
corner crying her eyes out from disappointment. Rather she dances with all
her might and tells them she knows she will get there! Lo and behold they
already have taken her out of two choruses and told her they had a good part
in reserve for her shortly after the show opens."

Kahn was also very pleased with the reading. Morton and his brother,
Edwin, were men of considerable means and influence, and Kahn believed
they could do great things for the work if only he could engage them in a
business deal. Kahn communicated as much in a letter he wrote to Edgar asking him to do all he could to remain in Morton and his brother's good favor.
In this same letter, however, Kahn revealed a weakness that would ultimately unravel his relationship with the Blumenthals.

Unbeknownst to Edgar, Morton had agreed to reimburse Dave Kahn for telephone and other expenses he had incurred in communicating with Edgar and to make a cash donation of $50 to Edgar beyond the cost of the initial reading if Dave agreed to match that amount. Morton paid the money to Kahn, who delivered Morton's $50, but only $25 dollars from himself, telling Edgar, "understand you have received the full hundred dollars." Apparently Kahn was tight himself and needed the other $25 for the monthly support he was sending his mother. Later, under a similar arrangement with Morton, Dave Kahn not only didn't pay his full half of the money, but kept a small portion of the Blumenthal money as well. It was years before Morton discovered the full extent of Kahn's business practices.

Although Kahn had been arranging readings for the Blumenthals since he had met them, neither Morton nor Edwin had yet made a request themselves. It wasn't until Edgar wrote to Morton early in August, telling him of the policy to only do readings when asked directly by the subject, that Morton made a request for himself.

The first reading was on a wide range of topics, but generally centered around Morton's physical condition, which for the most part was good. The Source cited a slight irritation of Morton's tonsils, a problem with his gums and teeth, and a general imbalance of physical activity. He had too much stress and not enough exercise. The reading also highlighted Morton's abilities as a businessman and his potential to bring good into the world. However, the Source admonished him that the "spiritual force" must "be kept apace with the development in the mental proclivities of the entity." Echoing Psalm 19 from the Bible, the Source added: "Ever keep the injunction in the faith of the entity's forces and keep the words of the mouth, the meditation of the heart, holy and acceptable unto Him."

However comprehensive this reading appeared to be from a physical point of view, Morton was surprised that it hadn't mentioned a recurring ear problem he had since his youth. A second reading, conducted on September 2, 1924, addressed this issue. Morton's ear problem, the reading indicated, *had* been addressed in the earlier reading. The assumption was that this problem was the result of poor circulation, and that this caused, among other ailments that were specifically noted in the earlier reading, trouble with his Eustachian tube, which could be remedied with osteopathic treatments. This explanation satisfied Blumenthal. He underwent osteopathic treatments, and his hearing problems, gum disease, and general health improved greatly.

In the days after his second reading, Morton put more questions to the Source. He wished to know whether he should come to Dayton to meet Edgar or Edgar should go to New York. The answer came: "Under the existing conditions, better that . . . Morton Blumenthal study such conditions from both viewpoints. First, see and know ... Edgar Cayce in the home, and the surrounding conditions. Then in ... Morton's own surroundings." Asked how he could best benefit the work of Edgar Cayce, the Source said: "In the capacity of trustee, director, or manager, from that viewpoint, and in the financial assistance that the body [Morton Blumenthal], is capable of rendering [in] such work."

Morton Blumenthal, apparently concerned that Dave Kahn had been exaggerating Edgar Cayce's abilities, asked about Kahn's accuracy and sincerity, to which the Source responded: "The endeavors, as has been outlined, are worthy of consideration. The enthusiasm of David E. Kahn can be capitalized upon, and such an individual as Morton is capable of doing so ... The exaggerations are almost nil, yet should be taken under advisement and well considered."

The type and number of questions that Blumenthal asked Edgar clearly revealed his growing interest in the work. In the days before and after his readings, he peppered Kahn with questions about Cayce and his family. Kahn, by this time, was living in New York and dating an actress named Lucille, who coincidentally shared his last name. Lucille Kahn and Miriam Miller had much in common, as did their respective boyfriends, so it was natural that the couples began to double-date and become better acquainted. Edgar and Gertrude would later get to meet Lucille when she came to Dayton as part of the traveling company of an Otis Skinner play. Edgar eventually gave readings for her and Dave as he now did for Miriam and Morton.

Earlier, in June, Kahn had been pushing Edgar to drop everything and come to New York to meet Morton. Gertrude had been putting pressure on Edgar to stay in Dayton, and Edgar was loathe to leave town when there was not even money to put food on the table at home. Besides, he had been busy with Tim Brown on his static eliminator readings and was waiting for George Klingensmith and Byron Wyrick to take the next step in their new partnership, despite the fact that the partner who had initiated it all, Arthur Lammers, had dropped out of the picture altogether.

Despite heavy pressure from Dave Kahn, Edgar had continued putting off the meeting. Now, Morton's interest had grown to the point that he proposed to pay for Edgar to make a trip to New York, along with giving him a modest stipend to cover household expenses while he was gone. Ignoring the advice given by the Source that Morton come first to Dayton, Edgar headed off to New York on October 4 for a meeting with Morton at the Hotel Cambridge.

Morton was everything that Dave Kahn had said he would be, and more. The handsome, dark-haired stockbroker had great charisma: he had a philosopher's love of beauty and the arts and a businessman's practical approach to life. And unlike Arthur Lammers, Morton actually listened to what Edgar had to tell him—not just out of intellectual curiosity, but with genuine interest in Edgar as another human being. He listened with fascination as Edgar told him stories of his early childhood in Beverly, of Bowling Green and his partnership with Ketchum and Noe, and of his frustrations in the Texas oil business. Morton was impressed by the stories and found himself charmed, though he later admitted to being put off by Edgar's obvious lack of education and his slow Kentucky drawl.

The next day, over dinner at the Plaza Hotel, Morton told Edgar about himself. He and his brother, Edwin, had been born in Altoona, Pennsylvania, where their father ran a small appliance store. When Morton's father died suddenly, the two boys supported their mother while working their way through college. Morton described how difficult school had been for him and how often he felt like a "dummy." His persistence, however, paid off. He studied economics and sociology at night at the University of Pittsburgh while he clerked at McCreey's department store during the day. The dean was so impressed that he arranged a special evening educational program for Morton, which he completed at Columbia University in New York while working at various menial jobs. Morton and his younger brother were still in their twenties when they joined the William E. Lauer brokerage house on lower Broadway in Manhattan. Edwin then married a wealthy society girl, while Morton led the life of a bachelor. Morton preferred to work in the office, researching investments while Edwin "worked the floor" of the stock exchange.

Morton's interest in psychic phenomena had begun when a close friend, in whom he had the deepest and most sincere trust, said he had been visited by a ghost. This experience prompted Morton to study spirit communication in various ancient and modern philosophical texts, as had Lammers. But Morton delved deeper than Lammers had in many areas, particularly in the field of current philosophy. His book-lined study included the works of Bergson, Ouspensky, William James, and Thomas Hudson. Morton not only studied these books, but kept copious notes in binders and on loose papers, which were stacked on his desk and on his shelves. It was his hope to someday turn it all into a book. Though he considered himself a Jew, and in fact briefly entertained the notion of becoming a rabbi, Morton had a far broader interpretation of what it meant to be Jewish than was commonly accepted. He acknowledged that Jesus Christ was an important prophet and a son of God, from whom much could be learned. At the end of Edgar's ten-day visit, on

October 14, Dave Kahn would conduct the first of what would be four life readings on Morton. No doubt Edgar, like Kahn and Morton himself, was eager to hear what the Source would tell them.

As in all previous life readings, the Source provided astrological information. Morton was said to be mostly under the influence of Mercury, with positive influences of Jupiter, Neptune, and the adverse influence of Saturn and Uranus. Given this configuration, and what could only be described as Morton's accomplishments in previous incarnations, he was said to be "a leader . . . regarding those of the mental understanding of conditions [He] may be led, especially through respect . . . or through the ennobling influence of . . . love . . . yet never driven in either. One given to have much of the worldly goods."

Further, the reading stated that in his thirty-fifth year—1930—he would have much worldly goods, though how he chose to use those goods would greatly determine whether or not they would remain in his possession. As later life readings revealed, Morton was advised to use his "worldly possessions" in the "correct manner," or as the Source said, to bring "satisfaction to self and others" as opposed to "distress."

Regarding previous incarnations, Morton was described as having once been a gatekeeper in the city of Jerusalem, where he had helped to rebuild and protect that city. Prior to that he had been the great mythic figure of Achilles, a man of exceptional abilities and great physical beauty, who led the Greek army's assault on the city of Troy. Edgar and the others couldn't help but note that Morton, in his incarnation as Achilles, had killed Arthur Lammers, who, as Hector the Trojan prince, was the commander of the Trojan army. In keeping with the description in Homer's legend, the Source said Achilles died from a wound to his heel inflicted by Hector's brother, Paris.

The Source also mentioned one other of Morton's incarnations, that of Aarat, described as a sage in an Egyptian religious cult who became an important advisor to the king. As would later become evident, Morton's Egyptian incarnation, and in his incarnation as Achilles, coincided with Edgar, Gertrude, Hugh Lynn, and Gladys's prior incarnations. He too had been part of the work since the beginning. And he, like his brother, Edwin, had been, as a later reading would reveal, one of the "little folk"—Edgar's "imaginary friends"—who appeared not just for Edgar's amusement, but to help prepare him for his life's work.

Perhaps the most interesting aspect of Morton's first life reading was the suggestion by the Source that he had developed to such a degree in his previous incarnations that he might not have to incarnate on earth again if he continued to be of service to God. He had great power, the Source indicated, to help the lives of countless others and to provide the world with insight into the "realm beyond." He had the potential to become a great teacher.

No doubt Morton was impressed by his life reading. In his excitement to learn more, he encouraged Edwin to request a life reading of his own. Edgar agreed, and with this reading, his connection to the work became even clearer. According to the Source, Edwin and Morton had worked together in previous incarnations, most notably in the rebuilding of Jerusalem. Like Morton, Edwin was described as having exceptional abilities, especially those of a psychic nature, which, if developed, might rival that of Edgar himself. Apparently, they too, had been a team for many thousands of years.

The truth of these readings, from Edgar's perspective, was not in question. Morton, and in turn Edwin, had such an intuitive grasp of the fundamental principles of Edgar's work that hardly any explanation of the readings was necessary. In fact, only a few days after Edgar presented Morton with a copy of the manuscript of the book that he and Lammers had begun, Morton was offering insights and editorial advice beyond anything Edgar himself had considered.

One of the most interesting and revealing of Morton's editorial notes was the suggestion that the word "psychic" not be used in the book because it did not adequately convey the full meaning of what transpired when Edgar went into trance. "The powers possessed by Edgar Cayce are such that the language of today does not contain a word to describe it," Morton wrote to Byron Wyrick, Edgar's friend in Chicago. "[Now] we use psychic for the want of a proper word ... To hear or read his thesis on trips that he makes into the realm of subconsciousness gives one a clearer understanding of what is meant by the visions or dreams of the prophets, our Lord, and his disciples. It permits an understanding, too, of the realness of the inhabitants of oracles in the old Greek temples and the bards of the separate tribes of mountain folk in the cradle of Christendom. Convince yourself by test, which is the individual's method of proof. Your conviction will give the Cayce Institute its desired impetus toward its avowed aim of service to mankind."

Not long after Edgar's trip to New York, Morton followed the Source's earlier advice to visit Dayton. When he arrived by train on November 2, 1924, Morton couldn't have been more stunned by the dichotomy of the Cayces' existence in Dayton. Though Edgar was giving readings for some of the city's wealthiest families, and his eldest son attended Dayton's most prestigious school, the Cayces were living in what Morton described as "sheer poverty." Morton had the impression that he was walking into the "bleak home of destitute people." Morton simply couldn't believe that a man with such obvious talents would live in such squalid conditions. He didn't look into the bedrooms, but noted that the sole furniture in the rest of the house consisted of a shabby sofa, a bare wooden table, four straight-back chairs, and a chest of drawers.

"Gertrude and the two boys, Hugh Lynn and Edgar [Evans], looked undernourished," Morton later said. "Gertrude was thin and wan, her fingers almost skeletal in appearance. The older boy, Hugh, was small, drawn, and bespectacled." The sight of the house and the physical condition of its occupants prompted Morton to excuse himself, visit the grocery store, and return with boxes of food and dry goods to fill the pantry. Gertrude proceeded to prepare a large meal, which, according to Morton, "the family promptly scarfed down."

After visiting Dayton, Morton invited Edgar, Gertrude, Hugh Lynn, Edgar Evans, and Gladys to be his guest in New York at the Hotel Cambridge in early January of 1925. For Gladys, who had never been to "the big city," and who already had begun to feel a special affinity for Morton, the trip was a "dream vacation." Morton was the kind of chaperon that existed only in fiction: a rich and debonair intellectual, with a showgirl for a girlfriend and a partnership in a New York brokerage company.

Morton took the Cayces and Gladys to visit the places that they had only read about, including what they termed a "shocking" Broadway play called *Ladies of the Evening*, which was about prostitutes. Morton admitted with embarrassment that he hadn't picked the show himself, he had just sent for tickets from his ticket broker for whatever show had seats available. Afterward, he took them dancing at the Silver Slipper, his favorite New York nightclub. The next day, Freda Blumenthal took Gladys and Gertrude downtown where she bought them new dresses, then treated them to lunch at an elegant restaurant.

Among Morton's friends whom Edgar met on this trip was Merryle Rukeyser, a newspaper columnist who had attended Columbia University with Blumenthal. Rukeyser was given a reading, along with Freda Blumenthal, Edwin, and Edwin's wife, Ruth. Although each of these sessions went well, the readings that made Morton a true disciple were given for the woman who would become Morton's wife.

Twenty-year-old Adeline Levy, the future Mrs. Blumenthal, was visiting New York from her home in the French Quarter of New Orleans when she and Morton met. Morton fell instantly in love with the petite dark-haired beauty. Her quiet reserve, deeply felt Jewish heritage, and love of home and family were a refreshing break from the fast-paced and career-driven people who surrounded him. And yet, she was by no means provincial. She had traveled the world, spoke French like a native, and was nearly as well read as he was, though her tastes ran more to popular fiction. Miriam Miller quickly disappeared from Morton's life.

There was only one problem. Unlike Miriam Miller, Adeline didn't approve of Morton's interests in the Cayces, nor did she put any worth in the readings. Her family thought "psychic powers" were nothing more than parlor tricks. Morton was reportedly so disturbed by the situation that he requested a reading to be conducted on the subject. To Morton's relief, the readings suggested that Adeline—despite her misgivings about his philosophical and more spiritual interests—was an ideal mate for him. According to another reading, she was none other than Helen of Troy in a previous incarnation, for whom Morton, as Achilles, had waged war on that city. Adeline was also said to have a personality that complemented Morton's, and she would have a calming effect upon him, although, if crossed, she could become vengeful and vindictive toward him.

Dave Kahn would later joke that Edgar and his trance advice was "so good at selling Morton on the idea of marrying the young lady" that he wanted Edgar to start "selling furniture for his company." Morton still needed to persuade Adeline that Cayce was legitimate and begged her to submit to a reading for herself. The two physical readings and one spiritual reading given for Adeline convinced her of Cayce's ability more than anything Morton could have told her about the man. They were married in June 1925.

Based on the success of these readings, Blumenthal decided to devote much of his time and energy to Edgar—not as a manager as suggested in the readings, but as his benefactor. He put Edgar on a retainer of $50 a week. Subsequently, Edgar was expected but not obligated to give readings for him and his brother, and later for his wife. Gladys would be paid $25 a week for transcribing the readings and handling communications between New York and Dayton. The assumption that Dave Kahn made was that the Blumenthals wanted Edgar to give readings on the stock market. And, indeed, Edgar did. But, intrigued by the apparent knowledge the Source had exhibited, Morton also had something much grander than the financial world in mind: he wanted readings on the life of Jesus Christ.

33.

✤

The Life
of Christ

Cayce's readings had already suggested the exalted position with which the Source viewed the life and teachings of Jesus Christ. References to the "Lowly Nazarene," the "Master," and the "Prince of Peace" appeared thousands of times during trance sessions, in ways that suggested that the readings' recipients should aspire to a greater understanding of God. Now that Morton Blumenthal's curiosity had been piqued by his own life reading, he naturally wanted to know if Jesus the man actually existed, and if the accepted details of His life as put forth in the Bible were accurate. The fact that Morton Blumenthal—a Jew—first raised the subject, made the search for the historical Jesus all the more unusual.

To Edgar's relief, rarely did the contents of what became known as the Jesus readings—nor the hundreds of life readings that were later conducted for people purported to have played a role in the events of the early Christian Church—overtly contradict what appeared in the Bible. More often than not these readings added clarity and a deeper, more three-dimensional picture of the life and times of Jesus Christ. However, like so much else that came through in trance, the readings on Jesus also challenged anyone who studied them. Perhaps the most intriguing information that came through

Cayce concerned the preparation for His birth, a topic on which the Bible provides few details.

In a particularly fascinating discourse on biblical history, the Source suggested that preparations for the coming of the Messiah were underway four hundred years before the birth of Jesus. According to Cayce, the group of people who were "preparing the way," and in whose midst Jesus was eventually born, were the Essenes, or the "Brotherhood." Cayce described them as "a [noncelibate] religious order within Jewry," whose primary function was as record keepers, interpreters of the prophecies, and channels for the Messiah to come. According to the readings, because of their belief in astrology, numerology, and reincarnation, they were also generally viewed by the greater Jewish population as rebels and radicals.

For modern historians, the Essenes have long been an enigma, primarily because there is little mention of the sect's existence after the birth of Jesus. Much of what is now known about the Essenes comes from the Dead Sea Scrolls, which were discovered in Qumran in 1947, more than a decade after Cayce first discussed the Essenes and two years after his death. The Dead Sea Scrolls, which are generally believed to have been authored by the Essenes, ultimately created more confusion about who the Essenes were. However, the information revealed by the scrolls bears a striking similarity to the descriptions from Cayce's readings, and provides the single most compelling evidence that the biblical history as presented by Cayce might indeed be true.

Although historians and the Cayce readings are in agreement that the Essenes were a Jewish sect, the Source went quite a bit further in describing the makeup of the community. "They took Jews and Gentiles alike as members [as they did both men and women]," Cayce said. "This was the beginning of the period where women were considered as equals with the men in their activities, in their abilities to formulate, to live, to be channels. They joined by dedication . . . a [matter of] free will." Perhaps most surprising of Cayce's claims was that the head of the Essenes at the time of Jesus' birth was a woman named Judy, who "had the experience of hearing voices and communication with the divine—voices, dreams, signs, symbols." The Source went on to say that Judy's birth was foretold by an angel who appeared before her mother and father. "That the entity was a daughter, rather than being a male, brought some disturbance [and] confusion, but was a decision from the powers on 'high,' and gave the first demonstration of woman's place in the affairs and associations of man, for [like] the teachings of Jesus [this] released woman from that bondage to which she had been held since the ideas of man conceived from the fall of Eve."

It appears from the readings that Judy, who broke tradition by becoming the female head of this sect, also had the "Divine" responsibility for recording and compiling much of what is now found in the Old Testament and in the ancient documents that comprise the Dead Sea Scrolls. According to the Source, the Essenes "labored in the preserving of records of His activities as the Child [and] the activities of the [Magi]. Judy had been the prophetess, the healer, the writer, the recorder." As this last reading would suggest, and the next would confirm, the Magi, who had come out of the East in search of the newborn Messiah, had actually been in contact with the Essenes even before His birth. The Magi were described as soothsayers, astrologers, interpreters of dreams and of palms, and also "those that were seekers for the truth, for [the coming Messiah]."

Not only did the Essenes devote themselves spiritually to the coming Messiah, but according to the Source, they took practical steps to bring about the event when their own astrological calculations, and those of the Magi, indicated that the arrival of the "Promised One" was fast approaching. This was a time, according to the Source, when the Essene sages earnestly began studying the teachings of Persia, India, Greece, Egypt, and the Hebrews.

According to Cayce, the study took place on Mount Carmel, near Galilee, and not far from Nazareth. "Thus in [Mount] Carmel, where the priests of this faith were, there were [twelve] maidens chosen that were dedicated to this purpose [as potential channels for the Messiah]." The twelve maidens were purported to be selected from "all of those who chose to give those that were perfect in body and in mind for the service." As stated in other readings, the parents of these maidens were all hopeful that their daughter would be ultimately chosen. It was Mary, the entity whom Cayce described as "an Aquarius—in its perception [and] perfection," who had been given by her mother at age "four," and "between twelve and thirteen [was] the one chosen."

Mary, like the other virgins, was put into training according to Essene tradition, which included "chastity, purity, love, patience, endurance—all of [which] would be termed by many in the present as persecutions, but [were] tests for physical and mental strength . . . These were kept balanced according to that which had been first set by Aran and Ra Ta." Although the point may have been initially lost on Morton and Edgar, here was not only a description of the education of the mother of Jesus, but the first of many references to the role that Ra Ta—Edgar Cayce, in a previous incarnation—played in "preparing the way."

According to the readings, Mary had been in serious preparation for three years before she was chosen by an angel to be the mother of the Messiah. The selection was made on "the temple steps [when the] maidens [were] going to the altar for prayer . . . As they mounted the steps, all were bathed in the morning sun, which not only made a beautiful picture but clothed all as in purple and gold. As Mary reached the top step [there was] thunder and lightning, and the [Angel Gabriel] led the way, taking the child [Mary] by the hand."

The Source confirmed that Jesus was immaculately conceived and stated that Mary herself was also divinely conceived, though in a somewhat different fashion. Like Edgar Cayce and Gladys Davis, Mary and her son Jesus were described as "twin souls" or "soul mates" separated at some early and as yet undefined period during Earth's "indwelling." Asked to explain the nature of Jesus' conception, the Source said: "The immaculate conception is the physical and mental . . . attuned to spirit as to be quickened by same [Many will] say 'Impossible!' They say that it isn't in compliance with the natural law. [But] it is a natural law, as has been indicated by the projection of mind into matter . . . Neither Mary nor Jesus had a human father. They were one soul."

According to Cayce, once the teenage Mary was established as the future mother of the Messiah, the Essenes quickly sought to find her a husband. A thirty-six-year-old widower named Joseph was chosen, and the wedding, which was performed in the temple at Carmel, "followed the regular ritual . . . not . . . in the Jewish temple but rather in the general meeting place of the Essenes." The Angel Gabriel again appeared in a vision and blessed the union. Mary then became pregnant.

As described in the Bible, the readings said Mary joined Joseph in Nazareth after the wedding, and "from [Nazareth] they went to Bethlehem to be taxed, or to register." The Source went on to fill in many new details: "Mary and Joseph's arrival [into Bethlehem] was in the evening . . . the weather was cool, and there were crowds on the way . . . from the hills of Judea." In another reading, the Source said: "In the evening . . . the specter of His star in the evening sky brought awe and wonder to all who beheld [it]. At twilight, Joseph approached the inn that was filled with those who had also journeyed there on their way to be polled for the tax . . . required by the Roman law . . . Both Joseph and Mary were members of the [radical] sect . . . and thus they were questioned by those not only in the political but in the religious authority in the cities. Then there was the answer by the innkeeper, 'No room in the inn,' especially for such an occasion. Laughter and jeers followed at the sight of the elderly man with the beautiful girl, his wife heavy with child."

Regarding the innkeeper, who has been generally portrayed as heartless, Cayce provided an interesting detail: "Much of that as has been recorded as we find is not . . . in keeping with [what] the [innkeeper] did [His name was] Apsafar, who was of the Essenes [He] knew of those things that had been foretold by the teachers . . . and made all preparations as near in keeping with what had been foretold." Apsafar therefore sent Mary and Joseph to a grotto behind the stables to protect them from the Romans, where according to the Source, the Child was born.

"[Just as the midnight hour came] the star appeared that made the wonderment to the shepherds . . . All were in awe as the brightness of His star appeared and shone, as the music of the spheres brought that joyful choir, 'Peace on Earth! Good will to men of Good Faith.' All felt the vibrations and saw a great light—not only the shepherds above that stable but those in the inn as well. To be sure, those conditions were later to be dispelled by the doubters who told the people that they had been overcome with wine."

The Magi, according to the reading, arrived at the grotto where the child was born through their own purported psychic powers and visions, carrying with them gifts that represented—in the metaphysical sense—the three phases of man's experience in materiality: gold, the material; frankincense, the ether or ethereal; and myrrh, the healing force. Although the Bible story suggests that after the Magi visited them the Holy Family left Bethlehem almost immediately, Cayce asserted that Mary, Joseph, and baby Jesus remained in Bethlehem for twenty-nine days.

As described in the Bible, en route to visiting the newborn Messiah, the Magi had stopped to visit with Herod and inquire of him the whereabouts of the infant Messiah. Cayce pointed out that visiting Herod, who was only second or third in command, instead of the Romans who were in charge, might appear to be a strange choice on the part of the Magi. The Source went on to say that this was orchestrated by Judy, who knew that Herod, a despot, would react violently to the news of the new King of the Jews, and would thus fulfill another Old Testament prophecy, of "Rachel weeping for her children." This suggested that the fulfillment of prophecies and the Essene practice of record keeping were actually one and the same: to provide evidence to seekers that Jesus was the Messiah, and to chronicle the life that He would live.

Just as the readings dedicated to the life of Jesus provided interesting insights into the arrival of the "New King," hundreds of life readings conducted by Cayce over the next two decades described other important events of the life of Christ from the perspective of participants in His story. A particularly insightful life reading was given for a woman purported to have been Herod's third wife. According to this reading, Thesea, as she was known in her earlier incarnation, was fourteen years old when she was wed to

Herod, who reportedly had chosen her not only for beauty and education, but because of the political influence that her family had with the priests in power. Caiaphus, the high priest in the Bible who presided at the trial of Jesus, was her brother-in-law and was described by Cayce as making "overtures to Herod in his proclaiming the closer relationship to the Roman rule." Thesea, according to the Source, was horrified by her husband's edict to kill the infants of Jerusalem and disassociated herself from his activities and later, like the Essenes, suffered great physical and mental cruelty at his hands. As the story was related, Thesea became a secret informant for the Essenes, conversed with the Magi, and took on the task of chronicling what happened. Her writings, like Judy's, were purportedly part of the records destroyed in the Alexandrian library, and a portion of those records, in some form, is also said to still exist in the Vatican library.

Herod's persecution forced the Holy Family to leave for Egypt, but before their departure, Judy appointed a girl named Josie—one of the twelve consecrated virgins—to become the handmaiden to Mary and Joseph. The journey took them "through portions of Palestine, from Nazareth to the borders of Egypt," the Source said. "Do not understand that there was only Joseph, Mary, Josie, and the child, for there were other [Essene] groups that preceded and followed [them for their] protection." Regarding the "four years, six months, three days" that the family reportedly would spend in Egypt, the Source noted that Jesus had already begun to manifest the gifts later ascribed to Him in the Bible. The "garments worn about the Child" were said to have healing properties, "for the body being perfect radiated that which was health, life itself." Cayce also stated that Jesus was not consciously able to perform "miracles" until He was twelve, when He stayed to converse with the rabbi in Jerusalem.

According to the readings, the family's return from Egypt was made to Capernaum—not Nazareth as stated in Matthew—and was done not only for political reasons, owing to the death of Herod, but for the continuing education of Jesus: "That there might be the ministry or teaching [to Jesus] that was to be a part of the Brotherhood—supervised in that period by Judy." Though nothing is said in the New Testament about Jesus between the time He was a twelve-year-old child in the temple in Jerusalem, and when He was a thirty-year-old man about to begin His ministry, the Cayce readings chronicle Jesus' life in this period, alleging that He went to Persia, India, Syria, and Egypt to complete His education.

In India, Jesus was purported to have studied the "cleansings of the body as related to preparation for strength in the physical as well as in the mental man." Apparently these teachings represented forms of fasting and meditation, practices meant to purify one's body, thoughts, and actions. Jesus was also said to have studied in Benares—a holy Hindu city—where He learned "teachings . . . combined from the Essene schools, but . . . not true Essene doctrine as practiced by the Jewish and semi-Jewish associations in Carmel." Jesus returned home and after His father's funeral was reported to have accompanied the man who would become John the Baptist "into Egypt for the completion of His preparation as a teacher." It was in Egypt, Cayce said, that "both [John and Jesus] became the initiates in the pyramid . . . [studying] what you would today call [the law of one]." Cayce added that "these [aspects of Jesus' education] should not be looked upon by students as unnatural conditions," suggesting, perhaps, that anyone preparing for ministry in the Essene community would have undertaken such an education.

Cayce also made reference to "the passing of the tests [in Egypt] by those who were of the Essene group, as they entered into the service." For these tests, Jesus was in Heliopolis—a now ruined city outside of Cairo, not to be confused with the modern city with the same name. Heliopolis, which means "city of the sun," was the center of sun worship in the pre-Christian Egyptian civilization and had also been known as the "City of Ra"—another reference to the deified Ra Ta named in Edgar's life readings. The reason the Essenes chose this spot, as Cayce stated in another reading, was that "the unifying of the teachings of many lands was brought together in Egypt [under the law of one]."

Cayce—in trance—said that the Bible does not tell of Jesus' youth and education because there were few, if any, supporting records: "All of those that existed were destroyed—that is, the originals—with the activities in Alexandria [although] there are some that have been forged manuscripts." Exactly what Cayce meant by "forged" is not clear, but what he may have been referring to were adulterated copies of the originals.

Cayce asserted that "Mary and Joseph took up normal married life about ten years after the birth of Jesus, when Jesus went to be taught by priests." They then had three children. According to the readings, Jesus was twelve when Mary gave birth to James. The next year, when Jesus began His studies in foreign lands, Ruth was born in Capernaum and then Jude was born. Although this information varies from the Bible, which refers to brothers James, Judas, Simon, and Joses as well as unnamed sisters, some historians assert that the siblings mentioned in the Bible were not Mary's, but Joseph's from a previous marriage, which would have been in keeping with Cayce's account of events.

There is very little in the readings about James, who Cayce confirmed was the head of the Christian church in Jerusalem after Jesus' death: "James was exalted to the position of the leader because the honor was to Jesus . . . to whom all honor and all glory are due." However, Cayce also asserted something that modern scholars dispute, that James, the brother of the Lord, and "James the Less," as referred to in the Bible, were one and the same person.

The Source yielded much more information about Jesus' sister, Ruth, who is not specifically mentioned in the Bible. Information on her comes through a life reading given for a forty-six-year-old wife of a labor-management mediator and the daughter of a man who, at the time, was one of the wealthiest and most influential men in America, and purported in the readings to have been Caesar Augustus in a previous incarnation. Ruth was said to have reached young adulthood when the Jewish people were questioning the veracity of the events relating to Jesus' birth. Despite the difficulties that arose when her brother returned to Egypt to complete His training, Ruth would eventually support Jesus and recognize Him as the Messiah. And after Jesus' death, she aided their brother James in heading the church and in convincing their younger brother Jude of the truth of Jesus' resurrection. Jude was described by Cayce as "faltering much" in his early adulthood.

On a few occasions, Cayce offered a physical description of Jesus as a young man, sometimes including interesting details: "The Master's hair is 'most red,' inclined to be curly in portions, yet not feminine or weak—strong with heavy piercing eyes that are blue or steel-gray. His weight would be at least a hundred and seventy pounds. Long tapering fingers, nails well kept. Long nail, though, on the left little finger."

Cayce confirmed that the first recorded miracle performed by the Master was when He turned water into wine at a wedding. According to the readings, the bride, named Mary, was a close relative of His mother, Mary, whom the Bible refers to as the "other Mary." Cayce described the miracle: "The day was fine and the evening fair, with a full moon. There was more and more wine drinking and more hilarity, and the dance—which was done in circles . . . The wine ran low. Mary, remembering how, upon their return from Egypt, food had been mysteriously provided when they got waylaid, was convinced that here might be an opportunity to experience such an increase again, especially with her son returning a man, starting upon His mission." In what Cayce described as one of the rare instances where Jesus performed miracles among his own kindred people, the water was changed into wine "as it was poured out of the jugs."

According to the Gospels, not long after this miracle, John the Baptist had been imprisoned by Herod for publicly condemning Herod for taking his brother's wife—or, as Cayce put it, "because John had spoken against that which answered to the aggrandizing of a fleshly lust." Although the Bible speaks of the death of only John the Baptist, according to Cayce, Roael Zebedee, the groom at the wedding and the elder brother of James and John the beloved, was also among these followers who would suffer persecution and death.

Although Luke's Gospel has Jesus returning home from the desert to Nazareth and then going on to Capernaum, according to Cayce, Jesus went straight home to Capernaum. Upon His return, on the first Sabbath, He went into the synagogue, and His sister Ruth "for the first time heard in the synagogue His first utterances, as to the prophecies of Isaiah, Jeremiah, and the teachings of the lesser prophets."

On her way home from this meeting, Ruth met her future husband, a thirty-year-old Roman tax assessor named Philoas. Ruth was described as not only beautiful but "active in those conditions that were accorded to those peoples in the less fortunate circumstances, which became part of the interests of this Roman." The two were introduced by the physician Luke, the apostle. Once Ruth got over her shyness with Philoas, the Source said she began to resent the advice given by her mother, who was unsure of the wisdom of her daughter's relationship. Ruth persisted in seeing Philoas because in her mind, "he bespoke of greater knowledge of the needs of human experience than that held to either by the Essenes or the orthodox Jewish people." Philoas' job put him into contact with many of the Master's followers, including Judy, the head of the Essenes, and many of the apostles. He was said to have eventually obtained the records that had been gathered by Judy in Carmel and delivered them to Alexandria.

When Passover came, Jesus went to Jerusalem, where many people had already heard tales of His activities. One of these was a Pharisee named Nicodemus, who according to John 3:2, "came to Jesus by night" to talk with Him and ask Him questions. An interesting point that Cayce made was that Nicodemus was married to an Essene named Martha. As a Pharisee, Nicodemus was never able to fully accept his wife's group, but he did accept his wife, in keeping with the Essene tenets, as a partner rather than as chattel.

As told in the Gospel of John, when Jesus left Judea to return home to Galilee, He stopped en route in a city called Sychar in Samaria. This is where He met the woman at the well—who according to Cayce was named Jodie— whom Jesus impressed with His intimate knowledge of her past. Jesus knew, for instance, that she had had five husbands. What's not recorded in the Bible is that Jodie and her sisters brought many new followers to Jesus since they were the family of a high-ranking nobleman. Jesus' visit that day went a long way toward developing a huge following in Samaria. As Cayce would say, "The teachings of the man of Nazareth of these peoples began with this household."

The Bible says that Jesus and His disciples traveled throughout Galilee teaching and healing. In regard to these healings, Cayce said, "There were many instances where individual healings by the Master were . . . instantaneous, as . . . when He said [to a man who was] sick of palsy, 'Son, thy sins be forgiven thee' . . . The recognition was that sin had caused the physical disturbance." Cayce noted that healing through forgiveness, described both in his cherished Bible and in the readings, could certainly be construed as an argument for the existence of karma.

About the healing of Mary Magdalene, Cayce had some very interesting things to say. Information about her came through a life reading done for Gladys's cousin, Mildred Davis, who would later join the work in Virginia Beach, and who, in a previous incarnation, had been Mary Magdalene. In contrast to popular opinion, Cayce said that this woman was the person described as Mary, the sister of Martha and Lazarus. A courtesan to the Romans, twenty-three-year-old Mary Magdalene was said by the Source to have been separated from her family in Bethany and became established in a brothel. As a lucrative sideline, she also traded on information she obtained as a paid companion to influential clients. According to the readings, when a crowd of people brought Mary Magdalene to Jesus, requesting that she be stoned for her many acts of adultery, Jesus bent over and wrote in the sand. Exactly what He wrote is not mentioned in the Bible. The reason, according to the Source, was that the words that Jesus wrote in the sand miraculously appeared differently to each person who read them. Each person reading the message read of the sins that he himself had committed. It is no small wonder, then, that the crowd immediately dispersed.

There was not one—according to Cayce—but two incidents in which a woman accused of adultery was brought to Jesus. This may account for variations in the stories told in the Gospels. The incident included in the Bible, in which Jesus said, "He who is without sin among you, let him throw a stone at her first," was described in the readings as that of a woman caught in the act of adultery with a Roman soldier. While Mary Magdalene had seven "devils" to be cast out, this girl was guilty only of self-indulgence. In this instance, too, Jesus stooped and wrote in the sand. This time He wrote "Medi, Medici, Cui," which was translated by the Source as an expression of mercy and not sacrifice.

Jesus' raising of Lazarus, according to the Source, was the event that completely convinced Ruth and Philoas of His identity as the Messiah. According to Cayce, Lazarus had died of typhoid fever before Jesus raised him from the dead. One of the things that impressed onlookers most, when Jesus arrived four days after Lazarus's death, was that "He wept with those of His friends, in the face of criticism [for coming late and] in the company of the great and near great." This experience, Cayce said, "brought about change, which made for a new life, a new understanding, a new conception of . . . God among the children of men."

Cayce confirmed that the raising of Lazarus was also the last straw in the minds of high priests who then began to plot His death in earnest. Like so many figures in the New Testament, no mention is made as to what finally became of Lazarus, although it does state that the high priests plotted his death, too. What is most interesting to note is that Lazarus, like nearly every person identified in the life readings as being healed by Jesus, allegedly developed healing abilities in that lifetime, and also in later incarnations. The man who had been Lazarus was said by the Source to be reborn in 1875 as Fredoon Birdi, in Puna, India, to Persian parents. Biographical sources independent of the life readings support such a claim: Dr. Fredoon Birdi, born in Puna, India, was a well-respected naturopathic healer in St. Petersburg, Florida.

Among the other "early Christians" reincarnated in Edgar's generation were several "Holy" women, many of whom were described in the readings as having once dedicated themselves to Jesus and His work. These women included Mary and her sister Martha, His own mother, and Maipah, the wife of Jarius, whose daughter was raised from the dead. The Source described these reincarnated souls as having traveled from place to place in advance of Jesus and His disciples, seeing to their needs and establishing "places of refuge" for those people who had been healed by Jesus and who desired to become teachers or ministers of the Master.

Aware of their danger after the raising of Lazarus, Jesus and His followers withdrew "unto a country near to the wilderness." It was here, as described in the Bible, that a rich young ruler came to Jesus asking how to inherit eternal life. Jesus replied that he should give up his possessions and follow Him. The young man went away. Cayce's readings said this man's name was Nicholas, referring to him as "that one about whom much speculation has been in the minds of many . . . But remember . . . the Master loved the young man . . . He hath not willed that any soul should perish. And the entity did just that. He came, later, and followed."

As Jesus prepared Himself to return to Jerusalem, where many of His enemies lay in wait, according to Cayce, there was "much disturbance among the disciples who were of Galilee and those who were of the Judean ministry." Cayce suggested that people from all over had heard of Jesus and had come to Jerusalem in the hope of seeing Him and witnessing His works. The Source noted that when Jesus entered Jerusalem, there was a "crowd of people, especially the little ones. For, though man would have most believe that there were great throngs, they were mostly women and children." Despite the glorious arrival of Jesus, much of the crowd was apparently disappointed "when that mighty force, that glorious creature, that mighty man among men was not proclaimed 'King.' And He seemed to exert so little of that necessary material application of a glorious power and might over those things in man's experience of sickness, of doubt, of fear!"

Perhaps the most startling revelation to come out of the Jesus readings was Cayce's description of the Last Supper. The description didn't appear in the same form as the vast majority of the Jesus material, but was given at the end of a follow-up medical reading when Cayce refused Gertrude's command to wake up from trance. Without being asked, Cayce reported what he was "seeing," which turned out to be nothing less than the Last Supper, witnessed, it seemed, in first person.

In trance, Cayce spoke in a stream of consciousness that surprised and delighted both Gertrude and Gladys as they gradually understood what it was that was being described: "see what they had for supper: boiled fish, rice, with leeks, wine, and [bread]. The . . . robe of the Master was not white, but pearl gray . . . the gift of Nicodemus to the Lord. The better looking of the twelve . . . was Judas, while the younger was John—oval face, dark hair, smooth face [the] only one with the short hair . . . The Master . . . merry—even in the hour of trial! . . . Judas departs. The last is given of the wine and loaf . . . Lays aside His robe, which is all of one piece—girds the towel about His waist . . . is dressed with linen that is blue and white. Rolls back the folds, kneels first before John, James, then to Peter—who refuses. Then the dissertation as to 'He that would be the greatest would be servant of all.' . . . And now comes 'It is finished.' They sing the ninety-first Psalm : . . He is the musician as well, for He uses the harp . . . "

Here, the reading, if indeed it could be considered one, ended. But there was far more information to come in another reading. Cayce, in trance, said that the most difficult time for Jesus was not the trial or even the crucifixion, but "those periods in the garden . . . the seeming indifference and the feeling of the loss of one in whom trust and hope had been given." In another reading, Cayce said that "the real test was [with] the realization that He had met every test and yet must know the pang of death." But Cayce also stated: "Remember, He even made the joke as He walked to the garden to be betrayed . . . He looked with love upon His disciple that denied Him."

While in the Bible, Judas Iscariot is depicted as turning in Jesus for the reward offered, the readings suggest that Judas was trying to force Jesus to "assert Himself as a king and bring in His kingdom." According to the Source, there were many who believed that if Jesus was the Messiah, He would deliver them from their enemies, and more specifically, their Roman occupiers and the burdens of their taxation. They were expecting a material deliverance, rather than a spiritual deliverance. Judas was apparently hoping to speed the process by forcing Jesus to save Himself. While in the Bible, Pontius Pilate's wife appeals to him that no harm should come to "that just man," the reason offered is that she has had a dream. Cayce suggested another reason, that Jesus had healed Pontius Pilate's son of epilepsy. Nevertheless, Pilate washed his hands of the affair and handed Jesus over to the crowds.

Cayce's readings confirm many of the details of Jesus' death on the cross. References were made to the sky darkening, earthquakes, and the tearing of the veil in the temple. Cayce said that Martha, Nicodemus's wife, was at the crucifixion, while the other Mary was at her left. Two of the original twelve consecrated maidens were also there, along with many followers as the Romans attempted to disperse the crowds. According to Cayce, the "rich young ruler," Nicholas, who had turned away when he had been instructed by Jesus to give up all he owned, was instrumental in prompting "Nicodemus to seek the Lord [and] those that cared for the body when it was placed in a new tomb yet unused."

Once Jesus' body had been taken down, several of the women present prepared the spices and wrapped His head. A woman reportedly named Veronicani, a follower of John the Baptist, and whose son would become the first Christian martyr, bathed the Lord's face. Ruth was not present for the trial or the crucifixion—she was with her new husband, who had been called back to Rome just before the trial. They returned, however, the day after the crucifixion and were reportedly with the others on the mount when Jesus reappeared three days later.

The Source said that many people—even those close to the Holy Family—now felt doubts that Jesus had been the Messiah, wondering if His mother, Mary, had somehow become confused about the events of her son's life. Given the amazing miracles that Cayce confirmed, and that many others had apparently witnessed them, highlighted for Edgar and others who studied the readings just how subjective these experiences must have seemed for the people of the times. Just as today, it was all too easy to talk someone into distrusting their own eyes and ears.

The Cayce readings suggest that most, if not all, of the women present at the crucifixion were also present on resurrection morning, when many doubters became disciples. The Bible tells of two disciples meeting up with Christ on a walk to Emmaus, shortly after the resurrection, giving only one name, that of Cleopas. Cayce described Cleopas as a Jewish man from Capernaum who collected taxes for the Romans and whose daughter would eventually become a deaconess in the church in Laodicea.

According to Cayce, there were actually three disciples on the road to Emmaus that day. The second disciple, Cayce said, was Philoas, Ruth's husband, and the third was Luke—"the beloved physician who was both a Roman and a Jew and of those same provinces in the Grecian rule that were under the Roman authorities." In another reading, Luke of Cyrenia was described as "the young physician that never finished and never practiced, yet was known as the physician [who was] close to the brother-in-law of Pilate."

Cayce confirmed the various meetings cited in the Bible between the resurrected Christ and His disciples, and affirmed that for forty days after the resurrection, Jesus would talk often with the disciples but also with many others in Galilee. In another reading, Cayce said that the ascension occurred fifty days after the resurrection, and Jesus was seen by as many as five thousand people.

The years following Jesus' death and resurrection would produce many tales of heroism and martyrdom, persecution and discrimination. Philoas, Jesus' brother-in-law, through his reports to Rome, would prove to be highly influential in having Pilate recalled and having him replaced by a Roman leader who was more sympathetic to the new teachings of Jesus and His disciples. Later he would be instrumental in saving some of the church leaders from death sentences, granting them exile instead. Another who would help the cause of Christianity was Cornelius, the converted Roman ruler of Caesarea.

Over the years, the information that came through Cayce about Jesus, His followers, and the early Christian church was enough to fill several volumes. How many historians have consulted this material is unknown. But for Edgar, Gertrude, and Gladys, who shared a deep feeling of love and reverence for the Master, the Jesus readings—which grew in depth and scope on an almost daily basis—became a means to better understand the often confusing lessons taught in the Bible, and perhaps more important, became the catalyst for a greater and more intimate relationship with their Maker.

For Morton Blumenthal, the Jesus readings were enough to bring about a cathartic experience. Formerly a practicing Jew, Morton would convert to Catholicism. He would also devote his considerable financial skills to lifting Cayce out of poverty and building the hospital dedicated to his healing arts.

PART SIX

A Home on the Beach

34.

◉

Life in
Virginia Beach

In the midst of giving the Jesus readings, the lives of the Cayces and Gladys Davis in Dayton continued to be filled with "trials and tribulations." Had it not been for the new-found help of Morton Blumenthal, their New York benefactor, the family's future would surely have been drastically different.

For Edgar, the most physically painful tribulation happened on a trip back to Hopkinsville in November of 1924, a day or two after he celebrated Thanksgiving dinner. As he later shared in a letter to Morton, he boarded the wrong connection back to Dayton and had to be let out a mile from the station. Rushing to catch the right train—lugging a suitcase and another large parcel in his hands—he exhausted himself. At age forty-seven, and not in the best of shape, Edgar would pay a dear price. "I just broke my fool neck trying to make it back in time . . . running through the train yards. I made it but ruined self . . . Can't stand on my feet much or walk." As late as the following spring, Edgar was still feeling the consequences of that exertion.

While Edgar was in bed recovering—during which time he described himself as an "extremely poor patient"—Gladys's father suddenly died and she had to return to Alabama to attend to her distraught mother and siblings.

As both Edgar and Gertrude admitted, she had every reason to never come back: life in Dayton had been hard on her, and her family needed her as never before. Judging from their correspondence, Edgar truly believed that she might not return. In the interim, he and Gertrude also came to appreciate the quality of Gladys's work, for stand-in stenographers didn't come close to her high standards. In one letter from Morton, who was frustrated at not being able to decipher the transcript of a reading taken during this time, he advised Edgar to not bother giving readings until Gladys came back.

Then, in March of the new year, Gertrude had an accident, falling as she walked down the basement stairs and landing on the side of her face. Apart from a terrible bruise to her cheekbone, she seriously injured her eye. Readings suggested that it would get better with treatment, but only a few years later she fell again, in her kitchen. This time the fall aggravated her prior condition, and she eventually lost the sight in her left eye.

More bad news came from Hopkinsville, where Edgar's mother had taken to bed suffering from colitis and asthma. Readings conducted for her in Dayton provided temporary relief for her pain, but her body had deteriorated to such an extent that it was doubtful that she would ever completely recover.

The only good news, it seemed, came from Morton. He now embraced the readings—both the spiritual ones and, increasingly, those being given on the stock market—to such a degree that he had begun to think in terms of the Cayce family's long-term needs. Of all the people who showed an interest in working with Edgar and in forming the Cayce Institute, Morton was the only one who urged him to listen to the Source. And in terms of where Cayce should carry on the work, Morton was emphatic: "If the readings say Virginia Beach, then that's where you should go." Other supporters of the work, even the ever-faithful Byron Wyrick, had tried to draw the Cayces elsewhere, but in the late spring of 1925, Morton increased Edgar and Gladys's regular salary and promised to rent them a house in Virginia Beach and provide $1,000 to get them there. Morton's grand gesture was much appreciated, though it would be several months—after Hugh Lynn and Edgar Evans had finished out their school year—that Gladys Davis and the Cayces finally left for what from then on became known simply as "the beach."

The Cayces vacated their Dayton apartment on September 1, 1925, and spent the next ten days at The Hill visiting family and friends, while their belongings were in transit. It was not an altogether happy reunion, for although the Cayces of Hopkinsville shared the family's excitement at the prospect of their move to Virginia Beach and their new-found benefactor, Edgar's mother's frail health made it unlikely that she would ever be able to join them. Leslie was of little comfort to her, for he had taken to bed with a severe cold, which was threatening to develop into pneumonia. Edgar paid for his mother's and father's medical treatments with money given him by the Blumenthals for the move, but it was his eldest sister, Annie, who became their primary caregiver and companion. As Edgar said upon his departure, leaving The Hill cast a "cloud over us that was hard to overcome [an] empty feeling that will not be filled."

From Hopkinsville, Edgar and his family continued by train to Nashville, accompanied by Gertrude's cousin Stella, who had volunteered to help with the move. In Nashville they stayed with Edgar's sister Mary, then went on to Richmond, Virginia, finally arriving in Norfolk on the evening of September 13, 1925, where they checked into the Southland Hotel on Granby Street.

Unsure of what to expect in Virginia Beach, Edgar decided that he and Hugh Lynn, who had just graduated from high school, would make the final leg of the journey first. They would leave the next morning. Stella, Gertrude, and Edgar Evans would stay behind at the hotel to claim the family's possessions, which had been shipped from Dayton, and to await the arrival of Gladys Davis, who would be joining them from Selma, where she had gone to visit her family. The following morning, the family awoke to the blast of a distant foghorn calling the Norfolk naval fleet back to port. Dark storm clouds hung in the sky over their hotel and high waves crashed along the shoreline. Gertrude naturally began to wonder what life on the Virginia shore was going to be like. Edgar did his best to relieve her concerns, but like her, he had doubts that their new environment—far from friends or family, and hundreds of miles from Kentucky—would be an improvement over the lush brown farmland of their youth. Edgar and Hugh Lynn bid her good-bye, promising a report on their new home as soon as possible.

The twenty-minute ride from Norfolk to Virginia Beach by train cost a nickel for each passenger. Except for a brief glimpse at the muddy brown Elizabeth River as their train rattled across the trestle at Broad Creek, Edgar and Hugh Lynn saw nothing but a wilderness of pine thickets and duck grass that clung precariously to the sandy brown loam covering the ground. The broad sweep of the Atlantic Ocean was not visible until the trolley conductor abruptly sounded the bell and the wheels screeched to a halt at an unpaved junction at the Virginia Beach city limits.

Edgar and Hugh Lynn didn't realize they had arrived at their destination until they saw the sign on a small post office with the name of the stop the conductor had told them to look for. From their vantage point on the southern edge of town, Virginia Beach consisted of little more than two- and three-story cottages and rooming houses, a pair of boarded-up souvenir shops, a boarded-up restaurant, and a hardware and drugstore, which Edgar later learned was owned and operated by the mayor and sometime post-master. The summer tourists had pulled out some weeks before, leaving Virginia Beach a virtual ghost town.

Little did they realize at the time, however, that the small village of Virginia Beach, which didn't seem like a destination at all, was beginning to undergo a great transformation. Over the period from the first of January until February of the next year, more than three-quarters of a million dollars worth of property would change hands. Less than a year after their arrival, Edgar would lament not coming to Virginia Beach when the readings had first told him to go. "Had I been able at the time," Edgar wrote his friend Lamar Jones in Selma, "the profits [on five hundred dollars of real estate] would have . . . built a two hundred thousand dollar institution."

Edgar and Hugh Lynn didn't stay to explore downtown Virginia Beach but caught a trolley that took them north along Pacific Avenue past more cottages and boardinghouses and the larger Princess Anne Hotel, with its ornate cupola. The cottages became fewer at Twenty-fifth Street, and except for the cars parked at a children's hospital for tuberculosis patients, there was no sign of life. The homes, like the barren wind-swept dunes to the east and the ocean behind it, looked completely deserted, a result of the storm warning that had sent the tourists to higher ground.

The trolley dropped Edgar and Hugh Lynn at Thirty-fifth Street. The moment they stepped onto the street they could see their new residence— it was the only cottage within three blocks of Pacific and Atlantic Avenues. The forlorn two-story white-frame cottage that Morton had rented for them, sight unseen, sat among a grid of empty lots on a weed-choked square situated halfway between the sea to the east and the pine barrens to the west. There was no driveway, no garage, not even a walkway to the cement steps leading up to the open porch and the front door.

On this first visit, Edgar and Hugh Lynn didn't stay more than twenty minutes in their new home. The impending storm sent them scurrying back to Norfolk on the trolley that same day and kept them confined to their hotel for the next three days. Gladys arrived from Selma, and the family, with the help of Stella, collected their things and then rented a livery wagon to take them to their new home. By October 19, the move was complete, and all of them seemed to find their new accommodations quite to their liking. Having spent the last two years squeezed into a hotel room, and later a one-bedroom flat and then a three-bedroom apartment, they felt a real sense of joy at finally having a home for themselves, even if it did cost the then large sum of $35 a month, and even if it seemed they were all alone in this isolated environment.

"I believe we're going to like this place all right," Edgar wrote to Gertrude's family back at The Hill soon after the move. "I'm sure it'll get mighty lonesome here in the winter, for of course nearly all the people are gone from here now, except at some of the hotels where tourists come for a few days at a time—but I think the ocean is fine."

The fact that the house had no central heating didn't seem to pose a problem. The fall nights were still warm, with a steady breeze coming off the Atlantic, and their large living room at first appeared to be comfortably warm and charming. It wasn't until November, when the cold winds blowing off the Atlantic began to rattle the windows that they found the lack of heating a problem. Their only source of heat was a single brick fireplace in the living room, which quickly became the most inhabited room in the house. Later that winter Edgar wrote to Morton asking for an additional $50 above and beyond his $200 monthly stipend and bought a portable oil stove. This would be replaced a year later when they were able to install a furnace.

A more pressing concern was the fact that they hadn't brought any food with them. That first day in their new house, the entire crew went by foot back into the village in search of a meal. The Casino, four blocks away, was the only restaurant they found open, and even then, the chef and single waiter were not prepared for the arrival of six people. There was only one item left on their menu: a seasonal local fish called spot—a type of flounder. The chef had just enough left to serve one to each of the newcomers. The next morning they found the Pender Market, which was eighteen blocks away, on Seventeenth Street. Shopping there made for a time-consuming outing, since the trolley only came along Pacific Avenue once every two hours.

Their first Sunday in Virginia Beach they ventured out for a second time. The boardwalk that ran along the beach had been torn up by the storm— all that remained of it were pieces of driftwood washed up onto shore—so the family strolled along Pacific Avenue, past the closed-up cottages and deserted boardinghouses. There was no Christian Church to attend, but there were three others to choose from—the Baptist, Methodist, or Presbyterian. Gladys and the Cayces voted to try out the Baptist Church first because it seemed to be closest to their own fundamentalist backgrounds.

They were there in time for the morning service, which they quite enjoyed. Afterward Edgar approached the minister about joining the congregation. The pastor said that he would have to discuss the matter with his congregation and asked them to step into the vestibule. Edgar felt offended that he and his family were not welcomed into the church with open arms as one would expect in a Christian church. Without further discussion, the Cayces left and never went back.

The following Sunday they attended services at the Presbyterian Church, which at the time was just a small mission under the supervision of a parent church in Norfolk. The minister, Dr. Frank Scattergood, and his congregation of forty, immediately welcomed the Cayces, and even held a tea party for them to meet the church elders and the rest of the congregation. Within a few weeks, the entire family was active in the church: Gladys joined the choir, Edgar started teaching a Bible class, Hugh Lynn took over a Sunday school class and even Edgar Evans got involved, joining a Boy Scout troop, which met in the church offices.

Although the church became the Cayces' main outlet for social activities during the cold off-season months, they also became part of other community events and impromptu meetings. They were surprised to find that even in this seemingly deserted place, there were still occasional weekend square dances, PTA meetings, and city council planning sessions. Eventually Gladys and the Cayces established a routine that continued for the next decade. The family took the trolley to Norfolk every Saturday to pick up supplies at Freeman's Stationery Store and other shops, they ate dinner in one of the seaside restaurants, and then went to the movies.

Most nights, the family played cards. Their favorite game was Five Hundred, also called Rook. Another game they liked was one that Gertrude improvised. Each family member would research some topic of interest about Virginia Beach and present their findings after dinner. There were presentations on the flora and fauna of the pine barrens, the life and times of the Chesapeake Indians, and historical anecdotes such as an account of the sinking of the Norwegian freighter *Dictator*, which had run aground at the end of the last century five blocks north of the Cayce home. One night, Hugh Lynn surprised the family with an even more interesting topic. Edgar was not the only psychic in Virginia Beach. There were a pair of boys living on the edge of town who allegedly had telekinetic power. A shop owner in Virginia Beach said he had witnessed the children put their heads together and knock row upon row of dry goods off his shelves without so much as raising a finger. This made Edgar feel better—by comparison, a man who could lie down and diagnose disease wasn't all that strange.

Once they were settled, Gertrude came to love Virginia Beach. Though she didn't take to walking the beach as Edgar did, she was quite content to finally have a home of her own to decorate and care for without the constant parade of strangers coming and going for physical readings. "It is certainly proving wonderful for Gertrude," Edgar wrote in a letter to Alva Jones, the wife of his good friend back in Selma. "I doubt if you would hardly know her."

Edgar was able to resume many of the activities he loved so well. In the spring he unpacked his toolbox, made repairs and minor additions to the house, including screening in the front porch and building a swinging chaise lounge where he and Gertrude could sit in the early evening and watch the sunset. Edgar spent time canning fruits and vegetables, he installed planter boxes in the front windows and he seeded a lawn. Though the lot was only a 50-by-150-foot rectangle, Edgar found space for a lovely garden where he grew flowers with seeds he ordered from a catalog. Among the many plants in his flower beds were bleeding hearts, peonies, jack-in-the-pulpits, Tom Thumbs, bachelor's buttons, hardy pinks, violets, pansies, gladioli, butter-cups, snowdrops, tulips, and foxglove. And, for the first time, Edgar took up ocean fishing, which proved to be quite an experience for anyone who ac-companied him.

A fishing buddy from the Presbyterian church once remarked that bizarre things invariably happened when Edgar took his host's small boat out of the Norfolk marina. Fishing was always good when Edgar was with him, and on the few instances when they didn't immediately catch a fish, all Edgar had to do was sit quietly and concentrate on the water around the boat. Inevitably the fish began to bite. Edgar's most rewarding activity, however, was not gardening or fishing, but walking alone along the beach, collecting driftwood and small shells, and daydreaming about the hospital he hoped would some-day bring hundreds of people—perhaps thousands—to these same shores.

Two weeks after arriving at the beach, seven-year-old Edgar Evans, whom they called Ecken, began grade school at Professor Francis H. Green's School for Boys. He adapted well to his new environment, demonstrating great me-chanical skills and a talent for writing. Where Hugh Lynn was idealistic, philosophical, and visionary, Edgar Evans was very literal and practical. He was also a brilliant student. By the time he was ten years old he was build-ing various kinds of mechanical devices in the basement, and at one point created a minor explosion when making his own gunpowder. With Edgar Evans in the house, the family would never need a mechanic. The boy was quite meticulous in all his endeavors and kept detailed records of his activ-ities, which included accounting for every nickel he spent. He eventually be-came valedictorian of his high school class, and his grade average over his four years in high school was higher than anyone who had ever before grad-uated from that school.

More than his older brother, Edgar Evans, like his father, would love walking alone on the shore and had a deep love and appreciation of the solitary beauty of the beach. As Edgar said in a letter, "We can't hardly keep him off of it."

Like his older brother, he sustained a serious childhood injury. His came in the form of first-degree burns to his hips and legs, which he suffered a little over a year after arriving at the beach. While playing one day, Edgar Evans got too close to the fireplace and a cinder popped out of the fire and onto his flannel pajamas, causing them to burst into flames. He rolled helplessly on the floor, screaming, until his shouts brought Gertrude down from upstairs. She grabbed him and wrapped a shirt around him that she had been carrying to the laundry. She managed to extinguish the fire but not before he was badly burned along the back side of his left leg, from ankle to hip, causing the muscles to contract and his left side to become permanently disfigured.

Edgar had no hesitancy in seeking trance help, for Edgar Evans's life reading had warned his parents of the likelihood of such an event. He and Gertrude quickly applied the various oils and ointments suggested in the subsequent readings. The doctors who examined Edgar Evans recommended that the tendon be cut. Doing so, however, would result in a limp for the rest of his life, but at least he would be able to walk. Although the leg was doubled up and could not be straightened, the readings stated that an operation was not called for and if the recommended treatments were applied, the boy would eventually walk normally again. A month after the accident, Edgar Evans still couldn't walk. "It's right pitiful to see him sliding around on the floor trying to do some of the things that he normally does," Cayce would write to his youngest sister back in Hopkinsville.

As in the case of the readings conducted for his older brother, the treatments recommended by the Source ultimately proved their worth. Edgar Evans was scarred for life, but the musculature completely healed, and he grew to become the most athletic member of the family, a football player at school and an avid golfer in later years. "I'm thankful to say there have been no complications," Edgar reported. "I believe it will be all right."

Upon arriving at the beach, Hugh Lynn, like his younger brother, also began school, enrolling in a one-year general course at Norfolk Business College, where he commuted by trolley. Both Edgar and Gertrude thought it was a good way for him to meet people, as well as hone some important skills, which included typing, taking shorthand, and improving his spelling. He put some of these skills to use the next summer when he got a job with a real-estate agency, but even so, did not return to the business school the next fall.

Morton Blumenthal counseled Hugh Lynn to look beyond Norfolk for his higher education, and generously agreed to pay his tuition and board at Washington and Lee University in Lexington, Virginia, which had been suggested to Hugh Lynn in a reading. There, the Source said Hugh Lynn would meet many associates from previous incarnations.

Not surprisingly, the first real friend the Cayces made in Virginia Beach was Dr. Scattergood, the minister at the Presbyterian Church they attended, who had come from a construction and engineering background. He was also the first resident at the beach to become aware of Edgar's psychic activities. In the years ahead, Scattergood would play an increasingly large role in the activities of the association that Blumenthal and others would form to support the Cayces and promote the work.

Another minister they would get to know was the Reverend Joseph B. Clower, from Norfolk, who occasionally came to Virginia Beach to join Dr. Scattergood at the Presbyterian Church. Hugh Lynn and Gladys attended his discussion group after one of his visits and ultimately challenged his beliefs as perhaps no one had before. Hugh Lynn asked him questions about karma: why were some people born crippled, blind, or poor while others were born healthy or rich or in other favorable circumstances? Like Dr. Scattergood, Clower became friends with Edgar and eventually joined the work, though he did so from Hampden-Sydney College in Hampden-Sydney, Virginia. He kept in touch with the Cayces through frequent letters and occasionally returned to the beach, including one trip to perform Hugh Lynn's wedding service and another to perform Edgar Evans's. He also made the long trek back to deliver the eulogy at Edgar's funeral.

Harry Holland, the postmaster of Virginia Beach, and his wife, Ruth, also became close friends of the Cayces. Holland's curiosity was naturally aroused by the satchels of mail and special-delivery letters that Edgar started receiving, and he eventually came to the house to witness a reading firsthand and became a lifelong admirer. Gertrude got to know his wife, Ruth, through church activities; Gladys became friends with his daughter, Dorothy Moore, the manager of the Pender Market; and the whole Holland family would eventually participate in the study groups that later formed around Cayce and the work.

While nineteen-year-old Hugh Lynn was still enrolled at the business school, he met a young woman named Olive Koop, who played violin in the Norfolk Symphony Orchestra and was taking courses with him at the business school. He fell head over heals in love with the twenty-three-year-old, despite what Hugh Lynn perceived as her aloof, cold exterior. As Hugh Lynn later admitted, he began dating her as a kind of challenge, to melt, as he said,

the "ice queen." Besides her abilities in music, she was a fine artist and busi-
nesswoman. She was also stunningly beautiful, with light brown hair and
ivory skin. The fact that she came from a rich New York family, on Long Island's "Gold Coast," also appealed tremendously to the status-conscious
Hugh Lynn. It was love at first sight and he proposed to her knowing her for
only a few months. Gertrude took Hugh Lynn's romance in stride, but she
would have preferred him to be interested in someone from her own town
of Hopkinsville and not a rich New York society girl. The fact that Olive was
four years her son's senior didn't help matters.

Although occasionally homesick for The Hill, Gertrude herself was
steadily putting on weight, a sure sign that her physical condition was improving. Photographs taken in September 1925 captured her smiling for the
first time in nearly four years, and by the end of their first month at the
beach Edgar began to joke that she was "going to get fat [living here]." By
June 1926, Edgar was saying how "wonderful" the beach was for her. "She
weighs now about a hundred and fifteen—maybe twenty—and you know
she has never gotten over a hundred [pounds] before in her life."

Unlike Gertrude, who was content to spend most of her time at home,
Gladys needed and wanted social outlets. Her favorite time of day was the
early morning, when she would go off to the post office to collect the mail
and send off the day's correspondence. Invariably she would stop along the
way to visit with friends or to pick wild grapes that grew in the tangle of
woodland just above the boardwalk. Then there were weekend trips to Norfolk with the Cayce family, or strolls out to the Seventeenth Street meadows
to pick wildflowers with Gertrude. Apart from church, the only other contact she had with other people was when someone visited the Cayces for
three or four days at a time. And she lived for these visits.

The first visitor was Tim Brown, who came down from Dayton, followed
by Morton, who was accompanied by his new wife, Adeline. Because space
at the Thirty-fifth Street house was limited, visitors stayed in nearby rental
cottages, or later, at the Cavalier Hotel, which was built in 1927. Dave Kahn
came to the beach, as would Lamar Jones from Selma, Leslie, Thomas and
Carrie House, and their son, Tommy, the boy whose life Edgar had saved
years ago in Hopkinsville. Byron Wyrick brought his good friend Franklin
Bradley, a Chicago paint manufacturer who embraced Edgar and the work
and provided financial help in the months to come. Gladys's favorite visitor
was her mother, who would arrive by horse and wagon, accompanied by her
cow. She would later send the family chickens, which Edgar raised in a henhouse he built in the backyard.

Beyond attending to the visitors and the Cayce's normal summer activities, there were many readings to be done. In retrospect, it is interesting that the Source suggested that the Cayces move to such a deserted part of the country, where their social contacts were primarily supporters and friends who had to come to them. It was easy for the family to lead lives of relative seclusion at the beach, outside of the public eye, and where Gladys and the Cayces could better focus on what the readings were teaching them.

For the most part, these early Virginia Beach readings were for Morton and his brother, Edwin, who, as promised, were paying all of the family's bills. Readings for the Blumenthals were the first order of business each day and the last to be discussed each evening. The Blumenthals would invariably ask about the rising and falling stock market, personal relationships, medical concerns, and for further information on Jesus Christ and other spiritual topics. However, soon after the Cayces' arrival in Virginia Beach, Morton began asking the Source to interpret his family's dreams: most specifically those relating to his and Adeline's unborn child. As Morton had been told back in Dayton, "pay more attention to dreams, for [this is where] truths are given."

Those truths, it became clear to Morton and Adeline, were leading the Blumenthals down a path of self-discovery that brought them closer to the Cayce family and the work that would occupy an ever-increasing portion of their time and resources.

35.

Dreams and
Reincarnation

The proof of the importance of dreams, from Edgar's perspective, lay not in current literature or philosophy, but in the Bible, most specifically, the experience of Joseph, the much cherished eleventh son of Jacob, who not only had the ability to remember and interpret his own dreams, but those of the Pharaoh. As Morton pointed out, Edgar, too, could provide such insights.

Although Morton and Edgar had experimented with doing dream readings as early as January 1925, it was not until June and July of that same year—in the midst of doing the life readings—that the first series of dedicated dream readings were conducted. In a reading conducted on July 28, Morton requested an interpretation of two of Edgar's dreams, which Morton believed were central to the work in Virginia Beach. In the first of these two dreams, Edgar and nearly everyone connected to his fledgling organization were on a large barge anchored off the coast of Virginia. In the center of the boat was an elegant dance floor, surrounded by a soda fountain, and Morton, Gertrude, and Edgar were sitting on the edge of the boat fishing. Gertrude caught a fish, and when she pulled it out of the water, it had the face of a man. In the second of Edgar's dreams, a physician from Hopkinsville, Dr. Thomas, who had been bitterly against Edgar and his endeavors, visits Virginia Beach to inspect a hospital dedicated to Edgar Cayce. Liking what he finds, he becomes a champion of the work and preaches its worth to fellow physicians.

At the beginning of the reading to interpret these two dreams, the Source castigated Edgar for not being more mindful of the importance of dreams. "For as has been given," the reading stated, "often there is presented to every normal body . . . those conditions through the subconscious forces of the sleeping state wherein truths are given, visions are seen of things to be warned of [or] that will be advantageous to the body, physically, mentally, morally, spiritually, and financially . . . Pay more attention to the dream of each and every one [connected to the work]!" Implicit in this response was the suggestion that all people had the capacity to interpret and act on subliminal communications. "All have the power," Cayce—in trance—said repeatedly.

As Edgar and Morton would soon learn, it wasn't necessary for the Source to be told the entire dream. The conductor had only to reference the particular dream by date, or give a brief description of its plot. Cayce, in trance, would then expand on the most salient points and sometimes describe elements of the dream that the dreamer himself may have forgotten. All that was necessary for the Source to interpret Edgar's two dreams was for the conductor to mention the shipboard party taking place off the coast of Virginia Beach and the appearance of Dr. Thomas at the hospital.

Interpreting the first of these two dreams, the Source said that the barge was emblematic of Edgar being directed to that place—Virginia Beach—where "the forces of this body may be the better directed." Fishing off the side of the boat signified the specific nature of the work, and the fish with the human head represented "something drawn out," or a lesson that was learned. The second dream was interpreted to mean that a transformation would take place in the people who were initially against the work. They would be won over, and through them the institution in Virginia Beach would be able to reach out and help the world. "Through many . . . may be acquired . . . monies and aid to many through . . . medicines, lessons, truths, [and] understandings that may be acquired . . . and given to many."

These dream interpretations were straightforward enough. But as the Blumenthals and the Cayces discovered, dream readings could be much more complex, requiring lengthy explanations of the symbols and lessons appearing in them. Ultimately, Edgar gave eight hundred readings to interpret over sixteen hundred dreams. Although seventy different people requested and obtained trance interpretations of their dreams, 90 percent of these readings were for four people: Edgar, Gladys, Morton, and Edwin.

Cayce's dream readings suggested that dreams were to be interpreted through signs, direct messages, and symbols, all of which were derived from an indelible record registered in the subconscious mind of the dreamer and composed of everything that the dreamer had seen, read, heard, imagined, or experienced in their present life or previous lives. In other words, the language and imagery of an individual's dreams were derived from his personal soul record, and as such, spoke only to that person. The dream's message however, came from a higher self, or the higher selves of others. According to the Source, messages could come from the grocery clerk at the market down the street, deceased family members, or Divine communications sent to protect or guide an individual. Understanding the message was only a matter of keeping the channel open, or recognizing that it existed in the first place. "Happy may he be that is able to say they have been spoken to through the dream or vision," Cayce—in trance—would say.

Apart from the dream's message, the Source identified nearly two hundred different symbols that often had one particular meaning. An arrow, for example, was a portent of an incoming message. A baby or newborn child represented a new business venture or activity. Blood represented the physical forces of the body itself and was indicative of the individual's health. Fire represented fear, and hair was the reasoning process. Ultimately, however, all symbols represented what the dreamer made of them, for the relevance of a vineyard to one person, could be the same as a school classroom to another.

Many of the dreams were interpreted by the Source as warnings, as was the case with a dream Edwin Blumenthal reported: "[I dreamed of a] leak of what seemed to be liquor on our foyer rug, out of a bottle . . . or keg." In the subsequent reading on this dream, the Source said: "As is seen, this is as the warning to the entity as respecting liquors in and about the place, and in the use of same . . . Let not these conditions become the stumbling block either to health, position, or influential surroundings." As indeed turned out to be the case, Edwin's wife had a drinking problem that had to be checked before serious damage was done to the family or herself.

Frequently, dream readings involved people close to the dreamer who had passed on and who used the dream state as a direct means of communicating with loved ones. This apparently was the case with a dream Gertrude had in early October of 1926, in which Edgar's mother was showing Gertrude through her house in Hopkinsville. As they walked through the rooms, Gertrude noticed that all the curtains in the windows were white. Eventually Carrie led Gertrude through an underground passage in which Gertrude had the impression of a subterranean river and felt she needed to reach her children and bring them to safety. She was also fearful of an impending explosion.

The subsequent trance reading stated that the white curtains and the underground passage were an indication that someone—presumably Edgar's mother—would soon be buried, that this person was reentering the stream of life, and "returning again to the first element." The dream was also apparently a specific call to help the children—Hugh Lynn and Edgar Evans—through what might otherwise be an explosion in the family. Carrie Cayce did indeed die later that month, on October 25, 1926. Edgar, who received a wire from his sister Annie that his mother was seriously ill, traveled back to Hopkinsville and was with her when she died. Their mother's death was a sad and trying time for everyone in the family, especially Annie—who had cared for Carrie during her long illness.

Not surprisingly, Annie repeatedly received dream communications from her mother from the "other plane." In one of Annie's dreams, Carrie wrapped her arms around her, and Annie asked her if she knew how much she had always loved her. Carrie reportedly replied, "Yes, you've proven it always." In a trance interpretation of this dream on September 3, 1927, a spirit alleging to be Carrie Cayce interrupted the reading to relay a message to Annie. This was a dramatic moment, for rarely had anyone other than the Source spoken through Cayce. Alf and Roger Butler's father had communicated through Edgar in a dream that Edgar had had while giving a reading in 1918, as had a former assistant in the Selma photography studio, but this was the first time that a Cayce family member had come through. In the middle of the reading, Carrie addressed her daughter as "sister," as she had when she was alive. "Mother sees, mother knows, mother feels those same feelings of that love which is in the earth that makes of the heavenly home," Edgar said in trance. The voice belonged to Edgar, but the tone and words convinced Gertrude and the others that the speaker was indeed Carrie Cayce.

The rest of Carrie's message was an affirmation of the love she felt for her daughter: "While I am in the spirit planes I am yet present in the minds and hearts of those who express to me the love . . . that the Master shows to all when He gave that He would prepare the home for those who would come after Him. Love those about you in the way that mother gave, and be that as mother would have you be—for mother does not leave you . . . For the life is the whole life, even as the Master gave that He was the life and the light of the world, in that same concept as shown in that felt as mother gathers [Annie] in her arms."

Readings such as this convinced Morton Blumenthal of the good that could come from dream interpretation and prompted him to request readings on dreams that he and his wife were having about their soon-to-be-born son, Morton Jr.

Premonitions of the birth of a son first appeared to Adeline in a dream she had on June 29, 1925, in which a "weak-minded" boy or child appeared to her, and a reading was conducted on July 1. Cayce, in trance, cautioned her to be extremely careful about controlling her thoughts, for the projection of those thoughts would be translated into the physical: by dwelling upon negative thoughts she might indeed have a "weak-minded" child. "Good and *only* good thoughts should be projected into the subconscious . . . for the body . . . becomes that upon which it feeds . . . Dreams are that of which the subconscious is made, for any condition ever becoming reality is first dreamed."

Adeline, with Morton's help, tried to maintain a positive attitude during her subsequent pregnancy, and many readings were conducted to help her overcome one crisis after another. First there was the sudden illness of a longtime friend, then the sudden death of her mother, and finally the suicide of her father—all within a period of nine months. Her spirits were temporarily raised, however, when she had another foreshadowing of the child to be born to her and Morton in a dream on November 25, 1926, which was interpreted by Cayce in a reading a few days later.

Adeline described her dream in a letter to Edgar: "I dreamed [my baby] had blue eyes and blond hair and was a boy. It had, however, a Jewish nose that I didn't like. I said to my mother who was there: 'It looks kikish—too Jewish.' My mother . . . bit her finger in characteristic fashion and beamed upon the baby. She said it was grand . . . I looked at my baby. It was then one or two days old as before, but instead of being partially homely it appeared to be a beautiful child with light hair, blue eyes, and healthy."

Cayce—in trance—interpreted the dream as follows: "In the birth there will be seen the boy . . . blue eyed, or dark gray—nearly blue, blond, and presenting something of the characteristic condition as seen [by the mother]."

Indeed, as would later be revealed, Morton and Adeline's baby, which was born on April 4, 1927, was fair-skinned, had blue eyes and blond hair, and would grow up to be bright, lively, and given to mischief. But as the earlier reading had warned, the child was "weak minded." Morton Jr. developed psychological problems that would later result in his confinement to a mental asylum.

Through dream interpretations such as these, Edgar came to understand that information from the dream readings didn't detract from the life readings. Rather, each kind of reading could enhance the other. Hugh Lynn launched a test balloon of sorts, in this field of research, when he requested a life reading for his fiancée, Olive Koop, who frequently appeared in his dreams.

The reading was conducted on April 3, 1926, when Hugh Lynn invited Olive home to meet his mother and father. As was the case with other people he had brought home to "meet the folks," she was skeptical and didn't quite believe what Hugh Lynn's father did for a living. However, she liked Edgar and the rest of the family immediately, and as they all got to know one another better, Edgar, suspecting that she was part of what he was now calling the "Egyptian crowd"—gave her a life reading. The reading confirmed that she and Hugh Lynn and Edgar had all known one another in ancient Egypt. During that incarnation, she accompanied the high priest, Edgar Cayce, when he was banished by the Pharaoh, Hugh Lynn, and she later returned to marry Hugh Lynn and give him a son. Rather than being put off by her life reading, as Hugh Lynn had originally been, Olive fell in love with it and eventually went on to write about her experience in a magazine article. Her acceptance of the reading only made Hugh Lynn want to know more than ever if the life readings were valid or just a figment of his father's imagination. He had his chance when Edgar did a reading for a high school classmate of Hugh Lynn's from Selma, Fred Batterson.

Hugh Lynn and Fred Batterson had once been quite close, often double-dating when Hugh Lynn went out with Fred's sister. A reading requested by Hugh Lynn said that he and Fred had been brothers in Egypt when Hugh Lynn had been the Pharaoh, and that a quarrel they got into over the girl who now was Olive had split the kingdom. With this information, Hugh Lynn thought that he and his family finally had a chance to test the validity of the life readings. If indeed Fred had been his brother and had fought over Olive, surely there would be some karmic energy at play when they all met. Without letting either of them in on his plan, Hugh Lynn invited Fred to visit Virginia Beach at the same time Olive and her mother would be visiting from Long Island. After their first meeting at the Cayce home, Hugh Lynn questioned Fred at length. "She's the worst you've ever picked," he told Hugh Lynn. "You can't marry this girl. She's as cold as ice."

A week later, Olive and her mother returned to Long Island. Fred stayed in Virginia for an additional week and unbeknownst to Hugh Lynn, made a detour to New York on his way back to Selma. He went to see Olive, whom he had already been secretly dating. To him, she was anything but "cold as ice." And as he later admitted to Hugh Lynn, Fred and Olive had begun an affair the first night they were introduced at the beach. A few days after Fred left, Hugh Lynn received his engagement pin back from her and an apology from them both. "By golley, these life readings are right!" Hugh Lynn announced to his father and mother. This knowledge, however, did not lessen the pain he felt at having been betrayed. His anger ran so deep, in fact, that it became the subject of further readings nearly two decades later when Hugh Lynn went through a period in which he choked on things he ate.

As Hugh Lynn would later describe his experience, the first thing he choked on was a piece of gristle, then on a stew bone, and again on a pill he was swallowing. On three separate occasions he would have to be taken to a hospital emergency room to prevent suffocation. After the last incident, he had a dream in which he saw his former fiancée's face. It was a scene right out of his life reading in which he was a Norwegian invader in England. Olive Koop, it turned out, had been his wife. In the dream, he choked her because she had become pregnant with someone else's child. As this dream suggested, his own fit of choking suddenly seemed to make sense. Following his father's advice, he prayed for the strength to forgive her and for forgiveness for himself for harboring ill will. Hugh Lynn awoke the next morning feeling as if "a great weight had been lifted." A few days later he unexpectedly received a call from Olive, his first contact with her in many years. She had married and divorced twice and was now working as a legal secretary in New York. She had called him on a whim to say, "I do hope you've forgiven me by now. I did treat you so disgracefully." Hugh Lynn forgave her, and the choking incidents ceased altogether.

Another reading Hugh Lynn requested during his early years in Virginia Beach admonished him not to handle firearms. This seemed puzzling to Hugh Lynn because all his life he had been quite adept at using them. He loved shotguns and pistols and was said to be so good with a gun that he could drive nails with a .45 pistol. Despite his prowess, however, the reading stated that guns would have an adverse effect upon him, and unless he curbed his tendency to surround himself with them, he would lose a part of his own body. Based on the accuracy with which his father described his son's relationship with Olive, Hugh Lynn promptly got rid of every gun he owned and did everything he could not to fight in World War II short of becoming a conscientious objector. Although he ultimately did fight in the war and was under the command of General Patton himself, he spent the war years in Europe distributing literature and coordinating entertainment activities for his fellow troops. He never suffered the injury he had been warned to avoid.

Hugh Lynn also requested readings for many of his new friends. By far the most important reading in the larger scheme of the work was for Tom Sugrue, one of the first people Hugh Lynn met at Washington and Lee University when he arrived in September of 1926. Like Fred Batterson, he was also a man with whom Hugh Lynn had much karma to work out.

The first time Hugh Lynn ever saw Tom, he was wearing a beanie, strumming a ukulele, and singing an Irish ditty. The short, redheaded young man from Naugatuck, Connecticut, asked Hugh Lynn where he was from. Hugh Lynn told him Virginia Beach and Tom responded with a disparaging remark that would set the tone for the rest of their relationship. An argument was begun that would not end for another twenty-five years.

Tom wanted to be a writer more than anything else. He had been out of high school for two years and was working at a Connecticut bank when the bank president asked him to write a story for the local newspaper about the company picnic. The article was well received and inspired him to enroll at Washington and Lee University. From the moment he and Hugh Lynn met they argued over practically everything, sometimes settling their disagreements with a fistfight that sent one or both of them to the school infirmary. They fought about the most mundane things, from the pictures each chose to hang on their walls to who would get the better grades each semester. They argued about where they would live, about fraternities, politics, and about which school dining club to join. Most important, however, they argued about religion.

Tom was an ardent Catholic and had once considered studying for the priesthood, but was "too much the rebel," as he later wrote in a letter to Edgar. Hugh Lynn taunted him with theories on reincarnation and karma, and the stories about Jesus that he claimed hadn't made it into the Bible. Hugh Lynn finally challenged him to meet his father, and Tom agreed to do so, he said, with the intention of proving that "Cayce was a fake." No sooner had he arrived at the beach in June than he began pontificating about the "ruse" of psychic research. Hugh Lynn and Gladys were quite happy to give him enough rope to hang himself, and on June 7, 1927, they conducted his first life reading.

As usual with the life readings, the Source discussed the influence of various stars and planets on Tom Sugrue's behavior before launching into a character analysis. Cayce described Sugrue as being "high minded," and a lover of the beautiful, whether in music, poetry, literature, or the outdoors. The Source said he was "one that is attracted to few, yet attracts many," that he was "eccentric in a manner . . . well seeing, well meaning . . . yet not well grounded."

The readings indicated that in one previous life Tom had been a monk in the Anglican Church, during which he studied music, which he liked, and chemistry, which he did not—something that exactly paralleled his current experience in college. The Source said that in the most recent incarnation he had been a crusader in the Holy Land and had aided many who had been taken prisoner. The Source said that this was why he had an innate desire to see the Holy Lands and write about them—which, in fact, he later would do. Tom's most relevant incarnation—to Hugh Lynn's mind—was as a conspirator in the rebellion that ensued from Ra Ta's expulsion from Egypt. Tom had taken Ra Ta's side in the priest's dispute with Hugh Lynn, who was the Pharaoh.

The reading made perfect sense to everyone but Tom. In the days that followed, however, Tom had a chance to read the other life readings, and his own started to make more sense. Edgar understood what the young college student was going through. "Becoming accustomed to the ideas [in the Cayce household] was like living with jungle tribesmen who do not wear clothes," Cayce wrote. "After a year or two you realize you are the funny-looking one with all your clothing."

Tom became an outright convert to the work when he received a physical reading on December 30, 1927, which revealed intimate details of his personal life that a normal person could not possibly have known. This reading suggested that he had been afflicted with gonorrhea—a fact that Tom had never disclosed to any of the Cayces—and warned that there would be dire consequences if he did not follow a special diet, injections of medication into his urethra, and what the Source described as "clean and pure living." In trance, Cayce counseled him not to worry, "for worry will bring the greater disturbances for the system."

Even Hugh Lynn could see how everything changed for Tom once he accepted his own readings. Hugh Lynn reported how his friend now began to study the hundreds of pages of previous readings that were on file and at night would join the group around the living room talking about the readings, and about reincarnation, astrology, and medicine. By the middle of the next year, Tom made the decision to devote himself entirely to the work in Virginia Beach. "I have decided to enter into the work as a life career," he wrote Edgar from college. "And since I have full faith in it and in you . . . I should at this time put myself entirely in the hands of 'it' both physically and mentally."

Tom eventually became like another brother to Hugh Lynn and a son to the Cayces. He came to stay at Virginia Beach for weeks at a time and later for entire summers. The readings became a subject of lifelong study to him, and in the years ahead, saved his life more than once. He also became Edgar Cayce's first biographer.

Another person who received a significant life reading was Dr. Thomas House, who, with his wife Carrie, also came to play a pivotal role in the Cayces' life in Virginia Beach. During the years that had elapsed since the birth of their son, Carrie and Thomas House had undergone a serious mental and physical crisis. Emotional turmoil—the result of the re-evaluation of his medical practices based on the precepts he had come to know and trust—left Dr. House suffering from bleeding ulcers, which Cayce was able to cure through a series of readings. Later, Dr. House again turned to Edgar to overcome the addiction he had developed to the morphine he had used to dull the excruciating pain of those ulcers. House credited his recovery to the good he had found in the readings. In early 1926 he decided to turn his life over to the work, and become, if Edgar and Morton agreed, the chief doctor in charge of their proposed hospital in Virginia Beach.

It was only natural that he should receive a life reading to help Morton and the others determine whether or not he was suited to take over operations at the proposed hospital. Edgar deemed the subsequent reading, conducted on August 7, 1926, as one of the most important given to date, for it documented House's continuing contribution to the work. As Edgar would later write to Tim Brown in Dayton, "[House's reading represents] one of our very important appearances in the affairs of the old world, and possibly may be just as important in the affairs of the present-day world."

The reading's most interesting revelation was that Dr. House and his wife, Carrie, had been together in the French courts during the revolution. Their child, then, as now, was Tommy House Jr., and had been taken from them to be imprisoned in the Bastille, where he had died without knowing the love of his parents. In their current incarnation, Dr. House and Carrie had been karmically tested again on that cold March evening in 1909, when Carrie called Edgar to The Hill. It was their demonstration of love and their trust in the "higher powers" that prevented the "entity" Tommy House Jr. from being taken from them again. Further, the life readings established Dr. House's positive relationships with Edgar and many of the others associated with the work in previous incarnations.

The hospital staff hiring committee, which requested the reading, couldn't have been more pleased. "A well-rounded individual has resulted, one with a fixed ideal and purpose . . . the highest possible, for it calls for the sacrifice of self for the betterment of mankind," the committee concluded. "There are many contacts, many friends, few enemies, few losses."

The position of chief administrator now belonged to Dr. House. Their decision appeared to be a good one, as evidenced by an insightful dream that Gladys had on November 27, 1926. In Gladys's dream, Tim Brown, Frank Bradley, the Blumenthals, and the other principal association members were sitting in the front room at the Cayce home on Thirty-fifth Street. They were called to the window to see Dr. House sitting behind the controls of an airplane taking off from what appeared to be a grassy knoll where Edgar frequently liked to walk. As the plane rose into the air above the Cayce home, Gladys and the others could see a rope hanging from behind the plane. Upon seeing the rope, Tim Brown, with whom there existed the most serious potential problems, dashed out of the house to the airfield, grabbed hold of the rope, and was pulled skyward.

In terms of dreams and the underlying karmic debt of the principal players, the building of a hospital seemed inevitable. It was only a question of when.

36.

Treasures Great
and Small

Morton and Edwin Blumenthal remained a constant presence in the daily lives of the Cayce family. They not only paid Edgar a stipend and covered Hugh Lynn's tuition and expenses at college, but they sent regular payments to Gladys, and made the Cayces' lives in Virginia Beach more secure and happy than at any other point in their lives. That first Christmas at the beach, the Blumenthals sent Gladys a check for $300, which she immediately used to purchase gifts for her family back in Alabama. And in February 1926, Morton and Edwin purchased the house for the Cayces on Thirty-fifth Street, for approximately $11,500, and also bought them the first automobile they ever owned, a brand-new Ford. Most important to Edgar, however, by the spring of 1926, the Blumenthals made their first serious attempts to raise the funds necessary to build the hospital.

Morton's plan, as outlined in a series of meetings in March and April of 1926, was to raise an initial $50,000 from the 1,160 names on the association mailing list that Gladys had been preparing since their days in Dayton, and then to raise an additional $100,000 from other sources. Toward this end, application cards were printed offering various types of membership in what they called the Association of National Investigators. Individual memberships could be obtained for a cost of $5, patron status could be had for $25, and life memberships for $100.

The first mailing went out in July 1926. In certain respects the campaign was considered a success, for it resulted in the association becoming something more than just a mailing list. An organization was in place, which had a permanent address, a standardized set of rules and procedures, and a plan for the future: the creation of a hospital where all members could receive the kinds of treatments recommended in the readings.

From a fund-raising point of view, though, the mailing was a dismal failure. Forty-nine people contributed a total of $5,500. The reason became clear from the numerous letters that poured into the association—the vast majority of people on the mailing list had had only minimal contact with Edgar, and some hadn't seen or heard from him in years. There were also people who had only recently received their first reading and felt offended that they were expected to participate in the building of a hospital. As one woman wrote from Pittsburgh, "The yell for money came so quickly after my reading that I have lost faith . . . in the whole thing, and fear it is only a money-grabbing scheme."

Undaunted by the initial response, Morton put another plan into action. He and his brother would use trance advice from their business readings to establish a dedicated stock market account, the profits from which would be used to buy property and begin construction of the hospital. Morton's thinking, as well as Edgar's, was that once the members saw an actual building going up they would contribute larger amounts that would defray the association's initial expenses. And once the hospital was built and operating, the patients themselves would support its continuance. Morton asked the association's most active members—Tim Brown, Franklin Bradley, Dave Kahn, and others—to join him and his brother in pooling a portion of their resources and investing in the association account. The stocks would be owned by the investors, but the profits would be put toward building the hospital.

The idea was warmly received, if for no other reason than that the Blumenthal brothers themselves had successfully used the trance advice to triple their own stock market holdings. Rarely did more than a day or two go by that Morton or his brother didn't ask for a reading on stocks in their personal accounts, and though the record is not clear as to how often they acted on Edgar's advice, they were making enough money on the stock market that they had generously opened an account in Edgar Cayce's name, which, in fact, had nearly doubled in value in less than one year.

Tim Brown made the most substantial contribution to the new association account by giving a total of $13,433 dollars. Dave Kahn gave $740. An estimated $5,000 was given by other members, which included a thirty-nine-year-old engineer from General Electric brought in by Morton Blumenthal, a thirty-seven-year-old vice president of a prominent leather goods manufacturing company, and Franklin Bradley's partner in a large paint company. Upon Cayce's trance advice, Morton purchased stocks in over twenty companies, which included Hudson Motors, General Electric, Atlantic Gulf, Pan American Petroleum, the Louisville and Nashville Railroad, Chrysler Motors, Pacific Gas and Electric, and IBM.

Perhaps the most impressive aspect of the more than two hundred stock market readings that were subsequently conducted was Cayce's astonishing trance ability to provide specific detailed trading information, not unlike the geological data he had previously provided at Desdemona and Rocky Pasture. As evidenced by the readings themselves, Cayce—in trance—could apparently quote figures on the daily stock market as if he were a ticker tape machine with a direct line to the floor of the New York exchange. However, it must be noted that the Source qualified all of its stock market advice by saying that the future was not certain, and thus, any predictions about the rising and falling market were only to be used as indicators for the future value of a particular stock given present market conditions.

During these readings, it was not uncommon for the Source to say that "Atlantic Gulf will advance from 57 to 80 [points]," that "Louisville and Nashville will go back to 132," or that "Chrysler Motors will split at the end of the month." In one particular reading about U.S. Steel, for example, Morton was told that the corporation "will sell off near to the 151½ [to] 152½ [mark] . . . [and] with the changes as come about, then, there will be seen . . . the advance to the 164 [mark] in this present week [and] the big change will occur about the third or fourth of February." During another reading, Morton asked if stock in Havana Electric was going up or down. The reply came: "Going down on Monday and up Tuesday and Wednesday."

In addition to the daily market indicators, the Source frequently mentioned the names and agendas of various CEOs and major shareholders whose actions would determine a particular stock's performance. In September of 1926, for example, the Source indicated that the Ford Motor Company would attempt to take over the management of Hudson Motors, and that Hudson Motors' stock would respond accordingly—which did, in fact, happen. In another reading, the Source discussed the impact that the raising of interest rates by the Federal Reserve would have on the New York exchange. The management decisions of Macy's Department Stores were a frequent topic of discussion, and the information that came through routinely referred to long-term plans, presumably unknown to the general public, to greatly expand the number of its department stores.

Perhaps the least understood and most misrepresented aspect of these readings was that Cayce's "higher self" was not the primary source for the market information. A host of other entities introduced themselves through Cayce to provide specific information, and in more than two-thirds of the stock market readings, Cayce—in trance—was not requested to report directly on a stock's performance but asked to interpret performance based on Morton or Edwin's dreams. The purpose of such readings, according to the Source, was not to interfere or give one individual an unfair advantage over another, but to help Morton and Edwin to develop their own intuitive abilities as they applied them to their lives and their work.

There were over one hundred instances in 1926 and 1927 of Morton or his brother dreaming that one or both were standing on the floor of the stock exchange watching the ticker tape on a particular stock rise or fall, or hearing "voices" quoting actual stock prices or describing trends. These entities primarily provided advice and guidance—from a spiritual perspective—on the stock market and business affairs, and were mainly the voices of four deceased souls: Morton's father, August Blumenthal; Marcus Loew; Elbert H. Gary; and Felix Fuld. All of these men—with the exception of Morton's father—had once been major international business or financial leaders. August Blumenthal had died in 1919. Elbert Gary, who helped to organize the U.S. Steel Corporation, had died three days before making his first trance appearance, in 1927. Marcus Loew, who had also recently died, was a motion picture producer and the owner of a chain of movie theaters. And Felix Fuld, best remembered as one of the founders of the Bamberger Department Store chain, appeared in the readings in 1929, the year that he died.

The entities introduced themselves during readings by saying, "We have Elbert Gary here," or "It is Felix Fuld," and Morton had been told in a dream that they had "united for a common purpose in the cosmic plane . . . to help . . . accomplish a certain purpose on earth." The dream continued, "Your father is the center of one group that seeks your better understanding and to aid your better application. Elbert H. Gary is the center of another group that seeks to aid you financially. He and the group are determined to make you a millionaire."

Unfortunately, the loss of the Blumenthal trading records during the Great Depression makes it impossible to now determine exactly what percentage of their income came directly from recommendations made in the readings. But a review of the trance advice given to the Blumenthals by

Fuld, Gary, and others in readings conducted between September 1924 and October 29, 1929—from when the first business requests were made to when the stock market suddenly crashed—is impressive by any standards. The record shows that the vast majority of stocks and bonds performed as described, and some of the Blumenthal holdings, such as Chrysler Motors, had grown well beyond the normal expectations in the "bull" market of the late 1920s. However, it should also be noted that the Source's daily predictions in which the "voices" were asked to cite the trading prices of a particular stock were wrong by at least one to two points in nearly three-quarters of the cases studied. This was apparently not viewed by the Blumenthals as a failure, but rather as a result of the Source's acknowledged inability to predict specific daily performance based on changing market conditions. The market was determined by man's collective will, and even God could not predetermine the will of man.

The fact that Morton and his brother became millionaires during the late 1920s is perhaps the best indicator that their association with the Cayces helped them to realize their goals. In three years the young traders went from being junior members at one firm to purchasing their own seat on the exchange for approximately $500,000 in 1928 dollars—the equivalent of owning a moderately large midtown Manhattan office building. They also had roughly that same amount in personal holdings, including an elegant town house in New York, where Edwin and his wife, Ruth, lived and an oceanfront house in Deal, New Jersey, where Morton and Adeline lived.

It is interesting to note that Edgar himself took little personal or professional interest in the stock market readings. He didn't study the rising and falling markets and left all financial decisions regarding his own holdings in the hands of Morton. Feeling compelled to broaden his base of support, and unable or unwilling to let the Blumenthal stock market readings entirely determine the fate of his dream to build the hospital, Edgar launched his own initiatives designed to generate income. These efforts were to locate hidden petroleum deposits, as he had done hundreds of times in the past, to find buried treasure, and to patent various inventions.

Among those people to offer their help in these endeavors was Frank Mohr, who had recently moved to Florida to join his brother-in-law and two other businessmen prospecting for oil and speculating in real estate. They urged Edgar to come to Florida to join them.

The principal financier of Mohr's syndicate was Thomas Peters, known in Miami as the "Tomato King" because he had earned his wealth from a large produce trucking operation. He had invested approximately $5 million in developing the Caribbean island of Bimini as an off-shore resort, hoping that American tourists would flock there in order to escape Prohibition, which had been in place since 1919. Peters built the Bimini Bay Rod and Gun Club as well as the Hotel Bimini, which featured a casino, a cocktail lounge, gardens and tennis courts. Altogether he owned approximately twelve thousand acres on the island, as well as vast tracks of land in Dade County, Florida. Prohibition, however, didn't make his hotel on Bimini the draw that he expected, and he had to temporarily close its doors in 1925. Less than a year later he reopened the hotel in partnership with real estate financier A. C. Preston.

Peters and Preston had heard about Edgar from Frank Mohr's brother-in-law, who also had a financial interest in Bimini. The first request they made for readings was in late July of 1926, to see whether or not oil could be found on their Dade County property. The subsequent reading said that only very small quantities of oil could be found, and these unfortunately, would be difficult to access because of large deposits of mud. Based on this reading, Peters and Preston decided not to drill in Dade County, but instead asked for a second reading, this time on their property on Bimini.

This reading was conducted on August 14, 1926. Cayce—in trance—located the island without difficulty. He didn't hold out much hope that they would find oil, for he said that the majority of the underground structure of the island consisted of coral. He was, however, far more hopeful about locating other treasures. "There are many that are hidden," the Source said, and these consisted of "gold, bullion, [and] silver."

In a reading that was as dramatic as any of the treasure readings Cayce had previously given, the Source described an incident in 1839 when a sailor named Bill Desmond committed mutiny on a ship, later robbed a storekeeper outside of Jamestown, and escaped down the coast and then to Bimini, where his ship was wrecked on a coral reef. Desmond and four others were described as living on a promontory in a lookout station they had built from the timbers salvaged from their ship. One of the sailors who had escaped with Desmond died of a snake bite and another died of food poisoning. The two remaining sailors had a fight over their cache of hidden loot. Desmond was wounded and died soon after the fight. The other took a portion of the treasure and tried to escape to the mainland on a small boat, but was lost in the surf and drowned. The Source said that the remains of Desmond's body were still in the hidden vault of buried treasure. This vault, according to the Source, contained nearly one hundred and twenty thousand gold coins and much silver.

This reading was enough to inspire plans for a massive search of the island. Peters and Preston made a thorough investigation and found Cayce's geography of the island and the environment around where they supposed the treasure to be "absolutely correct." Excited, Peters and Preston invited Edgar to become a part of their crew, promising him $10,000 should they find any of the treasure. Their first request that he join them came in late November 1926, just after Edgar Evans had had his legs burned. Due to his son's injuries, Edgar declined their invitation, but said he might consider making the trip later. Before committing to finally making the trip, however, Edgar consulted his old friend Byron Wyrick, who knew firsthand the kind of trouble that all too often resulted from readings of this kind.

Byron counseled Edgar to be careful, for the potential for failure was as great as all his previous ventures to raise money through prospecting for oil. "If all parties are consciously sincere and honest in their desire to produce wealth and recover treasures on [the] basis of equity to all concerned, then the efforts will succeed and you would be justified in going there and giving the readings. But if the parties concerned are selfish in mind [by] expecting the lion's share, then the project will fail."

Before Peters and Preston could take the matter any further, a great storm struck the Bahamas and Florida and devastated Bimini, where seven residents were killed and fifty-two homes and the island's only radio station were destroyed. The Bimini Hotel would never reopen—vandals stripped it of its furnishings and anything else that could be carried off. Peters and Preston pleaded with Edgar to come to Florida for more readings. The landmarks that Edgar had identified in the first reading couldn't be found after the storm—in one case floodwaters had completely covered the ground where a natural spring was supposed to be located—and they could not carry on without Cayce's help. Mohr was growing more excited by the day. "If this comes out all right," he wrote to Edgar, "you are fixed for . . . life."

He was finally persuaded to come to Bimini in person on January 20, 1927, accompanied by Gertrude, Edgar Evans, and Gladys, all expenses paid. Edgar believed that he needed to bring the whole "office" along, as he had a full schedule of readings to give and refused to delay them. "The time has [already] been given to others," Edgar would say by way of explanation, "and a promise is my bond." The truth, however, was more complex. Edgar didn't want to repeat what had happened in Desdemona and Rocky Pasture. By surrounding himself with those he knew and loved, he thought they might succeed where Thrash and the others had failed.

Peters and Preston met the Cayce entourage at the Miami train station with two Packard limousines to take them to the hotel. "The rooms were all arranged for us and are as nice . . . as we could possibly ask," Edgar wrote in a letter to Hugh Lynn, who couldn't join them because he was away in col-

lege. Left unsaid was his excitement at the prospect of digging for lost treasure and of visiting a foreign country for the first time.

On February 3, Edgar traveled with Peters, Preston, and Mohr to Bimini,
where they remained for three days. Edgar later described the experience as
quite wonderful, especially the trip over, when he saw the most fabulous
sunset he had ever seen. Unfortunately, this was the highlight of the trip. Although Edgar gave four readings on the island, the gold and silver were
never found, nor could the landmarks in the readings be located. However,
no one but Frank Mohr appeared to have been discouraged.

Returning to Miami, Edgar gave a series of readings to ascertain why
they were unable to locate the treasure trove mentioned in the earlier reading. The subsequent reading on February 7, 1927, faulted the group's purposes, even that of Edgar himself. It was "not because of information being
incorrect . . . but because the trouble lies within . . . For these sources from
which the information comes to the material world are from a universal
and infinite source, but the channel of same is of the carnal or material
place. Hence we know sin lies at the door, and in that information as has been
given respecting same, that the house must be set in order." Perhaps Edgar
himself knew in his heart that their motives weren't pure, but refused to acknowledge it because of his desire to be their partner.

Edgar was still in Miami at this point, staying at the Halcyon Hotel with
Gertrude, Gladys, and Edgar Evans. Peters and Preston kept after Edgar to
return to Bimini. He was reluctant to do so, for it would interfere with a
physical reading he had scheduled long in advance. Edgar asked the Source
to see whether or not he should further interrupt the work by forgoing the
physical reading and returning to the island to help the men find the treasure, which might—in the long run—provide the money for Edgar to carry
on his work in a much grander way and hence help the many. The answer
came: "Keep the engagement . . . for the physical reading [for as Jesus healed
the one and not the many], all be the gainers thereby."

This reading and subsequent others at the Halcyon Hotel would tell
Edgar to return to Virginia Beach and stressed the importance of seeking
"inner riches" first. The degree to which Edgar heeded this advice is debat-
able, for although he returned to Virginia Beach after Florida, he went immediately to New York to conduct stock market readings for Morton and to
attend a lecture that had been arranged by his New York supporters. Edgar
reported to Morton that "the trip [to Florida] has been really beneficial,"
even though "it was disappointing from a financial standpoint." To Edgar,
the best thing that came from it was the cooperation that developed be-

tween himself, Gertrude, and Gladys. "It made us all appreciate the part played by each individual and their relation to those seeking advice, help, and aid," Edgar said. "I am sure that this is almost like creating new blood in the work."

As for why the treasure hunt had failed, Edgar told Morton that "we can see, from our understanding, just why ... they have never located the treasure, for there are cosmic or psychic laws just as we have a penal law, and these people, I think, realize this ... Then they have gone about—even with all their other worries—to try to get their individual selves straightened out ... [They have] given up the idea of finding it until each one has come to the consciousness of making himself right with the Creative Forces."

Before bidding the Blumenthals farewell and returning to Virginia Beach, Edgar wrote Peters, outlining many of the same things he had told Morton. By the time that Peters received this letter, he and Preston were no longer getting along and would soon part company altogether. "[Peters] will not listen to common sense nor will he listen to his friends or those that pretend to be his friends," Preston wrote Cayce. "He did not want me to devote any of my time to anything outside of handling the rental of the [hotel and casino]."

For the time being, the demise of the partnership put an end to his search for the Bimini treasure. This however, did nothing to dampen Preston's interest in Cayce as a source of psychic information on hidden treasure troves. Before Edgar left Florida, Preston obtained readings on treasure hidden along Lostman's River, near the site where Ward Cawthon, Edgar's friend from the Selma drugstore, had already successfully dug.

In Preston's reading on the Lostman's River, conducted on February 14, 1927, at the Halcyon Hotel in Miami, the Source again discussed this Monroe County waterway as a good place to hunt for treasure. "This is rather a favored rendezvous ... though many ... changes ... have taken place in the development of the countries from which these people sailed, lived, escaped, or used these waters and the surrounding country as places of hiding—not only of ill-gotten gains by raids, but those that were actually taken—where people were even murdered for same, and on ... a portion of this river there may be found many places where various amounts have been put."

The spot that was recommended to Preston was some six miles above the mouth of the river, on an island near a bay where the river was divided in two. "There was once a very large tree here, on the end of the island [on] the southernmost end, and in this stump [is] this box or trunk ... and in this will be found much loot, much in gold, in silver, and in various ... jewels [about] five hundred thousand dollars worth in all." The reading went on to say that the spot on the island could be identified by a young tree that was growing out of the stump of the old tree.

In a second reading on this treasure, conducted at the Halcyon Hotel on March 3, 1927, Edgar provided a detailed explanation on how to reach the island by canoe and what equipment and supplies would be necessary to bring along when searching for it. The readings also cautioned Preston to be careful about the local inhabitants of the area and strongly urged Preston not to present himself as a treasure hunter, but for their own safety, to act as hunters, fishermen, or land developers.

Preston and a party of others did in fact make trips up the Lostman's River in July 1927, but had difficulty finding their way up the river and became lost. "There are thousands of islands in this river," he wrote Edgar. "Description of country was perfect and believe we will locate if we can find the proper island." He sporadically continued his search, always believing that he would find the treasure. In the process, his appreciation for Cayce and the work only grew more profound, prompting him to request a life reading, which revealed that he too had been associated with Ra Ta, and that the two had been exiled together to Nubia. Eventually, Preston would become the business manager for the Association for Research and Enlightenment, known as the A.R.E., which took over the activities of the original association that Morton Blumenthal formed in 1927. His former business partner, Peters, lost interest in the work, eventually went bankrupt, and died soon after. As for buried gold in the Bahamas, much was later found, though there are no known reports of gold being discovered in a hidden vault on Bimini. The only real exploratory effort on the island was an attempt to find oil, which proved unsuccessful, as the Source had foretold.

Although treasure had not been found, there was one unexpected reward that came from Cayce's readings on Bimini: an exact geographical location of the mythical continent of Atlantis. Had previous and future life readings not continually confirmed the existence of such a place, the Bimini reference would have been dismissed by the Cayces as a fanciful mixture of fact, fiction, and mythology. The information in the life readings, however, suggested this and much more: that the future destiny of the United States, and of the world, was in the hands of those who had once been entrusted with the welfare of Atlantis. Their failure to abide by God's laws had resulted in the destruction of the then civilized world, and these same souls would now, in America, be karmically tested again.

37.

◉

Atlantis and the
Future of Man

Details on the lost continent of Atlantis, or Poseidia, had been mentioned in the very earliest life readings. But until Edgar's trip to Bimini, no one involved with the work thought of Atlantis as a specific place, a former continent now vanished under the sea. In a reading conducted on March 2, 1927, at the Halcyon Hotel, the Source said that a temple of the "Poseidians" was once located near what was now the island of Bimini. This comment marked the beginning of what would become a lengthy, intensive inquiry into the subject and led to the compilation and study of six hundred life readings that made reference to Atlantis, Poseidia, or Alta, as the readings variously called the now lost continent. And early in 1932, Cayce's group conducted an intensive series of thirteen readings, which they hoped would make sense of a subject that had perplexed historians and scientists since Plato.

Fourteen-year-old Edgar Evans could take some of the credit for inspiring the committee to begin their research, for it was his life readings that first detailed events in the mythic Atlantean kingdom and suggested both the grandeur and tragedy of Atlantis' history. And just as Hugh Lynn came to embrace his own life reading and eventually devoted himself to a book-length study of reincarnation, Edgar Evans, in the years ahead, became the association's most adept student of the Atlantis readings, and he, too, eventually published his own book on the subject.

The first mention of Edgar Evans's connection to the "land of the Poseidians" was in his second life reading, which had been conducted in Dayton on February 27, 1925. The reading said that Edgar Evans had developed his considerable mechanical and engineering skills in Poseidia, skills that he had carried through all of his subsequent incarnations. As later readings revealed, talents he had developed in Atlantis would be much in demand in his present life, and how he would put his skills to use would play a determining factor in the course of future events. Thus it was natural for the inquisitive and scientific-minded Edgar Evans to want to know what that now vanished culture had been like.

Many of his questions were answered in the series of readings dedicated specifically to Atlantis, although some of the most interesting details would come through the life readings. In the 1932 series, begun on February 3, the Source made reference to passages in Plato's dialogues "Timaeus" and "Critias," which date to the fifth century B.C. in which Atlantis is described in a conversation among Egyptian priests as a large island in the Atlantic that sank in a volcanic catastrophe some nine thousand years earlier.

It wasn't until the third reading in this series that the Source came right out and said that Atlantis had existed and was once a large continent whose borders stretched between the Gulf of Mexico and the Mediterranean. "That the continent existed is [at the present time] being proven as a fact," the Source said, making reference to recent scientific and archaeological endeavors in Mexico. In another reading the Source said that evidence of Atlantis had already been found in the Yucatan in the form of a stone marker or tablet, which was at that moment purportedly on its way to a museum in Pennsylvania, though archaeologists hadn't yet understood the significance of what they had found. Evidence of the Atlantean culture was also said to exist in the Pyrenees Mountains, Morocco, British Honduras, Peru, and Central America. "There are some protruding portions within [these regions] that must have at one time or another been a portion of this great continent," the Source said. "The British West Indies or the Bahamas, and a portion of same that may be seen in the present . . . in Bimini and in the Gulf Stream."

These, however, were just landmarks, or anchors that the Source gave to better place Atlantis on the globe and to reveal how vast a region it had once encompassed. The fact that this description was not of an "island," as had been referred to by Plato and other later historical sources was explained in the readings: Plato's references were to what remained of the huge continent after successive waves of cataclysmic destruction had caused most of it to be submerged under the sea. To properly understand Atlantis, Cayce suggested, one had to look back millennia before Plato, to the dawn of man's incarnation on the planet. To Plato, Atlantis was merely an island. But to earth's first inhabitants, as purported by the Source, it was a cosmic incubator where "mind as builder" took on a significance far beyond anything Plato could have imagined.

According to the readings, the first soul or entity that God created was named Amilius. He was, along with the other souls that God created, described by Cayce as "pure light." And it was he, according to the readings, whom God was symbolically referring to in Genesis when He said, "Let there be light." The Source explained that God was not saying let there be physical light, or light from the sun, but rather, let there be the "light" of spirit in the entity of Amilius. And when God said, "Let us make man in our image," He was saying, according to the readings, that He and Amilius co-created man in their spiritual image.

The Atlantis readings describe how the first wave of souls to enter the earth experimented with matter and the physical realm. The Source said they built bodies for themselves "much in the way and manner as the amoebae would [appear] in the waters of a stagnant bay, or lake." Their reason for inhabiting the physical form, as metaphorically described in the Bible, and expanded upon in the readings, was to experience the earthly environment, or vibrations of "sound, taste, and touch" that couldn't be experienced in their non-three-dimensional realm. Most of all they desired carnal relations, and this, according to the readings, resulted in souls becoming trapped or "hardened" in various inferior physical forms. Amilius, who incarnated as Adam, the "first son of God," took it upon himself to enter the earth's plane to try to free the lost souls who had become trapped in materiality. Adam created a companion in Eve, the first "twin soul," and together they populated and subdued the earth with a superior "human" form, one that was capable, through the power of free will, to return to God.

The culture in Atlantis developed sooner than other indigenous cultures because it was where Amilius, as Adam, and many of his fellow "sons of God," first established a temple dedicated to the "Law of One." And, according to the readings, it was in this temple that the population of Atlantis developed a moral foundation far ahead of other cultures that co-existed on the planet.

The degree to which the Atlanteans eventually developed technology was altogether beyond anything that existed on Earth at that time. While nomadic tribes in one part of the world were presumably still living in caves,

Atlanteans had learned to cultivate and replenish the soil, construct canals and waterworks for irrigation and bathing, and produce various forms of lightweight metals. The capital city was named Poseidia, and was built on a hill that overlooked the sea. Unlike cities being built in other developing cultures described in the readings, Poseidia was not a walled fortress, but open on all sides. It was also designed so that river water was channeled into pools where residents bathed, played sports, and conducted religious ceremonies. There were also aqueducts or canals that, according to the readings, were kept constantly in motion so that [the water] purified itself in its course."

Over time, the Source said, "Divisions between those of the Law of One—the sons of God who had retained their purity—and the sons of Belial [arose]." The sons of the Law of One were described as those whose standard was "that the soul was given by the Creator . . ." But the standard of the Law of One was rejected by the sons of Belial. According to the Source, the sons of Belial sought "the gratifying, the satisfying, the use of the material things for self, without thought or consideration as to the sources of such, nor the hardships in the experience of others . . . They were those without a standard of morality. The sons of Belial had no standard, save of self."

According to the Source, "[The] first upheavals [in Atlantis] were brought about when the activities of the sons of Belial brought to the daughters of the children of the Law of One the abilities for enjoying the pleasures of excesses of every nature in human relationship as well as those related to same." This theme was repeated in another reading: "[They gradually began] polluting themselves with those mixtures that brought contempt, hatred, bloodshed, and those that build for desires of self without respect of other's freedom, other's wishes."

The Source made another important point concerning progress in Atlantean culture. The Atlanteans traveled or visited other developing peoples and shared with them some of their sophisticated advancements. And they, like their neighbors, had to contend with the menace of huge carnivorous beasts of the field and fowls of the air. The "sons of men" had actually created these creatures and then lost control over them "by influences of the powers of suggestion . . ." The creatures were described as great beasts or "prehistoric animals" that trampled the forests, destroyed the fields, and consumed vast quantities of food, making man's life miserable. The Atlanteans and people from other nations tried many approaches to subdue and destroy these beasts. Eventually, a great convention was held in Egypt, the one place on earth where the beasts had not overrun, to determine what was to be done about this menace. Perhaps because of their advanced technology, the Atlanteans took it upon themselves to eradicate the beasts. Thus, technology that had once only been used to harness energy for life-giving purposes and to communicate with their maker, was now used to develop weapons for hunting and slaughtering the beasts and fowls of the air, and ultimately would lead to the end of the first phase of life on the continent.

A technological invention, described as a huge "power station" fueled by a "firestone," was purported to have brought on the second phase of destruction in Atlantis, said to be around 28,000 B.C. According to the Source, the firestone was "unintentionally turned too high" and resulted in an earth-shattering explosion, which heated the ground and caused volcanic activity, leaving only three of the five islands, those named Poseidia, Aryan, and Og. The volcanic eruptions, or explosions, were of such great force that a tidal wave created a vast flood across large parts of the world, covering much of the land and resulting in many deaths. This event, according to the Source, was the great flood depicted in the Bible, for which Noah and his family built their ark. It was also a time when an evacuation of large segments of the Atlantean population, many of whom were associated with the Law of One, made their journey to other parts of the earth, most notably Egypt, the Yucatan, and Peru, where they would become high priests and spiritual guides among the developing cultures there.

No evidence exists to suggest that Cayce's group made an effort to corroborate the Source's depiction of Atlantis or the alleged archaeological discovery that was then on its way to Pennsylvania. Not until Edgar's death did Hugh Lynn and Edgar Evans launch a search along these lines, and their findings were generally dismissed as "pseudoarchaeology" or "New Age science." The likely reason that no effort was made in 1933 to verify the Source's claims was because the information that came through on the third and final phase of Atlantean culture was beyond rational belief and was hence deemed too far removed from serious consideration. However, given scientific developments in the 1940s, the information may not have been as implausible as originally thought.

According to the Source, the Atlanteans, who were now at war, purportedly learned to alter the molecular structure of atomic particles into a chain reaction, or "eternal fire." In the forty thousand years since the first earth changes had altered the social and geographical configuration of their continent, the Atlanteans had purportedly developed technology that was powered by a limitless source of electrical energy—a concentrated beam of light, much like a laser beam, emanating from what Cayce called "the mighty, the terrible crystal." The word "atomic" was used in many direct references to the type of "electrical energy" or "electricity" being harnessed by the Atlanteans to rebuild in the wake of the devastation at the end of the second destruction of Atlantis. The Source said that the Atlanteans used "rediscovered gases, and those of the electrical and 'aeratic' formations [those being charged with gas] in the breaking up of the atomic forces to produce impelling force . . . or of changing the faces or forces of nature itself." In another reading, the principle that was described as fueling the "eternal flame," was "such as we may find in those that make for the active forces in that of uranium."

There were other interesting revelations given in readings. For instance, according to the Source, persons who had incarnations in Atlantis, "are all exceptional . . . They either wield woe or great development. And their influences are felt, whether the individual recognizes it in himself or not."

A far greater revelation would come out of the Atlantis readings. According to the Source, just as Edgar as Ra Ta had subsequently incarnated several times to "help prepare the way," so had Amilius, the first created of God, who had incarnated as Adam. Only he had not returned to "prepare the way" as had Ra Ta. He *was* "the way." The entity once known as Amilius, and then Adam, was none other than Jesus in His last incarnation. And it was here, in a trance session conducted on April 5, 1932, that the hundreds of individual life readings could finally be viewed as parts of one giant mosaic depicting God's and man's activities on Earth, and providing testimony to a vision of Christianity quite unlike that understood by most practicing Christians today.

Edgar knew that many present-day Christians would be horrified at the concept of reincarnation, particularly as applied to the "Master of Masters." And yet, as the Cayces had been told by the Source when the topic first came up, reincarnation had fallen away from Christian theology as a result of attempts to take "shortcuts." As the Source said: "Much might be given respecting that ye . . . call the Bible. This has passed through many hands. Many that would turn that which was written into the meanings that would suit their own purposes, as ye yourselves often do." For Edgar, a great lover of the Bible, this would have been as difficult to accept as it would be for many other fundamentalists. He was relieved, however, when the Source went on to say: "But if ye will get the spirit of that written [in the Bible] there ye may find it will lead thee to the Gates of Heaven. For, it tells of God, of your home, of His dealings with His peoples in many environs, in many lands. Read it to be wise, study it to understand, live it to know that the Christ walks through same with thee."

However one chooses to view Jesus and the Atlantis readings, it was clear that Cayce had overcome a major hurdle in understanding the bigger picture presented in all the readings. Just as the soul of Amilius had incarnated as Adam and as Jesus to try to lead mankind back to God, the Source also conclusively stated that He would come again, not only in the hearts and minds of those who love Him, but "as ye have seen Him go in the body."

Confirmation of the second coming was both awe inspiring and frightening for Edgar, Gertrude, and Gladys. And it was in connection with one reading devoted to the second coming, in which Edgar's role in the "greater picture" was most clearly defined. Edgar was both humbled and proud to learn that the Source described him as "one who is to be a forerunner of . . . [the] Christ consciousness . . . that force or power into the earth that has been spoken of through the ages." In this same reading, the Source then admonished Edgar and the others to approach the work in humility and cooperation: "*Listen* while He speaks!"

38.

Gravity, Polarity, and Perpetual Motion

The continuing connective tissue in the readings constantly surprised, impressed, baffled, and confused Edgar Cayce and the others. No sooner had they finished placing one or two more pieces of the puzzle into place than they would discover that the picture itself had changed, or had become more comprehensive than they had previously imagined possible. Just as earlier readings had opened their eyes to a new fascination with history and religion, the Atlantis readings inspired interest in everything from mythology to geography, oceanography, archaeology, and even modern science and technology.

More than 650 people had life readings placing them in the technologically advanced Atlantis. The fact that, according to the Source, these specific individuals—among them Edgar Evans—were being incarnated in the present certainly seemed to explain the technological advances that were being made at an unprecedented rate in this century. Technological innovations that seemed preposterous in 1925 would become reality in the 1930s and '40s. Edgar and Gertrude themselves had gone from riding in a horse and buggy in Hopkinsville, Kentucky, to driving a Buick in Virginia Beach. Had Edgar and Gertrude lived beyond 1945, they, like Gladys, Hugh Lynn, and Edgar

Evans, would see a man walking on the moon within their lifetime. Edgar Evans himself, the son of a photographer who developed pictures on glass plates, would help to operate an aircraft radar system. In light of what was coming through in the readings about the technology of the Atlanteans, it was then no small coincidence to Gladys and the Cayces that a man who (in Edgar's mind) must have been a former Atlantean involved Cayce in an invention that seemed as improbable as anything said to have been created in that ancient kingdom: a perpetual motion motor.

Thirty-five-year-old Marion L. Stansell, an engine mechanic from Birmingham, came to the attention of the Cayces on a brief trip Edgar made to that city in early 1928 to stir up interest and support for the new Association of National Investigators, the ANI. Like Edgar B. Davis, who struck oil in Luling, Stansell's personal story is quite remarkable. And he too, like Edgar Davis, had a vision in which he allegedly received a direct communication from God.

Stansell had his vision while stationed in France during World War I, when he was in a hospital recovering from mustard gas poisoning. In the recuperation process, he contracted a flu virus, and in his weakened condition, suffered heart failure and was declared dead. Not unlike others who have reported near-death experiences, he claimed to have risen above his body and to have watched all the activities in the hospital ward around him. He then became aware of his family back in Alabama, who were praying for his safe return home. A "spirit guide" escorted him to what he described as a dimension inhabited by the recently dead. But Stansell didn't want to continue his astral journey. He asked to meet Jesus, with whom he then pleaded to be permitted to return to Earth to serve God. Christ told him he could go back, and that he would be given a formula for a mechanical device that would ultimately save the planet from certain environmental destruction in the next millennium. After twenty minutes of not breathing, Stansell reawakened to discover that doctors had already pronounced him dead. Physicians were not only shocked to find him living, but apparently fully recovered from both the flu and the effects of mustard gas poisoning.

A physical reading conducted by Cayce on February 1, 1928, confirmed that Stansell's body had undergone a miraculous healing process. Further readings indicated that Stansell had considerable "psychic talents," and that through dreams and visions he was able to view blueprints for a revolutionary type of motor. This motor, according to the readings, was designed in the spirit realm by De Witt Clinton, the deceased former governor of New York, who, in his last incarnation on earth, had been the prime creative force behind the development of the Erie Canal and other large-scale public engineering projects. The readings also suggested that Stansell needed the trance assistance of Edgar Cayce to relay precise technical information from Clinton to Stansell, and that Stansell also required a dedicated team of like-minded Atlantean entrepreneurs—such as Morton Blumenthal and Dayton auto parts maker Tim Brown—to see the invention through to completion.

The first of twenty-one readings on the Stansell motor took place on March 8, 1928, at the La Salle Hotel in Chicago. Morton, who conducted the first reading, asked for a description of the device to be built. "[The] motor . . . will develop power on its own action," the Source said. "The idea and the plans, as have [been] worked out [are] the better application of the created [or universal] energy."

The motor was to consist of a large metal tank containing water, in which a drum containing compressed air or vapor would be suspended. Around the sides and inside the drum were metal sprockets, called "sprankles" in the readings, much like pins inserted into a cushion, or spark plugs on an engine block. A "cam shaft" running through the center of the drum would be connected to a caterpillar-type drive shaft at the top of the tank. Positively charged particles expanding in the bottom of the vapor-filled drum would contract as they rose to meet negatively charged particles at the top, which would create a rotational force, causing the drum to spin. The action in the metal drum was compared to the rotation of the earth: once put in motion, the drum would spin indefinitely until it was physically stopped. The larger the motor, the more power it would produce. There would be no exhaust fumes, no dangerous emissions of any kind, and it would require no fuel beyond that necessary to initially put the drum into motion.

Cayce, in trance, also issued a warning to all participants in the building of this motor: "There must be perfect cooperation of the self and the will with those who would assist in perfecting this from the material side. Also there must be perfect cooperation with inner self to obtain that information that would give self knowledge . . . For [all] force is one."

Brown and Blumenthal jumped at the opportunity to help Stansell realize his dream. In the process, they naturally hoped to become rich themselves, for the technical revolution that a perpetual motion motor would create in industry could have unimagined consequences, not the least of which was an unlimited source of "clean" energy. The result was a contract that Brown and Blumenthal worked out to pool their resources and install Stansell at the Brickman Engineering Company, a state-of-the-art incubator for Detroit motor technology. It was also, the partners would discover, an expensive place to develop their invention. In the first few months of experimenting at Brickman, Brown and Blumenthal are estimated to have spent several thousand dollars putting together several nonfunctioning prototypes of the Stansell motor.

The original prototype of the motor—which looked something like a small evaporative cooler—was much discussed in trance sessions during the initial phase of product development, then scrapped in favor of starting from scratch using more precise tools and materials as specified in the readings. As a new model was being built, Brown requested and received numerous additional readings to explain exactly how and why the motor was supposed to operate. And just as Morton Blumenthal had embraced the mysteries of the "spirit" in the life readings, Brown was doing the same with the mysteries of the material world in the physics or scientific readings. Edgar himself had little initial interest in the technical aspects of the information coming through, yet he soon discovered that the scientific readings, more than the medical and life readings, provided insights into how he was theoretically able to retrieve information in a trance state.

The Stansell motor readings, which were conducted over a two-year period, might well be considered a continuation of the information presented to Thomas Edison and Nikola Tesla a decade earlier in Bowling Green. The important difference was that Brown and Stansell were not only compiling new theoretical concepts, but they were also building an actual prototype machine to test them. Perhaps in no time in modern history had engineers consulted a psychic in an undertaking of this sort.

The terminology that was being used in the Stansell readings was clearly not the same as found in engineering or physics textbooks, but the concepts were clear. "Life in [all] its manifestations is vibration," the Source stated. "Electricity is vibration." The type or "wave length" of vibration determines how it acts in a given environment. "Vibration that is creative is one thing [and] vibration that is destructive is another . . . yet they may be from the same source, as in the electrical forces . . . in the [human] body . . . Remember, life is vibration, [and] so is mind, so is matter."

According to the Source, "electricity . . . is the same energy . . . [that is called] God. Not that God is an electric light or an electric machine, but vibration that is creative [rather than destructive] is of the same energy as life itself." Further, the Source stated: "The lowest form of vibration electrically gives creative [building] forces, rather than the highest. It is the high vibration that destroys."

In trance, Cayce explained how one vibration affects another, as seen in the creation of chemical compounds or colors on a painter's pallet. The same was said to be true for sound. Just as two substances could be combined to form a third, sound vibrations could be combined into octaves, which create their own harmony. By virtue of the fact that man is subject to the limitations of his human body, his knowledge or awareness of the great range or spectrum of "vibratory scales" is extremely limited.

In Cayce's all-encompassing concept of vibration being the force of life, he would—in trance—introduce the concept of time as well as sound and color in its relation to vibration: "History will be seen to come in cycles . . . as in [the case of] energy, [for] there is seen the relativity of space and force as [it] is begun, and as [it] continues to vibrate [When] it vibrates in the same vibration, it shows as the same thing." In other words, history, or time, is governed by a specific range of vibrations that exist in a given environment. But time in one environment would not be the same as it might exist in another environment or dimension where the vibrational range is different or subject to a different set of laws.

As Brown and Edgar himself realized, the Source was confirming much the same theory as previously postulated by Einstein in his theory of relativity. However, the concepts put forth by the Source were given a Divine inspiration by the Source's suggestion that time, matter, and space were all one vibration begun by God. And it was, in a large sense, the "spiritual" aspect of vibration that made the Source's interpretation of natural phenomena the most relevant to a theoretical understanding of how Edgar Cayce was able to do what he did when he went into trance.

According to the Source, the fundamental difference between that which was of the "spirit" and that which was of "earthly manifestation" was the law of "polarity" acting upon the "First Cause," or God's energy force. In the Divine or spiritual realm, all energy was said by the Source to be positively charged, or expanding. Earthly or material manifestation was both positively and negatively charged. Negatively charged vibrational energy, according to the Source, contracts rather than expands.

As previous readings had suggested, human beings contained both positive- and negative-charged particles or vibrations, but due to one charge being greater than another, a person could be said to be positive or negative. Edgar himself had been told that he was positively charged, and thus would do his best work with a person who was negatively charged, as Gertrude was.

"Matter is that demonstration and manifestation of the units of positive and negative energy [or one being pulled into another]," the Source said. This theme was expanded upon in another reading that said: "Each [atom] of a physical body is made up of its units of positive and negative forces that brings it into a material plane . . . As a group may raise the atomic vibrations that make for those positive forces as bring Divine Force in[to] action [in the] material plane, those that are destructive are broken down by the raising of that vibration."

These concepts were crucial to understanding the motion of the Stansell motor because they were alleged to be the essence of physical law. The Source said that just as positively charged energy expands, negatively charged energy contracts, or draws positively charged particles to it. This action between the two was described as gravity, or that in which "everything . . . is drawn to a common center . . . [Gravity is but] the centralization of the vibratory force [on the material plane]." The Source further suggested that what was commonly understood as the magnetic attraction that a compass needle had toward earth's positive pole, was one and the same thing as gravity. An apple falls to the ground for the same reason that a piece of metal clings to a magnet. The Earth's rotation or "radial force" was a result of gravity too, or the displacement of "compelling forces."

The message being communicated, quite simply, was that gravity was the result of a combination of positive and negative vibrations acting in relativity to one another. By altering the combinations of vibrations, one could theoretically change gravitational pull on the various elements. The Stansell motor worked on the principle of alternatively changing the gravitational pull of vapor in the drum housing the motor. The "sprangles," or sprockets that were housed in the drum were nothing more than tuning forks that transmitted the vibrational level of the vapor in the drum and acted on the gasses trapped inside, causing them to alternately rise to the top of the drum and then sink to the bottom. This action was described as being the same kind of centrifugal force as found in nature, which theoretically would keep the drum spinning forever. By first setting the drum in motion, man was doing what God had done in the First Cause, when his "directive force" or release of vibrational energy created the universe and set the earth and other planetary objects spinning in space.

A natural question put to the Source was how the atomic structure of metal could be restructured as to prevent the gravitational pull of the positive into the negative. The Source was reluctant to reveal how this could be accomplished but indicated that it was possible. "There must be determined for what purpose these are to be used before ye may be given [this information]," the Source said.

Though reluctant to speak further on this subject, there were many inferences in the Stansell readings to the power of highly developed people to raise the vibrational level of matter to change or alter its composition by merely "thinking" or "concentrating" on an object or person. This concept was certainly another way of describing the concept mind as the builder on the material plane. The Source suggested that this principle worked on many different levels, such as "faith healing," or the combined forces of "groups of people in prayer." Further, highly developed people had the ability—to varying degrees—to tap into a greater range or spectrum of "vibratory scales." This, in theory, was how Edgar Cayce had the ability to obtain trance information. By subjugating his earthly or material self in order to enter the spiritual dimension, his astral body was no longer subject to gravity, time, and spatial relationships. Entirely different laws governed conditions in an environment where negatively charged energy didn't exist.

Tim Brown appears to have had a clearer understanding of the purported scientific principles being put forth in the readings than Edgar Cayce, for much of the correspondence from the lab in Dayton to Edgar in Virginia Beach was merely an attempt to explain what he thought the readings were saying. The problem was that however much Brown may or may not have correctly understood the theory behind the motor, putting that theory into practice proved to be a daunting challenge.

The readings provided a multitude of technical reasons why each of the early prototypes didn't work, not the least of which was the seemingly impossible task of assembling the motor parts in proper order while submerged in water and while maintaining the right pressure inside the drum. All of this had to be done in the correct sequence and accomplished in a relatively small window of time to prevent the mixing of negatively and positively charged gases in the drum. Further, the readings specifically said that the drum had to be put into motion when the device was precisely set along an east and west axis line, presumably because the Earth's positively and negatively charged poles would interfere with the action taking place inside the drum. The real challenge was not in keeping the motor running, Brown concluded, but getting it turning in the first place.

As the months passed, one prototype after another was built and then scrapped. Like finely honed tuning forks, the "sprankles" and the grooves cut into them had to meet exacting standards in order to properly transfer the vibration of the water in the tank to the vibration of the vapor in the drum. And just as the density of the steel with which they were made had to be taken into account, as did the thickness and surface contour of the metal with which the drum was made, the chemical composition of the liquid in the holding tanks also had to meet exacting specifications. In the case of the first two prototypes of the device, the metal drum proved to be too fragile and had to be strengthened. More readings were conducted to try and bring each successive model to the standards set in the previous reading. The challenges were formidable and tested everyone's patience.

Instead of growing frustrated with the lack of progress, Brown became increasingly more fascinated with the motor. He believed that the principles behind the Stansell motor would not only result in a technological revolution, but open the doors to a greater understanding of cosmic law. Confident that they were taking the necessary steps to reconfigure their most recent prototype, and that it was just a matter of time before they got it working, Brown, Blumenthal, and Stansell moved forward to have the device patented and requested a reading on March 7, 1929, to determine how much income their invention could generate. To their delight, the reading suggested a payout of $10,000,000.

Enthusiastic as Morton was at the prospect of making a fortune on the Stansell motor, he hardly needed the additional income. During the five years that had elapsed since he had met Edgar, the Blumenthals had become millionaires. And despite the lack of financial support by the vast majority of association members, the Blumenthals had amassed enough capital to build the hospital themselves.

PART SEVEN

The Cayce Hospital

39.

A Dream
Realized

During Edgar's long afternoon walks, he would inevitably pause at one spot along a remote stretch of wind-swept beach, one quarter of a mile up from his house. Looking inland he would stare up at a grassy knoll above the pines, the highest sand dune between Cape Henry and the city limits. It was here, in his mind, that he would paint a picture of the hospital that he had come to Virginia Beach to build, a hospital rising like a "lighthouse" over the sand and sea. Edgar hoped the institution would become an enduring example of the association's motto, which would be etched into its cornerstone: "That we may make manifest our love for God and man."

Edgar could therefore not have been more pleased and grateful when Morton and Edwin dipped into their personal account in February 1927 to purchase five adjoining parcels of land on precisely the spot Edgar envisioned for the hospital. The five parcels, along with improvements, which included a road leading to the south entrance and the installation of a water main, cost $10,000. Each parcel measured approximately 150 feet along Atlantic Boulevard at what is today Sixty-seventh Street and extended westward for 300 feet to Holly Avenue, just over the top of the sand dune and into a thicket of pine trees beyond. This totaled 225,000 square feet, or just over five acres.

The same month that the land was purchased, Morton hired the respected Norfolk architectural firm of Rudolf, Cooke, and Van Leeuween to begin designing the building, and two months later accepted a bid from the United Construction Company in Norfolk, to begin construction. A loan of $46,500 from the Definite Contract Building and Loan Association of Norfolk, secured by Tim Brown, Dave Kahn, and the Blumenthals, helped to defray a portion of the initial construction costs, estimated to be in the neighborhood of $52,000. However, even before construction was set to begin, the costs for the architect and contractor were already rising, and by the beginning of May had reached $65,000 as improvements and additional buildings were added to the contract.

However much the hospital was meant to be "a beacon of light" over troubled seas, the building itself was designed along the classical lines of a massive antebellum plantation house, with a wide porch at the front running the length of the second floor and around the sides. This main building would have four levels. The ground floor, or basement, would house therapy rooms and an X-ray and fluoroscope machine. The main entrance would be on the second floor, with stairs leading up to it from the outside. Inside the front door would be the lobby, and then a library, doctors' offices, a lecture hall, and treatment rooms. The third and fourth floors would house beds for thirty patients in wards and private rooms.

In keeping with the Source's recommendations to lead a balanced life of both work and play, there were also to be tennis courts, a croquet and shuffleboard park, a club room for card players, and bath houses on the beach, where the Source often sent people for the healing effects of the sea, sand, and sun. And because it had been Edgar's dream that the building wouldn't just be a hospital, but a place for patients to seek spiritual and mental help, a meditation garden was added behind the main building. Concerned that patients might turn the hospital into a shrine and worship Edgar and the work rather than the God within, the Cayces decided against building a chapel, something they would have no doubt loved to have had for themselves. But as the Source always reminded them, the body was the true temple of God.

In order to maintain an atmosphere of privacy, the Cayces decided that readings should be undertaken at home on Thirty-fifth Street. This would also allow Gertrude and Edgar to care for their home and family in between trance sessions. Gladys, single and sociable, would probably have preferred to work at the hospital, but working from home would not be without its delights. She had grown to be more and more like the daughter that Edgar and Gertrude never had, and like a sister to Hugh Lynn and Edgar Evans.

As plans were still being drawn up for the building, the finishing touches were being made to the charter establishing the ANI as a legal entity. The Association of National Investigators would receive its state charter in Virginia on May 6, 1927, as "an association for the purpose of psychic research and to provide for the practical application of any knowledge obtainable through the medium of psychic phenomena." The original officers of the association included Edwin and Morton Blumenthal; Morton's wife, Adeline; Lucille and David Kahn; Tim Brown; Byron Wyrick; Franklin Bradley; the Cayces; and Gladys Davis. One of its ten bylaws required any person requesting a reading to first become a member of the association, which meant acknowledging that the hospital's psychic research was purely experimental. This protected the association and its trustees from legal prosecution for "fortune-telling," which was a misdemeanor in the state of Virginia.

In the year between the purchase of the land and when construction finally began, in June of 1928, numerous readings were conducted to help fine-tune the blueprints, prepare budgets, obtain the necessary work permits, and order medical equipment that had to be specially made. Dr. House resigned his post in Hopkinsville and he, Carrie, and Tommy moved to the beach, along with Edgar's father, Leslie.

There was no formal ground-breaking ceremony, but the whole family was on hand as Edgar, dressed in overalls, witnessed construction crews clear the land in preparation for pouring the foundation. Although Edgar had been feeling, as he said, "under the weather"—again having lost his voice and suffering the headaches and other side effects of the adhesions resulting from the accident he had had as a child—there was no chance he would miss this momentous event. By 3:30 P.M. that same afternoon, he was back in his study on Thirty-fifth Street, preparing for the afternoon reading. Every day thereafter, Edgar and Gertrude came and watched the progress being made, with Edgar pitching in and helping out where he could. Within the next two months the foundation was laid and the carpenters began to frame the building.

Throughout the construction process, the Blumenthals, like Tim Brown, were constantly surprised and impressed with the skills Edgar demonstrated with a hammer and saw, for they had only known him in his capacity as a psychic, not as the Kentucky farm boy who had become as adept at building a barn as he was behind a plow. Climbing on the scaffolding that rose over the sand dunes must have added to Edgar's pleasure, for each day his long-time dream of building a hospital was becoming a reality around him. At his side were his twenty-one-year-old son, Hugh Lynn, and Tommy House Jr.

The first months of construction, in the summer and fall of 1928, were marked by an attitude of cooperation and harmony between the Cayces and the Blumenthals. Yet the readings at this time admonished Edgar to enter more deeply into the world of spirit and warned Morton of future problems that might arise from his feelings toward others in the association. This message came through especially clearly in a dream Edgar had in October of 1928, which provided a lesson for both Morton and himself.

In Edgar's dream, the voice of the Old Testament prophet Habakkuk spoke to him about his relationship to Morton and the work. Although the exact contents of the dream are unknown, a subsequent reading about this dream confirmed that Edgar was indeed visited by the spirit of Habakkuk. "Tell Morton to pattern much [of his work with Edgar] after that given in the lessons by Habakkuk," the Source stated. "Not his lamentations re-specting filial conditions, nor those of a lost people, but rather the good tidings that are in store for those who will listen to [that] which comes from within . . . Read [Habakkuk] and in the study of same will come as an experience which has never appeared to the body as yet. For the glory of Him who gave Himself in ransom will spread about same. Be true."

The reference was to the end of the Book of Habakkuk, where the prophet, after revealing, in trembling fear, the terrible punishment he saw ahead for the people who had strayed, declared: "The Lord God is my strength . . . and he will make me to walk upon mine high places." These verses, perhaps by no coincidence, also make reference to buildings—to the Lord in his Holy Temple, and to stones and building timbers that "cry out and are not heard."

The Source's warning, in the same reading, was not to take Edgar's psychic phenomena for granted—and not only as they were manifested in trance, but in dreams and in a waking state. The Source said: "Visions and dreams which come to the body should be applied in the light of . . . daily affairs . . . for the propagation of thought. Yet there is laxness in these considerations."

This may have been the first time that Edgar, in dream or trance, was visited by Habakkuk, but was by no means the last visitation by a prophet from the spirit world. As construction continued, Edgar could feel the presence of angels operating far beyond the limited scope of Elbert Gary or Felix Fuld, and these spirits indicated everyone involved in the construction process was on the right track and was doing God's bidding.

Perhaps the most dramatic visitation occurred a few months earlier, in July of 1928, when an unexpected announcement interrupted a reading that was in progress: "Hark! There comes the voice of one who would speak to those gathered here."

Morton, Gertrude, Gladys, Thomas House, and the others present sat in stunned silence as the Archangel Michael, the angel who stands before the "Throne of the Father," was announced by the Source. As Gladys later described it, they could instantly feel a "vibrational change" in the "energy forces" around them. She described how the panes of glass in the windows began to shake and how she felt as if the pad of paper in her hand was being pulled away from her just as if a gust of wind was blowing through the room. The people sitting in the room could feel the sting of tears in their eyes and shivers up and down their bodies as they sat, frozen in both awe and fear.

"I AM MICHAEL, LORD OF THE WAY!" Cayce proclaimed in an unusually loud voice. "BEND THY HEAD, OH YE CHILDREN OF MEN. GIVE HEED UNTO THE WAY AS IS SET BEFORE YOU IN THAT SERMON ON THE MOUNT . . . FOR EVEN AS THE VOICE OF THE ONE WHO STOOD BESIDE THE SEA AND CALLED ALL MEN UNTO THE WAY, THAT THOSE THAT WOULD HARKEN MIGHT KNOW THERE WAS AGAIN A STAFF IN DAVID . . . FOR IN ZION THY NAMES WERE WRITTEN, AND IN SERVICE WILL COME TRUTH!"

The group sat in silence as the Source quietly ended the trance session. Gertrude had to compose herself to attend to Edgar's needs, issuing the usual command to wake up. Edgar stretched and opened his eyes to see every one of them wiping away tears. Although the Archangel's words were biblical in content and allusion, their meaning was clear: those gathered to hear the reading were being given a great opportunity—and also the frightening responsibility—to serve God and their fellow man in a most uncommon way.

The money for the hospital, as promised, would be there. But the task that was yet to be accomplished—a task that required something more than hammers and nails—was to develop cooperation between those who would run it. Problems between the various members had been brewing since Morton first took the helm and came to a head at the first formal meeting of the association held in the newly built Cavalier Hotel in Virginia Beach.

In a letter inviting all members of the association to the gathering on August 4, 1928, Hugh Lynn warned the participants that many of them hadn't gotten along in previous incarnations, and it was incumbent upon all of them to enter into their work together in a spirit of cooperation. Many of the participants had been pitted against each other in Egypt—Hugh Lynn admitted that he himself was one of them, as were Morton Blumenthal, Dave Kahn, and Franklin Bradley. According to their life readings, these men had had many conflicts with each other.

The meeting started out on a happy note. According to Hugh Lynn, everyone was greeting and hugging one another. And yet, as Hugh Lynn later said, "within thirty minutes after they sat down and started talking, you could hear . . . Morton and Franklin screaming at one another." The initial argument was over whether a tin or shingle roof should be put on the twelve-car garage that was being constructed behind the hospital next to the tennis court. "Morton and Franklin were never on the same side of a vote from that time on," Hugh Lynn later noted. In some respects, the meeting marked the beginning of a very tense and troubled period in the association's history, although none of the participants realized the serious nature of what had been set in motion until three years later.

Another incident that marred the joy that Edgar was feeling in seeing the hospital built occurred when they were nearly finished, and Morton, wiring them from New York, called a sudden halt to construction. His reason, he said, was that the contractor was billing him for approximately twice what he had expected at this stage of the construction. Morton was told that significant alterations had been made to the plans, including adding a bath between each of the ten second-floor bedrooms, and another bathroom in the hall on the third floor.

Morton was so concerned about the changes that he hired a plane to fly him to Virginia Beach so that he could speak to Edgar and the contractor in person. He discovered that Edgar himself had authorized the changes, without seeking Morton's permission. Eventually, Morton agreed to go along with the changes but was visibly angry with Edgar. Up until that point, Edgar believed that he was in charge of the building operation, but from then on, he stepped aside and let Morton oversee the construction from New York City. And although Morton had castigated Edgar for making changes, he himself was responsible for $15,000 of improvements, which included grading the gently rolling knoll between the hospital and the beach and covering it with thousands of pounds of sod. This gave the Cayce Hospital the distinction of having the only lawn between the Cavalier Hotel and Cape Henry, and a huge one at that.

Edgar had long looked forward to opening day at the hospital, but now that it was approaching he looked on it with a certain trepidation. By October 25, 1928, when pressure to complete the hospital was highest, he wrote a friend. "I haven't been feeling able to do anything . . . while I have continued to be up and about, perhaps I should have quit trying to work, but

seemingly many things have piled in on us . . . [and] when we get so far behind, we are bound to make somebody feel neglected." Edgar was most concerned about Morton. In his effort to outfit the building he was not giving
the attention to Morton's daily readings, and sometimes two or three days
would elapse before he could address the Blumenthals' many questions.

The tension also made Edgar's temper flare. On one particularly bad day,
Gladys recounted that Edgar dictated a number of letters to her and, after
giving his morning reading, said he was going to the building site to see how
things were going. Gladys reminded him to take his raincoat. "I was going
to take it anyway," he snapped. Gladys then mentioned that Morton was
waiting for a dream reading. Edgar replied that he didn't have time to do it,
he had to talk to the gardener. When Gladys pointed out the importance of
the reading, Edgar fired back at her that *he* was in charge, *not* Morton, and
that she was fired, and then marched out of the room. Leslie, who was still
staying at the beach, tried to comfort her by telling her that Edgar didn't really mean what he had said. Later that day, when Edgar returned to the
house, he acted as if nothing had happened.

Gladys was feeling the stress also. In October of 1928, she discovered a
lymph tumor on her left breast and was experiencing weakness in her fingers and poor circulation. In a subsequent reading, she was told to stimulate
excretion, externally and internally, through steam baths and by using iodine
in the water. She was also to drink three or four glasses of water just before
the baths, after which she was to massage her breast and underarm with
Iodex, an iodine compound. The treatments proved to be successful: A little
over a year later, after a checkup reading, physicians reported that the tumor
had dissolved. It never reappeared.

As the hospital neared completion, the association held many meetings
to determine how it should best be operated. It was decided that overnight
stays in single rooms would be billed at $100 a night, double rooms facing the
ocean would be charged a rate of $65 and ward rooms would run $45 a
night. Treatments such as hot baths and osteopathy would be charged at the
rate of $2 each session. During this same meeting, the physicians' salaries
were set, amounting to $800 a month, and it was decided that these, along
with other operating expenses of approximately another $1,000, would be
jointly shared by the Blumenthals, Franklin Bradley, Tim Brown, and Dave
Kahn until the institution could pay for itself. Although it was generally assumed that the Blumenthals would carry the lion's share of the operating
costs, each of the other parties would be expected to make monthly contributions. In addition to the cash payments, donations of supplies, paint, and
equipment were hoped for and expected.

Two weeks before the scheduled opening of the hospital another meeting was held, in which a reading was conducted to see whether or not it would be appropriate for Edgar to give a psychic demonstration at the dedication ceremony. The response was a most definite "no." The Source said, "It would not be in keeping with [the hospital's] best interests . . . Let that as may be accomplished be well spoken of, and do not parade that that is holy."

The dedication ceremonies, conducted by Morton Blumenthal as president of the association, took place on November 11, 1928. Differences were put aside as the Blumenthals, the Cayces, the Kahns, and others proudly looked on the completed building with anticipation. Crowds of Cayce supporters from near and far filled the lecture hall. When Morton formally turned the hospital over to the association, Edgar was said to respond, "When your prayers are answered, you find out that prayers are about the only things that words are good for, so there's nothing to say, except to give thanks."

Morton, standing next to Edgar, was so moved by the moment that he leaned over to him and said, "[Here] rises our great oak, Edgar, from the earth heavenward." As Morton later wrote, "Here was a center for the distribution of God's blessing to the suffering. Here, perhaps, the life of two worlds [the earthly plane and that of the spirit] might meet in common endeavor and make more understandable the great truths of the universe."

Dr. William Moseley Brown, Hugh Lynn's psychology professor from Washington and Lee University who had been introduced to the work by both Hugh Lynn and Tom Sugrue, gave the address. This occasion, he said, "marks the consummation of the efforts of years . . . [of] work, perseverance, and consecrated devotion to a new and little-recognized cause . . . the visible results of the labors of those who had allied themselves with this association for the benefit of mankind."

Although the hospital was dedicated that day, there was still much to be done, and several months passed before the doors were officially opened. On February 11, 1929, they admitted their first patient—Charles Dillman— who was suffering from a chronic sinus condition. Nine days later, after receiving medicinal, osteopathic, and heat treatments, his condition was gone. As Edgar excitedly wrote on February 21, "Our first patient has already come and gone—cured!" By this time, their second patient had arrived, Elizabeth Gresham, a thirty-six-year-old woman who had been suffering from digestive problems for over a year. Two others would arrive before the month was out: Herman Drinkwater, a fifty-eight-year-old man with a tumor in his bladder and Elizabeth Meredith, the wife of a pharmacist, who had asthma, bronchitis, and gall bladder disturbances. Over the next ten months over forty more patients would be admitted, among them Dave Kahn's secretary's brother and Leona May Ringle, the oil driller's wife. Patients would come from all over the country, suffering from conditions ranging from tumors, to stomach ulcers, acute gastritis, general pruritis, colitis, syphilis, and optic neuritis. These patients stayed for days—sometimes months—and virtually all were reported to have been cured. "I shall be singing your praises," said one grateful patient upon his release.

Never before had Cayce given so many physical readings and never before had there been so many physicians on hand to treat the patients exactly as the readings recommended. During the first three months of the new year, Edgar gave 210 readings, and the waiting list for appointments grew to two months long. The difficult years in Dayton, when clients were few and money was tight, seemed gone forever. Cayce had every reason to believe that the greatest reward for his gifts was finally at hand.

40.

◉

The Healing Arts

Throughout the chaotic years of Cayce's medical partnerships in Hopkinsville and Bowling Green—before trance readings were properly recorded and indexed, and when the patient's detailed medical records were kept private by their doctors—it was nearly impossible to view Cayce's psychic contribution to medicine in the broader context of medical practices in the 1920s. Unless a patient experienced immediate recovery, little or no effort was made to trace a patient's progress or determine the effectiveness of the treatments Cayce recommended. Files containing letters of thanks offered the only insights. At the hospital, however, with a dedicated conductor and stenographer to supervise and record trance sessions, and a team of board-certified physicians to chart, study, and interpret a patient's progress over a long period of time, it was possible to see the scope of Cayce's contributions and to understand the general principles of health being communicated in the readings. As medical scholars would point out a generation later, Cayce's trance readings provided a primer on the emerging field of holistic medicine.

Although the information he imparted was often in keeping with the practice of both homeopathic and allopathic medicine at the time, it became clear by the late 1920s that Cayce also drew information from the medical knowledge of ancient cultures, especially those in Egypt and Greece. And a fair percentage of Cayce's ideas were entirely new at the time the readings were given. Some of Cayce's medical insights have been confirmed by modern medical science, while others have yet to be validated. None have yet to be dismissed as the fanciful products of an overactive imagination.

The greatest surprise of Cayce's health readings were the apparent causes given for various illnesses. The Source cited ideas that ranged from what now might be considered old-fashioned common sense, like not getting one's feet wet or avoiding colds by exposing oneself to the elements, to advice more unusual, like not washing one's food down with a drink before chewing it properly. The Source veered furthest from accepted medical philosophy in the era of cosmic-related physical conditions—such as the karmic repercussions of previous life experiences. Perhaps just as unusual in his time, Cayce frequently connected illness to the mental and emotional states of the patients. In one reading he was quoted as saying, "Thus you can [suffer] a bad cold from getting mad [or] from [cursing out] someone."

The fact that many of the treatments Cayce recommended were in keeping with the standard medical approach to illness made it easier for Dr. House and his successor, Dr. Lyman Lydic, to follow his advice. As a general rule, these treatments varied only in the combination of medicine and therapies and generally involved more hard work on the part of both the doctor and patient than has become the norm in modern medicine. Invariably, however, the hard work paid off.

In many instances, Cayce was clearly ahead of his time. He once recommended that an infant with digestive problems be kept on a strict diet of bananas, which in the 1920s was generally considered to be poisonous to infants. Now, the all-banana diet is standard medical treatment for celiac children. Cayce also described primary causes for physical disturbances, which then, as now, remain unrecognized by the medical profession. These included conditions such as psoriasis, which Cayce said was caused by the thinning of intestinal walls and the body's attempt to throw off toxins through another system of elimination, the skin; migraine headaches, which he said were frequently the result of congestion in the colon; and morning sickness in pregnant women, which he attributed to a lack of certain minerals needed to build the baby's body. He also said that spinal injuries could cause problems as diverse as asthma, stuttering, and even violent behavior.

In studying the readings, House and Lydic were forced to expand their understanding of the role that four basic processes played in governing the health of the body, which Cayce said affected the cells' ability to reproduce and function properly: assimilation, elimination, circulation, and relaxation.

Assimilation, which appeared in almost one quarter of the medical readings, referred not only to the body's intake of nutrients, but also to digestion. Cayce frequently warned against eating when upset, angry, or distressed, saying that due to the resulting physiological changes in the body, food would remain undigested and become toxic to the system. Cayce also spoke of avoiding certain food combinations, specifically those foods requiring different acids to be digested. If such foods were eaten together, Cayce said, one would be digested while the other would sit and ferment in the stomach. He also spoke of the balance of acid and alkaline in the body, which he said was affected by the foods we eat—an area of nutrition that was virtually unheard of in the 1920s, and has only recently become popular.

Just as mass-produced foods were beginning to appear, and decades before the whole-food movement became popular, Cayce was issuing warnings. He repeatedly stated that refined foods, sugars, red meat, and fried food were generally harmful to the body. "What we think and what we eat, combined together," Cayce said, "make what we are, physically and mentally."

Cayce did not just warn patients away from certain foods, he encouraged the consumption of others. For instance, in keeping with what is now known about the importance of ingesting active food enzymes, he recommended eating one meal per day primarily of raw vegetables. And although he didn't use the contemporary term phytochemicals—the nutritional element related to the color of foods—he often recommended foods of a certain color for particular ailments. He also consistently instructed patients to eat whole rather than refined grains, saying that refined products not only lacked nutrients the body needs, but that such foods, with all enzymes and other elements removed, are actually toxic to the human body.

Cayce's general diet guidelines recommended the consumption of 20 percent acid-producing foods, such as meats, starches, and sugars, and 80 percent alkaline-producing foods, such as vegetables, fruits, and dairy products. To a forty-eight-year-old woman, Cayce said: "The less physical exercise . . . the greater should be the alkaline-reacting food taken. Energies or activities may burn acids, but those who lead the sedentary life can't go on sweets or too much starches."

He also recommended that vegetables from below the ground, such as carrots, beets, and potatoes, should constitute only 25 percent of one's diet of vegetables, while above the ground vegetables, such as lettuce, squash, and tomatoes, should account for 75 percent. He recommended that only 10 percent of our diet be fats, another 10 percent proteins, 5 percent refined starches and sugars, and the other 75 percent complex carbohydrates such as vegetables, fruits, and grains.

Long after Cayce's death, many of the seemingly radical guidelines he offered in the 1930s would be seen as having merit. But some of Cayce's recommendations still seem strange to this day. For instance, he stated in several readings that while tomatoes contain more nutrients than any other single food, when not vine-ripened, were toxic to the human body. He also stated that carbonated drinks were to be almost always avoided, not just because they generally had sugar in them, but because they interfered with the equilibrium between the liver and the kidney. Cayce also said that apples should never be eaten raw, only baked or cooked, unless used for fasting purposes; only the peel of the white potato was of any real nutritional value; and coffee and tea became toxic when combined with milk or cream.

Poor elimination was cited as being at the root of a great number of illnesses, and references to it appeared in over half of Cayce's medical readings. Apart from taking in nourishment, human cells must also eliminate waste products and toxins to remain healthy and according to the Cayce readings, "[if] the assimilations and eliminations . . . [were] kept nearer normal in the human family, the days might be extended to whatever period as was so desired, for the system is . . . able to bring resuscitation so long as the eliminations do not hinder."

Cayce suggested many different aids to elimination. One of the simplest was to drink a cup of hot water with a squeeze of lemon juice each morning upon rising and before eating, which apparently helped the body eliminate the toxins thrown off during sleep. Similarly, he recommended doing deep-breathing exercises each morning to eliminate toxins pooled in the lungs from the shallow breathing characteristic of sleep. Dietary measures were recommended to improve bowel activity, which included eating leafy vegetables and stewed fruit such as figs and raisins. He also suggested drinking as much as six to eight glasses of water a day.

In extreme cases of toxemia, Cayce recommended enemas and colonics, adding that these could also be used by healthy people. "For everyone—everybody—should take an internal bath occasionally as well as an external one." Cayce also frequently recommended three-day apple fasts and occasionally four-day grape fasts or five-day orange fasts for more extreme cases of toxemia. While the apple fast in particular was intended to have a cleansing effect on the intestines, it would also, according to Cayce, "cleanse the activities of the liver, the kidneys, and the whole system."

The third aspect of sustaining good health, according to Cayce, was circulation. "The circulation . . . is the main attribute to the physical body, or that which keeps life in the whole system," he often said in trance, and references to which turned up in approximately 60 percent of the readings. Highlighting the role that circulation plays in assimilation and elimination, he pointed out that "there is no condition existent in a body that the reflection of same may not be traced to the blood supply, for not only does the bloodstream carry the rebuilding forces to the body, it also takes the used forces and eliminates same through their proper channels." In the same reading, Cayce made a startling prophetic remark: "The day may yet arrive when one may take a drop of blood and diagnose the condition of any physical body."

Cayce made reference not only to arterial circulation but lymphatic circulation, which he considered to be just as important. The Source referred to the fluid in the lymphatic system as "white blood" or "lymph blood," and pointed out that unlike the arterial system, which has both the heart and the muscle-lined wall of the arteries to move the blood along, the lymph system, which has no pump of its own, relies on other methods to move waste matter out of the body. One method Cayce recommended was massage. Although it was considered by many to be nothing more than idle pampering, Cayce saw massage as curative, particularly for the inactive.

The most natural way to sustain good overall circulation, both of the lymph and the blood, Cayce said, was exercise. As he pointed out in a reading for a forty-six-year-old woman, "Exercise is wonderful, and necessary— and little or few take as much as is needed, in a systematic manner." To another patient he said exercise "is not something merely to be gotten through or gotten rid of." Daily stretches, head and neck rolls, and walks, preferably of twenty minutes, were all recommendations Cayce gave.

The fourth process Cayce considered vital to good health was what he referred to as relaxation. In trance, Cayce stated that "the activity of the mental or soul force of the body may control entirely the whole physical [body] through the action of the balance in the sympathetic [nervous] system, for the sympathetic nerve system is to the soul and spirit forces as the cerebrospinal is to the physical forces of an entity." The nervous system was the vehicle through which Cayce's "mind as the builder" could most directly influence the body.

Cayce's physical readings divided the nervous system into three parts: the cerebrospinal system, made up of the brain and the spinal cord; the sensory nervous system, which included the sense organs; and the sympathetic nervous system, or the autonomic nervous system, over which a person has no conscious control. According to the readings, the sympathetic nervous system could be considered "the brain manifestation of soul forces in the body." Cayce also suggested that within this system habits, both good and bad, were formed and retained. These habits governed the links between our mind and our body. And apparently anyone could "correct habits by forming others! That [goes for] everybody!"

Although modern-day medical practitioners often look upon the power of "suggestion" as pseudo-science, Cayce often recommended that positive suggestion be a part of a patient's daily treatment. Cayce said that emotions, both positive and negative, moved as electric energies through the nervous system, affecting the entire organism. The message here was that the nervous system acted as a conduit, as it were, and carried impulses and instructions to every cell in the body. Positive and negative thoughts could therefore physically alter each cell's functioning. Again, Cayce was far ahead of his time in pinpointing the role that stress played in one's overall health. In one reading at the hospital, Cayce—in trance—stated that "worry and fear [are] the greatest foes to [a] normal healthy physical body." For another patient he said, "For thoughts are things! And they have their effect upon individuals . . . just as physical as sticking a pin in the hand!"

This same theme was expanded upon in a reading Cayce did for a forty-four-year-old physician who had sought a life reading. "While [it is] true [that] medicines, compounds, mechanical appliances, radiation, all have their place and are of the creative forces, yet the [ability] of arousing hope, of creating confidence, of bringing the awareness of faith into the consciousness of an individual is very necessary," the Source said. "Only when any portion of the anatomical structure of a human being is put in accord with the divine influences . . . may real healing come."

Cayce also said that a preoccupation with a particular illness could result in the manifestation of that illness in one's own life. To maintain health, Cayce suggested that "quiet, meditation, for a half a minute to a minute, will bring strength [if the body will] see physically this flowing out to quiet self, whether walking, standing still, or resting." Cayce also urged patients to find balance in their lives: "budget the time so that there may be a regular period for sustaining the physical being and also for sustaining the mental and spiritual being. As it is necessary . . . for recreation and rest for the physical, so it is necessary that there be recreation and rest for the mental."

To a forty-five-year-old man who suffered circulatory and elimination problems, Cayce admonished that he had "not enough in the sun, not enough of hard work." The Source continued by saying: "Plenty of brain work, but the body is supposed to coordinate the spiritual, mental, and physical. He who does not give recreation a place in his life, and the proper tone to each phase . . . will some day . . . be paying the price. It is well for people . . . to get their hands . . . in the dirt at times, and not be the white-collared man all the while!"

In contrast to the predominant view that doctors healed exclusively through medicine or surgery, Cayce's trance view was that "unless it be for a removal of conditions that have become acute by neglect or other causes of the same nature, all curative forces must be from within self and are of the whole of a physical being: for the human anatomical body is as the working of a perfect whole." In this sense, Cayce viewed the human body as a miracle of creation in its ability to heal itself. His view became more apparent in a statement he made to a group of entrepreneurial doctors seeking information on health products they wanted to produce. In this reading requested on their behalf by Hugh Lynn and Tommy House, Cayce said, "There is no greater factory in the universe than that in a human body in its natural, normal reacting state. For there are those machines or glands within the body capable of producing, from the very air or water and the food values taken into the body . . . any element at all that is known in the material world!" Cayce would also say, more than once, that "every cell of the body is a universe in itself."

In other readings, Cayce took the generative properties of the body one step further, to suggest that if a person were to maintain the proper attitude and to keep their organs properly coordinated with one another, they could live as long as they wanted: "For, as may be told by any pathologist, there is no known reason why any individual entity should not live as long as it desires. And there is no death, save in thy consciousness. Because all others have died, ye expect to, and you do!"

The ability of a human being to prolong his or her life, according to Cayce, depended on the proper functioning of the endocrine system. The glands, Cayce said, were "that which enables the body, physically throughout to reproduce itself." The glandular system also, according to Cayce, served as the physical point of contact between a person's nervous system and his or her "spiritual bodies." The readings identified seven glands, referred to as seven centers, or "chakras," which act as growth centers for the physical body and major spiritual centers. These seven include the gonad, the lyden—also referred to as the cells of Leydig—the adrenals, the thymus, the thyroid, the pineal, and the pituitary. In the 1930s, when Cayce did readings on these glands, their purposes were being hotly contested, and to a certain degree, none would be completely understood by the medical profession until a half century or more later.

As with the nervous system, Cayce described how a person's emotions affect the glands' activities: "For as has been indicated in some manners, some activities, there is an activity within the system produced by anger, fear, mirth, joy, or any of those active forces that produces through the glandular secretion those activities that flow into the whole of the system." These emotions caused secretions and could wreak havoc with one's health. "Anger causes poisons to be secreted from the glands," he said. "Joy has the opposite effect." On another occasion he noted: "No one can hate his neighbor and not have stomach or liver trouble. No one can be jealous and allow the anger of same and not have upset digestion or heart disorder." Perhaps the most radical assertion he made along these lines was to say that all disease was caused by sin, most notably the sin of fear, for that represented a lack of faith. "Fear is the root of most of the ills of mankind," he said in a reading given in June of 1928.

The Source would also state that while the spiritual body is not actually contained in the physical body, "there is the pattern in the material or physical plane of every condition, as exists in the cosmic or spiritual plane." It was for this reason, perhaps, that Cayce did not view illness as strictly caused by physical problems, nor did he see its cure only in the physical realm. Belief and anticipation played an important part in the healing process, too. He reminded patients that " . . . what ye ask in His name, believing, and thyself living, mind will build." He also said that "a good laugh, an arousing even to . . . hilariousness, is good for the body, physically, mentally, and gives the opportunity for greater mental and spiritual awakening." In another reading he said: "One is ever just as young as the heart and the purpose. Keep sweet. Keep friendly. Keep loving, if ye would keep young."

According to Cayce, the attitude that heals is the "Christ Consciousness . . . the only source of healing for a physical or mental body." As the Source once put it: "There are in truth, no incurable conditions . . . that which exists is and was produced from a first cause, and may be met or counteracted, or changed." In another reading Cayce said that "all strength, all healing of every nature is the changing of the vibrations from within, the attuning of the divine within the living tissue of a body to Creative Energies. This alone is healing. Whether it is accomplished by the use of drugs, the knife or [anything else], it is the attuning of the atomic structure of the living force to its spiritual heritage."

As much as Cayce advised his patients not to ignore spiritual matters when dealing with health challenges, he also warned them not to ignore their physical lives either. In one physical diagnosis, the Source said: "The body is made up of the physical, the mental, the spiritual," and that "each have their laws, which work one with another, and the whole is physical man, yet do not treat physical conditions wholly through spiritual or mental laws and expect same to respond as one."

Of all the physical treatments, Cayce regarded osteopathic therapy as the closest to the healing process of the human body. "There is no form of physical mechanotherapy so near in accord with nature's measures as correctly given osteopathic adjustments," he said. Osteopaths, designated as "D.O.'s," whose degrees are generally considered equivalent to those of medical doctors, emphasize the body's natural ability to heal and work through manipulation of the musculoskeletal system. As Cayce said, "The science of osteopathy is not merely the punching in a certain segment or the cracking of the bones, but it is the keeping of a balance—by the touch—between the sympathetic and cerebrospinal system. That is real osteopathy!"

In a particularly moving reading on May 24, 1934, in which he summarized much of his philosophy, Cayce discussed the beauty of being "one with God," in a spiritual as well as a physical sense. "When the earth was brought into existence or into time and space, all the elements that are without man may be found in the living human body," Cayce said. "Hence these in coordination, as we see in nature, as we see in the air, as we see in the fire or in the earth, makes the soul, body, and mind one coordinating factor with the universal creative energy we call God."

Just as Cayce talked about being one with God, he suggested that a body's cells must act in concert to sustain good health. In thousands of medical readings, Cayce offered physical treatments directed toward improving "coordination." Likewise, the theme of "vibration" was quite evident in his diagnoses. As Cayce had said in the physics readings for the Stansell motor: "Life in its manifestations is vibration, electricity is vibration." In this sense, Cayce suggested that the same principles of "harmonics" governing the release of energy were at play in the human body. All of Cayce's remedies had the intention of correcting the vibrations of the various cells of the body, whether through medicine, osteopathic manipulation of the spine, hydrotherapy, the application of heat and cold, electrical magnetic therapy, or the simple laying on of hands.

One of the most interesting concepts regarding good health and longevity put forth by Cayce was that "[there is no need] for a better body [unless it is] to serve thy fellow man the better." Similarly, when asked by a woman how many more years of life she should expect, Cayce responded: "How many do you wish [or need]? Let the prayer be ever: 'Father, so long as I may be useful as a manifestation of Thy love in the earth, and as I may be gentle and kind and true and pure to my fellow man, keep Thou, O Lord, me.'"

When asked "Who will aid me most in my work and daily life?" Cayce simply replied, "God." In another reading, the Source said: "The church is in thyself. For, thy body is the temple of the living God." And indeed, in addition to all of the advice he would give about diet, habits, physical treatments, mental states, attitudinal adjustments, and exercise in keeping the body healthy, there was always one underlying theme—a willingness to call on God's help through prayer and have faith that help will come. On this topic, Cayce would give perhaps his most inspiring and easily understood advice: "Never worry as long as you can pray. When you can't pray, you'd better begin to worry! For then you [really] have something to worry about!"

41.

Atlantic University

For thirty years, Edgar Cayce had delivered his message lying on his back while in trance. In Virginia Beach, in August 1929, prompted by Morton Blumenthal and Tim Brown, he stood on his feet, in front of an audience, and consciously presented the first of more than thirty lectures he would deliver on topics such as karma, astrology, auras, mental telepathy, and evolution. And it was the overwhelming success of these talks that reignited in Morton Blumenthal a dream to establish a college devoted to developing the mind, just as the hospital had been dedicated to healing the body. The result was an institution of higher learning called Atlantic University.

Although Edgar himself was credited with the idea of starting Atlantic University, Blumenthal had dreamed about starting his own school since he had attended Columbia University a decade earlier. Morton proposed the idea at the first formal meeting of the ANI in early 1927, before the hospital was built. At that time he outlined a plan to move a preexisting boys boarding school to Virginia Beach, but the idea was voted down in favor of first establishing the hospital. No sooner had the hospital become a reality than he presented the idea a second time—and now with Edgar giving his own lectures, he had a far grander vision of what could be accomplished. He wanted nothing short of an Ivy League university. "Harvard at the Beach," was how he described it to one potential student.

Morton didn't, in reality, have a school like Harvard in mind. While he did desire a school with academic prestige and stately, ivy-covered buildings, the institution he envisioned would offer what now might be termed as a "New Age" curriculum. Although there would be standard courses in math, science, and the arts, inventors like Tim Brown and Marion Stansell would introduce engineering students to new theoretical concepts, and Morton and his brother would create a series of "cutting-edge" courses on philosophy, metaphysics, spiritualism, and the esoteric sciences suggested in the readings. Atlantic University would be to the academic community what the Cayce Hospital was to medicine.

Tim Brown—himself an experienced teacher—had certain reservations about Blumenthal's plan from the outset and initially voted against Morton's second proposal, as did Dave Kahn. In their opinion, the ANI had its hands full with the hospital, and the added complications of hiring a faculty, building classrooms, and providing food and shelter for two hundred or more students in Virginia Beach would be a logistical nightmare. At a special board meeting held in the late summer of 1929 at the Blumenthal Brothers' New York brokerage company, Brown proposed an alternative plan to first offer continuing education courses, using the hospital as an administrative base of operations and renting additional classroom space at one of the Virginia Beach hotels as needed. They could gradually expand the program into a full-fledged college over a period of years. Morton, however, adamantly rejected the idea.

Besides a few statements by Brown and Kahn on the subject, there is no further record of the discussions that took place on this topic. The initial vote by the board was a deadlock, presumably due to Edgar's failure to cast the deciding vote for or against the proposal. Although he traditionally supported all of Morton's initiatives, he couldn't in good faith dismiss Brown and Kahn's financial concerns. A university would be as costly an undertaking as a hospital, and he, like Brown and Kahn, couldn't afford to put his signature on a banknote.

Rather than haggle with other board members, Morton put forth a revised proposition, which stated that he and his brother would foot the entire bill. The ANI would operate the university as an adjunct to the Cayce Hospital, but all financial decisions and any banknotes that had to be signed would be taken care of by the Blumenthals. The board decided in favor of Morton chairing a newly formed Educational Board, composed of himself, Edwin, and Tim Brown, which would develop and operate a university.

Though technically a part of the ANI, the Educational Board would answer to no one but its own members. Edgar had no real voice in the board's decisions, but his lack of involvement was neither a matter of his tight schedule at the hospital nor his initial reluctance due to the financial commitment. The truth, as later became apparent, was that Morton didn't consider Edgar Cayce an educated man. In Morton's memoirs, he repeatedly pointed out that Edgar had no schooling to speak of, and that it was he, Morton, who had raised the psychic out of "obscurity." Edgar wasn't called upon to give a reading on what the university's mission should be until the spring of 1931, nearly two years later, by which time classes were already being held.

The readings Morton requested during the early stages of the proposed university were focused only on the financial feasibility of his plans and whether or not his estimate of a $10 million profit on the Stansell motor was within reason. He was pleased to hear the Source confirm this possibility in a reading on March 7, 1929, since he was counting on this money to finance the university, which the Source referred to as "a university in every sense of the word." However encouraging this news must have been, the Source went on to remind Morton that "mind is the builder," and that proper thought must be given to how the institution would be created in his own mind. It was then, in the midst of this reading, that another one of Morton's spiritual guides introduced himself.

"This is Jeremiah speaking for the first but not the last time," Cayce said, presumably speaking on behalf of the Old Testament prophet. The message being communicated was one that had come through before: that decisions Morton made in the years 1931 and 1932 would determine what greater blessings were to come. "There has been seen the call for thee in such an undertaking, and indeed would there be a message for mine people who have long remained in bondage through superstition and through dogmatic relations as have been brought about by those that would teach 'as I see' and not as the individual may have awakened in them as to their abilities."

As promised, Jeremiah would indeed make another appearance—the very next day. The message was both one of encouragement and counsel. Morton was assured of assistance from the spiritual realm in this his present incarnation, as had purportedly been given when he and Edwin and other family members had joined together to build the wall around the city of Jerusalem in an earlier incarnation. Jeremiah didn't dwell on the financial feasibility of the plan to build a university, but on the importance of Morton not letting his ego interfere with the greater work he sought to accomplish.

"Be not led astray in any manner," Morton was told. "Be not dictatorial, nor lording in thine own activity. Rather humble in spirit . . . For even as the knowledge comes let it be disseminated among those who seek to know the Lamb that taketh away the sins of mine people, and their transgressions shall be remembered no more, and sickness and sorrow and tears shall be wiped away. For He who came in the flesh will establish His name there. Through thine efforts then my son, be faithful. I have spoken, I, Jeremiah, the servant of the King."

Despite the encouraging spiritual counsel that Morton and his brother were receiving at this point, an increasingly large number of stock market readings recommended caution and warned that an "upheaval" in the market was on the horizon. This was clear on March 6, 1929, when Morton asked the Source to interpret a dream in which he envisioned a bull chasing and harassing his wife, who was dressed in red. "Dreamed we should sell all our stocks, including [ones considered very safe]." The Source interpreted this dream to say that Morton should take the bull by the horns. The bull was a bull market on its way out. The red dress on his wife was a warning of danger. "Expect a considerable break [in the market]," the Source said. "[There will be trouble] between those of the reserves of nations and of individuals, and will cause—unless another of the more stable banking conditions come to the relief—a great disturbance in financial circles."

Edwin himself had a provocative dream on April 6, 1929, in which he was being unfairly blamed for the murder of a young man. A crowd of angry spectators sought restitution by injecting him with a deadly poison. "I felt a needle and expected death," Edwin said of the dream. Having become accustomed to interpreting his own dreams, Edwin said that this dream represented a fight currently being waged within the Federal Reserve Board, which would have a negative impact on the financial market. Investors, whom Edwin represented, would blame him for the depreciation of their stocks. A subsequent reading confirmed Edwin's interpretation. "The [Federal Reserve Board] is . . . divided [and if] allowed to run without a check . . . there must surely come . . . panic in the money centers."

During the same time that these readings were being given to Morton and Edwin, Dave Kahn and others were receiving similar warnings of imminent financial problems. In a later memoir of his years with Edgar Cayce, Kahn described a reading in which the Source specifically told him to sell all his stock by August of 1929. Kahn didn't act on the advice because the market appeared to be strong, and the Blumenthals, who had invested upwards of $35,000 in stocks for him—all purchased on margin—also didn't believe a crash would happen.

The Source's recommendation to move ahead with the plans to build a university must have seemed to contradict the warnings about impending financial upheavals. In the absence of trading records, it is difficult to know the degree to which the Blumenthals understood or took heed of the advice being given. All that can be said for certain was that Morton was inspired to move ahead at breakneck speed, believing that he indeed had control over the "dictatorial" aspect of his personality, and that his spiritual guides would not fail him during whatever upheavals were ahead.

In September, less than a month after the Educational Board had been formed, Morton and Tim Brown held a luncheon meeting in Dayton with Dr. William Moseley Brown, Hugh Lynn's former professor at Washington and Lee who had delivered the commencement address at the dedication of the Cayce hospital. Dr. Brown's reason for meeting with Morton and Tim was to raise money to make a run on the Republican ticket for governor of Virginia. Morton had something else in mind—making him the first president of what he referred to as "his" university.

As Morton well knew, there was much to recommend a partnership between himself and Dr. Brown, and the Source indicated that Brown understood he had been an aid to Achilles, a previous incarnation of Morton's. The two had worked well together then and would presumably work amicably again now. Morton also knew that Dr. Brown did not have the clout needed to defeat Democratic incumbent Harry Byrd for the governorship. Brown's campaign, Morton believed, would be over before it had started. Whether or not Dr. Brown admitted as much to Morton during their luncheon is not known. All that can be said for certain was that Morton's enthusiasm for starting a university was contagious. Before the end of their brief meeting, Dr. Brown agreed to become the university's first president at the annual salary of $10,000—regardless of the outcome of the election.

Morton didn't initially share this good news with anyone other than Edwin and Tim Brown, not even Edgar. Had they made their plans public, controversies that later erupted around the proposed curriculum and Edgar's involvement with the university might have been avoided. Although there had been much research and discussion previously regarding Dr. House's appointment as head of the hospital, practically no consideration had been given to Brown's appointment as president of the university, and his surprise appearance on the Educational Board would do little more than divide the interested parties into factions.

By the time Dr. Brown's appointment became formal, in August 1929, it was already clear that there was no coordinated effort to clarify what the university's policy and aims were to be, let alone where the campus should be erected. Without consulting either Dr. Brown or seeking a reading, Morton

had unilaterally hired the respected architect Lawrence B. Emmons to design two buildings, one to house administrative offices, and the other for
classrooms. The property he chose consisted of two lots situated between the
hospital and beach, across Atlantic Boulevard. This made for one long piece
of property stretching from the grove of pines at the top of the sand dunes
behind the hospital to the crashing waves on the beach, and broken only by
the boulevard. In keeping with the locale, Blumenthal now gave his institution a name: Atlantic University. While the blueprints for the school were
still being drawn up, Morton set the date for the school's opening—the fall
of 1930. Since construction would not be finished by then, he decided to rent
office space in Virginia Beach to serve as classrooms until the campus was
completed; he also hired a second faculty member, Dr. Job Taylor, of Roanoke
Rapids, Virginia, a noted spiritualist and world traveler, and the owner of an
ancient papyrus manuscript of the Egyptian *Book of the Dead*.

Unbeknownst to Morton, Dr. Brown was also putting together a faculty
and curriculum. Brown was excited and impatient to get started and had his
own vision of the physical grounds and academic environment that was to
become Atlantic University. Just how far afield Dr. Brown's plans were from
Morton's became evident in an article published that August in the *Norfolk
Virginian-Pilot*. In an interview given by Dr. Brown, who had now given up
on his bid for the governorship, he described a traditional liberal arts education leading to a bachelor's degree in the arts and sciences. He proposed
classes that would include English, English literature, economics, sociology,
government, philosophy, psychology, history, mathematics, astronomy, chemistry, physics, biology, physiology, public speaking, and dramatics. No mention was made of psychic studies.

Morton was flabbergasted upon reading the report and called for an
emergency meeting of the Educational Board. No notes remain from the
meeting, which took place in New York, but it resulted in another newspaper story, in the *New York Times*, as well as editorials in the *Norfolk
Virginian-Pilot*. Dr. Brown now announced an "alternative" course of study
for Atlantic University. Exactly what these alternative courses would consist
of, however, was not clear. But rumors circulating in the editorial pages of
the Virginia Beach papers suggested that Morton was demanding courses in
clairvoyance and spiritualism. According to the *Norfolk Virginian-Pilot*,
Brown had "relegated psychic research to a footnote" before Morton and his
brother had stepped in.

Brown and Blumenthal eventually resolved this issue. Atlantic University
would offer the standard regimen of pre-law, pre-engineering, and pre-
medicine programs, along with a special elective study program in a re-

search center for psychic study. This would be modeled after a similar program at Duke University in Durham, North Carolina, which was presided over by the famed psychic researcher William McDougal, formerly of Oxford and Harvard Universities. "The approach will be entirely scientific and the same general methods will be used as are utilized in all of the other sciences," Brown told reporters in the next interview he gave. "[The board is] most emphatically not interested in spiritualism, mediumism, clairvoyance, or any of the other commonly known quackeries."

It was now Edgar's turn to feel slighted. Although he never viewed himself as a spiritualist or medium, he couldn't exactly deny that this was what he was doing. The inference that the activities taking place across the street from the proposed site of Atlantic University could be lumped together with "quackery" shocked him. The tone of Morton's correspondence regarding this issue also didn't help matters. In Morton's own mind, it seemed, the work in Virginia Beach was being separated into two discrete endeavors, as indeed it later would be. "It looks like you will stand as chief guardian at the gate to the hospital, I at the gate to the university," Morton said of their respective roles. By way of apology for not including him in the decision-making process, Morton said: "I have never lost my affection for you, yours, or the work, nor do I want to usurp any bossy power that in any way would seek to take advantage of anyone. Yet, be patient until I can completely find my own self, which is not so easy in the terrific strain and pressure that is constantly upon me, even from men who would use me to take advantage of the work, or of you, and even from my own lower nature. I will find the rock, and with it, the way to use the divine agency to bring harmony and peace."

However much Morton was feeling the strain of running a brokerage company in New York and building a university in Virginia Beach, Edgar was under an equal if not greater strain acting, by default, as the administrator at the hospital, while at the same time giving readings and explaining them to doctors and patients alike. And then, in late September of 1929, Dr. House became ill with colitis and had to be admitted as a patient in his own hospital. Not only was House's condition seen by the readings as life-threatening, but the suggested treatments required a trained osteopath. Dr. House, in no condition to treat himself, and without another osteopath at the Cayce Hospital to supervise the treatments, had to be sent to Dayton, where the readings indicated he was to be put under the care of Dr. Lyman Lydic. Accompanying Dr. House was Carrie, who naturally wished to comfort and aid her husband in his time of need. Thus, the Cayce Hospital not only lost its resident physician and chief medical administrator, but the head of its nursing and housekeeping staff.

During Dr. and Mrs. House's absence, the pressures on Edgar and every-one else in the hospital increased dramatically. There was no mention in ei-ther Edgar's personal correspondence or his brief diary entries accompanying the readings of where Gertrude stood on the subject of the university, the hospital's activities, and Dr. House's declining health. There is also no indi-cation that she sought to involve herself in any meetings that took place. No doubt she supported her husband at home and gladly opened her door to the many people who did actively step in to help out in the hospital.

The people who came to Edgar's aid included Leslie, who began doing chores at the hospital, and Annie Cayce, Edgar's only unmarried sister, who had moved up from Nashville and took over Carrie House's duties. They were later joined by Gladys's cousin Mildred Davis from Oklahoma City, and Linden Shroyer, from Miami, who came to help run business affairs and to begin the long and arduous task of cataloging the growing volumes of read-ings and other hospital records. But even these new arrivals couldn't straighten out the panic and eventual disarray that set in when a letter ar-rived from Dayton on October 7.

"It is useless for me to try and find words to express my appreciation for your endless and untiring efforts to help Dad," Tommy House wrote. "Only God knows how Mother and I have prayed that he might get well, and if he does pull through, I feel that we will owe it all to you [But] Dr. Lydic still says that if Dad pulls through it will be a miracle. Poor old fellow, he is the gamest fighter that you ever saw, but he just seems to be lying there wast-ing away and I can't do anything for him." A day later, a wire arrived from Tim Brown, confirming how dire Dr. House's condition had become. Dr. Lydic gave him less than two days to live. An emergency reading conducted that same day, October 8, concurred. "Not much hope . . . in the present," the Source said, ending the reading.

Indeed, on October 12, 1929, after months of being bedridden, Dr. House, age sixty-two, died of kidney failure and was later buried in the plot that had once been reserved for the infant Tommy House. Edgar joined Carrie House in Hopkinsville for the funeral, sharing her sorrow at his passing and trying to convince her to return with him to Virginia Beach. A devoted friend, a for-mer financial partner in his photo studio, and perhaps the person who had unceasingly and compassionately supported the work longer than anyone else, Carrie decided to retire and live out the rest of her years at The Hill. As much as she desired to help Edgar and Gertrude meet the challenges that she knew would face them, she felt she couldn't continue her duties at the hospital without the companionship of her husband.

And challenges there were. Foremost among them was the void that resulted from Dr. House's passing. Osteopaths who were also medical doctors were in short supply, and it was next to impossible to find one who was also an experienced interpreter of the readings. For two months, several were tried and then let go. Finally, in late December 1929, Dr. Lyman Lydic was convinced to move from Dayton and take over for Dr. House. But as Edgar and Morton were later to note, however skilled Lydic was as a physician, osteopath, and administrator, he lacked a spiritual understanding of the readings. He would no more pray at a patient's bedside than he would enact a treatment on "faith," as Dr. House and Carrie had consistently done. Unless the treatment recommended in the readings agreed with his own, Lydic wouldn't prescribe it.

Edgar, morose and distracted, began suffering from neuritis, and for the first time had to wear glasses due to eye strain. This, no doubt, was the result of spending an increased number of hours at the hospital sorting out the books and making do without Dr. House and Carrie. Along with Linden Shroyer, Edgar was also attempting to collect money from former patients. No one, it seemed, had been watching the accounts and approximately half of the patients who had been admitted either didn't have the money to pay for their visits or hadn't kept their accounts up to date.

It wasn't long before Morton asked for a more detailed accounting of hospital expenses. Unhappy with what he received, Morton requested that expenses be cut and efforts be made to keep the budget in line with revenue. The problem, from his point of view, was that there was no single person in charge of business affairs, nor was there a central person in charge of purchasing supplies for the hospital, which resulted in a duplication of efforts and cost overruns. Although Edgar promised Morton and Edwin to put the books in order, there is no evidence that he did anything other than recommend that Leslie Cayce, or someone else, be hired as a central purchasing agent. And as one new hospital administrator after another was tried out, then let go, the situation only became worse.

Cooperation among members of the ANI—which was no longer the rule, but the exception—was a subject the Source expounded on in one of the most remarkable readings conducted that year. During a trance session held to better determine what each board member's role should be in the hospital, another heavenly visitor—believed to have been no less than the Master Himself—made an appearance. In language that could easily be mistaken for a passage from the Bible, the "entity," speaking through Cayce, stressed the urgency of working in accord before the situation got out of hand.

"Let each be mindful of that place, that niche, that [purpose] each is to fill," Cayce said in trance. "Cooperate with other individuals, working in their individual capacities, that the whole [purpose] may be as one, even as the Father and I are one in you. I speak not of myself, but that ye may know the truth, even as delivered in the day when I walked among men and became known as the 'son of man' and the savior . . . Here, my brethren, ye are come again to fulfill, in this place, a glorious principle, a glorious article of work among the sons of man."

It is not clear from the record or from subsequent correspondence who among the ANI board took this message to heart, for no one, it seemed—except perhaps Gladys—had the collective interests of the entire board foremost in mind. Dave Kahn sent his monthly payments to Virginia Beach, but his checks were written personally to Edgar, not to the ANI account. Gertrude conducted all the readings, but seldom ventured into the hospital itself to visit the patient for whom a reading had been given. Linden Shroyer, perhaps still jealous of the role that Gladys played as Edgar's chief confidant, held her accountable for the cost overruns and the poor state of the hospital books, even though keeping the books was not part of her job description. And in the midst of the crisis over Dr. House's health and eventual demise, Morton and Dr. Brown still couldn't agree about the university faculty or what they were hired to teach.

Dr. Brown submitted his proposed budget for Atlantic University, along with a portfolio of teaching contracts that had already been negotiated and signed. To Morton's astonishment, Brown had assembled a full faculty of twenty professors, at a budget in excess of $125,000—approximately twice the figure that Morton claimed Brown had discussed in a meeting in Washington, D.C. "I couldn't believe my eyes," Morton said after being presented with the proposed budget. Irate, Morton called a meeting of the Educational Board in late September and threatened to shut down the university before its doors had even opened. Had it not been for the intercession of Dr. Job Taylor, who was respected by both the Blumenthals and Dr. Brown, Atlantic University might never have had a single student. In a private meeting between Morton and Taylor, the much esteemed head of the university psychic sciences department vowed to help Brown cut his budget during the first semester of the school's operation.

Lack of cooperation—especially in regard to financial matters—continued to be a source of great discord as Atlantic University came closer to opening its doors. Hugh Lynn became the focus of such tension before his graduation from college in June 1930. As he prepared to come home from school, he naturally desired to get a job and was flattered by an offer from Dave Kahn to help him get established in New York upon graduation, where he could work part-time in Kahn's furniture factory and continue his education in graduate school. Morton, upon hearing that Hugh Lynn might soon be working for Kahn, became incensed that Hugh Lynn had not come to him first. After all, it was he who had paid for Hugh Lynn's education, not David Kahn. Morton wrote a note to both Edgar and Hugh Lynn on the subject and then made an extravagant proposal: to hire Hugh Lynn as Atlantic University's librarian at a salary of $150 a month, a job that he subsequently accepted.

However pleased Edgar and Gertrude were at the prospect of having their son home in Virginia Beach and employed at Atlantic University, Hugh Lynn's proposed salary caused a certain degree of consternation among various members of the hospital staff. Gladys was earning $50 less a month for her job as Edgar's secretary, stenographer, and the hospital's de-facto bookkeeper—for which she worked an average of ten to twelve hours a day—and Edgar was earning only $50 more a month as superintendent of the hospital, in addition to giving readings. As Morton became further preoccupied with the financing of Atlantic University at the expense of the Cayce Hospital, and as the "upheavals" described in the stock market readings became a reality, payroll checks to the hospital were delayed and routine bills were not being paid. At one point, Hugh Lynn got his paycheck, but Edgar and Gladys didn't get theirs.

Morton acknowledged the seeming disparity between hospital and university salaries but argued that it was Dr. Brown who was responsible for the Atlantic University budget, and that Dr. Job Taylor would be helping to cut expenses. And in fairness to Morton, he had every reason to believe that once the Atlantic University budget was cut, income from other sources would reduce the financial strain on everyone involved and put an end to what Morton termed "minor differences and other pettiness." In fact, as late as the summer of 1930, long after the Blumenthals had incurred serious financial losses at their brokerage firm, they remained steadfastly optimistic about their own future and the fate of the university and hospital.

In June of 1930, Morton was encouraged by the fact that student applications were arriving at a temporary administrative office in Norfolk at a rate of three or four a day and initial enrollment was projected at several hundred, with more applications expected once brochures were printed and distributed. Morton, his brother, and Tim Brown, were also still expecting rich rewards from the Stansell motor, which was alleged to be nearly operational.

Optimistic as Morton was at the time, nothing he counted on would become a reality. The latest model of the Stansell motor didn't rotate more than a few revolutions before grinding to a halt. In the midst of a campaign to lure more nonboarding students, news reached the Atlantic University of-

fices that the finest private college in the state—William and Mary—had
announced plans to expand their campus and begin holding classes in Norfolk. Hopes of increasing the number of day students were instantly dashed.
And despite claims to the contrary, the Atlantic University budget, like that
of the hospital, exceeded all previous estimates.

In the fall of 1930, when the first class of 209 students arrived at the two
Virginia Beach hotels that served as the boys and girls dormitories, Atlantic
University offered a curriculum consisting of thirty courses, taught by
twenty teachers, amounting to approximately one teacher for every ten students and seven students per class. In addition to the course work, the school
boasted a fully outfitted football team called the Seadogs, a woman's soccer
team called the Mermaids, a dance band called the Atlanteans, a newspaper,
library, fraternities, and a three-legged mascot dog named Tripod.

The timing could not have been worse for the university, the hospital, or
the Blumenthals. That first year, more than 40 percent of the incoming students would be unable to make their tuition payments, and over half the patients at the hospital would be unable to pay for services received. As Dr.
Brown greeted his freshmen class during an assembly held at the Presbyterian Church and the morning sun sparkled on the blue waters beyond
Cape Henry, the Great Depression loomed like a storm cloud over the proceedings.

42.

Irish Eyes
and Fallen Angels

Exactly how much money the Blumenthals lost during the Depression varies dramatically depending on whom one believes. Hugh Lynn claimed that the Blumenthals lost over a million dollars, and in the mid-1930s became destitute and were forced into menial labor. Morton claimed that their losses were closer to one hundred thousand dollars, and that they rode out the Depression in style. The fact that he and his brother didn't lose their seat on the exchange until 1937, and that Morton and Edwin respectively took trips to Europe and Havana just a few months after the stock market crash is evidence that their losses probably weren't as devastating as Hugh Lynn believed. And yet, however much Hugh Lynn may have exaggerated the impact the Depression had on the Blumenthal fortune, Morton's account of the events that transpired immediately prior to and following the stock market crash are in striking contrast to the records that do exist.

Morton and his brother made repeated claims in the years after the crash that the trance readings Edgar Cayce gave them didn't so much as hint at the events to come, and that it was the physical and business readings in the wake of the crash that led them to become disillusioned with Cayce and unable in good faith to continue to take his trance advice seriously or support any endeavor associated with him.

"I have often wondered if the money-crazed era of the twenties didn't have some effect on [Edgar] Cayce," Blumenthal later told a journalist with whom he collaborated on his unpublished memoirs. "People were making fortunes overnight and Cayce himself had moved rather quickly from the edge of poverty into a world of money and material plenty. It is just possible that this was the cause of some of his inconsistencies. At any rate, his psychic gifts seemed never to benefit his benefactors and they let me down at the moment when they could have been the greatest help."

The reference that Blumenthal made was to October 29, 1929, the day when prices on the exchange dropped ten points in the early morning, and by noon, there were no buyers for the stocks being offered. As that day wore on, and the situation drastically worsened, Morton reportedly became frantic. He and his brother watched as investors lost as much as $30,000 in less than ten minutes of trading. Desperate for an insight into what was happening, Morton reportedly called Virginia Beach and asked Edgar to take the train to New York. Morton claimed to have reserved a hotel room for him and made an appointment for a reading the next morning at 8 A.M. According to Morton's account, the subsequent reading indicated that the worst was over: that the bottom had been reached in stock prices and that the market would stabilize and soon start up again. Morton reported that it was his own idea to get out of the market that day—not Edgar Cayce's—and had he not taken immediate action in direct contradiction to the readings he would surely have been bankrupted as the market continued to plunge.

Evidence in the archival record does not support any of Morton Blumenthal's claims. Throughout the summer and the fall of 1929, Morton and his brother received numerous readings suggesting that an upheaval in the market was imminent. Morton had, in fact, traveled to Virginia Beach by train on October 26, 1929, for the express purpose of clarifying the latest warning of impending disaster. During that session, which was not only requested by Morton, but conducted by him, Cayce—in trance—was specifically asked for confirmation regarding a statement made by Morton's spiritual guide, Elbert Gary, that one of the Blumenthals' largest accounts, which was "well margined," could be "wiped out" the next day. The answer came: "[The information by Gary] is correct."

Morton then made the observation that since the stocks held in their largest portfolio were also the same stocks in the Blumenthals' own account, the result would be devastating. "That wipes us out also, and that is the end of the business," Morton said, obviously hoping that he had somehow misconstrued the remarks made by Elbert Gary through Cayce. But there had been no misunderstanding. "That . . . is the situation as is given here," Cayce said. In this same reading, the Source specifically said that it was "best to sell, and then buy [back] at the lower price [at a later date]."

For all intents and purposes, Morton had been given his marching orders. Due to the fact that the Blumenthal trading records were later destroyed, it is impossible to know for certain whether or not Morton and his brother acted on the advice given on October 26. All that can be said with certainty was that Morton returned to New York that night, or early the next morning, and did not contact Edgar again until the market had begun its steep decline. Edgar was next contacted by telephone in Virginia Beach on November 2, 1929, at which time Morton requested confirmation that he should be "out" of the market. The advice was the same. Morton was told to stay out of the market for the next few days, at which time he and his brother would be given further instructions.

"Let not the minds be troubled," the Source said. "Let not the bodies become overwearied. Let not the mental come unbalanced by the clamor or the unsettledness as is arising at this time." The Source also urged them to "get within themselves that stillness of purpose as comes from the constant prayer with those that would aid or guide at this time."

A subsequent trip Edgar made to New York, which Morton referred to in his memoirs as having taken place at the end of October, didn't actually occur until November 15, when Edgar was invited to stay as Morton and Edwin's guest at the Prisament Hotel. The reading conducted there began with a reminder to Morton and Edwin that the "union" they represented with Cayce, which had been "manifested in the material, moral, social, and financial matters," would be "envied by many," and that it was their responsibility to "honor" the trust that had been given them by remaining steadfast. "He that furnisheth bread for the brothers shall control many cities," the Source told them. "He that honoreth his God shall not go without full recompense, saith the Lord. For him that I have loved, him will I also raise up. Him that teacheth his brother the right way, shall not go unrewarded. Keep thy hands clean. Keep thy strength in me. Love the Lord. Forget not His benefits. Keep always that in shadow in thine remembrance, for I will repay, saith the Lord. I will protect thee."

As was suggested in the earlier reading, the Source advised Morton and Edwin to stay attuned to the spiritual guidance being offered. "In understanding, does strength, power, and might come. Take this and keep it with thee in thy heart, and in thine mind always. With power of money, with position, and wealth, comes greater responsibility."

At this point in the reading it was clear to the Blumenthals that Gary and Fuld, who had regularly communicated through Cayce when asked about the market, were not addressing them. Morton asked if the voice coming through belonged to Jesus. The Source replied, "He speaks with thee often in thy meditations and prayers." This indicated to the Blumenthals that Jesus Himself was indeed speaking to them, and that they could count on His help if they remained open to and mindful of His communications. They asked if Jesus would continue to guide them now, and in their relations with others. The Source replied: "Thou art [guided]. In the hour that thou speakest I put it into thine heart what to say. For oft in prayer do I speak with thee." Morton and his brother, apparently moved by the message that had come through, closed their session by saying a prayer. "Father, my brother and myself now bow our heads in gratitude for this beautiful reading, counsel, and guidance [and] pray we may live to merit . . . and carry out thy purpose."

Given the archival record of this reading, it is strange that Morton and his brother had such a remarkably different memory of what transpired between them and Edgar after the market crashed. It's extremely unlikely that the existing transcript was forged—this reading was not conducted at Virginia Beach, but in New York under the Blumenthals' auspices. Edwin was present in the hotel room, Morton was the conductor, and their company secretary was the stenographer. They kept a copy of the reading for themselves and sent Gladys a duplicate for the ANI records.

Later claims by Morton that he and his brother had long ago stopped requesting stock market advice were also not true. Morton and his brother obtained almost daily stock market and business readings for the five years immediately prior to the crash. And regardless of what the Blumenthals' "gains" and "losses" were in relation to those readings, there was an undeniable connection between their wealth and their work with Edgar Cayce. As Morton himself had earlier acknowledged, the Blumenthals and the Cayces were participating in the same "work of the Master of Masters," and any material gain that resulted belonged to Him, the "true cause of their wealth." Edgar was no more responsible for the Blumenthals' financial problems than Morton was himself. Morton must have known this to be true for work-related readings continued until March 30, 1930, five months after the crash, through which Edgar provided some of the most interesting business and stock market advice on record.

On November 18, for example, Cayce—in trance—was asked to interpret a dream Morton had had two days earlier. In the dream, Morton was at a train station on his way to Chicago when he realized that he had forgotten his suitcase "I had to hurry for the train was going to leave at eleven and was going to start in a big hurry and go through a tunnel," Morton said. The Source indicated that his dream was a message that the market was about to pass into the "lowest stage." During this trance session, Morton queried the Source about another dream he had had on November 16, in which he saw a diver going into the sea to save people from drowning. Again, the Source said the dream was related to the plunging stock market.

Morton and his brother received seven more readings before taking an extended holiday from their brokerage company, during which time Morton and his family traveled to France and North Africa, and Edwin and his wife went to Havana. In none of these readings, or the accompanying correspondence, is there a hint that they had suffered great losses or felt betrayed by Edgar in regard to the devastated market. Nor, according to the historical record, did they appear to feel misled by a physical reading conducted during this same period, which Morton was later to claim to the press was certifiable evidence that Edgar Cayce had lost his ability to give reliable trance information.

The physical reading in question was initially requested on October 7, 1929, for fifty-four-year-old Rosamond Blumenthal, the sister of Morton's mother, who had recently undergone a serious operation at a New York hospital and was not recovering properly. Edgar wrote Morton's mother directly, saying that he couldn't get to the reading for quite some time, due to the backlog of requests at the hospital. However, he said that her request could be expedited if Rosamond would come to Virginia Beach, because hospital patients were being given preferential treatment. Little did Edgar realize at the time that such a trip was out of the question—Rosamond herself had no faith in the readings, didn't approve of her nephew's involvement with the alleged Virginia Beach psychic, and wasn't aware that Edgar Cayce was being consulted on her case. Rather than alerting Edgar to the truth of the matter, Morton's mother asked her son to intervene on his aunt's behalf and obtain a reading without having to go through regular channels. Morton obliged. He called Edgar on October 22, 1929, and requested that his aunt's reading be tagged onto the end of his usual daily reading. Edgar said that he would see what he could do, but having just returned from Dr. House's funeral in Kentucky, he added that he didn't hold out much hope of getting to it for at least a week.

Edgar eventually gave the reading at 4:30 P.M. on October 30, 1929. Gertrude conducted, reading from the letter that Morton's mother had originally written on October 7. According to the reading, Rosamond was near death; her organs were still functioning, but under great distress. The recommendation was that she build up her strength before another reading could be obtained outlining the treatments necessary for her recovery. In order to build up her strength, she was directed to drink a solution containing wild cherry bark, sarsaparilla root, wild ginger, Indian turnip, ginseng, prickly ash bark, buchu leaves, and mandrake.

A copy of the reading was sent to Morton's mother, and another to Morton himself. Blumenthal called Cayce on November 2 to express his surprise at what it contained, for his aunt had died and was buried three days before the reading had been conducted. He hadn't told Edgar because he had been too busy with the activities on the collapsing stock market. Morton, however, had an idea about what might have happened and told Edgar that they could discuss the issue when he would be in Virginia Beach the next weekend.

Morton and his wife, Adeline, got together with Tim Brown and the Cayces to discuss the matter on Sunday, November 9. Edgar wanted to give another reading to see what might have gone wrong, but Morton didn't think it was necessary. He said that the readings had insisted that appointments be definite and that the individual requesting the reading be in a seeking, meditative attitude at the time of the appointment. Rosamond hadn't even known there was a request or an appointment for the reading, nor would she have approved had she been informed. Nor was she at the location when the reading was requested because she was already in the grave. And, having studied the reading, it was clear that the diagnosis applied to the patient's condition at the time the reading had been requested, not at the time the reading was given. The only psychic "link" that Edgar had to Rosamond was the letter that Gertrude held in her hand as she conducted the readings—a letter that was already twenty-three days old. Rather than reveal an "error" on the part of Edgar Cayce, Morton said, the reading revealed something of the process of requesting information from the Source. Cayce—in trance—literally stepped back in time to examine her condition.

Gladys's diaries revealed that Morton didn't appear to be upset by his aunt's reading. His attitude only began to change upon his return from Europe when his mother and other family members began to question the veracity of Edgar's work and Morton's involvement in it. Morton's mother thought her son foolish to be giving so much of his time and money to a psychic who had made such an obvious blunder, especially during such unsettled times. Morton may or may not have concurred. But one thing soon became clear. The upheavals in the market had shaken him and filled him with fear. And instead of turning to Edgar Cayce for help, or to his wife, he invited another woman into his life.

Patricia Devlin was an attractive twenty-five-year-old redhead, described by some people as voluptuous and by others as merely "chubby." She had

first come to Morton's attention in late 1928, when she was a switchboard operator in the building that housed the Blumenthal brokerage company.
There is no hard evidence that she eavesdropped on the telephone conversations between New York and Virginia Beach, but there is no doubt that she
had an intimate knowledge of Morton and Edgar's affairs long before Morton hired her as his personal assistant in 1929. Devlin claimed her source of
information was the same "psychic channels" that Edgar Cayce tapped into
and told Morton that she had only to close her eyes to enter a self-induced
trance state that permitted her to subconsciously travel to Virginia Beach to
see what was going on. Morton later reported "discovering" in Devlin what
he had seen in Edgar Cayce back in Dayton and said he was responsible for
developing the "precious gift" that Devlin allegedly possessed.

Exactly when she and Morton's relationship passed beyond that of employee and employer is not clear. By early 1929, she began to accompany
Morton to Virginia Beach and help him prepare lectures and take notes for
improvements he wished to implement at the hospital. Edgar expressed mild
interest in what he termed Morton's "protégé" when they were first introduced, and like Morton, encouraged her to develop her psychic talents. In December 1929, she delivered a talk in the hospital lecture series and soon began
to take over responsibilities as Morton and Edwin's new source of psychic
stock market and business advice. Edgar was not disappointed in this shift of
responsibility. To the contrary, he was noticeably relieved to have the pressure
of giving Morton and Edwin business readings twice a day taken off his
shoulders. The fact that Morton was certain of her powers and the help she
could give him and his brother made Edgar all the more pleased. He wrote
Tim Brown that there "certainly [has] been some wonderful things that Morton has been able to get through his helper and assistant there at the office."

Unlike Edgar Cayce, Patricia Devlin could and did remember the information that allegedly came to her during trance sessions, which allowed her
to discuss the communications she received in ways that Edgar was unable
to do. She also spoke in her normal voice while in trance, in clear distinct sentences without the repetitious use of pronouns and adverbs that sometimes
made Cayce's readings difficult to understand. Her plainspokeness, coupled
with her availability to give readings to Morton—both night and day—
made her more desirable in many respects than Edgar Cayce, whose responsibilities at the hospital made it impossible to devote himself to Morton
full time, as he had done in the past.

The confidence that Morton put in Devlin was everywhere apparent,
from the advice she began giving Tim Brown and Marion Stansell, in which
she described "seeing their motor operational," to her stock tips, in which she

allegedly begged Morton and his brother to get out of the market the very day that stocks began to plummet. It is curious, however, that Morton never requested a reading from Edgar on her psychic abilities, as he had requested a background check on Stansell. The closest that either of the Blumenthal brothers came to asking Edgar's psychic advice on Devlin was a question that Edwin asked on February 16, 1930, apparently concerned about problems he was having staying "attuned" when working with Devlin. In a particularly revealing response, the Source came right out and said that he should not put his "trust in powers made with hands," which was apparently a reference to Devlin.

The only trance session dedicated to Devlin was a physical reading conducted on January 11, 1931, to diagnose and recommend treatment for pains she was having in her back and solar plexus. Cayce—in trance—prescribed a standard treatment that consisted of a change of diet and the application of Epsom salts and castor oil packs, indicating that should she follow the recommendations her pains would disappear within two or three days.

Devlin had apparently begun influencing Morton before Atlantic University's doors actually opened. In early October of 1929, Devlin was reviewing university correspondence and discovered that unbeknownst to Morton, Brown had hired two more professors than they had agreed upon in an earlier meeting. Morton was justifiably upset. Devlin, however, was also irate. As Morton later said, "Pat nodded her pretty red head, put on her hat, and left, returning with a lawyer."

Devlin also recommended legal action after she reviewed expenditures. Morton took a more benign approach. He and Devlin visited the hospital and took Edgar aside, informing him that expenses had to be cut, and that this time, he would be in charge of making the necessary changes. In addition to cutting the expenses, Blumenthal requested that Edgar cut back on any "freebie" readings and concentrate on paying customers. When Morton and Edwin took their trips abroad in early 1930, Devlin was placed in charge of managing the hospital.

There is no evidence to suggest that Edgar or Gertrude particularly minded Devlin being temporarily put in charge of hospital affairs. Edgar may not have actually seen her during the month and a half that the Blumenthals were away, though she indeed made frequent trips to interview doctors and hospital staff. Edgar's main difficulty was trying to limit the number of readings given to patients who were unable or unwilling to pay for them. In a letter he wrote to Morton on January 13, 1930, Edgar found himself in the uncomfortable position of having to justify the fact that he couldn't abide by Morton's edict. "[No one] you or anybody else . . . can control the readings [You and I] may be able to control the times when we will give the readings, but who they are going to be for, and when they are going to be given—the minute we do that, we have lost the very . . . foundation of the whole work . . . Remember the Master didn't refuse to heal the whole ten lepers, though only two came back and said 'thank you.' "

Morton clearly understood what Edgar was saying, because he let the matter drop for the time being. But he, like Edgar, couldn't ignore the repeated plea for cooperation coming through the readings. When the hospital had been formed, the readings described cooperation as a "need." Now the Source indicated that all would be lost unless cooperation became their central "task" and "purpose." The message coming through was similar to what had been said in readings for another partnership, that of Edgar B. Davis and Frank Seiberling. As the Source had said then: "Unless there is a coalition of the interests . . . much of that which has been as a dream . . . will be lost. Rather than . . . magnifying the differences that have existed [act] in the manner of brotherly love . . . The law of the Lord is as the two-edged sword . . . Unless good is done to all, good cannot grow out of same. For what ye sow, ye reap!"

Edgar and Morton were still not getting along, and with the introduction of Patricia Devlin, the distance between the two men became considerably greater. Upon Morton's return from Europe on February 16, Devlin reported what she described as the "disillusioning" news that Edgar had failed him as never before and was in the midst of taking him for a "financial ride." Spending hadn't been cut at the hospital. Not only this, but Devlin's investigation had revealed a large number of nonpaying guests living at the hospital whose contributions to the work she found questionable. Among them were Tom Sugrue, who had been invited to help edit association publications, Gladys's cousin, Mildred Davis, who was helping with the secretarial work, and Leslie Cayce, who had moved into an upstairs room at the hospital. There were also two of Edgar's sisters, Annie Cayce, and Sarah Cayce Hesson, who came to the hospital to fill in for Carrie House. Finally, there was Booker Avery, the hospital's handyman and driver who, according to Devlin, used the hospital automobile for frequent all-night excursions.

Morton called Tim Brown and Devlin to an emergency meeting at the hospital that same month to study Linden Shroyer's bookkeeping. The meeting didn't get off to a good start. As Morton's party walked up the path to the front of the hospital, one of Devlin's high heels caught on something buried in the grass. They discovered that it was a pipe. Tim Brown traced the pipe and found that it ran from the hospital water line to a private home adjacent to the recently completed nurses building. Edgar was called in to look at the

pipe and admitted that he had let a neighbor tap into the hospital water supply rather than have the man go to the trouble and expense of finding his
own water source. The hospital, Edgar admitted, was not being compensated for their largess.

The rest of the afternoon, according to Morton, only got worse. He, Tim
Brown, and Devlin were reportedly shown all the hospital records except the
one ledger that detailed disbursements. Try as they could, the ledger couldn't
be found until sometime later that day, when Devlin led a search party into
the basement where the missing book was discovered under what Morton
termed a "pile of debris." How it had gotten there and whether or not Devlin used her alleged psychic powers to find it was never made clear.

According to Morton, the ledger revealed excess payments for food, ex-
traneous hospital equipment, and many personal expenditures by the Cayce
family and hospital staff. More irregularities were reportedly discovered
when the investigators consulted merchants from whom large purchases
had been made. Upon Devlin's recommendation, Morton stopped paying
the bills until the accounts were put in order and personal expenses were re-
imbursed.

"I'm [just] not that good a businessman," Edgar admitted when confronted by the ledger and Devlin's accounting. "It certainly does get my goat
to do my level best and then find I have fallen far short of what should be
done." And a reading, conducted later, also squarely put the blame on Edgar's
shoulders. "This present discord . . . has been . . . the extravagant expendi-
ture by . . . Edgar Cayce." Although the Source, when asked for specifics, suggested that this might only be viewed as an extravagance in material terms:
"[his extravagance can only be] judged by individuals. [But] not from here."

A special board meeting was held in Virginia Beach on September 16,
1930, attended by the Kahns, Cayces, Blumenthals, and all other board members. The mood was described as "somber." The hospital's outstanding debts
were calculated, and it was determined that $42,572 was owed to the build-
ing and loan association that held the mortgage on the hospital property—
for which Dave Kahn and the Blumenthals were jointly liable—and that the
association owed $14,420 in unpaid building loans and $19,724 in unpaid
commercial bills. Morton then made it clear that such amounts could not
possibly be covered by what little revenue was being generated by the hospital, and that should he have to cover interest on the loans and the hospital's other obligations, he and his brother would first have to have the
association's agreement that the Blumenthals would assume total financial
and managerial control of the hospital, and that Edgar would have no authority to pay bills or accept new patients without prior approval. In addition

to cuts in salary for the hospital staff, only the nurses would receive free room and board, all others would pay $30 a month. A device known as a "governor" was also to be placed on the hospital automobile to record and restrict its unauthorized use. Dr. Lyman Lydic was dismissed and replaced by Dr. Gena Crews, an osteopath from Richmond, Virginia, and Dr. James R. Parker, a general practitioner from Norfolk. Both Crews and Parker were to report directly to the Blumenthals. Morton made one other demand: that Dave Kahn was to receive no further readings.

This final demand came as a result of Devlin's review of the financial records, in which she discovered that Kahn, besides his initial $750 investment in the ANI stock fund, had not been making regular contributions to the association as he had agreed a few years earlier. Instead, he had been paying money directly to Edgar, who spent it as he saw fit. Equally serious was the revelation that furniture Morton believed to have been donated by Kahn, estimated to be worth $7,000, had in fact been invoiced by Kahn's company and paid for by Morton and his brother through the ANI account. Incredulous, Morton demanded to know how such a thing could have happened. Edgar said that he too had been surprised to have received a bill for the furniture, but had paid it because he didn't wish anyone to feel obligated to give to the hospital when they didn't want to. Donations were expected to come from the heart. Edgar's response didn't satisfy Morton. The long-simmering antagonism between Blumenthal and Kahn now became outright hostility, and Morton demanded that Edgar not give Dave Kahn any more readings without Morton's express permission.

Edgar, who had remained calm when earlier demands were placed upon him, exploded. He reportedly turned to Morton and said, "As much affection as I have for you, and as much as I appreciate all you have done for me, on the day that I cannot give a reading for Dave Kahn or any member of his family or anyone, is the day 'little Eddy' will be six feet under the ground."

In the heat of the moment, the reasons that had brought the board together appear to have been overlooked. However justified the Blumenthals were in accusing Edgar of extravagance, it was not an extravagance characterized by fancy cars, beautiful homes, or any sort of material excess. The extravagance that Edgar was guilty of was charity. His goal all along had been to give away his services in any way he could, and it was often beyond his ability to ask for money in return. Put simply, Edgar couldn't bring himself to demand payment for what he believed to be a gift from God.

Nothing more was said at the meeting on the subject of Edgar's poor management skills or his giving readings for David Kahn. The meeting ended, and Morton paid a portion of the hospital's most pressing debts. But by December of 1930, the Blumenthals had again stopped paying hospital bills, claiming that Edgar and the others were doing nothing to curb expenses. The ANI account was in arrears by approximately $10,000. Morton fired Linden Shroyer and put Dr. Job Taylor in direct charge of all hospital bookkeeping and disbursements. Perhaps even more serious, patients returning after the Christmas holidays found the doors temporarily closed to them while Morton and Dr. Taylor evaluated the current status of the hospital accounts. At a meeting, shortly afterward, on February 28, 1931, they would close the hospital doors forever.

Prior to the meeting, Morton approached Hugh Lynn—a voting member of the ANI board—to inform him that he would be requesting that the board turn ownership of the hospital over to him and his brother. Morton reminded him that it was he who had paid for Hugh Lynn's education, and it was he who had given him a job upon graduation. Morton told Hugh Lynn that if he didn't use his influence to see that the board approved the resolution, he would be fired from the university staff. Hugh Lynn was outraged that Morton should resort to such tactics and was determined not to let Morton have his way.

The meeting was held in the nurses quarters in the building adjacent to the hospital. As always, Morton and his brother were immaculately dressed. Edwin sat quietly in a chair off to the side as Morton stood up and gave a brief review of the financial history of the hospital. He then listed $10,000 worth of outstanding bills that had accumulated. Finally, he proposed that the ANI board formally turn the hospital property and all its assets over to him and his brother as a prerequisite for settling all outstanding ANI bills. The motion was voted down, with Tim Brown, the Kahns, Hugh Lynn, and Frank Bradley voting against it. Edgar abstained. Morton lost his temper. The association attorney, who was being paid by the Blumenthals, resigned his position and indicated that he now represented the Blumenthals personally.

Morton threatened to force an immediate closing of the hospital. Edgar then took the floor, and during what Hugh Lynn described as the "simplest and most beautiful" speech his father ever made, assured Morton of his faith and confidence in him and told him that if he wanted the hospital and its property that he would like to return them to him, that they would mean little without Morton's interest and cooperation. "Morton has given the property and if he needs it, we should turn it back to him," Edgar said. A second vote put the hospital property into the hands of the Blumenthals, the deciding vote being cast by Tim Brown, who believed that there was no point in continuing operations unless Edgar desired to be in charge.

Less than a month later, a second board meeting was held in New York in which the papers were signed that closed the hospital and disbanded the ANI. Edgar returned to the hospital one last time to collect the records of the trance readings, a clock that had been given to him by the carpenters who built the hospital building, and a picture of his mother, which had hung over the fireplace at the entrance.

Gladys and the other members of the now defunct organization quickly went into action, hoping to recapture the momentum of their earlier years. Hundreds of letters were sent out notifying Cayce supporters of what had happened and asking their help in forming an organization to replace the ANI. Readings were conducted to decide what should be done, culminating in a meeting on March 28, 1931, attended by nearly seventy people who crowded into the living room of Cayces' house on Thirty-fifth Street.

Unlike previous general membership gatherings for the annual ANI Congress, those who stood or sat shoulder to shoulder in the living room of the Cayce house were relative newcomers to the work. They included A. C. Preston, who had been with Edgar in Bimini to search for treasure, Esther Wynne, the high school teacher who had been drawn into the work after having attended one of Edgar's lectures, Frances Morrow, who had become an adept student of the readings since meeting Edgar on the steps of the hospital, and Reverend Frank Scattergood.

Except for Gladys, Leslie, Annie Cayce, Linden Shroyer, and Dave Kahn, virtually none of those gathered had been active in the work for more than two or three years. And none of the people in attendance were wealthy or influential, except perhaps Kahn, who was still dealing with lawsuits and the bankruptcy of his own company in the wake of the plunging stock market. Absent, but not forgotten, were Frank Bradley and Byron Wyrick, who would continue to support the work in the years to come and would help form a Cayce support group in Chicago. Tim Brown and Marion Stansell, now working with Patricia Devlin on the perpetual motion motor, didn't so much as send a card. Eventually, Stansell dropped from sight altogether, forever crushing the Blumenthals' dream of recouping their investment in his invention.

Edgar opened the meeting with a moment of silent prayer, then delivered a short, heartfelt speech: "Friends, I hardly know how to express myself at seeing each one of you here this afternoon. While we come together for a very definite purpose, I believe you will say when you have left the meeting that it was an unusual meeting. It is not that we may know how to carry on the work, but . . . that . . . we *shall* carry on the work."

Though the vast majority of members were new to the work, all expressed their encouragement and commitment to forming another organization. And unlike the small nucleus of people who had brought the ANI into existence, these people represented a wide spectrum of supporters—the "power base" that Morton had attempted to create when the Cayces first came to Virginia Beach. The new group may not have had the financial means to build a hospital or university, but their strength lay in numbers, and the fact that the future of their organization did not rest on the generosity and wealth of any one individual. No one addressed the question of how such an organization would be funded, but they did turn to the matter of what to call it. Hugh Lynn's cousin Gray Salter suggested they name it the "National Association of Research and Enlightenment." By the end of the meeting, it was decided to simply call it the "Association for Research and Enlightenment," or the A.R.E.

It was only a matter of months before the university also closed its doors. Morton first cut salaries in half, then refused to pay salaries or other expenses altogether, resulting in another $10,000 owed to local merchants and faculty members. Hugh Lynn described the situation as an "armed camp," with Dr. Brown and the faculty on one side and the Blumenthals on the other. Brown called a meeting with all remaining faculty and board members in the Cavalier Hotel. Morton and Edwin had been invited to join them, but were kept waiting outside the meeting room with their New York attorney while Brown held a private discussion with other faculty and board members. When Brown finally ended his private meeting and invited the Blumenthals into the room, it was not to ask for their input, but rather to demand an immediate payment of $10,000. Otherwise, Brown, as president, would close the university. Morton's attorney called Brown's bluff. Unless the Atlantic University board signed a document putting the university property into Blumenthal's name, not a single penny would be forthcoming. Brown refused, at which point the Blumenthals attempted to leave the building. They couldn't go out the front doors because a security guard had locked them. Angry, Morton marched over to one of the side doors, kicked in the glass, and left.

Unlike Edgar, who had simply turned the hospital over to the Blumenthals, Brown decided to put up a fight. He arrived at the Blumenthal brokerage company a few days after the Virginia Beach meeting, accompanied by a New York attorney who was also an important bank executive. Morton and his brother kept Brown and the banker waiting for more than an hour before they agreed to show them inside. Morton's attorney took the same approach they had taken at the Virginia Beach meeting. Unless Brown signed a document returning what the Blumenthals considered rightfully theirs, they would let Atlantic University go bankrupt.

"Up to this point the Blumenthals have left you to run the show and you have taken advantage of every privilege they have given you, beginning with the very opening of the school," Morton said his attorney told Brown. "You have broken every promise, violated even rules of common courtesy, and shut them out completely from the institution that only their money and generosity make possible. Mr. Brown, that college is ours—founded by our money and our organization and you are our employee."

Brown reportedly turned to his banker friend for help, at which point the banker said that he had not been properly informed about the matter and asked to be excused. Brown left the Blumenthal office, returning a day later to sign a document giving the Blumenthals everything they wanted. Atlantic University struggled on for two more semesters before Morton and Edwin closed its doors, leaving many of its professors and students stranded in the middle of a school year without any place to go.

As had occurred back in Hopkinsville three decades before, the partnership that had begun with the best of intentions, ended up in court. David Kahn, irate that the Blumenthals should blackmail the hospital board into turning the ANI's assets over to them, sued Morton and Edwin on behalf of Edgar Cayce and the Association for the return of the property. In a separate proceeding, Patricia Devlin sued David Kahn on behalf of Morton and Edwin for notes that he had countersigned for the hospital property and for stock options he had purchased on margin before the crash. Then Morton and Edwin sued Edgar in another civil suit for several hundred dollars they claimed Edgar had drawn in unauthorized expenses in the final months of the hospital's decline.

Edgar and Morton met for the last time on April 11, 1932 at the Princess Anne County Courthouse, a redbrick structure with a portico overlooking green lawns and sprawling shade trees. Inside, standing in the witness box, Edgar admitted that Morton had provided the money for the house he was living in as well as the hospital, whose assets had been turned over to the Blumenthals during a legitimate board meeting held by the ANI, of which Morton was then president. The judge settled the ANI case in favor of the Blumenthals, and another judge, in 1937, decided against Kahn for the $7,500 owed the Blumenthal brokerage company.

Edgar held out his hand to Morton in the hallway outside the court room when their own case was settled in 1932. "It's all yours, Morton," he said. Morton replied: "You mean our oak . . . It's fallen." He refused to take Edgar's outstretched hand.

Edgar and Morton never spoke again. Letters that Edgar wrote asking for a reconciliation went unanswered.

PART EIGHT

Called Back

43.

Begin at
the Beginning

Long walks along the deserted sand dunes or quiet meditations in his vegetable garden did little to remove the intense pain and depression that Edgar, now fifty-four years old, felt in the months after the hospital's closure. Gladys described her soul mate as "listless" and "unable to concentrate." Friends were disturbed to see him "bewildered," and "uncertain." They had every reason to be concerned, for his physical being was clearly reflecting his inner turmoil: Edgar lost his voice once again, he suffered from neuritis and severe constipation, and a simple cold took him the better part of a month to overcome. In less than three months, he was twenty pounds lighter, his usually tanned face was drawn and waxen. "Unless changes are made, this might become a very serious condition," a physical reading warned.

Had the readings not told him to remain on the Virginia shores, he most certainly would have packed the family's belongings and retreated to The Hill, where, at the very least, he would not have to look at the "great white ghost" that had once been the Cayce Hospital. And the Blumenthals wasted no time in liquidating what remained of the institution. They assigned Patricia Devlin to fire the hospital's doctors and therapists, cart away the records, and for pennies on the dollar, dismantle and sell the equipment.

Days later, as a crew of carpenters arrived to turn the hospital building into a hotel, Morton dispatched a Virginia Beach sheriff to the Cayce home with an eviction notice. Already involved in two lawsuits over the hospital's closure, Edgar wasn't about to initiate a third by fighting to keep the home he believed rightfully belonged to him and Gertrude.

Rentals were costly and hard to find at the height of the tourist season, and all the Cayces found within their price range was a drafty summer cottage at the foot of 105th Street, which looked out over the ocean on one side, and on the other side, the now defunct Cayce Hospital. Edgar's last chore was perhaps the most difficult: digging up a bed of violets for transplanting. A sense of gloom descended upon him as he shook the dirt off his hands and thought of the fruit and vegetables that had yet to be picked. Gertrude herself had to keep from crying, for she too had poured her creative talents into their house on Thirty-fifth Street—the first and only home that she and Edgar could have truly called their own during their twenty-eight years of marriage.

From the upstairs bedroom window in their new 105th Street cottage, the Cayces had a clear view of what the former hospital had been converted into: the Cape Henry Hotel, which was run by the brother of the man who operated the Princess Anne Country Club. Less than one year later, Morton and Edwin turned it into the Princess Pat Hotel, presumably named in honor of Patricia Devlin, who managed the property on their behalf until it closed four years later. Later still, it would be sold and turned into a nightclub, then an officers' club, and eventually a Masonic Temple.

One evening in the late summer of 1931, Edgar was sitting at his bedroom window in his new house when Devlin hosted a party for over one hundred friends and admirers to celebrate the grand opening of the hotel. The sound of music drifted out of the old hospital, and there was much dancing and drinking. Early the next morning, people were still spilling out onto the beach.

"No one but God knows the heartaches I have had over that place," Edgar admitted in a letter to Carrie House. "Am afraid they will never make a success of anything of it, except what it was built for. Too many people's heart's blood went into that building, and it was dedicated for another purpose than for just revelry."

The Cayces were once again in deep financial straits. Although Edgar continued to give readings, they barely had enough money to make ends meet. Though much had happened in the last seven years, both Edgar and Gertrude felt as if they were right back where they had been at Christmas of 1923, when Edgar had stuffed newspapers into his jacket to fend off the freezing cold in Dayton. Unbeknownst to either Edgar or Gertrude, Gladys sought to improve the situation by writing scores of letters to A.R.E. members requesting their help to find the Cayce family a more permanent home and a steady income. But in the winter of 1931, the Great Depression was well underway, and although their new association was high on enthusiasm, it remained short on funds. Gladys's letter-writing campaign eventually netted them several hundred dollars, barely enough to keep groceries on the table and wood in the fireplace during what proved to be one of the longest and coldest winters in the history of Virginia Beach.

The Cayces' economic situation soon got to the point where their credit at the local grocery store was canceled and their utilities disconnected. Without fuel oil, the Cayces had to collect driftwood and other debris on the beach to burn in their fireplace. But rather than try to pull himself out of his depression and do something about their financial plight, Edgar became all the more remote, and then irrational. Gladys reported that when a few dollars did come in, Edgar failed to act responsibly with the money. In one case he was dispatched by Gertrude to the grocery store to settle their account and returned with a new fishing pole and armful of tackle. Gertrude reportedly looked at him with despair. "Don't worry about it, Mother," he replied. "The money will turn up somehow."

In October of 1931 a few dollars did come, and this money was set aside to pay for round-trip train fare for Gladys and the Cayces to New York, where Dave Kahn and other association members had arranged for a series of physical readings. Cayce hoped that these readings would generate sufficient funds to tide them through the holiday season. For a time, it looked as if Edgar would be able to recapture some of the momentum of earlier visits, when the Blumenthals had treated the family to fine hotels and evenings at the theater. The appointment calendar was full for their entire two-week stay at the Victoria Hotel, and a lecture Edgar gave at the Theosophical Society garnered them many new supporters. The curtain fell, however, on November 7, the day they planned to give two final readings before setting off for Virginia Beach. Their trouble began when their three o'clock appointment was suddenly canceled, and Gladys agreed to an unscheduled reading for a hotel guest registered as Bertha Gorman, who had been begging for help from Edgar for several days, and who was offering three times the normal fee for membership in the A.R.E.

Mrs. Gorman, and her companion, Mrs. Anna McNamara, were vague about how they heard about Edgar Cayce or who exactly had recommended that she obtain a reading. All the forty-five-year-old subject of the reading said about herself was that she was an unemployed widow from Wilmington, Delaware, who was visiting the city to consult with doctors about an undisclosed ailment. There was nothing particularly unusual about their behavior except that neither she nor her companion wanted to sign the application to the association. Gertrude explained that signing was required, that Edgar gave trance readings under a Virginia-based charter that stipulated that only members could have readings. The trance reading wouldn't be given without their signatures. Mrs. Gorman and Mrs. McNamara read the application and allegedly signed it.

The reading was unusual in two significant ways. Unlike the vast majority of other readings, the Source was unusually vague about what exactly was ailing Mrs. Gorman. All the Source indicated was that the root of her problems lay less in the physical and more in the spiritual. Mrs. Gorman should, the reading stated, clarify her ideals and not let her material needs become her guiding principles. The Source further stated that Mrs. Gorman suffered from loneliness, alienation, and lack of faith, and these were termed as being of more concern than any physical difficulties or a home equity loan that she was worried about at that moment. Another curious aspect of the reading occurred when Mrs. Gorman asked about her sister's health. The Source said no sister could be found. Perhaps the most interesting aspect in the reading was that it suggested that Mrs. Gorman herself, if she wished, could develop some psychic ability.

The truth, as it was later revealed in court, was that the woman calling herself Mrs. Gorman didn't have a sister. However accurate the trance information may or may not have been, the contents of the reading had little bearing on what later developed. No sooner had the reading ended than Mrs. Gorman and her companion announced that they were undercover policewomen. A detective appeared at the door and arrested Edgar, Gertrude, and Gladys for "pretending to tell fortunes." To add to the indignity, someone had tipped off the press. As Edgar, Gertrude, and Gladys left the police station later that night, released on bail, a photographer from the *New York Daily News* snapped their picture. Hugh Lynn didn't get the news until the next day when he read the story in the tabloids and saw a picture of Edgar and his "pretty blonde secretary" being taken to jail. Gertrude, who was standing between Edgar and Gladys when the picture was taken, had been cropped out of the photo.

A trial was set for November 11. The coverage was overwhelmingly negative, but the Cayces would find at least one supportive reporter in Tom Sugrue, now working for the *Herald-Tribune*. His own undercover reporting of the subsequent trial revealed how the press had been tipped off, as well as the name of the person he believed had paid for "Mrs. Gorman's" eight-day hotel bill and A.R.E. membership fee: Morton Blumenthal. As Edgar wrote in a letter to Gertrude's mother: "Our good friends are still trying to torment us. I don't wish them any harm, but I only wish they would let me alone."

The Cayces' New York supporters, of which there were many, went into action. A New York businessman, whose brother owned Gallagher's Steak House, provided the bail and paid expenses for Gladys's and the Cayces' extended stays in New York; and a Norfolk attorney and his New York associate agreed to represent them at no cost. In the interim, Gertrude conducted a reading to see how best they should deal with the crisis. The reading came back saying that they should reply to the prosecutor's questions "simply" and "truthfully," and not to complicate or aggravate their situation. They were assured that the trial would end in their favor if they kept to the truth.

The state presented their case in the first ten minutes of the two-hour trial at the Seventh District Court. Bertha Conwell, the woman who had pretended to be Mrs. Gorman, told how she paid $70 in marked bills to be told her fortune, and this sum, along with Gladys's notes and other documents, were introduced into evidence. It was only under cross-examination that it was revealed to the court that the $70 was given to the Cayces as payment for her membership in the A.R.E. It was also pointed out that the membership application bearing her name and address, which the witness admitted to seeing in the hotel suite, and that she allegedly did not sign, could not be introduced into evidence because the police could not produce the document. The application had conveniently vanished from police files.

Dave Kahn was the first to testify in Edgar's defense. "This defendant Cayce has an unusual power," he told the court. "What it is, no one has been able to tell. I have had lawyers, doctors, presidents of universities in this city, the most prominent people, and not any man has been able to say anything but that it is perfectly remarkable and what he says is the truth . . . Our [association's] charter is organized for the purpose of investigation and . . . records are kept in our archives." Before stepping down, Kahn added: "The man is not commercializing it, and a poor man from the street can come in."

Gladys was cross-examined next and provided the only humorous moment during the proceedings. Asked if she was married, she reportedly replied "yes." Gertrude later elbowed her in the ribs and said, "You know that isn't true." Gertrude, of course, was right. Gladys was legally single. But Gladys—at least in the spiritual sense—considered herself married, if not to her soul mate, then to the work. Gladys, who was admittedly nervous and had to fight to keep from showing her panic, was next asked if she had solicited the reading. "Absolutely not," she replied.

Gertrude followed her to the stand, and her testimony was brief. Then

Edgar was called. He was asked to explain the trance process and said that he knew nothing about what he said or did during a session until after coming out of trance, at which point the conductor would tell him.

Minutes later Judge Francis J. Erwin handed down his verdict: "After seeing the people's witnesses and the three defendants and their witness on the stand, and observing their manner of testifying and after reading the exhibits in the case, I find as a fact that Mr. Cayce and his co-defendants were not pretending to tell fortunes and that to hold these defendants guilty . . . would be an interference with the beliefs, practices, or usage of an incorporated ecclesiastical governing body . . ."

Edgar just stood silently while everyone else was smiling and shaking hands. Dave Kahn gave everyone a big bear hug, while Tom Sugrue cheered. But no matter how much of a spin Kahn and others put on the episode, Edgar openly called it a "nightmare," and sank into an even deeper depression than he had been in before coming to New York. Upon his return to Virginia Beach, he suffered a severe bout of nausea and abdominal pain, which was diagnosed as cholecystitis, forcing him to cancel all but his most pressing appointments. One reading, while not suggesting that he was seriously ill, did say that things would get worse if the problem wasn't dealt with.

Nightmares haunted Cayce's sleeping hours. His visions sometimes consisted of small dark creatures Edgar called "imps," which tugged on his shirt sleeves or hung on his shoulders, constantly pulling him into the darkness or causing him to lose his balance and spin helplessly into a void. At other times he dreamed of doing battle with supernatural armies carrying spears, shields, torches, and helmets. In one particularly ominous dream, on November 30, 1931, he found himself standing in a forest clearing waiting to be joined by others whom he would lead into battle. Amidst great excitement and a thunderous clamor, a large horse appeared wearing a glittering harness. As the horse approached, Edgar was suddenly aware that he was the rider, and that he was at the head of a long procession of soldiers. The dream seemed to be telling him that the fight between the supernatural armies was over him. A subsequent reading said that the dream was a warning that Cayce would be drawn back into the spirit world unless he were held here by his friends: "[For] those in the spirit [world] would make such holds or demands as to bring about a separation from the body." At the end of this reading came an unsolicited message: "We are calling here. There are things to be done!"

Upon hearing this pronouncement, Gertrude, stricken with fear, leaned toward her husband—still in trance—and softly asked what could be done. The Source replied: "Conditions are to be met! There is much need in the spirit world for the activities of [Edgar Cayce]." Gertrude argued with the Source, saying that there were surely many more people in the material world that needed him, herself and their children included. The Source replied: "Then there should be such as would outweigh those calling [from the other side]."

Edgar's one consolation that year, and the thing that Gertrude and Gladys ultimately came to believe kept Edgar on the "earthly plane" during the months ahead, was the formation of a spiritual study group, which the Cayces called the "good circle," and which later would become known as the Norfolk Study Group. A smaller prayer group composed of many of the same members was formed about three weeks later, inspired by a dream Edgar had had. This group became known as the Glad Helpers, named after the outreach program Edgar had joined in Louisville many years earlier. Together, these two groups allowed Edgar and the others to feel more optimistic about the challenges they faced in the aftermath of the hospital closing and the New York arrests.

Members of the original prayer and study groups had actually been together since before the Cayces had even moved to the beach. In 1925, a local housewife, Edith Edmonds, had gotten together with her sister, Florence, a nurse, and their friends—among them Mary Louise Black, Esther Wynne, Hannah Miller, and Minnie Barrett—to study the great religions of the world by reading holy books. As Edgar frequently liked to say, they were composed of almost every "cult or ism" he could imagine. "[There are] Rosicrucians of three different schools . . . also a healer in the Spiritualist Church," Edgar would say. The majority of members, however, practiced standard Christianity. Eventually the group wished to expand their study, and in 1930, began attending the lecture series at the Cayce Hospital with the idea of exploring their own potential psychic abilities. Their enthusiasm for the message being put forth in Edgar's lectures brought them deep into the life of the association, and the Cayces subsequently invited them into their home whenever important or interesting people came to the beach.

After a short meeting of the informal group at a Virginia Beach coffee shop in August of 1931, Edith Edmonds, aware that the Cayce Hospital had been shut down and the Cayces had lost a major source of support, sent a handwritten note to Edgar on behalf of her and her friends asking how they could be of assistance. The note pleased Edgar greatly, and a month later a reading was conducted to answer that question.

During that first reading, held in Minnie Barrett's living room on September 14, 1931, Cayce—in trance—invoked Jesus' message as put forth in the Bible: "If two or three are gathered together in My name, there am I in the midst of them." It also offered them a promise: if they were sincere in their desire and commitment, they could give "light to the waiting world."

Everyone was pleased and excited as Edgar told how each of them could contribute to one another's spiritual development, and that their combined efforts would become a "light" in their own lives and in the lives of many others. The reading stated that each member of the group would come away with something different: "To some will be given those of prophecy, to some will be given those of teaching, to some will be given those of ministration." Asked to outline the steps they should take to become more of one mind, Cayce was quite clear. "First" he said, "learn cooperation!"

The members of the new group were so impressed and delighted by the reading that the very same day they made a promise to stay together to see where the readings would take them. They also pledged to live up to the strict regimen of prayer, meditation, and study that was to accompany the readings. Each member would meditate every morning in their own homes, conscious of the fact that the other group members would be meditating at the same time. They would also faithfully seek to apply the lessons and spiritual laws put forth in Cayce's readings. Asked what their next lesson should be, the Source admonished them not to move ahead until it finished with the first lesson. "Let's take one at a time . . . Begin at the beginning!"

On October 4, 1931, a third reading on cooperation was conducted and the group was given a prayer upon which to meditate. "Not my will but Thine, O Lord, be done in and through me. Let me ever be a channel of blessings, today, now to those that I contact, in every way. Let my going in, mine coming out, be in accordance with that Thou would have Me do, and as the call comes: Here am I, send me, use Me!"

On October 18, a fourth reading was given, also stressing the importance of cooperation. Esther Wynne, the group's secretary, had begun to compile Cayce's messages into a lesson plan, which each member could take home and study. By November 29, 1931, the Norfolk Study Group was able to present a summary of their first lesson, along with a suggested format for how this lesson and future lessons might be used by their group and others. Each meeting, it was proposed, would begin with a reading of the lesson as a whole. Next they would memorize the prayer given in the previous trance session, study the lessons by topic, and then meditate before trying to take what was learned out into their everyday life. The Source was pleased and indicated that they were ready to begin their second lesson: "Know thyself."

Edgar, Gertrude, Gladys, and Mildred would all become members of the study group, as did Hugh Lynn, who became one of its leaders. Hugh Lynn didn't hold out much hope that the group of "housewives," as he sometimes privately referred to them, would stay together beyond the first year or two, nor did he think they could support and protect the fledgling A.R.E. against the likes of the tabloid journalists and the Blumenthal brokerage company. But he did know that his father was benefiting greatly from the sense of comradeship and support he derived from participating in their trance sessions and attending their meetings. In contrast to the study group's activities, he and Dave Kahn believed that Edgar and the A.R.E.'s salvation was to be found in an entirely different manner: locating oil wells or lost treasure, or high-profile readings that would capture the attention of the press. Toward this end, both men pursued a variety of money-earning schemes, which probably only served to prolong Edgar's depression.

Hugh Lynn, who had not participated much in early treasure-hunting expeditions, had become as obsessed with finding hidden treasure as his father had once been obsessed with finding oil. This time the site was not in Florida or the Bahamas, but much closer to home, at White Horse Hill, in Virginia Beach, in an area once known as the Cape Henry Desert. Although referred to as a desert, the area was anything but barren, consisting of sand hills and swamps covered with rich green vegetation and hanging vines. Treasure hunters had long been interested in the area since some of the oldest settlements in the country had been nearby. Blackbeard, the pirate, was killed at Oregon Inlet in North Carolina, only a few miles to the south, and legend had it that he had buried a fortune in treasure on or near White Hill, along an old Indian trail that led from the beach. Hugh Lynn believed finding Blackbeard's treasure would be the answer to their financial difficulties, as did his cousin, Gray Salter, their friend Dr. Owen Snyder, and perhaps most significantly, A. C. Preston, the first manager of the A.R.E. At their request, and amidst what Hugh Lynn described as his father's grave "misgivings" to continue to involve himself in yet more treasure hunts, they conducted the first reading on this topic.

As with every other treasure reading, the Source prefaced its comments by stressing the need for the searchers to have the right mental attitude. "In seeking such information . . . much consideration should be given as respecting purposes, aims, and ideals," the reading began. Hugh Lynn and the others were thrilled to hear what came next. "As we find, there are—and have been—treasures, or moneys, jewels, papers, and such, that have been put in this vicinity." The Source went on to describe treasure in excess of $1,000,000 hidden in an old Indian burial ground ten to twelve feet southwest from a dead gum tree on the west side of White Horse Hill. Hugh Lynn had one more question to ask. Having come to realize that the Source for medical readings was not the same source as for business and other readings, he wanted to know who was providing this information through Edgar Cayce. The answer was quite revealing, for it suggested that the Source was now deceased Indians who desired that the treasure be removed from their sacred ground.

Excited, Hugh Lynn, Preston, Gray Salter, and Owen Snyder launched what amounted to an assault upon White Horse Hill. This proved rather problematical because the location turned out to be a state park. The searchers were faced with the choice of treasure hunting surreptitiously, or obtaining permission from the authorities. Hugh Lynn decided to go to the authorities and subsequently obtained a license to excavate for artifacts. But their initial forays to White Horse Hill turned up little more than a pile of tin cans left by careless campers. A more thorough inspection, however, revealed some other tantalizing artifacts. Gray Salter found an ancient musket wrapped in oilcloth hidden in a hollow tree, and not far away Snyder found the rusted blade of a sword buried in a stump. Their search continued through the winter as more readings were conducted. Their most significant challenge was the fact that White Horse Hill was home to not just one dead gum tree, but several. There was also a problem of depth. According to the readings, the cache of loot was buried "extremely deep." A veritable blanket of thick tree roots and undergrowth made even the shallowest of excavations a major undertaking.

Edgar Evans later picked up where Hugh Lynn had failed. He and his partners eventually invited a jeep salesman to join them, and using his connections, requisitioned the use of a four-wheel drive auxiliary fire truck, which the team forged through the swamp and up the side of White Horse Hill. In spite of the great logistical difficulties of getting the truck to their location, and the equally formidable task of getting it back, in a single day they washed more sand and earth off the hill than a dozen laborers could have shoveled in a week. Not a single Indian bone or gold doubloon was found, and the team decided at this point to give up the search. Whether they just couldn't dig deep enough, or the Source was wrong about the location, they never attempted to find out in a subsequent reading.

Dave Kahn would also temporarily step in to try and help relieve the Cayces' financial situation. But his solution, like Hugh Lynn's before him, was to involve Cayce in what promised to be an even more demoralizing experience than his failure to find buried treasure. The reading that Kahn requested was to locate Charles Augustus Lindbergh Jr., the infant son of America's most renowned pilot, who was kidnapped from the family's home in Hopewell, New Jersey, on March 1, 1932.

Kahn requested the reading on behalf of Major Thomas G. Lamphier, alleged to be a close personal friend of the Lindbergh family. To a certain degree, the request itself verged on fraud, for the Lindbergh family hadn't been contacted about the reading nor is it known if they would have put their faith in information coming from someone with whom they had no firsthand contact, let alone from a psychic. Although Kahn and Lamphier may have had the child's interest in mind, their motives were complicated by the publicity that they knew would be generated were Cayce to help investigators locate the child, as well as the $10,000 reward being offered for the successful return of the child.

The first reading was conducted on March 9, 1932. Cayce—in trance—didn't seem to have the slightest difficulty going back in time to provide the details: "Yes, we have the body here, Charles Augustus Lindbergh Jr.," he said. "7:30—8:30—he's being removed from the room—He is carried by a man. There is another waiting, and who takes the body as it is lowered to the ground. They immediately turn to the right and through those of the surrounding grounds leave [They go] northward, and through those of the outlying section [of town]. Now . . . another car is used in going . . . into Jersey City and through the tunnels. Then across the city in the morning carried into Connecticut, in that region of Cardova, and there the body is . . . not far from New Haven."

Cayce—in trance—went on say that the child's hair had been changed. The car was later described as a Mercer automobile whose license plate had been changed. The home where the child was being held was said to be a two-story frame building at 437 Scharter Street, described as having once been painted green, and was now a dirty brown. There were three men and a woman in the house with the child. The woman's name was said to be Madge Beliance. One of the men, described as the leader, was named Megleo.

Kahn and Lamphier apparently contacted authorities immediately, who were unable, if indeed they investigated Kahn's initial report, to locate the house. Thus, on March 10, another reading was requested. This time the location was again said to be Cardova. However, the Source pointed out that this was not an area found on the map, but one that was connected with a company that manufactured leather goods. Cayce gave further directions that indicated there was a sign on a rock on the corner of the road, partially covered, identifying it as Scharter Street. He went on to describe the house a second time, pointing out that there were two goats in the yard, one brown and one white. At the time of this reading, the leader, Meg, was said to be in the grill room at the Taft Hotel having a coke.

This time, Kahn and Lamphier drove out from New York and tried looking for the house themselves, but soon got lost in a section of New Haven where all the streets were numbered and many of the houses looked alike. Kahn and Lamphier briefly considered having Edgar join them in Connecticut, but argued over who would foot the bill for the train fare. Instead, they decided to wire Edgar for more explicit instructions. This time the Source became almost sarcastic, referring to them as "little minds," and castigating them for not following the directions as given. "The directions have been given . . . It will be too late after a while!"

Although Edgar was disappointed that the house had not been found, he was not surprised. After having walked the length of Bimini Island looking for landmarks that may or may not have washed away hundreds of years before, and spending tens of thousands of dollars drilling wells on land that didn't produce the oil that the Source claimed it contained, he didn't hold out much hope for answering a request that hadn't come directly from Charles or Anne Morrow Lindbergh. "I have always had my doubts about anything very authentic [coming through] on such matters unless it came of itself through individuals deeply concerned," Edgar wrote Kahn on March 12, 1932.

Edgar's lack of enthusiasm didn't prevent Kahn from requesting additional information. On March 12, Kahn got another friend of Colonel Lindbergh's involved. The reading this time indicated that Cardova was an area of New Haven where shoes, boots, saddles, and other leather goods were manufactured. The entrance to the manufacturing plant was described and the house was located in relation to this description. The Source identified a street near Scharter, Adams Street—a street, they later discovered was not even on the map yet because it had been renamed only two weeks before. Kahn and Lamphier were again unable to find the house and requested another reading on March 13. The answer came: "Turn right at new Macadam Road, on half street before end of Adams, two-tenths of a mile."

Yet another reading was given. Kahn took a different approach, asking more about the individuals involved. He was told to find the child, not to focus on the gangsters. Even so, some more information about the kidnappers was provided. One of them was a person called "Rosenblat" or "Rosenthal" who had served time in Sing Sing Penitentiary in 1922, and who was once employed by the Lindbergh family using a different name. "This was October 15, as we find, when [he was] dismissed—under another name . . . Douger or Dogan—when dismissed."

Kahn was still unable to find the street. By the time the next reading was requested and conducted, the Lindbergh child, according to the Source, had been moved to Jersey City by a car with the New York license plate, 2M 217. Directions to the house were not as clear as they had been for the location in New Haven. This time, Cayce described the location as being on a street that intersected Broad Street at the Jersey City Guaranty Trust Building. "It's three streets up from this bus terminal—goes down a hill—one little alleyway ... " Cayce said. The reading also indicated that the child was not well.

At this point Kahn didn't pursue his investigation. The primary reason was that Kahn was told in a reading on March 26, 1932, that he could do nothing to further the police investigation, and that he should drop the matter. Another reason, however, was that he had his hands full in his own company's bankruptcy proceedings, and with Morton Blumenthal, who was making efforts to have Kahn arrested for not paying the settlement owed him from the civil suit. Much to Kahn's embarrassment, he was eventually arrested and soon found himself the subject of two unfavorable articles in the *New York Times*, spent a night in jail, and was fined $250.

Kahn's decision not to pursue the Lindbergh investigation, however, was not the end of their involvement in the case, for by March of 1932—unknown to Kahn or Cayce—the FBI was investigating the police investigation of the Lindbergh kidnapping. Edgar Cayce's name, and that of David Kahn, were now considered part of the official Lindbergh file. Although the degree to which Kahn and Cayce were personally investigated is unknown, later communications between David Kahn and Harold G. Hoffman, the governor of New Jersey, in December and January of 1935, suggest that a possible reason that Kahn and Cayce were investigated was because some of Cayce's information had been accurate, though none of it pertained to Bruno Richard Hauptmann, the man who was arrested by the police.

In a letter dated December 30, 1935, 3½ years after Kahn had first initiated readings on the kidnapped child, Governor Hoffman requested answers to twenty-four questions. Among those questions was whether or not Hauptmann had acted alone, why Hauptmann didn't tell all he knew about the others involved in the crime, and whether certain pieces of evidence in the case had been planted. In keeping with the previous readings on the case, Cayce—in trance—stated that Hauptmann had some involvement, though apparently not as much as the prosecution's case suggested, and that he was not the only guilty party. The reading also suggested that those "parties" seeking the information were not necessarily looking for justice to be served, but had other motives. The Source said that if the "proper officials" would take responsibility for following the leads given—though it may bring criticism—help would arrive "through this channel."

Hugh Lynn sent a letter containing the reading along with an explanation to the governor. In it he explained how Cayce conducted his readings and how the "truth" could only be found if all the people involved were genuinely interested in its discovery. Hugh Lynn also asked that Cayce's name not be used in connection with the case regardless of the results. They heard nothing more from the governor, and Bruno Richard Hauptmann died in the electric chair on April 3, 1936, amid a cloud of controversy over whether or not he had acted alone and after repeatedly insisting that he was not guilty as charged. If there is any evidence to support the information that came through Cayce, it has yet to be made public.

44.

He That
Endureth

Though it did little to relieve his misery, Edgar concluded that the hospital's failure was not only a result of conscious choices made by himself and others, but that karma—that deep and abiding internal memory of relationships through time and space—had been everywhere present in the events leading to the closure of the hospital. Like an actor vying for the lead role in a drama, each person involved in the hospital had been too preoccupied with himself to accomplish the greater task of collectively staging the play. Their presumed director, the Master of Masters, knew the challenges confronting the group, along with the severe consequences that would come from their failure to trust in Him as the curtain was raised. The Source confirmed as much in a reading given to Edgar himself: "Do not expect that evil days will not come upon each and everyone, for—as was given—indeed [challenges] must come."

However willing Edgar was to shoulder the entire blame, another reading provided some consolation and suggested the degree to which various forces had been allied against him. In a reference to a paragraph in the Epistle of Jude, the Source noted: "For there has been the continued battle with those forces [the devil] as Michael fought *with* over the body of Moses. He

that leads, or *would* direct, is continually beset by the forces that *would* undermine [But] he that endureth to the end shall wear the Crown."

The Source offered other encouragement as well. With the closing of
the hospital and the severe financial strain that again beset the Cayces, it is
understandable that Edgar, Gertrude, and Gladys might think of their work
as a complete failure. But the Source indicated otherwise. Asked why the
Cayces were having such difficulties, the Source responded: "He that looketh
upon the monetary conditions as success looketh in vain! [The work has] succeeded beyond measure in the spiritual forces."

Encouraging as this reading must have been, Gladys and Gertrude were
still seriously concerned that Edgar was being called back to the spirit world.
Edgar's dreams foretold as much and even began to suggest that he was in
the process of being prepared for this transition. In one dream Edgar reported, he had met the "Angel of Death," who told him to prepare to leave
this world, and that he could take with him only that which he had "given
away." Hugh Lynn, seeking to raise Edgar's spirits, told him: "Dad, I'm
thinking they'll have to have an express [train] to carry all your baggage!"

Despite his humor, Hugh Lynn, like Gertrude and Gladys, knew that
something had to be done. Exactly what was "to be done" was not clear, but
the "unseen forces" speaking through Cayce clearly had something more in
mind than what was currently going on. As Hugh Lynn, Gertrude, and
Gladys later concluded, it was as if the goals of the work were being re-
evaluated, and the former plan to build a hospital or a research institute
had been abandoned in favor of some undefined task. Their first directive
from the Source was to find Edgar Cayce and the A.R.E. a more permanent
residence, a place that would indeed keep "Edgar at home."

The need for this would be heightened in early 1932, when just as Edgar
was preparing to do his spring gardening, the Cayces discovered that their
one-time "good friends," the Blumenthals, had made preparations to either
buy or lease the 105th Street home they were living in, forcing them to
move yet again. Thus, in March of 1932, the Cayces and Gladys settled into
two tiny cottages on Lake Drive, which ran along brackish Lake Holly in a
section of town called Pinewood, at the south end of the Beach. "Two for the
price of one!" Edgar declared, characteristically putting a positive spin on
their move. However, in terms of convenience and size, the two cottages left
much to be desired.

From a spiritual point of view, however, Edgar's dreams suggested that
things were looking up. He requested a reading on a dream he had in late
March that he described as follows: "Saw a little mound of dead leaves. As
I looked . . . [a] snake poked his head out and said, 'Don't hit me—and I won't

bother you any more.' " The Source interpreted this dream as indicating a "clearing of the system of those things that are vile" and the imminent arrival of "that peace as sought." Edgar felt he was on his way to earning that crown promised to "he that endureth." The Source had often said that there were many parallels between the Egyptian incarnations of Edgar, Gertrude, Gladys, and Hugh Lynn and their current lives. Recognizing this, and hoping to receive good news, they had asked the Source if the part of their lives "corresponding to the period of banishment" in Egypt was behind them. The encouraging response came: "[You] are entering that period of the gathering together for the development of the truths as may be ministered to others, or the ministry in Egypt, as has been given [and] was a *beginning* [of] an uprising, a settling, a ministry [You] are entering that of the ministry, still in the throes of the uprisings."

The "throes of the uprisings," apparently included continuing financial difficulties, and yet another move to a new home. Although the Cayces had taken a year's lease on their new property, a clause allowed the owner to prematurely cancel their lease if the cottages were sold. Just one month after moving in, the property was sold, and the Cayces were out looking for another home.

Around this time, the Cayces discovered a spacious but decrepit summer rental for sale across the lake on Arctic Crescent. The Source recommended they buy rather than rent it, and they decided to act on the advice. According to one account, Edgar—without so much as $100 in the bank—called the owner of the Arctic Crescent house and said he wanted to buy it. Edgar agreed to pay $500 in thirty days as a down payment, with a remaining mortgage—held by the seller—for $4,600. When the down payment came due, however, the Cayces still didn't have the money. Just as Edgar was going to give up on buying the house, the owner called him to apologize, saying that he would not be able to come with the necessary documents and collect their down payment until the following Monday. The owner wanted to know what time on Monday he should call. At random, Cayce said noon. And much to Edgar's relief, the morning mail on Monday brought the Cayces two checks from satisfied recipients of readings. A Hollywood film producer named Harry Goetz sent a check for $250 in gratitude for helping his son, a polio victim, and the other check came from Helene and Ernest Zentgraf, relatively new A.R.E. members from Staten Island, New York, who had received both physical and life readings. Although the down payment was not much money against the principal, it would, as Edgar wrote to Alf Butler, "after a few centuries," provide the family with "some equity in the place."

Edgar and his family were relieved to finally have a home they could call their own, even if they were a bit frightened by its forlorn appearance. Large unkempt bushes and tall weeds masked its outlines, and ivy had grown into the house through cracks in the walls. The lake at the rear of the property had encroached upon the yard and reeds and bull rushes grew within a few feet of the back steps. Despite its dilapidated condition and somewhat poor location—it was just down the street from a dance hall and amusement park and only a block from the jail—Edgar thought it had an air of quiet dignity and beauty, as well as a spectacular view. It was only two blocks from the ocean. "Imagine looking out one window and seeing the lake while looking out another and seeing the ocean," Edgar wrote a friend.

Most important to the family, the four bedrooms were large enough to accommodate everyone. Hugh Lynn and Edgar Evans shared a bedroom in the north wing, and Leslie Cayce—described by Edgar as having now become a "crotchety widower"—had his own room at the top of the stairs. Gladys and her cousin Mildred would share a third bedroom, and Edgar and Gertrude had the fourth.

No sooner had they moved than Edgar requisitioned the downstairs sunroom for his office and immediately decorated it with photographs of friends and family and a bookcase where he kept knickknacks and souvenirs from his career. Edgar had displayed photographs in all of his previous offices, but this time he put up nearly everything he had—more than sixty framed pictures, along the walls with two paintings and printed copies of some of his favorite prayers. In the A.R.E. office upstairs, Gladys, Hugh Lynn, and Mildred each had desks.

Edgar set about once again to make a garden from the plants that had survived three different moves. As he wrote to a friend, "Practically the only thing I've saved out of all the beautiful assortment is my violets. They have been moved so often that I suppose when they see anyone coming with a hoe they wonder where they're going next."

Edgar's new flower garden was in full bloom on June 29, 1932, when the A.R.E. held its first annual congress. Despite the generally poor condition of the house and grounds, the membership much appreciated having a place they too could call "home." During the four-day event, attended by over eighty people, groups of twenty or more at a time toured the house, collected on the lawn, and listened in rapt silence as Edgar gave readings. The focus of the readings and accompanying discussions was not the A.R.E. as an association, but rather the messages being communicated through Cayce. The questions put to the Source were formed from whatever was on the minds of those in attendance, which was perhaps why the subjects ranged from the proper care and education of children, to hidden chambers in the great pyramid at Giza.

Not long after the annual congress had ended, and with the modest infusion of money that came as a result, Gladys and the Cayces focused on making their new home a suitable place to carry on the work. In July and August the old paint was scraped off the house, doors and windows were repaired, and two decades of old growth was cut back. In the process, they continued to receive other signs that the "unseen forces" had a special undertaking in mind if only Edgar and the others had the courage and presence of mind to put the past behind them and move in a new direction.

Although Morton and Edwin Blumenthal might have believed that the Archangel Michael's visits had been specifically for them, Michael would return three times in readings that year to offer advice, counsel, and encouragement. In previous appearances, the Archangel had admonished Morton to be mindful of the importance of his task in building the Cayce Hospital, and later, he had addressed A. C. Preston, Hugh Lynn, and others to protect Edgar. Now, as the period described by the Source as the "ministry" began, Michael appeared again, beckoning the Cayces to move onward and rebuking them for lost time and thinking only of themselves. Michael would appear again.

Michael's first visit to Edgar's prayer and study group came in September of 1932, when they had just completed their first of seven lessons for that session. The title of the new lesson, "The Open Door," was aimed at preparing those seeking guidance from above to open their hearts and minds to the Lord so that they could become more adept channels for the divine work they were undertaking. Edgar, in trance, elaborated on the "open door" as being the entrance point of the holy spirit, as it sought expression through human life.

At the end of the brief discourse, the Archangel Michael introduced himself. "BE STILL MY CHILDREN!" the voice coming through boldly stated. "Bow thine heads, that the 'Lord of the Way' may make known unto you that you have been chosen for a service in this period when there is the need of that spirit being made manifest in the earth . . . [You who have] named the name make known thy daily walks of life, in the little acts of the lessons that have been builded in thine own experience, through those associations of self in meditation and prayer, that His way may be known among them: for He calls on all whosoever will may come . . . For today, will ye harken, the way is open. I, MICHAEL, CALL ON THEE!"

Two weeks later, when the group reassembled for their next reading,

Michael made another appearance. This time the voice came through so powerfully that many in the room were moved to tears, Gladys most of all. "BOW THINE HEADS, OH YE SONS OF MEN, WOULD YE KNOW THE WAY: FOR I, MICHAEL, [am] THE LORD OF THE WAY. WOULD THEE THAT THOU STANDEST NOT IN THE WAY OF THY BROTHER NOR ... [sit] IN THE SEATS OF THE SCORNFUL, BUT RATHER MAKE KNOWN THAT LOVE, THE GLORY, THAT POWER IN HIS NAME, THAT NONE BE AFRAID."

If the weekly study group meetings were not already thought provoking, it is hard to imagine that anyone in the group would miss the next session, where, as expected, Michael again made an appearance. According to Gladys, the presence of the Archangel brought tears, silence, and "beautiful attunement."

Michael, as he had done in the past began with: "HARK, OH YE CHILDREN OF MEN! BOW THINE HEADS, YE SONS OF MEN: FOR THE GLORY OF THE LORD IS THINE, WILL YE BE FAITHFUL TO THE TRUST THAT IS PUT IN EACH OF YOU! KNOW IN WHOM YE HAVE BELIEVED! KNOW THAT HE IS LORD OF ALL, AND HIS WORD FAILETH NOT TO THEM THAT ARE FAITHFUL DAY BY DAY: FOR I, MICHAEL, WOULD PROTECT THOSE THAT SEEK TO KNOW HIS FACE."

Michael was not the only angel to speak through Cayce. Approximately one year later, on October 15, 1933, a reading was conducted for the study group's fourteenth lesson, "Day and Night," whose title was described by the Source as being the spiritual symbols of good and evil. The subject matter was unusually profound, and the reading was remarkable for its clarity and the ease with which the group was guided toward a greater understanding of the significance of the opening chapter of Genesis. The reading ended with an unexpected message: "Come, my children! Ye no doubt have gained from the comment this day that a new initiate has spoken in or through this channel. Halaliel, that was with those in the beginning who warred with those that separated themselves and became as naught!"

The lesson presented in the reading was apparently so challenging that the study group didn't think to address the question of who or what Halaliel was for another three months, which they did during a reading on the subject of "Creation." Halaliel was, according to the Source, "one in and with whose courts Ariel fought when there was the rebellion in heaven." The reading went on to say that Halaliel's enemy, Ariel, was a companion to Lucifer, and "one that made for the disputing of the influences in the experience of Adam in the Garden."

Just as the Archangel Michael had led the study group through the complex issues in the "The Open Door," Halaliel—one of the heavenly combatants pitted against the forces of darkness—appeared to be the ideal entity for "Night and Day." And, like Archangel Michael, Halaliel increasingly became a presence in the readings and an influence on those who obtained them. For Edgar, the appearance of the angels coincided with a dramatic increase in the number of visions he had both in waking and trance states. It was as if the "unseen forces" were not only taking Edgar Cayce and the A.R.E. in a new direction, but Edgar was personally being granted powers and insights to help him lead them.

An indication of Cayce's visionary powers came on November 15, 1932, a little more than a month after Michael's last appearance, while Edgar was teaching his usual Sunday school class at the Presbyterian Church in Virginia Beach. Apart from the fact that only a few members of his class were in attendance, there didn't appear to be anything special about that morning. And yet, as he began his lesson that day—a biblical discussion of the admonition of Joshua—a strange phenomenon occurred. According to Edgar, the empty seats in the church began to fill with ghosts. Edgar's father, Leslie, who was attending the class that morning, couldn't see what Edgar saw, but from the look of astonishment on his son's face he knew that something unusual was taking place. After the class, Edgar explained to Leslie what he had seen: "I saw the entire section of the church fill with those disincarnate entities, people of many faiths . . . as was signified by their dress. Many I knew. Many I did not."

Edgar would have another curious experience of conscious clairvoyance on October 22, 1933, when Byron Wyrick, Edgar's close friend and associate, appeared before Edgar while he was sitting in his living room on Arctic Circle listening to his favorite gospel radio show. "I realized my friend was sitting there with me listening to the music," Edgar later said. "He turned to me and said, 'Cayce, there is the survival of the personality . . . but [the life of prayer] is the only life to live.' " What made this incident extraordinary was that Wyrick had been injured in an accident and died on April 28, 1933, six months before Edgar's vision.

Edgar was also now beginning to remember at least some of what went on when he gave readings. For instance, as he was giving a life reading for a fifty-one-year-old chiropractor on November 14, he could feel his spiritual body separate from his physical body and follow a stream of light to a building where the records of an individual's life were contained in large books. Edgar described what he had seen in a lecture he gave a month later in Norfolk.

"I see myself as a tiny dot out of my physical body, which lies inert before me," Cayce said, describing the experience. "I find myself oppressed by darkness and there is a feeling of terrific loneliness . . . I am conscious of a white beam of light. As this tiny dot, I move upward following the light, knowing that I must follow it or be lost. As I move along this path of light I gradually become conscious of various levels upon which there is movement. Upon the first level there are vague, horrible shapes, grotesque forms such as one sees in nightmares. Passing on, there begin to appear on either side misshapen forms of human beings with some part of the body magnified . . . I become conscious of gray-hooded forms moving downward. Gradually, these become lighter in color. Then the direction changes and these forms move upward and the color of the robes grows rapidly lighter. Next, there begin to appear on either side vague outlines of houses, walls, trees . . . As I pass on, there is more light and movement in what appear to be . . . cities and towns . . . I become conscious of . . . music, laughter, and singing . . . The houses are left behind, ahead there is only a blending of sound and color. Quite suddenly I come upon a hall of records. It is a hall without walls, without ceiling, but I am conscious of seeing an old man who hands me a large book, a record of the individual for whom I seek information."

Edgar's memories of such out-of-body experiences were not always the same, but nearly all of them involved the light, which he followed, and the house with the books. A trance interpretation of this vision suggested that Cayce's soul was passing from one realm to another to seek sources of information. Every image he saw conveyed to him something he could relate to from the material realm. Edgar saw books simply because that was his frame of reference. "To a mind that thinks books, literally books," the Source said, "[just as heaven] would require Elysian fields with birds, with flowers."

In April of the following year, Edgar obtained one further insight regarding his astral travels, this time during a reading for Dave Kahn. Upon waking, Edgar reported that he had been conscious of his physical self separating from his soul self and that he had the impression of his "physical self being encased in a box, like an alabaster or moonstone box, from a material I could not describe." He went on to say that "it seemed that the material manifestation of my physical and mental self was in the box. I gave the box to someone and felt, as I gave it, 'This is one [conducting the reading] that I can trust.' " Edgar described the box as being similar to what he imagined the Ark of the Covenant to be: a kind of temple that housed a sacred possession. This reading reaffirmed the importance of the conductor—not only to aid Cayce in his journey, but to protect what he would leave behind.

Given the unusual psychic phenomena Edgar was experiencing, it was no surprise that he should receive a return visit from the East Indian who had mysteriously shown up years earlier, when he, Ketchum, and Noe were signing their partnership papers back in Bowling Green. The East Indian appeared to him on October 28, 1933, while Edgar was visiting with the Zentgraf family at their elegant and palatial town house on Staten Island, in New York.

By this time, the Zentgraf's New York home was becoming much like The Hill had once been to him and Gertrude in Kentucky. It was the Cayces' home away from home, a place where Edgar could experiment and be assured of a friendly and safe environment. Edgar was especially impressed with Helene, who cared as much for her family's diet as their spiritual environment. He would later pay her a great compliment: "A wonderful thing it would be if all mothers contributed as much as you do toward the proper balancing of food to make strong minds and bodies! . . . If I had to choose one woman out of the world to pattern my life after, it would be you."

Edgar was standing alone in the library of the luxurious Zentgraf town house when the East Indian appeared to him in a vision. Hugh Lynn, Gladys, and others in the house never physically saw him, but they knew something unusual had occurred because Edgar was strangely silent, and without explanation, asked that his New York appointments be canceled. Edgar never revealed exactly what the turbaned man had told him, only that it was a warning he later heeded. This clearly had something to do with his health, for toward the end of his visit, Edgar was forced into bed by a terrible fever, stemming from a cold that had been plaguing him for three weeks. Ernest and Helene were so concerned that they called in a doctor, who diagnosed Edgar as having pneumonia and ordered that he be taken to a hospital immediately. An ambulance was called, and Hugh Lynn was sent upstairs to prepare Edgar for the trip. Edgar, however, refused to go. It seemed to Hugh Lynn that his father knew that if he were to visit the hospital, he might never return home.

As Hugh Lynn later told the story, Edgar seemed to have made up his mind to deal with this crisis privately, and he believed he would have spiritual help in doing so. He asked Hugh Lynn to lock the door and not let anyone in the room until he awoke. Hugh Lynn did as he was told. He watched as his father put himself into a trance. "It was just like he was giving a reading, except that he did it himself," Hugh Lynn said. "Almost immediately he began to perspire. It saturated the sheets and ran off the bed onto the floor in puddles." Before Edgar could come out of his trance, the ambulance had arrived and the doctor was knocking on the bedroom door. Hugh Lynn told him through the door that his father was asleep and was not to be disturbed.

The doctor pounded on the door. The Zentgrafs came upstairs and demanded that they be allowed in. Hugh Lynn refused to open the door. About twenty minutes later, Edgar awoke, dripping with sweat. His temperature had returned to normal and the congestion in his head and lungs had vanished. He got up and went in to shower, while Helene changed the bedding. Meanwhile, her husband attempted to explain to the confused doctor that Edgar had certain powers beyond most people's comprehension. The doctor finally sent the ambulance away. There was no point in taking a healthy man to the hospital.

Not long after Cayce's "rejuvenation," yet another series of visions occurred that further demonstrated Edgar's newfound abilities. This incident involved a young man named Mitchell Hastings, the son of a well-known New York socialite and theosophist. About the same age as Hugh Lynn, Hastings had received a life reading first in November 1933, followed by a physical reading in December for severe back and abdominal ailments related to a serious injury in which he had fractured a number of ribs. These readings not only prescribed treatments but suggested that Mitchell was a deeply talented and spiritual individual who had much to offer the world. At Edgar's invitation, Mitchell had traveled to Virginia Beach after Christmas and spent New Year's Day 1934 with the Cayces.

Mitchell's parents didn't doubt the veracity of their son's readings. At the time of the first physical reading, Cayce knew nothing of the young Hastings's ailments. His diagnosis proved to be accurate in every detail, and a year after the initial reading Mitchell was out playing golf and tennis. His life readings appeared to be just as insightful, for Cayce named him as one of the scientists in Atlantis who had had highly developed psychic powers and had helped to construct and maintain the "firestone" in the Atlantean power plant. Mitchell's parents believed this to be entirely accurate—their son had already been recognized as a genius in the field of electricity, had gained early admission to Harvard University, and, in later years, would become a pioneer in the development of FM Radio, obtaining patents on a number of devices that used crystals and gem stones to alter electrical frequencies. Over the next half century, right up until his death, at age ninety, Mitchell remained an ardent and committed supporter of Edgar Cayce, openly crediting him for the help he received in developing his unique gifts. Left unsaid was the help this young college student had provided Edgar at a critical moment in his life.

As part of the treatments for his back, the readings recommended that Mitchell should spend time in Arizona—to get out in the sun and dry air where he would mentally and physically recuperate. A physical reading

Cayce received for himself around the same time recommended that he also "get out in the sun and dry air." And in March 1934, the two decided to make the trip together. On very short notice, and like a schoolboy taking his first trip away from home, Edgar bid his family and friends good-bye and drove off with Mitchell in the Hastings's Pontiac. Gladys, able to take advantage of Edgar's absence, decided to go home for a visit and traveled with them as far as Selma. After that, Hastings and Cayce disappeared for parts unknown. It was only later that Gertrude and the others learned that they had traveled from Alabama through Texas, New Mexico, and Mexico before stopping at a ranch in Bonita, Arizona.

Edgar rarely spoke of their adventure together, and it was only through Mitchell's extensive correspondence with him during the later years of Cayce's life that anything is known about what happened. A jealous rivalry between Hugh Lynn and Mitchell may have contributed to Edgar's reluctance to speak of their relationship and may also be what made Hastings unwelcome in Hugh Lynn's home once Edgar was gone.

Based on the existing correspondence, it is clear that Hastings and Cayce had only to be in close proximity to share extraordinary visions. Hastings described them as mirages, in which people would ride toward them on horseback or strangers would approach them to impart a curious bit of information or advice. Perhaps the most astonishing and revealing of these visions was one they had in a field in New Mexico.

An apparition of Edgar's dead mother appeared and spoke to Edgar about the future. She urged him not to give up hope and not to worry about his precarious financial situation nor doubt the power and veracity of the information coming through him. In previous visionary experiences, Edgar had only seen or heard spirit visitors. But here in New Mexico, perhaps aided by Hastings's own power of mind, Edgar reportedly received a more physical manifestation of the visit. His mother handed him a silver dollar, and when she had faded from sight, the coin remained in the palm of his hand.

45.

❁

Beloved Teacher

B ack in 1931, shortly after the closing of the Cayce Hospital, Gladys Davis had had a prophetic dream in which all the people connected to the work were gathered in an upper room on the top floor of a building. "All sat and stood around waiting for an explosion, which we knew must come," Gladys remembered. "All understood that the building would crash, but none even thought of running away or getting outside [because] we had faith in some higher power . . . It seemed, too, that the explosion would open up a treasure buried beneath the building that we had heretofore not been able to locate, and those who survived the shock and remained faithful would receive the treasure."

That treasure, many people came to believe, was delivered through Edgar Cayce, starting with a trance session held on January 19, 1934, when the Source delivered an hour-long discourse on world affairs in what was arguably the most controversial reading of Edgar Cayce's career. Perhaps sensing that the reading they were about to receive would be important, Mitchell Hastings recorded it on an Edison phonographic cylinder.

Interestingly, this reading was not conducted on behalf of an individual, but, like those being given for the Norfolk Study Group, was given at the request of a small circle of New York friends and family members who had known, studied, and worked together for a number of years, and were, at that time, seeking to individually and collectively use their substantial resources to bring "truth" or the "word of God" to their fellow man.

"Each of you gathered here have your own individual development," Cayce said at the beginning of the world-affairs reading. "Yet as each seeks to be a channel of blessings to the fellow man, each attunes self to the 'throne of universal information.' And there may be accorded you that which may be beneficial, not only in thine own experience, but that which will prove helpful, hopeful, in the experience of others."

Although the Source of the information was not initially revealed, Cayce—in trance—prefaced his later remarks by saying that "many are present" desiring to give the information "whose names alone would bring . . . awe . . . even a wonderment." Given these introductory remarks, it came as no surprise that the group would be treated to something quite remarkable. They were, as it turns out, allegedly being given a picture of potential world events, the second coming of Christ, and the day of reckoning for planet Earth. Cayce's readings prophesied nothing less than Armageddon.

The Source announced that a new age of spiritual awakening would begin when the Prophet John, "beloved of all men in all places where the universality of God in the earth has been proclaimed," would return to the earth to become a channel "through which spiritual, mental, and material things [would] become one in the purpose and desires of that physical body," and usher in the "Day of the Lord." Left unsaid, but ever present in this discourse, was the suggestion that Edgar Cayce himself had been sent as a messenger, a "forerunner" or bearer of a Divine message calling for the brotherhood of man.

In trance, Cayce told the assembled group to look for material changes that would be "as an omen," or "a sign." He went on to describe this in detail: "The earth will be broken up in the western portion of America. The greater portion of Japan must go into the sea. The upper portion of Europe will be changed as in the twinkling of an eye. Land will appear off the east coast of America. There will be the upheavals in the Arctic and in the Antarctic that will make for the eruption of volcanoes in the Torrid areas, and there will be shifting then of the poles . . . As to times, as to seasons, as to places, alone is it given to those who have named the name—and who bear the mark of those of His calling and His election in their bodies. To them it shall be given."

The spiritual and physical changes, Cayce said, would touch everyone: "Those in lowly places [shall be] raised to those of power in the . . . ma-

chinery of nations . . . so shall ye see those in high places reduced and calling on the waters of darkness to cover them. [Through] those that in the inmost recesses of themselves awaken to the spiritual truths that are to be
given, and those . . . that have acted in the capacity of teachers among men,
the rottenness of those that have ministered in places will be brought to
light, and turmoils and strifes shall enter . . . Armageddon is at hand."

It was at this point in the reading that the Source referred to itself as "I,"
not the "we" that Gladys and the Cayces invariably had come to expect: "I
have declared this! That has been delivered unto me to give unto you, ye that
sit here and that hear and that see a light breaking in the east, and have
heard, have seen thine weaknesses and thine fault-findings, and know that
He will make thy paths straight if ye will but live that ye know this day . . .
Love the Lord thy God with all thine heart . . . Love thy neighbor as thyself."

The speaker then revealed "his" identity: "The weakling, the unsteady,
must enter into the crucible and become as naught, even as He, that they
may know the way. I, Halaliel, have spoken."

Finally, Halaliel suggested the mechanism that might trigger catastrophic
events and bring "material suffering" on a "troubled people." Halaliel said:
"The young king will soon reign!" The nation that would produce the "young
king" was identified along with his name. The country was "Germany."
The king was "Hitler."

Much has been said and written about the prophecies offered in this
reading, and about how many of these events actually came to pass. The shat-
tering earth changes would not manifest themselves. And yet the reading
was entirely accurate regarding Hitler's reign. Despite the major attention
that has been paid this and Cayce's other prophetic readings, an important
point has often been lost: the events foretold were ones that could *potentially*
occur given the state of world affairs in January of 1934, when the reading
was given. In trance, as in a waking state, Cayce repeatedly said that even the
"Lord of Lords" could not accurately predict future events because man's
will altered and defined the future.

As Cayce said in another reading less than a year later, "It is not the
world, the earth, the environs about it nor the planetary influences nor the
associations or activities that rule man. Rather does man—by his compliance
with Divine Law—bring order out of the chaos, by his disregard of the associations and laws of divine influence, bring those . . . destructive forces into
his experiences."

This idea was perhaps best illustrated in the same reading in which Hitler
was named king. Cayce was asked whether or not Franklin Roosevelt would
live out his term in office. In response, the Source said: "The greater period

for destructive forces to enter in . . . has passed. It will come again not in this year, but when there are changes in the next session. As to what will be the final outcome, [it] depends—as ever—upon what is done about that period . . . Make known that [Franklin Roosevelt's] ways are worthy of being considered, and pray ye with [Roosevelt] that if it be His will his hour [of danger] will pass. If he falters, then he must be removed."

Here, as with the reference to Hitler, Cayce was both astonishingly prophetic, and at the same time mindful of how the will of man—in this case Franklin Roosevelt's will—would determine his own fate. The reference to the "greater period for destructive forces" could be construed to mean Roosevelt's bout with polio. The reference to the "final outcome" suggests the challenges he would face in his second term or "session" in office during the months leading up to war. And his inability to meet those challenges suggested both the final outcome for him personally and the Divine forces at work during the international conflagration. Roosevelt was "removed" when he died in office in April 1945. Cayce—in trance—would say much the same for Hitler. Had the "young king" been permitted to realize his dream of world domination, perhaps the catastrophes specified in 1934 might have come about.

Gladys herself was quite moved by this and other prophetic readings, but like Gertrude, and eventually Edgar himself, she came to believe that the real "treasure" foretold in her own prophetic dream, was not the "world affairs" readings, or any of Cayce's prophecies. The real "treasure," to her mind, were the lessons still being delivered to the Norfolk Study Group each week, and which were now being circulated among other study groups forming in New York, Chicago, Detroit, and Miami. The members of the original Norfolk group had begun their journey by reading books about the great religions of the world. Now they were on a spiritual journey, guided by Cayce in trance, and under the direction, they believed, of the "Master of Masters," to create something that would go well beyond the confines of the small beach community from which they came. Gladys believed that this group was what the Source referred to as their "ministry," and represented Edgar Cayce's greatest and ultimately least recognized contribution as a Divine messenger. To her mind, Cayce's clairvoyant powers and the thousands of medical readings he had given were a means of getting people to pay attention to the message of love and the brotherhood of man that he was delivering to the study group, just as Jesus' miraculous "healings" had established His credibility as the Son of God.

Esther Wynne, an English teacher, was appointed by the group to be the official compiler of Cayce's lessons, which she did between meetings to permit Cayce, in trance, to comment on them in the next session. The transcripts, when complete, would then be forwarded on to the other study groups.

As Wynne later described the process, the most serious challenge the group faced was at the beginning, during their sessions on cooperation. The members were repeatedly told that they were not, in fact, applying the lessons they had been given, and that no further instruction would be given until they did. The root of the problem was bickering and friction about what each individual's respective roles would be within the group and jealousy between the larger study group and the smaller prayer group. Eight meetings were held before the group could move on to the next lesson, and in the process, two of the original members dropped out while others arrived to take their places. At one point they had as many as fifteen members. Eventually their membership would settle at a consistent twelve, which was, as Edgar noted, the same number as Jesus' disciples.

One member who added a great deal to the cohesion of the group was Ruth LeNoir. Ruth had attended some of their first sessions, but had been unable to continue until the group was in its fourth lesson, entitled "Faith." Her contribution, it appears, was to help the group to accept the concept of reincarnation, which to some members was the most radical doctrine being presented. During one meeting on the subject, when little progress was being made, Edgar demonstrated another example of his waking clairvoyance. He addressed each member of the group individually, revealing their innermost thoughts and true feelings on the subject being discussed—which they, out of courtesy, fear of embarrassment, or other reasons, had been reluctant to express in front of the others. As Edgar would later confide to a trusted friend, he had had the ability—in a waking state—to read a person's mind when he was a child back in Beverly, Kentucky. And only now, since the demise of the hospital, had that power again begun to manifest itself on a daily basis.

As Gladys, a full-fledged member of the group, undertook the daily regimen of prayer and meditation, she began to have visions and vivid dreams herself. One of her dreams indicated that her role in the new work was considerable—an especially important thing for the other members to know, for although it might be easy to downplay Gladys's role as a stenographer, Edgar and those closest to him were aware that no one before her had been able to do the job. Without someone able to record Edgar's messages properly, no "ministry" would even be possible. Edgar and Gertrude also knew that Gladys faced many personal challenges, not the least of which was the fact that Gladys's mother—a devout Seventh Day Adventist—disapproved of her daughter's participation in the study group, admonishing Gladys to seek the truth where she would most certainly find it: in church.

When the earliest readings on cooperation were being conducted, Gladys had a dream in which she arrived in New York harbor on a ship and saw the Statue of Liberty. A subsequent reading explained the significance of the dream to her: "That, as the statue stands for a spirit as is supposed to emanate from a nation, so do the activities of . . . [Gladys Davis] in recording that [which] . . . will be the formulative spirit in the minds, hearts, and souls of . . . the many thousands that may be reached."

By the middle of 1933, when the group had reached its twelfth lesson, several members were experiencing a deep spiritual crisis, none more acutely than Florence Edmonds. Florence had become haunted by unseen spirits in her dreams and in her waking life. She felt an unearthly presence in her home. Doors would creak open. Unusual sounds and noises could be heard throughout the house. She had become frightened, believing that the study group had gone too far in its research. Edgar was called to her home on June 25, 1933, to discuss the issue and conduct a reading to see what could be done. The Source suggested that Florence had been gifted with psychic powers, which by virtue of participation in the study group, were becoming more developed. The crisis eventually passed, and the "unseen forces" allegedly at work in the Edmonds home vanished. Florence became an even stronger presence in the group, and like two other members, became a healer, whose seemingly miraculous cures—through the laying on of hands—brought many people into her home.

Minnie Barrett, one of the group's original members, also experienced a spiritual crisis that manifested itself in "vibrations" she heard before going to sleep at night, including the sound of a bell ringing. The readings indicated that this was a sign to her that the door to her soul was opening, she had only to heed its call and step through. "As ye open the door, I will enter," the Source said. "Be not afraid."

The most serious crisis in the group occurred in the late summer of 1934, during a lesson entitled "Desire," at which time Edgar and the group as a whole were in a turmoil. Progress had reached a standstill. In trance, the Source seemed exasperated, repeatedly answering a question by saying: "As has been given . . . apply it." Out of frustration, more members left the group. Edgar himself admitted that the readings didn't seem to be taking them where they wanted to go. He confessed that he had to almost force himself to give more readings and considered calling an end to the study group activities.

Then, on September 9, 1934, Edgar announced that he felt good about the reading he was about to give. He didn't explain what caused the change in his attitude, only that he felt confident that the upcoming session would be productive. The reason, as later became apparent, was that Halaliel had appeared to Edgar in a dream the night before.

"That part thou hast chosen in such a work is born of truth," Cayce—in trance—told the group. "Let it come in and be a part of thy daily life. Look in upon the experiences, for, as will be seen, my children, there has been appointed one that may aid thee in thy future lessons, and he will be thy teacher, thy guide, [Halaliel] one sent through the power of thine own desires."

Halaliel appeared again in two subsequent readings, and it became clear that this spirit, or "Lord of Karma" as he was becoming known among Cayce's disciples, was offering his services to the group as its spiritual guide. Not only this, but the group was expected to decide if they wanted him to continue in that capacity. Halaliel literally put them on the spot, asking them if they could accept such a challenge. "Think ye well, then . . . and choose."

The problems of having such a spiritual guide were many, for no one knew exactly who Halaliel was, what his intentions were, or why his interventions in the study group readings, like those conducted on the world affairs, appeared to be increasing. Until that time, Edgar, like the others in the group, assumed they were being led by Christ, the "Master of Masters." To accept another spirit as guide, was similar, in a way, to accepting a teaching assistant in place of the professor. At the same time, however, it seemed clear to everyone in the group that the Master of Masters had directed Halaliel to come, and they were reluctant to send him back.

In retrospect, it seemed that the study group was being tested, and that Halaliel was being given free rein to exact a price for noncompliance with Divine Law. The readings appeared to be saying that the "Master of Masters" was not altogether pleased with their progress in 1934 and was telling them that if they didn't act on the lessons being given through Christ, the alternative was to learn from Halaliel, an intermediary who would address them in his own manner. The price for "understanding," as Halaliel said in a later reading, would be "heavy."

After weeks of discussion, the group voted to reject Halaliel's guidance. According to Gladys, the group's collective decision to put Christ first made all the difference. Their lessons began to progress smoothly. In a later session entitled "Knowledge," they were addressed by no less than the guiding spirit of John, "the Beloved," who, according to the readings would be the next true forerunner on the earth. "Not instead of thy Master, the Christ," the reading stated, "but as the beloved of Him in the earth, that ye may be one in mind, in purpose, that the day of the Lord may draw nigh."

Ruth LeNoir and the Edmonds became convinced that Edgar was ushering in a "new age of spiritual enlightenment" and "Christ consciousness." Gladys concurred, believing that Cayce was "preparing the way" for a future generation that would accept God's teachings. "It was as if all the previous readings were leading Edgar to this point in time," another A.R.E. member said. "The medical readings called attention to the fact that there were forces at play in the universe beyond our comprehension. Now that he had an audience that was prepared to listen, Edgar Cayce was delivering the real message of the work: that through Christ or Christ consciousness there was purpose and meaning in their lives."

In correspondence and in person, Edgar was now being frequently addressed not just as the Judge, or as Dr. Cayce, as others had come to call him, but as "teacher," or "beloved teacher." His letters to his patients and friends had always been thoughtful and considerate, much like one might expect from a country minister to a member of his congregation. Now they would begin to take on the poetry and spirit of the readings themselves—sometimes making it difficult to tell where the sleeping man left off and the waking man took over. In a letter to a patient of Dr. Henry Harding, in New York, Edgar wrote: "Many here are passing through a test period . . . Most are holding to the true light, that comes down to man from God, and all is well—For He is in His Holy Temple—our minds—and all is well. Just hold to something like this though in your own words: Father—God—let there be done in and through me that which will bring our brother to the awareness of the God within."

Just as Edgar Cayce was helping the study group to remain focused, he and the Source provided a similar message in a series of readings for the Zentgraf family, who underwent a crisis that threatened to tear them apart. The trouble began on April 18, 1934 when Ernest Zentgraf disappeared from home, taking with him a pistol. The next day, Helene, his wife, received a suicide letter, the result, she believed, of a depression stemming from Ernest's belief that he was a failure as a businessman, husband, and father. As was later revealed by other family members, Ernest had been the trustee for a $2 million inheritance, most of which he had lost in the stock market and other bad investments. Just before his disappearance, his sister, Marie, a beneficiary of the trust, had severely criticized Ernest for his handling of the family accounts. Ernest had last been seen at a small coffee shop in Reading, Pennsylvania.

Edgar knew something of the financial plight of his friends because the last reading he had given Helene was to help her find a job to support the family. Now she called him for help in saving her husband, if indeed he was still alive. It was clear in the first reading, however, that no one, not even Edgar, could interfere in what he described as a matter of Ernest's "free will." Edgar explained this in a letter he wrote Helene after the first reading: "The readings are given wholly from the mental and spiritual angle, as we have been told not to use these channels for forcing a person against his will to return—or to override another's desire . . . Even in a case like this where the man means so much to us, we are helpless. A man's will is supreme."

Edgar came up with an alternative plan that they believed would not interfere with Ernest's free will, but rather strengthen and support his own self-determination in a time of obvious need. They would sit together, as Edgar was doing for the Glad Helpers in Norfolk, and open a psychic channel through which they could receive advice and through which they could send their prayers—in this case to Ernest. Thus began what became the first of thirty-three readings that were conducted between April 19 and June 11, 1934.

All of the readings began and ended with prayers, sometimes lasting a minute or two, and at other times, up to half an hour. No two prayers were the same, yet each sought to communicate God's love and deep affection for Ernest. On May 8, Cayce, in trance, said: "Keep that thou hast had delivered unto thee, in making thy will one with His will. Though the shadows of doubt and fear assail thee, in Him is strength and light . . . Be not afraid." Six days later, Cayce said: "No soul, save one that has separated itself from the love of the Father, wanders alone."

During the third reading conducted on behalf of the Zentgrafs, the family received a hopeful sign: Ernest, they were told, was still among the living, though suicide still haunted his thoughts. In that same reading, the Source counseled against an individual taking one's life. "To desecrate the body that is the temple of the living God is to belittle self . . . To destroy same is to be weak and unworthy of those privileges that have been thine in thy relations in the earth . . . Put thy burden on Him, and He will sustain and guide and guard thee."

Two readings later, Cayce, in an undertone, muttered the word "Philadelphia," as if to suggest that this was where Ernest was at that moment. The next reading gave another tantalizing piece of information: "His cough is bad." In a reading a few days later, Cayce remembered—as if in a dream— seeing woods and water. On April 26, the message came through clearly that Ernest would return home. There were no specifics, only that he would return, and that Helene should continue her prayers. On April 28, Cayce said that Ernest had written a letter to his family, as indeed, they soon discovered, he had.

On May 14, Cayce—in trance—said that Ernest was "surrounded by green," suggesting he was outdoors, maybe in a forest. [Later it was revealed he had been standing in a cemetery.] Two days after this reading, Edgar awoke from another trance and reported that he had seen the Christ. In his vision he had seen Jesus walking toward the assembled group praying for Ernest's well-being. Jesus was smiling, apparently pleased by their activities. This session was followed on June 2 by a dream that Gladys had in which Ernest was sitting with the Cayces and his own family. The readings from this point on were far more upbeat in tone, suggesting that Ernest had come "into the light." At the end of the last reading, on June 11, a special message came through: "How beautiful the face of those whom the Lord, the Christ, smiles upon!"

Ernest Zentgraf returned home from Philadelphia a few days later, bringing great joy to his wife and family. In a letter he wrote to family members he chronicled some of his trials and tribulations, and his eventual turning to Christ for help in his time of need. Helene referred to the letter as a "holy thing," for it showed to her "the birth of a soul." The letter read, in part: "Five months ago my affairs seemed so hopeless, the tangle so muddled, that I could not see my way out . . . I made such a mess of my own affairs . . . I had been living in a 'Fool's Paradise' and needed this shock to cleanse my soul. I have confessed my errors to God and I know He has forgiven me, for wonders have happened."

The trance sessions had also touched Helene. As she later wrote Edgar: "I have through this experience learned much: the necessity of living every hour of life as clearly as possible. I am surer of God as Presence and Power than ever in my life. The Divine Law must be manifested through us, and this now is my work."

The Messenger

As much as the emergence of Michael and Halaliel as spiritual guides appeared to increase Edgar's powers of waking clairvoyance, the study group didn't prevent him from continuing the health readings. In fact, from the time he had started giving them, in 1901, up until the day he died, Cayce never stopped giving trance advice to people in medical need. Among the most famous recipients of Cayce's health readings were the film producer Jessie Lasky, one of the founders of Paramount Studios, and the composer George Gershwin, who requested readings in 1932. But like so many others who received readings, neither Gershwin's or Lasky's doctors acted on the treatments recommended—despite the fact, in Lasky's case, that Cayce's diagnosis of heart disease was deemed "perfect" by his physicians. In Gershwin's case, physicians didn't consider Cayce's dietary treatments as being relevant to the "mental depression" for which he sought relief. Gershwin died five years later from a brain tumor, and Lasky later dropped dead from a heart attack.

The reason the treatments were not implemented had nothing to do with the bad press surrounding the failure of the Cayce Hospital or Edgar's arrest in New York, but with rather a general lack of faith in the holistic type of medicine suggested by the readings. The discovery of penicillin in 1928 had already set into motion a popular abandonment of natural approaches to medicine. And by 1935 the media were portraying physicians as "scientists" who would eventually provide cures for whatever ailments and disease plagued the human race in a simple pill. The innovations the Cayce readings represented in diet, preventative therapeutics, and holistic health practices were increasingly viewed by the medical community as antiquated, or worse still, a dangerous alternative to "modern medicine."

There were many doctors, of course, who were unable to conform to the more fashionable dictates of their colleagues. Like Dr. Thomas House before him, Dr. Lydic had been touched by the readings in ways that made it impossible for him to turn his back on the methods pioneered in the hospital in Virginia Beach. Another convert to Cayce's view of medicine was Dr. Harold J. Reilly, a physiotherapist who would, more than any single physician in the two decades after the hospital's closure, popularize the value of the medical readings. Using trance advice and his own considerable charm and medical expertise, Reilly was able to relocate his practice from a small gym in the Bronx to a suite of rooms at Rockefeller Center, where his clients would come to include a number of famous business and professional people in New York and Hollywood.

A tall, husky man, Reilly specialized in all forms of drugless therapy, using techniques he had learned at the American School of Naturopathy, the American School of Chiropractics, and during a brief tenure in the U.S. Army, where he taught athletics and jujitsu. His unique medical knowledge and emphasis on physical fitness had been everywhere evident in his small gym, which offered a complete line of exercise equipment as well as many types of hydrotherapy, electrotherapy, and other forms of manipulative "therapeutics."

Reilly had been doing a brisk business in 1930 when one of his patients handed him what he considered to be a curious document. It contained a psychic diagnosis and recommended hydrotherapy and osteopathic manipulation. The source of the diagnosis, the Cayce Hospital of Research and Enlightenment, in Virginia Beach, had no meaning for him at the time. Having received instructions from equally unorthodox sources, including astrologers and spiritualists, he didn't give the matter much thought. Reilly provided the indicated treatment and was pleased by the results. He would not begin to take notice of the name Edgar Cayce until dozens of other readings, many of which specifically recommended Reilly to provide the treatment, made their way to his desk.

"The directions and the results were most remarkable," Reilly later noted. "I [just] could not understand how a man could go to sleep and give as good, or better advice, than I was able to give in my waking state and in my own special field, so I decided to get acquainted with this . . . magician."

Reilly's first meeting with Edgar took place in early 1931 when Edgar made a trip to New York in connection with the Blumenthals' closing of the hospital. Cayce visited Reilly in his gym and afterward had lunch with him. Reilly had envisioned meeting a man of commanding appearance, with piercing eyes and majestic gestures, perhaps even wearing a turban, but the man who introduced himself reminded Reilly more of a minister from a quiet country church.

Reilly became even more puzzled when Edgar ordered his lunch. To his surprise, his visitor from Virginia Beach asked for a meal heavy in fried fats and topped it off with a rich dessert and coffee. When the meal ended and conversation ensued, he proceeded to smoke one cigarette after another. Cayce, it seemed, paid no attention to the rules of diet and health put forth in the readings that Reilly had been studying for the past several months. Asked how this could be, Edgar explained that in his everyday life he had no special knowledge of diet or any other health measures. A strong believer in healthy eating, Reilly urged Edgar to begin taking his own advice and would later help him to lay out a strict regimen of diet and exercise, which, unfortunately, Edgar ignored.

His curiosity piqued by their first meeting, Reilly decided to look deeper into the Cayce phenomenon. He visited the hospital at Virginia Beach, attended lectures, and ultimately became a knowledgeable scholar of the readings. He also received his own trance advice. And unlike Edgar Cayce, Reilly did *everything* that was suggested. Later in 1931 he would move his operation to Sixty-third Street and Broadway, where he opened the Physicians Physiotherapy Service, which handled many of the patients who were subsequently shut out of the Cayce Hospital. In 1935, he relocated to Rockefeller Center, where he opened the Reilly Health Institute.

Another New York physician, Dr. Frank Dobbins, became involved with Cayce in much the same way. In October of 1932, Dobbins, an osteopath, had recently moved his practice from Maine to Staten Island. One day, Helene Zentgraf arrived at his office and handed him a copy of one of Cayce's readings, expecting Dobbins to treat her daughter, Margaret, based on what it said. Dobbins had obvious misgivings, but having just arrived in the city and having very few patients, said that he would take the reading under consideration after first examining the patient himself. Before studying the reading, he gave Margaret a complete examination. Later that night, he studied the reading and to his shock and surprise, Edgar's diagnosis tallied exactly with his own. When he got to the end of the reading, his shock turned into incredulity. Dobbins nearly fell out of his chair when he came to the part where Cayce, in trance, was asked where Margaret should go for treatments: "Find Dobbins!" Had the reading been given later, once Dobbins was more established, he might not have been quite so astonished. But at the time of the reading his name was not even listed in the phone book. Helene had had to ask all over New York to find him.

Dobbins would become a devoted fan of Cayce and reportedly used the readings to diagnose 95 percent of his cases. And, like Reilly, and another prominent New York physician, Dr. Henry Hardwicke, Dobbins would work hard to study and codify particular aspects of the health advice put forth in the readings. As part of their practices, Reilly, Dobbins, and Hardwicke took a particular interest in readings referring to nutrition and its relationship to the freshness of food and how it is prepared. They also studied references to the negative effects of smoking cigarettes and inhaling automobile and other toxic fumes, and even addressed subjects that were increasingly taboo, such as the chemical imbalance that resulted from taking antibiotics. Reilly in particular viewed all of these factors as "dangerous traps" that conspired to make it more difficult to stay healthy and avoid disease. "It is an old cliché to say that Americans take better care of their cars than they do their bodies," he told patients. "But it is none the less true. Less wax on the car and more peanut oil on the body should be the rule in households for a stronger, healthier country."

Reilly and his associates put their message across in numerous lectures in the New York and New Jersey areas. The most notable of these lectures was entitled "Three Physicians and a Psychic," delivered at the McAlpin Hotel in New York, which both Edgar and Hugh Lynn attended. In the course of the lecture, Dobbins told the story of a former New York postal employee who had been sent to an upstate mental institution, where doctors had diagnosed him as suffering from a stress-related mental illness. According to the patient's cousin, who had approached Cayce for a reading, the man had "gone crazy" after work one day, beaten up his wife, and nearly killed his child. At the time the reading was requested, the patient was being held in a padded cell and where the doctors could not safely examine him unless he was wearing a straightjacket. The subsequent reading said that the root of the patient's problem was an accident in which the patient had slipped on a patch of ice in front of the post office and injured his spine. Dobbins administered the osteopathic treatments recommended in the reading and after fourteen sessions, the patient recovered completely. To all the listeners this was an eye-opening story, as it illustrated how instances of apparent mental illness could have physical causes.

As Dr. Dobbins told the story, he had no idea that an unexpected guest was there in the room—his former patient, Thomas Scanlon, was sitting in the audience. To everyone's great surprise, Scanlon, described as a giant of a man, stood up at the back of the room and announced: "I am that man, and everything that the doctor said was true!" Scanlon had never met Edgar Cayce in person and now stepped up to the podium to shake his hand. Edgar had to fight back tears.

During the course of the lecture, a woman had come into the hall just to get out of the rain. Knowing nothing about the purpose of the meeting, she took a seat in the front row and began to listen. When the lecture was over, she ran to the front of the line forming to talk to Edgar. After hearing her story, Cayce took hold of Hugh Lynn's arm and told him to set up an emergency appointment for the next day.

The woman, who had just come from visiting her daughter at a hospital on Ward's Island, described behavior that was similar to Scanlon's. Her daughter, a New York artist, had been acting violently and irrationally ever since she had been the victim of an attack. One night, she had been followed home by a man who had purchased one of her paintings. The man beat her violently, threw her down on the floor, and raped her. Cayce's subsequent reading recounted this incident, and as in the case of Scanlon, said an injury to her spine was causing her seemingly insane behavior. Two days after the McAlpin lecture, Dr. Dobbins visited her in the hospital and gave her the spinal adjustments suggested in the readings. She recovered completely, and in thanks painted a portrait of Edgar that he would proudly hang in his study.

In the course of their relationship with Cayce, Reilly and his associates touched many lives, among them a growing number of celebrities. Patients of the Reilly Health Institute who received readings from Cayce included Mrs. Eddie Rickenbacker, wife of the famous pilot, RCA founder David Sarnoff and his wife, Dorothy, and band leader Vincent Lopez. Other Reilly clients who were treated with Cayce's therapies and who may or may not have been aware of it, included Governor Nelson Rockefeller, the labor leader George Meany, author William Saroyan, composer Irving Berlin, and actors Fred MacMurray, Eddie Albert, George Jessel, and Marilyn Monroe. During his lifetime, Edgar referred more than a thousand patients to Reilly and mentioned him an estimated three-hundred times in trance sessions. Although fewer patients were directed to visit Dobbins and Hardwicke, they too treated hundreds of people sent by the readings.

As Edgar was acutely aware, however, Reilly, Dobbins, and Hardwicke were the exception to the rule. The vast majority of physicians were adamantly opposed to what Edgar was doing, as the family would learn on a trip they took to Detroit to conduct a series of physical readings for new members. In November 1935, the Cayces, accompanied by Gladys, traveled to Detroit and stayed at the home of a wealthy family of A.R.E. supporters. One of the readings was conducted for Betty Ruth Mitshkun, a young girl suffering from asthma. This reading suggested using a technology referred to as a "wet-cell," as well as spinal manipulations to relieve her respiratory trouble. Two days later, on the morning of November 30, 1935, four officers arrived where the Cayces were staying to arrest Edgar, Hugh Lynn, Gertrude, and Gladys on charges of practicing medicine without a license.

As later became clear, Maurice Mitshkun, the father of the child suffering from asthma, didn't understand the reading. Nor did Dr. Hyman Cohen, the doctor treating the patient. According to Hugh Lynn, Dr. Cohen told the father that the reading was "worthless" and without consulting Edgar or giving the reading to one of the many doctors in Detroit familiar with Cayce's methods, promptly filed charges. Police investigators took Gladys's notebook and other pertinent paperwork and brought the four of them to the police station where they were fingerprinted and jailed. As was the custom, the police took all of their clothes and possessions, leaving them with just three dollars for candy and cigarettes.

In contrast to his earlier arrests, Edgar was more bewildered than angry. He could understand how this might have happened to him, but having his family and secretary treated as petty criminals was beyond comprehension. Later he looked on the incident more philosophically, reflecting on the unexpected good he was able to accomplish in the jail cell.

Gladys and Gertrude were taken to the women's section of the jailhouse and each put in a narrow cell furnished with a bunk and toilet. Edgar and Hugh Lynn were trundled off to the men's section, a large confined area in which there were a number of small cubicles, each with a double bunk. As Hugh Lynn would later recount the story, as soon as the two were locked inside, some twenty or twenty-five inmates gathered around them, the leader demanding the three dollars they had been allowed to keep. Hugh Lynn promptly handed it over, after which a very curious thing occurred. The leader of the group asked why Edgar and his son had been arrested. Edgar told them that he had been charged with practicing medicine without a license. The other prisoners wanted to know if this was true, and Edgar said that it indeed was true, but that it wasn't the real reason he had been locked up. "Like all of you, there is back of what you are accused of, the real cause, the real reason for your confinement," Edgar said.

As Hugh Lynn later related the story, Edgar diffused a potentially awk-

ward situation by using his power of clairvoyance in a conscious state, much
as he had earlier helped members of his study group overcome a challenging lesson by revealing their innermost thoughts. Edgar looked at the leader
of his fellow inmates and said, "You are accused of hitting a child with an
automobile. That's why you are here. But the real reason for your confinement is a conflict with your wife that's been going on for a long time. You
were very, very angry after an argument with her. Because of this anger
you got into your car and pulled out quickly without being very observant
and struck a child."

The man reportedly turned white, and several other prisoners who knew
him gasped. He then ordered the men to get Edgar and Hugh Lynn the two
best mattresses and put them in their cubicle. They never did use their beds
since the four of them were released on bail later that evening. Half the bail
was put up by the general manager of the Detroit Buick plant, who just the
week before had received a successful reading for kidney stones. The other
half was from Charles Dillman, who had been the very first patient at the
Cayce Hospital and was now a furniture dealer living in Flint, Michigan.
Each put up $400 to cover the $200 bail for each of them. Instead of spending the night in jail, they were treated to dinner and the theater.

A pretrial hearing had been set for the following Thursday, and Edgar was
so upset by the arrest and the police questioning that he could not give any
readings while awaiting the hearing. The Cayces and their friends discussed
the effect that publicity might have on the work. Hugh Lynn had called Tom
Sugrue, who prepared press releases emphasizing Edgar's long and well-
documented history of psychic research as well as a copy of the A.R.E.'s Virginia charter. Hugh Lynn favored calling the newspapers to tell them their
side of the story, but A.R.E. associates in New York and their lawyers in Detroit felt that such publicity would do them more harm than good.

Prior to the hearing, Edgar's attorney made a plea-bargain agreement.
The charges against everyone but Edgar were dropped. And when his day in
court came, Edgar pleaded guilty. The judge called Edgar to the stand and
explained to him that the situation was most unfortunate and he was very
sorry that it had happened. He suggested that since it was necessary to im-
pose a sentence, he would ask for either a return of the original membership
fee to the complaining witness or a short period of probation. Edgar accepted the latter, and was released on probation into the custody of a Norfolk parole officer.

Perhaps because the Blumenthals were not involved this time, not a single reporter showed up during the proceedings and nothing appeared in any
of the major newspapers. As luck would have it, Edgar's parole officer turned

out to be Esther Wynne's brother-in-law, a court officer and A.R.E. member in Norfolk, whom Edgar had helped overcome injuries suffered in an automobile accident the year before. As the official parole officer, he took great pleasure in making routine checks on his parolee throughout 1936 by traveling to Virginia Beach, during which time he also received readings on his diet, his career, and on a home loan.

Throughout the next year, the Cayces would be reminded again and again that "unseen forces" were taking care of them. This was clearly the case in the summer of 1937 when their financial situation became so dire that they believed they might lose their house on Arctic Crescent. A dream Edgar had in May suggested that they would be provided for just as they had been helped in the past.

In the dream, Edgar attended a concert in Paris, and afterward, as he was leaving the concert hall, he noticed that the Duke of Windsor and Mrs. Simpson were walking in front of him. The duke was dressed in top hat and tails and carried a cane. Mrs. Simpson was also well dressed. At this moment, an elegantly attired gentleman with a friendly smile approached them. Edgar recognized him as Christ, the "Master of Masters." He and Jesus walked arm in arm down the street until they came to a sidewalk café, where Jesus said, "Let's have a drink here." Then Jesus called out to the duke and Mrs. Simpson, who were still ahead of them, and invited them to join Him and Cayce. The four sat down and Jesus ordered champagne. It was served in beautiful stem glasses and they all drank with appreciation. The bill came to $13.75. When the waiter presented Edgar with the bill, he felt in all his pockets and found only three cents in the righthand pocket of his vest. He said with a great deal of feeling: "I can't pay this bill." Jesus slapped him on the shoulder merrily and laughed with much humor at Edgar's predicament. "Never mind," Jesus said at last, still laughing. "Here is $13.75 to pay the bill. Don't worry. On the wedding day of the two who have just left us, your troubles will be over."

Not long after Edgar had this dream, a complete stranger arrived at the Cayce house on Arctic Crescent and handed him a sealed envelope. She said that on a recent trip to Paris, a woman who was on her way to India had told her about a reading Cayce had given her in New York. The recipient of the reading had asked that Cayce be given this envelope. Edgar opened the envelope and found that it contained $1,375, precisely the amount he owed the bank on his mortgage. That same day, June 3, 1937, the Duke of Windsor and Mrs. Simpson were married.

There were many other curious phenomena that Edgar Cayce reported experiencing that same year. He lost his enjoyment in reading because he had only to read the first few paragraphs of letters or books to know their entire contents. He could sense a person's mood from a distance, and on at least one occasion, slipped into a church office before a parishioner, whose body was surrounded in a red aura, could tell him what was on her mind. "Come back to see me when you are not so angry," Edgar told the surprised woman before escaping into the church office. Perhaps the most discussed incidents took place on trips to New York when Edgar revealed two astonishing examples of his waking clairvoyance, which by now, were becoming a routine occurrence.

In one incident, which reportedly took place when Edgar and Hugh Lynn were dining at a hotel restaurant, Edgar stopped a woman as she was about to step out the door. He politely excused himself for intruding, explained briefly who he was, and urged the woman—whom he had apparently never seen before—not to ride in a car that day. Their entire conversation lasted no more than a few minutes, after which Edgar bid the woman good-bye and returned to his meal. The next day Edgar and Hugh returned to the same restaurant where they found the woman waiting for them. Hugh Lynn described her as nearly "breathless" as she hugged and blessed Edgar for saving her life. Only hours before she had received news that a relative, with whom she had intended to take a car trip to the country, had had a fatal automobile accident. Because of Edgar's warning, she had decided to stay home and had urged the driver—to no avail—to do the same. The woman carried with her a telegram confirming the accident.

Hugh Lynn recounted another strange incident that occurred when he and his father were about to step into a hotel elevator. When the door opened, Edgar looked at the people waiting inside, hesitated, and then told Hugh Lynn that they were going to take the stairs. Later, Edgar wished he had told the passengers to get off, for the elevator cable snapped, sending the passengers to their death. Edgar rarely spoke of this incident except to say that when he looked at the passengers in the elevator, he could see that they had "no future."

Edgar Cayce continued to give a wide assortment of readings in 1937. The most interesting reading that year, as far as Hugh Lynn was concerned, was for a schoolteacher, Sally Taylor, whom Hugh Lynn had fallen in love with and wished to marry. He asked if Sally Taylor would make a good wife for him. Hugh Lynn reported that the reading said "yes," but that the girl said "no."

The problem was not one of affection, for Sally found Hugh Lynn "irresistible." The problem was the boy to whom she was engaged to be married when she met Hugh Lynn. In subsequent readings Hugh Lynn learned of a long association she had had with Hugh Lynn in a previous incarnation in

Mongolia. "The choice is well," one reading said. "Ye were both very good Chinese!" The readings also clearly stated that they could build a life together, that "each might accomplish a great deal of that which has been seeking." That was enough for Hugh Lynn, and he would pursue her for the next four years, until she finally relented and agreed to set a wedding date.

Perhaps the best known reading Edgar Cayce gave during this time was for the pilot, Amelia Earhart, who disappeared with her companion in her airplane near Hawaii on July 2, 1937. Unlike the previous debacle involving Cayce's effort to locate the Lindbergh child, the request this time came from Earhart's husband, George Putnam, whose interest in psychic research was well documented—evidence that he was predisposed to receive help of this kind. Cayce gave the first reading on July 5, 1937, on behalf of Putnam and one of his friends, Myra Kingsley, an A.R.E. member deeply interested in astrology.

"Yes, we have the request, and the anxiety that is manifested in the minds of many at this time," Cayce said in trance. "As we find, . . . the conditions are rather serious." He went on, further stating that she and her companion, Fred Noonan, had run out of fuel and crashed their plane on a coral reef approximately ninety miles northwest of Howland Island. The reading also stated that Amelia Earhart was alive and doing "much better" since the crash, but that her companion was "panicky," that he was "not injured bodily so much as from exposure, and the mental condition." Their plane was damaged during the landing, leaving them stranded. However "serious" their condition, the reading stated that there was still time for rescuers to locate them. "Conditions, to be sure, are gradually growing worse all the time, but there should be the rescue with that set in motion, in the early morning of tomorrow . . . which is already beginning, but not fully complete yet, and more activity is being shown in the right direction now." Upon awaking, Edgar said he had had a vision of wire netting, suggesting that Earhart was being held captive.

A second reading was conducted on August 1, again at the request of Putnam, who had by this time joined the A.R.E. himself. This reading indicated that Earhart had died on July 21, three days after rescuers had given up the search. Years later, researchers found what they believed were Earhart's remains along with wreckage from a plane in approximately the location Edgar had specified in the reading. Anthropologists studying the bones reported, in accordance with Cayce's information, that she and her companion had lived for a time after the crash.

Cayce appears to have been equally accurate in a reading he gave that same year to Captain John Craig, a deep-sea diver who sought information that would help him salvage the *Lusitania*, the passenger liner that sank off the coast of Ireland in 1915 after having been torpedoed by a German submarine. In trance, Cayce correctly pinpointed the location of the wreck between Kinsale and Galley Head Point, approximately 11½ miles off the coast of Ireland. He described its position on the ocean floor and added interesting details that have proved to be correct, including wire fish netting snagged on the wreckage. The most important point made in the reading was the Source's assertion that one torpedo had struck the ship, not two, as was generally believed in 1937, and that the British government had not conspired to conceal from the public details about the ship's cargo, which did not—as researchers would later discover—contain a hidden store of munitions. The Source encouraged Captain John Craig to launch a salvage operation and suggested that he would receive "sympathy and help" in his exploration of the wreck from the "the souls of those whose bodies are here confined [in the wreckage]." Captain John Craig did indeed launch a salvage operation, but was interrupted by the war then in progress.

As interesting as these readings proved to be, the single most gratifying to Edgar, on a personal level, was one he would give for a forty-seven-year-old divorced secretary on December 15, 1937. Innocuous as this reading may have seemed to anyone other than Edgar, it shed light on a question that had perplexed Edgar for years and lent meaning to the entire body of readings given on the work. This reading would provide an explanation for Edgar's early and profound love for the Bible and demonstrate how far Edgar had progressed spiritually since the Dayton readings, the demise of the Cayce Hospital, and the difficult years during the early formation of the A.R.E. Most important, it clarified Edgar's relationship to Jesus Christ in a way that surprised and delighted him.

The subject of the life of Christ was one, of course, that the Source had covered extensively in the past. As Edgar had learned back in Dayton in 1923, Hugh Lynn had been Jesus' apostle Andrew; and a 1929 reading had revealed that Edwin Blumenthal had been a blood relative of Jesus in an earlier incarnation, although one whom the Bible has little to say about. Edwin was said to have been Jude, the younger brother of Jesus, who was in his late teens when Jesus was crucified and who authored the General Epistle of Jude in the New Testament.

In readings for the Blumenthal brothers, the Source had often been encouraging and complimentary, suggesting to them both that, if they so chose, they could become important teachers in the world. On certain occasions— such as the stock market crash reading in 1929, Edwin and Morton had even received communications suggesting that Jesus Christ Himself was speaking to them through Cayce. This was, as Edgar knew, an honor indeed, for the two young men had been seemingly conversing directly with the "only begotten son of God!"—a privilege denied Edgar himself by virtue of the fact that he had no conscious memory of communicating with the Exalted One, or with anyone else while he was in trance.

Edgar had also had the honor of doing readings for 500 or more individuals who—in previous incarnations—were described as having some role in the events in the first century A.D., which included Andrew, Jude, Jesus' sister Ruth, Mary Magdalene, Martha, and Lazarus. While Edgar felt a certain thrill at having access to such fascinating biblical material, he also felt mystified that no indication had been made in the readings that he, himself, had played any part in the drama of the birth, life, and death or resurrection of the Messiah, or the development of the early Christian church. Hugh Lynn, perhaps sensing his father's feelings of disappointment, had asked the Source during a reading in Washington, D.C., in 1935, what name Edgar Cayce had used in his incarnation during biblical times. The name that was offered, "Lucius," left Edgar and Hugh Lynn confused, but not entirely disappointed. A Lucius of Cyrene was mentioned in The Acts of the Apostles as a Christian ministering in Antioch. And in Romans, Paul sends greeting from his kinsmen, one of whom is named Lucius.

In December 1937, however, the Source surprised Edgar—at sixty years of age—with information that he, in fact, as Lucius of Cyrene, had played a substantial role in the events at that important time in world history. The Source first said that the divorced secretary for whom the reading was conducted had been a young woman married to Lucius. As described by the Source, Lucius had been well educated but was something of a ne'er do well. After meeting Jesus, he became inspired by His teachings and eventually became one of the seventy apostles, or Divine messengers, whom Jesus sent out to "prepare the way." Despite the initial concern of several of the other apostles, Lucius became the bishop of the church in Laodicea, one of the seven Christian churches of Asia, located near Antioch. The reading's most exciting revelation—and the one that thrilled Edgar the most—was that the author of the Gospel according to Luke and The Acts of the Apostles was Lucius of Cyrene, not Luke the physician, as generally believed.

Compared to the other three Gospels, which each tell in their own way the story of Jesus' birth, ministry, death, and resurrection, the Gospel of Luke is the most concrete and precise, told with almost first-person detail. Most Christmas and Easter stories come from this Gospel. Tradition has it that the author had come from Antioch in Asia Minor, north of the Mediterranean, and east of Greece, and he used polished and correct Greek, indicating his nonprovincial background. The Source said that Lucius of Cyrene, the true author, was known first as Lucius Ceptulus and was of Roman and Greek parentage, which would explain his proper use of Greek. The Source further claimed that he was not of Antioch, but from Cyrene, which was on the southern shores of the Mediterranean, on the African continent, even further west than Alexandria—near, in fact, the lands that Edgar, as Ra Ta, had been banished to in his Egyptian incarnation. Lucius's family had at some point however, moved to Laodicea, not far from Antioch.

Edgar, Gertrude, Gladys, and Hugh Lynn must all have wondered why it had taken so long for the Source to reveal this information. Toward the end of the first of several readings subsequently dedicated to the life of Lucius, the Source addressed this question before they had a chance to ask it: "It may be questioned by some as to why such an outstanding experience of the entity now called Cayce should not have been given [earlier]. If this had been [the case] there would have been a puffing up [of that entity's ego]."

Despite this somewhat insulting explanation, nothing could squelch the incredible exhilaration and excitement that Edgar felt with this new knowledge. Not only had he been a participant in the life and times of Jesus, he could read his own words in the New Testament! This was the best Christmas present Edgar would ever receive.

47.

❈

Peace and
Prosperity

The Cayces no longer entertained thoughts of returning to The Hill. By the late 1930s and early 1940s, membership in the A.R.E., and the resulting demand for readings, had increased to the point that the family was earning an income of approximately $300 to $400 a month—a modest amount but enough to meet their obligations and allow them to devote themselves to what they believed was their true life's purpose: the readings for the study and prayer groups, and the lectures and publications that would spread Edgar's teachings. Even Edgar Evans, who had grown up to be the most fiscally conservative of the Cayce family, was relieved to see his father, mother, brother, and Gladys on more stable footing. "This business," Edgar wrote in a letter to his son, "has [finally] run into real money these days!"

Along with the steady income came many purchases and home improvements that the family had long put off. Edgar and Gertrude bought the two building lots adjacent to their own property, where they hoped their children would some day build homes. They were able to buy a car, a 1940 Chevrolet, which they later traded in for a 1941 Pontiac. Most important, they completed renovations and landscaping on their Arctic Crescent home, transforming the property into a more suitable place to receive the many new members making the pilgrimage to Virginia Beach to obtain readings, attend the annual A.R.E. Congress, or just to visit the Cayce family.

Among the house's most impressive features were its lovely flower beds, fruit trees, and vegetable gardens. Although Edgar Evans, Hugh Lynn, and a helper named Bains, could be credited with doing a great deal of the manual labor of moving quantities of topsoil, composting, and transplanting, Edgar was given credit for the spectacular success of the grounds around the Arctic Crescent house. It was always Edgar, Hugh Lynn would say, who worked harder, stayed longer, and would touch and speak to each of the plants. Hugh Lynn jokingly said that Edgar had a personal name for each plant, though if he did, he kept those names to himself.

Edgar's vegetable garden had the reputation for having the earliest peas, the largest and most succulent strawberries, and the tallest and thickest asparagus that visitors had ever seen. Throughout the grounds Edgar had planted sixteen different varieties of fruit and flowering trees purchased from mail-order catalogs, including peach, pear, quince, crab-apple, and Formosa trees. Edgar also built a chicken coop, a henhouse, a rabbit hutch, and an aviary for canaries near the lakeshore.

Apart from the gardens, Edgar's favorite outdoor spot was the lake, which had been dredged and given a timber bulwark to keep the water from overflowing into the yard during the spring rains. Attached to the bulwark was a pier where Edgar liked to sit and fish for bass and crappy, and where he designed and built a rather ingenious invention to maintain shade during his afternoon fishing trips. Rather than pitching an umbrella, he planted a tree in a large wooden tub, which he floated in the lake and tethered to the pier. When he shifted his fishing spot, or the sun changed direction, he merely pulled his shade tree along with him.

It was here, at the end of the pier, under the shade of his floating tree, that Edgar once caught a bass with a small coin lodged in its mouth. Reminiscent of a tale from the life of Jesus, who, when asked to pay taxes, sent His disciples to catch a fish in whose mouth they would find a piece of money, this incident served as an omen for Edgar that no matter how difficult times were, he and his family would be provided for.

The Cayces also took pleasure in the proximity of their home to the Star of the Sea Catholic Church, just across the street. Gladys once wrote to Helene Zentgraf to say that the church's closeness had a positive effect on everyone in the house, for they constantly saw people coming for services and prayer. "It is very inspiring and I feel that we are at last in very spiritual surroundings, not just the church but all nature around us."

Father Brennan, the parish priest, got along famously with the Cayces and frequently brought them cakes and pies baked by parishioners. He also let the A.R.E. unofficially use the parish hall for meetings. On his many frequent visits to the house, he invariably sprinkled holy water in the rooms he entered—all the rooms, that is, except the one where Edgar gave readings.

Like the property outside, the inside of the Cayces' home was transformed. The walls were scrubbed and painted, the kitchen was extended and an apartment for Gladys was added. Perhaps most crucial—given the frequency with which various of Cayce's homes and studios caught fire—a reinforced fireproof vault was put in to protect the readings and what had now become Edgar's voluminous correspondence.

The downstairs of the house contained the dining room, kitchen, living room and, most important to Edgar, his office, where he could read, listen to the Emerson Radio that had been a gift from a supporter, carry on his correspondence, and give readings. Against one wall, Edgar had arranged his desk with all his photographs of friends and family members, the photos of his mother and father being most prominent. He said that he especially enjoyed seeing his mother and father's photos there because it reminded him of "days long gone by" and the "wonder of what life is all about." He also asked Father Brennan for a picture of himself, which the priest reluctantly gave Edgar, saying, "Now you must be sure, Edgar, you don't stick any pins in it." Against another wall was the sofa with pillows that had been crocheted by Carrie House, where Edgar gave readings.

In light of Edgar's heightened sensitivity to psychic phenomena in his waking state, it came as no surprise to family members that their home became a gathering place for "ghostly" visitors. Gertrude reported that Edgar carried on what appeared to be one-sided conversations so frequently that they became almost commonplace. Three such incidents are worth noting because they help to provide insights into why—to Edgar's way of thinking—discarnate spirits sometimes remained "earthbound," and how he could help them make the transition to another plane of consciousness.

In one incident, late in 1936, Edgar awoke to the sound of rapping on their second floor bedroom window. Gertrude also heard the rapping, but didn't see what Edgar saw when he opened the window. Hovering outside appeared to be a woman named Bunchie, whom the Cayces had once employed at the photo studio in Selma. Edgar reached out to touch her, but as soon as he did, she vanished, only to reappear a few minutes later. He invited her to come inside and went downstairs to open the door and let her in. Bunchie's ghost entered and she and Edgar proceeded to carry on an hour-long conversation, but based on what Edgar was saying, it became clear that Bunchie had come to seek medical advice. Edgar did not learn when or how she had died, only that she was dead, and that she didn't realize it. She apparently had no sense of time, either, and spoke of seeing Edgar's father in Selma recently, though it had been many years since Leslie had been there. She also told Edgar that she was still being treated for an illness by a Selma physician, Dr. Furniss, who Edgar would later learn had also passed away. Asked how she had found Edgar, she said she had overheard a conversation in Selma about his moving to Virginia Beach and had now come looking for him. Edgar told her that she had died, that she should stop concentrating on the illness that had obviously obsessed her, and that she should "look for the light" that would lead her to where she was supposed to go. Bunchie never returned to the Cayce home again.

A year after this incident, another ghost visited the Cayces, only this time it was permitted to remain for more than a month, during which time everyone in the household became convinced of its presence. The ghost was none other than Edgar's father, Leslie, who had died at age eighty-three on April 12, 1937, while on a trip to Nashville to visit his daughters, Annie and Sarah. A fire had broken out in the upstairs apartment of Annie Cayce's house, and while escaping the building, Leslie suffered burns on his head and neck, which, due to his advanced age, hastened his death. An emergency reading for Leslie, conducted immediately after the fire, began, "It is the end."

About a week after the funeral in Hopkinsville, family members began hearing strange noises in Leslie's former bedroom at the top of the stairs. Hugh Lynn swore he heard his grandfather's heavy breathing. Gertrude and Gladys also heard someone walking around. Edgar went into the room to see for himself. When he came out, he reported: "He's back. He'll be here for a few days." And then Edgar said, as if to casually explain the phenomenon, "In his mind he is trying to straighten out his papers before he died. He'll not be here long. Don't bother him because it will upset him and he can't communicate, can't make himself heard."

Hugh Lynn found it rather curious to have a ghost in the house and availed himself of the opportunity to see if nonfamily members could hear or see what was apparent to Gladys and the Cayces. He decided to use the mailman as a test subject. The mailman, whom everyone in the family knew quite well, was invited into the house and asked to walk up the stairs to see if he could hear anything unusual. According to Hugh Lynn, when the mailman was halfway up the stairs he too heard Leslie's breathing. He looked at Hugh Lynn very strangely and asked, "Isn't that where your grandfather stayed?" Hugh answered: "Yes." Then the mailman asked what the sound was that he was listening to. Hugh Lynn said, "It's my grandfather. He's back." The mailman allegedly turned white and ran out of the house. From that day on he wouldn't bring the mail to the door, but tossed it into the hedge, running as he left the yard.

One morning, a few days after the incident with the mailman, a great deal of noise began emanating from Leslie's room. Hugh Lynn was about to go upstairs to see what was the matter when his father told him not to. "Don't do that," Edgar warned. Hugh Lynn didn't listen to his father and rushed up the stairs anyway, and at the top of the stairs ran smack into what he believed to be his grandfather. "I could feel him," Hugh Lynn said. "Every hair on my head went straight up in the air. I don't know how I knew it, but I just knew it was my grandfather. It was cold, but quite a different chill, and it was like running into cobwebs in the dark woods, very fine when they touch you, but when you wipe them away there is nothing there."

A third incident involved the ghost of Frank Mohr, who had suffered a stroke in July 1937, brought on by arterialsclerosis, and who died on February 1, 1938. Soon after his death, Mohr began appearing to Edgar in dreams and visions. The first dream took place in July 1940, in which Mohr told Edgar that he would receive a letter from Mrs. Grace Wilson, a longtime friend of Mohr's who had received physical and life readings from Edgar in the late 1920s. A few days after the dream, Edgar did indeed receive a request from Mrs. Wilson for a reading for James Taft, her son-in-law, a musician who had recently been confined to a tuberculosis sanitarium in Monrovia, California. Owing to the intervention from the spirit of Frank Mohr, Edgar immediately did the reading, which recommended a treatment not unlike that which had saved Gertrude's life. James Taft's health improved greatly on following Cayce's recommendations but, several months later, his condition took a turn for the worse, and he died in April 1941. Edgar shared the family's grief and was at a loss to explain what had gone wrong. Frank Mohr answered that question in a dream Edgar had a few days after Taft's death. Mohr told Edgar that the reading had been a good one, and that the musician had died because he had neglected to follow through on the treatments.

Mohr visited Edgar once more in an even more dramatic way. This last appearance occurred during a reading for his wife, Ella, who had been suffering from a heart condition. In the middle of the session, Mohr appeared to Edgar, telling him, "No, No, Mr. Cayce, Ella wants to come on [to be with me on the other side]—don't prevent her." Ella Mohr died the day after the reading. In Edgar's heartfelt letter of condolence to Frank's daughter, Helen, he assured her that Ella, like Frank, lived on in another plane. "They have only gone through God's other door and we must not worry too much for them."

Apart from ghosts, hundreds of living people visited Edgar in his study, and from his desk Edgar kept a very active correspondence, sometimes writing as many as ten people in a single day. Letters went out to Los Angeles, Detroit, Chicago, Hopkinsville—all over the country—and although many were to family and friends, an astonishingly large number were to people Edgar had never met—often people who had written him for personal advice about a reading they had obtained. To a housewife in New York, married to an alcoholic, he humbly recounted his own struggle growing up in a home with a father who abused liquor, praising his correspondent for her strength and character in making the most of difficult circumstances.

To Edgar, the most important visitor to his study, with whom he carried on a long and detailed correspondence, was Beatrice Coffing. Beatrice was introduced to Cayce in September of 1940 by her fiancée, a violinist and music teacher in Altadena, California, whose sight Edgar had helped regain after many years of suffering from cataracts.

Studying her fiancé's readings had a profound impact upon Beatrice, and she subsequently requested both physical and life readings for herself and the man she wished to marry. The information that came through captured everyone's attention, for rarely had a life reading suggested as many prior connections between two people than Beatrice's between her and Edgar. The two had apparently been together during Edgar's sojourns as Ra Ta and Uhjltd, and even as recently as Edgar's present incarnation in Beverly, Kentucky. And yet, in the correspondence Edgar sent with the life reading, he remained unusually circumspect about how they had known one another in Kentucky. Nor was he apparently willing to discuss the subject with Gladys or Gertrude.

It was not until he had a chance to meet Beatrice in person, on September 17, 1940, that Edgar let the "secret slip out." He had to "see the truth" for himself before he could, as he later said, "be absolutely certain." That day, when Beatrice and her fiancé, Richmond Seay, arrived on the doorstep of the Arctic Crescent home, Edgar stood in the doorway, unable to move, or even speak to her as she raised her hand to greet him. Tears began to pour down his cheeks. He then said: "Little Anna . . . Little Anna, it's true."

The twenty-nine-year-old bookkeeper from Attica, Indiana, had read everything she could about Edgar before meeting him and though she believed him to be a "kindred spirit," she was not prepared for the outpouring of affection that Edgar showered upon her, or the curious way he addressed her. After they talked together awhile in his study, she began to understand what seeing her meant to Edgar, and also gained a startling insight into her previous relationship to her fiancé, Richmond Seay.

As Edgar had figured out from studying her life readings, Beatrice, in her most recent incarnation, had been Edgar's beloved childhood playmate, Little Anna Seay, who died when Edgar was only twelve. Anna had been the daughter of Barney Seay, who died the day after she did, and who, according to the readings, was reincarnated back into the same family, this time as Richmond Seay. Little Anna and her father Barney Seay, who had both died of pneumonia in Beverly, Kentucky, in 1887, were now, in 1941, Beatrice and Richmond Seay, soon to be husband and wife.

No sooner had she and Edgar begun to compare notes about their present lives than they realized how much they had in common. Both had an unusual affinity for flowers and gardening and frequently spoke to their plants. Each had spent many solitary hours alone in the woods as children, creating "forts" out of canopies of leaves and other materials that they had found there, and conversing with "imaginary" playmates. Most remarkably, the spiritual paths that she and Edgar were on had brought them to the same destination: a deeply rooted belief in both Jesus Christ and in reincarnation. From the moment of their meeting in Virginia Beach, Beatrice and Edgar were fast and devoted friends, and she and her future husband became active leaders in the A.R.E., even heading up a fund-raising effort to expand its headquarters. To Edgar, she was never Beatrice, but Little Anna, and to her, he was simply Eddy.

In a letter Beatrice wrote to Edgar two years after her first reading, she poured out her affection. "I have a great many things to be thankful for, Eddy, but I think you are one of the greatest and deepest of those things that I am thankful for, so I'm always so very grateful to you for giving us some of your time and blessedness," she wrote. "I've just finished reading through and pondering all of your letters since first you addressed me . . . Although at that time I had no idea that "Little Anna" or "Little Eddy" ever existed— something flickered even then. And what a wonderful revelation and what beautiful things have come out of finding a certain Mr. Edgar Cayce." Later, Beatrice would write again: "The beauty and wonder of it! I could not understand what pulled and tugged at my heart and soul from the moment I heard of you and your work, until little by little you have told me of experiences that have helped me to understand . . . It seemed as though you were part of my heart and soul."

In return letters, Edgar would pay her a most distinctive tribute. "You, [Little Anna], stand between the living and the dead, and the plague of doubt in my own mind is stayed . . . when [I] am with you . . . All doubt slips away, and when I allow myself to slip back to days long since gone, a part of the whole business of living, am just transported into another world. A world that one cannot help but see, feel, hear the goodness and the love of God. I now am never able to put into words what I feel, but it is there, and know I am better able to at least try and serve others better when I have been with you."

Around this time, Edgar met a fascinating young child, Faith Harding, a girl who Edgar and many others came to believe was one of God's chosen channels through which the next generation of Americans would hear divine messages. Although much of the story has been lost and what eventually was reported by the press has been for the most part dismissed as little more than a curiosity, Faith Harding's childhood, in certain respects, rivaled that of Edgar's own.

Edgar first learned about Faith Harding in a letter he received on February 22, 1940, from Leila Learned, an A.R.E. member in Connecticut who had been hearing all kinds of curious and fantastic reports about the child. The "Little Prophetess," as Faith Harding was called, had been born in Trucksville, Pennsylvania, the child of Harry and Virginia Harding. According to popular legend, Faith could speak in complete sentences at just eighteen months and was credited with remarkable powers of clairvoyance. In one incident, when Faith was only 1½, she demanded to be taken off a bus only minutes before it burst into flames. Doctors who examined the child were said to be confounded by her astonishing vocabulary, frequent biblical references, predictions of future events, and the highly unusual messages of love and hope she delivered. Faith so impressed Leila and Arthur Learned, a wealthy and prominent couple from Stamford, Connecticut, that they became Faith's devoted godparents, hosting her baptism at age 4½, in the Shinto temple they had imported for their Japanese garden. This was the same temple where Alice Bailey, a noted theosophist and writer, the Catholic archbishop William Francis, and Khahil Gibran, the Assyrian poet and author of *The Prophet*, had all given talks.

Less than a month after Edgar received this first communication about Faith Harding, another A.R.E. member, Josephine Buchanan, wrote Edgar asking that Faith be the subject of a life reading. Buchanan reported visiting the child in Pennsylvania and seeing in her "definite proof of the [Divine] guidance." She described her in nearly angelic terms: "lovely . . . natural, sweet, happy, and good and just radiating light and love. You simply must meet her!"

Virginia Harding, Faith's mother, had turned down numerous requests to have her child "psychically" tested, but at the urging of the Buchanans and other A.R.E. members, agreed to have Edgar do a reading. A thirty-minute trance session was conducted in Virginia Beach on March 30, 1940.

The Source said the child was "a chosen channel [through] which the Father hath bestowed upon the children of men," and that she was "a vessel through which the Prince of Peace would bring encouragement, assurance, and . . . messages of hope and of light to . . . those who are not only mentally but physically sick . . . to those who are ill at ease, rather than the diseased." Faith Harding would do this, the reading stated, by her own psychic ability to communicate with "patience," "love," and "kindness," and through the "laying on hands," a talent she would develop as she grew older. "He hath promised to stand in the places of those who are discouraged, disconsolate, who have lost a vision, lost hope: so may this entity be that channel through which many may take hope, many may be aroused to the awareness that the Lord is nigh, that He standeth at the door of thy consciousness, that ye may be awakened!"

According to the reading, Faith had been through many previous incarnations, and this fact would continue to serve her in the years to come. Most important were her incarnations as Elizabeth, the mother of John the Baptist, and as Saint Cecilia, who, during the Roman era, brought great hope, patience, and understanding to the world.

However gifted this child was in her present incarnation, the Source also admonished Faith's parents and those around her to nurture her in the "spirit of truth," to provide her with love, kindness, and gentleness of spirit in those things that bring "constructive, hopeful, helpful forces into the experiences of others," and to not let her experience "distrust," "envy," "malice," or "jealousy." The reading stated that given her "special nature," she would never experience "a normal world or normal environment," but that nevertheless the child should be provided with as typical a childhood as possible.

In closing, the Source said, "Let there *not* be a worshipfulness as of the body of the entity, but rather as of its abilities to arouse in the hearts and minds of others the knowledge that the day of the Lord is at hand!"

Edgar had an opportunity to meet the child and her mother on April 16, 1940, at the home of Milton and Irene Harrison in Bronxville, New York. Irene was the daughter of Frank Seiberling, and she and her husband, both members of the A.R.E., had been actively trying to foster a reconciliation between Seiberling and Edgar B. Davis, with the help of readings from Cayce. At the time, Faith and her mother, Virginia, were on their way to Tryon, North Carolina, to meet with the board of a foundation interested in helping to develop the child's gifts.

At their brief meeting, Edgar characterized the child as "darling," and found the mother extremely knowledgeable about psychic phenomena and the spiritualist movement. Although Edgar himself was convinced of the integrity of both mother and daughter, there were certain aspects of the mother's approach that caused him some concern. Like a typical Hollywood stage mother, Virginia Harding was all too eager to promote her daughter. Dave Kahn, of course, had beat the drum for Edgar in much the same way as Mrs. Harding did for her daughter, but there was an important difference, in addition to their ages. Apart from the stories Mrs. Harding told about her child, she carried with her a scrapbook of newspaper clippings and a file folder of signed affidavits. She also had a photograph purported to have been taken during Faith's baptism, which she claimed to be evidence of a Divine presence: Hovering near the head of the child were the shadowy and indistinct images of Mother Mary, Christ, Buddha, and a number of other images that Edgar recognized as holy men and women. Despite the fact that Edgar himself had once experimented with double exposures, and that Arthur Conan Doyle had been publicly humiliated by Houdini for having been fooled into believing in the authenticity of similar pictures, Edgar gave Gladys and Gertrude the impression that he believed the photo to be a genuine vision of Divine spirits gathered to bless Faith during her baptism.

While Edgar was in Bronxville, he gave a second reading for the child, and again the Source directed a warning to those "privileged to have the care, the attention of this entity in this material experience." The reading requested that the parents "heed those warnings indicated," and reminded them of the specialness of their child. Faith Harding, the reading stated, expressed the "voice of nature itself . . . in the laughter . . . in the look of its eye, in the movement of its body, in the patter of its feet, giving expression in a manner that brings to the minds and consciousness of those who seek to know God and God's ways with the children of men."

Near the end of this second reading, Cayce was asked if anything else could be said about this child. "Worlds might be filled with that as might be given!" the Source said. "But let each of you here so live the Christ consciousness as manifested in the Master that you may be counted worthy to be even as those who would gather the crumbs of wisdom that will be manifested through this entity!"

At this point in the reading, Gladys and others in the room became aware of an unearthly presence. Though the windows were closed, a wind blew through the room, and a vibration rattled the windowpanes. They knew that this was another visit from the Archangel Michael.

"HARK, YE FRIENDS!" Cayce suddenly announced in a voice that witnesses said had more force and fury than at any other time they could remember. "I MICHAEL, LORD OF THE WAY, WOULD GIVE THEE WARNING!" Cayce continued. "Bow thine heads, ye vile ones of the Earth!

Know what has been entrusted to thee! Live the life, lest ye be counted accursed for being unworthy of the trust given thee!"

It is not known how much or little Gladys and the Cayces knew about the circumstances surrounding Faith Harding or her parents at the time this reading was given, or whether they grasped the full meaning of this admonition from the Archangel Michael. However, in the months that followed, it became clear to everyone involved that the child's life was taking a tragic turn for the worse.

Edgar, Gertrude, and Gladys soon learned that Virginia Harding had erected a temple in Tyron, North Carolina, where initiates of "The Cross and Circle Foundation" would devote themselves to the "Little Prophetess" and her teachings. Many thousands of dollars had been raised to keep Faith and her mother housed in what has been described as a Greek temple and to have them driven around in a station wagon with the Little Prophetess's logo painted on its doors. Much of the attention lavished on the child was apparently generated by the story of a Greek laborer who appeared at the Harding's home. His son was allegedly very ill and having heard of Faith came asking for help. The Little Prophetess walked with him into the garden and after saying a prayer for the son's recovery, picked a flower and advised the man to place it beneath his son's pillow. The child reportedly got well.

Faith's father, Harry Harding, who earned his living in Trucksville manufacturing felt typewriter pads, was furious at his wife's behavior and accused her of exploiting their child for her own fame and notoriety. In letters and court declarations, Harry Harding detailed Virginia's misdeeds, including an allegation that she had embellished many of her daughter's psychic messages before they reached the public. He then hired a local doctor who diagnosed his wife as suffering from "madness" and sought a court order to retain sole custody of the child until the mother could undergo psychiatric therapy.

Despite the difficulties that were raging on around the "Little Prophetess," her predictions of future events were apparently uncannily accurate. Messages allegedly came out of the little girl in the form of automatic writing, which she did in the evening on long rolls of plain wrapping paper. The entity that communicated through her referred to him- or herself as "the Entity," and spoke in a language that rivaled Edgar's, using such words as "beeth and "beseechment." For many months, throughout 1939 and 1940, messages from the Entity were printed weekly in the *Nanticoke Daily Press*. Almost all included an encouraging message and made references to karma, reincarnation, and the arrival of a teacher who will enlighten mankind.

The Entity, through Faith, described how and when the war in Europe would begin and the battle that would determine the outcome of hostilities. She also described, in the fall of 1940, how America would be pulled into the war by what she said was an "act" of aggression by a small but unnamed Asian nation—a prediction that was also made in one of Cayce's later readings. Edgar himself was the subject of one of her last predictions. In the spring of 1940, he was told by Virginia Harding that the Entity had said that unless he immediately stopped giving readings and left on an extended retreat to "fast" and "rejuvenate," his dreams of his own death would become a reality, and mankind would sustain a "deplorable loss."

After a difficult court battle, Harry Harding eventually obtained custody of the child and set about raising her and her three older siblings, doing everything he could to put the past behind them. He divorced Virginia Harding in 1941 and shortly after she married another man and moved in next door to Harry and the children. Unhappy and suffering from humiliation and ridicule at school, Faith blamed her mother and, despite their proximity, would have nothing to do with her for the next eight years. Faith, with the help of her father, also did everything she could to block out "dreams, visions, and voices"—anything pertaining to the spirit world. She married young, shortly after meeting her husband, her marriage having been foretold in the one dream she could not block out. Her dream included such details as whom she would marry, the number of children they would have, and where they would live.

Edgar never learned the truth behind Harry Harding's allegations brought against Virginia Harding, but he nevertheless understood that the chaotic environment of Faith's family life had destroyed her incredible gift. Perhaps he now appreciated more than ever the protection his simple farm upbringing had offered him. When the readings urged that Faith be treated as normally as possible, Edgar immediately understood the importance of this, remembering how difficult it had been for him, even at age thirty-three, when the spotlight had first been turned upon him. Although Cayce came to believe in the authenticity of Harding's psychic power, he never did heed the warning that the Entity had made regarding his need for a retreat.

Quite to the contrary, Edgar continued to give readings at an ever-increasing pace. Gertrude said that readings were literally "pouring out of Edgar." Many of these readings were for the members of the Norfolk Study Group. Throughout the 1930s copies of the lessons were available for 10 cents each to any A.R.E. members who had formed or were in the process of forming their own study group. The Norfolk group had also considered preparing parallel study pamphlets on the study of dreams, auras, mental telepathy, power of thought, numerology, astrology, palmistry, spiritualism, and spiritual healing, but the readings steadfastly advised against it. In 1939, however, the readings revealed to the study group the ultimate purpose of their sessions together and the challenge in front of them now: the lessons were ready to be compiled into book form.

According to the Source, the reason this information hadn't been revealed earlier was that the members themselves had to first undergo transformation and enlightenment before their message could be taken outside their small circle of friends and supporters. Edgar himself couldn't help but consider the many failed endeavors—whether it was drilling for oil or building a hospital—during which he and others close to him had been asked to accomplish much the same personal transformation and, unable to reach the accord requested, had been denied their ultimate goal. Judging by what the Source was asking of them, Florence Edmonds and the Norfolk Study Group had succeeded where the others before had failed. For more than a decade, the group had been able to remain as a single unit, working together for the greater good that might come of it. Edgar viewed this as the supreme accomplishment of his career.

At the express wishes of the Source, the group compiled their completed lessons and presented them to Protestant, Jewish, and Catholic ministers for commentary. Records do not indicate if this was done for all three denominations, but one review remains from Joseph Clower, who had replaced Reverend Scattergood at the Presbyterian Church, who was asked to comment on the first six lessons on soul development. He reported: "Truth is truth, regardless of the Source from which it comes . . . True, I found a few implications here and there which I felt inclined to question . . . There is still much about them that I do not understand as more learned and careful observers than I are equally ready to admit, and there are some philosophical assumptions underlying the work that is being done which I find congenial, but which I have not yet been led to accept dogmatically. But with these exceptions I found nothing in the substance of the 'lessons' as such which, in my judgment could not appropriately be published with the imprint of my own church's denominational publishing house. The lessons are Christian in theme and purpose."

In their excitement and trepidation about what would come next, the question most on the study group's minds was what to call their lessons. After considering asking the Source for a title, in the end they settled on one themselves: *A Search for God*. Ever mindful of the book's origins, the group humbly offered its contents to anyone for whom the work could bring hope, peace, and a better understanding of their fellow man. "There is nothing new here," the group wrote in its introduction. "The search for God is as old as humanity. This book is passed on in the hope that through it, during the trying times ahead, many may glimpse a ray of light, that in other hearts it may awaken a new hope and vision of a better world through application of His laws in daily life."

The task of publishing proved to be a difficult undertaking. The group knew that the Source wanted them to find a serious professional publisher— one of the readings had even provided detailed instructions on the overall format of the book including the placement of an affirmation on a page that stood alone facing the title of each lesson. The reading instructed: "Do not print it in a form that is to be just thrown aside. It deserves a good house. Give it such."

Esther Wynne was given the task of finding it a "good house." She approached the William Byrd Press, in Richmond, and although they were reluctant at first, Esther prevailed upon them to print the first edition. She acted, as Hugh Lynn said, "like a little mosquito in their ear until they finally agreed to print it." They did so on the condition that ten members of the study group agreed to buy ten copies each for one dollar apiece. *A Search for God* was eventually published in two volumes, in 1942 and 1950, and became the most widely used educational material ever issued by the A.R.E. It is also generally considered to put forth Cayce's message better than any single publication. But it was not this book that made Edgar Cayce a legend in his own time.

In 1942, the same year that *A Search for God* was published, Henry Holt released the first edition of Tom Sugrue's biography of Cayce, *There Is a River*. The story of how *There Is a River* came to be written was perhaps as unusual as *A Search for God*. The creative process that went into writing it also made the book one of the most unusual popular biographies to ever see print. And while its author gave his talents to a project that he hoped would keep the Cayce story alive for generations of future readers, Edgar's talents literally kept its author alive so that he could write it.

The root of Tom Sugrue's physical problems was a case of gonorrhea he had contracted back in college. After following recommendations given by a series of Cayce's medical readings, the disease was eliminated. However, the readings also said that Sugrue should not let his immune system become weakened from drinking alcohol or taking drugs, and that he should follow a strict dietary regimen rich in vitamins and minerals. Above all, the readings stressed the need for exercise to eliminate toxins that would naturally begin to collect in his joints as the virus was flushed out of his system. The reading specifically warned that unless he followed the recommendations he would suffer from arthritis. "Do not overtax the body by too much of night study, or night living!" the Source said.

For the most part, Sugrue followed the advice set forth in the readings, but during the years he worked for the *Herald Examiner*, shortly after the closing of the Cayce Hospital, he began to heed the recommendations less and less. Later, he took a job as a roving reporter for *American* magazine for which he wrote one story a month on any subject of his choosing. He traveled widely to many exotic locales, including Europe, the Far East, and Egypt, writing on themes that ranged from monastic life in Italy to sheep herding in Turkey. During one of his European adventures he became seriously ill. In his weakened state, the side effects of his earlier problems with gonorrhea became evident, and arthritis set in.

Upon his return to the United States in 1935, he obtained physical readings indicating that the toxins that had collected in his joints had given rise to an infection, which was gradually spreading to the rest of his legs. Although the readings warned that this might develop into a serious condition, the pain he experienced was not so severe that he failed to act on the advice in a timely manner. The recommendations put forth in the readings required a substantial amount of time and energy, which, at that point, he preferred to lavish on a lovely socialite from Washington, D.C., named Mary Ganey, whom he intended to marry. He continued his daily activities, suffering from what he thought of as mild arthritis in his legs.

Later that same year, he took a new job as an editor at *American* magazine in New York, got married, and bought a home on Long Island. His wife, Mary, became pregnant. A devout Catholic and skeptical of the readings, Mary did what she could to keep Tom away from Edgar Cayce and Virginia Beach. Mary suggested that when she went to the hospital to deliver the child, Tom should have doctors treat his knees. It was a mistake they both lived to regret.

The hospital doctors diagnosed the same infection in his joints that Edgar had discussed in the readings, but their prescribed treatment was to put Sugrue in a heat cabinet, which raised his body temperature to a very high degree. From then on, as Hugh Lynn described it, he literally began to "wither" away. He left the hospital looking like a skeleton. Tom wished to have a reading, but Mary adamantly refused, saying he shouldn't have anything to do with Cayce. But as her husband continued to lose weight and his doctors could do nothing about it, she relented.

According to the reading they obtained, the high temperature in the heat cabinets had burned the lining of his intestinal tract, preventing it from properly absorbing food into the body. Tom was literally starving to death. The reading stated the severity of the condition, but also held out hope that his premature death could be prevented if he were to undergo a complicated series of treatments, including constant massage, injections of atomidine, and baths in Epsom salt.

Mary, with an infant child to care for and not predisposed to trust advice from a psychic, declared that she couldn't help Tom through the ordeal that would be necessary to bring him back to health. Hugh Lynn, who was living in New York at the time, volunteered to help; he moved in with the family and devoted several hours each day to helping his friend overcome his debilitating illness. A few months after Hugh Lynn arrived, Mary's father was diagnosed with a brain tumor. In June 1939, she and her child moved to Washington, D.C., to care for him while Hugh Lynn took Tom to Virginia Beach.

During the two years that Tom lived with the Cayce family his condition was precarious. His arms and legs were so thin that the outlines of his bones could be seen. Moreover, they were stiff from arthritis, making it difficult for him to change positions while he lay in bed, let alone stand. Cayce, who had now begun to give world affairs readings on Hitler and the hostilities in Europe, took time aside to give physical readings for Tom, sometimes as many as twice a day. One reading recommended that snake venom be used to loosen Tom's leg joints. Hugh Lynn called a local doctor who had never heard of using such a medication but agreed to look into it. Three or four days later he called and told Hugh Lynn that he had just received the latest issue of the *AMA Journal*, which, to his amazement, contained an article on the therapeutic use of snake venom. Tom was rolled to the doctor's office in a wheelchair and given an injection, which was viewed as a great success. But it was a long and difficult recovery period, during which time Hugh Lynn, who had learned massage therapy from Harold Reilly in New York, worked with Tom twice a day. With the help of volunteer Boy Scouts, Hugh Lynn took Tom out to the shore and put him in the water, where he paddled around as best he could and soaked up the sun.

In the midst of the recovery process, Tom began to write the story of Edgar's life. He had entertained the idea before, in 1936, and conducted a series of interviews, but time constraints and his inability to find a publisher had put the project on hold. Now he fully embraced the idea, and with trance help from Edgar, found an editor, William Sloan, and a publisher, Henry Holt and Company.

To everyone concerned, a biography seemed like the right idea at the right time, for as both Gertrude and Gladys said, it took Edgar's mind off the lives of the many young men who were being drafted into the military. By the time the project was underway, twenty-three-year-old Edgar Evans had graduated from Duke University and briefly returned to Virginia Beach to marry his first serious girlfriend, Kathryn Bane. He was also, as it turned out, viewed by the military as a prime candidate for the draft. On the advice of the trance readings—and, more specifically given what Edgar had learned about the demise of Atlantis and his own purported role in its destruction—Edgar Evans opted not to involve himself in the design or construction of armaments, but rather to attend officer training school in New Jersey for a commission in the Signal Corps. Hugh Lynn managed to avoid the draft for another two years by working for the government as the recreation director for Virginia Beach, where he arranged public relations events for officers and enlisted men in nearby army camps. The rest of his time was devoted to Tom's health and his father's biography.

The research and writing process went smoothly. All the important participants were readily available, and Tom's illness didn't prevent him from using a typewriter. Interviews began in earnest in 1940 and with them, a highly unusual editorial process was set in motion. Apart from having named the editor and publisher where the completed manuscript was to be sent, the Source didn't discuss factual or biographical details, but rather general themes about how Cayce's work was to be presented to the general public. In his waking state, Edgar deferred to Hugh Lynn and Tom as to what biographical details were to be included, and upon their recommendation, several controversial topics—Atlantis, Edgar's various incarnations, examples of Edgar's waking clairvoyance, among others—were excluded on the grounds that the public wasn't yet ready to hear the full scope of Cayce's psychic experiences.

Even with all this rigorous vetting, the first draft of the book was rejected by William Sloan on the grounds that the general public would find it too difficult to believe and that the book needed to be reorganized before he and the Henry Holt Company could move forward. Tom and Hugh Lynn had to rewrite hundreds of pages before it was finally accepted. But it was time well spent, for the manuscript ultimately captured the attention of many people at the publishing house, prompting the editor and the head of the publicity department to request trance readings. By the time the editing was complete, the book had the full support of the publishing house, and Tom had taken his first faltering steps out of his wheelchair. Although he still required treatments, Tom had recovered sufficiently to move to Clearwater, Florida, to be with his wife and daughter.

Hugh Lynn, to whom the book was dedicated, couldn't have been more enthusiastic about what he believed the book might do for his father's career and the future of the A.R.E. He was delighted to be living in Virginia Beach and working with Gladys to build the A.R.E. into a larger and more established organization. And as his father's readings had recommended, he was determined not to spend the war years with a gun in his hand.

During Tom's recovery process, Hugh Lynn's fiancée, Sally Taylor, also became an ardent believer in the readings. She finally consented to marry Hugh Lynn, and on October 7, 1942, she gave birth to an eight-pound, ten-ounce boy. At her and Hugh Lynn's requests, Edgar gave the baby a reading within a few hours of the child's birth. The Source suggested that the child be named Charles Thomas Taylor Cayce—"Taylor" being in honor of his mother's family name, while "Charles" was connected to one of his earlier incarnations in Sweden, which the reading made reference to. The "Thomas" was for both Tom Sugrue, as well as for Thomas Jefferson Cayce, Edgar's grandfather, who, the reading said, had just been reincarnated as Sally and Hugh Lynn's child! "You've given him so many names you won't have any left for the next one," Sally's family, the Taylors, teased their daughter and son-in-law.

Less than a month after Charles Thomas's birth, an advance shipment of the first edition of *There Is a River* arrived in Virginia Beach. Hugh Lynn emptied the shipping crate and excitedly drove through town announcing the news and giving away copies of the book. Having experienced first hand the adverse effects of media attention and his own intense dislike of deification, Edgar himself was a great deal more reticent to share in his son's enthusiasm and privately expressed his concern to Gertrude that the family would once again undergo scrutiny and an invasion of their privacy. Their lives together, it seemed, had finally gotten on an even keel. He wasn't ready for more potentially upsetting changes. No sooner had Hugh Lynn emptied the wooden shipping crate of books than Edgar took the crate outside and chopped it up for firewood.

Ultimately, although it would later bring a great deal of attention to the A.R.E., neither Hugh Lynn nor Edgar fully enjoyed the book's publication, for it coincided with Edgar Evans's assignment to a military post to build a radar station in Trinidad, and Hugh Lynn's draft into the special services division of the army and his departure for Europe.

In the spring of 1943, Edgar, Gertrude, Gladys, Sally Taylor Cayce, and infant Charles Thomas made their farewells to Hugh Lynn at the bus station in Norfolk, where he was to depart for Fort George Meade. Everyone got out of the car and stood on the sidewalk. Edgar held Charles Thomas as Hugh Lynn kissed Sally and then his mother good-bye. It was an especially bittersweet moment, for all were aware of something Edgar had told Hugh

Lynn just a few days earlier, during what would be the last of their father and son talks.

According to Hugh Lynn, his father had sat him down in the study and, referring to both himself and Gertrude, said: "Hugh Lynn, we won't be here when you get back." Surprised and annoyed, Hugh Lynn said: "Of course you will." Edgar then told Hugh Lynn that there were some things that he knew as a parent *and* as a psychic but couldn't explain. He only knew that Hugh Lynn wouldn't see his mother and father again—at least not in this lifetime.

48.

The Last
Reading

Edgar Cayce's most terrifying vision of America's involvement in the war came on August 30, 1941, more than three months before the bombing of Pearl Harbor. The vision was not only unique for the message it contained, but because it occurred while Edgar was in the middle of giving a business reading for a local Virginia Beach labor leader. Using language and imagery straight out of the Book of Revelation, the Source painted a grim picture of the destruction to come.

"I saw a great . . . white horse, with a man all dressed in armor and in flowing robes but black, [and] fringed around the edges in gold," Edgar said, describing his vision. "Then I saw another horse coming—a very red horse. As it came closer I saw that the rider . . . had on white and blue armor, and there were hordes of people following him. Then as the two horses came together, it seemed that [the rider] disappeared and the two groups clashed. The followers of the first horse were well armed, while the others were not. Yet there were such hordes following the red horse that they seemed to march right through the ranks of the well-armed group, though millions were slain."

This was not the first occasion, of course, in which Edgar's trance sessions had prophesied the arrival of war. Cayce had begun to discuss this possibility as far back as 1934. In that year he had a dream in which armed camps of men had begun to form on opposite sides of a small stream. On one side stood soldiers dressed in white, led by an angel with wings "like a dove." On the opposite shore were soldiers dressed in browns and blacks, led by the Devil, with wings "like a bat." In this dream Cayce was sent to deliver a message before a great fight was to begin, but the Devil interfered and Edgar couldn't remember the message he had been sent to give.

In a reading Edgar gave on October 7, 1935, long before America's experts had begun to perceive the political and geographical alliances that would soon involve nearly seventy nations, Cayce—in trance—said: "[International affairs] are in a condition of great anxiety on the part of many, not only as individuals but as to nations. And the activities that have already begun have assumed such proportions that there is to be the attempt upon the part of groups to penalize, or to make for the associations of groups to carry on same. This will make for the taking of sides . . . by various groups or countries or governments. This will be indicated by the Austrians, Germans, and later the Japanese joining in their influence—unseen—and gradually growing to those affairs where there must become, as it were, almost a direct opposition to that which has been the theme of the Nazis [or] the Aryan. For these will gradually make for a growing of animosities. And unless there is interference from what may be called . . . 'supernatural forces' and influences that are active in the affairs of nations and peoples, the whole world . . . will be set on fire by the militaristic groups and those that are for power and expansion in such associations."

In November 1939, two months after Germany invaded Poland and Britain had declared war on Germany, but two years before the United States was brought into the conflict by the Japanese, Cayce, in trance, said what "a sad experience [it] will be for this land [America] through forty-two and forty-three." Four months before Pearl Harbor, a young man deciding whether or not he should serve in the army or navy, asked how long hostilities would last. "Until at least forty-five," Cayce said.

Throughout all of these readings, the Source held out hope, knowing that future events would be avoided if individuals and nations prayed and "lived as they pray." In this sense, the readings seemed to emphasize not only the help available to mankind from the greater powers, but also how the spiritual life of individuals directly affected the values of nations and thus directed the course of human affairs on a global level.

The overriding message in these readings was that the collective will of mankind, and the extent of brotherly love in the world, would determine whether or not there would be war. Back in 1933, when Adolf Hitler was chancellor of Germany—before he had become "Der Führer"—Cayce gave perhaps his most controversial readings on this subject, suggesting that even Hitler had the potential to be a force for positive change in Europe if his personal will could be turned toward the brotherhood of man.

In one reading Hitler was described as being "psychically led," and as having been called for a purpose, "not only in the affairs of a nation, but as in the affairs of the world." Cayce admonished, "study . . . the impelling influence in the man, in the mind as it has acceded to power," and pointed out that, "few [men] does power not destroy." In one particularly controversial passage, Cayce suggested that the Jews had wandered "far afield, and their rebelliousness and their seeking into the affairs of others has rather brought them into their present position," and made reference to the resurgence of an old influence that would mark "the beginning of the return that must come throughout the earth." Cayce might have been referring to the return of the Jews to their homeland in Palestine, which would become the formalized state of Israel in 1948.

However, the Source specifically stated that Hitler would be a force for good only if he were able to avoid falling into the trap of the forces of "self-aggrandizement." From the outset, the Source tempered every positive statement about Hitler with qualifying clauses such as, "if imperialism does not enter in." By January 1934, Cayce stated that, indeed, "[imperialism] is entering." And in 1938, eighteen months before war had officially broken out, and just as Germany annexed Austria, the Source became vitriolic on the subject, referring to Germany as "a smear upon its forces for its dominance over its brother, a leech upon the universe for its own sustenance!" In 1939, three weeks after Hitler invaded Poland, when asked about Hitler's future, the Source answered succinctly: "Death."

Germany was not the only country singled out for criticism. After allying itself with Germany in 1935, Italy was described in the readings as "selling itself for a mess of pottage," and was later denounced for "forcing servitude" upon others. And Japan, which had invaded Manchuria in 1931, was referred to as "domination forces." Cayce also said that England held "ideas of being just a little better than the other fellow," that the sin of France "is the gratifying of the desire of the body," and that the sin of India is "the cradle of knowledge not applied, except within self." The Source did not leave America out, either. Americans, according to Cayce, *had* to begin to live according to that which was written on their dollar bill—"In God We Trust . . . That principle [is] being forgotten . . . and that is the sin of America."

Another controversial reference in a reading done around this time was to Russia, which Cayce, in trance, said would emerge as the greater "hope of the world," but "not as that sometimes termed of the Communistic, or the Bolshevistic." Here the Source stressed exactly what Russia would bring: "Freedom, freedom! That each man will live for his fellow man. The principle has been born. It will take years for it to be crystallized, but out of Russia comes again the hope of the world. Guided by . . . that friendship with the nation that hath even set on its present monetary unit 'In God We Trust.'"

As inconceivable as this declaration would have sounded to anyone at the time, the Source went on to clarify in a way that made it seem more plausible, adding that this freedom would not come about until it [Russia] "knew freedom" at home. "A new understanding has and will come to a troubled people," Cayce said. "Here, because of the yoke of oppression, because of the self-indulgences, has arisen another extreme. Only when there is freedom of speech, the right to worship according to the dictates of the conscience— until these come about, still turmoils will be within."

In 1939, Edgar also gave some highly prophetic readings on the subject of life in America. One reading specifically addressed changes that would result from growing racial and labor-related tensions in the United States. "Ye are to have turmoils [in the aftermath of war]" the Source told A.R.E. members assembled for their eighth annual congress in Virginia Beach. "Ye are to have strifes between capital and labor. Ye are to have a division in thine own land before there is the second of the presidents that next will not live through his office. [For a time there will be] a mob rule!"

Like the readings given on Hitler and World War II, the reference to the deaths of two presidents in office foretold actual events—in this case the deaths of Franklin Roosevelt in 1945 and John F. Kennedy in 1963. Likewise the statement about mob rule could be taken as a foreshadowing of the race riots that would take place in Little Rock, Birmingham, Chicago, and New York. "Then shall thy own land see the blood flow, as in those periods when brother fought against brother," Cayce said in another reading, given on December 2, 1941.

Along with commentary on the nightmare of World War II, which would ultimately leave over seventy-five-million people dead or wounded, the readings started down another morbid path, by raising the specter of Edgar's own death. For many people who had come to know and love the "sleeping prophet"—among them members of the Norfolk Study Group, who believed that "Armageddon" was near at hand—the suggestion that Edgar was being "called back" was in keeping with the idea that he would be a more effective force in the affairs of man from the "other side."

Throughout 1941 and 1942, readings repeatedly warned Edgar about his poor diet, high blood pressure, respiratory problems, and various lesions and other obstructions in his intestinal tract, suggesting that these would eventually lead to his demise. The warnings came as no surprise to Gertrude or Gladys, for Edgar himself had only sporadically practiced the health recommendations prescribed in the readings. He continued to smoke two packs of cigarettes a day, eat pork and other high-fat foods, and had long since given up his routine hikes along the shore. This, along with a lack of sleep and almost continuous worry over his children and other loved ones in the war, promised to be a deadly combination.

At times, the Source even appeared to be angry with Edgar's inability to take better care of himself. As Edgar's health grew more precarious, the readings progressively grew shorter, more to the point, almost abrupt. "Unless there are corrections made . . . the disturbances . . . will become rather a serious disorder and not much may be done if waiting too late." In one reading, when asked about certain treatments and diets Edgar needed to undertake, the Source asked, "How will you make him follow it?"

It was a tragic irony that Edgar didn't act on the health advice given. What largely prevented him from doing so were the ever-increasing demands being placed upon him for readings. The publication of *There Is a River* brought nearly a thousand new members to the A.R.E. in 1943 and a great deal of attention from both average citizens and influential figures in the world of psychic research. Among authors and journalists who conducted studies of Cayce's work were Homer Curtis, author of *Christian Mystics*, and Sherwood Eddy, whose book, *You Will Survive After Death*, detailed Cayce's life along with the lives of other prominent psychics, including Arthur Ford, Michael Thomas, and Pamela Nash. The piece of writing about Cayce that garnered the most attention was that written by Margueritte Bro, entitled "Miracle Man of Virginia Beach," which appeared in *Coronet*, one of the most widely read magazines of the 1940s. The issue in which her article appeared sold more copies than any in that magazine's history.

The deluge of publicity that Cayce received brought an estimated 4,500 requests for readings, and many tens of thousands of dollars in checks and money orders for memberships. Edgar's daily mail had to be delivered in sacks. During one six-month period in 1943 the A.R.E. received $18,000 and over three thousand letters. Telegrams came in parcels. The written requests were stacked waist high in the library, on the stairs, on the dining room table, and in the den. Gladys hired as many as eight assistants, mostly wives of servicemen, just to read and respond to the requests, and had to disconnect the telephone to prevent its incessant ringing. The waiting list for new appointments would eventually extend five years into the future.

As Edgar had done in Hopkinsville years earlier when his story ran in the *New York Times,* he was determined to send all the money back. He wanted people to pay only what was required and to know exactly what they would receive if time permitted him to grant their request. For this reason, each person seeking a reading would be sent a small booklet outlining Edgar Cayce's life and work and explaining the A.R.E.'s ideals and purposes. The greatest source of frustration and worry for Edgar was the number of people who genuinely needed his help and wouldn't receive it. There were, of course, fan letters and requests from people seeking only to satisfy their own curiosity, but the vast majority were from people who were deathly sick or sought help for a dying child or wanted to know about their sons at war.

On top of the strains all of this produced on Edgar's conscience, there were other unexpectedly adverse effects from the national publicity. One such problem developed at the First Presbyterian Church in Virginia Beach. The Cayces had been active members at that church for over sixteen years, during which time Edgar had taught Sunday school and Bible study. Rarely in those sixteen years had he missed a class. Once his story became widely known, however, influential members of his congregation complained that a "psychic" was not suited to be teaching the Scriptures in their church. In previous years, Reverend Clower would have intervened, citing the half century that Edgar had been active in the church, and the nearly four decades he had taught Bible study. But Clower had been replaced by a new minister in the fall of 1943. Edgar was unceremoniously "relieved" of his Bible class.

Hugh Lynn sought to console his father by explaining why he believed the minister and those in the congregation were fearful of him. "You are a symbol of principles which are not lived," Hugh wrote to his father in a letter from England. "I can understand such people [at the church], [and] so can you, and if you can continue to smile . . . you [will] live [to be an example of] what you talk about."

One of his few joys during this time was playing with Charles Thomas—whom he called Captain—and giving a reading for his second grandchild, Edgar Evans Jr., who was born June 29, 1943, while his father was stationed in Trinidad. The reading, conducted two days after Edgar Evans Jr.'s birth, indicated that the child, like his father, had been an Atlantean. It also stated that the child would be prone to serious accidents from his second to fifth year, that he would be short in stature, and would be capable—given proper development—of manifesting "unusual" psychic forces, such as levitation.

Like the life reading for his cousin, Charles Thomas Cayce, much of the information would turn out to be accurate. Despite his being an especially large baby, he did grow up to be short in stature. And a month before his fourth birthday, he had an accident in which the broken glass from a milk bottle severed one of his arteries. If he manifested psychic abilities, that fact is not known outside his immediate family.

Edgar found both Edgar Evans Jr. and Charles Thomas delightful company. "You should see these two grandsons," he wrote to a close friend back in Selma. "I know you would see Edgar Evans all over again in this bouncing boy of his. While he is not nearly so active as Charles Thomas . . . he is certainly the carbon copy of his dad . . . the smartest thing in the country."

Not long after giving the reading for his new grandson, and in the midst of his own declining physical condition, Edgar invited more trouble into his life by agreeing to hire a graduate student from the University of Chicago to help in the office. Harmon Bro, by all accounts, was a brilliant but deeply troubled young man, whose emotional outbursts, coupled with a tendency toward suicide, would add to the confusion in the Cayce household. Edgar had hired him at the behest of his mother, Margueritte Bro, the author of the article that had run in *Coronet*, who believed that Edgar's influence on her son might make all the difference. As it was later revealed in her life reading, Margueritte had in a previous incarnation been "the other Mary," at whose wedding Jesus had turned water into wine. Edgar, as Lucius, had known her in that incarnation. And in that same Palestine incarnation, Harmon Bro, identified as Thaddeus, had been Edgar's son. Although Edgar and Harmon's time together in Virginia Beach was relatively short, their relationship would develop many of the karmic resonances of their earlier incarnations together, which perhaps explains why the readings supported Edgar's decision to hire him as a secretary.

The months Harmon spent in Virginia Beach under Edgar's influence would, in fact, have a profound effect upon the young graduate student, for Harmon went on to become a much-loved and charismatic minister and author who praised Edgar and his work from the pulpit and in print. Unfortunately, Harmon's presence in the Cayce household was another challenge for Edgar. The months that Harmon and his young wife, June, worked with Edgar can only be characterized as a struggle of wills between Harmon and Edgar. One day, the two of them got into a shouting match that ended with the young man punching the sixty-seven-year-old in the solar plexus. It is to Edgar's credit that rather than banishing Harmon from the house, he tried to work with him.

Despite the tension between them, Harmon was able to use his pull with

Edgar to get readings for his friends without waiting in line behind the thousands of others who had requested help. The most interesting of these was conducted for a man seeking a lost treasure in Arizona. This was one of the only nonmedical and nonspiritual readings Edgar gave in 1944 and was the last of all the treasure readings Cayce ever conducted.

The reading was for Paul Lyon, an acquaintance of Harmon's who desired to obtain information relating to a cache of gold hidden in the Lost Dutchman Mine, allegedly located in a chain of mountains near Weaver's Needle in Pinal County, Arizona. As the story was related to Edgar, a Spanish prospector had first found gold in the 1840s and was working the mine with a party of other miners when they were attacked by Apache Indians. All the miners were killed in a short and bloody encounter. The location of the mine remained a mystery for another decade until a wandering prospector stumbled onto it. He kept the mine's location a secret and never filed a claim. But the quality and quantity of gold he brought out of the Needle mountains convinced everyone that the miner was sitting on a veritable fortune. According to popular legend, the prospector, an old Dutchman, blasted the mine's entrance closed in the 1870s because he realized he was dying and would never live to enjoy his wealth. Many prospectors died trying to follow the Dutchman's trail, and superstitions regarding Apache ghosts, the lost mine, and the Dutch prospector, emerged in subsequent years.

The reading on the Lost Dutchman Mine was conducted on February 1, 1944. It is remarkable for its brevity as well as the precision with which the information was delivered. Lyon was told to go to Needle Canyon, where he would find the entrance to the mine under an unusual-looking rock that was located exactly 37½ yards north of a cactus, which also had certain peculiarities. The reading also alluded to the special character of its location as a sacred burial ground, which was protected, Cayce said, by various spirit groups, presumably Apache Indians.

Correspondence does not indicate whether or not Paul Lyon acted upon this reading and searched for the mine, and to this day it is still considered lost. While Bro could take the credit, indirectly, for the last treasure reading, he himself was one of the focal points for the final—and the most terrifying—appearance of the Archangel Michael in the Cayce readings, which occurred not long after Harmon punched Edgar.

The reading on March 14, 1944, lasted only fifteen minutes. Harmon Bro sat at Edgar's side, Gertrude conducted, Gladys was the stenographer, and June Bro and four others were present in the room. The readings for that day began benignly enough, as hundreds of others before it.

"Yes, we have the body here, Edgar Cayce. This we have had before," the

Source said. "As we find there are, and have been, disturbing conditions in the general physical functioning of the body. These are rather multiple in their cause and in the reactions . . ." The reading went on to discuss gland secretions and congestion in the tissue of head, face, throat, bronchi, and through the lymph of the alimentary canal. The reading said that Edgar's mental and spiritual condition needed to be made consistent with the physical aspects of the entity.

As the Source continued, Harmon recognized a reference to his recent argument with Edgar: "Don't preach, don't act in one direction and then say or do those things in another direction. Be patient with those who are weak. Be kind to those who are even ugly." Here, Harmon reported feeling the blood rush to his face, realizing that could well mean him. To Edgar, the Source said: "Be gentle with those activities wherein there is the necessity that ye live consistently, that ye be consistent with that ye would represent among thy fellow men. For know, the Lord is in His holy temple. If thou hast, as His child, desecrated thy temple—in word, in act, in deed—know that ye alone may make those corrections, and that thy body is the temple of the living God. Act as though it were, and not as if it were a pigpen or a place of garbage for the activities of others."

At this point in the reading, Cayce's voice grew louder and his quiet whisper took on a sudden air of stern authority. The windows began to rattle and the force of the spiritual presence in the room brought Bro and the others to tears. "It felt as if a giant [vibrational] wave came crashing into the room to sweep us away," Bro later reported.

"BOW THINE HEADS, YE CHILDREN OF MEN!" Cayce's voice thundered. Immediately everyone's head went down. Gladys, determined to not lose a word, continued to take notes. Cayce—still in trance—went on speaking in the same booming voice: FOR I, MICHAEL, LORD OF THE WAY, WOULD SPEAK WITH THEE! YE GENERATION OF VIPERS, YE ADULTEROUS GENERATION, BE WARNED! THERE IS TODAY BEFORE THEE GOOD AND EVIL! CHOOSE THOU WHOM YE WILL SERVE! WALK IN THE WAY OF THE LORD OR ELSE THERE WILL COME THAT SUDDEN RECKONING, AS YE HAVE SEEN! BOW THINE HEADS, YE WHO ARE UNGRACIOUS, UNREPENTANT! FOR THE GLORY OF THE LORD IS AT HAND! THE OPPORTUNITY IS BEFORE THEE! ACCEPT OR REJECT! BUT DON'T BE PIGS!

The last phrase, Bro said, was "spat out with utter disdain," as if admonishing everyone in the room not to wallow in their own arrogance and conceit and to use the "unseen forces" as they were intended to be used. The reading ended in Edgar's quiet whisper, with instructions on how to speed

Edgar's recovery and to "keep the body-mind, the body-physical, clean in the sight of thy God."

According to Bro, when the reading ended, everyone quietly got up and scattered in different directions. Bro himself went away miserable, saying later that they were "wounded" to the very depths of their souls. "We were known. We were seen. [And] we were found wanting."

However, while Edgar was duly humbled by Michael's message and led the group of them the next day in prayers for forgiveness, not even Michael himself could, it seemed, motivate Edgar to take the steps necessary to care for his ailing body or act in better "attunement" with those who loved and cared for him. Instead of the normal three or four readings Edgar had been giving for years, he now insisted on doing as many as nine and ten in a single day. Gladys and Gertrude complained, citing previous trance counsel, which indicated that he should give no more than five readings a day, even in the best of health. The only concession Cayce made was not to give readings on weekends, and even then, he invariably felt compelled to give emergency and follow-up readings.

During this time, Edgar also gave one of the last life readings of his career. Grace Hall Hemingway, the mother of Ernest Hemingway, wrote Edgar to inquire about her past associations with various close friends, and about how she could help steer her son the novelist, "to be a power to move the world toward 'The Kingdom of God on earth.' "

Grace Hemingway was given a detailed life reading, which suggested she had been associated with various painters in previous incarnations, among them Raphael, to whom she had been "inspirational." Edgar went on to chronicle various other incarnations in which she had been previously associated with several of her current friends, such as Lillian and Albert Beath, Margueritte Bro, and Myrtle Walgreen. Grace was also told that she knew her son Ernest during an Egyptian incarnation, in which Ernest was a person who "contributed and added to the light through which, in which, he became the active force in tempering the lives of others."

As to how she could help steer Ernest and her other children toward God in their present incarnations, the Source advised her not to lecture and interfere, but to act as an example of God's grace and love. "By just living and being . . . Not by what you say but what you are. These are the things that will grow most in the experience of those to whom ye have given and do give spiritual and mental help." As for her relationship with Ernest, in particular, she was counseled to always "speak gently, never harshly." The Source further said that someday Ernest might come to her in "humbleness," to thank her for the support and example she had provided him. Grace was never known to have taken Edgar's counsel to heart, nor, unfortunately was Ernest ever reported to have thanked his mother for her example. Right up until the end of Grace's life in 1951, Ernest was still disparaging her as the "all-time bitch" or "all-American bitch."

Not long after giving the Hemingway reading, Edgar's physical condition began to seriously deteriorate. By February 1944, when Edgar was on the verge of collapse from a severe cold and cough, he agreed to take a short vacation to visit Tom Sugrue in Clearwater, Florida. He enjoyed fishing with Tom in the warm waters, but when he came back ten days later, he plunged back into the same schedule, giving four readings in one day and then nine the next. By the end of the month he was in bed with pneumonia.

Despite orders from his physician, Dr. Woodhouse, and recommendations in the readings, Edgar prescribed for himself a potent drug—a sulfa compound that he had once taken at the onset of a severe cold. The shock to his system left him in such a weakened condition that he was forced into bed and unable to give further readings until March 14, when he gave one for himself. Then, against the pleadings of Gertrude and Gladys, he began doing readings for a few friends in desperate need, and by March 20, he was back to giving nine readings in a single day.

Betty Allen, one of the secretaries Gladys hired to help with the vast amount of letters arriving each day, was so upset by the "depleted" state in which Edgar frequently found himself after giving readings that she referred to his trance sessions as the "drain machine," and urged him to stop. "Hour by hour, day by day I could sense some vital life sustenance ebbing from the body of a man whom I had come to admire and to love in some special personal way," she later wrote.

In the midst of giving physical readings, Edgar entertained many new visitors who came to the beach seeking his advice and counsel. Among them was an unnamed government agent who arrived from Washington, D.C., on May 30, 1944. At Edgar's request, Gladys led the visitor into the study, and the doors were closed. Edgar's only words about this visit were in a letter to Edgar Evans, in which Edgar described his visitor as "one of the higher-ups," who was "an advisor to those in authority, who were the ones that formulate the patterns about the inter-relations that are to be with all of the other countries after the war." Also around this same time, Harmon Bro reported answering a telephone call, which he put through to Edgar, from the office of Harry Truman, soon to be the vice president of the United States.

Gladys and Gertrude fretted that Edgar was not physically strong enough to be involved with government agents, let alone to keep up with all the physical readings he was giving. There seemed to be nothing that would slow him down until, that is, Edgar was stopped by a stroke in August 1944. The stroke left his right side partially paralyzed and his right hand was so affected that he couldn't use a pen or type on his trusted Remington. Heeding the advice of his physician, and another physical reading, he left on August 30 for Roanoke, Virginia, where he was put under the care of Dr. Harry Semones, an osteopath recommended in the readings. By arrangement with Dr. Semones, Edgar and Gertrude stayed at the Meadow View Inn in Cloverdale, which was owned and operated by the physician and his wife. Usually by this time of year, the doctor and his wife would have closed the inn and gone to Florida. Out of courtesy to Edgar and Gertrude, the inn was kept open, and this allowed Dr. Semones to make daily visits.

Back in Virginia Beach, Gladys wrote cheerful letters easing the Cayces' minds about matters at home and shielding them from economic worries, but Edgar suspected the trouble she was having running the A.R.E. by herself. Now that Cayce had stopped giving readings, the A.R.E. had no income. The extra help she had hired was asked to leave, and only volunteer staff answered the phones or kept the correspondence updated. To save money, Gladys gave up an apartment she had rented and moved back into the Cayce home. In a typical letter of explanation to A.R.E. members requesting readings, Gladys wrote Mr. H. B. Harrell, who had made an appointment a year in advance. "Mr. Cayce is suffering from complete exhaustion," Gladys wrote. "We are having to cancel appointments every day now for people who have been waiting way over a year for their readings."

Every day, Gladys called the Meadow View Inn and read letters to Edgar from the many people who wrote wishing him a swift recovery. Hugh Lynn, now stationed in France, wrote his father a heartfelt letter of encouragement. "I know, and it makes me glad, how easy it will be for you to slip away when you decide to do so," he wrote. "You must realize that you have done a magnificent job . . . It is not for any accomplishment for yourself that I ask you to continue, but for those of us who need your help a little longer *here*. The crystallization of our efforts lies just ahead, the molding of our work for the masses is shaping and needs your guidance, the influencing of several important individuals is needed—need I mention those close to you, your grandsons."

Edgar Cayce gave his last reading on September 17, 1944, for himself. There was little doubt in anyone's mind that the "Master of Masters" visited during this reading, and although he could not be seen, His presence was felt. In this reading, Gladys, Gertrude, Edgar, and his physicians were counseled to be at peace themselves. "Let not your hearts be troubled, neither let it be afraid, for, Lo, it is I, and I have promised to be with thee, even unto the end of the world." Recommendations were given for Edgar's physical comfort, but little else. "Would you advise us staying on here in Roanoke for a while?" Gertrude asked. "Stay on until you are well or dead . . . as has been given," came the reply.

A week after giving this reading, Cayce suffered another stroke, which resulted in complete paralysis of the entire left side of his body, from his neck to his feet, and further paralysis of his right side. He was, however, in good spirits, and on October 12, was sufficiently strong to dictate a list of instructions, which Gertrude relayed to Gladys by phone. "Appreciate you thinking things through," he told Gladys in answer to her letters explaining the various A.R.E. matters that had come up. He told her to let the accounts stand until he got home and that he wanted to see the new A.R.E. booklet that Tom Sugrue was writing. Gladys was to pay the car insurance, see about the heating bill, and rent the extra bedroom in the house. He also left instructions for Bains, the gardener, to dig a trench and plant his tulip bulbs.

Captain Edgar Evans Cayce, temporarily home on leave, arrived in Roanoke on November 19. He immediately grasped the severity of his father's condition. Heeding his father's desire to die at home, surrounded by the people and things he loved most, he bundled Edgar in blankets and checked him out of the Meadow View Inn for the journey home the next day. Sergeant Hugh Lynn Cayce couldn't join them because he was, at that moment, following General Patton's tanks into Germany.

In anticipation of Edgar's arrival, Bains, the gardener, worked overtime to see that the yard and grounds were in splendid shape, and Gladys and the others overhauled the house and did a spring cleaning. Despite their outward enthusiasm, however, they awaited Edgar's arrival with mixed feelings. The reports Gladys had received indicated that Edgar was on the mend, but she intuitively knew—as did Edgar Evans—that the end was drawing near.

Edgar himself knew that the end was approaching, and it was perhaps for this reason that he asked that the ambulance stop in Blackstone, Virginia, on their way to the beach, to see if Beatrice and Richmond Seay were home. He wished to see Little Anna one last time. Beatrice and her husband were gone when Edgar Evans and his father called. They too had sensed that the end was near and had driven to Virginia Beach in hopes of seeing Edgar. They left the beach just as Edgar and Edgar Evans were leaving Blackstone, and Eddy never got to say good-bye to his beloved Little Anna.

Edgar had to be carried into their Arctic Crescent home on a stretcher. The sight of Edgar on the stretcher, and his tears of joy at finally being home after three months away, was an emotional moment for everyone. "[He was] so glad to be home," Gladys wrote, "But heartbroken to be in such a fix."

In the comfort of familiar surroundings and the company of his friends and family, Edgar's spirits rose and he seemed to be doing better, although most of his body was still paralyzed from the neck down, and he could barely speak beyond a whisper. "I really think I have improved more since I have been home than in all the time since I have been sick," Edgar wrote to Hugh Lynn on December 2. On December 13, however, his condition got considerably worse and he went into a coma, which lasted through the night. Early the next morning he looked much better and his circulation seemed improved. But he had lost the alertness of his former days and couldn't sleep for more than thirty minutes at a time without waking. Catherine Patterson, a close family friend and recipient of many readings, provided round-the-clock nursing, aided by Gertrude, Gladys, and Edgar's sister Annie. Annie gave him daily massages until Dr. George came down from Wilmington, Delaware, and asked that the massages be discontinued. He diagnosed Edgar as suffering from pulmonary edema and administered doses of atropine made from belladonna, along with vitamins, a protein concentrate, and baby foods.

The Norfolk Study Group paid Edgar one last visit, as did Dave Kahn and a few other close friends. One member of the group, Jane Williams, a friend of the Cayces' since the demise of the hospital, was sitting with Edgar when he turned to her and told her about a dream that he'd had. He didn't go into detail but said that he believed he would be "rejuvenated" on January 5. Later that night he spoke of the power of faith and healing. "Faith, hope, and love—they are real," he told Gladys. "Faith is the substance of things hoped for, the evidence of things not seen, but it is more real than anything you can see. Love is universal, not personal. When it becomes universal, it is [a] creative [energy]. It can bring life just as surely as two bodies united become a channel for the entrance of a soul into the earth."

Edgar spent Christmas of 1944 in bed, and then sat up during the New Year when the midnight horns were sounded at the naval station. "Happy New Year!" Gladys told him. "We're going places and doing things in 1945!" Edgar replied: "Same to you . . . if the Lord is willing." Two or three times that night, Edgar would wake up saying such things as: "This world is in an awful mess, and we've got to control it. I just hope I am worthy."

Gladys vividly recalled Edgar's last night, January 2. Just after sunset, Edgar had a brief conversation with Gertrude, in which he told her that he loved her. Gertrude leaned over and kissed him. He said, "You know I do love you." Gertrude nodded, and he asked, "How do you know?" She smiled, then said, "Oh, I just know." Edgar looked at her with tears in his eyes. "I don't see how you can tell," he said, "but I do love you." After taking a moment to compose himself, he continued. "You know, when you love someone you sacrifice for [th]'em. And what have I ever sacrificed because I love you?" Gertrude broke into tears and left the room.

Later that night, Edgar awoke and told Gladys that he was conscious of someone in the room with them, though only Edgar appeared to see who it was. "He looks like a musical conductor," Edgar said. "[Playing] beautiful music." Gladys asked what kind of music was being played. "I don't know," came the reply. "I don't know much about music." Gladys begged to differ with him. "You know all about music," she assured him. "You know about the harmonies of the universe."

The next day Edgar was relieved of his congestion and reported the best night's sleep he had had in a long time. However, that afternoon, his pulse rate increased and he broke out in a clammy perspiration and had to be washed down. Annie Cayce came into the room with some oyster stew she had cooked in the kitchen and spoon-fed it to him. Gladys put an electric heating pad at his feet to keep him warm. They tried to get Edgar to use an oxygen mask, but he just pushed it away. From downstairs, in the dining room, Gladys could hear Gertrude sobbing. Edgar took two or three more sips of stew. It was seven o'clock. At seven-fifteen he stopped breathing.

Not long after the funeral, held on January 5, 1945, Gladys had a dream in which she saw Edgar's passing in a vision of a glorious sunset and a brilliant night sky. As the last rays of the sun shone through the heavens, a single star appeared in the gathering darkness. And then a second star appeared, connected to the first star by a thin thread of light. A third and a fourth star appeared—all connected together by threads of light—until hundreds of stars revealed uncharted galaxies and a vast interconnected universe in the now brilliant night sky. "I had no fear about Edgar or his legacy after I had that dream," Gladys told a friend. "The light he brought to countless thousands was just going to grow stronger."

Gertrude, herself, felt much the same way. But she too felt as if "a vital organ had been removed," and that life would never again be the same. She suffered not only from the emotional pain of her husband's death, but from the pain of a serious medical condition that had resulted from childbirth years earlier. Readings taken before Edgar's death indicated that Gertrude had been too soon on her feet during the recovery period. The injuries to her pelvis and uterus had never properly healed. Although she had felt well enough to walk, the weight of the body on her feet produced lesions and an overtaxation of the liver and spleen. Her engorged liver and spleen had begun to atrophy, and cancer developed. Physicians diagnosed her condition as terminal.

Too ill to run the household, Gertrude turned all business and financial matters over to Gladys and took to the same bed in which her husband had been nursed in his final days. Flowers, which had long been her love, arrived in great quantities and filled the house with their sweet perfume. That April the peach and pear tree in the yard began to bloom, and the bulbs that Bains planted opened their petals.

Through letters from home, Hugh Lynn—still in Europe—realized how grave his mother's condition was and wrote her a touching letter expressing his deep love and affection for "Muddie," the affectionate name he had called his mother since childhood. "It is important for you to realize how much fun it has been being your son," he wrote. "Many times I have seen you faced with problems [and] conditions that I have known to crumple up so many people, and you have risen above them and . . . carried others with you. These things Ecken [Edgar Evans] and I will not forget. To few people have been entrusted the guidance of so many lives—not in the outward way to be seen by men, but in the background where the going was tough. These things I know, and will not forget. Never had I known of such unselfish love for two human beings as you have always shown toward Ecken and me."

Gertrude would never get to read the letter, for it arrived a few days after her death, on Easter morning, April 1, 1945.

Epilogue:

The New
Tomorrow

Like Hugh Lynn and Edgar Evans, Gladys had been mentally preparing for Edgar's passing for many months. Although she and the others shared an unavoidable and unsettling sense of loss and grief, Gladys often felt as if he was still present long after his death. She would write him letters, and when she thought no one else would hear, spoke to him as if he were standing beside her in the same room. In a letter she wrote to Edgar soon after his death, which she recorded in her diary, she said: "Always I have discussed things with you before making decisions. As I look back I now realize that you said very little but you listened and after a while I could feel the right thing to do. Maybe this was the way it was with everyone else. Perhaps you acted as a mirror in which we could really see ourselves as we are . . . Dear Eddy Cayce . . . please still be that mirror for all of us."

In the year immediately after his death, Edgar Cayce appeared in the dreams of many who had come to know and love him. One of the most unusual dream visions was experienced by Dave Kahn on November 19, 1945, which he recounted in a letter to Hugh Lynn, who was still in Germany. "I saw hundreds of 'small people' about two inches high around him," Kahn wrote. "He stepped over and up to me [and] said, 'Well, here I am en route to Virginia Beach.' He was standing at Grand Central Station [in New York] He said . . . Dave, I must go down to the beach and help Hugh Lynn get straightened away. [Edgar] was dressed as I remember him thirty years ago—young and full of pep and promise. He was very well pleased with his trip, but did not tell me where he came from. A few minutes passed and your mother came up and [asked if I had seen Edgar]. I said, 'Yes, a few minutes ago.' She said, 'I want to go to the beach, too, and I have my money to pay my own car fare. [Gertrude] passed on [out of the dream] and your Dad seemed anxious to get away alone and passed me hurriedly looking for you. The little people just clamored all about him as if he was a king and they his subjects. Later, I saw a lot of Virginia Beach people around him, and they saw him greet Gladys . . . as if [he] had just returned from [a typical] trip to New York . . . I know he is with you and will follow with you to the beach. Keep yourself attuned quietly and he will counsel you."

However much Edgar may have been with Kahn and other A.R.E. members in spirit, Edgar Cayce's physical passing could not be ignored for long. Upon returning home from the war, Hugh Lynn and others had legitimate concerns that without Edgar to give more readings the A.R.E. would have to disband—not for a lack of love and enthusiasm for the work, but for lack of funds.

Except for the 14,256 trance readings stored in the vault, and the Cayce house on Arctic Crescent, Edgar and Gertrude's estate amounted to quite little. A joint savings account contained less than $2,000. The blue-book value of the family car, a 1941 Pontiac, was approximately $1,000. There was also a diamond ring and hair pin, a series E victory bond, household furniture, and a typewriter. By the time Gladys and her Norfolk accountant had paid funeral expenses and other minor debts, sold the car, redeemed the government bonds, and added in the value of the house, the estate amounted to less than $10,000.

Besides their lack of funds, the A.R.E. also had no defined purpose. As Harmon Bro remarked, the association was composed entirely of Edgar's friends. Trying to sustain those friendships without Edgar Cayce at its center was like "building an organization out of a dead doctor's patients." Many board members, among them Dave Kahn, said it couldn't be done and initiated discussions with Harvard University as a possible recipient of the readings and correspondence. Gladys refused to cooperate, believing that the Cayce papers must remain in the A.R.E. vault until she had guidance from Edgar as to their final disposition. She kept the key to the vault in her bosom, and at one point hid file boxes of correspondence that didn't fit in the vault under her bed. She adamantly refused to give the papers up and demanded

Hugh Lynn's promise that all of the readings and correspondence would stay in Virginia Beach until she—and Edgar—agreed to a new location.

The solution to their dilemma came to Gladys in a dream in which Edgar himself appeared and told her what to do. "It is time now to prove our big-sounding words and actually do some research on our files instead of just talking about it. Get the message out!"

Like Gladys, Hugh Lynn saw great wisdom in this approach. By putting the emphasis on the readings, and on the insights they offered on such diverse and broad subjects as biblical thought, prayer, medicine, and social transformation, the A.R.E. could become a resource center for individuals with varied backgrounds, beliefs, and interests, as had been the intent of Edgar and Arthur Lammers back in Dayton. Rather than build a cult around Edgar Cayce the man, the A.R.E. would encourage members of various faiths to remain in their folds while applying the spiritual wisdom and practical guidance found in the readings. This bold approach proved to be the most inspired decision that the fledgling A.R.E. would make with Hugh Lynn at its helm. Although Edgar Cayce the man would never be venerated as an icon to the same degree that Mary Baker Eddy or other founders of personality-driven religious movements have been, the message put forth in the readings ultimately touched the lives of many millions who might otherwise have turned a blind eye to the Kentucky farm boy turned prophet.

Tom Sugrue would move back to the beach from Florida to help Gladys and Hugh Lynn get started. They formed committees to study particular aspects of the readings and to prepare articles for publication and distribution. Many other people joined their ranks, among them Gina Cerminara, who became a respected author and historian, Judy Chandler, the broadcast journalist and playwright who had been Hugh Lynn's mentor, Mae Gimbert St. Clair, who provided first-person testimony of the power of the readings, and Esther Wynne, the retired schoolteacher and chief organizer of the first Norfolk Study Group. Like Tom, Gladys, and Hugh Lynn, all of these people had been identified in life readings as having been members of Edgar Cayce's "soul group" in previous incarnations.

Eventually the articles the A.R.E. staff and volunteers wrote and the readings the articles were based on came to the attention of a wide spectrum of educators, historians, theologians, medical professionals, and scientists. A large part of the attraction, as one Cayce scholar pointed out, was that regardless of the field of study, the readings continually proved to be decades ahead of their time. Readings for particular physical ailments such as arthritis, epilepsy, and cancer, were especially in demand, for the recommendations made in these readings could be found nowhere else. Later came interest in reincarnation, astrology, and the Bible readings, which would become staples of the burgeoning New Age movement. A newsletter, distributed to the many study groups that were forming across the United States and abroad, chronicled what was available.

As a result of these efforts, the A.R.E. survived its transition from an organization that produced psychic readings to one that studied and disseminated them. While the association didn't see the phenomenal growth it had experienced with the publication of a "Miracle Man of Virginia Beach" or *There Is a River*, there was a gradual, incremental growth built entirely on study and interest in the readings. Ultimately, interest in Edgar Cayce's work, and the estimated three million people who have consulted the readings, far outweighed the original membership of the association he had founded.

The A.R.E. Press, which had begun with a one hand-crank mimeograph machine, became what is now a major publisher with thousands of books and study materials distributed each year. Through Hugh Lynn's efforts, the A.R.E. study materials and two volumes of *A Search for God* have been translated into ten languages and would eventually capture the imaginations of such diverse fans as Elvis Presley, John Lennon, Shirley MacLaine, Ram Dass, Steven Spielberg, and astronaut Edgar Mitchell. They would also draw the criticism of prominent television evangelists, among them Virginia Beach's other favorite son, Pat Robertson.

Hugh Lynn spent more than three decades traveling the United States and abroad helping study groups get started, leading educational trips to Egypt and Palestine, and giving lectures at Harvard, the University of Chicago, Cal Tech, and more than two hundred other schools. The admission price for lectures was typically 25 cents. Hugh Lynn fondly remembered once going up to the desk to pay his hotel bill after one speaking engagement and handing the clerk two fistfuls of quarters, which he spread out over the desk. When the clerk protested, Hugh Lynn told her that it was quarters or nothing at all.

While Hugh Lynn focused his attention on building membership, Gladys was left with the formidable task of indexing and organizing the thousands of readings into a database available to the general public. Although great strides were made in the 1940s, the task would not be completed until forty years later. A typical reading might include as many as ten or more references to the Bible, various geographic locations ranging from Dayton, Ohio, to Paris, France, as well as ten or more medical terms and references to blood, physical ailments, and individual organs. Eventually, the readings were cross-indexed under approximately ten thousand different topics. All of the material was put on computer and is now available on a CD-ROM.

One person who would be instrumental in helping Gladys organize the readings was Albert E. Turner, a retired Pennsylvania stockbroker. Turner came to Virginia Beach to learn about Cayce and was immediately smitten with Gladys, who—at forty-seven years old—still was quite lovely. Gladys, however, had no intention of giving up the work. It was Turner who embraced her and the A.R.E., and he devoted himself to both. He and Gladys were married and by all accounts, had a happy life together until Turner's death sixteen years later. Gladys subsequently married a second time, to a retired Virginia farmer who had been one of Albert Turner's close friends. Sadly, Gladys, by then seventy-seven years old, would be widowed once again, five years later. "But her marriage to the work," as one staff member said, "continued uninterrupted."

The A.R.E. grew and expanded greatly under Hugh Lynn's direction. Perhaps the most daring financial move he and the others made was to buy back the old hospital building. Since the Blumenthals had sold the property in 1936, the building had been used as a nightclub, a home for army nurses, a Masonic lodge, and a summer theater. The realtor handling the property believed it to be cursed because of the frequency with which it had changed hands. In 1955, Hugh Lynn had heard that the building was going up for sale and proposed to the board that the A.R.E. buy it. "It was a wild dream," Hugh Lynn later said. "I had the entire board of trustees against me. It was voted down three times. But I kept on calling meetings to discuss it again." Eventually, the board caved in, and Margueritte Briggs, an A.R.E. member in Florida, put up the $5,000 down payment.

Most important to Hugh Lynn was the psychological victory. "Like troops retaking ground lost in an earlier skirmish, its spiritual soldiers enjoyed a sense of triumph," wrote A. Robert Smith, Hugh Lynn's biographer. Harmon Bro, a frequent visitor, concurred and said that "capturing it was a courageous and symbolic step." Gladys said that she could feel Edgar on the other side, "grinning from ear to ear."

Hugh Lynn made his office on the main floor, just off the lobby. A small library was established on the opposite side of the building. Gladys, the A.R.E. business manager, took over the lower levels, where a large vault was installed to house the complete collection of Edgar Cayce's papers. It was called the "dungeon," recalled Mary Ellen Carter, who worked as a part-time secretary to Hugh Lynn and became Gladys's biographer and the editor of the A.R.E. magazine, *The Search Light*. The upstairs was turned into a residential area and occupants included Ruth LeNoir, a widow and one of the early study group members. A story is often told about the night an intruder broke into the building and found a place to sleep, not knowing anyone lived upstairs. He was awakened by the sleepwalking LeNoir in her long, white, flowing nightgown. Shrieking, he made a hasty retreat.

With the same boldness with which he'd reclaimed the hospital property, Hugh Lynn also reopened Atlantic University in 1961, using the original charter, which Dr. William Moseley Brown had kept active since the school's closing thirty years earlier. The school grew gradually and underwent many changes, and in 1985, offered its own Master of Arts degree program. Atlantic University's curriculum currently includes a full range of courses that compare concepts from the Cayce readings with ideas in psychology, parapsychology, religious traditions, and other spiritual philosophies.

Under Hugh Lynn's auspices, the A.R.E. began building a library and conference center in the 1970s, which now stands adjacent to the former hospital on Atlantic Avenue, with a commanding view of the ocean. Along with complete transcripts of all the Cayce readings, the library houses one of the most extensive collections of metaphysical books and manuscripts in the world. The downstairs conference center hosts thousands of visitors each year to hear lectures on such subjects as ESP, dreams, holistic health, meditation, and life after death.

In addition to its efforts in Virginia Beach, the A.R.E. is the headquarters for thousands of study groups now in existence throughout the world, as well as for an active prison fellowship. The association also runs a popular summer camp for families and children, acts as a referral service for various physicians and medical clinics, and through some of its members, supports archaeology digs in Egypt and undersea exploration in the Bahamas.

However dynamic the A.R.E. has been in "getting the message out," the legacy of which Edgar himself would surely have been most proud is that of the many physicians and therapists who have successfully used his trance-induced recommendations to help thousands of patients. No university hospital or independent medical center has yet made a comprehensive study of the "truth" or "fiction" of the readings, but the statistical and anecdotal results for both Cayce's diagnoses and treatments speak for themselves.

In a study by journalist Sherwood Eddy, conducted five years after Cayce's death, eleven doctors who had consulted the readings were surveyed. Two of the physicians declined to participate on the grounds that they had handled too few cases to provide an accurate measure of their success or failure, but the nine remaining physicians gave answers that were consistently favorable. A doctor in Bronxville, New York, evaluated Cayce's diagnoses as perfect in all twelve of the cases in which he had treated patients who had received readings. A Detroit physician, who had treated twenty patients using the readings, estimated the accuracy of Cayce's diagnosis at 80 to 90 percent correct. An Albany, New York, physician stated that all five of the patients he had treated using the readings had received accurate diagnoses. A physician from Port Washington, New York, who had treated nine patients, also gave Cayce a perfect score. Yet another New York physician, who had treated at least one hundred patients, estimated Cayce's accuracy in the range of 80 percent. The only dissenting voice was from a Norfolk, Virginia, doctor who said Cayce's diagnoses would not be considered scientific, but nevertheless acknowledged Cayce's "extraordinary powers." Likewise, these nine doctors generally praised the recommended treatments and unequivocally stated that they universally brought good results. "Nothing short of miraculous!" said one doctor.

The only other recorded effort to analyze the accuracy of the medical readings was conducted by Hugh Lynn and Edgar Evans and was published in book form in 1971. Based on seventy-four randomly chosen readings in which patients followed the recommended treatments and follow-up reports had been filed by physicians or the patients themselves, sixty-five reported positive results, which reflected a success rate of approximately 86 percent. That figure may not seem remarkable when compared to the overall success rate that most physicians have in treating their patients, however it is quite astonishing given the fact that Edgar Cayce had never physically examined—and sometimes hadn't even met—the recipients of his readings. Furthermore, patients often turned to Edgar as a last resort, when no one else seemed to be able to help them.

Impressive as this aspect of the Cayce legacy may be, it is important to understand the limitations and challenges these readings present to medical practitioners today. Virtually all of the ten thousand medical-related readings given by Cayce in his forty-five-year career were conducted one at a time for specific individuals with particular ailments. Hence, what was true for one person in one situation may not necessarily be true for another. And a recommended treatment for a person living in a place like rural Hopkinsville at the turn of the last century, before the advent of pesticides, growth hormones, and genetically engineered foods, is not necessarily relevant or helpful to a person living there today. The true measure of Edgar Cayce's contribution to medicine rests in the holistic approach he brought to helping the people who came to him. "The body, physically, mentally, [and] spiritually, is one body," the Source had said. "Mind is the builder."

Another important aspect of the Cayce legacy, and one much discussed in the half century since his passing, were the many readings he gave on the history of early civilizations. Few aspects of these trance readings have been verified, most notably those regarding Atlantis. However, archaeological research in Peru, the Bahamas, and Egypt, topographical satellite and space-shuttle photographs of Africa and the Middle East, and discoveries on the western shore of the Dead Sea, in Israel, have provided tantalizing circumstantial evidence in support of Cayce's historical information. The most thorough attention has been paid to Egypt, where scientists have discovered evidence of an ancient river system—identical to one described in the Cayce readings—which once existed in what is now a barren desert. Egyptologists have also continued to roll back the clock on their appraisal of when the first pyramids were built. No leading archaeologist to date, however, has placed the building of those monuments as long ago as 10,500 B.C., the time period specified in the readings.

Much attention has also been given to Cayce's prophecies. Despite the fact that such predictions represent less than 2 percent of the trance information provided by Edgar, upward of two hundred books and magazine articles have been devoted to them. Despite the overwhelming attention paid to the prophecies, surprisingly little thought has been given to the spirit in which they were provided: that the future is uncertain because only mankind—as builder and co-creator with God—ultimately determines the outcome. And here lies what may be the most important and least appreciated aspect of Edgar Cayce's legacy.

The readings suggest that it was not by chance, but by design, that large numbers of individuals incarnating on earth at the end of the last century were described in the life readings as having had previous incarnations in Atlantis, Egypt, and then the Holy Land at the time of the Master. Many of these people in that previous incarnation were described as important figures in the development of the early Christian church. Among the hundred or more named in the readings were Andrew, Bartholomew, Matthew, Judas, Martha, Mary Magdalene, and Edgar Cayce's own Lucius of Cryene, author of the Book of Luke. John the Beloved was said to be returning soon, and that his arrival would indicate that "the way" was being prepared for the return of Christ Himself, the Master of Masters.

Like Faith Harding, the "Little Prophetess," the host of biblical incarnates who had arrived on the earth were described as forerunners or bearers of the Divine message calling for the brotherhood of man and the fatherhood of God. It is perhaps in such a role—as a prophet—that Edgar Cayce can best be understood. In this light, Cayce's clairvoyant powers and his thousands of medical readings can be viewed as a means of convincing people of his special powers so that his real message would be heard, just as Jesus' miraculous "healings" had established His credibility as the Son of God.

"Know that right, justice, mercy, patience—as was represented and presented by Him, the Prince of Peace—is the basis upon which the new world order must eventually be established before there is [lasting] peace," Cayce, near the end of his life, had told a thirty-six-year-old railroad freight agent in Norfolk. "Prepare self for 'cooperative measures' in all phases of human relations in this direction." In another reading, the Source said: "He that hath eyes to see, let him see. He that hath ears to hear, let him hear . . . Then make thy paths straight for there must come an answering." And another important message Cayce would offer was: "Raise not democracy nor any other name above the brotherhood of man and the fatherhood of God."

Edgar Cayce, in person and in trance, humbly sought to honor that brotherhood of man and fatherhood of God. His prayer was the one taken up by those seeking to follow in his footsteps: "Lord, here am I! Use me in the way and manner that [I am best] fit . . . That we may still be as one brotherhood, as one knowing Thou art near, as one manifesting Thy power . . . not for ourselves, but that others may see the glory. Even the one next to me. Even though he may curse, may swear, may do those things that are unseemly, let Thy power be manifest . . . that Jesus Thy son may indeed come into the earth, that all men may know that He is the Lord of my Heart."

Though this prayer reveals Edgar's distinct Christian orientation, the Source also pointed out: "As He has given, it will ever be found that truth— whether in this or that schism or ism or cult—is of the one source. Are there not trees of oak, of ash, of pine? There are the needs for these for meeting this or that experience." The Source went on to note that in "each experience" an individual should strive to be the best Jew or the best Hindu or the best Christian he or she could be.

The degree to which Edgar Cayce and his fellow biblical travelers succeeded in bringing this message to the next generation is a question whose answer is yet to be determined. That his own personal journey was worthy is not in doubt. That he will come again, many of his followers have taken for granted. His return would come, according to one reading, "when the day of the earth . . . is fulfilled in Him, this body, Edgar Cayce . . . shall be made free!"

Edgar and Gertrude, free from their physical bodies, had been the first of their immediate "soul group" to pass through "God's other door." Tom Sugrue would be next. After the publication of *There Is a River*, he obtained readings that led him to write a biography of Will Starling, Edgar Cayce's childhood acquaintance from Hopkinsville and the protector of five U.S. presidents. *Starling of the White House* was published in 1946. As predicted in a Cayce reading, the book went on to become a best-seller, and Sugrue became a much sought-after lecturer. He died of heart failure in 1953, following an operation on his hips, knees, and elbows.

Dave Kahn remained an active and dedicated member of the A.R.E. Before his death on December 7, 1968, from colon cancer, Kahn reported having a dream in which the oil wells he and Edgar drilled were finally producing.

"[Cayce] was standing in front of the mantle in my bedroom," Kahn wrote in a letter to Gladys Davis. "The entire mantle was covered with what seemed a thousand openings of gas holes and all were burning in bright flames about one inch wide. He said, 'my, we've got it at last and now we can do all the things we promised our people!'"

Lucille Kahn died in 1995 at the age of ninety-three. As predicted in the life readings for her and David's children, one son became an accomplished physician, the other a prominent attorney. And each in their own way provided testimony to the power and good that came from those readings.

Morton and Edwin Blumenthal never made peace with the A.R.E. or the Cayce family. They declared bankruptcy in 1946, moved permanently to Virginia Beach, and legally had their names changed to Martin and Edwin Kane. Before their respective deaths in 1954 and 1980, the former Morton Blumenthal operated the Patricia G. Devlin Printing Company, which sold specialized greeting and postcards on Atlantic Boulevard. Edwin worked briefly as a short-order cook on the boardwalk after Patricia Devlin's death in 1951.

Gladys Davis happened to meet Morton Blumenthal at a stoplight in Virginia Beach in 1947. His car stopped just as she was crossing the street. For a brief moment, it seemed to Gladys that she and Morton were "all alone in the world." After exclaiming how well each other looked, Morton asked what Gladys was doing with her life. She told him that she was working with Hugh Lynn on the "records." Gladys then asked him if he would be willing to stop by the A.R.E. office to offer some advice about how the readings could best be organized. He declined. The light changed and he drove on. That was the last she ever saw of him.

Devastated by his affair with Patricia Devlin, Adeline Blumenthal divorced Morton in the early 1930s, and later suffered a nervous breakdown, as did their son, Morton Jr. She became a nurse, and then a house cleaner. Their son joined the navy. Edgar was the last member of the immediate Cayce family to see him. Morton Jr. arrived unexpectedly at Edgar's Bible study class at the Presbyterian Church and then visited the A.R.E. office to get copies of his life readings.

Carrie House died at The Hill on July 1, 1949, at seventy-four. Her son,

Tommy House Jr., became the manager of a company that produced home health care remedies based on Edgar Cayce's readings. He later died of emphysema on March 20, 1972, and was buried alongside his mother and father in Hopkinsville.

After leaving Hopkinsville in 1911, Dr. Wesley Ketchum opened a successful medical practice in Honolulu, where he treated clients such as Sanford B. Dole, the first and only president of Hawaii. He and his second wife, Katy deTuncq, had a child and later moved to Los Angeles, where he worked as a medical examiner for the Metropolitan Life Insurance Company. In 1953, Ketchum celebrated his eightieth birthday at A.R.E. headquarters in Virginia Beach. He died in 1963 at his home in Palo Alto, California, at age ninety.

Hugh Lynn died of cancer on July 4, 1982, at age seventy-five. Charles Thomas Cayce, his son, and the fourth-generation Cayce to actively participate in the work, took over the reins of the A.R.E. and is a frequent lecturer.

Edgar Evans, now in his eighties, is still spry and articulate. He remains on the A.R.E. board.

On February 12, 1986, Gladys Davis was reunited with Edgar, who was described in the readings as her "twin soul." She was eighty-one. Her dream of a pantheon of interconnected stars lighting up the evening sky was brighter than it had ever been. As Jeanette Thomas, a friend and the woman who carries her legacy onto the next generation has aptly pointed out: "Gladys Davis's own star is among the brightest."

Acknowledgments

This book could not have been written without the generous support, companionship, and hard work of Nancy Thurlbeck, to whom this book is happily and proudly dedicated. Her research, insights, and contributions are everywhere present in these pages.

I also owe a debt of thanks to Jeanette Thomas of the Edgar Cayce Foundation in Virginia Beach. The loving care she has given to the great body of material under her supervision is an enduring tribute to her mentor, Gladys Davis.

Thanks must also go to Delbert D. Cayce III and William T. Turner of Christian County, Kentucky, who have devoted many hours to help preserve a past that is quickly slipping into obscurity; and to Charles Thomas Cayce at the Association for Research and Enlightenment in Virginia Beach, who has helped to bring the work of his grandfather into the twenty-first century.

There are many others whose contributions to this book were substantial: Dr. Paul Allen, Ray E. Bailey, Sam Benesch, June and Harmon Bro, Gus Brunsman, Edgar Evans Cayce, Joseph Dunn, Sue Ehret, Rielly Froh, Janet Gentry, Ralf Grey, Anne Butler Hall, Janet Hamilton, Faith Hope Charity Harding, Nancy Horlacher, Rosalie Horstman-Haines, Aurale Huff, Richard and Dr. David Kahn, Mary Kane, Alton Ketchum, Debra Lambert Ketchum, Betty King, Joanne Larson, Dan Leach,

Brooks Major, Sue Lynn McGuire, William Osborn, Judith Partington, Debra Pence-Massie, Michael Pinkava, David Rose, Brad Sorenson, Henry Vaughan, and Robert Warnock.

There are also many dedicated scholars of the Cayce readings whose work and personal insights have greatly contributed to my understanding of the Cayce material. Among them are Doris Agee, Juliet Brooke Ballard, Mary Ellen Carter, Gina Cerminara, Howard Church, Jim Dixon, Richard Henry Drummond, Christopher Fazel, Ernest Frejer, Jeffery Furst, Rob Grant, K. Paul Johnson, Robert Krajenke, Noel Langley, Gladys McGarey, David McMillin, Eric Mein, John Pagano, Herbert Puryear, Henry Reed, Douglas Richards, Lytle Robinson, Glenn Sanderfur, I. C. Sharma, A. Robert Smith, Lynn Sparrow, Mark Thurston, Kevin Todeschi, John Van Auken, and Louis Wilson.

I am also grateful to several old and new friends for their unfailing support: Alison Bingeman and Noah Blough, Bill Dear, Derek Dickenson, Jeremy and Mardesia Finch, Tony and Suzanne Marks-Nino, Ruben Miller, Elise and Phillip Stone, Dr. Kenneth Stoller, Jean Sharley Taylor, and John Ziska.

A note of appreciation must also go to my agent, Mary Evans, who believed in this project from its inception and steadfastly saw it through to completion.

Final, special thanks must go to Christopher Knutsen, my editor at Riverhead Books, who consistently provided insights on every aspect of this book's form and content, and whose advice, good cheer, and invaluable suggestions are much appreciated.

Notes

Unless otherwise indicated, the sources cited below are part of the archives of the Edgar Cayce Foundation [ECF] and the library of the Association for Research and Enlightenment [A.R.E.] in Virginia Beach, Virginia.

ECF and A.R.E. sources are designated by a one- or two-part number corresponding to the indexing system devised by Gladys Davis. The first number is the case number, which references the subject's name. The second number—separated from the first by a dash—is the sequence number, which designates the number of that reading in the series associated with that individual. All of the correspondence directly associated with a trance reading can be identified or located by using this numerical classification system. In cases where this has not been possible, correspondence has been referenced by the individual's name and date of that correspondence, and unless otherwise noted, can be located in Gladys Davis's general correspondence files in the ECF vault.

Extracts from the Cayce readings come directly from typed transcriptions housed in the A.R.E. library or found on the ECF CD-ROM and computer database files. The only liberties that have been taken with this material have been in connection with spelling, punctuation, capitalization, or paragraphing. These liberties—I believe—can be justified by virtue of the fact that readings have been given verbally and hence are not subject to the same editorial standards as other written material. In cases of variant editions of a particular text, I have used my best judgment to decide which is the most accurate.

The primary source for autobiographical material not contained in the personal correspondence files come from Cayce's three attempts to chronicle his life story: *My Life and Work*, written in 1935; *Personal Memoirs*, written in 1938; and *Edgar Cayce's Memoirs:* 1877–1924, which Cayce dictated to Gladys Davis in late 1924. A secondary source for unpublished autobiographical material was found in Cayce's several attempts to keep a diary: from October 15 to October 23, 1930, and from March 18 to May 20, 1938, and in Leslie Cayce's two unpublished sketches of his son's life, which are also housed in the ECF archive.

Additional sources of unpublished material are Morton Blumenthal's memoir, *The Fallen Oak*, edited by Gene Owens, and made available through the courtesy of Mary Kane, of Virginia Beach; the Christian County Court Records, Hopkinsville, Kentucky; the personal papers, photographs, and reminiscences of Delbert D. Cayce; special collections of the Dayton and Montgomery County Public Library; Gladys Davis's *Red Date Book*, notes and diary entries; Gladys and Mildred Davis's notes and diary reports of observations during readings; the FBI records that have been obtained through the Freedom of Information Act; genealogical holdings of the Filson Club Library in Louisville, Kentucky; the historical archive of the First Christian Church of Bowling Green; the historical papers of the First Christian Church of Louisville; the research and writing of Rielly Froh, biographer of Edgar B. Davis; the Genealogical and Historical Society of Caldwell County, in Luling, Texas; Dr. Rosalie Horstman-Haines's *The Past Life Historical Documentation Project;* Wesley Ketchum's personal memoir, *The Discovery of Edgar Cayce;* Robert W. Krajenke's research notes on the Texas and Dayton years; the library and historical collection of Liberty Christian Church; materials from the Pennyroyal Area Museum in Hopkinsville, Kentucky; the Princess Anne County Court Records in Norfolk, Virginia; research and writing of historian Dan Leach, of Cleburne, Texas; the Central Texas Oil Patch Museum, in Luling; the Historical Research Center, in Luling; the Moody Bible Institute in Chicago, Illinois; the Kenneth Silverman collection at the Houdini Historical Center of the Outagamie County Historical Society, Appleton, Wisconsin; transcripts and taped interviews with Hugh Lynn Cayce as conducted by Libbie and Robert Smith for *Hugh Lynn Cayce: About My Father's Business*, by A. Robert Smith, The Donning Company, 1988; Tom Sugrue's 1936 and 1940 interview notes for his Cayce biography, *There Is a River;* Earl Thomas of the Hopkinsville Electric System; records from the University Archive of the Western Kentucky University; the personal papers, photographs, newspaper archive, and reminisces of William T. Turner of Beverly, Kentucky; lecture notes by Robert Warnock, of Anniston, Alabama; the historical collection of the First Christian Church of Selma; the historical records of Woodman of the World Life Insurance Society in Omaha, Nebraska; and correspondence files in the Woodrow Wilson collection at the Seeley G. Mudd Manuscript Library in Princeton, New Jersey.

Interviews have been designated by an [I].

The following abbreviations have been used:

AB	Adeline Blumenthal
ARE	Association for Research and Enlightenment
EB	Edwin Blumenthal
HB	Harmon Bro
MB	Morton Blumenthal
TB	Thomas Brown
CC	Carrie Major Cayce
DC	Delbert D. Cayce III
EC	Edgar Cayce
EEC	Edgar Evans Cayce
GC	Gertrude Cayce
HLC	Hugh Lynn Cayce
LC	Leslie Cayce
MC	Mary Ellen Carter
TC	Thomas J. Cayce
GD	Gladys Davis
CH	Carrie Salter House
LMH	Lillian McAllister Hale
TH	Thomas House
DK	David Kahn
GK	George Klingensmith
SK	Sidney Kirkpatrick
AL	Arthur Lammers
FM	Frank Mohr
LS	Libbie Smith
RS	A. Robert Smith
TS	Tom Sugrue
JT	Jeanette Thomas
WT	William T. Turner
BW	Byron Wyrick
EZ	Ernest Zentgraf
HZ	Helene Zentgraf

Introduction: The Open Door

EC's appearance: [I] LMH to SK; the smell of photo chemicals: [I] HLC to Charlie Dillman in taped interview September, 17–19, 1979; journey through Hopkinsville: [I] WT and DC to SK; description of The Hill: [I] LMH to SK; EC reading for Thomas House Jr.: background report, 1005–1; "There are no shortcuts": 830–2.

PART I: A CHRISTIAN IN CHRISTIAN COUNTY

Chapter 1: A Most Unusual Child

TC's drinking: EC to Mae Ladd Hogen on March 26, 1926, EC Foundation; genealogy of Cayce family: *The Family of William and Elizabeth Garrett Cayce,* as compiled by WT, courtesy of WT; Virginia ancestors from Scotland: EC to Mrs. James Nash, November 23, 1941; TC's psychic powers: EC to TS, see notes in Book 1, spiral binder, provided to TS by EC; folklore of Christian County and vicinity: Oral History of Weather Signs and Other Folklore, courtesy of University Archives of Western Kentucky at Bowling Green; Dr. Schlatter: the *Kentucky New Era*, September 23, 1898; Blind Mary: Joe Dorris column in the *Daily Kentuckian*, January 1, 1987; background on LC: see report by Kenneth Cayce, Sr.; broke every bone in his body: GD's notes for 304–5; "I wish I could be as optimistic": EC to HLC on May 5, 1942; LC as playboy: EC to Luther Hesson, November 11, 1929; LC's binge on night of birth of Leila Beverly Cayce: from EC to Beverly Simmons on November 2, 1940; "the delivery went smoothly": EC to Laura Pratt, February 28, 1933; falling off fence post: ibid.; little folk behind Beverly Store: EC to TS on March 6, 1942; little folk as incarnations of EC's support group: see 900–422 and 294–008; "came alive in his hands": DC to SK; death of grandfather: *Memoirs,* by EC, unpublished, 1938, also [I] Brooks Major, WT, and DC to SK regarding TC's drinking and activities of Lester Major.

Chapter 2: Little Friends and Little Anna

EC's play activities: EC to Esther Wynne, November 16, 1932; Little Anna: background, see correspondence between Beatrice Seay and EC, most notably December 13, 1942; little folk conversations with Hallie Seay and playmates inside the haystack: EC to TS on March 6, 1942; additional Little Anna: EC to TS on March 6, 1942; "walked several miles to be with her": 2072–2; Beverly School: EC to Robert Cayce, January 4, 1933; EC's being whipped: EC to U. L. Clardy on January 3, 1938; Crazy Bill: *What Prayer Has Meant to Me,* talk given by EC on June 18, 1943; puncture of testicle: EC to Mrs. Laurie Pratt, February 28, 1933, also see 294–2 for medical description; reading the Bible: EC to LC, December 20, 1924; EC at Liberty Church: EC to TS on March 6, 1942; little house in the woods: EC to Anne Cayce, December 9, 1943; angel story: EC's memoirs.

Chapter 3: In the Company of Angels

"the voice of my uncle": EC's memoirs; spelling lesson: EC's memoirs; Congressman Jim McKenzie speech: Daisy Aldridge to HLC, as reported in the ARE Bulletin, September 1962; additional Jim McKenzie: Daisy Aldridge to HLC, April 30, 1948; B. F. Thom: material compiled by DC, in undated letter from DC to JT; Annie Cayce's account of EC being hit with baseball: undated newspaper interview, *Kentucky New Era,* circa 1964, found in 294 clippings file.

Chapter 4: A Voice from Beyond

Bessie Kenner: EC to Miriam Gregory, October 12, 1943; Bessie Kenner married: [I] WT to SK; date of family's move to Hopkinsville: Kenneth Cayce to Albert Turner; EC's dream: as related in a letter from EC to Ed and Louise Johnson on April 16, 1938.

Chapter 5: Hopper Brothers Bookstore

Hopper Brothers: see 294 "Early Years" file; Harry D. Smith ministry: [I] background material provided to SK by DC on February 3, 1998; Christian Endeavor: from articles in the *Louisville Courier-Journal* on January 31, 1938, and February 7, 1938; Dwight L. Moody: *Kentucky New Era*, March 29, 1898; Dwight L. Moody: background material of Hopkinsville visit courtesy of Walter Osborn, Reference Librarian, the Moody Bible Institute; Moody dream: see 5749–5, and EC dream record December 12, 1942.

Chapter 6: The Young Lady from The Hill

"uncouth and uneducated": 4907–4; meeting GC: EC's memoirs and additional material from EC's biographical notes to TS; about GC: [I] LMH to SK; additional GC and Salter family: 538 series.

Chapter 7: Margaret of Louisville

EC and the J. P. Morton Company: EC's memoirs and EC's journal sketches; additional information on J. P. Morton: J. P. Morton family records at the Filson Club Library, Louisville; E. L. Powell: from church ledgers at the First Christian Church of Louisville; James Phelps: conclusion drawn by a process of elimination after a search of the Louisville genealogical records at the Filson Library; "secret flame": EC to Charlie Daniel, June 29, 1944; EC plays the piano: LC's memoirs; GC's "decline": EC's notes to TS; dream in hall of records: 1107–2; what might have happened had he returned to Louisville: 294–8.

Chapter 8: Miraculous Recovery

"ashamed": EC's memoirs; LC's racism: see statement in folder 304 dated November 18, 1928; lost his voice: *Kentucky New Era*, February 12, 1901; "his strength and will to carry on": [I] LMH to SK; LC's debts: letter to landlord in Cadiz from LC, January 3, 1901; the Cayce boarding house: from an interview by George M. Draper of Addie P'Pool as contained in a letter to GD on March 24, 1991; Hart the Laugh King: background from notes to TS from EC on March 3, 1942; on display at funeral home: Joe Dorris's interview with Arthur N. Anderson as printed in the *Kentucky New Era* on October 23, 1967; EC's first reading: from LC's memoirs, additional material from Sarah Cayce and from interview in the *Nashville Tennesean*, December 8, 1968, and additional material from April 1, 1901, article in the *Kentucky New Era*.

Chapter 9: A Child in Need

background on Layne and his illness: see *Kentucky New Era*, March 1901; diagnosis on Al Layne: see reading 4238–1; early readings: from an interview by George

M. Draper of Addie P'Pool as contained in a letter to GD on March 24, 1991; "feel at home": notes by EC entitled "Mrs. Hollins Boarding House"; Louis J. Darter, secretary of the YMCA, has erroneously been referred to as Joe Darter; Louis Darter and other friends of EC: Mrs. Ford Wulfeck to EC, August 7, 1943; Tenth Street Christian Church: see "History of the First Christian Church of Bowling Green," in the archive of the First Christian Church of Bowling Green, also see *A Bit of History,* by Joe Ford, which can also be found in the archive of the First Christian Church of Bowling Green; The Pit game: *Kentucky New Era* and the *Hopkinsville Kentuckian*— the date of these clippings are lost, but the clippings themselves can be found in EC's clipping file at the ARE; life in Bowling Green: Grover Kemp to EC on August 12, 1943; details of Layne's involvement in Dietrich case: *The Discovery of Edgar Cayce,* by Wesley H. Ketchum; Dietrich case: case reading 2473, also see affidavits by C. H. and Minnie Dietrich for Noe/Cayce suit of 1911, papers property of the ARE; Layne's appearance in Bowling Green and offer of $2,000: The *Bowling Green Times-Journal,* June 26, 1903; Reading for Blackburn and Roup: *Bowling Green Times-Journal,* June 22 and June 24, 1903; nature of the relationship between EC and GC: Daisy Aldridge to HLC, April 30, 1948; seeking other employment: EC to the Triumph Information Company, in Dallas, Texas, on December 19, 1903; "very ugly": EC to Grover C. Kemp, August 18, 1943.

Chapter 10: Mind Is the Builder

photo studios: from EC's notes entitled "Details of the Studios"; "I don't know how he made Junior sit so still": from HLC and EEC as found in *The Outer Limits of Edgar Cayce's Powers,* by HLC and EEC, ARE Press, 1981; Elbert Hubbard: see EC's memoirs; "give his prints away": [I] LMH to SK; Al Layne reading with Percy Woodall: correspondence between Sunora Whiteside and EC, March 21, 1938, and March 23, 1938; Percy Woodall and Al Layne: see correspondence between Robert Emery and EC June 16, 1943; EC and mental telepathy: from "Telepathy," a talk given at the Cayce Hospital on Sunday, February 15, 1931; "Every thought is a deed": 3184–1; Bowling Green Business University: *Brief Historical Sketch of the Bowling Green Business University* as printed and produced by that university and housed in the University Archive of the Western Kentucky University; meetings with famous people: see correspondence with Byron King and 740–1; EC meeting Edison: from a talk given by EC at the Arlington Hotel, Washington, D.C. on February 3, 1935; on electricity: 440 series and 4489–1; destruction of files: [I] JT to SK; reporter seeing files: the *Birmingham Age-Herald,* see October 10, 1922; material on the Divine nature of electricity: see 440 series, especially 440–11, and background material on Thomas Jefferson Jackson, also comments contained in this file made by NASA scientists Dr. John H. Sutton; Tom Baugh: from Joe Dorris's *Watching the Parade* column on August 1, 1969, for *Kentucky New Era;* information on Hopkinsville power grid: [I] Earl Thomas of the Hopkinsville Electric System, Hopkinsville, Kentucky, to SK.

Chapter 11: Final Days in Bowling Green

EC pronounced dead: see spiral notebook prepared by EC for TS; Miss Daisy

Aldridge: interview in the ARE Bulletin, September 1962; final experiments: see correspondence between GD, TS, and Jack E. Tate on July 15, 1945; Dr. Sadler experiments: Dr. William Sadler to Harold Sherman in 1941, as detailed in *How to Know What to Believe,* by Harold Sherman, Greenwich, Fawcett, 1976; fire in studios: see GD's correspondence with TS regarding oversights of the "Thomas Hudson meeting"; possible causes of fire: 4135, see notes labeled "Conversations with Dr. W. H. Ketchum," November 12, 1962; readings for Hanberry: LC to EC on April 19, 1926; "I often feel": EC's letter to MB on May 9, 1927; Paul Cooksey: see readings 740; "to leave it [behind]": EC's memoirs.

Chapter 12: The Discovery of Edgar Cayce

"days and weeks and months": 4907–2; on the Putnam case: 4468–1; Dr. Posey: 4969–1; Anniston and the Russell Brothers: Harriet Sumner to GD on July 25, 1961, also see the *Anniston Star,* June 28, 1964; material on Andrew J. Hyde: EC to TS in interview notes; material on Ketchum: from taped interviews that HLC, George Abel, and Ronald Rosewood conducted with Wesley Ketchum at his home in Palo Alto in June 1959, and further interviews on November 12, 1962; background material on Ketchum's cases: 577–1, HLC to the ARE Staff, April 4, 1959, also see 3502–1; George Dalton: see 5779–1; press reports: the *New York Times,* October 9, 1910, and October 15, 1910, *Seattle Times,* October 15, 1910, the *Kentucky New Era,* October 15, 1910, the *Cincinnati Times-Star,* October 10, 1910; material on Ketchum partnership: *The Discovery of Edgar Cayce,* by Wesley H. Ketchum, also see Dr. W. Ketchum's talk about EC before one of the ARE Study Groups in California as filed in 5889–1, and *Reminisces of Hopkinsville* by Alton Ketchum, part of the ECF collection; first reading on the work: see 254–1.

Chapter 13: The Psychic Partnership

Noe, Ketchum, and Cayce partnership: see *The Discovery of Edgar Cayce* by W. Ketchum; for documents relating to the partnership and the demise of partnership: case #7394, in Civil order book #76, Edgar Cayce and Ex Al vs. A. D. Noe, Sr. And Ex Al; "the mysterious visitor"; EC to Dollie Herring, March 12, 1941; for the etheric body: 254–68; Source humor: 294–134; leaves the body: 835–8; advice for doctor: 947–2; need glasses: 404–4; details of relationship between EC and Frank Mohr: EC to Martin Conroy, December 15, 1938, also readings 948–1, 948–2 and 281–1; newspaper stories and Roswell Field: see *Chicago Examiner,* February 19, 1911, and EC's memoirs; secret sin and pregnant girl: *The Discovery of Edgar Cayce,* by W. Ketchum.

Chapter 14: Under Investigation

announcement of death of Milton Porter: *Kentucky New Era,* May 20, 1911; background on Milton Porter: EC to MB on May 9, 1927; GC's health and subsequent readings: 538–1, 538–53, and 538–4; Ketchum under investigation: *The Discovery of Edgar Cayce,* by W. Ketchum; Münsterberg's visit: see Dolly Dalrymaple's article for the *Birmingham Age-Herald,* October 10, 1922; Münsterberg background: *The National Cyclopedia of American Biography,* 1915; reading on Boehme: 134–1; Münsterberg background and testimony of student: see report of Kenneth Cayce Sr., August 5, 1972; additional on Münsterberg: EC to GK on May 26, 1924; EC's reaction to court decision: EC to Thomas Peters on April 9, 1927.

Chapter 15: Little City on a Big River

the Broad Street Studio: many details have come from annuals of the city of Selma, which were made available through the Selma Public Library; they adored him: [I] Dr. Paul Allen to SK; Bible, Christian Endeavor, and Sevenette Class: from the archives of the First Christian Church of Selma, with additional material from [I] Dr. Paul Allen to SK; hanging out at studio: Harry Bredin to HLC on May 9, 1956; DrinX: see DrinX instruction booklet and Library of Congress copyright requests for December 13, 1913; poetry: see EC postcard collection; woman with Alaska photograph: EC's memoirs, and report of reading 4961; Flora Butler: 4953; "organ transplant": 4971; account of the DeLaney reading: see 4974 and W. E. DeLaney to DK on January 22, 1921; "full of pep and promise": DK to HLC on November 20, 1945; background on David Kahn: 257 series; Dr. Gay's father: EC's memoirs.

Chapter 16: Trial by Fire

GC's need of apple brandy keg: EC to CH on April 2, 1940; HLC's eye problems: see the *Alabama Times Journal*, February 1913, [undated clipping] titled "Child Burned by Powder Flash"; appendicitis operation: 294–2; Williamson scenarios: 4907–1; Eddie Jones Smithson: 605 series; Kahn family and business readings: *My Life with Edgar Cayce*, by David Kahn, with Will Ousler, Double Day & Company, Garden City, New York, 1970.

Chapter 17: At Home and Abroad

Kahn readings: 257 series; background on the relationship between the Wilson cousins and EC: EC to Alfred M. Wilson, January 22, 1927; readings regarding President Wilson and/or League of Nations: 3976–12, 3976–23, 3976–29, 3182–1; EC's introduction to Alfred Wilson: see A. C. Beford's participation in Bible study as contained in Bible study files in the archives of the First Christian Church of Selma; world affairs reading: EC to TS, see notes in Book 1, spiral binder and 1936 notes for proposed biography of EC; Will Starling readings: see 3182 reports; "one-legged man in a kicking match": EC to DK on March 8, 1918; dream of Milton Porter and flower vendor: 294–15.

PART IV: RICHES FROM THE EARTH

Chapter 18: Lucky Boy

Thrash: there have been many erroneous reports that Thrash was from Cleveland, Ohio, and was the editor of the *Daily News*. There was no *Daily News* in Cleveland at that time; Thrash: see 3777–1; reading giving advice not to take "unfair advantage": 254–7; reading regarding motives and incentives in searching for oil: 254–3; automobile statistics: *Pan-American* magazine, 30:22–32, November 1919; descriptions of Cleburne: [I] Dan Leach to SK and [I] William Osborn to SK; Lucky Boy readings and Joseph Long: 3777–2; "the gushing promise of Texas oil": *My Life with Edgar Cayce*, by David Kahn, with Will Ousler, Doubleday & Company, Garden City, New York, 1970; no legal relationship with Sam Davis: EC's name never appeared on company stationery, lists of stockholders, or corporate records; Henry Orman readings: 3777–5; for phosphate: 3777–3; more oil readings on Lucky Boy: letter and affidavit by Jos. D. Long to EC, January 22, 1921; "ninety-nine-year leases": *My Life with Edgar Cayce*, by David Kahn, with Will Ousler, Doubleday & Company, Garden City, New York, 1970; material on Major Wilson: 195–38.

Chapter 19: Desdemona

life in "Ragtown": *Oil! Titan of the Southwest*, by Carl Coke Rister, University of Oklahoma Press, 1949, and *Tales from the Derrick Floor: A People's History of the Oil Company*, by Moody C. Boatright and William A. Owens, Doubleday & Company, Garden City, New York, 1970; Kahn's activities in Desdemona: EC to Curtis Willmott on April 8, 1935; Ringle family: 5628 and 3777 series, also see Robert Krajenke's unpublished article "Edgar Cayce and the Crucial Years: Texas and Dayton, 1919–1925"; EC and rainstorm: *My Life with Edgar Cayce*, by David Kahn, with Will Ousler, Doubleday & Company, Garden City, New York, 1970; scandals and con games: [I] William Osborn to SK; large number of delays: 3777 series; HLC's trip: HLC to LS and RS; Kahn's behavior at Desdemona: *My Life with Edgar Cayce*, by David Kahn, with Will Ousler, Doubleday & Company, Garden City, New York, 1970; the shooting incident: Curtis Willmott to EC December 3, 1923; additional shooting incident: EC's memoirs; "grasping, selfish, turbulent minds": Rudolph Johnson to DK on June 3, 1952; Ringle being fired: Robert Krajenke's "Edgar Cayce and the Crucial Years: Texas and Dayton, 1919–1925."

Chapter 20: Luling and Edgar B. Davis

Cayce Petroleum agreements: see September 20, 1920, and February 1, 1921, lease and shareholders agreements and contracts; decision to go to Luling: *My Life with Edgar Cayce*, by David Kahn, with Will Ousler, Doubleday & Company, Garden City, New York, 1970; Background material on Morris Rayor: *Edgar B. Davis, Wildcatter Extraordinary*, by Reilly Froh, The Luling Foundation, 1984; additional background material on EC and Luling: [I] Reilly Froh to SK, [I] Ray E. Bailey to SK, and [I] Aurale Huff to SK; the name Minnie Phillips has been deduced from Kahn's recollections in Luling and the name of his pharmacist in Lexington, Kentucky; connection between Edgar B. Davis and EC: DK to Rudolf Johnson on May 24, 1952; additional material about EC's Luling connections: Cecil Ringle to EC on August 4, 1936; Edgar B. Davis bio: I have supplemented the Reilly Froh material with two articles about Davis. "Where Are They Now," which appeared in the *New Yorker* on November 26, 1949, and "He Gives Away His Millions," which appeared in the August 1951 issue of *American* magazine; Edgar B. Davis reading: 1265; Frank Seiberling reading 1266–3.

Chapter 21: Harry Houdini and Cayce Petroleum

"lust for oil": *My Life with Edgar Cayce,* by David Kahn, with Will Ousler, Doubleday & Company, Garden City, New York, 1970; Bealle readings: 4958; Birmingham readings: see 4956–4960, also see Schanz affidavit included in 4959; cinder in eye: EC to Fannie Graham Cayce on June 11, 1924; details of Nashville trip: *My Life with Edgar Cayce,* by David Kahn, with Will Ousler, Doubleday & Company, Garden City, New York, 1970; Washington readings: EC's memoirs; "constant companion": *Starling of the White House,* as told to Tom Sugrue by Colonel Edmund W. Starling, Simon & Schuster, New York, 1946; New York "stag party": EC's memoirs; EC's meeting with Houdini and others: EC to Abigail Finlayson on February 21, 1933, see also 3630 series; EC and McDougal: EC to GK on May 26, 1924; EC and Hereward Carrington: 254–89 and press release entitled "Dr. Hereward Carrington on the Work of Edgar Cayce," in February 1936; Houdini's New York movie activities and description of Houdini's house: *Houdini!!!,* by Kenneth Silverman, HarperCollins, New York, 1996; Houdini's activities after Cayce reading: [I] Kenneth Silverman to SK.

Chapter 22: Rocky Pasture

The new role played by DK: EC's memoirs; drilling in Rocky Pasture: EC's memoirs; depth of hole in Rocky Pasture: EC to E. H. Reynolds on October 29, 1921; efforts to raise money by selling shares: see wires between EC and Martin Company in November 1921; Autry affair: HC to Hollywood screenwriter, [I] James Miller to SK; GC's "burden": [I] LH to SK; TH's visit: EC to TS, and HLC to RS and LS; Curtis Willmott: Curtis Willmott to EC on December 22, 1923; EC's failure to reach an accord: EC to Curtis Willmott on January 1, 1924; "First Purpose": see report of reading 294–93; "right with the creative forces": 900–302, also see 551–3; "the oil was there": 195–38.

Chapter 23: Birmingham and Dayton

in Columbus: EC's memoirs; in Denver: EC's memoirs, and *My Life with Edgar Cayce,* by David Kahn, with Will Ousler, Doubleday & Company, Garden City, New York, 1970; speaking engagement in Birmingham: EC to Gladys Dillman in June 1923; William Darling Jr.: 3751; stranger at magic show: EC's memoirs; EC's return to Selma: EC to Mary Gilmore on February 7, 1923; Penn-Tenn: 257–2 and 257–3; Tex Rice: 4945; DK's role in Penn-Tenn: 257–1; amusing ways: 257–2; prohibition readings: 3976–8; reading for McConnell's mother-in-law: 247; also see 638–2; Tex Rice and Penn-Tenn: EC's memoirs; sadness in EC's life: 294–6.

Chapter 24: Divine Law

AL's background: [I] Gus Brunsman to SK; AL's business interests: EC to Tex Rice on May 24, 1923; AL's personal interests: AL to EC on August 20, 1923; AL's early readings in Dayton: 3744, also see correspondence between JT and Tom Kay in December 1992; Divine law: 294–7; Cayce's interest in doing business with AL: EC to Fannie Cayce on August 7, 1924; EC's trip to Texas: 5628–2; potential investment by

AL: AL to EC on August 20, 1923; problems with Tex Rice: 269–3; EC's changing outlook on oil business: EC's memoirs; "work first, self second," 259–10 reports and
257–10.

PART V: VENTURE INWARD

Chapter 25: Miss Gladys and Mr. Cayce
"spook room": 254–2; Fay Autry unavailable: EC to Tim Brown on September 5,
1923; background on GD: *My Years with Edgar Cayce,* by MC with GD Turner,
Harper & Row, New York, 1971; details of first reading with GD as stenographer:
3875–1; Abrams machine: 400–16; AL's proposition: 5717–4; GC and menopause:
538–8 and 538–11; about GK: GK to EC on May 24, 1924; "I do love you": EC to GC
on September 30, 1923.

Chapter 26: Ruled by Jupiter
the Thrash astrology reading: 254–2; Evangeline Adams, background: "They
Hitched Their Wagons to the Stars," by Frederick L. Collins, *Collier's* magazine, May
15, 1926; the AL astrology readings: 5717–1; "first people to use astrology": 3744–3;
those who dismiss astrology: 5757–1; planets that affect emotions: 2501–7; differences between astrological systems: 275–25; soul arrives at different times: 457–10;
"thirty degrees off": 2011–3; "Righteous anger: 3416–1; Mercury and the mind:
1650–1; influence of Saturn: 1981–1; Uranus: 2571–1; "at other times very ugly":
1958–1; "the mountaintops": 3706–2; "lucky at any game of chance": 406–1; "entity's
'sojourn' ": 3744–4; different rate of vibration: 281–55; Harvard and Yale: 633–2;
"part and pattern": 5755–1; man's place in the universe: 262–86 and 5757–1.

Chapter 27: A Monk in His Third Appearance
AL's life reading: 5717–2; "Seventh manifestation": 294–7; July 1922 reading:
4811–1, see also 4841–1 and 4492–1; reading for GK: 4121–1; "appearance of these
four individuals": 5717–5; EEC's first reading: 487–1; GD's first reading: 288–1; Linden Shroyer's life reading: 5453–3; GK's life reading: 4121–2; GC's life reading: 538–5;
"crazy enough anyway": 5756–14; HLC's life reading: 341–1; dire situation in Dayton: HLC to RS and LS; the demise of Lammers Photo Productions: [I] Gus Brunsman
to SK; financial plight and outlook of EC: HLC to the ARE general membership in
newsletter dated December 15, 1949.

Chapter 28: Karmic Debt and the First Cause
HLC's letter to the ARE: HLC to the ARE general membership in newsletter
dated December 15, 1949; 1933 reincarnation readings: 5753 series; "that is worthwhile!": 5753–2; free will and bloodlines: 5749–14; EC, reincarnation, and the Bible:
see EC's memoirs and 1931 hospital lecture on reincarnation; "Yet he was Elijah":
1158–6; Gnosticism, reincarnation, and the early church: 5749–14; reading on child
with asthma: 3906–1; Yokohama prostitute: see 272 series and related background ma-

terial; glaucoma reading: 3524–1; New Jersey housewife reading: 852–12; "not to the willful disobedience in any manner": 3524–1; "there must be eradicated that of any judgment or of condemnation": 631–6; homosexuality: 1089; "in a causation world, have their cause and effect": 2927–1; "peculiar statement here, but true!": 364–6; "laws as pertaining to health: 2067–3; "karmic forces are [such that] what is meted must be met": 442–3; "is able to forgive thee": 3124–2; forgiving sins and reaping what you sow: 5000–1, 3376–25, 254–91; reading for businessman: 1901–1; "talk too much!": 5125–1; "an experience": 956–1; Cayce Jones as incarnation of EC's brother: 2722–5 and 318–2; "mighty meaningful to me": 2722–5.

Chapter 29: History and Hardships

continuing financial plight of AL: EC to Byron Wyrick on August 12, 1924; EC's emotional state: EC to Byron Wyrick on August 29, 1924; playing under the Dayton Bridge: HLC to RS and LS; "still eating—sometimes": EC to Byron Wyrick on March 17, 1924; EC's life reading: 294–8; LC's life reading: 304–5; successes in tracking down past-life information: see Dr. Rosalie Horstman-Haines, Past-Life Historical Documentation Project for the ECF; Virginia music teacher: 1861.

Chapter 30: Love and Marriage

EC's and GD's life readings: 294 and 288 files; EC's and GC's karmic bond: 294–8; "unity": 288–8; GD as virgin: [I] JT to SK; GD's medical records: see 288 report file on GD and cancer.

Chapter 31: Blessings to Come

"angels in disguise": EC's memoirs; screenplay for *Why?*: 4907; *Bride of the Inca* [L]: 4908 series; correspondence with Alf Butler: EC to Alf Butler in December 1924; other screenplays: 294–143 to 294–146; readings on the static eliminator: see 2492 series, also 317–4, 440–612, 1497–5 [7] [12] [14]; readings on fog lights: 137–38, 254–30; readings on "elastic glass": 254–30; forming an institute: EC to Dr. Lily Carpenter on June 3, 1924; first letter to Fannie Cayce: EC to Fannie Cayce on June 11, 1924; second letter to Fannie Cayce: EC to Fannie Cayce on August 7, 1924; GK's letter: GK to EC on August 7, 1924; finding a manager for the Cayce Institute: 254–11; special reading on the work: 254–8; work with Chicago people: EC to Fannie Cayce on August 7, 1924; "restless to become better established: EC to GK on July 28, 1924; Linden Shroyer's financial plight and decision not to become manager: GD's notes on December 9, 1925; Wyrick as potential business manager: EC to Wyrick on July 9, 1924; MB as potential manager: EC to DK on June 19, 1924.

Chapter 32: The Blumenthal Brothers

Miriam Miller: see EC's letter to MB on November 24, 1924, also see 4353 series; DK's letter about MB: from DK to EC on June 16, 1924; MB's background: MB to EC on January 27, 1925; MB's life readings: 900–6; 900–14; 900–38; 900–63; EB's life readings: 137–4; 137–12; 137–18; trip to New York: EC to Alf Butler on November 6, 1924; EC on early relationship with MB: EC to Lamar Jones on November 14, 1924;

MB's visit to Dayton: see MB's unpublished memoir, *The Fallen Oak;* readings and background on AB: 136–1 to 3; MB on Christ: 900–11.

Chapter 33: The Life of Christ

"preparing the way": 5749–7; "the Brotherhood": 1010–17; "a religious order within Jewry": 1602–4; Essenes viewed as rebels or radicals: 1851–1; history and significance of the Dead Sea Scrolls: *The Dead Sea Scrolls Deception*, by Michael Baigent and Richard Leigh, Touchstone, New York, 1991, *The Meaning of the Dead Sea Scrolls* by A. Powell Davies, Mentor, 1956, and *Dead Sea Scrolls*, Geza Vermes, Penguin, New York, 1968; on Essenes's role: 649–1; Essenes given to good deeds: 254–109; "voices, dreams, signs, symbols": 3175–3; Judy and her prophetic role: 2067–11; record-keeping activities: 1472–3; Judy as prophetess and healer: 1472–1; relationship to Magi: 1581–1; role of Essenes and Jesus as channel: 2505–1; channel of the prophecies: 2173–1; virgins: 1222–1; "These were kept balanced according to that which had been first set by Aran and Ra Ta": 5749–8; chosen to be the mother of the Messiah: 5749–7; Mary: 5749–8; Joseph: 254–109; the Angel Gabriel appeared: 5749–7; "Mary then became pregnant": 5749–8; immaculate conception: 5749–7; to Bethlehem to be taxed: 5749–8; "elderly man with the beautiful girl, his wife heavy with child": 5749–15; innkeeper's role: 1196–2; Jesus born in grotto: 587–6; Jesus' birth and birth place: 587–6, 5749–15, 2562–1, 519–1, 1859–1, 5749–15; Magi: 5749–7, 2067–7, 1908–1, 256–5; Herod: 1472–3, 775–1, 2067–2, 245–109, 587–3; documents in Vatican library: 2067–7; persecution: 1152–3; "For the body being perfect radiated that which was health, life itself": 1010–7; education supervised by Judy: 1010–17; Jesus' education and training: 5749–16, 5749–2, 2067–7, 5749–7, 2067–11; joining John: 5749–16; Jesus' education not unusual or unnatural: 2067–7; documents in Alexandria: 2067–7; Jesus' brothers and sisters: 5749–8, 1158–2, 900–427; Ruth: 1158–4, 1158–9; descriptions of Jesus: 5354–1, 5749–1; "Instead, he took a much more uncertain path": 1158–4; preparing the way: 587–6; water became wine: 3361–1; trouble with the Romans: 1158–4; on sin and healing: 5749–16; "a paid companion to wealthy or influential clients": 5749–9; "It is no small wonder, then, that the crowd immediately disappeared": 295–8; "Medi, Medici, Cui": 5749–9; "Lazarus died of the typhoid fever": 993–5; Jesus going to Jerusalem: 5749–10; witnessing His works: 681–1; "they were mostly women and children": 3615–1; "those things in man's experience of sickness, of doubt, of fear!": 1152–3; EC's description of the Last Supper: 5749–1; going to cross: 5277–1; Judas: 2448–2; healing of Pontius Pilate's son by the Master: 1207–1; Jesus could laugh in the face of the Cross: 3440–2; Mary at the crucifixion": 3175–3; consecrated maidens were there: 2425–1, 649–1; caring for Jesus' body: 2677–1; the first Christian martyr: 489–3; Jesus reappeared: 1158–9, 2067–11, 1152–3, 1877–2, 3615–1.

PART VI: A HOME ON THE BEACH

Chapter 34: Life in Virginia Beach

trials and tribulations: EC to Alf Butler on December 9, 1924; "Can't stand on my feet much or walk": EC to MB on December 11, 1924; sickness at home: EC's letters to Annie Cayce on January 1, 1927 and January 13, 1927; getting to VB: EC to Carrie Elizabeth on October 24, 1925; description of Virginia Beach: [I] Joe Dunn to SK; EC wishing he had invested in real estate: EC to Lamar Jones on February 2, 1926; details of move and heating problem: EC to MB on June 24, 1925; description of first day in new home: HLC to LS and RS; GC's enjoyment of Virginia Beach: EC to Alva Jones on June 29, 1926; EEC's school activities: 487–17 and 487–4; life at the beach: EC to Porter Smith on October 26, 1925; additional life at the beach: EC to Carrie Elizabeth Evans on October 24, 1925; EEC getting burned: see 487–8, also EC to Annie Cayce on January 1, 1927; GC happy: EC to Alva Jones, on June 29, 1926.

Chapter 35: Dreams and Reincarnation

dream interpretations of Joseph: Genesis 37–41; dreams as avenue or channel through which God might speak: 1904–2, 294–34, 295–15, 136–7; EC's dream of barge and Dr. Thomas investigation: 294–33; nature of dreams: 900–8, 294–15, and 1650 series; "Happy may he be": 294–15; EB's dream of liquor on a foyer rug: 137–97; GC's dream of Carrie Cayce's death: 538–22; about death of mother: EC to Annie Cayce on January 1, 1927; September 23, 1927 dream interpretation reading in which Carrie Cayce broke through: 243–5; premonition dream of Morton Jr.: 136–7, 900–226, 136–51; AB's birthing experience: 136–59; Olive Koop's life reading: 2486; Olive and Fred Batterson story: HLC to RS and LS; TS on being a priest: TS to EC on March 26, 1931; background on TS: TS to EC on April 12, 1929; HLC letter home about TS: HLC to EC on May 16, 1927; TS's first life reading: 849–1; "put myself entirely in the hands": TS to EC on June 11, 1928; August 7, 1926, reading and report on House: EC to TB on August 10, 1926; incarnations of Thomas House and report by the committee: see Report of the historical committee and connections of Dr. House, July 26, 1927; "catch hold of the rope and be pulled skyward": 195–42.

Chapter 36: Treasures Great and Small

MB's fund-raising activities: MB to EC on June 6, 1928; dollars raised: MB to EC on July 8, 1926; "money-grabbing scheme": EC to MB on September 13, 1929; U.S. Steel reading: 900–295; Havana Electric reading: 900–316; Ford Motors and Hudson Motors: 900–267; Federal Reserve decisions and stock market: 900–436; other entities giving stock market advice: 900–345; "determined to make you a millionaire": 900–376; the cost of a seat on the exchange in 1928 ranged from between $290,000 and $595,000 as reported by the New York Stock Exchange; MB's and EB's holdings: 900–442; FM and Preston partnership: see FM's letter to EC on July 7, 1926; readings on Bimini treasure: 996 series and reports; "absolutely correct": FM to EC on November 12, 1926; "the project will fail": Byron Wyrick to EC on January 22, 1927; "you are fixed for . . . life": FM to EC on December 6, 1926; "a promise is my bond": EC's letter to FM on March 12, 1927; details of Florida trip: 254–34; karma and treasure-hunting experience: 1770–4, 996–8, 2671–5, 996–11; reference to Poseidians and Atlantis: 996–12.

Chapter 37: Atlantis and the Future of Man

EEC's Atlantis reading: 487–4; series of readings on Atlantis: 364–1 to 364–13; "living in caves": 364–12; ability to push out of themselves: see lecture entitled *First Cause*, ECF archive; "much in the way and manner": 364–13; appearance of man in physical on earth's plane: 137–4; "when the morning stars sang together, and the whispering winds brought the news of the coming of man's indwelling": 294–8; Adam and Eve: 262–115; Amilius and God co-creating: 2879–1; description of Poseidia: 364–12; "sons of Men": 1416–1; Law of One: 877–26; beasts overrunning earth: 1210–1; carnal desire: 1999–1; relationship between the sons of Belial and the sons of God: 364–4; destruction of the material lands: 1292–1; the Atlantean power station: 440–5; gratifying of selfish appetites: 3633–1; the flood: 257–201; the crystal: 519–1; atomic power: 364–4; the Atlantean exodus: 5748–5; Jesus' purpose: 364–7; "attempts to take 'shortcuts' ": 5749–14; "would suit their own purposes": 262–60; the second coming: 5749–4, 364–7; "*Listen* while He speaks!": 5749–5

Chapter 38: Gravity, Polarity, and Perpetual Motion

Stansell background: MB to EC on March 30, 1928, also see 4666–2; first Stansell physical reading: 4666–1; Stansell motor readings: see 4666, 4665, and 195 nonphysical, nonlife reading series; "life is vibration, [and] so is mind, so is matter": 1861–16; "vibration that is creative": 2828–4; "It is the high vibration that destroys": 933–3; "vibrates in the same vibration . . . shows as the same thing": 254–47; vibration and matter: 195–70; positive and negative energy: 412–9, 281–3; 195–54; gravity and antigravity: 412–9; radial force: 4665–13; energy that is spiritual: 412–9; more motor readings: 4665–7 and 4665–12; "Be patient": 4665–5; advice on patent and stockholder shares: 4665–3; income from motor: 254–48.

Chapter 39: A Dream Realized

purchasing land for the hospital: see the Cayce Hospital files and expense reports; hospital layout: from the advertising brochure distributed during the hospital's first year of operation; "read Habakkuk": 294–114; "the most dramatic visitation": 779–15; other pertinent readings: 254–42, 900–422, 294–114, 294–71; problems brewing: MB letter to EC on June 6, 1928, also see MB to EC on July 8, 1926, and court documents of Princess Anne County, David Kahn, Franklin Bradley, and Max Mannerling vs. The Association of National Investigators, filed December 7, 1931; MB's trip by plane to the beach and negotiations with Edgar and contractor: see MB's unpublished memoir, *The Fallen Oak;* GD's being fired: GD to MC; GD's health: see 288–22; fees and donations: see court documents of Princess Anne County, David Kahn, Franklin Bradley, and Max Mannerling vs. The Association of National Investigators, filed December 7, 1931; "do not parade": 254–45; "great truths of the universe": MB's unpublished memoir, *The Fallen Oak:* "for the benefit of mankind": see Moseley Brown's dedication notes in 254 series; "went out feeling fine": 1100 correspondence file for

Charles Dillman; first group of patients at hospital: [I] HLC to RS and LS and first quarter's medical reports.

Chapter 40: The Healing Arts

"a bad cold from getting mad": 849–75; "what we think and what we eat": 288–038; "less physical exercise": 798–1; "eliminations do not hinder": 311–4; "internal bath": 440–2; "circulation": 4614–1; "no condition existent": 283–2; exercise: 654–7; sympathetic system: 5717–3; "sticking a pin in the hand": 386–2; medicines and compounds: 5083–2; meditation and rest: 3691–1; brain work and physical work: 3352–1; "no greater factory in the universe": 1800–21; "is a universe in itself": 1158–2; the ability to prolong life 866–1, 1475–1; the pineal and the Leydig: 294–142; "Joy has the opposite effect": 281–54; "Fear is the root": 5459–3; "pattern in the material": 5756–4; "keep loving": 3420–1; "each have their laws": 4580–1; "this alone is healing": 1967–1; "osteopathic adjustments": 1158–31; creative energy as God: 557–3; "serve thy fellow man the better": 1620–1; "keep thou, O Lord, me": 4055–2; "Cayce simply replied, 'God' ": 2444–1; "something to worry about": 3569–1.

Chapter 41: Atlantic University

MB's vision of Atlantic University: MB's unpublished memoir, *The Fallen Oak* and MB to EC on October 22, 1929; first Jeremiah reading: 254–48; second appearance of Jeremiah: 900–428; a great disturbance in financial circles": 900–425; panic in the money centers: 137–117; considerations for Brown's appointment: 204–1; "at the gate to the university": MB to EC on January 9, 1930; last reading on TH and correspondence regarding his passing: 5618–19; need for cooperation: MB to EC on October 22, 1929; the Jesus reading: 254–50; HLC's appointment at Atlantic University: HLC to RS and LS, also see 341 files; financial problems plaguing the university and hospital in 1930: MB's unpublished memoir, *The Fallen Oak*.

Chapter 42: Irish Eyes and Fallen Angels

HLC's account of MB and EB's losses: HLC to Albert Turner, see 900 reports; MB's account of events regarding the stock market crash: MB's unpublished memoir, *The Fallen Oak;* October 26, 1929 reading: 900–457; November 2, 1929 reading: 900–459; November 15, 1929 reading: 137–125; November 18, 1929 reading: 900–460; MB's two dream interpretations regarding the market: 900–46; Rosamond Blumenthal reading, and MB's initial analysis of what went wrong: 144–1; background on Patricia Devlin: MB's unpublished memoir, *The Fallen Oak*, and AB's divorce correspondence found in 900 and 142 series; more on Patricia Devlin: 3734; EC's attitude regarding Patricia Devlin: EC to Tim Brown on December 20, 1929; "Trust in powers made with hands": 137–27; Patricia Devlin physical reading: 3734–1; "returning with a lawyer": MB's unpublished memoir, *The Fallen Oak;* "though only two came back and said 'thank you' ": 900–464; Edgar B. Davis and Frank Seiberling reading on cooperation: 1266–3; "fallen far short": 900–464; "by the one in charge, Edgar Cayce": 254–51; details of hospital closing: 2504–20, also see 409–17; first organizational meeting and background on what became the ARE: see 254–52 to

254–55; account of the university closing: HLC to RS and LS; last meeting between EC and MB: MB's unpublished memoir, *The Fallen Oak;* desire for reconciliation: EC to MB on October 24, 1932.

Chapter 43: Begin at the Beginning

"unless changes are made": 294–128; details of hospital as hotel: *Norfolk Virginia Pilot,* February 18, 1968; "the heartaches I have had over that place": EC to CH on February 10, 1938; the serious nature of their financial situation: EC to EZ on August 27, 1934; "the money will turn up somehow": [I] HB to SK; New York arrest: 3871–1; MB and EB not letting EC alone: EC to Elizabeth Evans in March 1932; EC's attitude during arrest: 254–59; "they are discharged": see 254–59 for complete trial transcript; "on a technicality, rather than on its merits": EC to Mr. and Mrs. Levy on November 23, 1931; "sank into an even deeper depression": ibid.; horse and soldiers dream: 294–127; "there are things to be done": 294–128; efforts to keep EC on earth plane: GD to DK on December 11, 1931; "healer in the Spiritualist church": EC to HZ on October 27, 1934; first study group reading: 262–1; reading on October 4: 262–3; White Horse Hill treasure: see 3812 series; challenges while digging for treasure: 3812–6; HLC's account of digging for treasure: see *The Outer Limits of Edgar Cayce's Powers,* by HLC and EEC, Bell, New York, 1971; A. C. Preston: GD to Maurice Pereles in April 1932, also see 426–2; Lindbergh readings: 4191 series; "unless it came of itself through individuals deeply concerned": EC to DK on March 12, 1932; "drop the matter": 257–80; reference to FBI investigation: see FBI report of August 19, 1943, and February 25, 1944, as obtained through the Freedom of Information Act; Hoffman letter: 4191–7.

Chapter 44: He That Endureth

"evil days will not come": 254–54; "[But] he that endureth to the end shall wear the Crown": 2897–4; "carry all your baggage": 294–155; MB and moving to new house: EC to James Hough on March 8, 1932; period of the ministry: 254–60; purchase rather than rent: 254–62; "looking out one window and seeing the lake while looking out another and seeing the ocean": EC to Abigail Finlayson on October 21, 1932; moving to new house: EC to Alf Butler on June 6, 1932; details of the new house: GD to MC; "The ARE office was located upstairs": GD to Vaughn Hall on July 13, 1933; EC's garden: EC to Abigail Finlayson on October 21, 1932, and December 1, 1932; details of first annual ARE Congress: 5747–1, 5752–2 and 5748–6; aim of ministry: 254–61; "CALL ON THEE": 262–27; "NONE BE AFRAID": 262–28; "KNOW HIS FACE": 262–29; "Come, my children!": 262–56; "Adam in the Garden": 262–57; church experience of seeing ghosts: 1567–1; Byron Wyrick vision: 1567–1; "contained in large books": 441–1; astral travel: 254–68; "protect what he would leave behind": 257–130; "pattern my life after": EC to HZ on December 6, 1933; Mitchell T. Hastings readings: 440 series; "coin remained in his palm": 1770–7, also see HLC's correspondence with Minnie and George Hirn on September 23, 1959.

Chapter 45: Beloved Teacher

"would receive the treasure": 254–60; the young king and earth changes reading: 3976–15; "It is not the world": 416–7; "He must be removed": 3976–15; Woodrow Wilson and Jesus: 3976–8; "the many thousands that may be reached through that . . . recorded by [Gladys]": 262–2; "be not afraid": 69–1; the price would be heavy: 262–83; "day of the lord may draw nigh": 262–96; Christ consciousness and EC: Ruth LeNoir in taped interview by HLC, 1964; Dr. Harding's patient: 954–4; Zentgraf readings: 378 series.

Chapter 46: The Messenger

background on Reilly: see *My Forty-three Years with the Cayce Cures,* by Harold J. Reilly and Ruth Hagy Brod, draft of unpublished book as found in ECF archive; background on Dobbins: from a lecture by Lydia Shrader Gray on October 22, 1946; Thomas Scanlon reading: ibid.; "Edgar had to fight back tears": 1513–1; rape victim reading: 1789–1; incident regarding Detroit arrest: HLC to RS and LS; Jesus dream: 1468–1; "to know their entire contents": [I] HB to SK; "had no future": HLC in undated taped interview in 1964; Sally Taylor: HLC to RS and LS; Earhart readings: 1396–1 and 1396–2; *Lusitania* readings: see 1395 series; December 15, 1937 reading: 1468–2; EB's life reading referencing biblical incarnation: 137–121; "If this had been given in the first, there would have been a puffing up [of that entity's ego]": 294–192.

Chapter 47: Peace and Prosperity

descriptions of house and gardens: this is pieced together from a myriad of sources, but a good description is that given by HLC to RS and LS, and GD to MC; EC's state of mind: EC to Ola Crumb in undated 1941 letter; Bunchie's ghost: 1196–2, also recounted in letter from GD to HLC on May 13, 1976; "It is the end": 304–49; "there is nothing there": HLC to LS and RS; "follow through on the treatments": 2321 reports; Beatrice Seay: 2072 series; "You must meet her": Josephine Buchanan to EC on March 17, 1940; Faith Harding readings: 2156 series; "the child reportedly got well": see correspondence with Leslie Savage in 1561 series; "deplorable loss": EC to Josephine Buchanan on March 17, 1940; additional material on Faith Harding: [I] Faith Harding to SK; TS's readings: 849; TS's condition regarding arthritic problems: 849–10; last father and son talk; HLC to RS and LS.

Chapter 48: The Last Reading

vision out of Book of Revelations: 294–296, also see 1151–29; the message he had been sent to give: EC to HZ on February 23, 1934; "power and expansion in such associations": 416–7; "through forty-two and forty-three": 1151–24; "until at least forty-five": 984–4; brotherhood of man: 1152–29; Hitler and rise to power readings: see 3976–13 and 15, also see 257–203; "[imperialism] is entering": 3976–15; Hitler's future: 257–211; "selling itself for a mess of pottage": 1554–3; "forcing servitude": 3976–29; "knowledge not applied, except within self": 3976–29; sin of America: ibid.; "In God We Trust": 3976–29; prophetic reading on "mob rule" and death of two presidents: 3976–24; brother against brother reading: 2632–1; EC's declining health:

294–211; "How will you make him follow it?": 254–115; the deluge of requests for readings: 3588–1; "$18,000 in cash": EEC to GD on September 29, 1944; postal deliveries: EC to Evelyn Horton on September 20, 1943; "Edgar Evans Cayce Jr. reading: 3069–1; "the smartest thing in the country": EC to Bessie G. Taylor on April 12, 1944; Lost Dutchman Mine reading: 3638–1; last Archangel Michael reading: 294–208; Hemingway reading: 3954–1; EC's declining physical condition and the "drain machine": Betty Allen Curson to HLC on April 18, 1972; EC's visitor from Washington: EC to EEC on May 31, 1944; "need I mention those close to you": HLC to EC on October 11, 1944; "until you are well or dead": 294–212; "heartbroken to be in such a fix": GD's notes for November 21, 1944; "entrance of a soul into earth": GD to EEC on January 3, 1945; "what have I ever sacrificed": 294–8 supplement; "the light he brought to countless thousands": [I] JT to SK; "opened their pedals": GD to TS on March 19, 1945; HLC's last letter to GC: HLC to GC on March 30, 1945.

Epilogue: The New Tomorrow

GD's activities after EC's death: see GD's diary; DK's dream of EC: DK to HLC on November 20, 1945; HB's impression of challenges to come: [I] HB to SK; HLC's decision on the new focus of the A.R.E.: HLC to GD on June 3, 1945; "marriage to the work": MC in *Miss Gladys and the Edgar Cayce Legacy*, A.R.E. Press, 1972; HLC buying back the hospital: HLC to RS and LS; "prepare self": 416–17; "make thy paths straight": 364–7; "raise not democracy": 3976–24; "Lord of my Heart": 3976–25; GD meeting MB: GD's notes on June 15, 1947; stars in the evening sky: [I] JT to SK.

Index

For further information about Edgar Cayce and the Association for Research and Enlightenment, Inc., please write A.R.E., 215 67th Street, Virginia Beach, VA 23451, or visit the Website at *www.edgarcayce.org*.

In the Winter Dark

Tim Winton was born in Perth in 1960 and has written
novels, collections of stories, non-fiction and books for
children. He has won the Miles Franklin Award four times,
and been twice shortlisted for the Booker Prize, for *The
Riders* (1995) and *Dirt Music* (2002).

Also by Tim Winton

Novels

An Open Swimmer

That Eye, The Sky

Shallows

Cloudstreet

The Riders

Dirt Music

Breath

Stories

Scission

Minimum of Two

The Turning

In the Winter Dark

Tim Winton

PICADOR

First published 1988 by McPhee Gribble,
a division of Penguin Books Australia Ltd

First published in Great Britain 1995 by Picador in
The Collected Shorter Novels of Tim Winton

This edition published 2003 by Picador
an imprint of Pan Macmillan Ltd
Pan Macmillan, 20 New Wharf Road, London N1 9RR
Basingstoke and Oxford
Associated companies throughout the world
www.panmacmillan.com

ISBN 978-0-330-41259-9

Typeset by SX Composing DTP, Rayleigh, Essex
Printed in the UK by CPI Mackays, Chatham ME5 8TD

for Denise and Jesse

and for the Nannup Tiger
wherever you are

Acknowledgements

The author thanks the Literature Board of the Australia Council for senior fellowships in 1984 and 1987 when this book was written. Final revisions were made in Paris at the Australia Council Studio while the author was a recipient of a Marten Bequest Travelling Scholarship.

A portion of an earlier version of *In the Winter Dark* has appeared in *Antipodes*. Characters and events in this story are fictitious.

There is such a thing as the pressure of darkness.

Victor Hugo

It's dark already and I'm out here again, talking, telling the story to the quiet night. Maurice Stubbs listening to his own voice, like every other night this past year, with the veranda sinking and the house alive with solitary noises the way it always is when the sun's set on another day and no one's come to ask the questions they're gonna ask sooner or later. I just sit here and tell the story as though I can't help it. There's always something in the day that reminds me, that sets me off all hot and guilty and scared and rambling and wistful, like I am now.

This morning I found Jaccob down at his boundary fence drunk as a mongrel again, and I carried him up the hill to his place and lit him a fire, fixed some food, cleared away the bottles and that shoe he leaves around, and I left him there in that big old house before it drew breath and screamed my name. An old man like me can lift him now, for God's sake. He's always drunk or silent and skyward as a monk. There's only me and him left, but he doesn't speak.

So I'm the teller. But why don't I keep my mouth shut? Why? Because someone has to hear sooner or later. Because the bloody dreams don't go away. Because today I saw a real estate agent sniffing around across the valley at the girl's place. Because I'm alone, I'm alone here on the farm, the carrier of everyone's memories. So when the dusk comes, in that gloaming time of confusion when you can't tell a tree stump from a kangaroo, an owl hoot from a question in the night, the dark begins to open up like the ear of God and I babble it all out, try to get it straight in my mind, and listen now and then for a sigh, a whisper, some hint of absolution and comfort on the way.

This is what I remember, but it's not only my story. It happened to Ida, too, and Jaccob and the girl Ronnie. It's strange how other people's memories become your own. You recall things they've told you. You go over things until you think you can see the joins, the cells of it all. And there's dreams. I have these dreams. Dead people, broken people bleed things into you, like there's some pressure point because they can't get it out any more, can't get it told. It's as though the things which need telling seep across to you in your sleep. Suddenly you have dreams about things that happened to *them*, not to you, as if it isn't rough enough holding down your own secrets. I don't know how it works – I'm no witch-doctor – but I know I remember things I can't possibly know. I'm not mad. Not yet.

They call this valley the Sink. Well, they did when I was a young man. From my veranda of an evening you can see mist on the dark sheen of the swamp and the river bend below. Ducks spatter round the old white bridge. Frogs come on with the sound of marching. The jarrah forest takes the westering sun as a prick of blood on its brow. There's still only three houses. On the stony pasture across the valley there's the little house surrounded by fallen fences where no one's lived since Ronnie, the girl. Weird thing is, I got to like her in the end, but everyone likes the helpless and the vanquished. To the left, on the slope just up from here, Jaccob lives in the limestone place that's been there nearly as long as I can remember. We used to call it the Minchinbury place. God, how I hate that house. Jaccob's chimney smoke rising like a spirit against the gloom. He'll be sober enough to start drinking again by now. Since the day we dug a grave and drove to the hospital, the day we sat together like friends and drank half a case of Japanese Scotch and talked and talked it all out, we haven't said a word to one another. It's a year.

My neighbour Murray Jaccob used to push a lawnmower for a living. Just before it sent him deaf, he retired to nurse his crusty little crop of skin cancers. He sold up the business, left the city, and came here. Jaccob wanted to devote his retirement to the growing of grass. He was a big man in his late forties with streaky bleached hair, a kind of worn-out stooped look about him, and a way of looking at you as though he could never be quite certain where you fitted in; it might have been the way he squinted, or the habit he had of speaking to a point just to the left or right of you. But I could understand that after twenty-five years of cutting lawns, a man'd want to grow long, scruffy, weedy grass, the sort you could wade through and see lapping in the wind. He never wanted to see lawn again as long as he lived. He bought the old Minchinbury place amidst run-down orchards, some good pasture, and a lot of uncleared thickets and forest. When I was a boy, a Doctor Minchinbury made it his country residence. When he died, he left his daughter there to grow old and crazy. I remember her too well. The house had to be rebuilt since her day – the wooden bits, anyway, but it's still the same grand, fatuous-looking joint dominating the hill with its wide timber veranda and white-washed stone. There's nowhere you can be in the Sink where you'll miss seeing it.

Jaccob was no farmer. I noticed how late he got up. He had a policy of doing nothing. He was rigorous about it. From his place the river bend was obscured by a hump in the lower slopes of his land, but as he walked daily between rows of scourged fruit trees he could see the black sprays of birds rising from it to curve out over the swamp. It was a kind of ritual, that walk in the morning. The rest of the day he'd involve himself in trivial tinkerings that chewed up the time and left him at dusk, looking down through the broken ranks of orchards with the satisfaction of knowing that he hadn't done a damn thing all day, hadn't begun to put the place to order, hadn't learnt any more about orchards, and above all, hadn't had his ears thrashed by a machine and his nose stung by two-stroke fumes while his brain broiled in the sun. One more lawn-free day.

Jaccob was the first to notice something. I know it so well now, it's like I'm there myself.

Walking in the orchard late in the day, Jaccob saw the flash of a windscreen across the valley. The few months he'd been here, he'd kept clear of his neighbours. Ida and me seemed friendly enough in a stiff sort of way. We were the old couple who'd been around for ever. Jaccob felt the amusement of those yokels, the way they saw his presence, his kind of life. But he couldn't know what hatred there was in me, what fear.

His other neighbours, across the valley, were a young pair. He wouldn't have called them hippies; they were kind of modern types from the city. He'd spoken to them a couple of times. The girl was pretty enough, though she wore clownish clothes and had her hair in spikes. The boy wore overalls, but you could tell he belonged in a leather jacket. Jaccob didn't know a thing about them and he was not curious, though that afternoon as the sun caught the windscreen of his neighbours' car over the valley, he watched it wind down to the road. He heard the unreasonable note of the engine and the muffler grinding as the station wagon left the gravel and pulled away towards town. He caught himself staring after it and it made him laugh. An event! Good Gawd, he thought; what a life to have found.

He turned to go back up to the house. The light was failing and he had wood to chop. He set off, but something stopped him still as a stump. Between the trees he saw something. A movement. A silhouette. It was travelling. *Loping*, that was the word that came to him. He squinted. All around him, birds were roosting, or stirring, or something. He heard the tick of his own body. The shadow seemed to stop, slip sideways between apple rows. And then there was nothing.

It was the evenings that took getting used to. Jaccob was teaching himself to do very little and to be content. In the city he'd spent evenings by the TV with a beer and a buzz in his ears. As he'd got older, it took more beer, more repeats of *High Chaparral* to soften his nerves. His bones ached, his sunburn stung, blood chugged in his ears. And the last couple of years there was that other twinge too, but only dreamless sleep could rid him of that.

Here at night, Jaccob was becoming a reader. To his new life he'd brought his carved jarrah rocker, some old Marty Robbins records, and a pile of big novels by people he'd never heard of. With its great awkward stylus like a plough, his ancient hi-fi was probably, he thought, the only agricultural implement he was ever likely to use.

That night he made a fire, put old Marty's 'El Paso' on repeat, and sat rocking with *Look Homeward Angel* over his knee like a fat little lapdog. He was good at not letting shadows and suspicions ruin everything. He was new to the country; there was no point worrying. He poured some whisky. Before long he slept.

There was a dream he had, an old one flashing the colour of lightning in him. A yowl of grief, the panic rising in his chest like locusts on the wing as, in another life again, he threw the newspaper aside and began to run for the nursery door. Now Marjorie was screaming, shaking the cot as he came. I know this dream. It's Jaccob's, but I have it too, these days.

Jaccob slept on.

As that station wagon wound down the gravel drive in the sunset, someone else had been watching too. She saw her great herd of Muscovies scatter from its path. She saw the KEEP MUSIC LIVE sticker on the rear window – she'd stuck it on herself. The car left in the only direction it could – away. There were no passers-by here, no through traffic. These farms form a cul-de-sac at the end of a back road. The car disappeared around the first bend and was gone. The young woman found herself standing alone out in the cold, hugging herself until her breasts hurt. Her name was Veronica Melwater, though the man who'd just left her called her Ronnie.

She shivered. The kind of shiver you have when you cut yourself, in that moment before the blood springs, when

there is only the shock of the open wound and the anticipation of pain or maybe outrage.

She'd helped him load guitars and amplifiers into the car,
listening to him say how it was only a couple of weeks. We
need the cash. You don't wanna go back to the suburbs, do
you? Jesus, it's not like the old days, you know. Be reasonable, Ronnie.

Her Muscovies scuffled behind the troughs for night
shelter, and she could hear the geese somewhere coming up
from the river. There was the goat to milk and night was
ready with the sun setting the trees afire up behind the old
people's place over the way, but she stayed there until it
flared briefly and went out altogether. She looked up to the
great white house on the hill, the Minchinbury place. Now,
that was a place, all right. Mist formed on the valley slopes
below it. Looks like a movie set, she thought. But her eyes
wandered and her mind came back to the huge empty space
she seemed to be walking in. Who the hell needed to empty
their wardrobe for a two-week trip? She knew what that
meant. She wasn't stupid. Well, not in that way, boy. She
knew things weren't like they were in the old days. Didn't
she, though.

It was dark when she went inside. The little house had
been an old soldier settlement place they'd repaired and
filled with potted plants and posters. There were a few
lumpy hand-woven rugs, a spinning wheel she'd never really
learnt to use, a pot-belly stove, some simple furniture. The
walls were scabby with stripped wallpaper. They'd never got
around to finishing it off and putting some bright paint on
the walls.

'Ah, Ronnie,' she told herself aloud in that dark, small
place, 'don't panic. It's all right. It's just two weeks.'

She rested her low, full belly against the windowsill in the front room and felt the baby slip and kick inside her. All the Valium made her light enough to move without muscles, to float, like him or her, in warm fluid. She looked out into the dark and suddenly she was afraid. She had no car, for Godsakes. How would she get to town if she needed to? What was he doing to her? The money was gone, sure, but what else was going on? What about the staying out of music, what about the promises? Oh, Ronnie, you are so dumb, girl.

The room was dark and the faces of dead musicians and dead actors peered down at her. She held her belly. It was sinking in and it was like the pills were great white clots in her veins. Too many, Ronnie. She didn't even know how many she took, these days. But any of it had to be too much.

She felt this swimming creature in her, and she wanted to speak to it, to explain it all, but she was ashamed. She'd read the books, she knew what she'd been doing. Jesus, she thought; one minute you're paying some rich bastard to cut one out of you, and the next thing you're wanting one and you poison it.

Out in the dark she saw the anaemic cheek of a full moon rising from the forest. Stumps, windrows, clumps of gravel queued behind their own shadows.

Stuck. With everything, with everybody, she was stuck. It was quiet and she stood there feeling the strength go out of her. Always, she thought. Always when everything looks like coming together, just when you get up some guts, you get stuck. In the old days there was no problem. Then there was always a bit of acid to drop – keeping tabs on yourself, she called it. You stepped sideways and said fuck it. Ah, the old days.

It gave her an idea.

In the bedroom she knelt and pulled out a drawer beside the bed. She took it right out and put it on the floor. She reached into the hole it left and felt around the frame of the cabinet until she felt the little cellophane package taped to the wood. Old stock. A memento, really. She looked at it a while. No, things'd have to be black. She sat on the bed, getting strength back. She wanted this place, she wanted this baby, and she was gonna have them both. She made a fist in the half-light until she couldn't even see the tab in front of her. And then everything crumbled and went the taste of shit in her mouth, the taste of blotting paper. Fuck it, she thought; I deserve something.

When the walls began to breathe, Ronnie got up off the bed and went outside. It looked nicer out there. She felt the cold in an academic sort of way. Mist sifted past. It was like walking in the clouds. Better than breathing walls.

The sounds of the night were sharp. Crickets sounded like weapons being cocked. Her boots hissed in the grass. The bloated moon followed over her shoulder; she didn't like to look. The incline steepened toward a ridge of granite. The rock fairly pulsed in the blue light. Ronnie heard her own gasps, too loud to be hers.

The twisted trunks of redgums walked past, writhing. The ground was billowing now. Never do it alone, Ronnie. Oh, you never needed to in the old days.

She came to a delicious bank of grass and lay down in it. Up through the shreds of mist and the towering wet blades, the stars glowed. No, she saw, they glowered. I know, she thought; I know, you don't have to tell me. Cold beneath her, the earth soaked up her heartbeats and the stars showed blood in the dark contusion of sky. She heard a snapping, slapping deluge of footsteps, and turning her head she saw an army of ghosts marching upon her. They shrilled and squawked and sprayed shit.

'Oh, God! Nick? Nick!'

They closed on her with their great infernal pink bills pointing down at her from the end of looping white necks. And wings, evil white wings. There was purple fire in their eyes. She knew what they were, but they were more than that, you only had to use your eyes. She covered her belly and then they were gone. She got up and ran.

Ronnie stumbled through the granite boulders.

This wasn't the proper world. Tiny marsupials smashed through the bush. All the colours, all the dyes came unstuck and she walked through them.

A dam, huge pore in the flesh of the earth.

A fence. She plucked a riff crawling through.

There was forest.

There was forest.

Forest.

Forest.

Half the night there was Ronnie and there was jarrah forest, and yet it was no time at all.

There were places here the moon could not follow. No time at all but fast-time, quick-time, hurry-time that she dawdled in. She came to thickets. Thickets and thickets of thickets.

A year into the night there was sudden pasture again. Fog still. She coughed. Someone's hack. She swam through grass, played fences, began to find an incline. Big white house full of music. Trees like a graveyard. The road was a ribbon in the wind. She climbed aboard and surfed it, rode road bronco. It was fun enough to die. And in mid-step she fell asleep and went down into a softer dark. No, it wasn't like the old days.

Ida and me were married thirty-six years. We thought of ourselves as good country people; we knew what we knew, and tried to mind our business, or at least to be discreet when we minded someone else's. That night, as Jaccob slept, as Ronnie lurched around out there, Ida and me waited for dinner to cook. It was late because I'd worked through till dark, fooling with a fuel line in the ute.

She was a cunning woman, Ida, and I liked that about her. It was cunning that got her married to me. Our families look grim in the wedding photos. Everyone, including me, thought our Ida was with child. Her people disliked me, and now they had the chance to hate me, but there was no way they could avoid a marriage. Or so they thought. Lord, didn't we all get a surprise! There was no baby in *that* girl's belly – not for a year or two.

Pork chops spat and sizzled on the stove. It was warm in our big kitchen tonight. You could tell Ida had ideas for later when she cooked pork, but after nearly forty years of falling for it every time, a man has to pretend he doesn't know when he's being seduced. In those days, after a hard day's work and before a good meal, I liked to get by the stove with a volume of my *Pictorial History of Australia at War* and a bottle of beer and some bread and butter so I could get inside myself, all sullen with pleasure. I spread the big book on the table and listened to the urn hiss on the stove and sank into the comfort of history, the terse outlines, the facts, the bare black and white photos. I was never in a war, but my interest was deeper than that. In a way I've lived my life by the weather (that faithless bitch), and history, it seemed to me, was something solid, truthful, unswerving. Well, that was those days. I sat there airing my feet in their socks, and Ida tinkered with the chops in the pan.

Outside, the dog whined. It wasn't a farm dog, but a silky terrier, that useless kind of dog with a yap that sets a man on edge.

'What's that dog chained up for, woman?'

Ida sniffed. 'He's done business here on the lino and I'm punishing him.'

'I warned you about buying that dog.'

'Gawd, that was ten years ago, Maurice. He's old, that's all.'

'Well, there's three hundred acres out there he can crap all over.'

'I'm aware of the problem, Maurice. It's all in hand.'

I shifted in my seat, smoothed a page, and the dog found a keener note to whine upon. It was dark outside, and cold, and if it hadn't been for the dog and the chops and the stove and our crotcheting, you might have heard the water-snore of the valley, that strange sound of the river moving and the damp air settling on it in the hollows.

Ida sighed and served up the pork chops with a splash of peas and a hillock of mashed potato, and we ate in the silence we were used to. The food was good. I could feel the irritation and the weariness back off. Neither of us had really got going before the scream began. It wasn't a long scream; it stopped before I got to the door. Ida bellowed the dog's name, and the cold backhanded me as I stumbled outside.

I turned the light on. Saw the chain trailing down off the edge of the veranda.

'Maurice, what was it?' she said, sounding like she'd made the effort of being calm.

I heard her coming from behind me, and I kept my back to her. I held the bloody dog-collar in my hand.

'Get the shovel, love,' I said. I heard the awful quietness in my voice. 'Keep away. Go and get the shovel.'

I heard a thick noise in her throat, and as she moved away I looked out into the darkness. There was a light on up at Jaccob's, but no lights from across the way. My palm was hot with blood. In my hand was the severed head of Ida's silky terrier, still with nerves enough to flex its jaws foully in my grip. That was how I found it, the head left in the collar, the chain snapped, blood pushing out hot. And nothing else.

I heard Ida coming back and it struck me of a sudden that maybe we should never have stayed on here, maybe I should have taken Ida out of this valley thirty years ago and never come back. To spare her the hardships, the hidden things, this night.

We'd spent some time together, me and Ida. The children had grown and gone, and over the years Ida had fattened up. She sort of spread, like a garden gone wild. I think she was richer, better for the years. She'd developed a big, wide laugh and her memory was gentle. She wanted the best for people, to think the best of them. She gave me the benefit of any doubt, and she'd had a few, because, looking back on it, I see I'd grown in, gotten smaller, meaner with age. But she stayed, even so, though sometimes I wonder why. We loved each other, but I gather sometimes it's less than enough. Things had been cool between us sometimes, even stony quiet, but never in thirty-six years had there been an evening of such sick silence as this turned out to be.

We went to bed early, in the end. We lay beside each other, straight as coffins. Moonlight forked in through the curtains. We were there like that about an hour, maybe two, before Ida spoke.

'Was it a fox, you think?'

I listened to our breathing.

'I don't know.'

But she heard me open the bedside drawer, and she heard in the dark the heavy metallic sound as I placed the rifle bolt on the table. It was the only way I could tell her what I thought and not lie.

I dreamt I ran downhill full of holes in the creeping blindness of night, aflame and screaming. I lit up the valley like a torch and everything saw, everything knew I was being punished. I found the river, dived in, but it was just fuel to the flames. My mouth was a hole. There was nowhere to go.

We all dreamt that night – the four of us – as though our insides were all tight and grinding with rent chunks of secrecy shivering up to the surface.

I remember every dream from that night: Ronnie's floating nightmare, Jaccob's terrible memory, I even know what Ida dreamt. Like that old Bible story about the wild man chained up in the tombs, ranting and foaming in all those voices. Call me Legion, he says, because we are many. And the pigs screaming down into the water, remember that? What was he having, delusions? Or was he having everyone's recollections, was it history that tormented him? What had the wild man done in order to be mercilessly visited by everybody's dreams? Well, I can't speak for him, but I think about that poor bastard when I sit out here talking to the dark, or when I wake in the night from a dream that belongs to someone else. The wild man had someone come to cast out his demons. But here tonight, like every night, I sit here, and no one comes.

Jaccob went through his orchard in the light of the morning. He looked about, but he most definitely did not search. His neck was sore and his bones ached from sleeping in the rocker. From over the Stubbses' place he heard the low gearing of a motor. Kookaburras whipped up a brassy chorus back in the trees, and he saw fresh roo scat between the fruit trees which he ground moist into the earth with a smile. He smelt grass. He remembered the day he retired, the day he was a little mad with sun, when he mowed that rich bastard's lawn and then his herb garden, and his azaleas, made his garden gnomes into amputees, until the place looked like a UFO had landed on it in a careless manner. Yes, it was good to have at least one memory where you took destiny into your own hands.

He went down to the roadside boundary from where he could see birds engraving the platinum surface of the river. The little bridge shimmered in the sun, and he could smell the muddy sweetness of the swamp. He knew this place was good. Even if he died here alone, it would be good. It was morning, light had come and he had nothing to do but live his life.

He stopped, though, when something caught his eye. Something red. The wet-stiff grass seemed to shiver. Jaccob reached for a stick. As he climbed through the fence, the stick snagged in the wire and he fumbled a second and left it there. From across the road, in the tall grass, he heard panting. Well, it might have been panting. He stood there in the road, wishing he could just walk away, but he was afraid to turn his back. Whatever it was, it was moving again. He could see its slow passage through the grass. As he crossed the road he listened to the stones mashing underfoot, then the quietness of the macadam. A duck bawled in the distance. Jaccob hardened up. He saw everything quite clearly: gravel at the edge of the road, wild oats, the black gloss of beetles. And, knowing it was a stupid thing to do, he waded into the grass. He felt weirdly calm, or perhaps calmly weird. It was morning and there was light and sound and it was his land.

It hit him behind the knees so hard he went down like a sack of wheat, steeling himself, even as he fell, for the pain to come. It had hold of his legs, but his nerves hadn't caught up yet. His nose ploughed the ground, his mouth was full of grass stalks, and he tasted whisky at the back of his throat, waiting in that awful timeless calm before the pain.

'Dad?'

Jaccob lifted his face from the dirt.

'Daddy, is that you?'

'What the bloody—'

He twisted over and saw behind him, grafted to his calves like a rugby player, the girl from over the valley. Her hair was wet across her blue-pink face, snarled in drifting snot. Her red parka was torn and twisted. She was a mess.

'Jesus Christ!'

'Don't go.'

He felt laughter and relief gushing up in his throat and he hit her.

Ronnie didn't dare breathe. Sometimes the man carrying her looked like her father and sometimes he didn't at all. His face seemed to grow and shrink. The ground raced below her, like a runway. Yes, he hit her, he was her father all right. Yeah, now he'd take her up to her room and beat her and that hopeless twat of a mother'd shout at him but not stop it and he'd leave her in the room and she'd tear her clothes and smack her face against the wall while they ate their dinner downstairs.

There was a big place coming up, all elephantine and distorted. White. A white place. Oh, God, not a hospital! No, not this trick. Oh, they had it all organized. So this was the doctor. With his knife, his fish scraper, his pig-sticker or what-the-hell-ever.

She was inside, like it swallowed her. White walls, dirty white walls. So why did he put her on the floor? On a rug? Sometimes the rug was all crawly and sometimes just a rug. She lay there. No she couldn't let them, but she couldn't move any more, no she couldn't. Here came those great shudders again, and then she was hot and prickling and there was orange light and the doctor was pulling at her parka. Oh, God in heaven must know she didn't deserve this; she didn't deserve much, but this . . . this! This all went purple and grey and this became that. Or something.

*

On hands and knees I went over the wet grass, combing the ground beyond the veranda. I smelt woodsmoke and eggs, heard birds, felt the angry drive of blood in my ears. I was looking for tracks and getting madder. Everywhere I found my own stockinged footprints where last night I'd trampled the place like a fool in a fit. There was a rut where grass and dirt had been uprooted: something stopping fast. I laboured on for an hour. I cursed myself, I felt the old back and knees complain, but in the end I did find a single, clear print. Fifteen feet away from the veranda. I sat there on my haunches and set my teeth to just look at it.

At breakfast, a beeswax cast of the print stood between Ida and me on the table. We ate in silence. The early cold blue of the sky was giving way to grey and it felt as though a westerly was due. The footprint tilted, catching a bit of light. I could smell honey from it. I caught Ida looking at it. She sipped her tea. She brewed the stuff strong enough to shrivel your tongue.

'It'll rain d'rectly,' she said. 'Better get to it.'

I watched her get up and push into her gumboots by the door. I saw the blue veins of her legs and felt grateful and sad and as old as hell.

That morning we drove around the property, moving from one minor task to the next, putting some feed about when it wasn't really needed, shifting steers from paddock to paddock. Ida drove the ute and I got out for the gates. The pastured hills were the colour of the sea, and the sheep and steers like islands on it. Crows hoyed from the trees. We saw Jaccob on the edge of his orchard. He was stiff and small in the distance. We rode the boundaries, as they say, and we didn't know quite what else to do.

On the northern boundary closest to the forest we came

upon the carcass of a roo caught in the fence. It was a doe, fresh-dead with its neck broken in the wire. I motioned Ida to stop and I pulled the skinning knife from its sheath beneath the dash, thinking of meat for the dog, but Ida just looked at me and drove on and it caught me stunned a moment before I sank back like a fool, too ashamed even to say sorry.

Jaccob got the fire going and felt it hot on his face as he began to undress the girl who lay rigid with cold. Her eyes were wide, pupils like bullet holes. All she seemed able to do was shake her head. She was blue as a bruise. He peeled two shirts from her and her small breasts moved like . . . like things. Her jeans and boots were slicked with mud and his fingers had become fat and clumsy, but he got everything off and threw it on the hearth. He felt her eyes on him as he shucked down her panties, the way he might have done if she was his child, and the thought hurt. From upstairs he brought the feather quilt to wrap her up. The fire cracked and spat.

Jaccob sat down and thought. No, he wouldn't call a doctor, not yet.

The girl began to cry.

All morning Jaccob tended the fire while the girl slept. He was agitated like he hadn't been for a long time. He tried not to prowl and pace lest he wake her, so he confined himself to the rocker. Hell, this was his neighbour, naked on his living-room floor. He didn't know her, and he sure as eggs didn't want trouble. He rocked by the fire. This was not good, but it was no reason to panic. It was just something silly and unexpected. Nothing.

Late in the morning when the girl still hadn't woken, he hid his whisky bottle and his novels before going out into the chill to clear his head. He felt like he had a decision to make. Like maybe something was happening and he should identify it in order to square it away and get on with being happy and alone.

At noon, he bundled the girl's clothes up and took them out to the wash-house. They stank of sweat and stale deodorant. Cleaning the small, silly-looking boots, he caught himself smiling; it reminded him of his own father. He remembered his father used to clean all the children's boots. It was like a devotion, and the thought made him unaccountably happy. He knew he'd wanted it for himself. There'd be no little shoes to polish now. The sudden warmth went and there was bitterness in him. He scraped swamp mud from the little green pointed toes.

By the fire, the girl slept white lipped and muddy in the quilt. He knew he should take her up to a bed, but it seemed somehow just too much.

Now and then she moved a limb. Once, a white foot slipped out from under the cover to reveal ragged toenails and a crusty heel. He wondered if maybe he could get her in the car and take her home. Surely she'd wake up soon.

After lunch I went up to the northernmost reaches and into the forest. The smell of a good stand of jarrah is enough to make a man sing. Sink people over the years came to call the scrofulous bald patch on our side of the valley Dick's Hill, after my father. Dad was a tearer and burner, cleared damn near everything he could find, but he had to stop at the northern boundary because it's state forest, Crown land.

He was frightened of trees, my old man. Never sleep in the forest, he would say; everything is above you. And I know what he means. I've seen twelve-foot boughs fall and spear so deep into the earth that they looked like small trees in their own right. Being under that in your plastic tent – imagine. The old man had his practical side, but there was more to his feeling about the forest than that. Well, there's all those fairy tales for a start, all those stories we brought with us from another continent, other centuries. Whatever it was, the old man did what he could to bash and burn it into submission.

You get that big church feeling up there in the forest. We were running out of fuel early this winter, so I took the chainsaw with me to feel like I was working and not just farting about. I dawdled the ute along the muddy tracks in the broken light, looking for windfalls. It didn't take long to spot a toppled tree. I stopped and got out. The wind sounded like a choir way above. I grabbed the axe from the rear tray, picked my way through the undergrowth with its crush of bracken and creepers and ferns and bright orange fungi and beds of soft wet pungent bark, and when I came to the tree, I scrambled up its great flank and stood panting a moment.

The axe rang out sweet and clear, and I made a bigger notch than I needed to, just to feel the weight of the axe and hear that *thock!* a few times more. The timber was good and dead, the colour of honey.

I went back for the chainsaw. The air was full of the smells of eucalyptus and gravel and mud and dew. As I hefted the saw off the ute, I saw something along the track, something red and quickly gone and I felt a thump of excitement in my chest. This was it. I put the chainsaw back on the tray and reached into the cab for the rifle.

I moved as quick and quiet as I knew, cutting an imaginary line through the timber to where I thought I might get another sighting. Birds shuttered away up into the wind. My feet sweated in the clumsy gumboots. I remembered to cock the .243. I didn't understand my sudden anger. Things began to happen too quickly; everything was breathless.

When I saw that red blur ducking away in the bracken only forty metres away, I got off two shots in a hurry. The forest rippled with the noise and I heard a slug smack home. Strange, but the first thing I did was pick up the shells from the ground and sniff the cordite. As though I was putting off any investigation. Up there in the bracken, there was a scraping sound.

When I got close I saw blood, a smear on a fan of bracken. Ground litter rustled. I went forward behind the barrel of the gun. Then I all but trod on the quivering body of a fox, and I leapt back with a shout, and then let out a nervy little laugh. The beast had terrible mange, which would make it look bigger and stranger from a distance. I'd hit it twice: in the front paw and in the back hip. It shook with pain and didn't even look at me. I killed it with another shot and heard the crack tear up into the light. Then I went back to sawing wood.

Ida Stubbs heard shots and flinched enough to drop the preserve jar and it smashed at her feet. She leant against the sink a moment and looked out the window to the forest up the hill. Another shot; she heard it soar over the valley and it gave her a flittery feeling she didn't often get any more, that sense of being small, of not really belonging. She'd had it in her chest the day she'd come here after the wedding. And she got it each time she brought a baby back from the district hospital. She'd stand here at the window and feel new and strange, as though maybe she should get back in the car and take this helpless child to a town, a city, somewhere where the trees didn't stand over you, where the swamp didn't sit there brewing at your doorstep, where people might drive past occasionally and wave on their way to somewhere else.

She tucked a wisp of hair behind her ear and sniffed. That gun's just a bit big for our needs, Maurice, and besides, you couldn't hit a barn with a handful of gravel.

Ida didn't like guns. Her father went out one day five years after we were married and shot himself dead. And there were always accidents, stupid things. She had a cousin (an old man now) who blew his own ear off climbing through a fence.

She got on her knees and swept up the slurry of chopped apple and splintered glass. That was another thing; she hated waste.

What was that fool of a hubby doing up there?

I have an Ida dream all the time. Some nights I have it so bad it has me waking up thinking I *am* Ida. In the dream she stands at the last rise before those thickets which web the hills just beyond here. The children are there, picking mushrooms. They call out and throw cowpats and are happy. She holds their cardigans and watches them play, but in an instant she imagines them being drawn into the thicket, snagged deep beyond the light, as though the place will not yield and if it will not yield it won't be still. She stands there shuddering with apprehension. She clutches their sweet-smelling garments and watches her children. I am not there, not anywhere in the picture. She never told me about this fear. Maybe I wouldn't have listened. You understand yourself late enough to discover you're the sorriest bastard who ever was.

Jaccob woke at the sound of the shot. He got out of the chair and went out into the grey afternoon light. He waited but there was nothing else. Before long he heard the bawl of a chainsaw and he relaxed a little.

Guns. Jaccob had a rifle of his own, a .22 repeater which the estate agent had given to him as a sign of goodwill when he handed the keys over. To Jaccob it seemed an odd gesture of goodwill, and he'd never even fitted the magazine to it. He kept it in his wardrobe.

Jaccob yawned. Strange, but he was bored. With someone else around all day, just being uselessly there, the day seemed truly long and pointless. He poked in all the sheds behind the house with their chaff and rodent and diesel smells. He fed his pullets and watched them scuffle and bluff. He pocketed eggs. He chopped wood in the hope the noise might wake the girl up and it would seem accidental that he should disturb her, so he chopped until his back ached and he felt like a complete dolt.

The light went. Jaccob slunk back into the house and showered. Then he resolved to be neighbourly and set about roasting the leg of lamb he'd been saving the past few days. A roast dinner, a bottle of red, that might do. He crept around in the kitchen, basting meat and peeling vegetables, mixing mustard and finding some mint for the sauce.

But the dinner cooked and the girl slept on.

Jaccob ate alone as always, only now with someone else in the house he felt more lonely than he'd felt in all his months here. Mostly he'd been all right here on his own. Only a couple of times, usually when drunk, he'd given in to sadness and taken out the photo albums and looked at the pictures of Marjorie and him, Marjorie and the baby. But not tonight; he was damned if he'd cave in tonight. He listened to the sounds of his cutlery. Oh, how the clink of knife and fork spoke its own language. Yes, he remembered those evenings at dinner after the shit had hit the fan, when they were still married but with nothing between them but grief and recrimination, when her scraping knife would say: it wasn't my fault, so don't look at me like that, and his fork would rattle and mutter: for Christ's sake, leave it be.

Jaccob pulled his novel down from behind the old kitchenette and opened it beside his plate so he could read and make some normality. He took a mouthful of wine. The novels were Marjorie's. She read serious books and listened to serious music, and late in the piece she didn't even hide her contempt for his penny-dreadfuls and his country music. When they were packing to separate, he saw a brace of books she'd earmarked for the local opp. shop. Some were by Leon Uris and Morris West, but there was a pile by a Thomas Wolfe with swaggering titles and plenty of exclamation marks, and he took them. Marjorie sneered. A bit much for you, I would have thought, darling. Though thick enough, maybe.

He took them anyway and tonight he kept up his assault on *Look Homeward Angel*. As he read and ate he heard the girl snore in the next room.

And when the bells broke through the drowning winds
at night, his demon rushed into his heart, bursting all
cords that held him on the earth, promising him
isolation and dominance over sea and land, inhabita-
tion of the dark . . .

Sounded fine to him. He read on until he sensed that the
fire in the next room needed wood, and when he got up and
went in he found it was all but out. As he was rekindling it,
he heard the girl's voice behind him.

'What? The. The. What the fuck is this?'

He turned and saw her sitting up, breasts exposed, until
she realized and opened her mouth in surprise before claw-
ing the quilt around her. She was wild and angry looking.

'Oh.' He straightened up, wiped his hands. 'You're
awake.'

'Yes, I am. What the hell is this? What's happening here?
What've you been doing?'

'Listen, I—'

'Where's my clothes?' Her nest of crumpled spiky hair
made her look feisty and mean. Her face was smeared with
mud and the warrior-look it gave her took him aback.

'I'll go get them.'

'What've you done to them?'

'Washed them.'

He went out into the black cold to the wash-house. It was
quiet out there and he felt like staying, but he went across to
the clothesline in the yard outside and unpegged her clothes.
They were still wet.

'You'll have to dry them by the fire,' he said when he
went back in.

She looked hard at him. He backed some chairs up to

the fire and draped her clothes across them, avoiding till the very last the pair of plain white panties. Then he added a few split lengths of jarrah to the fire and sat in his rocker.

'Something to drink?'

'No.'

With its turned posts and mirrors, the mantel glowed like an altar in the light of the fire.

'Hungry?'

'No.'

'I can't believe that,' he said with a grin.

'I don't give a stuff what you believe.'

Jaccob shrugged. It stung all right. He left the room a moment and came back with a glass of wine for himself.

'How did I get here?'

'You're asking me?' He almost got up and stood over her, but he took a drink and tried to be calm. 'Are you sick? You were delirious as far as I could tell. Found you down there across the road from my place. Lucky you didn't go into the river.'

'Ah. No, I'm not sick. I remember.'

She seemed to soften a moment, as though it wasn't a good memory to have. And suddenly it was obvious to him.

'Listen, I don't know what you took, but it can't be much good for you if you've gotta ask where you've been.'

Drugs. He didn't know much about that business. It made him nervous, made him feel old.

'Pass me the clothes, will you?' She was abrupt. With one hand she pointed, with the other she held the quilt to herself.

'Wet, you mean?'

'Listen—'

'OK. Fine. Here.'

29

The wet jeans fell in a dollop on her head. The blouse and parka landed near by, and the panties fell well short.

'You gonna watch me dress as well?'

Jaccob left the room. He sat in the kitchen and bit a cold potato. Anger was slow in him these days, but he was beginning to simmer. Should have thrown her out the moment she opened her bloody mouth, he thought.

When he went back, she was shivering and lacing her newly polished boots. He put Marty Robbins back on the turntable and set the plough into the furrow. She looked up and wrinkled her nose at the first bars of 'White Sport Coat'.

He suddenly saw it. 'You're pregnant.'

'Bye.' She walked out. She was back in a moment. 'Where's the fucken door?'

Jaccob pointed. She went down the hall and was gone.

Ronnie walked out against that big slab of dark cold. The sky was starless and without a moon. Her feet were dead in the wet boots. She felt as though her bones were constricting in the chill. Her clothes moulded to her flesh. She couldn't even see her own house across the dark. She had no torch. She sensed a quavering, a faintness. She was hungry. Her teeth ached. Of course I'm bloody pregnant, she thought; what did you think it was, you dumb old prick, a pillow?'

She thought of the way he'd handled her panties. No, he was safe enough, nothing had happened. Stoned, Ronnie, you were wrecked. You idiot! She started to shake. A hard cold rammed her cheek. The house behind sloped away at an angle and a blade of dewy grass ran across her nose. It took a moment to know she had fallen. Oh, shit, what a mess.

She got up and went back into the lighted house.

I left the .243 leaning against the wardrobe and got into bed. Ida's buttocks were cold against me. I knew I wouldn't sleep for a while; every nerve seemed alive and awake tonight. I was surprised to feel Ida turn and move to me. I felt her lips against my throat. She rose from beneath the fug of blankets and her long breasts fell against me, and, strangely, I thought of our daughters, and their daughters. Women. Strangers. But soon my mind was swept clean of any thought but the grip we had on each other, the configuration we made in the dark, and I knew I was alive and my blood moved in me.

Jaccob watched her eat in silence. His old sweater was too big for her by half, and she felt like trash, scoffing and gulping the way she did. She wiped up congealed gravy with a potato, looked at him no more than a second.

'How old are you?' she asked.

'How pregnant are you?'

Their chins came up in unison.

Ronnie wondered about him. He had a look about him, like he was someone in need of kindness. That defeated air might have attracted her once. He was old and burnt; the sun-wrinkles in his face were like dry creekbeds. His mouth was small and set, and he had a permanent squint. Jeans fifteen years out of date, elastic-sided boots, flannel shirt, the whole thing. He looked like the sort of bloke who delivered your firewood in the city. But she liked the way he seemed perpetually embarrassed. He was always shifting his hands about.

'Sorry I hit you.'

She regarded him with surprise.

'You were going berserk down by the road.'

'How come you live here on your own?'

He smiled patiently and she squirmed. Yeah, he thought she was rubbish all right. She gulped some wine and spluttered. He laughed.

'I'll drive you home.'

She fisted up inside again. To hell with him.

In his small car she could smell him, and it made her think of her father. The smell of wood, linseed oil, some damn thing.

'Why are you driving me? It's only five hundred metres?'

'I'm being polite and neighbourly. It's cold and you're not well. Why, do you wanna get out?'

The headlights showed rising mist as they drove along the river before heading uphill along her gravel drive. The place looked lonely tonight. In the hard lights of the car, the house was sad and rickety, just too pathetic for words.

'Where's your friend?' he said, pulling in and swinging the car round in the yard.

'S'pose you wanna come in now?'

'Gawd no. Just be careful, all right?'

'What?' She got out and glared at him, saw his face green in the dash lights. 'What do you mean?'

'The baby.'

She clapped the door shut and walked away.

Later that night Ida slept in the crook of my arm as I lay awake and waited for my pulse to ease off. Outside, something coughed. A cow? A starter motor? I felt full of blood, bursting with it as my heart kept at it. Pretty soon something from a long while ago came to me. Blood.

Blood comes hot out of a boy's face. Two brothers carry him across sloping pasture in the twilight, the crash of the shotgun still in their ears. Their pockets are stuffed with apples from the orchard and the crazy old woman is shouting from her place up the hill. She's framed in the doorway of the big white limestone house, waving her fists. The boy moans: can't see . . . can't see. The brothers lift him across the fence, hear the wire ping away in the gloom. Stars are coming out. They get him on to the kitchen table and in the lamplight see the blood in his eyes and the pieces of shot. Their father does not look surprised. He sees the bulges in their pockets. He pulls an apple out of one boy's pants and squeezes juice from the pock-holes. He sits down and looks into the fire. The boy weeps blood. It seems a long time before the father goes out to the truck . . .

History. Yes, that was when history started in on me. The day after the dog was taken, the day Jaccob found Ronnie half-crazed down by the river. If only we hadn't had so many things to hide, so many opportunities for fear to get us. You can keep it all firm and tidy in you for a time, but, Godalmighty, when the continents begin to shift in you, you can't tell tomorrow from yesterday, you run just like that herd of pigs, over the cliff and into the water.

As I stumbled into the light-shafted bathroom, I came upon Ida before the mirror with the make-up box on the basin and her face half-painted. She had on her dark woollen suit, her pearls, and a pair of stockings. Her hair had that hard sprayed look I hated. Before I could even open my mouth, I saw her eyes in the mirror and I knew to shut up. She was going to church. She hadn't been to church since Christmas, and only then because Jennifer, the most pious of our daughters, was visiting to diminish the joy of the season.

I knew Ida believed in something – she was a convent girl after all – but church on a Sunday?

'There's a cup of tea on the stove,' she said.

'Can I've a shower?'

'You'll fog up the mirror.'

I slapped her on the arse and got a pained look. I went for my cup of tea.

The morning was cool and bright with the sky blue from one rim to the other. In the yard, the red circular blocks of jarrah I'd sawn yesterday lay steamy in the light. Hens, magpies, insects moved out there.

'You want to come?' Ida said, clacking in on her heels.

I shook my head.

'I'll have the car. What'll you do?'

'Oh, maybe go down the river.'

'Fishing?' She laughed.

'Well, you're going to church.' Somehow I couldn't meet her gaze as she kissed my brow and went out tinkling the car keys.

The Sink is the kind of place that's always failed to deliver. Soldiers came to this wet little valley thinking it might do good by them, all hidden away, but nothing came of their visions. Before the soldiers, before the wars, my father bought our side of the valley and he saw families come and go. In the end there were only three properties, though. Us, the Minchinburys, and the place across the valley where some hopeful always seemed to be setting up for a fall.

I've always lived here. When we married, Ida and me lived with the old man. My brother lived with us too, but he died a year after we married. He didn't have much to live for anyway. We used to string lines out in the yard for him to walk along. He was a strange sight, feeling his way along, him and his black eye-patches. He just died in his sleep one night, as though he'd decided enough was enough. The old man stayed around a few years more. He wasn't hard to live with – he hardly even spoke any more. He moved out to the truck shed after Wally died. Then he was sick a long time and he died in the district hospital. I never knew my mother.

By the time the farm had become my own, my second brother was a big success in the wheat-belt, and he wasn't interested in this place. So I stayed. I had no other ideas.

Ida was expecting a baby. We'd worked hard here. I didn't think to leave. Now I can't and poor Ida never will.

That Sunday morning I walked down the pastured slopes to the river. Paperbarks dunked their heads into the water all along the bank amid long grass and rooty tangles where insects hummed. I walked along to the bridge where I sat and watched the water roll slowly under. Caused a lot of trouble, that fancy little bridge. Old Doctor Minchinbury built it when I was a boy, and he wanted us to pay half, but we didn't have that sort of money. The rich think everybody's rich. That's their sin, forgetfulness. Oh, how I hated them, the Minchinburys, them and their fancy city talk, the cars and the parties, and the sight of the fruit dropping to rot on the ground up there by that big white house. By the time I was a teenager, there was only the daughter left. She always seemed old and terrifying, but she can't have been more than thirty, maybe forty. She was mad, at least we thought she was. Good God, maybe she had dreams too. I can't even think of it.

Sitting on that bridge, I had the feeling that I'd somehow missed my chance. Thirty years living like a hillbilly in your father's house. I got bitter thinking about it.

It was still only nine in the morning. Jaccob was back in his dream. He twisted and buckled beneath the blankets, and in the dream the cat springs up silent, settles in against the baby, that warm bundle to purr against. The little girl-child shifts. Pastoral scene, pretty moment for calendars. But now look. That little petal mouth against the fur as the cat snuggles closer. Ticklish. She breathes it deep, dark-thick, giggly a moment in slumber, then stifling. The family cat purrs. The only child smothers without even time to wake and cry. To wake and shriek. Wake up! Wake!

Jaccob heard the crash at the door and he came to. He knifed out of bed and stood in his room a moment, naked and hot with panic from the dream. He pulled some jeans on and went down.

He threw the door back and saw it was the girl, his neighbour. She looked sallow and sick. Yes, she was obviously an addict; he wished he'd never come across her. She could do what she bloody well liked. She could rant and bellow and he couldn't care less. He'd have nothing to do with her from this second onwards and he stepped back to close the door, but she seized him by the arm. He felt her fingers in his flesh. It was cool out here. He wrenched his arm away.

'Please?'

'What? Why'nt you just—'

'Listen to me. Everything's dead.'

'Yeah, I know, God is dead and so are Mum and Dad. The answer is blowing in the wind.' He laughed.

Then he saw the blood she'd left on his arms. It was on her hands, on her jeans.

The girl's yard was full of carcasses and they were stiff. White ducks and geese lay in drifts, like the remnants of an alpine thaw. Jaccob wandered amongst them, gingerly feeling their necks, finding some punctured, most broken. Many had open abdomens. Their shit and guts and gore all over. The girl took him behind the shed and showed him the disembowelled goat. It lay buckled and open eyed, as though still being pursued.

38

'It's eaten the guts out,' she said, but he saw it clearly enough. The animal was tethered.

He touched the wound. It was a fairly clean incision. He'd been expecting a mauling gash.

'There's a hole in its head,' she said. 'Two holes. Awgh. Horrible.'

'Teeth, you think?'

She shrugged.

'Been dead a while, I'd say. You hear anything?'

'No. I was asleep.'

'You're a sound sleeper.'

'I was tired. That's all. Oh, shit, look at this. Everything we had. It's scary. I mean, what would do it?'

It was his turn to shrug.

'I thought cockies knew everything about the bush.'

'Hell, I'm no farmer.' He thought of that silhouette in the orchard.

'It's wild dogs or something. Must be. Oh, God, it's my fault. One day alone and this happens. What do I do?'

'S'pose you ring someone at the shire office.'

'Haven't got a phone.'

Damn her, he'd have to do it himself. She was looking at him; what did she expect, middle-aged resolve?

'Don't s'pose you'll be able to bury this lot by yourself. You got a shovel, I imagine?'

As he dug in the gravelly earth with the sun on his back and the stink of blood and bowels rising from the awful pile with its weaving net of flies, Jaccob tasted red wine from the night before and he felt his faint headache get a hold, mounting with his anger and the exertion and the worm of worry in him. The girl looked on, biting the skin behind her fingernails in a way that made him sick. When he'd finished, an hour later, he threw the shovel down and went to his car without a word. He needed a shower. He saw her with her fists by her sides in the mirror as he swung away.

The shower took the dirt off him, but not the rest. He had to notify somebody, but it was Sunday. No use phoning the shire. In any case, over the phone he'd sound like a fool or a drunk – or both. Maybe he could go in and see somebody.

He made himself drive slowly on his way to town. He had no idea what to do or where to start. He wondered if perhaps he was overreacting. Someone'd lost some stock – it happened. He was just upset about losing privacy, that's all. And that dream; he could have done without that. His empty stomach churned.

Town was a cluster of shops and houses along the highway the Sink road eventually ran into. It was an apple town on the wane, a small, hopeless little place. Jaccob was a stranger here. Nothing was open on a Sunday except the churches, Protestant and Catholic, with their smattering of parked cars. In the park beneath the Anzac memorial by the river, some families picnicked. They looked like weekenders passing through. He saw the ugly war statue and its message LEST WE FORGET.

He pulled up outside the Bridge & Beam pub. A fat old woman with silver hair piled back off her face was sweeping the veranda. Half-dressed people straddled windowsills on the second floor to get a bit of sun. Jaccob sat there in his car. He didn't know anyone here, which was how he'd always wanted it, but who could he talk to? He'd met the estate agent a few times, but it was pointless talking to him. What could he say, anyhow? He felt his mind bog down with it all. He felt a little faint. Things shimmered at the edge of his vision. He needed something in his stomach, that's all. He'd taken a hiding from that red wine – and the whiskies on top.

A car passed, covered in a homely patina of gravel dust. Local plates. Normal, regular. Nothing unusual, nothing out of kilter. The interior of Jaccob's car warmed in the sun. He got out for some air.

He stood awkwardly under the gaze of the hotel guests above and wiped the sweat off his face. He set out along the forlorn main street. In the windows of the shops were little notices written on cardboard from old Cornflakes packets. FARM HELP WANTED . . . PRAM FOR SALE – IN GOOD NICK . . . CLEAN METHODIST GIRL NEEDS ROOM AND FACULTIES . . . Faculties, he thought; I could do with faculties. Everything in the shop windows seemed faded and forgotten. Stale insect strips, old Coke and Bushells ads, curling paperbacks (*Love Nest*, *Truckin' Man*), the desiccated bodies of flies and silverfish. Jaccob walked. He couldn't sustain a proper thought. Some kids tore by on bikes. He felt bile at the back of his throat.

Ida Stubbs came upon her neighbour puking in the street. At first she thought he was a drunk from the pub, but when he finished his quick little retch and came up for air, she saw his sun-cured face and she recognized him.

'Are you all right?'

He nodded, looked up, seemed puzzled a moment.

'Oh. Mrs Stubbs.'

'Too early for a hair o' the dog on a Sunday.'

He tried to smile.

She got him back down the street to the milk bar and bought him a drink. She sat him at a Formica table by the window.

'Thanks. But . . . a spearmint milkshake?'

'They're out of strawberry and vanilla. They never have chocolate and the banana's well worth avoiding. Anyway, the milk'll put a lining on your stomach.'

'My mother used to say that.'

Ida smiled, but it stung a little. Coming out of the church with the smell of incense on her, she'd felt younger than she had for years. My mother, indeed.

'I didn't know you were a churchgoer, Mr Jaccob.'

'Oh.' He left off sucking the green milk. 'I'm not.'

Some blood had returned to his face. It wasn't a bad-looking face, really, all beaten and burnt. It made him look older than he was, though he was still young enough to be her son. Sons. She'd missed not having boys.

'I got married in a church,' he said, 'went to a funeral or two. But that's about all the church I've had lately.'

Ida laughed. 'I think you missed my point. That was a polite country way of asking what brings you to the metropolis.' She laughed again.

The man looked embarrassed. This was the most they had spoken since he'd moved here. Outside, kids weaved up and down on grotesquely modified bikes. She knew some of them – the banker's boy and the little pain those new teachers had brought with them. All townies.

'Listen, would you mind if I left this stuff and just had a soda water?'

Ida laughed. 'Course not. Give it here – I'll drink it.'

She got him another drink and watched him sip meekly.

'How do you get hold of someone from the shire council

on a Sunday, do you think?' he asked. 'S'pose I should have come across and asked you and your husband before I drove in.'

Ida looked at him. He wasn't just embarrassed, the man was frightened. He looked crook. The council? She became careful.

'On a Sunday? I'd say it was a dead loss.' A lie so soon after confession, but she felt something out of whack here. 'I thought you'd be after a chemist, the way you look. Is it urgent?'

'I don't . . . really know.'

He seemed to be considering something, sizing her up.

'Actually, I don't know what it is at all.'

'Maybe you'd best tell me. After all these years I reckon I must know a thing or two.'

He tried a thin smile and looked into his drink. 'Well, the other night . . . It sounds stupid to a farmer's wife, I imagine . . .'

She shrugged.

'One; the other night I thought I saw something in the orchard. Only a shadow, it was too dark to see, but I sort of felt, knew, sensed that it didn't fit. Like it didn't belong. I had the idea it was long and bigger than, you know, native animals. I just thought I imagined it, you know, man alone, new to the area, city slicker. And then two; last night the couple across the valley, the young people, they lost ten big birds – those Muscovies they've got – and a goat.'

'Well, stock goes astray. Birds especially. You—'

'When I say lost I meant killed, mutilated. Disembowelled, I guess you'd say.'

Ida felt her chest tighten. 'Ah.'

43

He opened his hands in a gesture of uncertainty.

'I just thought we might be in for a dog problem in the valley. Wild dogs. Maybe the shire could lay baits for us or something.'

Ida got him up and out of there before he knew what was happening, and on the street he looked flabbergasted.

'What I suspect,' he said, 'is that we've got trouble on our hands.'

'Keep your voice down, Mr Jaccob!'

A slight breeze lifted dust along the street. In summer this place was like a desert and Ida hated coming in here to buy anything at all. She walked him across to the river to give herself some time to think.

'What about the Agriculture Protection Board? Someone told me once—'

'Look, you don't want those twits out there.'

'I just—'

'You're not a farmer, are you, Mr Jaccob?' She found herself fiddling with the brassy little brooch on her lapel. Maurice had given it to her, the occasion slipped her mind.

'No. I'm not, but I don't see—'

'What you should be able to see is that it's a Sink matter. We'll sort it out ourselves like neighbours should.' Listen to you, Ida, she thought; like neighbours indeed! But she thought of that little dog and the bloody collar on the chain. Something was wrong all right, but Maurice wouldn't want anybody tramping about in uniform on his land. The sight of an officer of any species was enough to get him sweaty. His family was like that. Of course it's rubbed off on me too, she thought; I don't want busybodies poking around my home.

She just needed a moment to think. Her wool suit seemed tight and prickly all of a moment.

I was still sitting on the bridge mooning when Ida came thrash-arsing around the bend, and only the sorry slack flesh that passes for my backside kept me from going into the water. The ute walloped across the bridge and skidded to the other side of the road. She backed it up with a tearing of gravel. She threw open the passenger door.

'Shit and corruption, woman, what're you doing? You been hearing the wrong gospel, or what?'

'Get in.'

She looked dead serious. I obeyed.

Ronnie saw the car pull in and she picked up a scarf and went out to meet him. As she got in she heard the mournful country music and she could barely keep from grimacing.

'They said seven,' he murmured, as though to apologize for being late. 'What's your name, anyway?'

'Ronnie.'

'Jaccob. Murray Jaccob.'

She didn't quite shrug. She felt all splintery and nervous and her rounding belly felt suddenly obvious and awful. Going up to the neighbours' place for dinner wasn't her idea, that's for sure. But anyway, here she was, being dressed, fed, nursed, and chauffeured by someone she didn't even know, who was taking her to more old strangers, and it was clear he wasn't getting a thrill out of it either.

'This whole thing is really weird.'

He didn't reply. She wished her mouth didn't run on ahead of her so much. Her mouth was never any use to her when she needed it. As they drove she thought about this old guy, Murray Jaccob. She still hadn't thanked him for the other night. He had done her a favour, after all. But, shit, everything was so miserable right now she wondered if he might have done her a bigger favour by not finding her down

46

there and letting her freeze to death. Oh, violins, Ronnie. But things were shitty, you couldn't pretend otherwise. She felt the pull of the car twisting up the gravel drive of the Stubbses' place where the house lights spilled out on to the grass and the silhouette of a man stood in the doorway.

I was washed and dressed and nervous as a heifer. Their lights cut their way toward me. Jaccob's little Toyota turned in and when the engine shut off the only sound was the creeping up of the night. No yapping dog. Just the night. Jaccob got out first. The girl seemed to hesitate.

Inside in the light, I saw that Jaccob wore a sports jacket with a pair of dark trousers and suede shoes. It wasn't a bad outfit, though it made me self-conscious, not having dressed up. The girl had on a pair of jeans that looked as though they were made of PVC. She had a torn windcheater and oil in her hair. My daughters were prissy little misses when they were young, and in a way I hated their smart frocks and sensible shoes, but I guess I had more to be grateful for than I knew.

I brought Jaccob and the girl into the living-room with the fat grey sofa. Ida came in smeared with sauce of some kind, and with cords of hair hanging steamy over her face. She saw Jaccob's clothes and blushed.

'Anyone for a drink?' I asked.

'What do you have?' the girl asked.

'What would you like?' I cranked up a smile.

'Oh, sherry'll do.'

'That'll suit me too,' Jaccob added, and I knew he was lying, but nervous.

'Sherry.' Sherry!

I found some sherry in the cooking cupboard in the kitchen and as I pulled it out, Ida raised her eyebrows at me and I grinned. When I got back I noticed that the space between Jaccob and the girl on the sofa was enough to land a plane on. I wondered how the girl had gotten herself into those jeans. She was obviously pregnant. Where was the boyfriend? I looked at Jaccob. Surely not.

No one said much. We quaffed our sherry. La-de-da.

For dinner Ida served up potato pie, and we all managed to slum long enough to drink beer. I used to brew my own. It tasted good and it hit like a hammer. The girl, who I discovered was called Ronnie, had what people used to call an elfin face – kind of perky and well made. All through the meal I kept thinking about where the bloke was, where her parents came from, what she was doing at the Sink anyway? She didn't look like any farm girl to me. She ate like she was used to some higher life. It caught Ida's attention too, and our eyes met and Ida's brows went up again.

'So how are you finding your place, Mr Jaccob?' she asked, as if she didn't already know.

Jaccob looked caught. 'In general, you mean? It's a beautiful old house.'

'Yes,' Ida replied, as though it really hadn't occurred to her before. 'Yes, it's always been the grand place of the valley.'

'Yeah,' I said. 'It's a nice place to watch the fruit drop.' I could barely keep a grip on myself when I thought of that house – that great white thing. It was like an object that wouldn't let itself be destroyed.

Jaccob laughed uneasily.

I poured more beers. Everyone was drinking quickly out of discomfort.

48

'When I was a kid,' I said, 'it was full of cats.'

'Cats?' The girl moved her cutlery like she was performing a brain operation.

'Yeah. The woman who lived there was pretty keen on them. She had hundreds of 'em. She lived alone.'

'Funny,' Ida said, 'how lonely people often keep cats when they're such uncompanionable – is that the word – unfriendly sorts of animals. No loyalty. You wonder what comfort that can be.'

'Yeah.' The girl smiled. 'They are their own masters, aren't they?'

'Clean sort of animals, though,' Ida murmured. 'Still, they're not my cup of tea. You see those women on TV with Siamese cats on the backs of their chairs, and you'd swear the cats knew more than they let on. Untrustworthy. Not like a dog.' She seemed to darken in the face a little then and there was a silence. 'Apple pie?'

While Ida was out of the room getting the dessert, the girl said:

'Over at Bakers Bridge there's some weirdos who have this strange thing about cats.'

'Bakers Bridge is nothing but weirdos nowadays,' I said. 'They all come down with their dole money and sit on good farmland and let it go to waste. Bloody vermin.'

'Which weirdos are these?' Jaccob asked the girl. 'I mean which particular brand of weirdo are they?' He laughed. He seemed to be loosening up a little. 'There's orange ones and ones that think the world is gonna blow up just after the flying saucers lift them off. There's even the old hippies, still there going grey in—'

'These are serious types,' Ronnie said.

'They're serious about cats,' I said, trying to catch

Jaccob's eye for a laugh. 'What do they do, turn 'em into handbags?'

She smiled a little.

'Close. They kill 'em. For blood. Sacrifices, you know. They're sort of witches.'

I laughed, but no one else seemed to think it was funny.

'Sick bastards,' I said.

Ida came in with the pie.

We ate and didn't talk much until the girl launched into it.

'Well, let's get to the point then.'

There was an awkward pause.

'Yes,' said Ida, 'why not.'

'Well?'

I ate my apple pie. Jaccob put his spoon down.

'I hear you lost some stock,' I said to the girl.

'Two geese, eight Muscovy ducks, and a goat.'

I kept on eating my apple pie. The log fire had begun to burn down a little.

'They had their guts torn out,' said Jaccob, 'even the goat.'

'You buried them?'

'Yeah,' she said.

'Pity. Would have been useful to have a look.'

'And leave fresh meat lying about when something's lurking around out there?' She looked at me with proper contempt. 'You must be kidding.'

'Was its throat cut?'

'No,' Jaccob said. 'Two holes in the head.'

'Bullet holes?'

'Looked like teeth marks to me.' He shrugged. It annoyed me, him doing that.

'What do you think it was?'

'A big dog? A few of them?' Again, he shrugged.

'Any tracks?'

He looked at the girl. She looked disgusted.

'We didn't think to look,' she said.

'If it'd been a dog,' I said, wiping cream from my lips, 'the birds would have been mauled and there'd be feathers everywhere. The whole place would be covered in 'em. There'd be tracks and scuffs all over. You,' I said to the girl, 'couldn't have slept through it if you were dead. If it was dogs.'

The girl looked me straight in the eye. 'There was barely a feather out of place. Their necks were broken, some with punctures. I didn't hear a thing.'

Jaccob looked grey.

'Well,' I murmured.

'Maurice.' Ida's tone was disciplinary. I knew it was my time to speak.

'We had some trouble too. The other night.' I poured myself some beer. 'We had a dog torn off its chain. A small dog. There wasn't anything left except the head in the collar.'

'Fuck,' said the girl, and Ida flinched.

'There wasn't a sound. Except for the dog screaming.'

As I looked around the table, I knew something had begun to roll forward – I didn't know what – and it was big and quiet and definitely to be worried about.

'I got a print in a cast. I looked all morning for some trace.' I pulled it out of the sideboard drawer behind me and put it, sweet and honey-smelling, on the table before them. They both held it like it was made of glass. 'What we're looking at here is not dogs. Funny we should be talking about cats earlier on, because that's what we've got on our hands.'

'Maurice?'

'A what?'

'Some kind of cat.'

'That's ridiculous!' the girl yelled.

'What would you know?' I yelled. 'How long've you lived here?'

She drank off her glass of beer and glowered, mouth puckering as though she tasted something foul.

Ida got up and came back with more bottles of beer.

'Let's keep this civil, shall we?' she said. 'All neighbours here. What kind of cat, Maurice?'

'Something wild or outsized or maybe foreign. My guess is it's a feral breed of house cat.'

'Oh, bullshit,' the girl said. 'A house cat turned wild is still a house cat. This thing killed a goat, for God's sake. How could a house cat do that?'

'I'm not talking about a cat that used to belong to Mrs Bloggs that's decided to go walkabout and decides he likes the wild outdoor life. This is a cat whose ancestors were house cats maybe two hundred years ago. They grow bigger than you think, bigger than we know.'

Jaccob seemed to stir at this. 'I had a friend once who had a skin, a pelt from a bush cat that covered the bonnet of his Datsun.'

I whistled. 'You ever see it?'

He shook his head. 'People exaggerate, I s'pose.'

'Now if that goat was killed by teeth in the skull, and we have to take this young lady's word for it—'

'Then the teeth'd have to be an inch long or more,' she said. 'Ever seen a cat like that?'

I shook my head. 'Not yet.'

'We're talking about tabby cats!'

'Any schoolkid knows that our house cats come originally from wild stocks from India and Europe. In the beginning, this is.'

'But that's ancient history.'

'There's no kind of native animal on this continent that can do anything like what we're talking about here. It has to be something foreign, something introduced.'

'Oh, but that leaves dogs, pigs, foxes—'

'You know damn well that this isn't a dog or a bloody pig. Look at this pawprint. That's a cat. A big cat. Two hundred years of breeding in the bush from strays. The big ones, the fast ones, the mean ones survive. The quiet ones. They slowly get bigger, faster, meaner, quieter. You know, it's what they teach at school these days. You know how many litters a cat has a year. Hell, the way we walk through the bush, the big ones'd be well warned, that's why we don't see 'em. God knows how big they get; they're lords of the bush.'

I fell back breathless. The whole thing seemed more plausible every word I said.

'Well, whatever it is,' the girl sighed, 'we should tell the authorities.'

'It won't help, and there's no point. We've got it out into the open amongst ourselves. We've had our losses and that's the end of it. Just to satisfy ourselves, Mr Jaccob and I will go out and take a look around tomorrow night. Agreed?'

Jaccob stared at me a moment, then nodded.

'Right then.'

'Is that all?' the girl demanded. 'Is that all you're going to do?'

I got up, barking the chair back on the boards.

'I'm going out for a bit.'

And I left them all there at the table, around the stand of brown bottles, and I went out hoisting my coat on. The fire was out. They all looked grim as mourners.

On a winter's night down this way, the cold darkness is like two black sheets of glass pressing you breathless. My throat burned. Stars peppered the sky. I hugged myself, not knowing where to go. I walked up the hill a little way, got to the first wire fence and heard it bulleting down the line in the dark as I pushed down the top strand. For a few moments I stood listening to that eerie sound in the dark and I was overcome by how vulnerable I was, here out in the night alone. And the sound of that wire fence took me a long way back in the past. Did they remember? The cats? Was that what this business was all about?

I stumbled back down the slope. Or was I just a bit pissed and ratty with nerves?

In the tractor shed I smelt the good regular smells of diesel and hessian. Rodents tinkered in the dark behind piles of junk. That business about the mob over at Bakers Bridge was a bit of a shock. Witches. I thought we didn't have that stuff any more. That girl . . . no, she didn't look the type. But what is the type? What do they look like? I started to shiver.

Before long, the voices of Ida and Jaccob could be heard from the front of the house, and a few moments after, the car started. I saw a stray beam of light as they turned around. I could hear the little Jap motor winding across the valley and then come back our way and climb a little to stop at Jaccob's place.

Quiet. Cold. I heard the faint clunk of dishes from the house. I went back in, forcing myself not to trot like a child frightened of the dark.

With the father gone for the doctor in the truck, the two brothers leave the whimpering boy on the kitchen table, go out to the tractor shed, and take a can of petrol across the paddock to the fence. They wait in the orchard beside their neighbour's house. In the light of the windows, they see the cats poised on the sills, gently brushing aside the filmy curtains which used to be so white and grand billowing there on hot afternoons. In time, a black tom comes out to look at them. It pads across fallen leaves and fruit and it rubs itself greedily, arrogantly against their knees, then purrs in their arms. One boy takes off his shirt and pours petrol on it. His brother holds the cat while he strokes its back with the wet shirt. The cat squirms a little, begins to spit and scratch as they tie the petrol-soaked shirt to its tail. The match flares. The cat shrieks and then explodes.

When they pulled up outside Ronnie's house, she didn't get out. She hadn't left any lights on. The place was lonely looking. She felt jittery and weak with anger.

'Good grief, what an evening.'

Jaccob nodded in the green light of the dash. He looked preoccupied. For a moment she wondered what that shit-head man of hers was doing tonight – probably playing in some hopeless joint with some hopeless bunch of characters who remembered him from the old days when everybody just had to recognize him. Probably be some hopeless-looking woman sitting beside the sound desk trying to look unmistakably connected to him and the band – oh, she knew all about that.

The engine was still running, Jaccob was waiting.

'Listen,' she murmured, 'I can't face this place tonight. I'm, you know, a bit spooked being on my own after all this business.'

He said nothing.

'Well, could I . . . stay at your place?'

Jaccob shrugged and turned the car around.

Ronnie woke at three in the morning and went down the cold wooden stairs to find Jaccob rocking in the dimness by the long glass doors through which she could see only the darkness of the valley. He turned a lamp on. He had a glass in his hand. She didn't know how to read the look on his face.

'You OK?'

He just rocked.

'I felt a bit strange then,' she said. 'I don't know. As though I was about to have a nightmare, as though I was about to slip into it. But I stopped myself. I woke up.'

'Lucky you.'

'What d'you mean?'

'Nothing. It's nice to be able to back out of a nightmare.'

She pulled the blanket tight around herself.

'That stuff about those people over at Bakers Bridge,' he murmured. 'Were you serious?'

'Yeah.'

'How do you know about them?'

'Oh. I met them once. It's only fifteen or twenty miles.'

'Did you see it happen? That stuff about the cats?'

'Cats! You don't think I'm one of them, do you?'

'What, a cat or a witch?'

'A friend saw it. She was kind of interested.'

'You don't think maybe they've got something to do with this, do you? I mean,' he tried to laugh a little, 'the goat and everything. All those birds with their bellies open.'

'You don't know much about it, do you?'

Jaccob smiled. 'I don't even know if it exists.'

'Black magic? Of course.'

'Black cats and everything, eh?'

She sank back against the sofa. 'Oh, cats again. Listen, what do you think is killing the animals?'

'Stubbs may be right, it could be a feral cat, or more than one. Jesus, for all I know it might be a Tasmanian tiger.'

She didn't laugh. 'Yeah, people talk about that still, don't they?'

'I s'pose it doesn't sound so stupid really, a marsupial cat, or is it a dog?'

Ronnie looked at him. He wasn't a happy man.

'I don't know you at all,' she said.

'Neither you should. We're strangers.'

He got up and went to bed and Ronnie sat there in that dim room with its mismatched furniture and bare walls.

I sat in the dark, shivering with cold and memory.

Running, one boy sees over his shoulder the ball of light cometing around the yard, the cat afire and screaming like an evil spirit, cutting back across its own path.

The morning was cool and overcast and Ronnie spent the day with Jaccob. They helped each other in a stiff, self-conscious way with the chores, first at his place and then at hers, where the cow had to be disentangled from the fence it had demolished in mad pain from an engorged udder.

In the shed where she milked there was a big bench stacked with picture frames she'd half stripped of their ugly red varnish. Jaccob, who was watching her with a look that she took to be amusement, picked up a frame and ran his hand over it.

'Oak.'

Ronnie peered along the length of the cow.

'Found them in an old shop in Balingup. Promised myself I'd do them up one day.'

Hiss of milk. Far away, the petulant song of a crow. Ronnie put her cheek against the warm side of the animal and she began to hum as a strange sadness came upon her. She kind of liked this bloke. He was awkward but not stupid. She was the one who felt stupid.

The headache got bad so Ida put herself back to bed. It was the kind of headache she used to have at school, the night before a spelling test. The pain would be like a hand clamping down on her skull and she could almost feel fingers creeping in under her scalp going hot and cold in waves that made her too frightened to move her eyes. She was no squib when it came to pain. Oh, the kinds of pain she'd lived with. Years of periods (now mercifully gone), and childbirth (let no one tell you it didn't hurt), secret pains she kept until the last minute like the cartilage in her knee she hobbled around on, keeping the house running and the children and Maurice in their routine until the day she couldn't even walk to the toilet. Ah, those were just everyday pains; but the headaches, she hated the head-aches. She pulled the blankets up to her chin and wedged her head between the pillows to keep it still. She lay with her eyes closed and the hot colours burst before her.

Now and then during the day the pain would slacken and she would have some respite for a while. She didn't get up for fear of bringing back the pain before schedule, so she had time to think, and what she thought about was Ronnie. She liked the girl in a way. Of course she was rude and disrespectful, but she was so alive and energetic, at least for a girl who looked so pale and badly fed. Reminded her of her younger days. She'd been cocky herself once, but girls in her day could barely even think the things that Ronnie was saying last night. Was she deserted? Did she have money? She was small; she'd take a hiding getting a baby out. She wondered what the dickens a girl with all the advantages was doing here. It seemed so wasteful that it made Ida angry and she felt the fingers tighten on her skull and then the colours cracking like fireworks.

Through the fizzing and spurting, a memory came to her.

It just arrived, blurring and ghosting but now and then coming clear despite the pressure.

Rain hits the windscreen of the truck. A woman – that familiar young woman – drives with her eyes slitted in concentration. Two small girls sleep on the seat beside her, mouths black with liquorice. Windscreen wipers labour against the torrent. The road is pelted with leaves and twigs, furred with the impact of water. As she rounds a bend near a rail-crossing, she sees an overturned semi and its garishly painted trailer jack-knifed at the side of the road. Behind a spear of light, the vision fades a moment and she sees only the heat of pain, but quickly it's back again and she sees the zoo-like bars on the trailer, some twisted wide apart. Great sods have been turned up in the accident. Someone is backing a tractor up to the overturned truck, and another man is hauling up a chain. The woman pulls in beside him and winds the window down. Rain spatters in on the children.

'Everything all right?'

The tractor driver looks over. He seems sick. A man in overalls comes across, steps up to the window.

'No problem, lady.' He has a beard and an American accent. DENVER BROS CIRCUS is embroidered over the pocket of his overalls. She can almost feel his gaze, as though he sees she's only a farm wife from some lost valley. She brushes the skirt across her knees. 'Nothin's happened. Drive on.'

'But is anyone hurt?'

'No one's hurt. Look, this never even happened.'

She gives him her coldest look. The girls begin to stir. She winds the window up in his face and drives on . . . Lord, she'd forgotten all about . . . the reds and flamebreaks shot in from every corner. Ida lay dead still.

Jaccob stood by while Ronnie skimmed the cream from the turning milk. Bulbs of sweat hung on her brow. The afternoon sun rested on the windowsill and dust motes twisted about. It had been a long day with their curiosity and their caution; nevertheless it had been a good day's work for a retired man and a girl who looked as though a day's work'd kill her. It stopped him thinking about things. She seemed like maybe she was a decent sort after all, this girl, just frightened, that was all. He started to wonder how she was going to get on alone.

'What does your . . . boyfriend do?' The sun was warm on his back.

'Oh, he plays guitar. Used to be in the Clever Young Boys in Black.' She said the name with an upward intonation as though she expected him to be familiar with it.

'When's he coming back, you reckon?'

She shrugged. It was an obvious effort to be nonchalant. You had to admire her guts.

'It's tough luck about your birds. I like Muscovies.'

She smiled.

The sun began to die on its soft bed of trees. At the bottom of the valley the river went coppery and the swamp glittered. Smoke rose perpendicular from the Stubbses' chimney over on the west side. Sun caught their windows as in a mirror. The wind was already dead.

'If you need a lift to the hospital any time, just let me know. I mean if your boyfriend isn't around.'

'Don't worry, you'll hear me screaming. Thanks. Anyway, he'll be around.'

He looked at her through the veil of steam.

'So. Tomorrow night you have to go a-hunting?'

He nodded.

'Men!'

He shrugged.

'Do you know anything about shooting?'

'No. Not really. I shot rabbits when I was a kid.'

'Why the hell are you going, then?'

'I don't know. Stubbs seems to think it's important. And,' he laughed, 'I didn't want him to despise me.'

'Boy. I don't understand men.'

You said it, love, he thought.

Jaccob and the girl came after dinner when it was dark and the paddocks were moony and still. He brought his .22 but he had no ammunition for it, so I went to the bedroom for a couple of boxes and left him with the women who chatted quietly. In the bedroom I found some bullets, pocketed them, and looked out the window, but all I could see was my own face, eyes narrowed like shutters. When I returned to the kitchen Ida was laughing with the girl over some joke I'd come in too late for and Jaccob was standing by the stove with a blank cast on his face. I put the box of longs in his hand and he looked at the women.

'No prizes for guessing who'll be enjoying tonight's proceedings.' He tried to smile. He was worried.

'Come on.'

He followed me out to the ute. The women didn't even say goodbye, and I felt like a fool for feeling miffed about it.

The air was hard and metallic.

'You should have worn some warmer clothes,' I said. I gave him the .243. 'I'll drive. You hold this.'

Jaccob juggled the two rifles a moment and settled them across his lap.

I drove slowly down towards the girl's place with the window open. The moon lit some patches of pasture well, but it also made the sort of shadows that cause you to wonder. A rabbit stared up into the headlights. I smelt the swamp and the night-wet stands of grass as I took us down by the river and slowly up the gravel drive to Ronnie's place.

In the yard beside that shoddy little joint, I got out and rigged up the spotlight on the roof of the cab.

'You know what to do?' I asked.

He got out.

'You just stand up here and move the light slowly. Sort of search the paddock, you know. If you see anything, just knock quietly on the roof and I'll stop.'

'Yeah, I did it when I was a kid.'

'Can you shoot?'

'I s'pose you mean can I hit anything?'

'It can be helpful.' I switched the light on. The motor idled.

Jaccob shrugged in the reflected light.

'Well, I'll shoot from the cab.'

I got down and he jumped up on to the tray. From inside the cab I could hear his elbows on the roof. I put the ute in gear. Jesus, I thought; here we are looking for something we don't know anything about. I knew something was out there, something that didn't belong, and I wanted to kill it and nail its pelt to a tree so all the hidden eyes could see it. I wanted things to feel right again.

We jolted up the rocky pastured slopes. The beam of the spotlight reached out like an arm to make a hot white oval that moved from stump to fence to rock, to climb the trunks of trees and send shadows spilling across the ground. It was cold. We ground along soft firebreaks and lit up meadows of spiders' eyes, and the sound of the motor in low gear grew stranger as the night went on. Out in the dark there was no definition, no assurance, nothing familiar, no sign, beyond that floating oval disk, that we hadn't stumbled off the edge of the world entirely. I couldn't be sure the world was anything but that oval disk. My eyes followed it. I drove automatically and the ute thumped and rattled tools as the wheel bucked in my hands.

Now and then a roo floated by like a ghost, or a fox hid arrogant behind the blaze of its eyes as it retreated deeper into the bush. The night was eyes, and I wondered if I'd recognize the right eyes when I saw them.

We lurched and jerked and tossed on the hard and slew and swayed in the soft. We lay weals upon the night, the way we always do in this country, making enough noise you'd think we were warning every secret and fearful thing to beware and flee.

As we came to the top of the property where a hoard of boulders rose from the side of the hill, each stone a sleeping beast in the light, there was a sudden thump on the roof from Jaccob and I flinched and stomped on the brake, ready to see some white shadow turning its flank to me, when all I saw was Jaccob as he rolled down over the windscreen to land with a crump on the hood. The motor idled. I stared. Jaccob lay before me with the light tilted full in his face, and I began to laugh.

'What the fuck?'

Laughter had a good hold of me and I put my head on the wheel, jerking silently, until my leg gave out on the clutch and the motor stalled and Jaccob was rolled off the hood and I could hear myself half choking in the still of the night.

Jaccob got in beside me, rubbing his elbow.

'I wanted a break, not a fracture.'

I got hold of myself, sighed, and sat back.

'It's bloody cold out there,' he said.

He mashed his fists to get some blood into them.

'What the hell are we looking for, anyway?'

'Eyes,' I said. 'You know what cats' eyes look like?'

'I know what a cat's eyes look like.'

'Well, that's what we're looking for.'

'Cats don't kill dogs and goats.' He said it out of anger. It was clear he wasn't so sure.

'You don't know anything about cats.'

Jaccob's teeth showed in his shadowy face. 'Oh, I know enough, old man.' It seemed to cost him something to not go wild. I realized I didn't know a damn thing about him.

'I'll spell you on the light,' I said.

Ida looked at Ronnie and Ronnie looked back. In the end they smiled again. They were enjoying themselves. They turned glasses in their hands.

'We're very different,' Ida said. 'I know what you're thinking.'

Ronnie grinned and put on an expression of mock outrage. 'I wasn't thinking that at all. I was wondering how you kept your age so well. Geez, you've done all right.'

'You don't even know how old I am,' Ida said with a

laugh. 'Why is it that women flatter each other and men ignore us? Well, I'm sure they wouldn't mean it, either. Anyway, you're a fibber. You were thinking how different we are.'

Ronnie took a drink.

'S'pose you're right.'

'I'm from the farm and you're from the city. We may's well be from different planets.'

'You really reckon?'

Ida got up and went to the window, though all she could see was herself reflected. It was warm inside. This was her place, this was what she knew, and it wasn't so bad.

'You think we're getting a bit tipsy?'

Ronnie drained her glass. 'I'd say there'd be some truth in that.'

'Well, I'll tell you a joke and it'll explain the way we're different. Oh, maybe it's more about Maurice than me. You eat pork?'

'Yeah, I shouldn't, I guess.'

'Oh, fiddlesticks, of course you should. See?'

'No.'

'Good. That settles that then.'

'We *are* getting a bit wrecked here.'

'Wrecked. Now that's a young person's word. See, you're young and I'm old.'

'But you're not!'

'I am too, but that doesn't mean I'm not stronger than you. I could box your ears, girl.'

'Tell me the joke.'

'*Then* I'll box your ears.'

'Oops, sorry about the carpet.'

'Here, one for me, too.'

'Now the joke.'

'Oh yeah, the joke.'

Ida got herself back into the sofa and hyperventilated a little while Ronnie snorted into her glass. Their shoes were off and their eyes narrowed from resisting laughter.

'Right, the joke. Now there's this bloke, see, and he's driving along a country road and he goes past a piggery and sees all the normal signs of piggeries – which probably means he was looking with his nose – and then he sees this big porker leaning up against the fence with a cigarette in his mouth, looking kind of handsome and thoughtful, and *then* as the driver slows down, he has to take a second look, because, lo and behold, not only is the pig dragging on a Marlb'ro, but he's got a bloody wooden leg. Excuse me. Anyway, anyway, a wooden leg. This pig's got a wooden leg.

'Well, the passer-by, he's pretty amazed by all this, so he stops the car and goes up to the farmhouse and gets hold of the farmer and says does he realize that there's a pig in his yard with, with, with a prosthetic piece—'

Ida took a drink and disciplined herself a moment before going on. To Ronnie, it was a wonderful dream.

'Anyway, the farmer says, "Yairs, yairs, that's a beautiful pig that, a most flamin' amazin' pig. A pig like ya never met before. I could tell a few stories about that pig down there. That pig is my greatest companion, my loyal friend, and I owe that pig more than a man can repay."

'The visitor's fairly dumbfounded and he asks him, you know, to elaborate.

' "Oh," says the farmer, "one time my kids were asleep

in the house and the wife was away shopping and I was down at the boundary putting in a few strainers and the house starts burnin' down. Course, I knew nothin' about it, but the pig was knockin' off the rosebushes in the front garden and he sniffs out a fire and quick as a wink he tears inside, drags the kids out of bed, gives them mouth-to-mouth on the front lawn and then gets the garden hose and single-handedly puts out the fire before I've even woken up to the problem. I owe that pig my children, the fruit of me loyens.

'"But that's only one story. There's a dozen others. That pig carried me home one day from the back paddock when I broke me leg. Just carried me back and put me down beside the phone. That pig helped me shear five hundred head o' sheep last year. That pig worked me out of debt. That pig sorted out marriage troubles 'tween me an' the wife. It opens the car door for her when she gets home from town. That's a sensitive pig; clever, compassionate – geez, it's damn near human!"

'The passer-by is really touched by this, you see. And he comes back to the pig's wooden leg. "I s'pose," he says, "the wooden leg is a souvenir from one of those adventures then, sort of a wound in the battle of friendship?"

'"Oh, no," says the farmer, "nothing like that."

'"Oh," says the passer-by, "then how do you explain the wooden leg?"

'"Well," says the farmer, "a pig like that, it'd be a shame to eat it all at once."'

Ronnie sat a moment and felt herself fill with sick, shocked laughter. And then Ida exploded into shrieks and giggles and they both fell to the floor, writhing.

'That's it,' Ida said, with her head under the coffee table, 'that's the difference between us and you. *We're* farmers.'

'You ever been resuscitated by a pig?'

'Only by the smell of one, dear.'

'We can't be that different,' Ronnie said, still lying on the floral carpet.

'Well, maybe not that much for us. We're girls.'

'Are you scared?'

'Right now? No. See, I've remembered this other joke.'

'No, no,' Ronnie pleaded. 'I'll die laughing.'

'Well, then you'll owe me a favour, dear. Can we drink lying down, you think?'

Up on the back with the cold handle of the lamp in my fingers and the wind in my eyes and cutting through my clothes, the night and the darkness seemed closer and I felt less protected by the car. I braced against the back window of the cab and rested on the roof, pushing the light back and forth, sighting along the beam until I felt like I was in it, that it was my eye, that the light was me.

Stumps, fallen trunks with upsearching grey arms, the broken teeth of Jaccob's fences, the dam with its startled covey of wild duck, the fruit trees like a stood-down regiment of old soldiers – everything melted in and out of vision in a dreamy, dislocated way where things were created out of darkness, yielded themselves up to the oval disk, and ceased to be a moment later. I found myself sinking into a matrix of tiny lights, fine black holes, and there was no telling space from matter.

A blur settled into view. Big white blur. It brought stillness – there was no vibration.

Jaccob shook my leg. He stood on the ground and was tugging at my trouser leg.

'What's up? What's the matter with you?'

He snorted.

'Don't tell me you were asleep.'

I looked down at him and then up at his house.

'C'mon,' he said, 'let's get some coffee.'

'I drink tea.'

I ran an icy hand over my face.

'Think you better try coffee.'

The spotlight made an eye out of one of the house windows. I switched it off. As I got down I felt the blood move in my legs; my knees felt like someone had knocked two-inch nails through them.

I stood there looking at the old Minchinbury house, and though it might've been the cold, I knew I'd never quaked like I was quaking now. There it was, the place I hated with its bull-nosed veranda and long scroll-silled timber windows, the limestone blocks rendered and painted white at the front. Even rebuilt, it was the same thing I remembered. A big, beautiful, pointless, idle place. Walking up those timber steps, I made myself breathe and I did not obey the messages my legs sent me; I did not fall down.

I'd never been inside before. It was a mess. That comforted me, in a way. Furniture was haphazard and covered in dirty crockery and clothes. Smudged glasses and an overflow of ash stood on the hearth. So this was how the rich lived.

In the kitchen Jaccob put the kettle on a gas ring and looked fidgety.

'Got the feeling we're not going to find anything, you know.'

He was right, I knew, but I said nothing.

'Whatever we're looking for won't be stupid enough to blunder into our light. If it's not been seen before, it won't show itself now, tonight. How do you think it got so big?'

I felt myself getting angry. He was right, but this thing was meant for me, and I was going to get it myself, I knew it.

'Why don't we get a professional hunter down here,' he said. 'We don't know what we're doing.'

'I know what I'm doing.'

Jaccob was silent a moment. The kettle growled.

'We don't even know what it is,' he said.

'I've told you what it is.'

Jaccob shook his head. He was smiling as though I was a crazy bastard, and my skin prickled hot and I felt my mouth run away from me.

'And another thing. Take some advice from an old man. Don't get involved in that girl. There's no use in it. She's a loser.'

He had me against the kitchen wall before I could draw breath. Where he grabbed my jacket I felt his knuckles against my ribs.

'I reckon you should mind your business,' he said through his teeth.

'We're neighbours,' I said, fighting for air.

He let go of me and stood back.

'Jesus Christ, now I can see how feuds get going down this way.' He looked a little shaken himself.

'No,' I murmured. 'You don't know the first thing about it.' I went cold as well, saying that. My heart was hard with fright.

'Veteran feuder, are you, Stubbs?'

I could still see poor Wally on the table, tearing at his pulpy eyes, and the cat squealing off in flames. I'd started it all, this whole nightmare.

He looked straight at me where I was, still against the wall, and very slowly he broke into a thin smile.

'Reckon I'm not the warrior type, son,' I said.

He took the kettle off the gas ring after a moment and made coffee. With that bloodless grin on his face, he gave me a mug, and I realized that I liked him. Not because he could be tough and push an old man around, but because suddenly it was clear that he had things twisting darkly in him too. It wasn't what was out there that frightened him most, it was something more secret. He didn't look right in this house, as though he hadn't gotten it beat into place yet. I thought maybe, if one day we could swap stories, he might understand mine and me his. I was right, but a lot happened before I was to find out.

We went out again in the ute and saw nothing. After his place we gave up. When we pulled up outside my house, every light was burning and Slim Dusty played flat-out on the radio, pouring into the yard.

The women were in the kitchen, pissed as sticks.

I started shouting.

Jaccob picked up the girl like she was a kid and took her out.

I heard his car start, even over my own bellowing.

Ida sat with her eyes closed to me. I felt utterly without hope.

'What the bloody hell do you think you're—'

My voice gave out. I didn't have the strength or the words to keep yelling. I followed Ida to the lounge-room. I looked at her. I held my fists like they were animals.

She rolled on to the sofa, lit a cigarette, which I hadn't seen her do for fifteen years, and said:

'Go to hell, Maurice.'

The night is full of stories. They float up like miasmas, as though the dead leave their dreams in the earth where you bury them, only to have them rise to meet you in sleep. Mostly the scenes are familiar, but sometimes everything is strange, the people unknown.

A boy sits in his father's lap out on the back veranda as the sun makes its way down among the trees. He smells tobacco and neatsfoot oil on his father and he listens to the creak in his chest. The carcass on the fence is still now. The boy strains, listening for the sound of a horse. The man from the paper is coming. Inside his mother is singing. She thinks they are going to be rich. But the sun rests in the jarrahs and no one comes.

This is not my memory. It comes to me now and then and I see it clear and sharp as though I am there, but it's before my time, things don't look right. These people ride horses. Their clothes aren't familiar, and yet when I dream it everything feels in its proper place, and sometimes I think this is one of my father's memories. I have no way of telling. It's terrifying to think you can remember things you shouldn't possibly be able to. It's like that childhood fear of having your soul slip from your body in your sleep. The darkness, those black sheets of glass sliding over you, upping the pressure, pushing you through the glacier of time and space and story.

After Jaccob went up to bed, Ronnie went out on to the veranda. It was cold and she hoped it would clear her head, but it just made her teeth ache. She stood at the rail and looked out into the darkness. They weren't kidding themselves – something was out there. She wished the memory of those people from Bakers Bridge hadn't come to mind, but it was all that talk about cats. She knew there was no point in telling Jaccob or the others what she'd really seen that night over at Bakers Bridge; they'd think she was one of the weirdos, they'd think she was sick and depraved for even being there, and sometimes she wondered if it wasn't true. But she hadn't known about it. It was all such a lark to Nick – that bastard. She liked old Mrs Stubbs, and she didn't want to frighten her off. The old girl had guts and she was pretty smart in her own way. Geez, hadn't they hit the piss tonight. Ronnie'd talked like a maniac and Ida was spilling secrets all over the place, about the days when her and Stubbs used to screw in a hollow log down in the paddock so his old man wouldn't hear them, about how they used to steal honey from the wild bees at the edge of the forest, and the days they used to row downriver out of the valley and haul an unsuspecting sheep off the bank at some distant neighbour's place and row it back up here laughing like larrikin kids, so they could butcher it and barbecue it for themselves. They went through all the beer in the house – even that vile homebrew – and then they'd knocked off the sherry. It was sad that Ida had never had the son she wanted. The daughters sounded awful. Ida showed her photos of them: greying, sensible mothers in running shoes and corduroys and styleless haircuts. They looked like they ran church youth groups; their smiles hadn't the least trace of fun in them. They looked like slaves to common sense and she felt sorry they were all Ida had.

Ronnie wished she'd known about Ida a long time ago. She couldn't help thinking she wouldn't be in such a bloody mess if they'd been able to talk last year when she first moved in. She looked out into the bitter cold night.

She wondered if you could be held responsible for something you saw but didn't take part in. Why had Nick taken her to that place? God, she hadn't even thought about it for six months and now she couldn't get it out of her mind.

Ronnie swayed in the dark.

Out there, something moved. She heard it step across leaf litter. The trees beside the shed; it had to be there. She looked around for something stout. Beside the back door was a furled umbrella, one of those yellow ones people give out at agricultural shows. She focused on it well for a moment, but it tended to reproduce itself a little. Ronnie, she thought, you're pisseder than you think. But bugger it. Some prick was out there scaring people and she was going out to give him a spanking.

As she felt her way down the steps in the reeling night she was barely able to suppress a giggle. Common sense and sensible shoes, that's what you need, Ronnie Melwater.

*

Ida felt the bed churning through space. She held the edge of the mattress and kept her eyes closed. The headache was coming back and she knew it'd be worse by morning, compounded by the worst hangover a body could anticipate, but all she could concentrate on now was the way the bed, the room, the house spun crazy through the dark. With her lids squeezed shut until moons burst into view behind her eyes, Ida Stubbs prayed that this spinning would take her away, out of this place for ever.

The thump was clear enough to wake him in a moment. Jaccob lay still and listened. There was another sound, a muffled rattle from out in the yard. He pulled on some jeans and went to the window. He could see nothing. The moon was cloud smothered. Opening the wardrobe he pulled out the .22. He turned no lights on as he went downstairs, and he slipped a bullet into the breach. The metal was cold against his hands.

At the back door he paused a moment to even out his breathing. As he pulled it open, he felt the jarring cold and slid the barrel out before him. Straightaway he heard the sound. It was a kind of hissing-scraping noise, quiet but distinct. Jaccob was suddenly full of breath again and for a few seconds he couldn't move. When he could make himself work, he cocked the gun and stepped out.

Hiss. Scrape. There it was.

Hiss. Scrape.

And panting. There was the faintest hint of something panting and it made his skin rise.

Jaccob eased himself on to the side veranda, and it took him some time to be able to distinguish the orchards and paddocks, the shadowy lines of fences and sheds in the dark. He heard the river and the swamp. He heard the blood in him. He heard the tiny click of the screen door as he let it come to.

He saw something light, but he'd barely registered it. He stepped out to the veranda rail. The wood was rough with cold.

Hiss. Scrape.

He looked down along the limestone foundations where the grass grew long against the house, and saw that light-coloured blob reeling across in an arc with the panting close now, and he brought the rifle to bear as it came.

He fired. The umbrella shook. The dull crack sounded up and down the valley and Ronnie cried out like a wounded rabbit.

He lowered the rifle as a poisonous rush of fear billowed up in him.

Ronnie continued her shuffling dance with the yellow umbrella until she came to the wooden steps.

'There's nothing out there.'

Jaccob made a weak little noise and went inside.

I stumbled in the dark to the window. There were no lights on up at Jaccob's. It was his .22, I guessed. That typical flat smack they made. Ida snored mercilessly. I waited. A light came on. I shivered in my pyjamas. The light up there went out. I figured a kill or a disaster would cause more ruckus than that, so I went back to bed and spent the rest of the night failing to sleep.

'Let the dead bury their dead,' Ida mumbled some time before dawn.

I shoved her in the ribs.

'You won't be soundin' so bloody smug in the morning, my love.'

'And milk,' she said.

You can't argue with a sleeping drunk.

This is Ronnie's dream, though it might as well be mine nowadays, I have it so often. It's quite short, and like the others, always the same.

There is firelight. There are voices raised. They are hammering in the nails and the tree is soft and the cat is mad with pain as they dance. Blood is like tar in the flickering light and suddenly the cat tears itself down and comes at Ronnie, pawing her belly until her shirt is open and there is only laughter.

When I dream this, I get up and find Ida's old Bible and the stuff about demons and spirits and miracles will make sense to me for minutes on end until the fear wears off.

Jaccob heard her scream and he was awake again, sweaty and awry in his bed. She was sobbing now; he could hear her in the room down the hall. He sighed and pulled on his trousers. He listened to the sound of her retching as he dragged on a shirt and blundered his way downstairs, bruising his shins on furniture until he thought to turn a light on to help find her a bowl. But when he got to her, Ronnie was back on the pillow, finished, and the sour-sweet stink of her puke was in the blankets. She groaned at the sudden light.

'I'm crook,' she said.

'Don't say.' He wiped her face with the edge of a sheet.

'No one's takin' this baby . . .'

Then she was asleep again.

She looked so pitiful. He turned the light out and sat by her. She was just a kid. He didn't know anything much about her. She was as silly as a wheel, though you could tell she knew more than she let on, maybe more than she herself realized. Plenty wasn't being said. Shit, she didn't have a chance, this one.

He put a hand on her. A curve of her calf muscle had exposed itself, and he ran his hand down the smooth warmth of her skin. It was a woman's flesh, all right. She might be eighteen, twenty maybe. He knew he should take his hands off her, but he ran a palm up her thigh and across her cotton panties. Her little belly was round and hard as fruit, and Jaccob sat there aching with his hand on her till the first cautious bird broke into song, and the light showed the mist rising on the slopes and the sorry lump in his jeans. He saw the hopeful, childlike outline of her face, and he felt the kind of pity he'd always reserved for himself. Little by little, the sun came up on him.

Ida Stubbs held her head and closed her eyes against the light. Even her teeth ached. She could hear Maurice moving about in the kitchen, but there was no way she'd be getting up before noon. Oh, Lord, maybe she'd never move again. She thought about last night. She thought carefully and was ashamed. That poor girl Ronnie. I let her drink so much – and her with a baby coming, what was I thinking? Where was my brain? Right now her brain felt as though it'd been cooked and eaten, and Ida pulled the blankets to her chin and felt old and stupid and sad and pathetic and irresponsible, and, and everything.

She wondered about the men. For all she knew they might've killed whatever'd been causing the trouble. But she remembered how angry Maurice had been and how quiet Jaccob was, and she knew it couldn't be. She lay still and let her mind roll with the morning. The grip on her head was terrible. Sometimes she slept light and dreamless, but when she woke again it would still be the morning and Maurice could still be heard putting wood in the stove, and she'd continue thinking about the last few days.

She couldn't recall a time like this. There'd been bush-fires and cockeyed-bobs, some floods and droughts and grasshoppers here before, but they were the kinds of things which announced themselves; terrifying because you knew what they could do – but this, this was worse. There was no knowing what might happen, what it was all about, and it seemed to Ida as though everything in the valley had stopped and nothing could go on until they knew what was out there.

There had to be something out there. Unless they were all imagining it, unless they'd dreamed up all those ducks dead, and the goat. But she'd never seen those herself. Unless. Maybe Maurice was right – they'd been relying on the word of people they didn't know, people who weren't farmers. Though there was the dog. Poor Coco. God, how it hurt to have him gone. Ida turned on the pillow. No, they weren't imagining it, but . . . but it could be a trick. Come to think of it, she hadn't actually seen poor Coco's . . . remains. Maurice had hid it from her. Out of kindness. Or. No, she'd heard the scream. But still, she couldn't say she'd seen it with her own eyes.

The sherry taste in her mouth became sickly and unbear-able. Ida reached across to the water jug by the bed. Beside the jug was the honey-smelling cast of the print. She picked it up and sniffed it. It made her shudder, it was so puke sweet. She turned it over in her hand. Now this was some-thing definite. This was no imagination. Nor was it a wild pig or goat – nothing hoofed. Some memory, the edge of something in the past, floated at the back of her mind. Rain. A rainy day. On the road. A dream? Something. It was hard to keep a thought alive with a head like this.

Ida slipped her fingers into the depressions in the cast. Each was big enough to rest a full knuckle in, and if she bent her hand into a loose fist, the curves fitted snugly. For a moment it made her smile. If she had a bigger hand, like a man's hand . . . She pulled her knuckles out and then slipped them back in. My God. A man could do that. A big hand could make this footprint!

She sat up and winced at the pain.

Someone was trying to frighten them. She thought as clearly as she could. Now where was that music-playing boyfriend of Ronnie's? Where was he? He'd never been what you'd call well disposed. Sometimes when he deigned to wave as they passed in their cars, Ida had the feeling he was laughing at them, sending them up. Funny how he'd been gone only a few days and this business had begun to happen the same time. Or. Or that talk about witches at Bakers Bridge. What was Ronnie up to? Should she trust her? What kind of a baby was she having?

Ida's mind galloped and swayed on and her blood packed her flesh until it almost hurt and it became hard to get her breath.

The men. Could it be the men frightening the women? No, that was stupid. Maurice hated practical jokes as much as he hated impractical people. Now. Now. Now, was it something or someone?

She drank some water. Her head constricted and it cramped up the muscles in her eyes. Everything tightened. She looked at the penny-spots on the backs of her hands and began to weep. Back on the pillow she felt the tears running back into her hair, across skin that almost hummed. She heard the rain coming across the valley and it sounded ominous and unpleasant though a long way outside of her.

She listened to the rumble of tears across her drum-flesh and tried to breath.

I sat there all morning on the sofa where I'd slept. The bloody house was full of beer bottles and lipstick-smeared glasses, and I was damned to hell if I was about to clean everything up. My eyes were sore and my back ached, and I didn't have the willpower to do much more than sit and look down the slope to the black bend of the river as drizzle turned to rain and swallowed up the light so the valley blurred like the grey end of a dream.

Toward noon I saw Jaccob walking down in the rain to the road. He trudged in the softening pasture and when he got to the road he headed for the girl's place. He looked dark and small with all that land and sky and rain around him, and before long he disappeared into it, and there was just the valley and the distance to look at.

I wondered what he'd shot last night. If it was the girl, he was certainly in no hurry to confess. Maybe, I laughed to myself, he's looking for a shovel. I shocked myself, thinking that way.

There were some scones left going stale on a tray near me and by noon I was hungry enough and lazy enough to eat them. Then I cleaned and oiled the .243 to keep my hands busy. Mostly I didn't think. I waited. Looking back, I suppose I'd been waiting for this half of my life. Something was going to happen.

The cat burns. The boy stops to watch a moment, and then he's running with a great and sudden light erupting behind him. Something has happened, and it can't be undone. He'll remember. It'll always be done. When he's an old man, it'll still be happening: over and over and over and over.

Jaccob didn't know much about milking a cow, but he'd watched Ronnie do it yesterday and he remembered the general idea. He made a fair job of it, and the cow seemed pleased to be out of the rain and she left no doubt about what hurt and what didn't. She smelt like a farmhouse, that cow, and the milking soothed him.

Coming back he realized he should have covered the bucket. Rain dimpled the milk's surface as he sloshed along with it steaming in the grey noon light. The valley was quiet but for the sound of the rain and the occasional disgruntled cry of a bird he wouldn't know the name of.

Jaccob saw no movement from the Stubbses' place and he figured that, like his own, it contained one snoring, sick woman in it, and that things would likely be that way all day. She was a good woman, Ida Stubbs. He thought perhaps she might be of help to Ronnie in the next few months. The girl was going to need a lot of it.

Jaccob walked and the ground squelched beneath him as the rain found its way into his eyes and down his collar.

Babies.

He felt that stony feeling in him again. The memory of that little box slipping into the hidden fire as the wailing relatives hugged one another and looked at him with pity and wonder. Strange, but it was only after the funeral that he felt anger. Marjorie was soggy with tranquillizers and dozing in the bedroom when he went out and gassed the cat. He could still feel it bucketing around in the bag. Jesus, it felt good making something pay. The yowl reached a pitch of fury as the monoxide and the motor and the heat filled the garage. Cot death, they reckoned. Kids die. It's a mystery syndrome. But he'd seen the cat leaving the nursery that night before Marjorie got up to check. Oh, it sauntered out casual as you please, and he thought nothing of it until he saw the fur on the pillow where the face of his daughter had been, warm as blood, not long before. But it was years now. Five? Six? Sometimes he wondered if he'd simply needed to think it was the cat that smothered his daughter, that a mystery, a syndrome just wasn't enough.

He stepped up on to his veranda and shook off some of the water. He looked at the milk and thought it must be rather diluted by now. He kicked his boots off and went in. The moment he was inside he felt he was back in a maze. That old feeling he'd come down here to escape.

The girl was up.

Ronnie got out of his rocker as soon as he came in. He had water in the wool of his sweater and the milk rolled in the bucket.

'Did the cow,' he said. 'How you feeling?'

'Shithouse.'

'You look it.'

Well bugger you, she thought.

The deep marks in his face stood out hard in the afternoon light. He looked old and sad as hell. He went into the kitchen and she heard him pouring the milk down the sink.

'Thanks a heap!'

'It's full of water,' he called back.

He came in again and stood by the window.

'Anyway, I did it for the cow, not for the milk.'

'Not to be neighbourly, then?'

He looked at her a moment. 'You're a silly little bitch.'

'Well, fuck you too.'

'Tell me, why do you have a she-goat and a cow when you're never in a fit state to milk the poor bastards?'

'You seem to forget that I don't have a goat any more. Anyway, who are you to tell me how to run a farm? You don't know the first thing about it.'

'Run a farm? You couldn't run a bloody tap, girl.'

'You're a prick.'

'And you're a spoilt twat. You'll kill that baby, you know.'

Ronnie tried to rub the dried spew off her sleeve. She set her teeth hard as a rabbit trap, but it was no use. She was going to cry, shit on it, she was gonna melt in front of this old creep.

'You'll never know, mate. You'll never have to carry one. You're a fucking male and you wouldn't know what a baby was if it crept up and bit your balls off! You're a fucking bastard!'

She got down the stairs to the back door with him yelling behind.

'I nearly shot you last night, you little idiot!' she heard him call as she got into a run and felt the jarring in her spine. She didn't remember. She didn't know. She didn't know what she'd done. He'd probably raped her and abused her and everything and she didn't give a shit. She ran out in the rain and the weight in her jugged around and the ground spread and slimed and skidded beneath her and the rain was in her face.

*

86

The weather set in. The river bed fattened. A cold southerly burrowed through the lupins on the slope. I emptied a box of shells into my lap and felt the smooth, brassy jackets with my fingertips. The valley soaked up rain and light and all sense.

When a man dreams things from the past, you'd think he'd be able to rearrange them in new sequences to please himself. You'd think your unconscious mind would want to do it for you, to spare you the grief and shame. But no. In my dreams, it all happens as it happened, and I see it and be it again and again and the confusion never wears off.

After a shower and a fistful of aspirin, Ronnie lay in her bed as dusk came on and she scrutinized the cracks and crazes times had left in the plaster of the ceiling. They'd never gotten around to fixing it up – that or anything else – and to look at it was to remind herself of what a joke the whole business had been. She could see now how Nick'd just been marking time, letting her have her fantasies until it was time to shoot through. It was like some lousy film. He'd left her high and dry.

She felt like hell. Head, limbs, even her mouth ached. She saw it all again, her dancing across the paddocks like that, knowing all the time she was having herself on, getting fuel enough from the booze to kid herself that she knew what she was doing. She must have been out of her mind! And that snail-slug of a bullet slowly turning across the dark at her to smack a hole in the umbrella just near her head. Yes, she remembered now. The breeze it made. Oh God, Ronnie, you're hopeless. There's no one now. Only you and this poor deformed little bastard in you, soaking up the poison. You'll lose him, you know. Him too. A woman can feel it. Mother's instinct. She laughed. Oh, Mother dear. It was bitter between her teeth.

For a while late in the day, Ida was able to read a book, but mostly the headaches were too much for her. The light of the bedroom was melancholy. She tried to find an explanation for the way life had come to a halt, but instead she came up with old memories. Like those stories she'd heard about American subs surfacing off beaches near here to get rid of mascots that had grown too big to be kept. Cougars, mountain lions, that sort of thing. And those prints someone'd found in the caves at Margaret River. And everybody the last few years talking about the thylacine, the marsupial dog or cat or whatever it was, coming back from extinction. And what about that time she'd come across that circus truck in the rain? Yes, she remembered that now. She'd had the feeling something dangerous had escaped there. Oh, there were so many things. Those thickets that ran all the way to the coast, and the miles and miles of forest. There were places for hidden things to breed. If they flourished, wouldn't they widen their territory? For a moment she thought she could make some sense of things, but her head thrummed like the engine room of a ship and there was still that creeping feeling of a trick. She knew she was old and silly. Could it be a cruel game?

Now and then Ida thought she would suffocate just thinking of it.

*

In the end I couldn't bear to see the steel-dark rain breaking up the earth, beating everything down, and so I went in to see Ida.

I saw myself in the mirror. I looked insane, I guess, not right, and Ida looked suddenly terrified.

'Ida, you ever wonder why Wally was blind? I mean what the real story was?'

She gazed up. She looked pretty damn wild herself.

'Everything makes me wonder. That brother of yours. He used to take the patches off to scare me. I s'pose I secretly thought your father'd poked them out for him.'

That got me. It took a moment to recover from that. It wasn't the moment for defending the old man, poor bugger.

'I sort of wanted to tell you. The real reason.'

Her jowls were all jumpy. She sat up in bed.

'I don't want to speak to you.'

'I just wanted to tell you. It'll explain things a bit.'

'Don't speak to me until you're prepared to tell me what's going on here, Maurice!' She couldn't hear. She was too frightened to listen. 'What is it, what's going on here? Who are you kidding? What kind of sick game, what is it?'

She fairly reared up in bed and her breasts rolled about in her nightie as she reached for the wax cast and I felt it hit me in the belly as the shouting got louder and I fell back against the door jamb. Then she began to scream without any words at all and the sound of it hit me harder than anything she could throw. It sent me back out of the room, that high squeal putting ice in me, coldness from another place and another time, it was the crazy woman's scream pursuing me from the flames. I stood in the living-room and heard it refuse to stop and I went hot and cold and shimmery and saw the gun and reached for it and put a shell in it and went back to the sound. I went in there. I shot upwards in that melancholy space and saw her mouth go wide and silent as plaster sprinkled on to the bedclothes. I put the gun aside and lay on the bed.

'That was a bit strong, don't you think?'

Her eyes shone madly and then fogged over with weeping.

I lay there listening.

In a beautiful Guy Fawkes curve the burning cat finds the open door. The old woman shouts in surprise and the white house swallows up the cat. And the curtains, how quick the curtains take, spitting and crackling like fuse-coil, licking up the timbers, the panelling, the drapes. Now, listen to the awful keening noise, the cat sound of her burning. The Minchinbury house roars. The sky drinks it up, the noise and light, the smells of cooking flesh and fur. It's the sound of hell, you know. She's burning and her cats are burning, and he's running, that farmboy, the silhouette, the flat shadow boy, he's running. There I am, here I am, with my chest fat with panic. A silhouette. Light and heat behind. This is the light to which the dreams come like moths. They come from everywhere, to beat themselves against the white heat inside my head.

There was still light in the sky when Jaccob drove across to Ronnie's with some soup and a lumpy little loaf he'd baked from a CWA cookbook. No lights were on. He stood on the veranda. The cow looked at him dolefully from across the fence. He'd made a friend there. He looked at the door a moment and decided to let himself in. It was a small place. Even in the twilight he found the bedroom quick enough. Ronnie was sitting up in bed. She must have heard the car. She looked afraid.

'Sorry,' he said. 'I didn't know if you'd be sleeping. I brought you some food.'

'I don't want anything.'

'You have to,' he said, trying to sound gentle. 'For the baby.'

'There's no baby any more, it's dead.'

Her voice was toneless. In a flurry, he put down the food and whipped back the blankets to reach for her. Ronnie squirmed away.

'Oh. I'm sorry.' He felt like a fool.

She looked amused. 'Nick'd never do that.'

'I'm sorry.' He looked at the bone-coloured wall. 'Can't you feel it kicking, or something?'

'Yeah. Yes, I can. I was being stupid. I think I'm going crazy.'

Jaccob got off the bed and went to the window to hide his face from her. She'd scared him. He didn't even know her, and the idea of her losing this baby made him panic. The room was almost without light now. Outside, the rain was hammering the ground into mud.

'Haven't you ever done anything bad?' she asked. 'When you knew you couldn't help yourself, wouldn't help yourself? That's what I do. Do you? Or are you always calm and smart and kind?'

He turned to face her. She sounded so young, but he'd heard that kind of sarcasm before. Was it sarcasm or innocence?

'I've done things.'

At this she smiled, and Jaccob turned his back to face the grey-blue evening light.

'No use looking out there,' she said. 'It's us.'

Then they heard the sound of the shot from down the hill. They saw each other in the gloom.

In the morning I woke to the water thunking on to the end of our bed. I'd made a nice old hole in the roof with that shot. The water made such a miserable sound that it drove me out into the day. Ida had slept nervously beside me as though I might cut her throat in the night. I could feel her relief as I got out into the morning chill.

Fowls hung grimly to their roosts, shaking themselves in the rain, and up on the pasture steers stood unmoving in the mud. The forest stood like a fortress behind. I got into my raincoat.

The lower pastures were miry, and I moved everything up to harder ground, leading them up with a few bales of feed on the back tray of the ute. It was cold and lonely moving around out there. I knew it'd be better out there with Ida. I loved that complaining chit-chat we could keep up in the cab when there were things to be done.

I drove slowly and let the stock follow and they snuffled and slapped tails and smacked mud and crud about. It was lonely, but peaceful enough.

Up at the northernmost reach of the property, in the stumpy pasture before the thicket country, I found twenty sheep with their bellies torn open and their skulls punctured.

It was a long day for Jaccob. Ronnie was determined to stay at her own place and he felt anxious for her in a way he couldn't explain to himself. He kept out of the rain, pacing, reading Thomas Wolfe, puzzling.

At dusk the rain stopped. Jaccob went out to split kindling for the fires. Under the lean-to by the machinery shed he got some pleasure for himself seeing the hard-grained jarrah stripped down to sticks.

He rested on his axe and smelled something burning. It smelt like carpet. Like wool. The wind was coming around from the west again. Now there was the smell of burning flesh. He bent and took an armful of wood in, and when he came out the light was gone. He sorted the kindling into another manageable load and smelt that whiff of barbecue. Lights were on down at the Stubbses'. He stood still and felt his skin prickle. Everything was hard to pick out in the dark. Jaccob made slits of his eyes and tried to pare the darkness into parts.

'Anybody there?'

What a rube he felt, saying that.

The drip of sagging gutters. No stars, no moon.

He must have known when to turn because he caught the movement out behind the shed, though it was less than he'd seen before.

He flinched. The phone was ringing inside the house. He hugged the wood to himself and ran.

For a moment I thought he wouldn't answer. Plenty of things rolled through my mind. But he answered. Breathless, sounding scared as hell. I stood there smelling of petrol and scorched meat. Those sheep had made a lousy fire. Ida looked at me as though she hadn't heard what I'd just told her.

'It's you, then,' Jaccob said.

'What's up? You sound a bit shaky.'

'I think I just saw something.'

'Jesus.'

'What?' He was getting his breath back. 'What's up with you, then?'

'Twenty sheep, that's what.'

He took a moment to let it register.

'Come over,' I said. 'Bring the girl.'

'Go to hell. You come here. I'd drive if I was you.'

It was raining and Ida noticed it. She could smell manure and upholstery and Maurice's shaving soap in the cab of the ute. The hot apple pie roasted her thighs through the tea towel. There was a strange electric taste in her mouth. It was what her old mum used to call a queer feeling.

'Here we are driving next door,' she said.

'Yeah, well. Under the circumstances . . .'

He looked normal enough. He had the gun behind the seat. She saw him put it in.

'Why didn't we have any sons, Maurice? Sons would have been nice.'

She saw the lights of the big white house through the scarecrow regiments of fruit trees. Maurice looked nervous now.

'Sons? We weren't given any, I s'pose.'

'You think they're given?'

'Gawd, woman, I don't know.'

'Because if they're given, then, you know, they're not given as well. Withheld, I mean.'

'That what they tell you in church once a year?'

She decided to let this pass. Her cheek rested on the cold window.

'You think we've done something?' she asked. 'Like "the sins of the fathers" and everything?'

He stopped the car. Right there. Right then.

'Ida, I've tried to tell you. The answer is yes.'

He drove on and she felt all breathless and confused and the serenity was gone and she knew she couldn't trust him.

That great looming white place looked at me as though it remembered. I could still feel that fourteen-year-old hysteria, thinking the fire would chase me down the hill right to the river itself. I thought: this night has been waiting for you all your life, Stubbs.

*

Ida noticed how dirty everything was. The big dining-room table was in need of a polish. The walls were bare and wanting paint or paper, she thought, and some nice things hanging, like a picture of a waterfall, or men on horses. It was the kind of place Ida imagined people took piano lessons in. Jaccob didn't look right in it, as though he wasn't quite master of the place. Maurice looked like something was about to bite him. And Ronnie. Ida had the urge to tidy her up a bit too. You could see the blue shadows of veins in her, she was so pale. She seemed grubby tonight, and cool. The coolness caught Ida unawares. It made her careful; it made her look closer at everybody.

'What are you grinning at?' Maurice murmured as they were shown into the living-room.

'Nothing, dear, what?'

'You were grinning like an idiot. What's funny?'

'Was I?' She felt a thrill of panic. The queerest feeling. She had no idea.

Jaccob and Ronnie came in behind them and everybody found chairs. This was a meeting. Ida felt away from it all.

'Why don't I fix us a cup of tea?' she asked, before anyone could speak. 'I brought an apple pie.'

Jaccob looked at her strangely. Perhaps I sounded too cheerful, she thought. They were all looking at her the way they really shouldn't be. Ronnie's eyes were narrowed. Maurice looked puzzled. She didn't like it. She got up and found the kitchen anyway and heard them talking tensely out there. The kitchen was a real bachelor's effort. Everything looked wrong, badly organized, unhygienic. She stood in the kitchen while the billy boiled and she could hear their voices coming and going. Now and then the pitch would be raised a little. Ronnie used some strong language; heard that plain enough. They prefer it this way, she thought; there's things they don't want me to hear. She planned to surprise them. When the tea was in the pot she found a tray and some spoons and plates and she ran the water and left it running as she crept back to the living-room.

'Well, let's get a dogger out here, straightaway,' Jaccob was saying. 'This has gone far enough. Someone's got to tell the authorities and get—'

'Authorities, authorities!' Maurice yelled. 'People suddenly want to be told what to do. This isn't the city, mate.'

'Oh, cut all the country bullshit. At least we could get someone out here who knows what they're doing. This thing could go mad, it could kill people. We need someone from the shire or the government. This is serious.'

'They don't know what they're on about. They'll tell you it's a dog and they'll take some notes and set some baits and tramp over our land with their badges and uniforms, putting their noses where they're not wanted. They'll laugh at us, you fool. It's just bloody interference.'

'Let 'em laugh,' Jaccob said. 'What's a bit of pride, for God's sake? What've you got to lose?'

'Or hide?' asked Ronnie tonelessly.

The room got quiet. Ida stood in the doorway, holding the tray. Her arms were beginning to shake with the strain. Yes, she thought. What have you got to hide, Maurice? And then she looked at them all. Their faces were hard with fear and secrets, she could see it straightaway.

'Nothing,' Maurice said. 'Not a thing.'

He was lying. What he said in the car. He was lying.

'Come on,' Jaccob said, softening. 'You might as well tell

us. Like you say, we're in this together.' His mouth twisted a little with irony. 'Neighbours, and everything.'

Ronnie smiled. 'He's growing dope in the forests.'

Jaccob looked startled.

'It's not true,' Maurice protested. 'You need your arse kicked, girl.'

'Face it,' she said with a laugh, 'you haven't got the legs for it.'

Ida felt herself harden up against Ronnie. No, it wasn't drugs. Maurice didn't know the first thing about them, not like this tart. Ida could see she looked the sort.

'Well, you must admit,' Jaccob said, 'that from where we stand you're sounding a bit paranoid. We've got something dangerous here and you don't want to do anything about it.'

Maurice was floundering now, she could sense it. He was holding his hands up against their innuendo like an old politician.

'It's only natural for us to think that we're not quite in the picture,' Jaccob said.

Natural! Ida thought. None of this is natural. Something is going on here. The whole land, the night, the valley is poisoned. What have these people been doing? What have they meddled with? What weird rites have they fiddled with? Why did you people come here? she thought.

Ronnie curled her lip in a sneer.

Then she saw their hands. They all had tumblers of whisky in their hands.

Maurice stood up and emptied his glass. He notice Ida then, saw her at the door, and he looked at the empty tumbler and then at the tray she was holding.

'I have done something about it,' he said. 'I set fire to those carcasses up on the hill. I thought it was time to bait them up. Tonight we'll cut some saplings to make a blind and we'll drive up to the back of my place, camouflage the ute, and wait until it shows. Or them. There's a lot of meat out there. Anything that comes will be startled a few seconds by the headlights, long enough to give us a good shot.'

'A good shot? You must be insane!'

'It's here!' Ronnie shouted. 'Jaccob saw it just now out the back and you've left all that meat out there? Ow. Ouch. Oh, shit.'

No one spoke. They looked at Ronnie. She'd gone way back in her chair with her hands on her thighs. She looked a long way away. Ida felt herself going away. This was all a trick. Leave here, a voice told her. Get on the bus, say the Our Father. She was slipping.

'Is that a contraction?' Jaccob asked after a while when all of them seemed to be going away down the wrong end of a telescope.

'How would I know what a fucking contraction is?' Ronnie shouted up the lens.

Ida shook. She looked at Maurice. She didn't know him. Not the way a wife should know a husband. There was a terrible cold rushing into her, a winter wind blowing right through. She was a stranger here, and they were impostors. There was just a hollowing wind and she was going.

Jaccob didn't move. He watched Ronnie who wore a ludicrous expression of rapture, as though she was the bleeding Virgin Mary herself. Ida Stubbs looked like she had heartburn, standing there with the tea tray, and for once the old man seemed to be out of his depth without pretending he wasn't. This should be a funny scene, he thought, but I'm as scared as shit. If we locked the doors, maybe if . . . now there's the cellar . . .

Ronnie felt the baby flexing his muscles. It was alive in there. It hurt, but she was keeping it alive on her own, with her blood and her water, with everything she had, and it worked. She was a mother. Nothing could stop her being a mother. She had the house, the land, she could grow things. There wasn't anything else.

I was seeing my shadow running down the hill with the flames behind, my guilty silhouette swallowed up in the night, my real form gone for ever while that firelight was behind me. I was always that shadow. With that burning house, that fact, I'd always be a silhouette.

The girl regarded her belly and I tried to get Jaccob's eye. I had to let him know I wasn't mad.

'You can't have that baby right now, you know,' I said. 'You'll have to wait for the authorities.'

Ronnie looked at me in great surprise.

Jaccob thundered with laughter. He would come around, I knew.

And when Ida dropped the tray and the tea and the pie and the whole business, and went barrelling through the house towards the door, no one moved.

The fire was out. The room was suddenly cold. I looked at the wash of broken crockery and food and liquid on Jaccob's jarrah boards, and I wondered what had brought me to this place, this still moment.

'Stubbs?'

I looked up at Jaccob. I liked him.

'Is she all right? God knows it's not safe out there.'

'Probably just needs some air,' I murmured. 'I'll get her. It's a bit unnerving for everyone, this whole business.'

Jaccob watched the old man leave the room. He poured himself another Scotch, a good one this time. He wanted to be calm.

'What a mess,' he said.

Ronnie looked up from contemplating herself.

The old man was out there shouting. 'Ida! IIIdaaaa!'

'Oh, Christ.'

In a single jerk, as though she'd abruptly returned to reality, Ronnie got to her feet and began to hiss.

'Get her in here, dammit, she'll die out there!'

Jaccob got up. Stubbs met him at the door.

'She's probably gone home,' Stubbs said. He had a gloss of sweat on his cheeks. 'I'll drive down and see that she's all right. Stay indoors.'

Jaccob watched him jog out to the ute. God, what a fiasco, he thought.

He went in and sat with Ronnie. He got up again and found the .22 and left it by the door. When he came back in Ronnie stood up and sat down again. She looked as though she was about to cry. He put his hands in his lap and looked at them. Maybe the old girl had the right idea – just climb back into bed with a hot toddy and goodbye. But something was out there and he began to believe it would kill them if they didn't kill it first. It's gonna come into our beds, there's no use going to bed over it.

He heard Stubbs's ute skidding back into the yard.

The old man came running in.

'She's buggered off.' He caught sight of Jaccob's rifle. 'Bring this.' Glancing at Ronnie, he waved a hand and said: 'Lock the house and stay here.'

'You're kidding! I'm not staying here on my own.'

The old man looked at Jaccob. 'Get her in the ute, then.'

Ronnie sat wedged between the two men, buffeted by their shoulders as the ute thrashed up the paddock. She felt it sway and judder in the waterlogged pasture. They slid to miss stumps and hummocks. Wet grass glittered in the lights. Every time Stubbs changed gears on the column-shift he clipped her breast with his elbow and she barked at him. What she saw ahead was a crazy rushing dream.

'Slow down, dammit!' Jaccob yelled.

'Can't see her anywhere. Where the hell is she?'

'Look out, Stubbs! For pity's sake!'

Ronnie saw the grass sliding away to the side as they skidded in a great curve and fishtailed back on line.

'She can't have gone far.'

'This is bloody madness.'

Ronnie felt something capsize, like a juggernaut rolling in her. She had a baby in there. This shouldn't be happening.

Jaccob braced himself against the dash as the old man drove crazy and hard and the ute crunched and rattled with the cab filling with the stink of their sweat. Roos stood still out there. The eyes of birds, rabbits, spiders showed in the mad light. He knocked shoulders with Ronnie and felt her knee against his. It was all over. He might as well forget the place now. The new life was over.

They topped the crest and the north gate loomed much too quick. Posts, wire leaping into largeness. He should have warned . . . Stubbs was standing on the brakes, he could feel it, and he pressed his own feet to the floor as they drifted sideways in a skid. Clods of dirt hammered under them. Should have bought a set of bloody golf clubs and a flat in Cottesloe by the sea, like any other harmless retired bastard.

They were going to go right through the fence. Jaccob covered his face, hunched to protect himself, felt Ronnie sag against him, but there was no shock. It just became quiet. He looked out. They'd stopped broadside to the fence, a foot away. The engine was stalled. Jaccob heard three people breathing.

'Shit a brick, Stubbs! Take it easy.'

Jaccob got out. Wind hustled in the trees up in the distance. The forest. There were great trenches in the mud from their four-wheeled skid.

From higher ground he heard the throaty sound of a nightbird.

The old man slocked over in the mud. 'You hear that?'

'A cough? Or a growl. From up there.'

Stubbs pointed north-west along the other side of the fence.

'What do you think?'

'My wife's out here somewhere, boy, what'm I s'posed to think? Open the gate. I'll rock us out.'

Somewhere. She was somewhere. Cold. Mud. Bog. Break. Bend. Fence. She kept running. Get in there. See and not be frightened, right into the thickets up there and see for herself. She wouldn't be tricked and frightened. She didn't care what they all were or who they worshipped – she was gonna see for herself. Ida felt the thrill of sense in her as she rode over the ground, blowing fog out before her. It was high time she faced it. It was only bush, only soil, only sky. There was nothing to be afraid of.

Jaccob took the spray of mud in the chest as the ute's wheels spun in the firebreak. He pushed until lights burst behind his eyes. It rocked and whirred and the tyres bit firmer earth and the whole shaking mess floated up on to hard ground. The mud was cold and he gasped and tasted monoxide. The brake lights glowed. The old man stuck his head out the window.

'We're right now. Come on.'

Jaccob ran to catch up.

I gunned the ute through the gate and across the other firebreak into the stumpy ground of Jaccob's back paddock. Up there, at the far limit of the headlights, were the forest and the thickets and the places a man couldn't go. Don't be up there, Ida, I thought. Just don't be there.

I drove hard. No one spoke. I just kept it up towards where we thought we'd heard something. In a moment, the ground turned to slush. I was feeling strong as a boy, not even touching the earth. Dreamy with weightlessness. She knows, I thought. She's cunning, old Ida. She's leading us to it. We belong here. We are strong.

Then I heard Jaccob shout. The wheel was gone from between my fingers and the world turned and my head went flat and it put burn behind my eyes.

I was cold.

I saw the stars return. The whole sky.

Jaccob crawled out on to the muddy ground. The front tyre was above him against the cloudy sky. There was wind and he found he could get up. The ute was upside down. He saw, across the exposed driveshaft and tangled exhaust, old Stubbs on his back, muttering in the dirt. Out in front the headlights made ragged white furrows in the earth.

And somewhere something else moved.

*

When it all stopped turning, Ronnie felt the pressure in her neck. Somehow she could see her left nipple in the dark; it was close enough to push into her eye. Her feet were above. No, up and behind. No seatbelt. This was her clearest moment before the world began to end, before the crushing heat and dark came upon her, squeezing juice out through every orifice and wrapping its rough tongue around her belly in a welter of spasms that forced her ribs into her lungs into her pelvis into her baby. There was no air for screaming. That dark thing in the dream, that angry crucified thing was coming at her for every bad thing. You could call it pain, something told her.

Jaccob stood in the crooked dark and saw the old man move, reaching into the upturned cab. For the girl? All he could see was a foot against the windscreen. Why couldn't he just make himself bend in and pull her out? Why couldn't he move? It was the sound from out in the dark, that's why.

The old man had his rifle.

'Urgh.'

Here it came.

'Bloody thing.' Stubbs's voice was quaking. 'Bastard stinking mongrel sick of a thing.'

'Curgh.'

Jaccob heard him cock the rifle. It was moving steadily out there, coming at them.

The old man had the weapon up. Jaccob could see the shadow of him aiming. This was the moment. Jaccob's body was suddenly sore and shaking. He knew he should get the girl out but there was Stubbs pointing the gun into the dark where the low, throaty grunt was coming from. Yes, it was coming. Yes. Yes.

But a sniff? A weepy sniff? No. This had happened before to Jaccob. He knew this. No! Wrong!

Jaccob turned. He saw the silhouette rearing up and he realized that the car was between him and Stubbs.

I heard it breathe and I knew I had a moment to kill the past, to fight it and wipe it away. The gun was all buck and flash and I was still strong.

Crack! Ronnie heard a tendon snap. Crackack! Brain, soul, something. She was on her way.

Jaccob made it round and drove the old man down in a tackle as the third shot went off. The barrel ploughed mud and muzzle flash. Stubbs's head rang against the upturned fender. Jaccob hit him and thought nothing and heard the hollow gurgling from out there and he knew the sound belonged to death.

Up in the mud and the furrows of light, my Ida drowned. She felt the heat and the wind in her throat. Blood was her only voice. For perhaps a second she had hold of a thought, a memory.

Ah, but you, Darkness, you know all this. I tell you night after night. Nothing will shock you. Maybe I go on at you in the hope that there's something beyond you. Some nights I sit here and talk and sob and stare out into the blackness thinking that if I look hard enough I'll see the light behind. But I stay out until the break of day, waiting, hoping, and there's only the sunrise again. I suppose there's some comfort in the fact of the sunrise. People used to take it as a sign that everything was under control.

Nobody comes out here. There's been no blue lights, no detectives, no curious social workers. It's almost a year.

Some afternoons I got down to the river and drag out the old bondwood dinghy I keep on the bank, and I row myself around the bend a little where the sun comes through the paperbarks to light up the water so bright you can barely see. I'll just drift along from there, maybe put a line over for bream, or maybe even a marron, or perhaps I'll read a querulous and dutiful letter from one of the daughters asking why her mother doesn't write back any more. I say she's having her change of life when I write back, sitting there with the light and water all around, balancing the pad on my knee. It's only a matter of time before they find out.

That's how I live now, knowing I'll only have this time for a little while. I should have known earlier to always live like that. There are small times of pleasure and I'm in no hurry to lose them before they're taken away by force.

I think about fear and panic a lot. I have quite a bit to do with them. You see I've known panic and I've been dead rational and I don't like either of them. Oh, maybe panic has a moral sense about it. When you're hysterical, you at least believe in what you're doing, however bloody stupid it is. But being rational is all about overriding what you believe in.

The moment I saw what I'd done that night, I became calm. I was suddenly sober. I measured things up. I planned. Surely this is possession! Jaccob was the same.

That night we stood by and watched the girl push out a dead baby. She didn't bleed much, though we worried. She didn't know who she was. We fed her pills and she slept. It happened very quickly. We buried Ida and the child in the forest. It was hard work but we dragged and dug without fuss. We discussed the options. We were at one purpose. We required certain things to be done. I do not have dreams about this. I barely recognize myself in my recollection.

It was two hours' drive in to the port town. Ronnie slept or was unconscious or in a coma. I know she was alive. Jaccob drove carefully. We rehearsed what we would do in our minds. We saw no other cars.

There was mist and we were grateful for it.

Just before five we coasted into the emergency admissions entry at the regional hospital with our lights out, motor idling. We took the trouble to wear some of Ida's pantyhose on our heads. Lights were on but no one was around. We hit the bell and left her at the door. Her head was on the thick rubber mat, her feet together in the blanket.

Jaccob drove smoothly and leisurely out of town through the mist and neither of us looked back. I was full of respect and terror. He wanted his time alone, he said. When everything caught up he'd go quietly, but he wasn't going to help anybody speed up the process. I knew what he meant.

At dawn we ran Jaccob's car into the river. Then we got drunk on Japanese whisky and told our stories. We made our vows of silence.

Now he drinks and I dream. It's killing the both of us.

My dreams are not symbols, they are history. Even the ones I don't understand, the ones I don't even know the characters in, they are all full of the most terrible truths. They settle on me, the guilty running silhouette. Yes, call me Legion for we are many.

I pay my bills. I buy my groceries and Jaccob's. I burn the letters that she sends him, those warped, crazy love notes. I go into the forest and look up to see if maybe some bough might fall my way. I learn things from books. Now and then I find a suspicious carcass or a pawprint, or I see a shadow between trees, but I go about my business.

The Americans have found bauxite in the forest. They'll be digging before long. That estate agent was across the valley the other day. I suppose that musician boyfriend could come around. It's a matter of time.

I can't redeem myself. That's why I confess to you, Darkness. You don't listen, you don't care, though sometimes I suspect you are more than you seem.

I live my life.

I am an old man.

Listen to me!

TELL THE WORLD
THIS BOOK WAS

| Good | Bad | So-so |

Very disturbing